The Battle of Kursk

The Battle of Kursk

David M. Glantz
Jonathan M. House

Maps by Darin Grauberger

University Press of Kansas

Published by the University Press of Kansas (Lawrence, Kansas 66049), which was
organized by the Kansas Board of Regents and is operated and funded by Emporia
State University, Fort Hays State University, Kansas State University, Pittsburg State
University, the University of Kansas, and Wichita State University

Library of Congress Cataloging-in-Publication Data

Glantz, David M.
    The Battle of Kursk / David M. Glantz and Jonathan M. House ; maps
  by Darin Grauberger.
      p.   cm. — (Modern war studies)
    Includes bibliographical references and index.
    ISBN 0-7006-0978-4 (cloth : alk. paper)
    1. Kursk, Battle of, 1943.   2. World War, 1939–1945—Tank warfare.
  3. Operation Citadel.   I. House, Jonathan M. (Jonathan Mallory),
  1950–   . II. Title.   III. Series.
  D764.3.K8G53   1999
  940.54'21735—dc21   99-22209

British Library Cataloguing in Publication Data is available.

Printed in the United States of America

10 9 8 7 6 5 4 3 2

Contents

Maps, Tables, and Illustrations

TABLES

ILLUSTRATIONS

Following page 78:
Marshal G. K. Zhukov
Colonel General M. M. Popov
Marshal A. M. Vasilevsky
Army General N. F. Vatutin
Colonel General V. D. Sokolovsky
Army General K. K. Rokossovsky
Colonel General I. S. Konev and his chief of staff, Lieutenant General
    M. V. Zakharov
Lieutenant General V. M. Badanov
Lieutenant General M. E. Katukov
Lieutenant General A. G. Rodin
Lieutenant General P. A. Rotmistrov and his staff
Lieutenant General R. S. Rybalko with his chief of staff, General V. A.
    Mitrofanov, and Lieutenant General I. I. Iakobovsky
Field Marshal Erich von Manstein
Field Marshal Guenther von Kluge
Colonel General Hermann Hoth
Colonel General Walter Model
General of Panzer Troops Werner Kempf
General of Panzer Troops Otto von Knobelsdorff
SS Obergruppenfuehrer Paul Hauser

Following page 196:
The T-34 Model 1943, the principal tank of the Red Army during the
    Kursk fighting
The crews of the T-34 Model 1943 of the 5th Guards Tank Corps prior to
    the outbreak of fighting in the Kursk area, July 1943
A Lend-Lease American M3 Lee medium tank burning after having been
    hit by German fire
A Churchill infantry tank, used in combat by at least one Red Army heavy
    tank regiment at Kursk in 1943
The KV-1S, the standard Soviet heavy tank in 1943
The T-70, the standard Red Army light tank in 1943

Preface

For more than fifty years, historians and readers alike have been fascinated and dazzled by the fabled Battle of Kursk. Buried amid the relative obscurity of World War II on the German Eastern Front, the battle's immense scope, ferocious nature, epic consequences, and staggering human and material costs have earned for it such superlatives as the "greatest" tank battle in history and the "turning point" of the war on the Eastern Front. As famous or infamous as it was, however, many of the details of the Kursk struggle have remained obscure because of the paucity of reliable Soviet sources. The battle, as described by a host of postwar historians, has been largely one-dimensional, with a well-defined German Army struggling against a mighty but faceless Soviet host. This fact alone has often made Kursk the subject of myth and misconception.

Superb books have described the course and outcome of the battle, but since only German sources have been readily available, most of these convey only German details and German perspectives. Many sound surveys of the war, including Earl Ziemke's scholarly account of the war, Albert Seaton's groundbreaking study, and Paul Carell's stirring, emotional, and immensely personal view of the struggle, contain chapters on the monumental conflict. While these relate the battle from the German perspective, Malcolm Mackintosh, John Erickson, and a few others have surfaced what we know from the Soviet side.

German generals who participated in the violent struggle wrote memoirs that concentrated primarily on assessing political and military blame for the unprecedented German defeat, whereas Soviet generals placed the battle within the context of the inexorable Soviet march to victory. Single volumes, too, have tackled the task of describing the immense battle. Geoffrey Jukes and Martin Caidin captured the drama of tank combat on an unprecedented scale, Janusz Piekalkiewicz exploited a variety of new Soviet sources in his panorama of the battle, and Mark Healy shaped a concise and attractive survey of the battle.

Yet the sheer drama of the battle juxtaposed against the limited quantities of exploited Soviet source materials has given rise to a certain mythology that has surrounded the battle. This mythology has accepted the German framework and definition of the battle and maintains that it took place from

5 to 23 July 1943. In so doing, it ignores the essential Soviet framework for Kursk, which placed the defensive battle in the Kursk salient within the proper context of the Soviets' two-month-long Kursk Strategic Offensive Operation.

Further, the mythology asserts that had Kursk been fought in May, as originally planned, it could have resulted in German victory. This myth argues that Kursk was a battle of tank against tank, that Kursk was the famous battle of Prokhorovka and little else, that the tank clash at Prokhorovka was the greatest tank battle in history and Prokhorovka was the field where Germany's wartime fate was determined. Historians have consistently exaggerated both the scope and the importance of Prokhorovka. Thus, while Seaton wrote that "nearly 1,300 tanks, assault guns and SUs were employed" at Prokhorovka, Carell weighed in with the dramatic declaration that "some 1500 tanks and assault guns were racing, firing, exploding, burning, thundering, and smoking on that minute sea of hills and valleys around Prokhorovka." As dramatic and appealing as these descriptions are, they are but a single fragment of the mythology that still envelops the fabled Battle of Kursk. Nor did the victorious Soviets have any incentive to debunk the myths in their numerous accounts, for to do so would have been to reduce the scale and drama of their victory.

Today, newly available Soviet and German sources permit a reevaluation of every aspect of the Battle of Kursk and, in fact, the war as a whole. Now the mythology can be stripped from the battle to reveal what actually occurred and why. That is the purpose of this volume.

This study synthesizes the massive existing detail on the battle with newly unmasked Soviet archival and semi-archival materials. It adds unprecedented new detail to what has already been written and places the Battle of Kursk in its proper wartime strategic and operational context. It attempts to capture the complexity of combat and places the famed Prokhorovka tank battle in its necessary context as one albeit dramatic segment of an immensely complex struggle. Finally, while assessing the costs and staggering consequences of the battle for the contending sides, it analyzes the military detail of the battle to describe how blitzkrieg ended at Kursk. In so doing, it strips away the myths associated with the struggle and restores Kursk to its proper place in the vast panorama of combat on the German Eastern Front.

ACKNOWLEDGMENTS

The authors owe special thanks to Soviet (Russian) authorities for making available the sources without which this study could not have been written. Specifically, in the late 1980s the Gorbachev government of the Soviet Union began lifting the veil of secrecy that had shrouded Soviet official and archival accounts of the war. To some extent, the post-1991 Russian government has continued this positive policy. This material can now be used to validate or invalidate the numerous, but often inaccessible, works prepared by earlier Soviet historians.

Others warrant special mention and thanks for their contributions to this study. Steven J. Zaloga offered his special talents as preeminent authority on wartime German and Soviet weaponry to review and correct the book and to provide the valuable photographs that illustrate it. George M. Nipe, Jr., and Niklas Zetterling shared their unique perspectives on the costs of the battle in tank and human terms. Mary Ann Glantz, as usual, endured the travails of her husband's research and thoroughly and skillfully edited the manuscript. Through our and their efforts, this volume took shape to join and supplement the imposing array of existing literature about the Battle of Kursk.

The Battle of Kursk

Prologue: Munich, 3 May 1943

For three quarters of an hour, Adolf Hitler lucidly summarized Operation Citadel, Germany's plan for a renewed offensive against the Soviet Union.[1] Around the long map table, the commanders of the Eastern Front and the principal staff officers of the Third Reich listened with varying degrees of concern, irritation, or resignation.

Colonel General Kurt Zeitzler, Chief of the Army General Staff, was the nominal author of the Citadel plan, although in truth the idea was so obvious that anyone at the table might have proposed it. After two years of struggle with the Red Army, the German *Wehrmacht* no longer had the resources to launch a full-scale offensive in the East. Instead, under Citadel the available German forces were supposed to concentrate on the Kursk salient, a portion of the front line that bulged westward into the German center. The brash, loud-mouthed Zeitzler had planned for two different forces to converge on Kursk, pinching off the bulge. Field Marshal Guenther von Kluge's Army Group Center would attack southward toward the Russian city of Kursk from the area of Orel while Field Marshal Erich von Manstein's Army Group South would attack northward into the southern flank of the bulge. If successful, this converging attack would encircle large Soviet formations and shorten the German lines, freeing troops for further offensives or, more practically, for a prolonged defensive campaign.

Such, in essence, was Zeitzler's plan. Its principal weakness was that it was so obvious; the longer the Germans delayed, the more probable it was that the Soviets would develop defenses to thwart the attack. Colonel General Walter Model, whose Ninth German Army would conduct the principal assault on the northern face of the salient, was convinced that the Reds had done just that. The day before the conference in Munich, Model had bypassed his commander, von Kluge, to present his concerns to Hitler. Model had laid out dozens of aerial reconnaissance photographs of the Kursk bulge. These photos showed mile after mile of elaborately prepared Soviet defenses in the exact path of the proposed offensive. Model argued that the opportunity to attack had passed, that the Soviets would slowly grind down and destroy the spearheads of Ninth Army without permitting a breakthrough. Citadel must be either radically revised or completely abandoned. At the very least, Model demanded two additional panzer divisions, a host of specialized units, and thousands of replacement soldiers to fill his ranks.

1

At Munich, Hitler presented both Zeitzler's plan and Model's objections to that plan. His audience, who had learned to read the dictator's moods, recognized that he was impressed by Model's arguments. Field Marshal von Manstein shared these misgivings; he believed that the Germans should have attacked in April, before their opponents had recovered from the defeats of late spring. Yet, as in so many conferences during the war, von Manstein hesitated to make his case. In private, he was often scathingly critical of German strategy, but he was so overawed by Hitler's personality and intuition that he often stumbled when talking to the dictator.

Field Marshal von Kluge argued strongly for a continuation of Citadel as Zeitzler had conceived it. He was irritated by the fact that Model had bypassed him and remained convinced that the Germans could bull their way through any Soviet defenses. Indeed, the unspoken assumption of most German commanders was that their army would always be able to penetrate enemy positions, regardless of how carefully prepared those positions might be. In addition, von Kluge appealed to Hitler's fascination with technology by insisting that the newly designed Panther and Tiger tanks would overcome any obstacles.

At this point the Inspector-General of Panzer (Armored) Troops, Colonel General Heinz Guderian, asked Hitler's permission to comment. Guderian was responsible for reconstructing the armored units of the German Army, and he warned against destroying those units in a bloody frontal assault on Kursk. The tanks necessary to replace such losses would be better employed in Western Europe, where the British and Americans were certain to invade eventually. Albert Speer, Minister for Armaments and War Production, supported Guderian with production figures, and both men noted that the Panther tanks were still suffering design problems because they had been rushed into production without adequate testing. Both the reliability and the production of new tanks were expected to improve by June, but that implied further delays in the offensive.

Guderian was adamantly opposed to Citadel, but his passion was increased by a continuing resentment against von Kluge, who had contributed to his relief from command at the gates of Moscow in 1941. The personality clash between the two generals was so great that after the conference von Kluge asked Hitler to act as his second in a duel with Guderian!

The conference itself, like the proposed duel, never reached a decision. For two days the participants considered the three options of an immediate offensive, a delayed offensive, and total cancellation of Citadel. The Luftwaffe (Air Force) Chief of Staff, Colonel General Hans Jeschonnek, spoke for many of those present when he argued for an immediate attack because it was no longer possible to conceal preparations for the offensive. According to his own recollections, von Manstein warned Hitler that a delayed Citadel would eventually have to be canceled when the British and Americans invaded the continent.[2] This prophetic comment, if it was in fact made, did not register with Hitler. In fact, as so often in the latter half of the war, Hitler seemed incapable of making a timely decision. Ultimately, the conference adjourned without a consensus. The Citadel plan remained in effect, but no starting date was set.

On 10 May Hitler summoned Guderian to Berlin to discuss tank production. After the meeting Guderian urged the dictator to abandon the plan for an attack in Russia in order to conserve resources for the defense of Western Europe. Field Marshal Wilhelm Keitel, Chief of the Armed Forces Staff, insisted that an attack must occur for political reasons—Germany could not afford to appear passive but had to resume the offensive to reassure its allies and its own population.

Guderian scoffed, "It's a matter of profound indifference to the world whether we hold Kursk or not. I repeat my question: Why do we want to attack in the East at all this year?" Hitler's reply was uncharacteristically honest, "You're quite right. Whenever I think of this attack my stomach turns over."[3] Still, the German preparations for Citadel continued inexorably, while every week the Soviet defenses became stronger.

DRAMATIS PERSONAE

Antonov, Colonel General Aleksei Innokent'evich: 1st Deputy Chief of the Red Army General Staff and *Stavka* member.

Badanov, Lieutenant General Vasilii Mikhailovich: Commander, 4th Tank Army, which participated in Operation Kutuzov, the Soviet counteroffensive against the Orel salient.

Guderian, Colonel General Heinz: Inspector-General of Panzer Troops.

Hoth, Colonel General Hermann: Commander, Fourth Panzer Army, which made the principal German attack on the southern face of the Kursk Bulge and defended in Operation Rumiantsev, the Soviet offensive toward Khar'kov.

Katukov, Lieutenant General Mikhail Efimovich: Commander, 1st Tank Army, which defended the southern face of the Kursk Bulge in Operation Citadel, the German offensive at the Kursk Bulge, and spearheaded Operation Rumiantsev.

Keitel, Field Marshal Wilhelm: Chief of the Armed Forces High Command (OKW).

Kempf, Colonel General Werner: Commander, Army Detachment Kempf, which attacked the southeastern shoulder of the Kursk Bulge and defended in Operation Rumiantsev.

von Kluge, Field Marshal Guenther: Commander, Army Group Center, which attacked the northern face of the Kursk in Operation Citadel and defended the Orel salient in Operation Kutuzov.

Konev, Army General Ivan Stepanovich: Commander, Steppe Front, which counterattacked in Operation Citadel and attacked in Operation Rumiantsev.

von Manstein, Field Marshal Erich: Commander, Army Group South, which attacked the southern face of the Kursk Bulge in Operation Citadel and defended in Operation Rumiantsev.

Model, General Walter: Commander, Ninth German Army, which attacked the northern face of the Kursk Bulge in Operation Citadel, and later acting commander of Second Panzer Army as well as Ninth Army in the defense of the Orel salient in Operation Kutuzov.

Popov, Colonel General Markian Mikhailovich: Commander, Briansk Front, which attacked the eastern face of the Orel salient in Operation Kutuzov.

Rodin, Lieutenant General Aleksei Grigor'evich: Commander, 2d Tank Army, which defended the northern face of the Kursk Bulge in Operation Citadel and attacked the southern face of the Orel salient in Operation Kutuzov.

Rokossovsky, Army General Konstantin Konstantinovich: Commander, Central Front, which defended the northern face of the Kursk Bulge in Operation Citadel and attacked the southern face of the Orel salient in Operation Kutuzov.

Rotmistrov, Lieutenant General Pavel Alekseevich: Commander, 5th Guards Tank Army, which spearheaded Steppe Front's counterstroke at Prokhorovka and the *front*'s offensive in Operation Rumiantsev.

Rybalko, Lieutenant General Pavel Semenovich: Commander, 3d Guards Tank Army, which spearheaded Briansk Front's offensive against the eastern face of the Orel salient in Operation Kutuzov.

Sokolovsky, Colonel General Vasilii Danilovich: Commander, Western Front, whose 11th Guards and 50th Armies participated in the attack against the northern face of the Orel salient during Operation Kutuzov.

Vasilevsky, Marshal of the Soviet Union Aleksandr Mikhailovich: Chief of the Red Army General Staff and *Stavka* representative on the southern face of the Kursk Bulge.

Vatutin, Army General Nikolai Fedorovich: Commander, Voronezh Front, which defended the southern face of the Kursk Bulge in Operation Citadel and attacked during Operation Rumiantsev.

Zeitzler, Colonel General Kurt: Chief of the Army High Command (OKH).

Zhukov, Marshal of the Soviet Union Georgi Konstantinovich: Deputy Commander of the Red Army and *Stavka* representative for the northern face of the Kursk Bulge in Operation Citadel and for Operation Rumiantsev.

PART I
BACKGROUND

CHAPTER 1

Barbarossa to Donbas: The German Army in the East, 1941–1943

Adolf Hitler's dilemma did not develop overnight: in order to understand the German strategic problem, one must consider the two years of Soviet-German struggle that preceded Kursk. During this period both the battle lines and the strategic initiative swung back and forth like a pendulum.

BARBAROSSA, 1941

When Germany attacked the Soviet Union on 22 June 1941, the German *Wehrmacht* was at the top of its form, while the Red Army was caught in the middle of a number of difficult transitions. As a result, Operation Barbarossa was a triumphal German advance that nearly achieved victory in less than six months.

In its previous campaigns in 1939–1940, the *Wehrmacht* had developed blitzkrieg (lightning war) from a propaganda theme into a practical set of tactics. The German Air Force was able to destroy much of the larger, obsolescent Red Air Force, freeing German aircraft to provide close air support for the ground advance. This ground advance, led by armored and motorized units, sought to penetrate, disorganize, and surround the enemy defenses, capturing entire field armies. Time after time the German mechanized forces created such pockets, but the foot-mobile infantry did not arrive in time to seal the perimeter of these encirclements. Many Soviet troops, especially the irreplaceable staff officers and commanders, escaped to become guerrillas or to rebuild new units in the rear. At the same time, these delays meant that the panzer units had to mark time while the Red Army assembled new defenses between the Germans and Moscow.

Ultimately, Operation Barbarossa failed because of German logistics and Soviet perseverance. The vast, roadless spaces of European Russia defeated German efforts to refuel, rearm, and repair their spearheads. The highly centralized German maintenance system, which relied upon returning vehicles to the factory for major repairs, could not keep pace with the demands of the Russian campaign. Panzer divisions that began the campaign in June with 120 to 130 tanks ended in December with no more than a dozen functional tanks. With limited rail and truck transportation, German logisticians

7

chose to delay shipment of cold weather clothing in order to supply their troops with fuel, ammunition, and spare parts for the final advance on Moscow. With two-thirds of all German motor vehicles immobilized, the advance sputtered to a halt in the first week of December 1941.

Meanwhile, the Red Army had to overcome enormous institutional problems while fighting vainly to halt the invader. Between 1937 and 1940, Iosif Vissarionovich Stalin had executed, imprisoned, or dismissed almost half of his professional officer corps, leaving inexperienced and demoralized junior leaders in command.[1] The Red Army's doctrine for offensive, mechanized warfare had fallen into disrepute because it was associated with the purged commanders. At the time of the German invasion, Soviet mechanized units were undergoing their third major reorganization in two years and were caught with a mixture of worn-out, obsolete tanks and poorly understood new ones. Moreover, Stalin had been so concerned to avoid conflict in 1941 that he had forbidden all defensive precautions until the night of the German attack.

Given these circumstances, the Red Army performed a miracle by simply surviving the German invasion, let alone halting it. The senior leadership of the armed forces, including Chief of the Red Army General Staff B. M. Shaposhnikov and *Stavka* (High Command) "troubleshooters" like G. K. Zhukov and A. M. Vasilevsky, had to retrain their subordinates under fire in the most basic principles of tactics and logistics. Each time the German commanders won another battle, their Soviet opponents learned another expensive lesson in modern warfare. More surprisingly, the Soviets were able to field new divisions faster than the Germans could destroy them. By 31 December 1941, the Red Army had created 385 new divisions and 267 separate brigades, more than compensating for the loss of at least 229 division equivalents in battle. Whereas prewar German intelligence had estimated an enemy of approximately 300 divisions, by December the Soviets had fielded almost three times that many units.[2] Most of these new units were poorly trained and equipped, but destroying them cost the Germans more casualties, fuel, ammunition, and time. The dogged perseverance of the Soviet soldier contributed markedly to the German failure in 1941.

On 5 December 1941, Stalin launched a counteroffensive, using carefully hoarded reserves to attack the overextended Germans outside Moscow. The attacks were relatively weak and crude, but the fact that the Red Army could attack at all shocked the Germans. At first, Hitler refused to approve any withdrawals, and numerous senior commanders, including Heinz Guderian, were relieved when they insisted that they must retreat to save their troops. Eventually, even Hitler was forced to accept some withdrawals. Meanwhile, however, Stalin was so elated by his initial successes that he attempted to expand the counteroffensive into a general advance along the entire front. In fact, the Red Army was still too weak and inexperienced to achieve such a major objective. The Germans quickly recovered their nerve and their mobility, fighting the first Soviet winter offensive to a standstill by February 1942.

TO STALINGRAD, 1942

For the rest of the winter, both sides rebuilt their forces. Hitler reluctantly recognized that the Soviet war had become a long-term commitment, and Germany belatedly began to mobilize itself for total war. Meanwhile, the shattered Soviet mechanized forces were reborn with the creation in May 1942 of the first tank corps, division-sized units of 7,800 men, 98 T-34 medium tanks, and 70 other, lighter tanks. The Red Army formed 28 such corps in 1942. These tank corps, joined in August 1942 by the slightly larger mechanized corps of 13,500 men and 204 tanks, were the basic building blocks of the new armored force.[3]

Unfortunately, I. V. Stalin was still tantalized by the near success of his winter counteroffensive and therefore failed to recognize that the Germans were also regaining strength. In May 1942 Stalin insisted that his untried mechanized forces launch an offensive in the Khar'kov region, approximately midway along the extended battlefront. The result was a disaster in the second Battle of Khar'kov, which only cleared the way for a renewed German offensive.[4]

Despite their recovery in early 1942, the German armed forces were no longer capable of resuming the offensive along the entire front. Instead, the 1942 offensive, code-named Operation Blau (Blue), concentrated most of the available panzer forces on the southern half of the German lines. Hitler's objective was to clear the eastern coast of the Black Sea and to seize the Soviet oil fields in the Caucasus. The attack jumped off on 28 June 1942 and, at first, achieved the same type of successes seen in the previous year. Again, however, the Germans stretched themselves over hundreds of kilometers, relying on poorly equipped Italian, Hungarian, and Rumanian satellite troops to protect the flanks of their advance. By the end of August 1942, the Germans had become decisively engaged in a struggle for the industrial city of Stalingrad, a struggle in which both sides were bled white.

Throughout the second German summer offensive, Soviet staff officers had planned for a renewed counteroffensive when the opportunity arose. After a year of war, Stalin had finally learned to trust his professional subordinates in matters of this kind. The new Chief of the General Staff, A. M. Vasilevsky, kept a small group of staff officers at work on a series of counteroffensive plans. The most famous of these plans was Operation Uranus, a classic encirclement operation designed to trap the Sixth German Army at Stalingrad. Uranus was to be preceded and accompanied by the equally ambitious Operation Mars, personally directed by Deputy Supreme High Commander G. K. Zhukov against German Ninth Army in the Rzhev salient, which menaced Moscow from the west.

Although Mars was delayed by bad weather, the Red Army launched Uranus on 19 November 1942, sending its new tank corps racing to encircle Sixth Army and part of Fourth Panzer Army. Yet the encircled Germans held out until the end of January 1943, tying down Soviet forces that might otherwise have exploited the huge holes torn in the German front.

More significantly, the Soviet High Command (*Stavka*) intended Mars and Uranus to be but the first steps in a strategic plan that would shatter the entire German front. On 25 November 1942, Marshal Zhukov finally launched Operation Mars, which attempted to repeat the Stalingrad success farther north, against Army Group Center. In this region, however, German forces were not overextended as they were in the south, and the Germans possessed significant reserves to counterattack. In two weeks Zhukov's forces suffered over 300,000 casualties and lost over 1,400 tanks without significant territorial gain.[5]

Despite this setback, the *Stavka* launched a series of operations, spreading gradually along the front to the northwest and south of the stricken German forces at Stalingrad. In two offensives during December (Operation Little Saturn and the Kotel'nikovsky Operation), the Southwestern and Stalingrad Fronts° destroyed the Italian Eighth Army and halted Fourth Panzer Army's attempts to relieve the Stalingrad garrison. The Voronezh Front followed suit on 13 January, launching the Ostrogozhsk-Rossosh' operation, which severely damaged the Hungarian Second Army. Then, without pause, in cooperation with the Briansk Front, the Voronezh Front continued its victorious headlong march westward, pressing the Second German Army in the Voronezh-Kastornoe operation.

OFFENSIVE AND COUNTEROFFENSIVE

By the end of January 1943, the surrender of Stalingrad was only a matter of days away. The *Stavka* launched two improvised offensives, Operations Gallop and Star, striking southwestward to exploit the apparent vacuum west of Stalingrad. The goal was to reach the Black Sea, cutting off all German forces south and east of Stalingrad. In Gallop, which began on 29 January, General M. M. Popov led an improvised group of tank corps in a deep raid that eventually became the model for future, large-scale mechanized operations. Three days later, on 2 February, the Voronezh Front, attacking to the west of Popov, began Operation Star, which threatened the key transportation centers of Belgorod, Khar'kov, and Kursk.

°A Soviet *front* was roughly equivalent to an army group.

Encouraged by the initial success of these attacks, in early February Stalin and his commanders aimed even higher.[6] The surrender of Stalingrad freed six field armies for operations farther north, against the junction of German Army Group Center and South. This provided Zhukov with the opportunity to complete the failed work of Operation Mars, the destruction of German Army Group Center. The ambitious strategic concept called for two encirclements. First, Colonel General K. K. Rokossovsky was to redeploy the victorious Stalingrad armies to become a new Central Front, which, in cooperation with the Briansk and Western Fronts, was to encircle the German forces around the city of Orel. Once this succeeded, the newly formed 2d Tank and 70th Armies, together with the veteran 21st Army, would plunge even farther to the west, linking up with other Soviet forces in a gigantic encirclement extending from Briansk to Smolensk. These offensives, in cooperation with continued attacks farther south, were supposed to propel Soviet forces to the Dnepr River by mid-March (see Map 1).

Planning such a strategy was far easier than implementing it. In fact, the Red strategic plan foundered due to a combination of Soviet ineptitude, appalling weather and terrain conditions, and the enduring military capacity of the German Army. First, the Soviet staff planners were hopelessly optimistic in their estimates of the time and transportation facilities necessary to redeploy forces from Stalingrad to the new Central Front. Rokossovsky was a brilliant commander, but even he could not move five armies 200 kilometers along a single rail line in the ten days (5 to 15 February 1943) allotted and then conduct a major offensive. Ultimately, the *Stavka* had to give Rokossovsky an additional ten days to prepare, and even then his troops attacked piecemeal as they arrived in their new area of operations. In the interim, the other Soviet forces attempted to attack without Rokossovsky and accomplished little against rainy weather and stubborn German resistance. Once Rokossovsky was able to attack on 25 February, his forces achieved considerable success against the weak Hungarian and German units south of Orel. His 11th Tank Corps, in coordination with cavalry and partisan units, conducted a daring raid 160 kilometers into the German rear, reaching the Desna River on 7 March. In the process, however, the Central Front's forces became strung out along the few available roads, leaving them vulnerable to a German counteroffensive that was developing to their south.

In the crisis of Stalingrad, Field Marshal von Manstein had received control of the surviving Axis forces in the region. He had failed in his efforts to relieve the encircled Germans, but in the late winter of 1943 he again demonstrated his mastery of mechanized warfare, launching a series of counterstrokes that eventually halted and bloodied the victorious Soviets.

In February von Manstein was hard-pressed to halt the raids of Mobile Group Popov and other exploiting Soviet tanks corps in Operation Gallop.

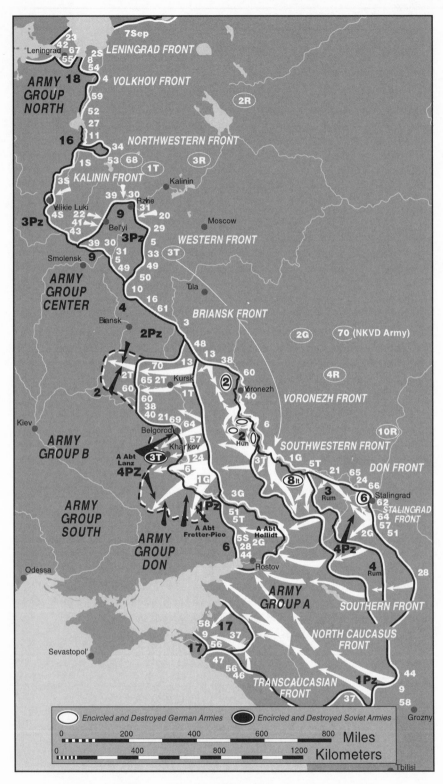

Map 1. The Winter Campaign, November 1942 to March 1943

During the last ten days of February, however, he mustered enough mobile forces from First Panzer Army, which had just barely escaped from the Caucasus, to strike back at the exploiting Soviet armored host. The threadbare divisions of von Manstein's III, XXXX, and XXXXVIII Panzer Corps mauled Group Popov south of Slaviansk and destroyed another Soviet tank corps marching on the Dnepr at Zaporozh'e. By 1 March Hitler had given Manstein sufficient mechanized forces to launch a full assault by the reorganized Fourth Panzer Army northward toward Khar'kov and the Northern Donets River. In five days of heavy fighting, Fourth Panzer Army utterly destroyed the Soviet 3d Tank Army south of the city of Khar'kov.[7] In addition to the XXXXVIII Panzer Corps, Fourth Panzer Army now threatened Khar'kov with the lavishly equipped SS Panzer Corps, consisting of the SS Panzer Divisions *Leibstandarte Adolf Hitler, Das Reich,* and *Totenkopf.* Meanwhile the German Fourth Air Fleet, under the charismatic Wolfram von Richtofen, had regrouped and repaired its aircraft, flying an average of 1,000 sorties per day in late February and early March. For perhaps the last time in Russia, the Luftwaffe provided undisputed air superiority for a major German mechanized operation.

Soviet commanders were slow to recognize this new threat from the south. At first, the *Stavka* simply diverted two of Rokossovsky's field armies (62d and 64th), still redeploying from Stalingrad, to reinforce Voronezh Front in the Khar'kov region and Southwestern Front's shattered forces along the Northern Donets River. In connection with this, on 7 March Rokossovsky received new orders, abandoning the original deep objectives around Briansk in favor of a shallower encirclement of the German forces around Orel. Rokossovsky dutifully began this new attack on 7 March but was unable to develop sufficient combat power both because his forces were scattered and also because German Second Army chose the same day to launch its own counterstroke against the exposed Soviet spearheads on the Desna River.

More significantly, on 6 March von Manstein struck directly at the transportation hub of Khar'kov, and by 15 March the SS Panzer Corps had recaptured the city. Two days later German Fourth Panzer Army and Second Army attacked the Soviet forces around Belgorod, seventy-five kilometers north-northeast of Khar'kov.

The *Stavka* belatedly recognized its danger and, to contain the German offensive, assembled forces north of Belgorod, including the 21st Army, which had just arrived from the Stalingrad region to reinforce Rokossovsky's offensive. In fact, von Manstein's panzers had reached the end of their tether, and bad weather as well as exhaustion brought the Germans to a halt. Soon the spring thaw and *rasputitsa* (the muddy or roadless season) made further operations impossible.

Von Manstein had wrecked the Soviet strategic plan, but he was reluctant to abandon the initiative in the Khar'kov-Kursk-Orel region. When Hitler visited von Manstein's Zaporozh'e headquarters on 10 March, the field marshal pressed the dictator for a commitment to resume the offensive as soon as the *rasputitsa* ended. Four days later, when the SS Panzers entered Khar'kov, von Manstein tried to persuade von Kluge, as commander of Army Group Center, to cooperate in an immediate attack against Rokossovsky's forces in the newly formed Kursk Bulge. Von Kluge refused, insisting that his troops needed to rest and refit.[8]

Meanwhile, the Soviet forces used to contain von Manstein around Belgorod had been diverted from the Central Front's revised offensive, effectively ending Rokossovsky's opportunity to take Orel. In fact, the *Stavka* canceled other significant planned offensives to dispatch reinforcements to the Kursk region.

These reinforcements included the newly formed 1st Tank Army, which had been designated to spearhead a Northwestern Front deep operation south of Lake Il'men' in late February to relieve the siege of Leningrad. Thus the front lines assumed the shape of a huge, backward "S," with a German salient bulging eastward around Orel, a Soviet salient pushing westward from Kursk, and von Manstein's forces holding their positions around Belgorod and Khar'kov (see Map 2). The stage was set for Operation Citadel.

REBUILDING THE GERMAN ARMY

Guenther von Kluge was correct about one thing—the German Army certainly needed a facelift. After continuous operations from June 1942 to March 1943, most German units were worn out.

The most pressing need was for manpower. Paradoxically, the totalitarian dictatorship of the Third Reich had been much slower to mobilize its population than were the Western democracies or the shattered Soviet Union. Adolf Hitler had steadily resisted radical disruptions of German life, such as reductions in consumer goods and using more women in factory work. In January 1943, however, he reluctantly appointed a committee of three men to find 800,000 new recruits for the armed forces, with half of this draft to come from nonessential industry. Field Marshal Keitel, Martin Bormann, and career civil servant Hans Lammers represented the armed forces, the Nazi Party, and the civil government, respectively.[9] In consultation with Albert Speer and others, this committee found military manpower without disrupting war production. Fifteen-year-old students manned antiaircraft guns in Germany to free more troops for the front, while *Volksdeutsch* men in occupied territories were reclassified as sufficiently reliable

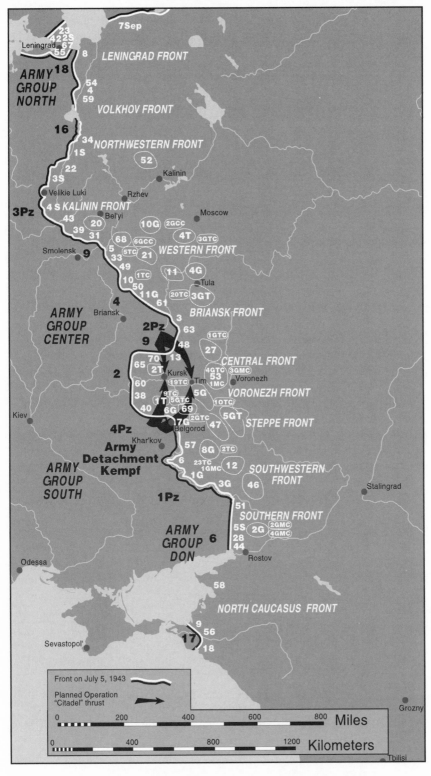

Map 2. Situation on the German-Soviet Front, 4 July 1943

to serve in the uniform. One million of these newfound replacements went to Western Europe, to flesh out the German units reconstituted after Stalingrad. Nevertheless, by 30 May 1943, this enormous effort had brought the German armed forces to their highest strength (9.5 million) of the entire war.[10]

In February 1943 Hitler recalled Heinz Guderian from disgrace to oversee the reconstruction of the mechanized forces, on which everything depended. Guderian had virtually created the panzer arm in the 1930s, and now he repeated his performance as Inspector-General of Panzer Troops. The competing bureaucracies of the Third Reich impeded his efforts, but with Hitler's backing and Speer's cooperation he achieved miracles of production, organization, and training.[11] Beginning as soon as the *rasputitsa* halted active operations, Guderian poured replacement troops and equipment into the panzer divisions of the Eastern Front. Most of these divisions were withdrawn from the front and given the time to retrain and rebuild. Guderian's own goal of 400 tanks per division was never even approached, but by June 1943 many panzer divisions once again possessed 100 to 130 tanks each, thereby regaining much of the combat power of previous years.

Guderian also attempted to increase the supply of self-propelled assault guns, which were a cheap form of armored support for infantry troops, and of armored half-tracks, so essential for the reconnaissance and infantry troops of mechanized divisions. The demands for high-grade steel for the new tanks meant that some of these assault guns were constructed with lower quality materials.

Such specialized equipment rarely filtered down to the average infantry or even panzer division. Germany's system of competing political fiefdoms was reflected in competing elite units, of which the most important were the Waffen (combat) SS divisions. The actual organization of these divisions changed frequently, but in general such units had more and better equipment than their counterparts in the regular German Army. In 1943 a typical Waffen SS division generally had more than 150 tanks, including the newest tank designs discussed below. In addition, an SS division usually had a battalion of self-propelled assault guns and enough armored half-tracks to mount most or all of its infantry and reconnaissance troops. The Panzer Grenadier Division *Grossdeutschland,* while not part of the Waffen SS, was equally favored in assault guns and armored personnel carriers. By contrast, an ordinary panzer division often had only one company of assault guns and one or two companies of half-tracks, with the remainder of its troops mounted in vulnerable trucks.[12] Such a division included two or three battalions of Panzer III and IV medium tanks, five battalions of infantry, and three battalions of towed medium artillery, plus specialized units of combat engineers, antitank gunners, and signal troops. Although nominally authorized at 13,000 to 17,000 men, the average 1943 panzer division, despite all Guderian's efforts, was probably closer to 10,000 or 11,000.

At the bottom of the pecking order, the infantry divisions that made up most of the German Army were steadily losing their combat capabilities. In the spring of 1942, sixty-nine of the seventy-five infantry divisions in Army Groups North and Center had been reorganized to reflect these losses. The old structure of nine infantry battalions and artillery batteries of four guns each was replaced by an organization of six infantry battalions with three-gun batteries. In essence, therefore, these divisions were expected to perform the same missions with two-thirds of their previous combat power.[13] By the spring of 1943, this reduced organization became almost universal on the Eastern Front, and an infantry division was fortunate to have 8,000 effectives, supplemented by up to 1,000 unarmed Russian "helpers." Continuing reductions in available horses and motor vehicles made this infantry division far less mobile than its 1941 predecessor. Soviet attackers sometimes overran German artillery batteries because the guns could not be moved, and German infantry units had to use bicycles for reconnaissance and local counterattack forces.

To complicate matters further, German infantry divisions were almost helpless against concentrated Soviet armor. The 37mm antitank guns with which they had entered the Soviet Union were largely ineffectual against the standard T-34 Soviet medium tank. In 1942 most divisions had received a limited number of new, 75mm antitank guns, but ammunition for these guns was often in short supply. Thus, the German infantry division was reduced to a passive role, holding long stretches of the front line with only limited offensive or defensive capability.

TIGERS, PANTHERS, AND ELEPHANTS

Like many amateur soldiers, Adolf Hitler was fascinated with new weaponry.[14] Throughout the war he frequently interfered in weapons' design and then placed exaggerated confidence in the results of his interference. Nowhere was this tendency more apparent than in the development of new tanks in 1943. Quite apart from the resurrection of the German Army, Hitler was convinced that these new designs would ensure victory at Kursk.

The sudden surge in new German tanks entering service in the summer of 1943 was the belated outcome of the "tank terror" that had gripped German troops in the summer of 1941 after the first encounters with the Soviet T-34 medium tank and KV (Klementi Voroshilov) heavy tank. In the short term, the two existing German medium tanks, the Panzer III (Panzer Kampfwagen—Pz.Kpfw.III) and Panzer IV (Pz.Kpfw.IV), were gradually upgraded with more effective guns and added armor. By the summer of 1942, the Panzer

IV was fitted with a long 75mm gun, which made it capable of penetrating the T-34 and KV tanks' armor. The Panzer III tank had too small a turret ring to permit such a weapon to be fitted; when production ended in February 1943 its chassis was used instead for the production of the Mark III (Sturmgeschutz, or StuG III) assault gun for infantry support. Although overshadowed by the more glamorous tanks, the Mark III assault guns provided the essential direct fire support for *Wehrmacht* infantry attacks. Quite apart from such assault guns, there were still some 432 Panzer III tanks of the later types with the long 5cm gun with the German units participating in Citadel; these could penetrate the T-34's frontal armor at ranges under 500 meters when using improved ammunition.

The upgunned Panzer IVG was the most common German medium tank type in service during the Kursk offensive, with a total of 841 tanks. It was roughly equivalent to the standard Soviet tank, the T-34 Model 1943. The Panzer IV had a superior gun, superior fire controls, a better three-man turret layout, and better radios. The Soviet T-34 had better armor and mobility. Both tanks could destroy one another at typical battle ranges, and the outcome was determined by tactics, training, and circumstance more than technical features. Prior to the Kursk operation, both the Panzer III and Panzer IV were fitted with side armor skirts to minimize the effects of the ubiquitous Soviet antitank rifles, which could otherwise penetrate their thinner side armor at close ranges.

The *Wehrmacht* began developing a heavy breakthrough tank prior to the 1941 encounters with the T-34. This entered series production in the autumn of 1942 as the Tiger I heavy tank (Mark VI). Armed with a version of the formidable 88mm antiaircraft gun and fitted with armor that was impervious to contemporary Soviet tank and antitank guns, the Tiger I was the most lethal tank on the battlefield in 1943. It could stand off and decimate Soviet tank formations from ranges of over 1,000 meters, where it was invulnerable to Soviet return fire. For example, on 5–6 July 1943, two companies from the 505th Heavy Panzer Detachment (battalion) destroyed 111 Soviet tanks for a loss of only 3 of their own.[15] Soviet tactics were to close with the Tigers as rapidly as possible and engage their thinner side and rear armor. These tactics were difficult to execute and the two Tiger detachments (battalions) during Citadel lost fewer than 10 tanks in combat while destroying several hundred Soviet tanks.

But each Tiger required more than 300,000 man-hours to build and only 1,354 were produced during the entire war, equal to less than a month of T-34 production. This enormous investment in scarce resources might have been better expended in producing simpler, more plentiful tanks, as was done by both the Soviets and Americans. Moreover, during the critical winter battles of 1942–43, Hitler sacrificed technological surprise by ordering the premature commitment of early-production Tigers to battle. A handful of the new tanks had little effect in the Stalingrad sector. Worse still for the Germans, on 14 January 1943, a Tiger tank was captured by the Red Army near Leningrad.

Although alerted to this deadly new threat, the Red Army did not have sufficient time to develop a suitable antidote to the Tiger. The first Soviet tanks capable of handling the Tiger, such as the KV-85 heavy tank, did not appear until after the Kursk battles. In the interim, the Soviets fielded a heavy self-propelled gun, the SU (*samokhodnaia ustanovka*, or mechanized mounting)-152. In only twenty-five days during January 1943, Soviet engineers married a 152mm field gun to an obsolescent tank chassis. The new weapon entered series production immediately; by May 1943, the first four heavy tank-killer regiments, each initially having only twelve SU-152s, were formed and sent to the front. In the coming battle, the SU-152 earned the nickname of *Zveroboi* (animal hunter) for its ability to defeat the new tanks, known as Tigers, Elephants, and Panthers.

However, there were few Tiger tanks available at the time of the Kursk battles. Walter Model's Ninth German Army had only two companies of 14 Tigers each (the 505th Heavy Panzer Detachment). In the south, von Manstein's Army Group South had a separate unit of 45 Tigers (the 503d Heavy Panzer Detachment), plus one Tiger company each in the *Grossdeutschland* Division and in the three SS divisions, for a total of 102 Tigers in the Army Group.[16]

The Tiger was deployed in special heavy tank units and was never intended to become the standard *Wehrmacht* tank. This mission was allotted to the new Panzer V, or Panther medium tank, which was developed as a direct response to the Soviet T-34. Originally, the Germans considered developing a close copy of the T-34 but instead decided to trump the Red Army by fielding an even heavier and better-armed tank. By the time of its initial deployment in the summer of 1943, the Panther was more than 50 percent heavier than any contemporary medium tank and would have been designated a heavy tank in any other army. The Panther's new long-barreled 75mm gun could penetrate any Soviet tank of the period, and its thick frontal armor was impervious to the standard Soviet 76.2mm tank gun. Its tactical vulnerability was its thinner side armor. Moreover, the Panther had been rushed into production and suffered serious teething problems in the spring of 1943. When first fielded in May, the Panther proved to be prone to engine fires and other breakdowns. Working feverishly, a special factory near Berlin rebuilt and reissued approximately 200 Panzer Vs in time for Kursk. These tanks were concentrated into two detachments (the 51st and 52d Panzer Detachments controlled by the 39th Panzer Regiment), but the design was still immature. During its first five days of fighting in July 1943, Panther strength was reduced to only 10 tanks; 123 were lost or damaged by enemy action and 46 to mechanical breakdowns.[17] The Panther developed a miserable reputation among German tankers during the Kursk fighting, but as the design matured through 1944, it would become the best tank of World War II. Yet, like the Tiger, it was woefully expensive and complicated to operate. Only 5,976 were built during the entire war, equal to only three months of Soviet tank production.[18]

Both the Panther and the Tiger went on to become superb weapons, but the same cannot be said for the third new design of 1943, the Elephant tank destroyer. This strange design was also known as the Ferdinand or Porsche Tiger, after its designer, Dr. Ferdinand Porsche. The Elephant had begun life as an unsuccessful entry in the design competition that Henschel had won with the Tiger I. Then Hitler asked for a new version of the Tiger that would carry a longer-barrelled (L71) version of the 88mm gun. Designing a turret to accommodate this gun was a time-consuming process, however. As an immediate response to the dictator's requirement, the long 88mm gun was mounted in a fixed armored casemate, producing a nonturreted assault gun on the Porsche chassis. While it was an adequate improvisation, the Elephant reflected the German penchant for diverting resources from the mass production of mundane but essential weapons in favor of the illusory advantages of small numbers of super-weapons. Hitler insisted upon fielding the Elephant in time for Kursk, and thus seventy-six of these strange vehicles were issued to the 653d and 654th Heavy Tank Destroyer Detachments (battalions). Moreover, because its intended role was to penetrate enemy armor at long range, the sixty-seven-ton Elephant was not equipped with any machine guns to protect itself against Soviet infantry with short-range antitank weapons.[19] As such, the Elephant had to remain in an overwatching position, well to the rear of the battle.

In May 1943 Speer and Guderian between them pushed tank production to a new monthly high of 988 vehicles, including 300 Panthers. Thereafter, production fell again because of production problems with the Panthers. Of the 1,866 tanks actually in the Kursk region in July, only 347 were these new wonder weapons, while the majority of tanks were the older Panzer III and IV. Hitler and Zeitzler were counting on the technical superiority of recently fielded, unreliable weapons. Despite frequent delays to allow further production and repair, only a few hundred of these new tanks, primarily the unreliable Panthers, were available for Citadel. To plagiarize Winston Churchill, never in the field of human endeavor has so much been expected by so many from so few.

WHY KURSK?

The defeat of Stalingrad, together with the Allied capture of North Africa in 1942–43, cost Germany more than just the troops who surrendered there.[20] Germany was visibly losing the initiative in the war, and its allies began looking for graceful exits. Italy and Rumania put out peace feelers, and Turkey finally decided not to attack the Soviet Union in the Caucasus. Tokyo had its hands full in the Pacific and clearly intended to respect its nonaggression agreement with Moscow. German foreign minister Joachim von Ribbentrop warned the Helsinki government that Berlin would never approve of a separate Finnish peace with the Soviets.[21]

Under the circumstances it was politically impossible for Germany to surrender the initiative on the Eastern Front. Although only fanatics believed that the Soviets could be decisively defeated, most senior leaders recognized the necessity for a renewed offensive.

Given von Manstein's brilliant successes in a mobile, mechanized defense, some of the German leadership considered deferring a renewed offensive until after they had absorbed the next Soviet offensive, an option that was sometimes described as hitting the Reds "on the backhand." Yet there was no guarantee that the Red Army would obligingly attack when and where the Germans wanted. In fact, the general impression among commanders like von Manstein was that the Germans had ended the winter campaign with a relative advantage over the Reds, an advantage that should be exploited by a renewed offensive as soon as the *rasputitsa* ended in April or early May. Thus, the concept of an immediate offensive "on the forehand" became common among German commanders and staff officers.

Even the optimistic Hitler had to recognize the limits of German combat power, though, especially if the new attacks would be launched after only six weeks of rest. In 1941 the German Army had been able to attack all across its front and had dissipated its efforts in too many directions. In 1942 Germany was still strong enough to economize in the north and attack in the south. Now, in 1943, Operation Citadel emerged as the most important in a series of limited offensives designed to consolidate the German defenses while inflicting sufficient damage on the Red Army to delay any Soviet offensive. Citadel in particular was expected to destroy two Soviet fronts while shortening the German defensive line by 120 kilometers.

On 13 March 1943, the German Army High Command (*Oberkommando des Heeres,* or OKH), as the responsible headquarters for the Eastern Front, issued Operations Order 5 (see appendix E for the full text). The order set the strategic context:

> It can be anticipated that the Russians will resume their attack after the end of the winter and the mud period and after a period of refitting and reconstitution.
>
> Therefore, the time has come for us to attack in as many sectors of the front as possible before he does—at least in one sector of the front, for example, in the Army Group South area of operations.

We must let them crash against the other sections of the front and bloody them. Here we must strengthen our defenses by committing heavy defensive weapons, by constructing positions, laying mines, establishing rear area positions, by maintaining mobile reserves, etc.

In addition, preparations must be made in all army group areas of operations. The attack formations must be refitted with personnel and equipment, and they must conduct training. Since the mud period is expected to end earlier this year than usual, each day must be used properly for the preparations. The army groups must report each week (every Monday) on the status of their preparations. The OKH will deploy the necessary equipment and heavy defensive weapons.[22]

In subsequent paragraphs Hitler detailed the specific missions assigned to each of his army groups, stating:

In detail, I order:
1. Army Group A . . .
2. Army Group South: . . .
On the northern flank of the army group a strong panzer army must be formed immediately, no later than mid-April, so that it will be ready for commitment at the end of the mud period, before the Russian offensive. The objective of this offensive is the destruction of enemy forces in the front of 2d Army by attacking to the north out of the Kharkov area in conjunction with an attack group from the 2d Panzer Army. Details on this attack, the command structure and force deployments, will follow in a special supplement.
3. Army Group Center:
First, the situation between the 2d and 2d Panzer Armies must be straightened out, then the defensive fronts are to be strengthened and equipped with antitank weapons as planned. This is especially important near Kirov, in the region north and northwest of Smolensk, as well as at Velikie Luki. Then an attack group is to be formed to attack in conjunction with the northern flank of Army Group South.[23]

Thus, by mid-April Army Groups Center and South were to assemble panzer forces on the flanks of the Kursk Bulge. A two-pronged attack to pinch off that bulge would begin as soon as the muddy season ended. To prepare for this offensive, German Army Group A, trapped in a Black Sea bridgehead in the far south, was ordered to transfer a number of divisions to von Manstein's Army Group South.

On the same day in March, Hitler began planning a series of other operations to accompany or follow Citadel. He instructed General Alfred Jodl, the operations chief of the Armed Forces High Command (*Oberkommando des Wehrmacht,* or OKW), to send a mountain division to Norway and to reinforce a panzer division being formed there in case Germany had to occupy Sweden. He also hoped to capture Leningrad, both for reasons of prestige and to shorten German lines in the north.

In late March Hitler seriously considered a series of operations (Habicht and Panther) to the southeast of Kursk, designed to push Soviet forces back from the industrial area of the Donets River (see Map 3). However, Hitler was unwilling to have these offensives interfere with the centerpiece attack at Kursk, and they were eventually canceled. Nonetheless, the twin operations retained a certain deceptive value.

On 15 April Operations Order 6 notified all participants to be ready to launch Citadel on six days' notice at any time after 28 April (see Appendix E for the text of the full order). In part, the order read:

> I have decided, as soon as the weather permits, to conduct "Zitadelle," the first offensive of the year.
>
> This attack is of the utmost importance. It must be executed quickly. It must seize the initiative for us in the spring and summer. Therefore, all preparations must be conducted with great circumspection and enterprise. The best formations, the best weapons, the best commanders, and great stocks of ammunition must be committed in the main efforts. Each commander and each man must be impressed with the decisive significance of this attack. The victory at Kursk must be a signal to all of the world. I hereby order:
>
> 1. The objective of the attack is to encircle enemy forces located in the Kursk area by rapid and concentrated attacks of shock armies from the Belgorod area and south of Orel and to destroy [the enemy] by concentrated attacks . . .
> 2. We must insure that
>   a. The element of surprise is preserved and the enemy be kept in the dark as to when the attack will begin.
>   b. The attack forces are concentrated on a narrow axis, in order to provide local overwhelming superiority of all means of attack (tanks, assault guns, artillery, rocket launchers, etc.) to insure contact between the two attacking armies and closure of the pocket.
>   c. The attack wedge is followed by forces from the depths to protect the flanks, so that the attack wedge itself will only have to be concerned with advancing.
>   d. The enemy will be given no respite and will be destroyed by prompt compression of the pocket.

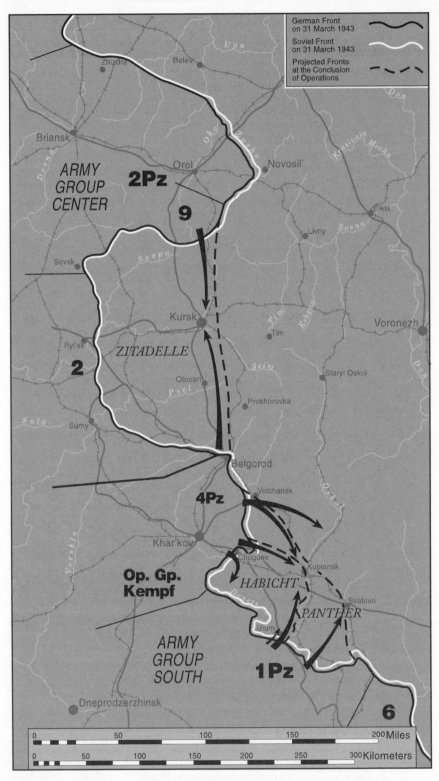

Map 3. Proposed Operations Habicht, Panther, and Citadel

e. The attack is conducted so quickly that the enemy will be denied the opportunity of . . . deploying strong reserves from other *fronts*.

f. Additional forces, particularly mobile formations, are freed up by quickly constructing a new *front*.

3. Army Group South sets out from the line Belgorod-Tomarovka with concentrated forces, passes through the line Prilepy-Oboyan, and makes contact with the attacking armies of Army Group Center east of and near Kursk. To cover the attack from the east, the line Nezhegol-Korocha sector—Skorodnoye-Tim is to be reached as soon as possible without threatening the concentration of forces on the main effort in the direction of Prilepy-Oboyan. Forces will be committed to protect the attack in the west, and they will later be used to attack into the pocket.

4. Army Group Center launches a concentrated attack from the line Trossna-north of Maloarkhangelsk with the main effort on the eastern flank, passes through the line Fatezh-Veretenovo, and establishes contact with the attacking army from Army Group South near and east of Kursk. . . . The line Tim-east of Shchigry—Sosna sector is to be reached as soon as possible. To protect the attack in the east, however, the concentration of forces on the main effort is not to be disturbed. Secondary forces will be committed to cover [the attack] from the west. . . .

5. The preparation of the forces from both army groups is to be conducted under the best possible deception measures. . . . The earliest date for the attack will be 3 May. . . .

6. To deceive the enemy, preparations for "Panther" will continue in the Army Group South area of operations. This is to be reinforced by all means available (conspicuous reconnaissance, deployment of tanks, assembly of crossing equipment, radio, agents, rumors, commitment of the Luftwaffe, etc.) and be kept up for as long as possible. These deception operations are to support the effective increase in the defensive strength of the Donets front. . . . Deception operations of this scale are not to be conducted in the Army Group Center area of operations, however, all means are to be employed to blur the enemy's picture of the situation.

SUSPENSE 24/4

[signed] Adolf Hitler, Lieutenant General Heusinger[24]

The same order also indicated that Citadel would be followed by Panther.

Thus, from its inception, Citadel was supposed to be launched as soon as possible after the end of the rainy season. The earlier the attack, the less prepared the Soviets would be, and the more time would be available for follow-on operations such as Panther and the capture of Leningrad.

However, the two reinforced armies designated to conduct Citadel—Ninth Army of Army Group Center and Fourth Panzer Army of Army Group

South—represented Hitler's entire strategic reserve in the East and could not be replaced if the offensive failed. Even a gambler like Hitler hesitated to roll the dice unless every possible precaution had been taken. On 30 April OKH issued the first of several postponement orders, in this case because of continued rains. As May turned into June, Hitler and his commanders repeatedly revisited the issue but failed to reach agreement. Time after time, the Germans prepared to launch Citadel, only to stop short.

CHAPTER 2

The Red Army in 1943

STALIN, ZHUKOV, AND SOVIET MILITARY STRATEGY

On 16 March 1943, Marshal of the Soviet Union Georgi K. Zhukov received a telephone call at the headquarters of the Northwestern Front, where he had been coordinating a major operation designed to raise the siege of Leningrad.[1] I. V. Stalin told his deputy supreme commander, "You may have to go to the Khar'kov area," where von Manstein's brilliant Donets Basin offensive was coming to a climax. By the time Zhukov reached the Voronezh Front two days later, however, the SS Panzer Corps had overrun Khar'kov, and the best he could do was to micro-manage the efforts of the local defenders who blocked a further German advance to the north.[2]

On the surface, this was just one of the innumerable fire brigade missions that Zhukov performed throughout the war. He was the most famous and most effective of the "*Stavka* representatives," the "fixers" who went from crisis to crisis making decisions and stiffening resolve. Zhukov's style was to be brutally frank with everyone, from Stalin on down, and then to insist on continuing an operation even when both sides seemed exhausted. He had learned that victory often went to the side that committed the last battalion, but implementing that lesson required incredible ruthlessness. For his part, Stalin tolerated Zhukov's ruthlessness and often overlooked his failures, for although casualty tolls were high in his operations, he was a proven "fighter."

In this case Zhukov's arrival at Kursk brought him back to the general arena of his greatest failure, the Mars offensive of the previous winter. Stalin had never voiced criticism for this disaster, even though both men knew that Mars had cost fully a half million casualties and had contributed indirectly to the creation of the Kursk Bulge. Despite the defeat in Mars, Zhukov and Stalin still shared a preoccupation with German Army Group Center. As long as that Army Group remained a solid mass poised along the Minsk-Smolensk-Moscow axis in European Russia, Moscow would never be entirely safe and the German Army would never be.ejected from the Motherland. Zhukov had failed to destroy Army Group Center in the Moscow Counteroffensive of 1941–42 and again in Operation Mars the following winter. Zhukov's preoccupation with Army Group Center would persist until its final destruction in the summer of 1944. In the case of Kursk, however, this myopic concern caused Zhukov and his peers to focus on the northern flank of the bulge, somewhat neglecting the threat from Army Group South.

In outline, the German plan for Citadel was as obvious to the Soviets as it was to the Germans. The central question for the *Stavka* was how to respond to near-certain German offensive action. Soviet planners had debated their future strategy since German planners had begun their work in early April, and at least initially there was no unanimity. Stalin and some of his more bellicose *front* commanders, like Vatutin, argued for a resumption of offensive action in early summer to preempt German action and to regain the offensive momentum lost in March 1943. Chastened by earlier experiences, however, Zhukov, Vasilevsky, and various General Staff officers urged caution and recommended that the Red Army remain on the defensive until the Germans had expended their offensive strength. Once the German thrust was halted, they argued, the Soviets could launch its decisive strategic offensive.[3]

A 2 April 1943 directive from A. M. Vasilevsky, Chief of the General Staff, to all *front* and army commanders reflected this strategic debate. On the one hand, the directive ordered commanders to "use the period of the spring *rasputitsa* to organize better defensive positions, particularly antitank, to develop defenses, and to create reserves on main axes, and also to improve force combat training." On the other hand, the directive ordered them to 'pay primary attention to matters of organizing and conducting offensive battles and operations and, in particular, to coordination among types of forces.'"[4]

The following day Vasilevsky ordered *front* commands and intelligence organization at every level to intensify their intelligence collection effort. Disturbed that the spring thaw and cessation of major operations had "reduced the receipt of information from force intelligence" and "obscured enemy regrouping," he added: "I ask you now to pay the most serious attention to all types of reconnaissance, and it is obligatory that you capture prisoners of war so that you can constantly follow all changes in the enemy grouping and determine in timely fashion the axes on which the enemy is concentrating his forces, in particular, his tank forces."[5]

This directive began a massive and vital intelligence collection effort that would endure unabated until the very day of the German attack. This effort embraced the entire Soviet intelligence apparatus at home and abroad, both in the air and on the ground, as well as the extensive collection network in the German rear area, which was controlled by Central Partisan Headquarters. The focal point of all intelligence collection was the timely identification of force concentrations at the tactical, operational, and strategic levels and the movement of operational and strategic reserves between German army groups and forward from the German strategic rear (Germany, France, etc.). While the *Stavka* was primarily concerned with potential German action in the Kursk region, however, it avoided its errors of previous years by surveying German activities and intent across the entire Soviet-German front. As the victims of earlier surprises, in 1943 the *Stavka* was acutely aware that surprise was a superb teacher.

Soon after, as was the custom, Stalin and Vasilevsky solicited strategic assessments from key *Stavka* members. The 10 April directive to *front* commanders, signed by the 1st Deputy Chief of the General Staff and Chief of the General Staff's Operational Directorate, Lieutenant General A. I. Antonov, read, "I request that you report your assessment of the opposing enemy and his possible operational axes by 12.4.43."[6] On 8 April Zhukov responded, predicting that the Germans would first attack at Kursk, then attempt to encircle Soviet troops south of the bulge, and finally turn against Moscow (see appendices for full text). He counseled caution, concluding: "I do not consider it necessary for our troops to mount a preventive offensive in the next few days. It will be better if we wear the enemy out in defensive action, destroy his tanks, and then, taking in fresh reserves, by going over to an all-out offensive, we will finish off the enemy's main grouping."[7] Zhukov underscored the most important attack indicator—the movement and concentration of German armored forces.

Two days later, Lieutenant General M. S. Malinin, Chief of Staff of the Central Front, whose forces were poised along the northern shoulder of the bulge, submitted his and *front* commander K. K. Rokossovsky's strategic appreciation. Malinin predicted the same sequence of events, with the German offensive to begin by mid-May (see Appendix F for key Soviet documents). Malinin assessed that the offensive would materialize along the Kursk and Voronezh operational axes, adding, "There is hardly likely to be an enemy offensive in other sectors."[8] He hinted that the *Stavka* could take preventive action against German forces concentrated in the Orel salient by mounting an attack on Orel with forces of the Western, Briansk, and Central Fronts. In any case, he urged the *Stavka* to establish strong strategic reserves disposed from Elets in the north to Voronezh in the south.

On 12 April Vatutin and his Voronezh Front staff weighed in with their assessment (see appendices for the full text). Vatutin noted German armored concentrations and also predicted a German attack against the flanks of the Kursk Bulge from Orel and Belgorod toward Kursk. Although he added that German forces could then attack southeastward into the Southwestern Front's rear area (reflecting German plans Panther and Habicht), he considered a subsequent northeasterly thrust toward Moscow more likely, with secondary attacks to the south. Like Rokossovsky and Malinin, Vatutin urged the *Stavka* to create strong reserves and to deploy them along the entire threatened front.[9]

On 12 April Zhukov, Vasilevsky, and Antonov met in Moscow to argue their case with Stalin. Armed with Vatutin's and Rokossovsky's appreciations, the three convinced Stalin of the necessity of conducting an initial defensive phase of the summer strategic offensive. Major General S. M. Shtemenko, then 1st Deputy of the General Staff's Operational Directorate, later wrote of these meetings: "Ultimately it was decided to concentrate our main forces in the Kursk area, to bleed the enemy forces here in a defensive operation, and then to switch to the offensive and achieve their full destruction. To provide against eventualities, it was considered necessary to build deep and secure defenses along the whole strategic front, making them particularly powerful in the Kursk sector."[10]

Consequently, after mid-April Red Army headquarters and troops in the Kursk region began to prepare their defenses against the expected German attack in accordance with *Stavka* instructions. These preparations signaled Soviet intentions to undertake a deliberate defense before launching the general strategic counteroffensive. At this stage it was fairly clear that the Voronezh, Central, Southwestern, and Briansk Fronts would likely be the focal point of initial defensive efforts. While the *Stavka* prepared its definitive operational plan, it paid particular attention to deploying strategic reserves to cover any eventuality. Zhukov later described the rationale for distributing these reserves so widely:

> At the same time, it was decided in which sectors the Supreme Command's reserves should be concentrated. It was intended to deploy them in the Livny-Stary Oskol-Korocha area, where defenses were to be organized should the enemy break through in the Kursk bulge area. Other reserves were to be stationed behind the right flank of the Bryansk Front in the Kaluga-Tula-Yefremov area. The 5th Guards Tank Army and a number of other formations of the Supreme High Command's reserves were to prepare for action beyond the junction of the Voronezh and Southwestern Fronts, in the Liski area.[11]

Shtemenko, on the General Staff, attested to Stalin's caution:

> No one had any doubts that the Central and Voronezh Fronts would play the main role in the defensive actions. It was not impossible that the Briansk and Southwestern Fronts would also participate in this. Zhukov and Malinovsky were convinced that the Southwestern Front would be attacked. Since its own reserves were not strong enough, they insisted that an army, or at least a tank corps, from the GHQ reserves should be stationed behind its junction with the Voronezh Front.[12]

With preliminary planning complete, on 21 April 1943, the *Stavka* issued directives implementing its strategy for the summer campaign. The *Stavka VGK* directive of 21 April 1943 to Rokossovsky's Central Front read:

As a result of our forces' advance during the period of winter operations in 1942/1943, a number of *fronts* have violated the requirements of the *Stavka* directive of 15.10.1942 concerning the establishment of a frontal zone of twenty-five kilometers in which the residing and access of the civilian population is prohibited. All *front* commanders will in timely fashion undertake measures to create new frontal zones which conform to the altered situation of the *front*.

The *Stavka* of the Supreme High Command Orders:

1. Establish a frontal zone . . . and, by 10 May of this year, complete the evacuation of the entire civilian population to the rear beyond the bounds of a twenty-five-kilometer zone from the formerly occupied front lines, including [the population of] Maloarkhangel'sk, Ponyri, Korenevo, Dmitriev-L'govskii, and L'gov.

Establish the rear boundary of the frontal zone for the Central Front along the line: Griaznoe, Viazovatoe, Vas'kovo, Voinovo, Topki, Khmelevaia, Lukovets, Goriainovo, Nizhnee Smorodnoe, Gor'ki, Khlynino, Mikhailovka, Krupets, Kuznetsovka, Arbuzovo, Shustovo, Sherekino, Ekaterinovka, and Pogrebki—all points inclusive for the frontal zone.

2. Immediately set about constructing two [to] three military defensive lines, following one after another, in the frontal zone and accommodate all population points in this zone for defense.

Prepare all towns and large population points in the frontal zone from which the civilian population must have been evacuated for defense, irrespective of their distance from the front lines. . . .

3. Immediately report fulfillment of this directive.

[signed] Stalin, A. Vasilevsky[13]

Analogous orders went to all participating *fronts*.

To bolster forward defenses and to provide forces necessary to convert temporary defense into a decisive strategic offensive, Stalin ordered the formation and deployment of strong strategic reserves. The nucleus of this reserve force was the newly formed Steppe Military District, commanded by Colonel General I. S. Konev, which during the upcoming operation was to deploy into combat as the Steppe Front.[14]

On 23 April 1943 the *Stavka* issued Konev his instructions:

1. During the period of its formation, simultaneous with its missions of combat training, Steppe Military District forces are assigned the following missions:

    a. In the event the enemy assumes the offensive before the district's forces are ready, care must be taken to cover firmly the following axes: Livny, Elets, and Ranenburg; Shchigry, Kastornoe, and Voronezh; Valuiki, Alekseevka, and Liski; Roven'ki, Rossosh', and Pavlovsk; and Starobel'sk, Kantemirovka, Boguchar, and the Chertkovo region, and Millerovo.

In accordance with the force grouping, the commander of district forces will organize careful study by unit and formation commanders and their staffs of these axes and the capabilities for developing positions.

    b. Undertake, study, and prepare to defend a line along the left bank of the Don River from Voeikovo, through Lebedan', Zadonsk, Voronezh, Liski, and Pavlovsk, to Boguchar. The line must be ready by 15 June 1943.

    c. Carry out reconnaissance of a defensive line along the line Efremov . . . to the Northern Donets River to determine the state of defensive installations along it . . . and to select that line correctly. . . .

    2. Forces, headquarters, and commanders will prepare mainly for offensive battle and operations, for penetrating enemy defensive zones as well as for executing powerful counterstrokes with our forces, for rapidly fortifying positions which we have captured, for repelling enemy counterstrokes, for countering massive tank and air strikes, and for night operations.[15]

This directive placed armies of the Steppe Military District in position to counter German offensive action across a broad front from Orel in the north to Voroshilovgrad in the south. So disposed, Konev's forces covered all potential German attack axes and, not coincidentally, countered all three German operational plans (Citadel, Habicht, and Panther).

Soviet planning intensified in May as *front* commanders implemented the *Stavka* directive. While honing their defenses, they also pondered the offensive actions that had to follow. Goaded on by nervous senior commanders, staff officers and commanders at every level methodically worked out the myriad of problems associated with strategic-level positional defense, while reserve and mobile force commanders studied how to implement maneuver defense if it became necessary. To a greater or lesser extent, commanders, staff officers, and common soldiers were haunted by the terrible realization that never before had the Red Army halted a determined German offensive short of the strategic depths. At Kursk this was the unprecedented mission assigned them by Stalin.

Given this extensive Soviet planning, almost from its inception, the Citadel plan had no chance of strategic surprise. The most that German commanders could hope for was to catch the Soviets before they had recovered from the defeats of late winter. Despite this loss of surprise, however, few German commanders or soldiers questioned their ability to achieve tactical and operational success. Where they existed, German doubts concerned the *Wehrmacht's* ability to sustain victory to strategic depths and the nagging fear of what would transpire if they did not. The twin specters of Moscow and Stalingrad fueled these doubts.

SOVIET FORCE STRUCTURE

The German commanders who prepared for Kursk thought of their opponents as tenacious but inept fighters who had difficulty coordinating the many ingredients necessary for modern warfare. Yet, as in the previous two years, the Red Army of 1943 continued its metamorphosis of structure and procedure. Special staff officers compiled historical after-action reports within weeks of the conclusion of the winter campaigns, and the lessons learned from previous mistakes were disseminated throughout the hierarchy. The Red Army's commanders, even those as experienced as Zhukov, continued to make mistakes to the very end of the war, but their average level of performance improved continually.

The Germans had several surprises waiting for them at Kursk. First and foremost was the continued development of Soviet mechanized forces. The Stalingrad operation and the winter campaign had proven the utility of the tank corps and mechanized corps structure, and V. M. Badanov's and M. M. Popov's deep raids in command of several such corps had proven the value of creating a larger structure capable of independent mechanized operations.[16]

Although various "tank armies" had participated in the 1942 campaigns, these had been ad hoc, mixed formations of armor, cavalry, and infantry. On 28 January 1943, the State Defense Committee (*Gosudarstvennyi Komitet Oborony,* or GKO), the highest body in the Soviet defense structure, took the next logical step. Decree No. 2791 directed the creation of tank armies of homogenous composition, with all elements able to move cross-country at the same pace.[17] In theory, each tank army consisted of two tank corps, one mechanized corps, and various supporting units for a total of approximately 48,000 men and 450 to 560 tanks. The actual organization of the five (later six) tank armies varied considerably. The principle involved, however, remained decisive. For the first time in the war, Germany's opponents were creating large-scale armored and mechanized forces capable of independent, deep operations. The tank army was equivalent in size and capability to the panzer corps that had spearheaded the blitzkrieg campaigns. For the remainder of the war, the Soviet tank armies became steadily more important until their success or failure generally determined the success or failure of an entire campaign.

The basic building blocks of the Soviet armored and mechanized force were thirty-four tank and thirteen mechanized corps. Some of these were merged into the new tank armies and others provided mobile armored support for field armies. Both type formations were in the process of reform in summer 1943. The tank corps consisted of three tank brigades, a motorized rifle brigade, and an increasing array of supporting arms. Depending on the strength of their component tank brigades (53 or 65 tanks organized into two or three battalions), the corps contained from 168 to 204 tanks and, sometimes, a varying number of self-propelled guns. Three types of mechanized corps existed ranging in strength from 204 up to 224 tanks depending on their armored complement. Mechanized corps armor was organized into three tank regiments or one or two tank brigades.

These sophisticated mechanized units required sophisticated mechanized commanders, and by 1943 the Red Army had grown its own armored leaders. Commanding tank units in the midst of battle required initiative, a willingness to make snap decisions without contacting higher authority. Such traits clash with the traditional German and Western stereotype of Soviet soldiers, yet in fact Stalin found and nurtured a number of such independent commanders. Typical of these men was Pavel Alekseevich Rotmistrov, who received command of the newly formed 5th Guards Tank Army in February 1943, at the age of forty-two. Short, bespectacled, and with a small mustache, Rotmistrov looked like a college professor, and indeed he had taught at the Frunze Staff Academy and written articles on tank operations. Yet Rotmistrov had also fought in the Civil War, the Finnish War, and the undeclared war with Japan. Between 1940 and 1943, Rotmistrov had commanded, in succession, a tank battalion, a tank brigade, a tank corps, and an ad hoc group of three such corps. Summoned to see Stalin on several occasions, Rotmistrov had bluntly described the advantages of German panzer organizations and disadvantages of earlier Soviet tank structures. His style as a commander was to use deception, surprise attack, and unconventional tactics whenever possible. He was called upon to use all his skill in the climactic struggles of Kursk.[18]

Change in the 1943 Red Army went far beyond the elite tank forces. The task of halting the upcoming German offensive belonged primarily to the conventional rifle (infantry) formations of the Soviet Union, and these formations were also in the midst of a transformation. In the crisis of 1941, when specialized weapons and qualified staff officers had both been in short supply, the *Stavka* had adopted a very simplified structure that represented stark reality. Rifle divisions were reduced from an authorized strength of 14,843 soldiers to just under 11,000, a bare-bones organization of nine infantry battalions with twenty-four guns for minimum field artillery support. The division also lost 64 percent of its authorized wheeled vehicles. Antitank, antiaircraft, armor, engineer, and most field artillery units were centralized under control of the rifle army, a structure that often consisted of only four or five rifle divisions plus a few specialized support regiments and brigades. The rifle corps, which in most Western armies was a tactical grouping of three or four rifle divisions, was almost eliminated as a luxury the Soviets could not afford.[19]

In the course of the year 1942–43, the Red Army finally acquired sufficient weapons and qualified officers to make its combat organization more sophisticated and elaborate. In some field armies, the rifle corps reappeared as a headquarters between division and army levels.[20] At every level of command, artillery, antitank guns, mortars, engineers, and infantry support tanks became more plentiful. Communications equipment, a recurring weakness of the Red Army, also became more plentiful and reliable, at least at the rifle army and *front* levels.

For example, von Manstein's efforts to relieve Stalingrad in December had come to nothing when he encountered the 2d Guards Army, one of the first multi-corps field armies in the Soviet force structure. Such a high-priority army often consisted of three corps of three divisions each, plus artillery, antitank, engineer, and infantry support tank brigades. A few favored rifle armies also controlled a separate tank or mechanized corps for local counterattack or short-range offensive action. Still, numerous rifle armies in unimportant sectors remained almost unaffected by this wealth of resources because the emphasis was always given to formations with high-priority missions.

Similarly, in the spring and early summer of 1943, the Reds formed the first antiaircraft artillery divisions, antitank artillery (destroyer) brigades, and artillery penetration divisions and corps. For the rest of the war, such formations, each of which contained multiple regiments and brigades with hundreds of gun tubes, were frequently redeployed to support rifle armies and *fronts* making the main attack or principal defense of a campaign. The whirlwinds of shrapnel that engulfed German troops and aircraft were made possible only by such ruthless prioritization of effort.

RED ARMOR, TRUCKS, AND ANTITANK WEAPONS

Compared to Germany, the Soviet Union took a fundamentally different approach to armored vehicle design and production.[21] The Red Army started the war with two tanks that were clearly superior to German tanks of the period, the T-34 medium tank and the KV-1 heavy tank. The Soviet military-industrial policy of the year 1942–43 maximized tank production at the expense of tank modernization. Technical improvements to the T-34 and KV-1, except those connected with increasing production, were intentionally minimized and Soviet tank design stagnated. The Soviet tank inventory rose from 7,700 tanks in January 1942 to 20,600 tanks at the beginning of 1943, in spite of massive combat losses in 1942, largely as a result of this highly successful industrial program. In contrast, German tank inventories rose far more modestly during the same period, from 4,896 in January 1942 to 5,648 in January 1943. As a result, the Soviet tank force during the Kursk battles had a substantial numerical advantage over the German panzer force. In comparison to the new German tanks, though, the Red tank force was at its lowest qualitative level of the entire war.

Technically, the Soviet tank force in the summer of 1943 was not significantly different from the summer of 1942. The Soviet tank plants were turning out T-34 medium tanks in increasing numbers, and this tank had become the staple of the Red Army's tank and mechanized corps. It was still armed with the same 76mm gun as in 1942 and protected by the same level of armor. The KV-1 heavy tank had proven a disappointment in 1942, having no firepower advantage over the T-34. Nor was its armor invulnerable to German antitank weapons as it had been in 1941. Its weight caused mobility problems without conferring relative invulnerability, and it was plagued by lingering technical problems, especially a poor transmission. As a result, its armor thickness was actually reduced in 1942, and in the autumn of 1942 the KV-1 was removed from the tank corps and segregated into separate tank regiments (with twenty-one tanks) for infantry support.[22] A portion of the heavy tank production lines at Cheliabinsk shifted to T-34 production, and consideration was given to ending heavy tank production completely in favor of the T-34.

The Red Army's one major attempt during the year 1942–43 to reconfigure its tank designs was a dead end. In June 1942, the Red Army embarked on a new "universal tank." The idea was to combine the better armor of the KV-1 with the superior mobility of the T-34; the tank gun remained the same. The universal tank would replace both the T-34 and the KV-1. The heavier armor was necessary as the advent of the German long 75mm gun in May 1942 had made the T-34 vulnerable for the first time to the standard German Mark IV tank at normal combat ranges. Two designs were competitively developed, an up-armored and improved T-34 called the T-43, and a reduced-weight KV called the KV-13. While the idea of standardizing on a single type was desirable, the focus on armored protection proved to be a mistake.

A universal tank might have entered production in the summer of 1943 but for the arrival of the excellent new German tanks. Tiger Is were encountered in small numbers on the Leningrad front starting in January 1943, and one was promptly captured by the Soviets and examined. It was clear that the Tiger's heavy firepower and thick armor completely undermined the universal tank designs, which were unceremoniously canceled. This decision came too late for the Soviet tank plants to develop a better armed medium tank to challenge the Tiger on more equal footing. As described in Chapter 1, a small number of improvised tank destroyers, the SU-152, were created by mounting a 152mm gun-howitzer on the KV-1 chassis. The inadequately armed "universal tank" requirement indicated that the Red Army did not anticipate the German shift toward heavier, better armed tanks and was unprepared with a new tank gun capable of dealing with them. As a result of the Kursk battles, the policy was changed, and the Red Army began receiving the up-armed T-34/85 medium with a new 85mm gun and the IS-2m heavy tank with a 122mm gun by March 1944.

In the area of light tanks, in 1943 the T-60 light tank was being joined by the modestly improved T-70 light tank. Both types would have disappeared but for the fact that the automotive factories where they were built did not have heavy machinery capable of turning out T-34s. By the spring of 1943, their production was coming to a close. Red Army needs for light reconnaissance tanks were being satisfied by Lend-Lease types such as the Anglo-Canadian Valentine light tank, while the T-70 tank chassis was better employed as the basis for a new assault gun, the SU-76M. The SU-76M combined the hull of the T-70 with the ubiquitous 76.2mm ZIS-3 divisional gun. The resulting armored vehicle was intended for direct fire support of the infantry, much like the German Mark III assault gun, and it would become the second most numerous type of Soviet armored vehicle of World War II after the T-34 tank. Kursk saw the first large-scale deployment of the SU-76M.[23]

Lend-Lease tank shipments from Britain, Canada, and the United States amounted to 16 percent of Soviet wartime tank production. The Red Army held a generally disparaging view of Allied tanks, comparing them very unfavorably to the T-34. The American M3 Lee medium tank was the subject of special derision, being sardonically called the "grave for seven brothers." This opinion was shared by U.S. and British troops still using this archaic design in Tunisia in 1943. Yet, British and American light tanks were no worse than the Soviet T-60/T-70. According to German intelligence, in 1943 about 20 percent of Soviet tank brigades were of mixed Soviet/Lend-Lease composition, and another 15 percent were equipped entirely with Lend-Lease types.[24]

Although Lend-Lease tanks did not play a substantial role at the time of the Kursk fighting, Lend-Lease trucks and jeeps made a major contribution. By June 1943, the Soviet Union had received over 17,000 jeeps and more than 90,000 trucks from the United States alone. These shipments were especially important since the Soviet automotive industry had been shifted over to light armored vehicle production and Soviet wartime vehicle production was inadequate. Furthermore, the U.S. vehicles were immeasurably superior to existing Soviet trucks, which were mostly license-produced copies of mid-1930s U.S. commercial trucks. U.S. trucks and jeeps became the backbone of Soviet logistics, moving Soviet troops, guns, ammunition, and supplies. Without such transportation, the Red Army would have been hamstrung in its efforts to conduct a sustained offensive, being forced to stop for lack of supplies after only a few days of battle. In a battle of attrition such as Kursk, this logistical support proved critical to victory. It is therefore not surprising that even today "Studebaker" and "Villies" are familiar words to Russian veterans of the Great Patriotic War (as it is known there) and virtually synonymous to "truck" and "jeep."

The Red Army's antitank weapons in 1943 were a mixed bag and generally inferior to the *Wehrmacht's*. By the summer of 1943, the Red Army was finally beginning to receive the excellent ZIS-2 57mm towed antitank gun, deferred for political reasons in 1941. It was more than adequate to deal with the standard German tanks of the day such as the Panzer IV. However, it was inadequate in frontal engagements against the new German Panther or Tiger tanks. As a result of the 57mm's delayed entry into service, the Red Army was still dependent on large numbers of the prewar 45mm Model 1932 antitank gun, which by 1943 was completely inadequate to penetrate the front of any German medium tank. In 1943, a modernization program was begun on these weapons resulting in the 45mm Model 1943 antitank gun, which had some modest capabilities against lighter German armored vehicles.

The Soviets organized their antitank guns into antitank battalions, regiments, and brigades assigned to divisions, corps, armies, and *fronts,* respectively. The antitank regiment contained twenty-four antitank guns of varying calibers, while the brigade consisted of seventy-two guns.[25] In general, army antitank regiments supported first echelon rifle divisions or corps, and the brigades supported armies.

The Red Army's greatest area of weakness was in infantry antitank weapons. By 1943, most major armies were fielding lightweight antitank rocket grenade launchers with shaped charge warheads capable of penetrating existing levels of tank armor. These included the German *Panzerfaust/ Panzerschreck* (literally, "panzer fist"), the British PIAT, and the American bazooka. Although the Red Army had been pioneers in this field in the 1930s, the purges had killed off the principal designers. As a result, the Red Army's infantry was still armed with the embarrassingly obsolete PTRD 14.5mm antitank rifle. These antitank rifles were organized into battalions under *front* control. During combat the *fronts* allocated these battalions to armies for use in support of defending first echelon rifle divisions. Although this rifle could still penetrate the thinner side armor of older German tanks at very close ranges, the lack of a modern lightweight antitank weapon made the Russian infantry particularly vulnerable to German tank attack. The German use of armored skirts on their tanks in 1943 undermined the effectiveness of the antitank rifles, and the Red infantry was forced to employ almost suicidal tactics, such as improvised explosive charges, when confronted with tanks.

RED WINGS

The Red Air Force of 1943, like its ground counterpart, had seen important improvements since 1942.[26] The Iliushin IL-2 *Shturmovik* was an effective ground-attack aircraft known for its durability and armored protection. It was built in larger numbers than any other combat aircraft of World War II and was the bane of the *Wehrmacht* in the later years of the war as Soviet pilot skills and tactics improved.

The Red Air Force had been handled ruthlessly by the Luftwaffe in the first two years of the war, due to Soviet technical inferiority in equipment and training. By 1943, the Red Air Force was finally getting fighter aircraft equivalent to standard Luftwaffe types. The new Lavochkin LA-5FN entered service in the summer of 1943 in time for Kursk and had speed equivalent or better than the German FW-190A-4 and Bf-109G-4.[27] The Yakovlev fighters were also improving in quality with newer types such as the Yak-9. In general, the Soviet fighters had a better performance at lower altitudes, while the German aircraft tended to have better high-altitude performance and were often more heavily armed. Ironically, some of the top Soviet aces flew Lend-Lease aircraft such as the P-39 Airacobra that most air forces would have considered obsolete.

As on the ground, the Reds enjoyed a significant numerical advantage in the air. By 1943 the Luftwaffe was stretched thin. The bulk of German fighters and antiaircraft guns were concentrated in Germany to defend the Reich from Allied strategic bombing. From March 1943 onward, German fighter losses in the West consistently exceeded those in the East, even at the height of the Kursk battle.[28] The few Luftwaffe aircraft that remained in the East were short of fuel and in constant demand to provide close air support to the German Army in the field. The only advantage Luftwaffe commanders had was the Freya tactical radar system, which could provide warning of incoming aircraft at a range of twenty-four kilometers. This range was barely sufficient for interceptor aircraft to scramble in response.[29] In short, the Luftwaffe was no longer able to guarantee air superiority in the East. Soviet pilots were often able to achieve significant results, but only at great cost of men and machines.

THE PLANNERS AND THE FIGHTERS

Unlike Hitler, Stalin avoided large conferences; the Soviet mania for security usually meant that future planning was initially restricted to a handful of senior commanders. But that planning process now involved far more extended consultations than it had in the past. The all-powerful Stalin could and did relieve, replace, and intimidate his generals, and his commissar cronies like L. Z. Mekhlis still plied their insidious trade, although with far less power than during the initial two years of war.[30] Stalin's arbitrary decisions had contributed to the military disasters in 1941 and 1942, when the specter of defeat and his distrust of even his finest generals brought out the worst in the dictator. By 1943 the crisis had passed and ultimate victory seemed certain, if remote. Stalin knew which generals he could trust, and his position of authority was sufficiently secure for him to recognize his limitations as strategic planner and Red Army Generalissimo. Hence, he sought and often heeded the counsel of his *Stavka* comrades and key military subordinates, particularly those who had passed the test of war. Among that number were men of considerable capacity.

The most important figures in Stalin's inner circle were the assertive Zhukov, the calm and rational Vasilevsky, and the penultimate planner and staff officer, Lieutenant General A. I. Antonov, Chief of the General Staff's Operations Directorate. While Zhukov, Vasilevsky, and others represented the *Stavka* at the front, Antonov frequently acted as Chief of Staff in Moscow.

At the age of forty-seven, Marshal of the Soviet Union Georgi Konstantinovich Zhukov, Deputy Supreme High Commander, 1st Deputy Commissar of Defense, and premier *Stavka* representative, was foremost among the emerging galaxy of battle-tested commanders surrounding Stalin.[31] A veteran cavalry officer of Russian Civil War fame, hero of the 1939 battle against the Japanese at Khalkhin Gol, and commander of the Kiev Special Military District in 1940, Zhukov had begun the war as Chief of the Red Army General Staff. During the terrible fighting of summer and fall of 1941, Zhukov orchestrated the furious if futile Soviet counteroffensive at Smolensk, which had contributed to the German High Command's decision to halt its drive on Moscow and, instead, to encircle Soviet forces stubbornly defending in the Kiev region. Zhukov had crossed swords with Stalin over the necessity for defending Kiev, and when his recommendation to abandon Kiev was overruled, Zhukov found himself exiled to Leningrad. In the disastrous October days, when the Germans resumed their advance on Moscow, Stalin summoned Zhukov to Moscow to stave off the looming disaster. Commanding in succession the Reserve and Western Fronts, Zhukov restored order from confusion and was instrumental in halting the German advance at the gates of the Russian capital.

In close coordination with Stalin, Zhukov organized and conducted the December 1941 Moscow counteroffensive and in January 1942 expanded that offensive into a grand but futile attempt to destroy German Army Group Center. Thereafter, Army Group Center became his nemesis, and Zhukov remained preoccupied with its destruction. Throughout spring and summer 1942, Zhukov strenuously argued that the Western Direction was the most critical axis for future operations. Overruled in May 1942, when Stalin approved the disastrous Khar'kov offensive in southern Russia, Zhukov remained in command in the north as the German armies spread into the depths of southern Russia.

While the drama unfolded in the south, Zhukov launched offensives against German forces near Briansk and Rzhev in July and August, all the while urging the *Stavka* to authorize a major new offensive to expel German Army Group Center from the distant approaches to Moscow. In October 1942 the *Stavka* finally acceded to his wishes. It approved the twin operations Mars and Uranus designed to defeat German forces at both Rzhev and Stalingrad and to alter decisively Soviet fortunes on the Eastern Front. Zhukov supervised the former and Vasilevsky the latter.

Zhukov was an energetic, stubborn, and often ruthless commander who approached war with dogged determination. His force of will, often combined with an utter disregard for casualties, propelled Soviet forces through their trials in the initial period of war and, ultimately, to victory. Like the American General Grant, he understood the terrible nature of modern war and could endure its effects. He demanded and received absolute obedience to orders, he identified with and protected key subordinates, and, at times, he stood up to and incurred the wrath of Stalin. There was little finesse in his operations, and he used the Red Army as a club rather than a rapier. His temperament was admirably suited to the nature of war on the Soviet-German front, and Stalin knew it. For this reason alone, Stalin could tolerate Zhukov's occasional failures.

Chief of the Red Army General Staff, forty-eight-year-old Colonel General Aleksandr Mikhailovich Vasilevsky, was arguably the Red Army's finest senior staff officer.[32] An infantryman who did not enjoy the benefits of being a member of Stalin's "cavalry clique," Vasilevsky rose through sheer merit and joined the General Staff after his graduation from the General Staff Academy in the purge-truncated class of 1937.[33] His critical work developing defense and mobilization plans in the months preceding the war made him the favorite of Chief of the General Staff B. M. Shaposhnikov and his heir apparent. Sheer merit explained Vasilevsky's rise from colonel to colonel general in the brief span of four years.

In August 1941, after being promoted to major general in June, Vasilevsky became Deputy Chief of the General Staff and Chief of the General Staff's Operational Directorate. The following June he succeeded Shaposhnikov as Chief of the General Staff, and in October he joined Zhukov as a Deputy Commissar of Defense. Vasilevsky's finest hour came in late fall when he served as principal planner and *Stavka* coordinator for Operations Uranus and Little Saturn, which tore the heart out of the *Wehrmacht* in southern Russia. Chastened somewhat by the strategic failures of February and March

1943 in the Donbas and around Khar'kov, on the eve of Kursk, Vasilevsky was ready to apply the lessons he had learned in those failures to forthcoming operations around Kursk, this time as *Stavka* coordinator for the Voronezh and Steppe Fronts.

Vasilevsky's even temperament and intellectual keenness balanced the sheer power, crudeness, and even brutality of Zhukov. Throughout the war, the two formed a superb team of effective *Stavka* troubleshooters, representatives, and commanders. Unlike Zhukov, whose fixation on German Army Group Center made him a "northerner," Vasilevsky's strategic vision spanned the entire front. Clearly junior to Zhukov at this stage of the war, his views were influential but not yet as decisive as they would come to be. In short, he lived with Stalin's and Zhukov's views but tended to moderate their excesses.

Unlike Zhukov and Vasilevsky, forty-six-year-old Colonel General Aleksei Innokent'evich Antonov, the future leading figure in the Red Army General Staff, had begun the war in relative obscurity.[34] A veteran of the World War and Civil War, Antonov remained relatively unknown until attending several Frunze Academy courses in the early 1930s, where he was recognized as "an excellent operations staff worker." His superb performance as Chief of the Khar'kov Military District's Operations Department during the 1935 Kiev maneuvers earned the praise of Defense Commissar K. E. Voroshilov and an appointment to the General Staff Academy, where he graduated with Vasilevsky in the class of 1937. Antonov next became Chief of Staff of the Moscow Military District under Stalin's favorite marshal, S. M. Budenny, and was posted to the Frunze Academy to replace purged faculty members.

Promoted to major general in June 1940 (like Vasilevsky), during the wholesale command changes of January 1941 Antonov became Chief of Staff of the Kiev Special Military District, where he was serving when war began. He survived the ignominious defeats of 1941 and at Khar'kov in May 1942, when he was serving as Southern Front Chief of Staff. In December 1942 Vasilevsky recognized Antonov's superb performance during the Battle for the Caucasus and brought Antonov into the General Staff as Chief of the Operational Directorate. There he would earn everlasting fame and praise from all who knew or worked with him.

It was this group of accomplished advisors who tempered Stalin's natural rashness during planning for the Kursk operation. Although Stalin occasionally wavered during the planning process and suggested the utility of preemptive action, he ultimately yielded to the compelling logic of their arguments. While accepting the defensive first phase of the Kursk operation, however, Stalin and his three generals unanimously agreed that the Kursk operation in particular and the summer campaign in general would be fundamentally offensive in nature. Even though they agreed to absorb the initial German attack, they were determined to seize the strategic initiative as quickly as possible. Just as the Kursk Bulge and German desperation to regain the offensive initiative dictated the German strategy of Citadel, so the ambitious strategic aspirations of the *Stavka* shaped Soviet offensive plans.

As was the case with the German High Command, the curving configuration of the front near Kursk inexorably drew Soviet attention to the Kursk sector. The *Stavka* saw to it that its most accomplished and promising leaders commanded in these key sectors. To the north of Kursk, the German salient around Orel was a natural objective for Soviet offensive action. A well-timed attack on Orel could derail Army Group Center's attack out of that salient toward Kursk, and thus Colonel General V. D. Sokolovsky's Western Front and Colonel General M. M. Popov's Briansk Front were almost as important as the forces in the Kursk Bulge itself.

Forty-five-year-old Vasilii Danilovich Sokolovsky was a close associate of Zhukov whose military career spanned both world wars and the Cold War.[35] A veteran of the Civil War and a 1921 graduate of the RKKA (Workers and Peasants Red Army) Military Academy, during the interwar years Sokolovsky fought the Basmachi guerrillas in Central Asia and served in key staff and command positions in several rifle divisions, a rifle corps, and in the Volga, Ural, and Moscow Military Districts. In February 1941 Zhukov appointed him as his deputy chief of the General Staff. After war broke out in 1941, Sokolovsky became Zhukov's chief of staff in the Western Front and Western Direction and again his chief of staff during the Battle of Moscow.

Sokolovsky assumed command of the Western Front in February 1943, replacing I. S. Konev, who in June 1943 took command of the Steppe Military District. Sokolovsky's reputation as a superb organizer must be tempered by his role in the Mars defeat of November–December 1942 and by his subsequent removal from *front* command in April 1944 for his poor performance and the heavy losses incurred by his *front* in operations in eastern Belorussia.[36] The survival of Sokolovsky's reputation during the war and his prominence in the postwar years (as Chief of the General Staff, Minister of Defense, and author of *Military Strategy*) was due, in part, to his association with Zhukov.

Forty-one-year-old Colonel General Markian Mikhailovich Popov, who had a well-earned reputation as an audacious fighter, had also served alongside Zhukov earlier in his military career.[37] Popov entered the Red Army in 1920 and fought as a private during the Civil War. During the interwar years he attended the *Vystrel* command course and the Frunze Academy and rose to command in the fledgling Soviet mechanized forces in the late 1930s as chief of staff of a mechanized brigade and the 5th Mechanized Corps. In 1939 he joined Zhukov in the Far East as commander of the 1st Separate Red Banner Army. When Zhukov became Chief of the General Staff in January 1941, Popov assumed command of the Leningrad Military District.

After war began in 1941, Popov commanded, in succession, the Northern and Leningrad Fronts and 61st and 40th Armies before serving as Chief of Staff of the Stalingrad and Southwestern Fronts during the Battle of Stalingrad. After a brief stint in command of the newly formed 5th Shock Army, in January 1943 Popov formed and led the experimental mobile group that bore his name. After helping to organize the Reserve Front and Steppe Military District, Popov was appointed, on Zhukov's recommendation, to command the Briansk Front in June 1943. A former associate, who was sparing of praise for Soviet generals, lauded Popov's capabilities and demeanor:

> Popov . . . was yet another distinctive individual. Popov was tall, with good posture, blond hair, and fine features. He was young-looking, communicative, and jolly, and an ardent sportsman. Popular with both officers and enlisted men, he had a quick, logical mind; yet he was unlucky in the war. Yes, he met with success on the battlefield, extraordinary success at times, but he was not liked by those close to Stalin. Perhaps Stalin himself did not like him. Popov was twice removed from command over a front, and, for the rest of his life, he served under the most talentless, tactless, and crude of the commanders, Chuikov. . . . I retain the greatest respect for this man.[38]

To the south of Kursk lay the critical transportation hubs of Khar'kov and Belgorod, and beyond them the industrial resources of the Donets Basin. To recapture this region, the Soviets would have to wear down von Manstein's spearheads and distract his reserves by supporting attacks farther to the south. Such an ambitious plan required enormous reserves and considerable flexibility on the part of the Soviet commanders. In addition to the two *fronts* defending in the bulge, Army General R. Ia. Malinovsky's Southwestern Front would play a key secondary role in the forthcoming offensive south of Khar'kov into the Donbas region.

Army General Rodion Iakovlevich Malinovsky had seen service in the World War and Civil War, and during the former he had fought with and deserted from a Russian expeditionary force in France.[39] Returning to Russia through Vladivostok, Malinovsky rose through the Red Army ranks in fighting in the Far East, commanded at the battalion level in the 1920s, and attended the Frunze Academy in 1930. Thereafter, he served in cavalry staff and command assignments until "volunteering" for service in the International Brigade fighting in the Spanish Civil War. After his return from Spain in 1938, he miraculously escaped the purges and taught at the Frunze Academy.

When war broke out in 1941, Malinovsky commanded the Odessa Military District's 48th Rifle Corps. He excelled in the difficult defensive fighting of summer and fall of 1941 in corps command and as commander of

6th Army, and, for his performance, in December 1941 he was appointed Southern Front commander. Despite his controversial role in the Khar'kov disaster of May 1942, Malinovsky remained in *front* command throughout the summer of 1942 and then commanded the Don Operational Group and 66th Army defending along the approaches to Stalingrad. He then led the powerful 2d Guards Army when it repelled German attempts to relieve their encircled Sixth Army. Resuming command of Southern Front, in March 1943 the forty-five-year-old general was appointed to command the Southwestern Front.

Malinovsky, a future Minister of Defense of the Soviet Union, was a competent but not flashy commander. Steady and thoughtful, he rose to and retained command due to his reputation as a tenacious fighter in the mold of Zhukov. In the words of one biographer, Malinovsky "while unusually able, courageous and keenly intelligent, was also headstrong, ambitious, prone to vanity, and, at times, ruthless when the occasion warranted. Once his mind was made up, nothing could shake his determination to do things his way."[40]

Despite the *Stavka's* concern for the flanks of the Kursk Bulge, the bulge itself would be the focal point of the Kursk battle. Here the *Stavka* positioned its strongest *fronts* and most competent *front* commanders. Opposite German Army Group Center's Ninth Army on the northern half of the bulge was Army General K. K. Rokossovsky's imposing Central Front, with Zhukov as the resident *Stavka* representative responsible for coordinating the operations of the Western, Briansk, and Central Fronts.

Army General Konstantin Konstantinovich Rokossovsky, appointed to Central Front command at age forty-six, had fought in the World War as a common soldier and junior officer and in the Civil War as a cavalry squadron, battalion, and regimental commander.[41] During the 1920s he had commanded cavalry regiments and brigades, attended the Frunze Academy, and participated in the 1929 Sino-Soviet conflict in Manchuria. Continuing his cavalry service, after 1930 Rokossovsky commanded the 7th and 15th Cavalry Divisions (Zhukov was a regimental commander in the former) and then the Leningrad Military District's 5th Cavalry Corps. There, in 1937 he was arrested on charges of "sabotage" and "impairing combat effectiveness." Although tortured and held in prison for three years on the trumped-up charges, in March 1940 he was released and soon regained command of 5th Cavalry Corps. Promoted to major general, Rokossovsky took part in the 1940 invasion of Rumanian Bessarabia and, in October 1940, took command of the Kiev Special Military District's newly formed 9th Mechanized Corps, which he commanded when war broke out in June 1941.

In wartime Rokossovsky demonstrated his combat skill and bravery, leading his corps in a fruitless counterattack against German armored spearheads in Ukraine. In early July he was summoned to the critical western axis, where he commanded, in succession, a special operational group during the Battle of Smolensk and the 16th Army in the critical defense of Moscow. There, under Zhukov's direction, he played a key role in the defense of the capital and the subsequent Soviet counteroffensive. After a brief stint as Briansk Front commander, where he organized several unsuccessful offensives against the Germans, in September 1942 Rokossovsky took command of the Don Front and led it with distinction through the Battle of Stalingrad. In February 1943 he led the Central Front in the audacious but unsuccessful offensive west of Kursk. Given his familiarity with the key Kursk region, he was the ideal commander to defend the northern sector of the Kursk Bulge.

Rokossovsky had a good reputation among Soviet generals and soldiers alike, and many senior German commanders viewed him as "the Red Army's best general." One biographer appropriately stated: "Of the leading Red Army wartime commanders, Rokossovsky combined outstanding professional ability with self-effacing modesty and a sense of traditional military values. There were times during the war when, amid the destructive urge for bestial vengeance on both sides, Rokossovsky displayed humanity and compassion for the suffering of the once powerful adversary and the hapless German population."[42]

On the southern half of the Kursk Bulge, opposite von Manstein's forces, was Army General N. F. Vatutin's Voronezh Front, with Vasilevsky as *Stavka* representative responsible for the operations of the Voronezh and Steppe Fronts. Vatutin was the "boy wonder" of the Soviet High Command, having risen rapidly through key staff positions to command Southwestern Front forces at Stalingrad. An army general at the age of forty-two, he garnered the well-deserved reputation as the Red Army's most daring fighting general.

Army General Nikolai Fedorovich Vatutin joined the Red Army in 1920 and saw only minimal service in the Civil War.[43] After serving in staff, school, and infantry assignments during the 1920s, he graduated from the Frunze Academy, where he attracted the attention of Shaposhnikov, the academy's director. After graduating from the truncated General Staff Academy 1937 course, Vatutin served as Chief of Staff of the Kiev Special Military District Chief of the General Staff's Operational Directorate, and 1st Deputy Chief of the General Staff.[44] Described by his contemporaries as a consummate staff officer, Vatutin long cherished a desire to command. The energetic Vatutin planned the incursion into Poland in September 1939 and into Rumanian Bessarabia in June 1940. While on the General Staff, he was instrumental in war and mobilization planning under Zhukov's and Shaposhnikov's guidance, and when war broke out, over Vatutin's objections, Stalin used Vatutin as his personal representative in key operational sectors.

As Stalin's representative, Vatutin orchestrated the Soviet counterstroke at Staraia Russa in August 1941, which slowed the German advance on

Leningrad, and throughout the fall and early winter Vatutin coordinated Northwestern Front operations during the Battle of Moscow and encircled two German corps at Demiansk. In May 1942 Vatutin returned to Moscow to become Vasilevsky's deputy on the General Staff, and in the critical days of July 1942 Vatutin requested and received command of the Voronezh Front. He commanded this *front* and the Southwestern Front during the ensuing Stalingrad operation, and this operation and the subsequent impetuous Soviet advance into the Donbas reflected both the positive and negative aspects of his audacity. Recognized and valued for his skill as an organizer and his fighting nature by both Zhukov and Vasilevsky, Vatutin was ideally suited to defend and then attack along the southern flank of the Kursk Bulge.

Vatutin's hallmarks were a keen appreciation for the intricacies of staff work and an audacious enthusiasm for command. His opponent, the German armored specialist W. F. von Mellenthin, once noted, "Certainly in men like Zhukov, Konev, Vatutin, and Vasilevsky, the Russians possessed army and army group commanders of a very high order."[45] Unlike many commanders, Vatutin was also well thought of by his subordinates and soldiers.

East of the bulge, standing behind these two *fronts* and far to the south, was the equally massive Steppe Front, commanded by Army General I. S. Konev, a former political officer whom Stalin eventually groomed as a political counterweight to Zhukov. Konev's mission at Kursk was to provide reinforcements and additional depth to the defenses while at the same time planning for the eventual Soviet strategic offensive.

Army General Ivan Stepanovich Konev was a World War and Civil War veteran who after 1916 fought as a junior officer in the tsarist army.[46] Joining the Red Army in 1918, he served during the Civil War as a commissar in an armored train, a rifle brigade and division, and the People's Revolutionary Army in the Far East. At war's end he took part in suppressing anti-Bolshevik uprisings in Moscow and at the naval base at Kronstadt. After serving as commissar in the 17th Coastal Rifle Corps and 17th Rifle Division in the 1920s, he attended the Course for Perfecting Red Army Command Cadre (KUVNAS) and was then assigned as a regimental and deputy division commander. During the following decade Konev attended the Frunze Academy and rose to command a rifle division, rifle corps, and the 2d Red Banner Far Eastern Army. Although accused during the purges, he avoided the fate of many of his colleagues, and in 1940 and 1941 he was assigned to command, in succession, the Trans-Baikal and the North Caucasus Military Districts.

Shortly before war began, Konev secretly moved his 19th Army forward to the Kiev region with orders to strike the flank of any German force advancing on Kiev. The headlong German advance prompted the *Stavka* to redeploy Konev's army northward, where German forces ground it up during the early stages of the Battle of Smolensk. After leading ad hoc formations in the Battle of Smolensk, in September Konev was appointed to command the Western Front shortly before it was overrun and largely encircled at Viaz'ma in October 1941. With Zhukov's help Konev was saved from prosecution for the disaster, and then, under Zhukov, he commanded the Kalinin Front in the defense and counteroffensive at Moscow. Again serving with Zhukov, Konev led the Western Front in the fall of 1942 and saw his *front* suffer serious defeat in November and December during Operation Mars. Once again Zhukov intervened to save Konev from disgrace. After commanding the Northwestern Front briefly in the spring of 1943, on Zhukov's recommendation, Konev was given command of the Steppe Military District in June. Only then did Konev's fortunes change for the better.

Noting that Konev was known as emotional and hot tempered, one biographer stated: "Personal courage and energetic initiative in difficult circumstances were characteristic of Konev as a military leader throughout the war. . . . Konev was particularly taken with military history, and, throughout his life, he regarded it as an integral component of success. On the other hand, others noted that Konev was often harsh with his subordinates, vain, and prone to jealousy of his peers."[47]

Another Red Army veteran noted that Konev "was swift in his decisions and actions and unrestrained with his subordinates." Although "his behavior was acceptable," at times it was "somewhat frightening for the target of his wrath. . . . However, those who fought under him all commented on his temper. Still, they did not accuse him, as they did Chuikov, of being insulting."[48]

Stalin was convinced that his best commanders would do battle with the Germans at Kursk. All that remained was to provide them with the requisite forces and arms. Then, only time and fate would tell whether the new Red Army could at last halt the *Wehrmacht* on a single field of battle. If so, it would be the first time!

PART II
THE GERMAN ASSAULT

CHAPTER 3

Preparations

THE GERMAN BUILDUP

Wehrmacht commanders took all the usual precautions to disguise their offensive intentions around Kursk. On 30 March 1943, the headquarters of Ninth German Army, having abandoned the bloody Rzhev-Viaz'ma salient, moved south into Orel under the assumed name of *Festungsstab* (Fortress Staff) II, a fictitious designation that implied a purely defensive mission.[1] To support this deception, front-line German troops labored to construct trenches in full view of the enemy. Yet, as indicated in Chapter 2, the Soviet High Command was not deceived.

The German buildup continued throughout the spring. By the time the battle began, five German armies in two distinct fronts were involved. In the north, von Kluge's Army Group Center controlled three of these armies. Second Panzer Army, the lineal descendent of Guderian's vaunted Second Panzer Group, defended the northern and eastern flanks of the Orel Bulge. Despite its panzer designation, the approximately 160,000-man army consisted of fourteen understrength infantry divisions and a single panzer grenadier division (the 25th) organized into three army corps (LV, LIII, and XXXV), backed up by two panzer (5th and 8th) and two security divisions.[2] This weakness proved critical in mid-July, when the Soviets launched their counteroffensive to seize Orel. Worse still, Second Panzer Army was commanded by Lieutenant General Rudolf Schmidt, a career soldier who had made no secret of his contempt for the Nazi regime. Schmidt was relieved of command on 10 July, depriving Second Panzer of leadership when it was needed most.[3]

The main German attack in the north fell to Ninth German Army, whose commander, the unflappable Walter Model, had already expressed his doubts frequently and eloquently to von Kluge and Hitler. Ninth Army, which numbered 335,000 men, controlled a total of twenty-one German and three Hungarian divisions, including six panzer (2d, 4th, 9th, 12th, 18th, and 20th), one panzer grenadier (10th), and fourteen infantry divisions (see Appendix A: German Order of Battle), and was assigned 590 tanks, primarily obsolescent Panzer III and IV vehicles, and 424 assault guns, but all were not operational when the battle began.[4]

Five corps headquarters controlled most of Model's forces, with the XX Corps (four infantry divisions) in the west, XXIII Corps (three and one-third infantry divisions) in the east, and three panzer corps—XXXXVI, XXXXVII, and XXXXI—in the center. General of Panzer Troops Joachim Lemelson's XXXXVII Panzer Corps had the responsibility for the main attack into the teeth of the Soviet Central Front, using the 2d, 9th, and 20th Panzer Divisions and 6th Infantry Division. In addition, Lemelson controlled the 21st Panzer Brigade, which consisted of the 505th Panzer Detachment, equipped with two Tiger companies (31 Tigers and 15 Panzer IIIs), and the 36 assault guns of the 909th Assault Gun Detachment. General of Infantry Joseph Harpe's XXXXI Panzer Corps was assigned to support this attack with 18th Panzer Division, the 86th and 292d Infantry Divisions, two Elephant units, the 653d and 654th Heavy Tank Destroyer Detachments with 5 tanks and 105 Ferdinand SP antitank guns, and 3 assault gun detachments (177th, 244th, and 216th Heavy). In addition, the four infantry divisions of General Hans Zorn's XXXXVI Panzer Corps participated in the main panzer thrust.

Lemelsen, Harpe, Zorn, and the other corps commanders of Ninth Army corps were veteran leaders who had struggled successfully with superior Soviet forces in the Rzhev-Viaz'ma salient just months before.[5] They harbored few illusions about the difficulties ahead of them. In addition to these five corps, Model had assembled an ad hoc reserve consisting of the 4th and 12th Panzer and 10th Panzer Grenadier Divisions, with a total of 184 tanks.

On the western "nose" of the Kursk Bulge was Colonel General of Infantry Walter Weiss's 96,000-man Second German Army (not to be confused with Second Panzer Army). These eight infantry divisions and three antitank detachments organized into the XIII and VII Army Corps remained on the defensive throughout the battle, acting as a thin connection between Army Group Center and the neighboring Army Group South.[6]

In addition to the committed forces of Second Panzer, Ninth, and Second German Armies, von Kluge had a number of forces assigned to rear area security against the persistent Soviet guerrilla effort, especially in the Orel Bulge. These troops, including four security divisions, elements of the three Hungarian light infantry divisions assigned to Ninth Army, and the 1st SS Cavalry Division, lacked much of the artillery and other heavy equipment necessary to be effective in mechanized combat.[7]

In Army Group South, von Manstein concentrated a much stronger force consisting of Colonel General Hermann Hoth's 223,907-man Fourth Panzer Army and General of Panzer Troops Walter Kempf's ad hoc 126,000-man Army Detachment Kempf.

General Hoth's aristocratic profile reflected his background as a Prussian officer and General Staff planner since World War I. After commanding a panzer corps in the Polish and French campaigns, Hoth headed one of the spearhead panzer groups that invaded the Soviet Union in 1941. In the ensuing two years of seesaw battles, he became one of the few early panzer commanders to retain his reputation.

Hoth was not blind to the difficulties facing him at Kursk. Still, when compared to Model, his counterpart in the north, Hoth had a much better chance of success. Fourth Panzer Army controlled three corps with a total of ten divisions, including three panzer divisions (6th, 7th, and 19th) plus the lavishly equipped Panzer Grenadier Division *Grossdeutschland* and three SS panzer grenadier divisions.[8] On the left, Hoth placed three infantry divisions under General of Infantry Eugen Ott's LII Corps to defend half his assigned sector so that he could concentrate his attack farther east. In the center, General of Panzer Troops Otto von Knobelsdorff's XXXXVIII Panzer Corps controlled 3d and 11th Panzer Divisions, 167th Infantry Division, and Panzer Grenadier Division *Grossdeutschland* with a paper strength of 535 tanks (including 200 Panthers of the 10th Panzer Brigade) and 66 assault guns. Von Knobelsdorff would share the main attack in the south with II SS Panzer Corps, commanded by SS *Obergruppenfuehrer* Paul Hausser. Hausser's three SS panzer grenadier divisions—the 1st *(Leibstandarte Adolf Hitler)*, 2d *(Das Reich)*, and 3d *(Totenkopf)*—had a line strength of 390 tanks and 104 assault guns between them, including 42 of the Army Group's 102 Tigers.[9]

On the right or eastern flank of Fourth Panzer Army stood Army Detachment Kempf. Originally intended as a flank guard, this improvised force would assume major importance because, unlike Ninth and Fourth Panzer Armies, it was attacking through the shoulder of the Red defenses rather than directly into their strong points. Werner Kempf's crewcut, spectacles, and forthright eyes radiated competence. He had been a Marine Corps officer throughout World War I and was associated with the growing panzer arm from 1934 onward. He had performed brilliantly as a division and corps commander but had never held a higher post before his ad hoc headquarters was created during the bitter fighting of February 1943. By June Kempf had three corps headquarters—III Panzer Corps, Corps Rauss (XI Army Corps), and XXXXII Army Corps—with a total of nine divisions. General Hermann Breith's III Panzer Corps was the main striking force. It contained the experienced 6th, 7th, and 19th Panzer Divisions with a total of 299 tanks, plus the 45 Tiger tanks of the 503d Panzer Detachment, an assault gun detachment, and the 168th Infantry Division.[10]

In addition to Fourth Panzer Army and Army Detachment Kempf, Army Group South had the veteran Walter Nehling's XXIV Panzer Corps in reserve, including 17th Panzer Division and 5th SS Panzer Grenadier Division *Wiking* with a total of 112 tanks. Overall, von Manstein's forces at Kursk included twenty-two divisions, of which six were panzer and five were panzer grenadier. Even without XXIV Panzer Corps, on paper his shock force included 1,269 tanks and 245 assault guns, although daily operational strengths varied.[11] It was a formidable assembly of combat power, but it was facing an even greater enemy force.

LUFTWAFFE FORCES

Sixth Air Fleet, commanded by Colonel General Ritter von Greim, supported Army Group Center. During World War I, von Greim had scored twenty-eight "kills" in air combat and had joined the Luftwaffe when it was activated in 1934. Yet experience could not make up for shortages of aircraft and aviation fuel. Von Greim's air fleet headquarters had direct control of various specialized units, such as a night fighter group and a long-range photo reconnaissance unit. In addition, von Greim supervised General Hermann Plocher's 1st Air Division, containing 730 combat aircraft. This impressive total included only three groups of aging JU-87 Stuka dive-bombers, plus a limited number of antitank and medium bomber aircraft. Worse still, Sixth Air Fleet generally received only two-thirds of its required levels of aviation fuel, a common problem as Germany became cut off from most of its petroleum sources. This shortage of fuel had a serious impact on the Luftwaffe's ability to support the German Army at a time when close air support had become essential to success on the ground.[12]

Sixth Air Fleet also included the 12th FlaK (Antiaircraft Artillery) Division and the separate 10th FlaK Brigade. German ground forces depended heavily on the antitank capacity of these Luftwaffe guns, especially the legendary 88mm. More than 100 88mm guns provided direct support to Ninth German Army, leaving the Luftwaffe with scant resources to defend airfields and other vital installations.[13]

Fourth Air Fleet, commanded by General Otto Dessloch, supported the German attack in the south. Like his counterpart in the north, Dessloch was one of the most experienced aviators in the Luftwaffe, having commanded a fighter squadron during World War I and every possible type of air force formation in the early years of the second war.[14] Under Dessloch's headquarters, VIII Air Corps controlled the air elements of Fourth Air Fleet, totaling 1,100 German and Hungarian aircraft. Although the number of aircraft was impressive on paper, seven groups of aging JU-87 Stukas had to provide the bulk of close air support in an increasingly hostile air defense environment. Fourth Air Fleet also included the I Flak Corps (Lieutenant General Richard Reimann), which again had to provide one regiment as antitank support to Fourth Panzer Army.[15]

OFF AGAIN, ON AGAIN

The initial start date for Operation Citadel had been 4 May 1943, but at the last moment Hitler postponed the attack until 12 June in order to allow more new tanks and self-propelled guns to reach German units.[16] When the Allies completed the conquest of Tunisia on 13 May, the dictator again delayed the attack until the end of June in order to prepare for the defense of Italy against a forthcoming invasion. For a few weeks, he apparently considered canceling the offensive completely and did, in fact, redeploy certain units, such as 1st Panzer Division, from Russia to the Mediterranean.[17]

Hitler's doubts were shared by many of his military subordinates, who voiced them repeatedly during May and June.[18] It was typical of his personality that such criticism had the unintended effect of strengthening his resolve. On 16 June, for example, Guderian asked Hitler for further delays in order to rebuild the panzer forces, while von Manstein and von Kluge urged an immediate attack before the Soviet defenses became any stronger. Hitler insisted that German aerial reconnaissance had given a greatly exaggerated image of Soviet defenses and that the offensive should proceed on schedule. On the 18th the OKW Operations Staff recommended to Hitler that he abandon Citadel in order to free strategic reserves for defense in both East and West. Hitler replied that he was determined to attack on 3 July, a date that was eventually moved back to the 5th.

Because of the two-month delay before attacking, the original idea of a springtime offensive had moved to high summer, when the world would inevitably compare its feebleness with the strong German offensives of the previous two years. Anticipating such an unfavorable comparison, as well as the possibility that Citadel might fail, General Alfred Jodl, OKW Operations Chief, instructed the armed forces propaganda office to portray Citadel as merely a limited counteroffensive.

On 1 July, Hitler sent a special order of the day to all commanders down to battalion level explaining his reasons for launching the offensive. Stripped of his rhetoric, this order indicated that Hitler's main goal was to influence the morale of the Germans, their faltering allies, and their long-suffering Soviet opponents.

THE SOVIET BUILDUP

While the German panzer forces re-equipped and retrained for battle, the Red Army underwent an equally massive preparation to defend the Kursk Bulge.[19] In comparison to the manpower shortages of their German opponents, most Soviet units in the Kursk area were closer than usual to their full authorized strengths by the time the battle began. Although rifle divisions still lacked their full complement of 9,354 (10,585 for guards divisions), those assigned to the Voronezh and Central Fronts averaged 8,400 and 7,400 men respectively, far higher than at any time before.[20] Some guards divisions were even closer to full strength. Often, this influx of replacements to combat units was possible only because rear echelon units were stripped of personnel.

On the northern face of the Orel Bulge, Colonel General V. D. Sokolovsky's Western Front fielded two armies opposite German Second Panzer Army, supported by elements of Soviet 1st Air Army. Lieutenant General I. Kh. Bagramian's powerful 11th Guards Army was deployed in the critical Zhizdra-Bolkhov sector northwest of Orel, prepared to spearhead Western Front's decisive thrust toward the vital Briansk-Orel rail line. The experienced Bagramian had begun the war as chief of staff of the ill-fated Soviet Southwestern Front and had been severely censured by Stalin for his role as Southwestern Direction chief of staff in the disastrous Khar'kov operation of May 1942. Thereafter, however, he regained the dictator's favor. A sound workhorse general and leading postwar Soviet military historian, Bagramian was assigned to command 16th Army in July 1942 and led it in the winter campaign of 1943 against German forces defending Orel. He then presided over the transformation of this army into 11th Guards after 16 April 1943, a transformation that German intelligence failed to note until Bagramian's army struck in July 1943.[21]

Bagramian's new host was based upon twelve rifle divisions, of which nine were the stronger guards formations, organized into three rifle corps. These armies were reinforced by four tank brigades, two tank regiments, and an imposing array of artillery and other supporting units. By 12 July Bagramian's army fielded 135,000 men, 648 tanks and self-propelled guns, and over 3,000 artillery pieces and mortars, including two fresh tank corps (1st and 5th) provided by Sokolovsky. As was the case with all Soviet forces, not all tanks and self-propelled guns were operational at any given moment.[22]

On Bagramian's left flank, Sokolovsky deployed Lieutenant General I. V. Boldin's 50th Army to support 11th Guards Army's main offensive effort with its 54,062 men, 1,071 guns and mortars, and 87 tanks and self-propelled guns. Boldin was also an experienced commander. He had begun the war as deputy commander of the Western Front and then 50th Army commander and had orchestrated harrowing escapes from German encirclement near Minsk in July 1941 and at Briansk in October 1941. Boldin survived to lead the 50th Army in the Red victory at Moscow and had since retained his command, no mean feat in the rollercoaster of defeats and victories in 1942. In July 1943 his army consisted of a single rifle corps headquarters, seven rifle divisions, and a tank brigade.[23]

The *Stavka* accorded a critical role in collapsing the Orel salient to Colonel General M. M. Popov's Briansk Front, whose 3d, 61st, and 63d Armies would all play an important role in the operation. Lieutenant General A. V. Gorbatov's 3d Army crouched opposite the nose of the German Orel salient ready to strike westward toward Orel from the Novosil' region. A World War and Civil War veteran, Gorbatov rose through division and corps command during the first two years of war to assume command of 3d Army in June 1943. He led this army until war's end, in the process earning the title of Hero of the Soviet Union for his army's superb performance in the 1945 East Prussian operation. In July 1943 Gorbatov's 3d Army counted a single rifle corps headquarters, a total of six rifle divisions, and supporting armor and artillery, for a strength of about 60,000 men and 100 tanks and self-propelled guns.[24]

On 3d Army's right flank was Lieutenant General V. Ia. Kolpakchi's 63d Army, which shared the responsibility for the direct assault on Orel in the counteroffensive phase. With seven rifle divisions and a strength of around 70,000 men and 60 tanks, Kolpakchi's army had been formed in July 1942 from 5th Reserve Army and had subsequently fought with distinction during the Battle of Stalingrad under the Stalingrad and Don Fronts. Kolpakchi, a tested World War and Civil War veteran, had commanded 18th, 62d, and 30th Armies earlier in the war and had attracted Zhukov's attention as a fighter. He assumed command of 63d Army in May 1943 and would also earn the title of Hero of the Soviet Union in 1945 for the tenacity of his troops along the Oder River.[25]

Rounding out the Briansk Front's shock force was Lieutenant General P. A. Belov's combat-tested 61st Army, which was deployed between 63d Army and 11th Guards Army, opposite German defenses at Bolkhov. Raised in November 1941 in the Volga Military District, during the Soviet Moscow counteroffensive 61st Army had formed the linchpin between advancing Soviet Western and Southwestern Front. Thereafter, as part of Briansk Front, throughout 1942 it had repeatedly pounded away in vain against German forces defending Orel. In July 1943 the army of 80,000 men and 110 tanks, organized into eight rifle divisions and supporting forces, hoped to complete the job of taking Orel under its daring and experienced commander, General Belov.[26]

An experienced cavalry officer, Belov had already earned a reputation for extreme tenacity and daring. The Civil War veteran had commanded 2d Cavalry Corps from the war's beginning and had led his reinforced corps (then redesignated 1st Guards) deep into the rear area of German Army Group Center during the Moscow offensive of January–February 1942. Although unable to seize his objective with this frail cavalry organization, Belov confounded German attempts to destroy this force, and in June 1942 he led his surviving cavalrymen back to the safety of Red Army lines. Belov was then assigned to command the 61st Army. In July 1943 he too relished the opportunity to gain a modicum of revenge against his old nemesis, German Army Group Center. Although Belov frequently quarreled with Zhukov, the latter appreciated his fighting talents.[27]

General Popov's Briansk Front was supported by its organic 15th Air Army and by imposing forces provided by the *Stavka*. These included the reserve 25th Rifle Corps, Major General M. F. Pankov's experienced 1st Guards Tank Corps, two full artillery penetration corps, and a wide range of other supporting arms. Thus reinforced, Popov's *front* numbered 433,616 men, 7,642 guns and mortars, 847 tanks and self-propelled guns, and about 1,000 supporting aircraft.[28] In addition, the *Stavka* earmarked other powerful new formations to support the Western and Briansk Fronts, including Lieutenant General I. I. Fediuninsky's 65,000-man 11th Army, Lieutenant General P. S. Rybalko's powerful 3d Guards Tank Army (731 tanks and self-propelled guns), Lieutenant General V. M. Badanov's 4th Tank Army (652 tanks and self-propelled guns), the 20th and 25th Separate Tank Corps, and the 2d Guards Cavalry Corps.

Along the northern flank of the Kursk Bulge directly opposite the Ninth German Army, Army General Konstantin Rokossovsky, commander of the Soviet Central Front, deployed three full rifle armies—Lieutenant General I. V. Galanin's 70th, Lieutenant General N. P. Pukhov's 13th, and Lieutenant General P. L. Romanenko's 48th—to man the first and second army defensive belts. Rokossovsky anticipated that Model's main attack would fall on the 13th Army, whose troops were therefore arrayed along a narrow, thirty-two-kilometer front and formed into three successive defensive layers of four, three, and five divisions, respectively.

General Pukhov's 13th Army consisted of twelve rifle divisions, of which three were guards and three were elite guards airborne, organized into four rifle corps. These infantry were supported by a separate tank brigade, five tank regiments, and the 4th Artillery Penetration Corps, with 700 guns and mortars.[29] As commander of this force of 114,000 men, 2,934 guns and mortars, and 270 tanks and self-propelled guns, Pukhov was an experienced combat veteran of the Civil War. A division commander in 1941, he rose to command the 13th Army in January 1942, during the height of the Moscow counteroffensive. He had earned the plaudits of the *Stavka* for his army's role in the defeat of the German Second Army along the Don River in January–February 1943 (the Voronezh-Kastornoe operation) and during the subsequent Soviet exploitation toward Orel in spring 1943.[30]

In the prospective German attack sector north of Kursk, Pukhov's 13th Army was flanked on the left by General Galanin's 70th Army and on the right by General Romanenko's 48th Army. Neither army had yet lived up to its advance billing, nor had their commanders. The 70th Army, which now consisted of eight rifle divisions and three tank regiments, had been formed in the late fall of 1942 from elite NKVD (People's Commissariat of Internal Affairs) border guards from the Far East and Trans-Baikal Military Districts.[31] During the decisive Stalingrad operation, the *Stavka* had retained the army in reserve to exploit opportunities for developing the winter campaign westward. Its moment of glory was supposed to come in February 1943, when it was ordered to join General Rokossovsky's new Central Front in a thrust designed to cap the winter campaign by cleaving the German front in half. Rokossovsky's *front*, consisting of the newly formed 2d Tank Army, the elite 70th Army, and several other armies freed up by the surrender of German Sixth Army at Stalingrad, was to advance westward via Kursk to seize Orel and Briansk and reach the Dnepr River. Spring mud and tenaciously skillful German resistance, however, had forced the offensive to abort short of its intended goals, and 70th Army had joined the Soviet host thereafter lodged in the Kursk Bulge.

The 70th Army commander, General Galanin, had taken command in April 1943. He was a Civil War veteran and the experienced commander of 12th, 59th, and 24th Armies. With 96,000 men, 1,678 guns and mortars, and 125 tanks, Galanin hoped to redress his army's lackluster reputation at Kursk.[32]

General Romanenko's 48th Army, deployed on 13th Army's right flank, consisted of a single rifle corps headquarters and a total of seven rifle divisions, six tank and self-propelled artillery regiments, and supporting arms for an effective strength of about 84,000 men, 1,454 guns and mortars, and 178 tanks and self-propelled guns. The 48th Army had been formed in April 1942 from a nucleus of the 28th Mechanized Corps and had subsequently served in the Briansk and Central Fronts.[33] Romanenko himself was an armored officer who never achieved the fame of his counterparts like Katukov and Rybalko. After commanding the 7th Mechanized Corps during the prewar period, when war began he commanded the 17th Army in the Trans-Baikal Military District. Reassigned to armored forces, he successfully commanded 5th Tank Army at Stalingrad and then, less successfully, the 2d Tank Army during Rokossovsky's spring 1943 offensive. Thereafter, he was assigned command of the 48th Army, which he led for most the war.[34]

The Central Front had two other armies—Lieutenant General I. D. Cherniakhovsky's 96,000-man 60th (six rifle divisions, two separate rifle brigades, and a tank brigade) and Lieutenant General P. I. Batov's 100,000-man 65th (nine divisions, one rifle brigade, and four separate tank regiments)—defending much wider segments on the western nose of the bulge, facing German Second Army.[35] Although Cherniakhovsky and Batov were Rokossovsky's most capable fighting commanders, neither would play a significant role in the Kursk operation. However, their time would come during the Soviet counteroffensive. In reserve, Rokossovsky held a wide variety of armored and artillery units, including one of the new model tank formations, the 2d Tank Army, and the 9th and 19th Separate Tank Corps.

The 2d Tank Army, commanded by Lieutenant General A. G. Rodin, consisted of the 3d and 16th Tank Corps and 11th Guards Tank Brigade, but no mechanized corps. Its strength was approximately 37,000 men and 477 tanks and self-propelled guns.[36] Rodin was also an experienced commander and armored specialist who had graduated in 1937 from the Red Army Motorization and Mechanization Academy. During the first year of war, Rodin commanded in succession a tank regiment, brigade, and division, and in 1942 he rose to command 26th (later 1st Guards) Tank Corps. For the performance of his corps at Stalingrad, Rodin was made a Hero of the Soviet Union and assigned to form and command the new 2d Tank Army. Held in high regard by opposing German commanders, Rodin's armored field service ended in early August during the Battle of Kursk, when Rodin fell seriously ill and was replaced as army commander by Lieutenant General S. I. Bogdanov. Thereafter, Rodin served in a less arduous position as chief of armored and mechanized forces for a number of *fronts*.[37]

Army General N. F. Vatutin's Voronezh Front fielded six armies in the southern part of the Kursk Bulge, supported by 2d Air Army. His *front* totaled 625,591 men, 8,718 guns and mortars, and a powerful armada of 1,704 tanks and self-propelled guns. The armored nucleus of his force was the 1st Tank Army's 646 tanks and self-propelled guns. Lieutenant General N. E. Chibisov's 38th Army with six rifle divisions and two tank brigades and Lieutenant General K. S. Moskalenko's 40th Army with seven rifle divisions, two tank brigades, and a heavy tank regiment defended wide frontages to the west and southwest, opposite German Second Army.[38] Chibisov's army numbered 60,000 men, 1,168 guns and mortars, and 106 tanks, while Moskalenko's army counted 77,000 men, 1,636 guns and mortars, and 113 tanks (see Table 1 for opposing orders of battle).

The main task of defending against Fourth Panzer Army and Army Detachment Kempf fell to two compact, multi-corps rifle armies—Lieutenant General I. M. Chistiakov's 6th Guards and Lieutenant General M. S. Shumilov's 7th Guards Armies. Each of the Guards armies had seven divisions, organized into two rifle corps, a variety of tank and antitank artillery units, and more than twenty artillery regiments for a combined strength of almost 16,000 men and 401 tanks and self-propelled guns.[39] Each of these armies had been built around the experienced staff of an army that had survived the crucial battles of 1942. Five of Chistiakov's and six of Shumilov's divisions bore the "Guards" designation, which most had earned at Stalingrad. However, in comparison to the extremely narrow frontage assigned to the 13th Army in the north, both the 6th Guards and 7th Guards Armies had fewer resources to defend wider areas (sixty and fifty-five kilometers, respectively).

Table 1. Opposing Order of Battle on 4 July 1943

German Forces	SOVIET FORCES	
	Front Forces	Reserves
Orel Axis		
Army Group Center (Field Marshal Guenther von Kluge)		
Second Panzer Army (Lieutenant General Rudolf Schmidt)	Western Front (Colonel General V. D. Sokolovsky)	
LV Corps	50th Army	
	11th Guards Army	11th Army
	1st Tank Corps	
	5th Tank Corps	
	1st Air Army	
	Briansk Front (Colonel General M. M. Popov)	
LIII Corps	61st Army	4th Tank Army
XXXV Corps	63d Army	20th Tank Corps
	3d Army	3d Guards Tank Army
	25th Rifle Corps	25th Tank Corps
	1st Guards Tank Corps	2d Guards Cavalry Corps
	15th Air Army	
Sixth Air Fleet (Colonel General Ritter von Greim)		
Kursk Axis		
Army Group South (Field Marshal Erich von Manstein)		
Ninth Army (General Walter Model)	Central Front (Colonel General K. K. Rokossovsky)	Steppe Front (Colonel General I. S. Konev)
XXIII Corps	48th Army	4th Guards Army
XXXXI Panzer Corps	13th Army	3d Guards Tank Corps
XXXXVII Panzer Corps	70th Army	27th Army
XXXXVI Panzer Corps	2d Tank Army	53d Army
XX Corps	9th Tank Corps	3d Guards Cavalry Corps
Group von Esebeck	19th Tank Corps	5th Guards Cavalry Corps
Second Army (Colonel General W. Weiss)		7th Guards Cavalry Corps
XIII Army Corps	65th Army	4th Guards Tank Corps
	60th Army	3d Guards Mechanized Corps
	16th Air Army	5th Guards Army
	Voronezh Front (Army General N. F. Vatutin)	10th Tank Corps
VII Army Corps	38th Army	1st Mechanized Corps
Fourth Panzer Army (Colonel General Hermann Hoth)		
LII Army Corps	40th Army	
XXXXVIII Panzer Corps	6th Guards Army	
II SS Panzer Corps	1st Tank Army	
	69th Army	
	35th Guards Rifle Corps	
	2d Guards Tank Corps	
	5th Guards Tank Corps	
Army Detachment Kempf (General of Panzer Troops Walter Kempf)		
III Panzer Corps	7th Guards Army	
Corps Rauss (XI)	2d Air Army	
XXXXII Army Corps		
	Southwestern Front (Colonel General R. Ia. Malinovsky)	
	57th Army	5th Air Army
	2d Tank Corps	5th Guards Tank Army
	17th Air Army	47th Army
	Southern Front (Army General F. I. Tolbukhin)	
	8th Air Army	

In reserve, behind the 6th Guards and 7th Guards Armies, Vatutin had the 1st Tank Army, with the 6th and 31st Tank and 3d Mechanized Corps commanded by the audacious Lieutenant General M. E. Katukov, the 69th Army (five divisions—52,000 men), led by Lieutenant General V. D. Kriuchenkin, and the separate three-division 35th Guards Rifle Corps (35,000 men). *Stavka* also placed the 2d Guards and 5th Guards Tank Corps and an imposing array of artillery and other support troops at Vatutin's disposal.

Vatutin's chief lieutenants were all accomplished and experienced commanders. Chistiakov had commanded at brigade, division, and corps level before leading 1st Guards and 21st Armies in the Battle of Stalingrad, for which in April 1943 his army received the Guards designation.[40] Shumilov, likewise, had extensive command experience and had led the 64th and, later, the 62d Army at Stalingrad. His army, too, became a Guards army in April 1943.[41] Moskalenko, a former armored commander and commander of an antitank brigade in 1941, commanded 40th Army successfully through the Stalingrad period. In 1953, Moskalenko would earn fame for his defense of Communist Party leaders against the NKVD head Lavrenti Beria as first commander of Soviet Strategic Rocket Forces and for his excellent war memoirs.[42] Kriuchenkin of the 69th, a former cavalryman, commanded at army level throughout the war and had already led the ill-fated Soviet 4th Tank Army in combat with the Germans on the approaches to Stalingrad.[43]

Finally, in Katukov, Vatutin possessed one the Red Army's most accomplished and experienced armor officers. Katukov had begun the war as a tank division commander, and after the destruction of the fledgling Red Army armored force in the initial stages of the war, he commanded a tank brigade at Moscow and a mechanized corps (the 3d) during Zhukov's abortive Rzhev operation. His successes, even in adversity, earned for him command of the new 1st Tank Army, which was formed in January 1943. Thwarted in his chance to raise the siege of Leningrad in February 1943, his army subsequently helped rescue Rokossovsky's failed February–March 1943 offensive and remained south of Kursk as the armored nucleus of Vatutin's Voronezh Front.[44]

Behind the Briansk, Central, and Voronezh Fronts stood Colonel General I. S. Konev's Steppe Front, which included five rifle armies (4th and 5th Guards, 27th, 47th, and 53d) with a total of thirty-two rifle divisions, plus Lieutenant General P. A. Rotmistrov's 5th Guards Tank Army with the 18th and 29th Tank Corps and 5th Guards Mechanized Corps. Additionally, Steppe Front disposed of three cavalry corps (3d Guards, 5th Guards, and 7th Guards), the 4th Guards Tank Corps, and the 1st and 3d Guards Mechanized Corps. Supported by 5th Air Army, as of 1 July Konev's *front* fielded 573,195 men, 8,510 guns and mortars, and 1,639 tanks and self-propelled guns.[45]

The Steppe Front performed two essential functions. First, it was Stalin's insurance policy. Deployed along a broad front from east of Orel to Voronezh, it was to insure that German forces did not advance into the operational and strategic depths as they had in every previous major German offensive. However, only a portion of Konev's forces would be employed to contain German forces in the defensive phase of the Kursk operation, since *Stavka* was relying on Konev's forces to spearhead the planned counteroffensive.

The commanders of Rokossovsky's, Vatutin's, and Konev's forces were in some ways as valuable as the forces themselves. The once-inexperienced leaders of 1941 were reaching their prime in 1943. By contrast, their German counterparts, who on average were almost twenty years older than the Soviet generals, were beginning to show the strain of incessant warfare with little hope of final victory.

Most of the Red Air Force was directly subordinate to senior ground commanders for purposes of this battle. Central Front was supported by 16th Air Army with 1,034 aircraft, including 455 fighters, 241 ground attack aircraft, 334 bombers, and 4 reconnaissance craft. Similarly, 2d Air Army was assigned to Voronezh Front with 881 aircraft, including 389 fighters, 276 ground attack aircraft, 204 bombers, and 10 reconnaissance aircraft. The 735 aircraft of 17th Air Army, attached to Southwestern Front immediately south of the Kursk Bulge, were also available to support Voronezh Front.[46] Steppe Front had its own air support in 5th Air Army, and the *Stavka* controlled a number of additional aircraft, including seven long-range aviation corps and two fighter divisions of the National Air Defense Command *(PVO strany)*.[47] Individually, Red aircraft might be inferior to their German counterparts, but they were certainly sufficient in numbers to deny the Luftwaffe undisputed command of the air.

SOVIET DEFENSIVE PLANNING

During the first two years of the Soviet-German war, the invaders had rarely been forced to conduct a frontal attack through well-prepared Soviet defenses. The 1941 invasion had caught the Soviets totally unprepared, while Stalin's preoccupation with the defense of Moscow and the conduct of preemptive offensives (at Khar'kov and in the Crimea) had allowed the Germans to achieve considerable surprise during the 1942 offensive. At Kursk, for virtually the first time in the war, improved intelligence collection and analysis permitted the Red Army to predict almost exactly the strategic focal point of a major German offensive. This prediction goes far to explain the ultimate failure of Operation Citadel, as the blitzkrieg never succeeded in penetrating into the strategic depths of the Soviet defenses.

These defensive preparations went far beyond simply assembling a huge number of men and machines, although that in itself should have deterred the German attack. Far more important were the ways in which Soviet military experience, implemented by millions of man-years of backbreaking labor, made the Kursk Bulge all but impenetrable.

The strength of these defenses depended on a number of factors, some of which have already been mentioned. First, the Soviet commands allotted forces and defensive frontages according to the perceived probability of German attack, with the expected attack sectors boasting the largest number of defenders concentrated on the narrowest frontages. In the Central Front, for example, the overall density per kilometer of defensive front was 870 men, 4.7 tanks, and 19.8 guns and mortars. However, in the sector of Central Front's 13th Army, this density increased to 4,500 men, 45 tanks, and 104.3 gun tubes per kilometer. The Voronezh Front, as already noted, was somewhat weaker, perhaps because of Zhukov's preoccupation with Army Group Center. Even here, however, the density per kilometer along the critical frontages of 6th Guards and 7th Guards Armies was 2,500 men, 42 tanks, and 59 guns and mortars.[48] Moreover, Vatutin arrayed his forces in depth, and they were backed up by even deeper defense lines occupied by Konev's forces.

It is an axiom of military theory and a studied product of Soviet combat analysis that the attacker should outnumber the defender, ideally by at least three to two strategically. With artful concentration, such an overall superiority can produce an operational superiority of between 3 and 5 to 1 and tactical superiority at the main points of attack of between 8 and 10 to 1. Yet, by Soviet calculations, at Kursk the Red Army actually *outnumbered* the attackers by about 2.5 to 1 in men and exceeded the Germans in tanks and guns. These ratios were somewhat less favorable to the Soviets in the narrow sectors where the Germans focused their main attacks, but no amount of German tactical and technical superiority, real or perceived, could guarantee success under such circumstances. However, there was a psychological qualification that tempered this comforting reality. Red Army commanders understood that in previous German offensives the Red Army had outnumbered the Germans; yet in no instance had the defenders halted the German advance short of the strategic depths. The fact that previous German thrusts had only been stalled at Moscow and Stalingrad, after an advance of hundreds of kilometers, had a sobering effect on even the most optimistic Soviet commander and encouraged the most pessimistic German (see Table 2).

Central and Voronezh Fronts alone contained more than 1.3 million men, 19,794 artillery pieces and mortars, 3,489 tanks and self-propelled guns, and (including 17th Air Army) 2,650 aircraft. Behind them stood the additional resources of Steppe Front.[49]

The second aspect of the Soviet plan was the extreme depth of the defenses (see Map 4). The armies just described occupied only the first three of as many as six major defensive belts, with each belt being subdivided into

Table 2. Correlation of Forces, Battle of Kursk: Defensive Phase

	Soviet Forces	German Forces	Correlation
Central Front			
Men (committed)	510,983	267,000°	1.9 : 1
Total	711,575	383,000†	1.9 : 1
Tanks	1,785	1,081	1.7 : 1
Guns and mortars	11,076	6,366°	1.7 : 1
Voronezh Front			
Men (committed)	466,236	300,000°	1.6 : 1
Total	625,591	397,900†	1.6 : 1
Tanks	1,704	1,617°	1.1 : 1
Guns and mortars	8,718	3,600°	2.4 : 1
Steppe Front			
Men (committed)	295,000‡		
Total	573,195		
Tanks (committed)	900		
Total	1,551		
Total			
Men (committed)	1,272,219	567,000°	2.3 : 1
Total	1,910,361	780,900	2.4 : 1
Tanks (committed)	4,206	2,696°	1.6 : 1
Total	5,040	2,696	1.9 : 1

°Based on classified Soviet assessments of committed German forces checked against German strengths.
†Includes one half of the Second Army.
‡Includes forces committed by 15 July (5th Guards Tank Army, 5th Guards Army, and 27th Army).

two or three layers. Generally speaking, the first two belts were fully occupied with the third and fourth belts being occupied by units held in reserve and the final two belts largely unoccupied. Still, even if the Germans succeeded in pinching off the Kursk salient, they would still have confronted several additional defensive belts constructed to the east of that salient under the direction of Konev's Steppe Military District (later Steppe Front). Thus, it is only a slight exaggeration to describe the Soviet defenses as being 300 kilometers deep.

One weakness that Soviet analysts identified after the fact was a shortage of cut-off positions, that is, diagonal defensive lines that would facilitate containing the flanks of any German penetration. The absence of such cut-off lines, especially in the area of the Voronezh Front's 7th Guards Army, made it much more difficult for Vatutin to halt the penetration of Fourth Panzer Army and Army Detachment Kempf.[50]

The Soviet main defensive belt consisted of battalion defensive regions, antitank strong points, and an extensive network of engineer obstacles. The thirty-seven rifle divisions manning the first defensive belt formed more than 350 battalion defensive regions, of which two to three arrayed in single or

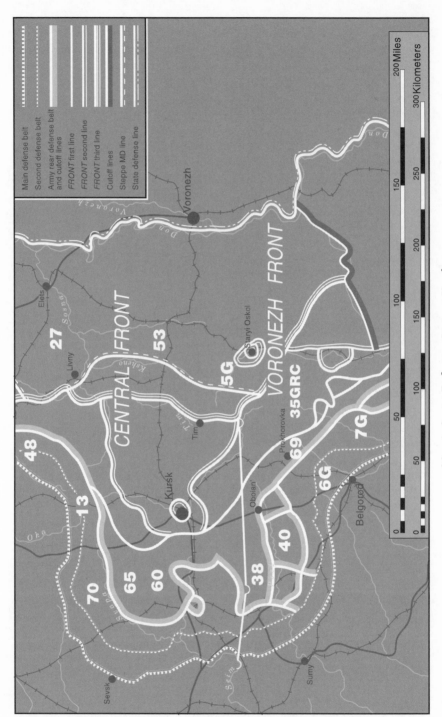

Map 4. Soviet Defensive Lines at Kursk

double echelon formed a regimental defensive sector four to six kilometers wide and three to four kilometers deep. Division defensive sectors averaged a width of fourteen kilometers (from six to twelve kilometers in especially threatened sectors to twenty-five kilometers in secondary sectors) and a depth of five to six kilometers.[51]

Each defensive position was a maze of trenches and blockhouses. Towns in the forward area were evacuated, and more than 300,000 civilians, mostly women and old men, labored for months on military construction projects. In the Voronezh Front alone, 4,200 kilometers of trenches and 500 kilometers of antitank obstacles were built from April through June. In the sectors of 13th, 6th Guards, and 7th Guards Armies, the defenders installed 2,400 antitank and 2,700 antipersonnel mines per mile of front. Thus, 6th Guards Army emplaced 64,340 antipersonnel and 69,688 antitank mines in its main army defensive belt and 9,097 antipersonnel and 20,200 antitank mines in its second army belt.[52] Artillery shells were buried with remote-control devices to act as additional mines. Most of these mines were located in the first two defensive belts, however. Rearward positions were not as densely protected.

In addition to infantry positions, the primary focus of the Soviet effort was antitank defense. Particularly along the expected avenues of German advance, forward rifle divisions and corps constructed special antitank strong points and regions and manned these regions with infantry, antitank rifle, and antitank artillery units. Sixth Guards Army alone had twenty-eight such strong points, eighteen in the main defensive belt and ten in the second belt, each carefully sighted and camouflaged on the best possible ground. Soviet planners in 7th Guards Army arrayed twenty-seven antitank strong points along six likely tank approaches into the army's defenses.[53]

A typical antitank strong point contained an antitank rifle company or battalion, a sapper platoon equipped with explosives, an antitank artillery company with four to six antitank guns, and two to three tanks or self-propelled guns. Recognizing that antitank rifles and 45mm antitank guns would have little effect on the thick frontal armor of the Panthers, Tigers, and Ferdinands, the Red Army incorporated self-propelled tank destroyers as well as 85mm and 152mm artillery pieces in these strong points, intended to engage German tanks with direct fire. In addition, some antitank strong points also included camouflaged positions for T-34s, giving them ready-made firing positions that exposed only their turrets. Two to four of these strong points operating together to cover a single armor axis formed an antitank region. Rifle regiments constructed three to four such strong points, for a total in each division of nine to twelve.[54]

Each forward rifle regiment, division, and corps also fielded an antitank reserve designated to act in concert with the antitank strong points and regions. These ranged in size from two or three antitank guns, an antitank rifle platoon, and an automatic weapons platoon at regimental level, through an antitank company or battalion at division level, to an antitank artillery regiment at corps. Antitank reserves were supplemented by a tank reserve, which normally consisted of a tank company for a rifle battalion, a tank battalion for each forward regiment, and a tank regiment or brigade for each forward division.[55]

Combat engineer (sapper) forces installed antitank mines and engineer obstacles to halt the German tanks in a designated "kill zone," where every possible antitank weapon from short-range antitank rifles through artillery pieces could ambush advancing German armor. In addition, rifle commanders at every level created engineer mobile obstacle detachments equipped with antipersonnel and antitank mines that could quickly deploy to key threatened axes and erect new obstacles while fighting raged. Normally a sapper squad performed this function for each regiment, while several sapper platoons and a sapper company performed similar services for rifle divisions and corps. Soviet commanders also placed reserve antitank regiments and brigades at varying depths to the rear of forward forces; these units would deploy forward to meet any developing German breakthrough.

The Soviet commands stiffened this dense antitank defense with an imposing array of supporting artillery, multiple rocket launchers, and mortars. Artillery was deployed in depth and concentrated along key German attack axes to fire preparations and counterpreparations, to engage advancing German forces, and to support counterattacks, counterstrokes, and the two planned counteroffensives. Soviet planners, as was their custom by mid-1943, incorporated variants for a wide array of counterattacks and counterstrokes in their original defensive planning.

SNAPSHOTS OF THE SOVIET DEFENSES

General Vatutin assigned General Chistiakov's 6th Guards Army the task of defending the key approach into Soviet positions west of Belgorod along the south flank of the Kursk Bulge. Chistiakov arrayed his army in single echelon, with his 23d Guards Rifle Corps on the left covering the main road northward from Tomarovka to Oboian' and Prokhorovka and his 22d Guards Rifle Corps on the right defending routes northward from Borisovka to Oboian'. Each corps defended with two divisions forward and a division in second echelon occupying key terrain roughly ten kilometers to the rear. A mobile corps of General Katukov's 1st Tank Army prepared to reinforce the defenses of each corps' second echelon division and if possible counterattack.

Major General P. P. Vakhrameev, the 23d Guards Rifle Corps commander, deployed Colonel I. M. Nekrasov's 52d Guards Rifle Division in the most critical corps sector astride the key road running northward from Tomarovka through Bykovka and Pokrovka and, ultimately, to both Oboian' and Prokhorovka in the Soviet operational rear (see Map 5).[56] Vatutin, Chistiakov, and Vakhrameev correctly judged that this would be one of the most important German attack axes northward. Between fifteen and twenty kilometers to Nekrasov's rear General Chistiakov erected his second defense line and manned it with Major General N. T. Tavartkiladze's 51st Guards Rifle Division of 23d Guards Rifle Corps, backed up by the 200 tanks of Major General A. G. Kravchenko's 5th Guards Tank Corps. Kravchenko's armor occupied protected assembly areas to the rear and was to deploy forward to support the 51st Guards once the German assault had commenced.

Colonel Nekrasov deployed his division's three regiments abreast along a fourteen-kilometer front extending east and west of the Tomarovka-Oboian' road, with his right flank anchored on the high rolling and partially wooded ground west of the Vorskla River and his left flank on the northern slopes of the Erik River. On his left flank and center, 155th and 151st Guards Rifle Regiments deployed all three of their battalions on line, and his 153d Guards Rifle Regiment astride the Vorskla River formed with two battalions forward. Reserve positions extended to a depth of four to six kilometers and were manned by the division's second echelon rifle battalion and training battalion. The forward battalions that formed the 52d Guards Rifle Division first defensive belt deployed two rifle companies forward and the third one to two kilometers to the rear. These forward battalions anchored their defenses on the northern slopes of ravines that traversed the front and incorporated into their defenses the villages of Zadel'noe, Berezov, and Gremuchii just to the rear.

The division created a security zone that extended three to five kilometers forward across the rolling and generally open terrain forward of the main divisional defensive belt. The security zone consisted of platoon strong points and outposts dispatched forward by each first echelon rifle battalion. These platoon positions, which often incorporated antitank rifles and, sometimes, a single antitank gun, exploited the defensive value of ruined villages like Iakhontov, the deep ravines that crisscrossed the open front, clumps of trees, and, on the division right flank, the rough terrain along the Vorskla River. The security zone confused the Germans regarding the true location of Soviet forward defenses, prompted extensive German reconnaissance before the attack, and were designed to make advancing German forces deploy into assault formation prematurely. Since the Germans employed similar outposts, Soviet and German main forces were separated by distances of up to ten kilometers.

The 36 76mm and 122mm guns of the 52d Guards Rifle Division's 124th Guards Artillery Regiment and the 167 battalion, regimental, and divisional mortars organic to the division provided fire support for the 3 rifle regiments.

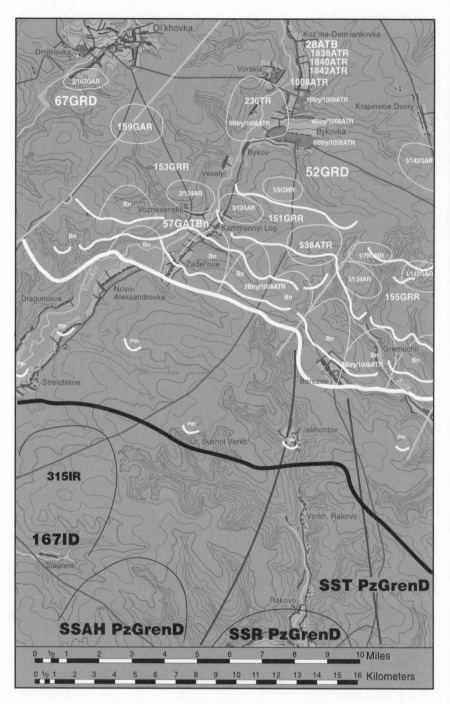

Map 5. "The 52d GRD Defense," 4 July 1943

One artillery battalion from the 124th Artillery Regiment deployed three to four kilometers to the rear in direct support of each rifle regiment. In addition, two battalions of the 142d Gun Artillery Regiment, two guards mortar (Katiusha multiple rocket) batteries and elements of the 159th Gun Artillery Regiment, assigned by the 6th Guards Army, provided additional artillery support.

For antitank defense, Nekrasov had his own divisional assets, including 36 antitank guns organic to his regiments and battalions and the 12 guns of his divisional 57th Guards Antitank Artillery Battalion. The Army headquarters had also assigned him an antitank rifle battalion (for a total of about 270 antitank rifles) and the 538th and 1008th Antitank Artillery Regiments, each with 24 guns. In addition, *front* had promised to allocate him the three-regiment, 72-gun, 28th Antitank Artillery Brigade, should the need arise.[57] Using these weapons, Nekrasov formed an antitank defense anchored on four antitank strong points. His 151st Guards Rifle Regiment, covering the main road running northward from Tomarovka, formed two such strong points, the first anchored on the village of Zadel'noe and the second astride the main road. These incorporated regimental and divisional rifle, antitank, and sapper forces and the four guns of the 2d Battery, 1008th Antitank Artillery Regiment. Each of Nekrasov's flank regiments formed one antitank strong point. On the division right flank, the 153d Guards Rifle Regiment employed the divisional 57th Guards Antitank Artillery Battalion to form an antitank strong point near the junction with the neighboring 67th Guards Rifle Division. The 155th Guards Rifle Regiment sited its antitank strong point along the high-speed road approach into the regimental sector and incorporated in it the obstacle value of the village of Berezov. It employed the four guns of 3d Battery, 1008th Antitank Artillery Regiment, as the nucleus of its antitank strong point.

To add depth to his antitank defense, Nekrasov positioned the twenty-four guns of his 538th Antitank Artillery Regiment astride the main road three kilometers to the rear. Its orders were to support forward battalions and contest any German armored advance along the corridor. Another four kilometers to the rear in and around the village of Bykovka, Nekrasov deployed the 1008th Antitank Artillery Regiment's remaining four batteries with orders to engage German armor should it penetrate northward along the highway. Here he also planned to commit the 28th Antitank Artillery Brigade should it be released to his control.

For armor support Nekrasov had the thirty-nine tanks of the 230th Tank Regiment. While he used some of the regiment's twenty-three light T-60 and T-70 tanks in a reconnaissance role, he retained the bulk of the regiment's twenty-three T-34 medium tanks as a divisional tank reserve in conjunction with batteries of the 1008th Antitank Artillery Regiment to counterattack against penetrating German armor. The gruesome reality was that these infantry support tanks would be sacrificed early to exact whatever toll they could on enemy armored spearheads.

In fact, such a defense was based on the premise that Nekrasov's entire 52d Guards Rifle Division would sacrifice itself by exacting maximum attrition on advancing German forces. Realistically, no one expected the guardsmen to prevail. By fighting and dying forward, however, they would erode German strength and condition subsequent Soviet victory deeper in the defense. This realism was underscored by the fact that Nekrasov's 8,000 men would face the full brunt of German II SS Panzer Corps' superbly equipped three panzer grenadier divisions.

Major General A. I. Baksov's 67th Guards Rifle Division of 22d Guards Rifle Corps, deployed on Nekrasov's left flank, faced an analogous situation.[58] He was defending with his 8,000-man division astride the main road that ran from Borisovka northward through Butovo and Cherkasskoe to Oboian'. His right flank was covered by the corps' 71st Guards Rifle Division and, ten kilometers to the rear, Colonel V. G. Chernov's 90th Guards Rifle Division, backed up by the 6th Tank Corps of Katukov's 1st Tank Army, had erected corps second echelon defenses along the meandering Pena River. The 67th Guards Rifle Division defended in a fourteen-kilometer sector along a low, generally treeless ridge line rising westward from the lightly wooded Vorskolets River valley. The division's left flank crossed the Vorskolets and joined with the 52d Guards Rifle Division defenses on another ridge running north from the junction of the Vorskolets and Vorskla Rivers. Its right flank linked up with 71st Guards Rifle Division defenses on the high open ground just southeast of the town of Korovino.

To Baksov's front the terrain sloped downward, gently on his right toward the main east-west rail line six kilometers distant and ever more precipitously in the center and on the left toward the villages of Butovo and Iamnoe and the Vorskla valley. The slightly tilted billiard table approach on his right was marred by a ravine and associated dry marsh, which marked the course of the rivulet Berezovyi, less than a kilometer to the front. In the center clumps of trees and in the east the ground forward of the division's defenses was heavily cut up and gouged by ravines and stream beds sloping southeast to the Vorskla and the village of Kazatskoe. Clearly the main routes into his positions ran northward along both sides of Butovo. The main German positions were invisible to the naked eye between four and six kilometers away, extending across the rail line from Loknia through Iamnoe to Kazatskoe.

General Baksov created a security belt that ranged from two to four kilometers forward of his main defenses and was anchored on the village of Butovo. Here elements of the 3d Battalion, 199th Rifle Regiment, supported by the divisional 73d Guards Antitank Battalion, formed a strong point that covered the main road north and could fire on forces advancing past the village's ruins. Smaller platoon-size outposts manned other security positions along the front and in the Vorskolets valley. On his open right flank, he emplaced an extensive minefield in the Berezovyi valley and covered it with automatic weapons, antitank, mortar, and artillery fire. Baksov's troops strung twenty-one kilometers of barbed wire in front of their positions and emplaced more than 30,000 antitank and antipersonnel mines.[59]

The 67th Guards Rifle Division's main defenses were formed in a single echelon of regiments with a reserve consisting of the 3d Battalion, 199th Guards Rifle Regiment (when and if it returned from its security mission), two batteries of the attached 611th Antitank Artillery Regiment, and a battery from the attached 1440th Self-propelled Artillery Regiment. In addition to normal artillery support provided by the 138th Guards Artillery Regiment, Baksov formed a long-range artillery group from the 159th Gun Artillery Regiment and two battalions of the 163d Gun Artillery Regiment, which were attached to the 67th Division by 6th Guards Army.

As did his neighboring 52d Guards Rifle Division, Baksov formed four antitank strong points, each with eight to ten antitank guns. Two of these covered the approaches into the village of Cherkasskoe on the division right flank (the 196th Guards Rifle Regiment sector), and one each protected the most trafficable approaches into his center 199th and right flank 201st Guards Rifle Regiments. The attached 868th and 611th Antitank Artillery Regiments provided the additional antitank guns for these strong points. A sapper platoon equipped with 250 mines formed his mobile obstacle detachment.

South of the town of Lukhanino and eight kilometers to the rear, Baksov positioned his tank reserve, which comprised the 245th Tank Regiment and remaining guns of the 1440th Self-propelled Artillery Regiment, which was equipped with twenty-one 76mm self-propelled pieces. These would deploy forward into battle once the German attack commenced, supposedly along with the twenty-four-gun 496th Antitank Artillery Regiment and the seventy-two-gun 27th Antitank Artillery Brigade, which army and *front* promised to commit in his sector.

Baksov's chief concern was for the viability of his defense in the division center and right flank. Once an enemy force was past Butovo and the Berezovyi valley, it could bypass the Cherkasskoe strong point and had a clear path northward down the gently sloping open terrain to the banks of the Pena River. Once that occurred, however, it would be Colonel Chernov's and the 90th Guards' task to continue the defense with Katukov's tankers.

Baskov's concerns were very real, for the Germans were about to commit *Grossdeutschland* Panzer Grenadier Division, 11th Panzer Division, and two infantry regiments of the 167th Infantry Division against his defending 67th Rifle Division guardsmen.

DECEPTION, INSPECTION, AND TRAINING

In addition to these defensive positions, the Soviets implemented an elaborate strategic, operational, and tactical deception *(maskirovka)* plan to confuse the Germans as to their true strength, dispositions, and intentions.[60] On the one hand, the Soviets attempted to conceal their troop concentrations and defensive dispositions by a variety of active and passive means, including the construction of kilometers of false trenches, dummy tanks and artillery, notional tank dispersal areas, and false airfields.

More importantly, the *Stavka* and lower echelons sought to conceal the size, scale, and direction of their most important force regroupments and concentrations, particularly strategic regrouping associated with the assembly of Konev's Steppe Military District *(front)*. Over the course of a month, the *Stavka* moved its 27th and 53d Armies from the Northwestern Front to the region east of Kursk and its 46th and 47th Armies from the North Caucasus Front to the region east of Khar'kov. German intelligence failed to detect these armies prior to the beginning of the Kursk operation and had an imperfect appreciation of the true correlation of forces (see figure, facing page).[61] At the same time, the *Stavka* assembled forces in more conspicuous fashion for planned diversionary actions in other front sectors to draw German attention away from Kursk. The most important of these diversions were to occur farther south along the Northern Donets and Mius Rivers in Southwestern and Southern Fronts' sectors.[62]

Similarly, Soviet commanders sought to conceal operational and tactical regroupings. When 7th Guards Army moved into the sector of 69th Army in late June, for example, all communications used the radios of the units being replaced, so that German radio intercept units would not detect any change. All troop and rail movements were conducted at night or when visibility was limited to thwart German aerial reconnaissance. Similarly, visitors and foot traffic were restricted around headquarters so as not to attract attention. It was impossible to hide the extensive activities completely, but such techniques caused the Germans to seriously underestimate the strategic strength of their enemies. While German intelligence detected all major Soviet forces within the Kursk Bulge including Major General Nekrasov's 52d Guards, Major General Baksov's 67th Guards, and Colonel Chernov's 90th Guards Rifle Divisions and their supporting armor of Soviet 6th and 5th Guards Tank Corps, it failed to detect the defensive preparations of Steppe Military District. Moreover, it had little idea of the size, composition, mechanized capabilities, or offensive potential of General Konev's force.[63]

The peculiar greyish-yellow topsoil of the Kursk region both facilitated and hampered all attempts to conceal and camouflage the gathering host; turning over even a single shovel full would expose black Russian earth under-

Kräftegegenüberstellung
Stand: 1.4.43

	Deutsche Kräfte				Sowj. russ. Kräfte			
Frontabschnitt	Reserven i.d.Tiefe	Front u. frontnah			Front u. frontnah	Reserven i.d.Tiefe	Verbleib unbekannt	Gesamtsumme
A		8 J.D. 9 / 1 Pz. ⚐~	⚑		44 S.D. / 2 Pz.	2 S.D. / 7 Pz.		46 S.D. / 9 Pz.
		321800	⚙		388000	23500		411500
		43 (35)	▭		45	100		145
		581	✝		1749	87		1836
Süd	davon in Auffrischung: 4 J.D.	26 J.D. 39 / 13 Pz.	⚑		97 S.D. / 51 Pz.	43 S.D. / 43 Pz.		140 S.D. / 94 Pz.
		548000	⚙		1008000	524500		1532500
		887 (389)	▭		765	655		1420
		928	✝		3799	1815		5614
Mitte		70½ J.D. 78½ / 8 Pz.	⚑		152 S.D. / 56 Pz.	10 S.D. / 11 Pz.		162 S.D. / 67 Pz.
		1221000	⚙		1429500	131000		1560500
		396 (181)	▭		1210	165		1375
		2732	✝		6327	508		6835
Nord		42½ J.D.	⚑		115 S.D. / 34 Pz.	5 S.D. / 18 Pz.		120 S.D. / 52 Pz.
		642000	⚙		1166500	51000		1217500
		10 (7)	▭		735	165		900
		2119	✝		4771	172		4943
Ostfront gesamt		147 J.D. 169 / 22 Pz.	⚑		408 S.D. / 143 Pz.	60 S.D. / 79 Pz.	36 S.D. / 29 Pz.	504 S.D. / 251 Pz.
		2732000	⚙		3992000	730500	429500	5152000
		1336 (612)	▭		2765	1085	400	4240 / +1800 6000
		6360	✝		16646	2582	1455	20683

Zahlen in ( ) = davon einsatzbereit

German estimate of the correlation of forces on the Eastern Front, 1 April 1943 neath, causing any construction to stand out in an aerial photograph. Thus, while it was relatively easy for the Soviets to create the illusion of construction activity, it was most difficult to conceal actual construction and troop concentrations.

Such elaborate defenses would be useless without communications to permit the defenders to respond to German threats. Communications had been a persistent problem for the Red Army, but the long German delay at Kursk permitted the Soviets to lay thousands of kilometers of communication wire, establishing a flexible and resilient system that could summon reserve forces or artillery fire to any threatened sector. Communications tests were conducted twice each day. Similarly, Red Army engineers repaired and improved the roads and railways throughout the Kursk Bulge, although the Germans still controlled the elaborate networks radiating from Orel and Khar'kov.

All these defensive preparations were subject to frequent and minute inspection by higher headquarters. During the month of May 1943, for example, the two *front* staffs checked every detail of the defensive preparations on one of the three battalions in every rifle regiment. Instead of standard briefings in headquarters buildings, senior commanders and staff officers frequently reviewed progress by walking the actual terrain to be defended. A general would appear unannounced at a forward command post, designate a target location, and measure the speed of artillery response to the hypothetical threat. Such inspections paid unexpected dividends during the battle, when higher headquarters were intimately familiar with the problems of their subordinate units.

Simultaneously with the construction of these defenses, the Red Army undertook a massive program of staff exercises, war games, and troop training to prepare for the battle.[64] Headquarters attempted to foresee the possible evolution of the German attack and then develop detailed plans to respond to such contingencies. Reserve units, especially the tank armies, received midnight alert orders to move along unlighted routes they might have to follow in battle. Every headquarters developed preplanned targets for artillery and automatic weapons. The Soviet infantry underwent intensive training to overcome the natural fear of tanks and to learn the weaknesses of Tigers and other German vehicles. A typical front-line infantry company or artillery battery spent one day each week at specially developed training ranges, firing live ammunition at targets and drilling on different defensive tactics. Typical drills included counterattacking enemy infantry following behind tanks, withdrawing to an intermediate defensive position, and fighting while encircled. Meanwhile, combat engineers practiced a concept that later became a hallmark of Soviet defenses—mobile obstacle detachments, assigned to move to a threatened sector and build hasty antitank obstacles in

front of a developing German penetration. Moreover, all soldiers had to practice chemical defense, wearing uncomfortable gas masks for up to eight hours
at a time in the increasingly warm weather of early summer.

FALSE ALARMS

These elaborate preparations were frequently interrupted by alerts of imminent German attack. Such alerts were often, although not always, based on
intelligence that was accurate at the time; only Hitler's vacillation made these
warnings false. Prior to the German assault Soviet intelligence organs at all
levels constructed a fairly accurate picture of German intent. Strategically,
information from Soviet agents in Central Europe, including the famous "Red
Orchestra" (Rote Kapelle) spoke clearly and unambiguously about German
intent to launch a summer offensive. In April 1943 British intelligence passed
similar information obtained through ULTRA (British code-breaking communications intercepts) means to the Soviets (without revealing the source),
but this information soon dried up due to an apparent British decision to halt
the passing of such information. Meanwhile, Soviet agents controlled by the
army's GRU (Main Intelligence Directorate) and force intelligence organs
collected extensive data that confirmed these agent reports. While strategic
information was valuable, ordinary combat intelligence and reconnaissance
permitted the Soviets to make fairly accurate predictions of operational and
tactical aspects of the planned German offensive. Despite this extensive intelligence effort and the mountains of data obtained, the Soviets were not
able to determine the precise location and strength of the German assault
south of Kursk.[65]

The *Stavka* issued at least three such warnings during May, on the 2d,
8th, and 19th.[66] On 8 May, for example, Stalin insisted that the entire region
be brought to a complete state of readiness in anticipation of a German offensive by 10 May. When the attack failed to materialize, on 26 May an impatient Vatutin and his political "Member of the Military Council," Nikita
Sergeevich Khrushchev, urged a preemptive attack on Khar'kov, arguing that
the German offensive had been canceled. Once again, Vasilevsky, Antonov,
and Zhukov risked Stalin's displeasure by arguing strenuously for the need
to wait for the German offensive. The Soviet dictator saw the wisdom of their
arguments but could not escape a nagging fear that Soviet defenses would
collapse as they had done so often in the previous two years.[67]

Meanwhile, the two sides sparred with each other in the air and on the
ground. Between 6 and 8 May, anticipating a German offensive in the near
future, the Red Air Force bombed seventeen German airfields. After the
initial surprise, these attacks were relatively ineffective. Nevertheless, in three

days Red aviators flew 1,400 sorties, destroying 500 German aircraft for a loss of 122 of their own. On 22 May and 2 June, the Luftwaffe in turn attacked the Kursk railroad junction, seeking to disrupt the logistical buildup of the defenders. The Germans even attempted some strategic bombing, such as long-range raids on the Gorki tank manufacturing plant.[68]

At the same time, Soviet reconnaissance teams and partisans operated throughout the German rear areas, gathering information and sabotaging the logistical buildup for Operation Citadel. During June alone, partisans operating behind Army Group Center destroyed 298 locomotives, 1,222 railroad cars, and 44 bridges. Every day railroad tracks were cut in thirty-four places, causing the Germans endless difficulty as they moved supplies and ammunition forward. This vast network of agents gave the Red Army far more accurate intelligence about German capabilities than the Germans had about their opponents.[69]

Both sides became increasingly high-strung and strained as the date of the German offensive obviously approached. Soldiers and junior leaders, whether Soviet or German, privately suffered the self-doubt that so often precedes combat. No matter how confident the Soviet defenders might have been, they all realized that no one had ever halted a deliberate blitzkrieg offensive before. The same thought must have comforted the German troops as they studied the labyrinth of defensive positions in front of them.

Beginning on 1 July, the Red Army defenders were on constant alert, waiting in their bunkers and positions for the first sign of attack. Neither side got much rest in the short nights and long, hot days of the Russian summer.

Marshal of the Soviet Union G. K. Zhukov, Representative of the *Stavka* to the Western, Briansk, and Central Fronts.

Marshal of the Soviet Union A. M. Vasilevsky (left), Representative of the *Stavka* to the Voronezh Front, with Lieutenant General I. D. Cherniakhovsky, 60th Army commander.

Colonel General M. M. Popov, commander, Briansk Front.

Army General N. F. Vatutin, commander, Voronezh Front.

Colonel General V. D. Sokolovsky (far right), commander, Western Front, with Marshal of the Soviet Union G. K. Zhukov (1945 photo).

Army General K. K. Rokossovsky, commander, Central Front.

Colonel General I. S. Konev (right), commander, Steppe Front, and his chief of staff Lieutenant General M. V. Zakharov.

Lieutenant General V. M. Badanov, commander, 4th Tank Army.

Lieutenant General M. E. Katukov, commander, 1st Tank Army (1941 photo).

Lieutenant General A. G. Rodin, commander, 2d Tank Army.

Lieutenant General P. A. Rotmistrov (center), commander, 5th Guards Tank Army, and his staff.

Lieutenant General R. S. Rybalko (right), commander, 3d Guards Tank Army, conferring with his chief of staff, General V. A. Mitrofanov (left), and 91st Tank Brigade commander, Lieutenant General I. I. Iakobovsky (center).

Field Marshal Erich von Manstein, commander, Army Group South.

Field Marshal Guenther von Kluge, commander, Army Group Center.

Colonel General Hermann Hoth (center), commander, Fourth Panzer Army.

Colonel General Walter Model, commander, Ninth Army.

General of Panzer Troops Werner Kempf, commander, Army Detachment Kempf.

General of Panzer Troops Otto von Knobelsdorff, commander, XXXXVIII Panzer Corps.

SS *Obergruppenfuehrer* Paul Hauser, commander, II SS Panzer Corps.

CHAPTER 4

Frontal Assault,
5–9 July

THE FIELD OF BATTLE

The Orel-Kursk region forms a rolling plateau called the Central Russian Uplands, which extends from the Bolkhov-Mtsensk region in the north to the Rakitnoe-Belgorod region in the south.[1] The Uplands are bordered on the east by the Oka and Don River basins beyond the cities of Elets and Staryi Oskol and on the west by the Dnepr River and Desna River basin west of Sevsk and Sumy. The Uplands are drained by several major rivers, including the Oka, which runs eastward into the Don River, the Northern Donets, and its tributaries, the Lipovyi Donets, Koren', and Korocha, which run to the south, and the Desna, Svapa, Seim, and Vorskla, which run west and southwest into the Dnepr River basin. German forces occupied an extensive salient in the northern portions of the Uplands around the city of Orel, while the Soviet Kursk Bulge dominated the Upland's southern region.

The Red Army anchored its defenses along the northern edge of the Kursk Bulge on ridge lines north of the Svapa River valley and along the southern bank of the Oka River north of Kursk. Along the southern flank of the bulge, Soviet defenses extended along the higher ground north of the cities of Sumy and Belgorod. These ridges, however, were only several hundred feet above the valley floors, and the terrain adjacent to the rivers was gentle, rolling, and punctuated with scattered ravines and small groves of trees. In short, the terrain resembled that of southern Ohio or Surrey, England, and it was excellent tank country.

Soviet defenses north of Kursk ran parallel to the small streams and rivers that traversed the region, and these waterways, although dry in July, tended to fill rapidly with water during the frequent summer thunderstorms. Thus, the streams and associated ravines assisted Soviet forces in their defense. South of Kursk, several rivers and many associated streams that ran from north to south cut through the Soviet defense lines. These included the Northern Donets River and its tributary, the Lipovyi Donets, just east of Belgorod, and the Vorskla and its tributary Vorskolets River, which cut from north to south through the main Soviet defenses west of Belgorod. Although some of the river valleys offered easy approaches into the Soviet defensive positions, other tributaries running from east to west and adjacent ravines reinforced these defenses, particularly during and after rainstorms. The banks of these rivers were low, and the rivers were generally fordable, with one notable exception. The Northern Donets River south of Belgorod had high western banks (up to 300 feet), which loomed over the lower plains extending eastward from the river's eastern bank. German positions on these heights dominated Soviet defenses on the river's east bank to a depth of more than ten kilometers.

The city of Kursk nestled along the banks of the Seim River in the center of the Soviet Kursk Bulge. Kursk was a key rail and road hub whose communication sinews spread to the periphery of the salient. Loss of this city would render the Soviet salient indefensible. To seize Kursk German forces would only have to penetrate the high ground north or south of the city. Once Kursk fell into German hands, the vast expanse of the Don Basin offered several broad routes for subsequent operations northeastward toward Moscow or eastward to the Don River.

Outside the city, the Soviet bulge was punctuated by scattered large and small farming hamlets, most of which the Red Army fortified and integrated into their successive defensive lines. These population centers were flanked by rolling farm country and abandoned fields. The narrow streams that dissected the Uplands were invisible a few hundred meters away, but they were generally fordable by armored forces. Entering and exiting the stream beds was often difficult, however, since in some areas their banks and approaches were earthen, marshy, and, during rains, swampy. The streams themselves were generally narrow, slow-moving, and relatively shallow. The most obvious exception was the Northern Donets River in the southeast, near Khar'kov, which was a major water obstacle for both sides.

Clumps of trees punctuated the rolling landscape, particularly in the stream valleys and around stream junctions where small hamlets often rested. Although these hamlets formed excellent strong points, they could easily be bypassed by forces advancing along the adjacent ridges.

The famous Russian "black earth," which characterized the soils in the region, was extremely fine, producing considerable dust when dry and then dissolving into a muddy morass after a rain. As in most of the Soviet Union, the roads were largely unpaved, dirt trails that could not support heavy wheeled vehicle traffic, particularly in wet weather. The only paved route was the main road running from Orel to Kursk and then southward from Kursk through Belgorod. For this reason, forces often operated along rail lines and rail rights-of-way, which were more extensive than the road system. Tanks and other tracked vehicles could usually move across country, but the folds of the plateau provided natural cover and concealment for defenders, and the streams and ravines formed excellent antitank positions.

Although the climatic conditions of high summer offered a welcome respite from the appalling weather and terrain conditions of the spring *rasputitsa* (thaw), summer posed challenges of its own. Warmer weather meant temperatures reaching 90 degrees Fahrenheit (over 30 degrees Celsius), oppressive humidity, and frequent afternoon and evening thunderstorms. While relieving the heat and ubiquitous dust, these storms instantly transformed dry streams, ravines, and dirt roads into temporary morasses.

PRELIMINARY MOVES

Shortly after 1600 hours on 4 July 1943, as was their custom prior to a major offensive, German forces along the southern face of the Kursk Bulge launched a reconnaissance-in-force (see Maps 6 and 7). The purpose of these limited actions was to eliminate the combat outposts, battalion-sized strong points, and observation posts in front of the Voronezh Front's first main defensive belt, to determine the precise location of the Russians' forward defenses, and, if possible, to gain a lodgment in those defenses so that the full weight of Fourth Panzer Army could strike the Soviet defenses at first light on the following morning.

Forward battalions from General von Knobelsdorff's XXXXVIII Panzer Corps initiated the reconnaissance along a front from Zybino to Pushkarnoe in an attempt to overcome the already identified Soviet outposts at Gertsovka, Gertsovka Station, Butovo, and Streletskoe. Advanced battalions from the 11th Panzer Division and from *Grossdeutschland* Division's Grenadier Regiment struck the outpost defenses of the Soviet 52d Guards Rifle Division's 3d Battalion, 151st Guards Rifle Regiment, defending between Streletskoe and Berezov. In the ensuing fight, which lasted several hours, the grenadiers succeeded in encircling most of the Soviet battalion and sweeping the remnants back from their forward positions and into the hills around Dragunskoe.

An even fiercer fight raged for possession of Gertsovka and Gertsovka Station. The 3d Battalion of *Grossdeutschland's* Fusilier Regiment and the 1st Battalion of 3d Panzer's 394th Panzer Grenadier Regiment ran into heavy resistance from the Soviet 2d Battalion, 210th Rifle Regiment, at and around Gertsovka and the 2d Battalion, 213th Rifle Regiment, near Novaia Gorianka. Heavy Russian antitank and mortar fire from Gertsovka pinned down the attacking Germans and severely wounded the Fusilier battalion commander and one-third of the men of his 15th Company, including the commander's replacement. The ensuing three-hour struggle was a portent of things to come. By 2100 hours, the grenadiers had finally cleared Gertsovka, but the human cost had been high.[2]

Meanwhile, to the east, advanced battalions of *Grossdeutschland's* Grenadier Regiment and 11th Panzer Division seized the treeless ridge lines east and west of Butovo but left the defending Russian battalion isolated in the

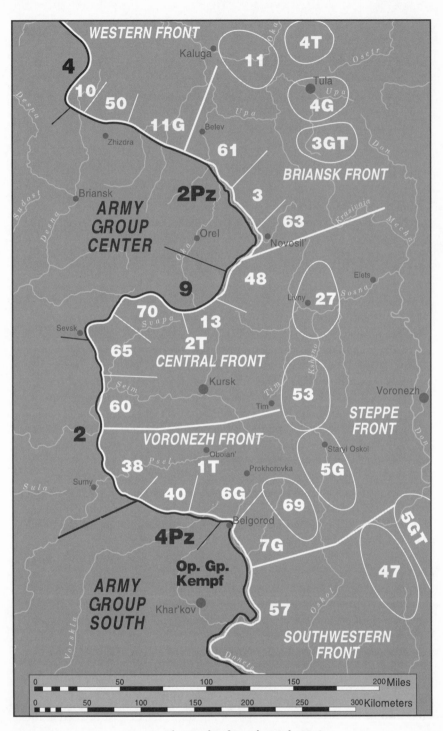

Map 6. The Battle of Kursk, 4 July 1943

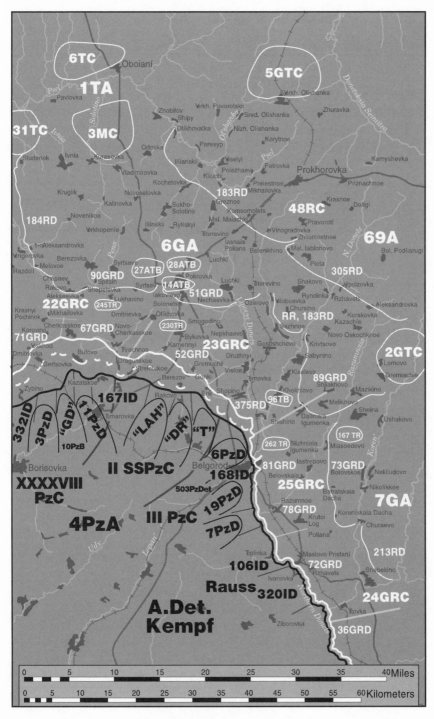

Map 7. Voronezh Front, 4 July 1943

low ground around Butovo village, where its threatening antitank guns could not inflict damage on the advancing Germans.[3] A group of riflemen from the Soviet 67th Guards Rifle Division's 3d Battalion, 199th Guards Rifle Regiment, commanded by Senior Lieutenant A. I. Starchikov, defended Butovo for seven hours, often in fierce hand-to-hand fighting. Although the group "perished in unequal combat, they did not abandon their positions."[4]

Thinking that the Soviets' defense had been rent, the Germans dug in to await the artillery bombardment and the general tank and infantry assault. They were optimistic, since before them they observed only open terrain punctuated by a shallow ravine a kilometer to their front. As darkness fell, the main force of *Grossdeutschland's* Fusilier and Grenadier Regiments, side by side, moved into assembly areas just south of Butovo, backed up by the division's Panzer Regiment and the lumbering Panther tanks of General Lauchert's 10th Panzer Brigade, while 3rd and 11th Panzer Division troops and armor moved silently forward into jumping off positions on their left and right flanks.[5]

Twenty kilometers to the east, where Soviet positions were closer to the German front lines, advanced battalions of *Obergruppenfuehrer* Paul Hausser's II SS Panzer Corps began its reconnaissance-in-force at 0115 hours on 5 July. Although fierce fighting also characterized their advance, by 0300 hours they had seized Soviet forward positions at Iakhontov and on the southern slopes of the Erik River valley.[6] Fourth Panzer Army's reconnaissance destroyed about half of the outposts in front of 6th Guards Army and forced many of the remaining outposts to withdraw. The Soviet battalions and platoons did so later in the evening, in the full knowledge that they had begun the battle in appropriate fashion. Because of the Northern Donets River barrier, the German reconnaissance in the 7th Guards Army zone was much weaker than elsewhere. The smaller German patrols had little impact on the Soviet defenders.

Although the sounds of battle faded after midnight, the expected lull before the planned German morning bombardment never materialized. Heavy thunder, violent lightning, and torrential rains bedeviled the assembling German host. To make matters worse, Soviet artillery fire soon joined the cacophony of sound that announced the beginning of the Battle of Kursk. The sudden and intense Soviet artillery fire confirmed what many Germans feared: the assault would not surprise the Red Army.

That evening, a combat patrol from the Soviet 6th Guards Army in the south captured a private from the German 168th German Infantry Division who told his captors that the offensive would begin at dawn on 5 July.[7] Other prisoners had made similar statements throughout May and June, but in connection with the afternoon's preliminary attacks, Vatutin and his advisors were convinced that the great struggle was finally at hand. Marshal Vasilevsky, as the *Stavka* representative to the Voronezh Front, authorized the defenders to begin their counterpreparation, a preplanned artillery barrage that was aimed at known and suspected enemy assembly areas. Vasilevsky passed the information on to Marshal Zhukov, his counterpart in the Central Front. Soon after 0200 hours the next morning, the commander of 13th Army, Lieutenant General N. P. Pukhov, informed Zhukov that his troops had captured Lance Corporal Bruno Fermella, a German combat engineer from the 6th Infantry Division, apparently engaged in clearing minefields in preparation for the offensive. This prisoner had also predicted an offensive beginning at 0300 hours on 5 July. Zhukov immediately instructed Rokossovsky to have Central Front begin its own counterpreparation. Only then did Zhukov telephone Stalin with the news: the battle was finally beginning.

Thus, at 0110 hours (Voronezh Front) and 0220 hours (Central Front), the Soviet counterpreparation roared out all across the front. Some weapons, particularly antitank units, remained silent to avoid disclosing their positions, but otherwise the Red artillery did its utmost to disrupt the German offensive before it ever began.[8]

This counterpreparation had mixed results. Wherever the Soviets fired at known German artillery positions, the effect was devastating, catching German gunners in the open, preparing to fire their own concentrations to support the offensive. Elsewhere, however, the Soviet guns were aimed at large general areas and often missed their intended targets, the German troops in their final assembly areas. Across the board, however, this artillery fire undoubtedly disrupted, if it did not destroy, the German forces. When informed of the situation, OKH reluctantly agreed to move back the scheduled start time for the attack by two and one-half hours in Army Group Center and three hours in Army Group South. Even then, the initial German attacks were somewhat staggered and uncoordinated.[9]

The Red Air Force's simultaneous attempt to destroy the Luftwaffe on its airfields was less successful. Early on the morning of 5 July, *Freya* radars reported incoming large groups of hostile aircraft, and numerous Me-109s rose to intercept in the grayish haze of early morning. Because of their limited capacity for night navigation, the Soviet fliers attacked in a rigid pattern at altitudes of 7,000 to 10,000 feet, making them easy prey for both fighters and FlaK (antiaircraft) gunners. First Air Division in the north shot down approximately 120 Soviet aircraft, while in the south VIII Air Corps claimed to have destroyed 432 enemy planes on 5 July for the loss of only 26 of its own. These figures were undoubtedly as exaggerated as most such claims for aerial combat, but certainly the Luftwaffe survived relatively unscathed and was able to support the initial ground attacks as planned.[10]

THE NINTH ARMY ATTACKS, 5–6 JULY

At 0430 on 5 July, after the thirty-minute Soviet counterpreparation had ended, Ninth German Army began an eighty-minute artillery preparation of its own, focusing on the first four kilometers of Soviet defensive positions (see Map 8). First Air Division also began to bomb these positions as well as the Red airfields around Kursk.[11] To weaken the effect of the German artillery preparation, General Pukhov ordered 13th Army to repeat its artillery counterpreparation at 0435 hours, five minutes after the German firing began. The 967 Soviet guns and mortars reduced but could not defeat the German artillery preparation. At 0530 the German ground attacks jumped off.[12]

As a recognized expert on defensive tactics, Walter Model was acutely aware of the vulnerability of his armored vehicles—particularly the Elephant self-propelled guns—to short-range attack by determined infantrymen in prepared defensive positions. To reduce this vulnerability, he had insisted that his armored spearheads be accompanied by dismounted infantry. This tactic undoubtedly reduced his tank losses but only at the expense of higher infantry casualties.

The first German attack by General Johannes Freissner's XXIII Corps on the eastern flank of Ninth Army was primarily an infantry action designed to confuse the Soviets about the real focal point of the German attack. This secondary effort failed to make a major penetration. Attacking at the vulnerable boundary between 13th and 48th Armies, Freissner's corps tried to seize the town of Maloarkhangel'sk, a road junction that would permit rapid advances to the east, west, and south, toward Kursk. The soldiers of the German 78th, 216th, and 36th Infantry Divisions, supported by Stukas and a limited number of tanks, pushed approximately 1.5 kilometers into the first defensive belt manned by the 13th Army's 148th and 8th Rifle Divisions (of Soviet 15th Rifle Corps) and by the 48th Army's neighboring 16th Rifle Division. The defenders not only halted this attack but also launched local counterattacks, so that the XXIII Corps made little progress toward Maloarkhangel'sk.[13]

The main attack by the XXXXVII Panzer and XXXXI Panzer Corps had more success. Three panzer and four infantry divisions, supported by a constant stream of airstrikes, assaulted the defenses of the 29th Rifle Corps' 15th and 81st Rifle Divisions northwest of Ponyri. The 120 tanks and assault guns of the 20th Panzer Division of General Lemelsen's XXXXVII Panzer Corps, the only German panzer division committed to the initial assault, breached the 15th Rifle Division's forward defenses by 0900 hours. Supported by vicious artillery fire and air strikes, Major General Mortimer von Kessel's division advanced five kilometers, routed the defending Soviet 15th Rifle Division's 321st Rifle Regiment, and seized the village of Bobrik. There it was halted by intense fire from

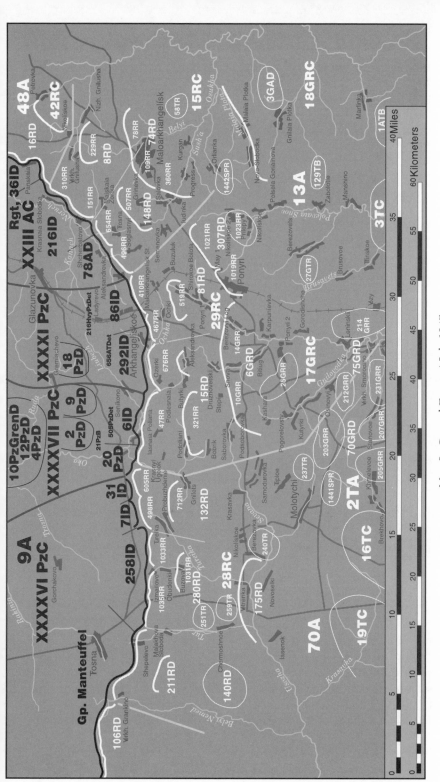

Map 8. Central Front, 4 July 1945

the 17th Guards Rifle Corps' 6th Guards Rifle Division, which was dug in along the ridges to the rear of the 29th Rifle Corps.[14]

A Soviet source vividly described the intense fighting in the 29th Rifle Corps sector:

> It was difficult to verify that anything remained alive in front of such a steel avalanche. The sky blackened from smoke and heat. The acrid gases from the exploding shells and mines blinded the eyes. The soldiers were deafened by the thunder of guns and mortars and the creaking of tracks. Their motto became the words "Not a step back, stand to the death!" . . . The first to enter the struggle were the artillery units, which fired concentration, mobile, and fixed barrage fire from concealed positions. As the Germans neared the forward edge, antitank artillery and antitank rifles opened direct fire on their tanks. Mortar and machine-gun fire concentrated on the enemy infantry. Our assault and fighter aviation appeared over the field of battle. Lunging forward, the penetrating enemy tanks began blowing up in the minefields. The tanks' movement slowed from the difficulty of overcoming the dense curtain of artillery, mortar, and submachine-gun fire. More and more frequently the infantry began to hit the dirt. Only by 0900 hours did the enemy succeed in penetrating into the dispositions of Major General A. B. Barinov's 81st Rifle Division and Colonel V. N. Dzhandzhgava's 15th Rifle Division.
>
> All of the weapons of the infantry, and the antitank strong points and artillery groups supporting these divisions, entered the battle to repel the enemy blows. Soviet soldiers heroically struggled with the attacking groups of enemy. The infantry skillfully destroyed his tanks with grenades and bottles filled with mixtures of fuel. Under a hurricane of fire they stole up to the enemy vehicles, struck them with antitank grenades, set them on fire with incendiary bottles, and laid mines under them. Overall, during the course of the day, the sappers emplaced an additional 6,000 mines in the army sector, which became a dreadful threat for enemy tanks and self-propelled guns.[15]

To the east, the German 6th Infantry Division, supported by two Tiger tank companies of the 505th Heavy Panzer Detachment, smashed through a defensive screen of T-34 tanks and antitank guns and penetrated the defenses of the 15th Rifle Division's right flank 676th Rifle Regiment. The fierce assault propelled German forces to the village of Butyrki and threatened the neighboring 81st Rifle Division with envelopment on its left flank. Simultaneously, on the 81st's right flank, the German 292d Infantry Division of General Joseph Harpe's XXXXI Panzer Corps, supported by the Elephants of the 653d Antitank Detachment, had already torn into the Soviet defenses northwest of Ponyri and threatened to collapse the 81st Rifle Division's defensive front.[16]

Farther east, along the rail line running south to Ponyri, the XXXXI Panzer Corps' 86th Infantry Division, supported by a regiment of the 18th Panzer Division and the Elephants of the 653d and 654th Antitank Detachments, lunged southward along the rail right-of-way toward Ponyri Station. To bolster the sagging 81st Rifle Division defenses, Pukhov committed his 129th Tank Brigade and 1442d Self-propelled Artillery Regiment. Although the Soviet defenders of the 29th Rifle Corps turned back the Germans four times on the morning of 5 July, on the fifth attack the corps' forward regiments had to withdraw. In order to maintain contact with its neighbor, the undefeated 148th Rifle Division, northwest of Maloarkhangel'sk, also had to pull back.[17] Meanwhile the XXXXVI Panzer Corps launched a supporting attack to the west of the main struggle. In intense fighting, the 7th and 31st Infantry Divisions inched forward toward Gnilets against determined opposition by 132d Rifle Division riflemen, but the 285th Infantry's advance ground to a halt after only minimal gains.

Rokossovsky responded by sending 350 Red aircraft to support 13th Army and gave Pukhov control of the 13th and 1st Antitank Brigades, an artillery brigade, and the 21st Separate Mortar Brigade from the Central Front reserve. The 74th Rifle Division, 15th Rifle Corps' second echelon division defending Maloarkhangel'sk itself, had to move forward to hold the eastern flank of the German penetration. Pukhov tried to choke off this penetration by deploying two mobile obstacle detachments, his reserve 27th Guards Tank Regiment, and combat engineer units from all parts of 13th Army.[18] A process had begun that would characterize the fierce fighting along the northern flank of the Kursk Bulge. Pukhov and Rokossovsky responded to the inexorable German advance by committing to combat a seemingly endless stream of armored, antitank, artillery, and engineer forces. As soon as the blazing cauldron of fire had consumed one force, another would arrive to replace it and stoke the flames of combat. This was attrition war with a vengeance. Unless the German armored spearheads achieved operational freedom beyond the Soviet tactical defenses, resources and sheer willpower would determine the outcome of this bitter struggle. Model was resolved to achieve that operational freedom; Pukhov and Rokossovsky were equally determined to deny him the opportunity.

As fighting continued on the morning and early afternoon of 5 July, the 15th Rifle Division was severely mauled as it withdrew its forward regiments to a line of ridges west of Ponyri. During the withdrawal the division's 676th Rifle Regiment was encircled and had to fight its way back to the positions of the second echelon 6th Guards Rifle Division.[19] This withdrawal also exposed the right flank of 70th Army, immediately to the west of the 15th Rifle Division. The easternmost division of 70th Army, Major General T. K. Shkrylev's 132d Rifle Division, then became a focus of renewed German air and ground attacks by the 7th and 31st Infantry Divisions of German XXXXVI Panzer Corps and was itself forced back with heavy losses. Pursuing German forces were finally halted by dense minefields covered by intense antitank fire.

While the ground fighting swelled, an intense air battle took place over the compact battlefield. Soviet after-action reports recorded, "Large numbers of aircraft were continuously on the battlefield in this narrow front sector, and, as a result, intense air combat almost never ceased along the entire front from dawn until darkness fell."[20] At 0425 hours more than 150 German bombers escorted by fifty to sixty fighters struck Soviet forces and troop installations across the entire front, but especially around Maloarkhangel'sk Station. The initial assault was followed by waves of bombers striking every fifteen minutes. By 1100 hours the Germans had delivered about 1,000 sorties against Soviet defenses.

The intense German air assault forced 16th Air Army forces to depart from their original plan and Soviet fighters conducted an "episodic" struggle against attacking German aircraft, which amounted to only 520 sorties by noon on 5 July.[21] Although Soviet 16th Air Army returned to its planned operations at 0930 hours on 5 July, on the first day of battle that plan was largely ineffective. Small groups of Soviet fighters contested with German aircraft over the battlefield and attempted to clear the way for Soviet ground assault aircraft. Despite their efforts, few assault aircraft took part in combat on 5 July, and the attrition in Soviet fighter aircraft was high.

It was already apparent to German general and infantryman alike that this battle was unlike any previous encounter. As one observer poignantly noted:

> The Soviet infantry refused to panic in the face of the roaring Tiger and Ferdinand tanks. For weeks on end the Russian troops had been trained in antitank tactics by Party instructors and experienced tank officers. Everything had been done to inoculate the troops against the notorious "tank panic." The result was unmistakable.
>
> The Russian infantrymen allowed the tanks to rumble past their well-camouflaged foxholes and then came out to deal with the German grenadiers in their wake. Thus the battle continued to rage on in sectors that the forward tank commanders believed already won.
>
> Tanks and assault guns had to be brought back to relieve the grenadiers. Then they had to be sent forward again. And pulled back once more. By evening the grenadiers were exhausted, and the tanks and assault guns were out of fuel. But the attack had pushed deep into the Soviet defences.
>
> Battalions and regiments reported: "We're getting there! Not easily, and the battle has been bloody and costly. But we are getting there."

And one other thing all commanders reported unanimously: "Nowhere has the enemy been taken by surprise. Nowhere has he been soft. He had clearly been expecting the attack, and numerous statements by prisoners of war have confirmed this."

That was a nasty surprise. Nevertheless, all along the front of XXXXI Panzer Corps, there was a firm belief: "We'll dislodge Ivan."[22]

By the close of 5 July, Model's forces had broken into the first defensive belt at the junction between the 70th and 13th Armies, creating a lodgment approximately fifteen kilometers wide and, at its greatest extent west of Ponyri, eight kilometers deep (see Map 9). The Red Air Force had lost almost 100 aircraft over the Central Front, and although it claimed to have shot down 106 German aircraft, it was unable to counter the German close air support effort. In the process, however, about two-thirds of the over 300 tanks and assault guns that the Germans committed to battle were put out of action due to enemy fire or mechanical failure.[23] Although some of these vehicles could be repaired at night, Model had lost at least 20 percent of his total armored striking power on the first day, when his troops were at their strongest.

In response, the Central Front commander, Rokossovsky, ordered his subordinates to prepare a counterattack for the next day, attempting to use plans drawn up during previous war games. The divisions of the 17th Guards and 18th Guards Rifle Corps, occupying the second defensive belt, were to push the Germans out of their penetration and restore the first defensive belt. They were supported by the 2d Tank Army's 3d and 16th Tank Corps, commanded by Major Generals M. D. Sinenko and V. E. Grigor'ev, respectively. To assist Lieutenant General Rodin's 2d Tank Army in this task, Major General I. D. Vasil'ev's 19th Separate Tank Corps was attached to it and moved behind the threatened right flank of 70th Army. Finally, Major General S. I. Bogdanov's 9th Tank Corps, then in *front* reserve north of Kursk, was to move forward into assembly areas from which it could reinforce 2d Tank Army's counterattack.[24]

Considering the enormous residual power of the German offensive, this proposed counterattack was premature. Vasil'ev's 19th Tank Corps wasted so much time in reconnaissance and in passing through Soviet infantry defenses in the darkness that it was not ready to support the attack the next morning. Nor was Sinenko's 3d Tank Corps in position by dawn to participate in the attack. Thus, when the 4th Artillery Penetration Corps fired a barrage at 0350 hours on 6 July, only Lieutenant General A. L. Bondarev's 17th Guards Rifle and Grigor'ev's 16th Tank Corps were prepared to counterattack. The 19th Tank Corps was to join the fray as soon as it arrived in its jumping-off positions, and the 3d Tank Corps was to take up defensive positions south of Ponyri Station. Thus, fewer than 200 of 2d Tank Army's 465

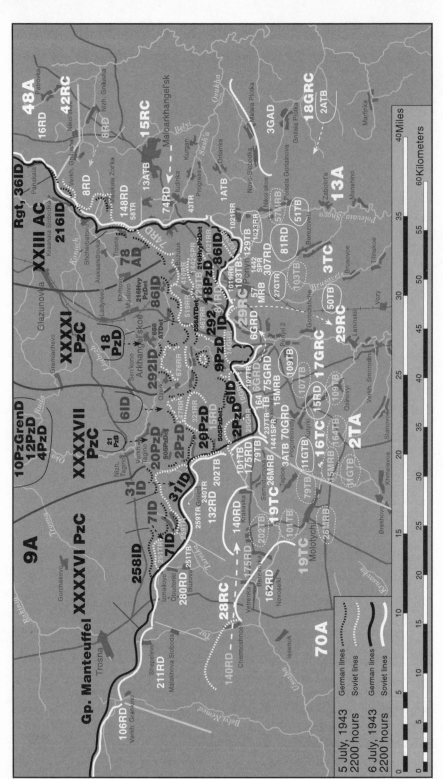

Map 9. Central Front, 5–6 July 1945

tanks would see action on 6 July. This new armor, coupled with German commitment of the 2d and 9th Panzer Divisions into battle (supported by the 505th Tiger Detachment), upped the ante and began an immense tank battle that would rage for four days along the barren ridges west of Ponyri Station. Between Ponyri and the small village of Saburovka, an armada of over 1,000 tanks and self-propelled guns, accompanied by massed infantry and artillery firing over open sights, struggled mightily and bloodily for possession of the key fortress villages of Ol'khovatka, Samodurovka, and nearby Hill 274. The ferocity of the fighting was unprecedented, and its potential consequences immense (Map 9).

Attacking toward Butyrki at the deepest point of German penetration, Lieutenant Colonel N. M. Teliakov's 107th Tank Brigade, leading the 16th Tank Corps, fell into an ambush of the Tiger-equipped 505th Panzer Detachment. In a matter of minutes, the Germans knocked out 46 of Teliakov's 50 tanks, and Lieutenant Colonel N. V. Kopylov's supporting 164th Tank Brigade, attacking on the 107th's left, was also heavily damaged, losing 23 tanks.[25] After repelling this counterattack, the XXXXVII Panzer Corps pursued the withdrawing Soviet troops, making a limited further advance up to the 13th Army's second defensive belt, where it ran into the entrenched riflemen of the 17th Guards Rifle Corps' 70th and 75th Guard Rifle Divisions. At 1830 hours that evening, the over 150 tanks of the 19th Tank Corps belatedly joined the attack, striking the nose of the advancing German 20th and 2d Panzer Division armor and infantry in the Bobrik-Samodurovka sector.[26]

While this struggle raged along the 13th Army's left flank, to the east General Harpe's XXXXI Panzer Corps again tried to split the 13th and 48th Armies apart. Late on 6 July, however, the combined assault force of the 292d and 86th Infantry Divisions and the 18th Panzer Division ground to a halt on the outskirts of Ponyri, their advance now blocked by the 29th Rifle Corps' second echelon 307th Rifle Division, which was dug in around Ponyri Station.[27] Thus the most that the first Soviet counterattack achieved was to delay the German advance for another day. By nightfall, the attacking tanks of the 2d Tank Army no longer represented a cohesive armored force. Committed in piecemeal fashion, they now fought desperate fragmented battles in support of the hard-pressed Soviet infantry. Soon Rodin would replicate this unfortunate use of Rokossovsky's precious armor by committing General Sinenko's 3d Tank Corps into battle, again in piecemeal fashion.

Although still tense, the air situation improved for the Soviets on 6 July. Despite their numerical superiority, Soviet fighters were not able to paralyze German air activity. Soviet fighters did, however, make it possible for assault aircraft to begin engaging German ground forces. The Soviets later claimed to have shot down a total of 113 German aircraft at a cost of 90 of their own planes.[28] The intensified air combat forced the Germans to commit fresh air forces from other front sectors to meet the Soviet air onslaught. Deprived of overall air superiority, the Germans concentrated their bomber and fighter assets to strike specific targets. In this manner they were able to achieve and barely maintain local air superiority at the critical points.

THE ATTACK IN THE SOUTH, 5–6 JULY

Three hours behind schedule, Colonel General Hermann Hoth's Fourth Panzer Army began its offensive on the morning of 5 July (see Map 10). The XXXXVIII Panzer and II SS Panzer Corps made their main attacks up two converging roads, leading to the north through Pokrovka and Oboian' toward Kursk. Many tank commanders in these two corps chose to lead with their new heavy Tiger tanks, reducing the exposure of the obsolescent Panzer IIIs and IVs but also exposing their best equipment to the full effect of a coordinated Soviet antitank defense. This tactic gave up the long-range armor penetration advantage enjoyed by the Tigers, bringing them close enough for the defending T-34s and antitank artillery to penetrate the thick German armor.

These massive assaults fell primarily on General Chistiakov's 6th Guards Army and particularly on Colonels Baksov's and Nekrasov's 67th Guards and 52d Guards Rifle Divisions defending northeast of Belgorod at the junction of the 22d and 23d Guards Rifle Corps. General Otto von Knobelsdorff's XXXXVIII Panzer Corps, 464 tanks and 89 assault guns strong, struck, with its 3d Panzer, *Grossdeutschland* Panzer Grenadier, and 11th Panzer Divisions attacking abreast northward from the positions they had secured the night before, supported on the flanks by grenadiers of the 332d and 167th Infantry Divisions. As spectacular as the initial German advance was, however, it was marred by difficulties that would come to characterize German frustration throughout the entire operation. Moreover, the Germans were unable to fulfill their initial mission of seizing crossings over the Psel River south of Oboian' by the end of 6 July.

Grossdeutschland's Fusilier and Grenadier Regiments, supported by 350 tanks and assault guns, advanced northward in a sector only three kilometers wide, led by the Fusiliers across the open ground fronting the ravine formed by the Berezovyi stream, and the Grenadiers astride the track leading from Butovo to the fortified village of Cherkasskoe, the anchor point of the 67th Guards Rifle Division's defenses.[29] Colonel Kassnitz's Fusilier Regiment, supported by a tank battalion of *Grossdeutschland's* Panzer Regiment and by the bulk of Colonel Lauchert's Panther Brigade, ran into minefields and deep mud in the ravine to its front. There, the regiment's advance stalled amid the din of exploding mines and withering fire from Soviet antitank guns and artillery firing over open sights from Soviet defensive positions on the heights

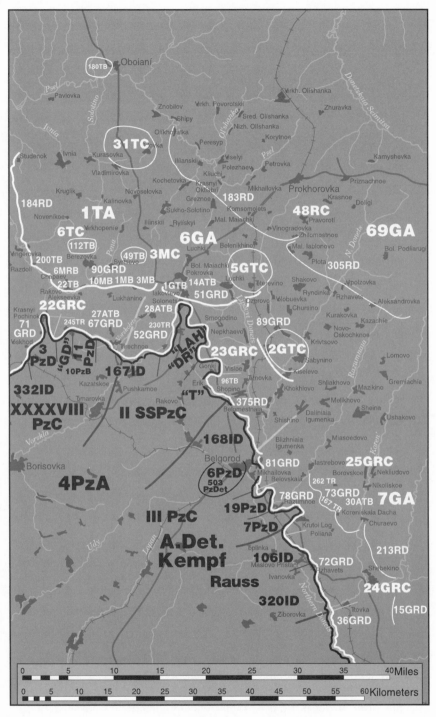

Map 10. Voronezh Front, 5 July 1943

to their front. For hours, sweating engineers labored in vain to clear the mines and open a route that the frustrated attackers could use to escape the bloody trap and withering hostile fire. *Grossdeutschland's* division history described the gruesome scene:

> The infantry left its positions and attacked, but there was something wrong with the fusiliers. The Panzer Regiment GD and the panther brigade were supposed to attack with them, however they had the misfortune to drive into a minefield which had escaped notice until then—and this even before reaching the bolshevik trenches! It was enough to make one sick. Soldiers and officers alike feared that the entire affair was going to pot. The tanks were stuck fast, some bogged down to the tops of their tracks, and to make matters worse the enemy was firing at them with antitank rifles, antitank guns, and artillery. Tremendous confusion breaks out. The fusiliers advance without the tanks—what can they do? The tanks do not follow. Scarcely does the enemy notice the precarious situation of the fusiliers when he launches a counterattack supported by numerous close-support aircraft. The purely infantry companies of III Panzer-Fusilier Regiment GD, or the 11th, 12th, and 13th Companies, walked straight into ruin. Even the heavy company suffered 50 killed and wounded in a few hours. Pioneers were moved up immediately and they began clearing a path through the mine-infested terrain. Ten more hours had to pass before the first tanks and self-propelled guns got through and reached the infantry.[30]

A lieutenant in *Grossdeutschland's* Panzer Artillery Regiment took up the bloody tale:

> The enemy fire is especially heavy before the attack lanes of the fusiliers, but the tanks? Where are our tanks? . . . Aren't they supposed to move out with the infantry? Then the bad news arrives: they're stuck in the minefield and cannot move. Any movement can bring further losses. First pioneers must come and remove the mines.
>
> Meanwhile we observe the fire with our naked eyes. Everything is shrouded in dust and smoke. The enemy observation posts certainly can't see anything. Our barrage is now over. The firing has become calmer and now is distributed over the specific areas as per the firing plan, at the same time it has wandered from the forward trenches farther to the rear. Are the infantry there? We can see some movement, but nothing specific. . . .
>
> General depression! My high spirits are gone. Then finally we get some good news: the grenadiers have taken advantage of the fire, have broken the bitter Soviet resistance in the trenches and are now advancing rap-

idly toward the hills. The general immediately moves the fusiliers to the right wing and sends them in behind the grenadiers. Everything is going to be all right after all.

Suddenly tanks appear behind us, more and more of them: they have a very long gun, a completely new type. Oh yes, the new Panther! Once again, however, our enthusiasm is dampened straight away: our tanks which have been able to free themselves from the minefield are now bogged down in a swamp which extends along a small stream. Patrols out at once! The available pioneer resources are totally inadequate for this job; it will take hours.

The breakthrough at the point of the main effort is therefore out! My lovely barrage! In view of this situation the corps transfers the point of main effort to the right where the 11th Panzer Division has made better progress than we. Quite contrary to expectations! Not until the afternoon do we get moving again, after first overcoming the unfavorable terrain and the enemy resistance.[31]

While the Fusilier Regiment was suffering its bloody rebuff, the Grenadier Regiment pushed northward along the Butovo-Cherkasskoe road, driving before it the remnants of the Soviet battalion that had been defending in Butovo. Despite ferocious resistance and near constant fire from Soviet defensive positions to the front, the Grenadiers and troops from the 11th Panzer Division's lead regiment (Combat Group Schimmelmann), attacking northward to the east of Butovo, smashed through the Soviet defenses and reached the outskirts of Cherkasskoe. Now the frustrated Fusilier Regiment and the critical armor of the Panther Brigade could extricate themselves from their marshy trap and join the march northward. This force swung to the east and followed the victorious Grenadiers into the heart of the Soviet 67th Rifle Division's defenses. Yet they made this march without the Fusilier commander, Colonel Kassnitz, who was seriously wounded while leading his troops in the fight to escape Berezovyi ravine, and also without thirty-six tanks that lay as smoking hulks in the deadly ravine.[32]

Pressed by *Grossdeutschland's* and 11th Panzer Division's relentless assault and by the 3d Panzer Division, which was attacking the 71st Guards Rifle Division on their right flank, the forward regiments of the 67th Guards finally gave way. The 196th Guards Rifle Regiment, reinforced by the blazing antitank guns of the 611th Antitank Regiment, made its last stand in the smoking ruins of Cherkasskoe village, and then, after nightfall, the pitiful remnants of the regiment escaped northwestward. The adjacent 199th and 201st Guard Rifle Regiments also caved in to the immense pressure. Reinforced by new antitank guns from the 1837th Antitank Regiment and armor from the 22d Guards Rifle Corps' 245th Tank and 1440th Self-propelled

Artillery Regiments, the shaken riflemen regrouped on the northern outskirts of Cherkasskoe. There they stubbornly defended for hours, their depleted ranks exacting a murderous toll on the advancing Germans.[33] All the while they prepared to conduct a fighting withdrawal to the northeast and the temporary safety of the 90th Guards Rifle Division's lines along the Pena River.

General Chernov's riflemen of the 90th Guards Division, in the 22d Guards Rifle Corps' second echelon eight kilometers from the front, could hear the intense fire reverberate to the south. As the sounds of battle grew throughout the afternoon, instinctively, they knew their turn was next. Late that afternoon and into the evening, they watched in silence as columns of tractors, trucks, antitank guns, and artillery sped southward toward the front, clear evidence that higher commands were responding to the challenge. Indeed they were! On the night of 5–6 July, Voronezh Front commander Vatutin released Lieutenant Colonel N. D. Chevola's powerful seventy-two-gun 27th Antitank Brigade to Chistiakov's control.[34] In turn, Chistiakov ordered two of the antitank brigade's regiments to assist the faltering 67th Guards Rifle and the third to reinforce the 90th Guards along the Pena River. These regiments joined the stream of reinforcements racing southward to close the breach in the Soviet defenses.

To the west of the *Grossdeutschland* Division, the 3d Panzer Division attacked due north from Gertsovka toward Korovino with the 394th Panzer Grenadier Regiment in the lead and the ninety tanks of the 6th Panzer Regiment poised to exploit a breach in Soviet lines. The attack struck and severely damaged the 210th Guards Rifle Regiment of Colonel I. P. Sivakov's 71st Guards Rifle Division, which was defending along the 67th Guards Rifle Division's left flank.[35] Although Sivakov's remaining two regiments successfully parried the German advance along the rail line west of Gertsovka, the division could not halt 3d Panzer's precipitous drive toward Korovino on the division's right flank. Panzer grenadiers of the 394th Panzer Grenadier Regiment overcame heavy antitank defenses covering the town, seized the key high ground in front of Korovino, and at dusk expelled the 210th Guards Rifle Regiment troopers from the bristling antitank strong point. Although Colonel Pappe, commander of the 394th, was wounded in the heavy fighting, his determined regiment prevailed. In late afternoon, the 2d Battalion, 6th Panzer Regiment, raced forward at the junction of the 71st and 67th Guards Divisions and seized the village of Krasnyi Pochinok, five kilometers deep in the Soviet rear. This daring German thrust penetrated the 71st Guards Division's second echelon defenses and forced Sivakov to pull his division back and reinforce his left flank to seal the yawning gap in his sagging defense line. Soviet forward defenses in this area were irrevocably breached. Fortunately, the impetus of the German advance was northward, and this permitted the 71st Guards to erect new defenses along a line facing east from its original positions to the Pena River and to prevent further German encroachment westward.

Nevertheless, von Knobelsdorff's panzer corps had torn a huge hole in the Soviet 22d Guards Rifle Corps' defenses, and the hole was too large to be repaired. Now the 3d Panzer, *Grossdeutschland,* and 11th Panzer Divisions prepared to complete the breakthrough and to wheel their armored spearheads northward and northeastward toward the Pena River. The question was whether von Knobelsdorff's victorious armor could now breach the Soviet second echelon defenses along the Pena on schedule and continue the headlong advance toward Oboian'. Vatutin resolved they would not and quickly reinforced his Pena defenses with heavy armor.

Despite having a number of antitank and tank units attached to it, Colonel Nekrasov's 52d Guards Rifle Division was even more hard-pressed by the II SS Panzer Corps' attack. *Obergruppenfuehrer* Paul Hausser's three SS panzer grenadier divisions, with 356 operational tanks and 95 assault guns, and supported by an entire *Nebelwerfer* multiple rocket launcher brigade, struck shortly after 0400 hours.[36] The 1st SS Panzer Grenadier Division *Leibstandarte Adolf Hitler,* commanded by SS *Brigadefuehrer* Theodor Wisch, advanced with guns blazing up the main road toward Bykovka, flanked on the left by the infantry from the 167th Infantry Division's 315th Grenadier Regiment. The 2d and 3d SS Panzer Grenadier Divisions *Das Reich* and *Totenkopf* were echeloned to the right, their advance oriented on the Soviet village strong points of Berezov and Gremuchii. Despite the SS Panzer Corps' spectacular advance, the stubborn Red defenders, as well as the mechanical unreliability of the Tigers, took a steady toll on the attacking panzers. An observer recorded the ferocity of the fighting: "The Tigers rumbled on. Antitank rifles cracked. Grenadiers jumped into trenches. Machine-guns ticked. Shells smashed sap trenches and dug-outs. The very first hours of fighting showed that Hausser's divisions were encountering a well-prepared and well-functioning opposition."[37]

Despite this opposition, *Leibstandarte's* two grenadier regiments smashed through the antitank defenses of the 151st Guards Rifle Regiment and commenced a grinding advance northward along the road to Bykovka. Soviet riflemen, antitank riflemen, and antitank guns of Lieutenant Colonel Kotenko's 1008th Antitank Artillery Regiment hotly contested every meter of ground, as did the neighboring 538th Antitank Artillery Regiment.[38] Deployed amid antitank strong points integrated into forward Soviet defenses along the road, the 1008th Regiment's 2d Battery, commanded by Senior Lieutenant Ratushniak, destroyed six German tanks, including three Tigers, before being itself overrun. The 3d Battery similarly contested *Das Reich's* advance on Berezov. Thereafter, throughout the afternoon the antitank regiment's remaining 1st, 4th, 5th, and 6th Batteries deployed in successive lines along the road to Bykovka and in the town itself and contested the headlong German advance. By late afternoon the regiment counted a toll of thirty-three destroyed German tanks, including seventeen Tigers. The intense fighting, however, decimated Kotenko's regiment. With twenty-one of its twenty-four guns destroyed and over half of its men killed, the survivors fought as infantry during the final defense of Bykovka.[39] As *Leibstandarte's* lead elements lunged on toward Bykovka, the Soviet 1st Battalion, 5th Guards Mortar (Katiusha) Regiment, leveled its multiple rocket launcher tubes and fired over open sights at the advancing Germans. This novel and terrifying use of Katiushas would become commonplace over the ensuing days.

By late afternoon, *Leibstandarte's* panzers and panzer grenadiers prevailed. At 1610 hours Bykovka fell to the 2d SS Panzer Grenadier Regiment, and without halting the 2d and 1st SS Panzer Grenadier Regiments marched northward through the 52d Rifle Division's remaining defenses, with orders to reach and cross the Psel River by nightfall. However, this was easier said than done. By 1800 hours the SS panzer grenadiers had advanced another six kilometers and seized the town of Koz'ma-Dem'iankovka, within striking distance of the division's first objective, Pokrovka. At this juncture Wisch ordered his 1st SS Panzer Regiment to begin its northward exploitation. However, as it raced toward the key road junction of Iakovlevo, the tanks ran headlong into a new Soviet defense line, which bristled with tanks, antitank guns, and dug-in infantry.

Leibstandarte's divisional history described the evening's frustration: "At 14.30 hours [1630 Moscow time], Panzergruppe LAH received orders to make its way through the second enemy lines east of Jakowlewo on that same day (5 July) and to establish a bridgehead across the Psel. At 18.00 [2000] hours, the Panzergruppe crossed the frontline near Hill 234.8 and just as the night was falling, ran into an antitank front near Jakowlewo. The Division ordered the Panzergruppe to stop and to resume its attack in the morning."[40]

Here the tired attackers halted to prepare for a subsequent advance to the Psel River the next morning. *Leibstandarte's* spectacular advance had torn apart the Soviet 52d Guards Rifle Division's defenses, destroying many troops and 15 enemy tanks in the process. The cost, however, had been high, as the 1st SS Division itself lost 97 dead, 522 wounded, 17 missing, and about 30 tanks.[41]

On *Leibstandarte's* right flank, SS *Gruppenfuehrer* Walter Kruger's 2d SS Panzer Grenadier Division *Das Reich* smashed Soviet defenses at Berezov, and by nightfall its forward elements had severed the key Oboian'-Belgorod road, cutting off the Soviet 155th Guards Rifle Regiment from its parent 52d Guards Rifle Division.[42] Farther south SS *Gruppenfuehrer* H. Priess's 3d SS Panzer Grenadier Division *Totenkopf* seized Gremuchii, wheeled to the right, and drove the defending 155th Guards into the right flank of the Soviet 375th

Rifle Division.[43] The 155th held fast along the Belgorod-Oboian' road thanks to its quick reinforcement by the 96th Tank Brigade, which had been dispatched in haste from the neighboring sector of the 375th Rifle Division. Its prompt arrival and strenuous efforts prevented *Totenkopf* from enveloping the 375th Rifle Division's right flank. This, in turn, prevented timely German seizure of Soviet defensive positions north of Belgorod and would cause considerable future grief to both Fourth Panzer Army and Army Detachment Kempf.

Thus, by early evening on 5 July, Hausser's SS troopers, supported by the VIII Air Corps, had split the 52d Guards Rifle Division in half and penetrated almost twenty kilometers to the minefields and obstacles in front of 6th Guards Army's second defensive belt. Although the 52d Guards had suffered more than 30 percent casualties, its defending regiments fought on, the 155th Guards covering the eastern flank of the German penetration along with the 375th Rifle Division, and the 151st and 153d Guards holding the ever-extending western flank along the Vorskla River.

In response to the initial German successes in the 6th Guards Army's sector, Chistiakov prepared the second echelons of his army and subordinate corps to meet the renewed German onslaught. After reinforcing the shaken 52d Guards Rifle Division with elements of the fresh seventy-two-gun 28th Antitank Artillery Brigade, he ordered Colonel Chernov's 90th Guards Rifle Division, in the 22d Guards Rifle Corps, to defend the corps' second echelon positions from Aleksandrovka No. 1 State Farm eastward along the north bank of the Pena River through Syrtsevo. To the east, Major General N. T. Tavartkiladze's 51st Guards Rifle Division, in the 23d Guards Rifle Corps' second echelon, dug in along the high ground between Syrtsevo and Nepkhaevo on the Lipovyi Donets River, with orders to block any further German advance on Pokrovka along the main Belgorod-Oboian' highway. It was Tavartkiladze's infantry and the 28th Antitank Brigade guns that halted *Leibstandarte's* advance late on 5 July.[44]

More significantly, in the late morning of 5 July, Vatutin also ordered Katukov's 1st Tank Army and the separate 2d Guards and 5th Guards Tank Corps forward to reinforce the rifle divisions in the 6th Guards Army's second defensive belt and to launch coordinated counterattacks against the advancing German armor to expel them from the main defensive belt. Shortly thereafter, Katukov began moving his army forward. Major General A. L. Getman's veteran 6th Tank Corps, with 169 tanks and self-propelled guns, was to occupy positions along the Pena River behind the 90th Guards Rifle Division's center and left sectors, with three brigades on line and a fourth in reserve.[45] At the same time, Major General S. M. Krivoshein's 3d Mechanized Corps, equipped with 250 tanks and self-propelled guns, would deploy eastward in positions extending from the Pena River valley to Syrtsevo, backing up the 90th Division's left flank and the right flank of the 51st Guards Rifle Division.[46] Krivoshein would retain a tank brigade in reserve. Katukov ordered Major General D. Kh. Chernienko's 31st Tank Corps, with 196 tanks, to remain in second echelon, well to the rear, ready to respond to whatever threat materialized.[47] Meanwhile, Major General A. G. Kravchenko's 200-tank-strong 5th Guards Tank Corps moved forward into assembly areas behind the 51st Guards Rifle Division, and Major General A. S. Burdeiny moved his 2d Guards Tank Corps, with an additional 200 tanks, into the Gostishchevo region east of the Lipovyi Donets River, on the right flank of the advancing German II SS Panzer Corps' penetration. All told, these movements brought more than 1,000 Red tanks into the fray against Fourth Panzer Army.[48]

Initially, Katukov's mission, like that of General Rodin's 2d Tank Army to the north, was to launch a concerted counterattack to repel the German armored spearheads and restore the front lines. While his 6th Tank and 3d Mechanized Corps would strike directly at the advancing XXXXVIII Panzer Corps, the 2d and 5th Separate Guards Tank Corps were to strike the nose and flank of the II SS Panzer Corps' penetration. Unlike Rodin's tank army counterattack, however, Katukov's blow never materialized. By late afternoon on 5 July, it was apparent that the 6th Guards Army's forward divisions would not be able to halt the German advance; nor could they successfully defend the army second defensive belt. Considering it inadvisable to launch Katukov's army into the teeth of a largely undamaged German armored force, Vatutin altered the army's orders. Now, 1st Tank Army was to establish a firm defense along and east of the Pena River with the defending rifle divisions and halt the German advance. Katukov could go over to the offensive only when the German advance was stopped.

At about the same time, Katukov had received the first reports from the front about the nature of the armored fighting, in particular, the German use of massed Tiger and Panther tanks. In part, these reports came from the lead elements of his army (1st Guards Tank Brigade), which had encountered the lead elements of the SS Panzer Corps south of Pokrovka. The news of the large numbers of German Tiger and Panther tanks and new self-propelled guns was a bit unnerving. Given the unanticipated German strength, Katukov recommended his army simply defend in the second defensive belt. Vatutin approved his request.[49]

Thus, much of Katukov's force went into battle, like Rodin's 2d Tank Army in the north, in an infantry support role rather than as a massed mechanized attack. Moreover, movement difficulties and German preemptive action on the morning of 6 July seized whatever initiative Katukov retained. Only Burdeiny's 2d Guards Tank Corps struck as planned, while Katukov's other corps and Kravchenko's 5th Guards Tank Corps found themselves waging a desperate defense against advancing German armor. This misuse (according to existing Soviet regulations) of the new tank and mechanized forces caused considerable controversy both at the time and later. Zhukov and Stalin were highly critical of this development but deferred to Vatutin, Vasilevsky, and *front* commissar N. S. Khrushchev, who were on the spot.[50]

Despite the fact that the planned Soviet counterattack never materialized, Vatutin's use of his precious armored resources began a pattern that would endure throughout the subsequent battle. While half of his armored force functioned in a purely defensive role to grind down and blunt the forward progress of advancing German panzers, the remainder struck repeatedly at the flanks of the German armored armada. Almost inevitably, these incessant flank battles distracted the Germans from their ultimate objectives of Oboian' and Kursk, wore down the German panzer force, and finally canalized it to the fateful fields of Prokhorovka.

While the Fourth Panzer Army struggled against the 6th Guards Army, General Werner Kempf's Army Detachment began its artillery preparation on schedule at 0330 hours on 5 July. After thirty minutes of shelling, five German divisions conducted assault crossings at different points along the Northern Donets River and from the German Mikhailovka bridgehead, across the river from Belgorod. Almost immediately, it became clear to Kempf that the 168th Infantry Division could not crack the Soviet 81st Guards Rifle Division, whose defenses contained German forces in the Mikhailovka bridgehead. Therefore, his plan to commit the 6th Panzer Division via Mikhailovka aborted, and the panzer division had to redeploy to exploit opportunities farther south.[51] South along the Northern Donets, Kempf's force had greater success. At 1100 hours, Lieutenant General Rudolf Schmidt's 19th Panzer Division achieved a small penetration across the river opposite the Soviet fortified village of Razumnoe. Exploiting the opportunity, Schmidt's 73d Panzer Grenadier Regiment lunged forward two kilometers at the junction of the Soviet 78th and 81st Guards Rifle Divisions.[52] By nightfall the 19th Panzer's 27th Panzer Regiment joined the grenadier regiment on the river's east bank and completed routing the Soviet 228th Guards Rifle Regiment, whose remnants dug in around Razumnoe.

The assault by Lieutenant General Freiherr von Funck's 7th Panzer Division was even more successful. At 1300 hours the division's 6th and 7th Panzer Grenadier Regiments thrust forward from Solomino across the Northern Donets. They advanced quickly across the rail line running south from Belgorod, split the defenses in the center of the Soviet 78th Guards Rifle Division, and with the 25th Panzer Regiment in the lead, pushed on for six kilometers along the high ground between the fortified Soviet villages of Razumnoe and Krutoi Log.

Major General A. V. Skvortsov, the 78th Guards Rifle Division commander, committed his 81st Guards Antitank Battalion to reinforce his shattered forward regiments and to halt the German armored onslaught. Still, the appalling terrain and the vigor of the 7th Panzer's advance thwarted his efforts. The division's sector was an absolutely level flood plain crisscrossed with small tributaries of the Northern Donets and Razumnoe Rivers and dotted with small villages scattered along these rivulets. The Germans dominated the terrain from the heights west of the river to a depth of over ten kilometers, and the first defensible ground lay along ridges well to the east. Therefore, Skvortsov's defending riflemen quite naturally gravitated into defenses around the small and often sunken villages, which soon turned into traps. Fortunately for these riflemen, the shortage of accompanying German infantry permitted many of the encircled forces to escape these traps.[53]

By day's end on 5 July, Army Detachment Kempf had captured a bridgehead from three to six kilometers deep and up to twelve kilometers wide, which tore gaping holes in the 7th Guards Army's first defensive belt. Although the Soviet defenses were not irrevocably torn apart, ominously for Skvortsov and his army commander, Lieutenant General M. S. Shumilov, by nightfall the 6th Panzer Division was deploying southward from Mikhailovka to exploit its sister panzer divisions' success. Equally ominous for Field Marshal von Manstein at Army Group South headquarters, Army Detachment Kempf had made only limited progress and was as yet unable to perform its primary mission of protecting the right flank of General Hoth's advancing Fourth Panzer Army.

To bolster the 7th Guards Army's defenses, on the night of 5 July, the Voronezh Front commander, Vatutin, ordered the 69th Army to transfer control of its 111th and 270th Rifle Divisions to the 7th Guards Army.[54] These divisions, together with the 7th Guards Army's 15th Guards Rifle Division, were to man an army second defensive belt east of the Koren' River and to the rear of the 24th Guards Rifle Corps. As additional insurance against a breakthrough by the II SS Panzer Corps and its linkup with Army Detachment Kempf, Vatutin dispatched the 93d Guards Rifle Division, part of the 35th Guards Rifle Corps that constituted the *front's* reserve, to occupy yet another defensive belt east of the Lipovyi Donets River and southwest of Prokhorovka. By morning this corps joined the 69th Army's 183d Rifle Division, which was already defending in the region. At the same time, the 35th Guards Rifle Corps' remaining two divisions (the 92d and 94th Guards) prepared to reinforce the 7th Guards Army.

The failure of the Soviet air attacks on German airfields early on 5 July disrupted the Soviets' ability to contest German air power over the battlefield on the remainder of 5 July. The Soviets counted almost 2,000 German sorties throughout the day, most concentrated against Soviet tactical defenses and important rear installations and along the advance route of the German panzer corps.[55] The Soviets committed the 2d Air Army's 5th Fighter Aviation Corps at 0600 hours, and it was joined later in the day by the main fighter aviation force. By day's end the Soviets had committed all available fighter aircraft in a costly but indecisive struggle. The bulk of the fighters engaged German fighters and were forced to allow German bombers to do their deadly work. Although by day's end Soviet fighters were finally engaging German bombers, the delay facilitated the rapidity of the German ground advance. The Soviets claimed to have achieved air equilibrium, but the price in pilots and aircraft led to sharply reduced air activity on both sides during subsequent days.[56]

Despite the strenuous Soviet defense, Hoth's armor was indeed making progress against the Voronezh Front (see Map 11). Having paused to rest and refit, von Knobelsdorff's XXXXVIII Panzer Corps resumed the offensive at mid-morning on 6 July. After a ninety-minute artillery preparation, the 3d and 11th Panzer Divisions, with the *Grossdeutschland* Division between them, attacked to the north and northeast, completing the rout of the forward Soviet defenders. Assisted by 200 sorties of close air support, the German force pressed back the 67th Guards Rifle Division until this division was fighting back to back with the 52d Guards Rifle Division, which was still trying to hold the shoulder against the SS penetration farther east.[57] By evening, this salient had been squeezed out, and Chistiakov had to authorize the remnants of the 67th and 52d Guards Rifle Divisions to withdraw to prearranged defensive positions in and behind the second defensive belt. Von Knobelsdorff launched at least eight unsuccessful attacks up the Oboian' highway against the second defensive belt held by Colonel Chernov's 90th Rifle Division, supported by General Krivoshein's 3d Mechanized Corps. As the Germans strove for a clean penetration, the combat only increased in intensity, yet success eluded von Knobelsdorff.

After smashing remaining Soviet defenses in the Cherkasskoe sector, by mid-afternoon the 3d Panzer Division's reconnaissance elements reached the banks of the Pena River near Rakovo. While heavy fire rained down on the Germans from the low heights on the river's north bank, the 3d Panzer troopers soon found that, although the river was shallow, the muddy and abrupt river banks and adjacent swampy terrain made it unfordable by armored forces.[58]

Accordingly, the 3d Panzer and the exploiting armor of the *Grossdeutschland* and 11th Panzer Divisions now reoriented their advance northeastward through the more favorable tank terrain between Alekseevka, Lukhanino, and Syrtsevo along the Tomarovka-Oboian' road. In late afternoon, after a spectacular advance from Cherkasskoe to the Pena River line, *Grossdeutschland's* and 11th Panzer's forward elements engaged General Krivoshein's deployed brigades of the 3d Mechanized Corps and Colonel Chernov's dug-in 90th Guards infantry along the Lukhanino River. In the meantime, Vatutin had re-

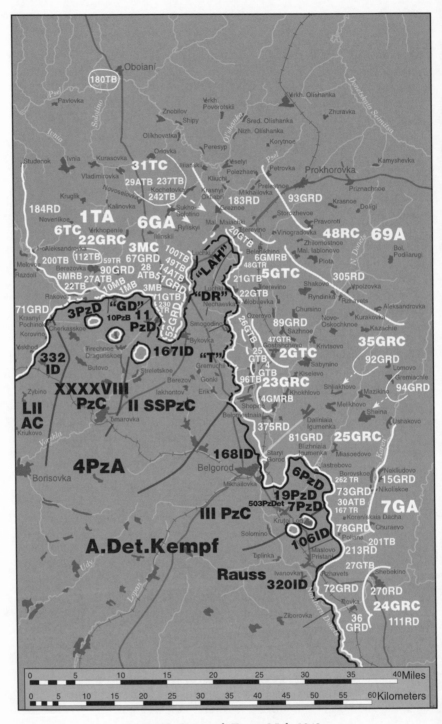

Map 11. Voronezh Front, 6 July 1943

inforced Krivoshein's mechanized corps with yet another antitank regiment (the 35th), and the fighting along the Pena and around Alekseevka and Lukhanino raged with unabated ferocity. One German observer later acknowledged the unprecedented violence of the first two days of fighting:

On the second day of the attack [5 July], we met our first setback, and, in spite of every effort, the troops were unable to penetrate the Russian line. "Gross Deutschland," assembling in dense formation and with the swamp in its immediate front, was heavily shelled by Russian artillery. The engineers were unable to make suitable crossings, and many tanks fell victim to the Red Air Force. During this battle Russian aircraft operated with remarkable dash in spite of German air superiority. Even in the area taken by the German troops on the first day, Russians appeared from nowhere, and the reconnaissance units of "Gross Deutschland" had to deal with them. Nor was it possible to cross the stream and swamp [the Pena] on the night of 5/6 July. On the left flank, the attacks by 3d Panzer Division against Sawidowka [Zavydovka] were as unsuccessful as those of "Gross Deutschland" against Alexejevka [Alekseevka] and Luchanino [Lukhanino]. The entire area had been infested with mines, and the Russian defense along the whole line was supported by tanks operating with all the advantages of high ground. Our assault troops suffered considerable casualties, and the 3d Panzer Division had to beat off counterattacks. In spite of several massive bombing attacks by the Luftwaffe against battery positions, the Russian defensive fire did not decrease to any extent.[59]

Grossdeutschland's history recorded the ferocity and costliness of the struggle against the 3d Mechanized Corps:

There [to the east], at about 11.45 [16.45 Moscow time], I Battalion, Panzer-Grenadier Regiment GD, and the panzers reported that the advance was proceeding smoothly and that the area south of Dubrova [on the Lukhanino River] could be taken. However, a heavy tank battle developed in the broad corn fields and flat terrain there against the bolsheviks grimly defending their second line of resistance. Earth bunkers, deep positions with built-in flame-throwers, and especially well dug-in T-34s, excellently camouflaged, made the advance extremely difficult. German losses mounted, especially among the panzers. The infantry fought their way grimly through the in-depth defensive zone, trying to clear the way for the panzers. Finally that evening the brave panzer-grenadiers of I Battalion under Major Remer were able to advance by Dubrova and take Hill 247.2 where they dug in. There I Battalion, Panzer-Grenadier Regiment and the panzers of the Strachwitz Group set up a hedgehog defensive position. All in all, however, it appeared that the breakthrough had not yet succeeded; instead the attackers were still sitting in the midst of the enemy defensive zone.

The regimental headquarters of the Panzer-Grenadier Regiment followed during the night and pushed its units, in particular II Battalion, as close to Dubrova as possible. The objective of this was to expand the penetration of the enemy positions into a breakthrough the next day and thus finally reach the open field of battle. Numerous Panthers had already been put out of action; the panzer regiment was forced to abandon many of its tanks on account of hits or track damage inflicted by mines and leave them for the following repair echelons for repairs.[60]

Soviet accounts confirmed the intensity of the fighting:

All attempts by the Germans to continue the offensive in a northern direction were thwarted by the stubborn resistance by units of Colonel V. G. Chernov's 90th Guards Rifle Division, and by 1st Tank Army's 6th Tank and 3d Mechanized Corps, which had occupied prepared defenses in the second line.

In the Lukhanino, Syrtsevo, Hill 247.2 sector, the enemy undertook eight attacks during the course of the day, simultaneously throwing [into combat] up to 250 tanks and infantry. All attacks were repelled by the 3d Mechanized Corps' 1st, 3d, and 10th Mechanized Brigades. In the region of Hill 247.2, separate groups of tanks succeeded in penetrating into our defense and filtered through the combat formation of Colonel A. Kh. Babadzhanian's 3d Mechanized Brigade. While separating the enemy infantry from the tanks, the brigade's soldiers did not waver and, by means at hand, they destroyed the penetrating machines. The enemy lost several tanks and, failing to achieve success, he was forced to withdraw to his jumping-off positions. During the course of the day, the 1st Mechanized Brigade was attacked eight times from the Ol'khovatka region by an enemy force with up to 100 tanks, but it did not abandon its positions.[61]

By nightfall on 6 July, the XXXXVIII Panzer Corps had once again failed to reach its objective of the Psel River. It was, however, positioned to thrust decisively northward on 7 July, albeit obviously against tougher opposition than anticipated. Opposite von Knobelsdorff's armor massed along the Oboian' road, Vatutin and Katukov faced a major decision. With the German armor spearhead shifting east of the Pena River opposite the 3d Mechanized Corps, the precious armor of the 6th Tank Corps deployed to the west along the Pena now faced a reduced threat. As yet, however, Vatutin did not order

General Getman to reposition his tank corps to the east. Vatutin was thinking more about countering the operational threat posed by the II SS Panzer Corps, which on 6 July had begun a precipitous advance northward into the heart of 6th Guards Army's defense.

The new threat materialized to the east, when Hausser's II SS Panzer Corps resumed its advance, tore through the 51st Guards Rifle Division's defenses south of Iakovlevo and, despite the intervention of Kravchenko's 5th Guards Tank Corps, continued a rapid advance to the northeast. After a late-morning artillery bombardment, Hausser's *Leibstandarte Adolf Hitler* on the left and *Das Reich* on the right pressed forward, overran the remnants of the 51st Guards Rifle Division, seized the Soviet strong points at Iakovlevo, and then pushed defending Soviet infantry and armor aside into fortified positions around the large towns of Pokrovka and Bol'shie Maiachki.[62] While *Leibstandarte's* two panzer grenadier regiments contained these Soviet strong points, other division elements raced forward up to twelve kilometers to seize Luchki and Teterevino as darkness fell.

General Kravchenko's 5th Guards Tank Corps counterattacked as ordered into the teeth of the German assault and over-optimistically claimed to have knocked out ninety-five tanks and several Elephant self-propelled guns belonging to *Das Reich*.[63] Despite these claims, the SS thrust shattered the Soviet defenses, and, like tenpins, Kravchenko's armored brigades were forced to withdraw precipitously to the northeast and east, together with the survivors of the 51st Guards Rifle Division's 58th Guards Rifle Regiment. The remainder of the 51st Guards Rifle Division, together with the tanks of the 3d Mechanized Corps' 1st Guards Tank Brigade and surviving infantry and antitank units from earlier battles, clung grimly to Pokrovka and Bol'shie Maiachki on SS Panzer Corps' left flank.[64]

With the 6th Guards Army's second defensive belt now punctured, the II SS Panzer Corps had an open route open to the northeast, with only a motorized brigade (the 6th Guards) of Kravchenko's shaken tank corps to their front. It was an opportunity, however, that Hausser and his corps could not exploit. First, his orders were to advance northward to Oboian', not to Prokhorovka in the northeast. Second and more important, powerful undefeated Soviet forces hugged his overextended flanks. With no infantry yet available to secure his flanks, he had no choice but to fight to defend those flanks until infantry arrived to permit his armor to resume its headlong advance. In the meantime, Hausser instinctively permitted his forces to continue marching along the path of least resistance. Accordingly, his advanced elements pushed farther north along the road to Prokhorovka.

A German account captured the mixture of exhilaration and concern generated by the II SS Panzer Corps' headlong advance:

At 16.30 [1830 Moscow time], the Panzergruppe had moved through Lutschki [Luchki] and was attacking Teterewino [Teterevino]. Untersturmfuehrer Guehs, leader of a Kampfwagenkanonenzug [armoured gun platoon] in the III. (armoured)/2., reported on the attack as follows:

"Elements of the Panzers and of the Aufklarungsabteilung [recon detachment] were in front of us. We turned northeast and attacked at top speed with all of our Schutzenpanzerwagens [armored personnel carriers]. On a broad front, we rode next to the Aufklarungsabteilung and the Panzers in an attempt to reach the Pssel [Psel]. Suddenly, it seemed over for us. There were mines all over the road and the open ground. There were antitank guns and tanks behind a tank trench on the hill in front of us. Four of our Panzers hit mines. The air support officer traveling with us in his Schutzenpanzerwagen also flew into the air. We could still capture Teterewino. But could we stay there? It was getting darker. We were worried about our flanks, so we set up defenses. I stayed at the Battalion headquarters for the night. At 01.30 [0330 Moscow time] hours, there was a call from the 12. Kompanie [company] (under Obersturmfuehrer Preuss). They had six Russian tanks in front of them. The 13. reported even more. Remarkably, we hardly got excited. We defended ourselves. In the morning, the Russians took a beating. We destroyed five of his sixteen tanks. Six Russians deserted and came to us. They said they belonged to a Tank Corps which had only moved out from Moscow on 3 July."[65]

Even more disconcerting for Hausser, on 6 July the Soviet 2d Guards Tank Corps had launched its offensive across the Lipovyi Donets River against his corps' right flank in concert with another tank attack (by 96th Tank Brigade) to the south.[66] This event too caused concern in II SS Panzer Corps headquarters:

At 19.15 hours [2115 Moscow time], the Chef of the Generalstab [General staff] of the II. Panzerkorps informed the Ia [operations officer] that a crisis situation was building. The enemy had moved strong tank forces from the northeast into the area Rhoshdestwenka-Krzjukowo-Nowje Losy [Rozhdestvenka-Kriukovo-Novye Losy], and numerous tanks with infantry had been moved across the Donez near Nepchajewo, a fact which had not been noticed at first.

The Korps [Corps] ordered a reinforced Bataillon [battalion] under the command of a Regimental commander to set out immediately for northern Lutschki [Luchki], where it was to provide cover for the march route to the west and northwest and establish contact with the Panzergruppe in Teterewino [Teterevino]. For the rest, the Division's orders remained the same.[67]

Although the Soviet assault was repelled by the Luftwaffe and General Burdeiny's 2d Guards Tank Corps was severely maimed in the process, the Soviet attack required that SS Panzer Division *Totenkopf* engage the new threat until relief by infantry could be arranged.[68] As in the XXXXVIII Panzer Corps' sector, obscure battles along the flanks were already quietly assuming decisive importance.

During the late afternoon and evening of 6 July, Vatutin and Katukov again adjusted their defenses to meet the new German threats. While Vatutin poured more antitank units into the struggle, Katukov, the commander of 1st Tank Army, ordered the three tank brigades (100th, 242d, and 237th) of General Chernienko's 31st Tank Corps to seal off the II SS Panzer Corps penetration from the west. General Krivoshein had already ordered the 2d Battalion of his second echelon 49th Tank Brigade to reinforce the beleaguered Soviet defenders at Pokrovka. Arriving just as German forces entered the town, Captain G. S. Fedorenko's battalion destroyed six German tanks, including one Tiger, and drove the Germans back.[69]

By late afternoon Colonel N. M. Ivanov's 100th Tank Brigade also reinforced Soviet defenses at Bol'shie Maiachki, and the remaining brigades of the 31st Tank Corps followed, with orders to contain the SS Panzer Corps' advance. With the arrival of the fresh armor, Vatutin ordered the tattered remnants of the 52d Guards Rifle Division be withdrawn to new defense lines well to the rear.

Farther south, in the critical sector just north of Belgorod defended by Colonel P. D. Govorunenko's 375th Rifle Division, elements of the SS Panzer Grenadier Division *Totenkopf* pressed on eastward toward Shopino and Ternovka on the Lipovyi Donets River in an attempt to reach the river and, ultimately, link up with Kempf's forces east of Belgorod. Reinforced by Major General V. G. Lebedev's 96th Tank Brigade and the 496th Antitank Artillery Regiment, the 375th clung firmly to its defenses and repulsed *Totenkopf's* forces well short of the river.[70] Govorunenko's stubborn and successful defense in this seemingly backwater sector would have a major but as yet unforeseen impact on the outcome of Operation Citadel. It was unforeseen because, at the time, all German eyes focused anxiously on the progress of Army Detachment Kempf south of Belgorod.

On 6 July Kempf's troops finally burst forth from their bridgehead across the Northern Donets River, posing a serious threat to the viability of the 7th Guards Army's defense. As before, the 7th and 19th Panzer Divisions led the assault, but in late afternoon General von Hünersdorff's 6th Panzer Division joined the fray.[71] General Schmidt's 19th Panzer Division, supported by the follow-on regiments of the 168th Rifle Division, wheeled northwestward against the left flank and rear of the 81st Guards Rifle Division. Despite heavy resistance by the 81st and elements of the supporting 114th Guards Antitank

Regiment, the Germans succeeded in seizing Kreida Station and the key town of Belovskoe in the Soviet rear. The 81st Guards Rifle Division had to deploy hastily its training battalion near Iastrebovo to halt the German thrust.[72]

Meanwhile, spearheaded by its 25th Panzer Regiment, General von Funck's 7th Panzer Division lunged forward from between Razumnoe and Krutoi Log, brushed aside the 78th Guards Rifle Division's second echelon 233d Regiment and the supporting 81st Guards Antitank Artillery Battalion, and trapped a Soviet regiment in Krutoi Log before running headlong into the newly deployed Soviet 73d Guards Rifle Division. The night before, General Shumilov, the 7th Guards Army commander, had ordered Colonel S. A. Kozak's 73d Guards Division, then deployed in the 25th Guards Rifle Corps' second echelon, to move forward and occupy new positions to block any further German advance eastward from Krutoi Log. Shumilov reinforced Kozak's guardsmen with the 167th and 262d Tank Regiments and the 1438th Self-propelled Artillery Regiment from army reserve and with the powerful seventy-two-gun 31st Antitank Brigade dispatched by Vatutin at *front*. Kozak occupied his new positions by 2200 hours on 5 July and erected a hasty antitank defense.[73]

Throughout the next day, the 7th Panzer repeatedly attacked headlong into the 73d Guards Rifle Division's defensive positions and, in extremely heavy fighting, bent but could not break the Soviet lines. In late afternoon the 6th Panzer Division finally arrived, rolled over Kozak's right flank regiment, and occupied a key position between the 19th and 7th Panzer Divisions. Kozak withdrew his center and right flank regiments to new defenses anchored along the low ridge northward from Gremiachii through Batratskaia Dacha. With the 111th, 270th, and 15th Guards Rifle Division now deployed to their rear and the fresh 94th Guards Rifle Division marching to their assistance, Kozak's forces managed to hold along their new defense line and even to counterattack. In fact, Army Detachment Kempf now faced the twin problems of developing and sustaining its northward drive while worrying about its right flank. For days Kempf's armor would be tied down on the flank, while Army Group South searched for infantry to fill in his beleaguered and overextended lines.

Thus, by the end of the second day of battle, the XXXXVIII Panzer Corps had linked up with the neighboring II SS Panzer Corps near Iakovlevo. Together, they had achieved a dangerous penetration into the Soviet second defensive belt, a penetration that pointed like a menacing danger northward toward Oboian'. In the process, however, Hoth had lost at least 300 of his armored vehicles to enemy action and to the mechanical unreliability of the new designs. *Grossdeutschland* had only 80 of its 350 supporting tanks still operational. As usual, some of these vehicles were later repaired, but the German spearhead had been seriously depleted.[74] The Soviets estimated that the Fourth Panzer Army had lost 10,000 soldiers killed and wounded. Moreover, the relative failure of Army Detachment Kempf to keep up with Hoth's northward thrust meant that SS Panzer Division *Totenkopf* now had to act as a flank guard, facing eastward against the 2d and 5th Guards Tank Corps rather than widening the penetration to the northeast. Likewise, Army Detachment Kempf's 7th Panzer Division was enmeshed in a similar security mission to the south. Most important, the German offensive was woefully behind schedule and significant Soviet forces remained to be overcome; in fact, there were more such forces than the Germans assessed.

Of equal significance was the strain placed on the VIII Air Corps. Two days of maximum effort had cost the Luftwaffe more than 100 aircraft in this sector, while seriously depleting its supply of aviation fuel and degrading the maintenance status of the surviving planes. Because close air support took precedence over air superiority missions, the German fighters could no longer intercept all the Red Air Force strikes. The diversion of FlaK guns to ground action further weakened German air defense. Henceforth, the German commanders would have to husband their dwindling air assets, and some attacks would suffer from the absence of air support. Soviet reports recorded 1,278 daylight sorties to 873 German sorties on 6 July.[75]

Vatutin also faced significant problems, not the least of which was the gaping hole in his front. By nightfall on 6 July, he had committed all of his *front* reserves, except three rifle divisions of his 69th Army, to assist the first echelon or to reinforce the rear defensive belt. He had also shifted forces from the 38th Army to reinforce the 40th and 1st Tank Armies. While Soviet forces still occupied two and, in some cases, three defensive lines along the Prokhorovka and Korocha axes, along the Oboian' axis the Soviets manned only the army second defensive belt. It was imperative, thought Vatutin, that this belt be held firm, for once through it, German forces would achieve operational freedom.

During the afternoon of 6 July, Vatutin formulated a solution to this defensive dilemma and presented it to *Stavka* representative Vasilevsky. He proposed that powerful counterattacks be launched against the Germans' east and west flank using fresh tank forces from the *Stavka* reserve. However, by late afternoon the rapid subsequent German advance had rendered Vatutin's plan irrelevant. At 1830 hours Vatutin reported to Vasilevsky and the *Stavka* "that six German panzer divisions were operating in front of the 6th Guards Army and that the enemy was continuing to bring up fresh reserves."[76] Therefore, through Vasilevsky, Vatutin requested that the *Stavka* reinforce his *front* with four fresh tank and two aviation corps. Vasilevsky appended the following personal note to Vatutin's request:

The situation at the front at 1700 hours corresponds to what was reported. On my part, I consider it expedient for further dynamic operations to reinforce the *front* with two tank corps, sending one of them to the Prokhorovka region (thirty kilometers southeast of Oboian') and the other to the Korocha region. Zhadov's [5th Guards Army commander] 10th Tank Corps could be used for this, and Malinovsky's [Southwestern Front commander] 2d Tank Corps from Valiuki could be used for this purpose. In addition, I consider it necessary to move Rotmistrov [5th Guards Tank Army commander] to the Oskol River and to the region south of Staryi Oskol.[77]

Later in the day, Stalin personally telephoned Vatutin to provide his reply. He began by ordering Vatutin "to exhaust the enemy at prepared positions and prevent his penetration until our active operations begin on the Western, Briansk, and other *fronts.*"[78] This clearly indicated that Stalin's attention was focused on the larger context of the Kursk battle. While Stalin focused on the broader offensive aspects of *his* Kursk operation, he did agree to release the two additional tank corps to Vatutin. Realizing that the success of the Soviet strategic offensive depended directly on defensive success at Kursk, Stalin also ordered General I. S. Konev, the Steppe Front commander, to begin the forward deployment to the Kursk region of General Rotmistrov's 5th Guards Tank Army.

Released at Stalin's command, Rotmistrov's armored host closed into the Staryi Oskol area on the morning of 8 July.[79] In the meantime, Major General V. G. Burkov's 10th Tank Corps and Major General A. F. Popov's 2d Tank Corps, equipped with 185 and 168 tanks and self-propelled guns, respectively, were marching toward Prokhorovka and the region to the southeast.[80] Both would be ready to join battle on 8 July.

Acting on the new *Stavka* instructions, Vatutin then formulated a revised plan to defeat the Germans with his existing forces and to finish them off with the two new tank corps once they had arrived. His decision was: "to defeat the enemy in a defensive battle at earlier prepared defensive positions, having reinforced the 7th Guards Army's endangered axis with 35th Guards Rifle Corps' units, and the Iakovlevo-Prokhorovka axis by moving two tank brigades and one antitank brigade into the junction between the 1st Tank Army and the 5th Guards Tank Corps. All of the Voronezh Front's air power would attack and destroy enemy tanks and personnel on the Oboian' axis, and Southwestern Front aviation would be used against the enemy operating against the 7th Guards Army."[81]

For Vatutin's plan to succeed, it was essential that the 1st Tank Army's 31st Tank Corps, then completing its march forward toward the II SS Panzer Corps' right flank, and the 2d and 5th Guards Tank Corps, deployed between Prokhorovka and Druzhnyi on the German corps' left flank, stop the inexorable northward march of the feared and hated black-shirted panzer force.

Katukov's remaining 6th Tank and 3d Mechanized Corps would have the task of halting the XXXXVIII Panzer Corps' northward advance up the Oboian' road. Hoth's two panzer corps, behind schedule, bruised but not blunted, were equally determined to prevail, as they always had in the past.

CRISIS IN THE NORTH, 7–10 JULY

At dawn on 7 July, General Model's Ninth German Army renewed its attacks to penetrate the Central Front's second defensive belt around the town of Ponyri and north of Ol'khovatka, ten kilometers to the west (see Map 12). The seedy village of Ponyri and its railroad and motor-tractor stations dominated the critical rail and road approach into Kursk from the north, and both Soviets and Germans appreciated its tactical significance. German participants in the battle later noted: "Ponyri, a strung-out village, and Hill 253.5 were the Stalingrad of the Kursk salient. The most fiercely contested points were the tractor station, the railway-station, the school, and the water tower. The railway embankment and the northern edge of the settlement had been captured on the first day of the attack. But after that began a savage struggle in which the 18th and 9th Panzer Divisions, as well as the 86th Infantry Division, participated."[82]

Five times, the 18th Panzer and 292d Infantry Divisions assaulted the town itself, only to be thrown back by Major General M. A. Enshin's 307th Rifle Division. Artillery fire and mines destroyed the tanks, and the attacking German infantry, held up by elaborate wire and other obstacles, suffered heavy losses from their Red counterparts. General Pukhov, the 13th Army commander, had provided the 307th Division with a full spectrum of large caliber guns, self-propelled tank destroyers, and engineer mobile obstacle detachments, whose deadly work left the landscape dotted with smoking German armored vehicles.[83]

At 1000 hours German infantry, supported by fifty tanks, penetrated the northwestern outskirts of the town but were thrown back by a 307th Rifle Division counterattack. A subsequent German attack by two battalions and twelve tanks captured the May 1st State Farm on the eastern outskirts of Ponyri and gained a lodgment in the northern section of the town. Almost simultaneously, just west of the town, the German 9th Panzer Division had even greater success, pushing back the 6th Guards Rifle Division to occupy part of a forest by 1230 hours. Despite this advantage, it took the Germans the rest of the day, with numerous, costly attacks, to finally wrest half of Ponyri from the 307th Rifle Division. During the struggle Colonel Enshin committed his second echelon 1023d Rifle Regiment into the fiery cauldron, retaining only the regiment's 2d Battalion in reserve. General Pukhov also upped

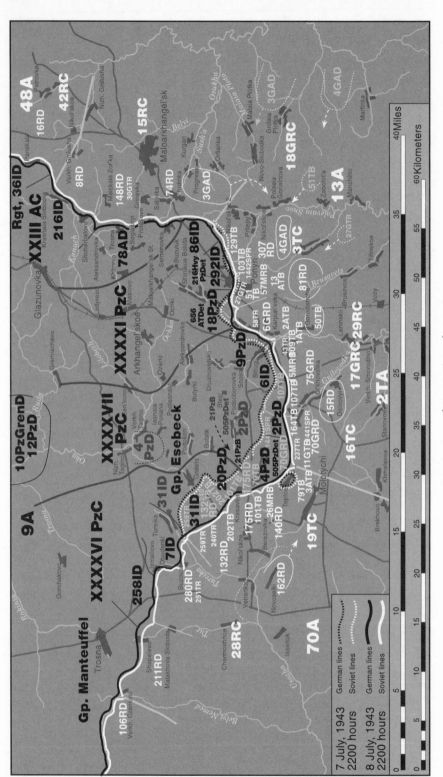

Map 12. Central Front, 7–8 July 1945

the ante as he sent his 129th Tank Brigade and 1442d Self-propelled Artillery Regiment into the battle, along with additional elements of Colonel S. P. Sazanov's 13th Antitank Brigade and a brigade of the 3d Tank Corps.

To the west, in the afternoon, the 2d and 20th Panzer Divisions of General Joachim Lemelsen's XXXXVII Panzer Corps, accompanied by grenadiers from the 6th Infantry Division, lunged southward toward Ol'khovatka, a position Model considered key to his army's success. A perceptive German observer noted:

The prize was the high ground of Olkhovatka with its key position—Hill 274.

These hills were Model's immediate objective. Here was the crux of his plan of operations, here was the key to the door of Kursk. What was the particular significance of these hills?

The chain of hills of Olkhovatka formed, from a strategic point of view, the middle section of the Central Russian ridge between Orel and Belgorod. On their eastern flanks was the source of the Oka as well as the sources of numerous lesser streams. From the hills there was clear view as far as Kursk, situated about 400 feet below Olkhovatka. Whoever commanded this high ground would command the area between Oka and Seym [rivers].

Model wanted to seize this high ground around Olkhovatka. He wanted to move his reserves into this area to engage the Soviet troops, above all Rokossovsky's armoured corps, in a terrain unfavorable to them, defeat them, and then thrust on to Kursk to link up with Hoth.[84]

Rokossovsky, however, fully appreciated Model's intent. Therefore, by nightfall on 6 July, the Central Front commander had already committed the 16th and 19th Tank Corps of Rodin's 2d Tank Army and Colonel V. N. Rukosuev's 3d Destroyer Brigade to the defense of the Ol'khovatka sector. Although the tank corps counterattacks had failed to achieve the decisive results Rokossovsky had sought, the tanks and antitank guns, fighting as battalions, companies, and platoons with the second echelon infantry of the 70th and 75th Guards Rifle Divisions, exacted a terrible toll on attacking German armor.[85]

Having failed to break through at Ponyri, in mid-afternoon the 2d Panzer Division's 140 tanks and 50 assault guns, with the 505th Tiger Detachment and 20th Panzer Division on the right, renewed their headlong assaults on Soviet defenses between Samodurovka and Ol'khovatka.[86] These attacks also failed, and the advancing Germans continued to suffer appalling losses for limited gains against this key sector of the Soviet 13th Army's second defensive belt. It was a similar story on the German right flank in the sector of

General Hans Zorn's XXXXVI Panzer Corps. Major General A. Ia. Kiselev's 140th Rifle Division, for example, committed from second echelon to bolster the defenses on the right flank of General Galanin's 70th Army, repelled thirteen separate German attacks. Efforts to turn the flank of these defenders and to widen the penetration were halted by massed tank destroyers and artillery firing over open sights.

On 7 July the air situation over the Central Front abruptly changed. The Soviets were able to implement fully their air plan and all required command and control measures. As a result, large groups of fighter aircraft could routinely patrol the battlefield and more aircraft were on call to respond to emergencies. German losses rose as the increased number of Soviet aircraft were brought to bear. Sortie rates increased and the Soviets achieved general and often local air superiority, which persisted throughout the remainder of the operation.[87]

The eighth of July proved to be the crisis point in both key sectors of the Soviet defense north of Kursk (Map 12, p. 115). At 0800 hours Model committed the 101 tanks of General Dietrich von Saucken's fresh 4th Panzer Division to support the 20th Panzer Division in the struggle for Samodurovka, while the 118 tanks of Lieutenant General Vollrath von Lubbe's 2d Panzer Division once again struck at Soviet defenses covering Ol'khovatka.[88] The XXXXVII Panzer Corps' 20th and 4th Panzer Divisions launched four successive attacks in the vicinity of Samodurovka, seeking to penetrate the ridge line of defenses at the junction between the 70th and 13th Armies. Lieutenant General A. L. Bondarev's 17th Guards Rifle Corps bore the brunt of this attack. Bad weather prevented Luftwaffe support for much of the day. Time after time, groups of 60 to 100 tanks with supporting German infantry stubbornly advanced against Samodurovka, Hill 257, and the ridge north of Ol'khovatka. A German observer captured the desperate nature of the fighting:

> The grenadiers of 20th Panzer Division fought a . . . furious battle on 8th July near the village of Samodurovka under a scorching sun. Within an hour all the officers of 5th Company, 112th Panzer Grenadier Regiment, had been killed or wounded. Nevertheless the grenadiers swept on through cornfields, capturing trenches and encountering new ones. The battalions melted away. Companies became mere platoons. . . .
>
> The famous battle of materiel of El Alamein, where Montgomery employed 1,000 guns to bring about the turning point in the war in Africa was a modest operation by comparison. Even Stalingrad, in spite of its more apocalyptic and tragic aura, does not stand comparison in terms of forces employed with the gigantic, open-field battle of Kursk.[89]

Meanwhile, in intense fighting, tanks and assault guns of the 4th Panzer Division smashed through Soviet defenses at the junction of the 175th and

70th Guards Rifle Divisions, and the panzer division's 2d Battalion, 33d Panzer Regiment, seized the small village of Teploe. Rokossovsky and Pukhov responded by committing the 140th Rifle Division and 2d Tank Army's reserve 11th Guards Tank Brigade to plug the gap. Strive as they did to clear the Russian defenders off the ridge south of Teploe, the Germans simply could not dent the stubborn Soviet defense.[90] Another German account captured the seesaw nature of the bitter struggle:

> The battalion [2d Battalion. 33d Panzer] had already lost 100 men. But the divisional commander did not want to give the Russians time to gather their wits. The 3d and 35th Panzer Regiments were lined up on the edge of the village. Armoured troop-carrying vehicles joined them. Dive-bombers shrieked overhead toward the Russian main positions.
>
> "Now!"
>
> On the opposite slope were the 3rd Anti-Tank Artillery Brigade. Moreover, T-34s had been dug-in. Their flank was covered by a Soviet rifle battalion with anti-tank rifles, simple but highly-effective weapons against tanks at short range. Their handling, just as that of the later German Panzerfaust, required courage and coolness.
>
> The assault on the high ground began. The Russian laid down a curtain of defensive fire.
>
> After a few hundred yards, the German grenadiers lay pinned to the ground. It was impossible to get through the Soviet fire of a few hundred guns concentrated on a very narrow sector. Only the tanks moved forward into the wall of fire.
>
> The Soviet artillerymen let them come within five hundred, then four hundred yards. At that range even the Tigers were set on fire by the heavy Russian anti-tank guns.
>
> But then three Mark IVs overran the first Soviet gun positions. The Grenadiers followed. They seized the high ground. They were thrown back by an immediate Russian counterattack.
>
> For three days the battle raged in the field in front of Teploye. The 33d Panzer Grenadier Regiment stormed the ground. They were dislodged again.
>
> Captain Diesener, the last surviving officer, assembled the remnants of 2d Battalion, and led another assault. He took the high ground. He was forced to fall back again.
>
> The neighboring 6th Infantry Division similarly only got to the slope of the hotly-contested Hill 274 at Olkhovatka.[91]

Soviet classified assessments of the day's fighting laconically, but accurately, recorded:

Having brought up more than 400 tanks and more than two infantry divisions to the Snovo, Podsoborovka, Saborovka region during the night, at 0800 the enemy again shifted to the offensive and attempted to penetrate our defense on a front from Ponyri 2 to Samodurovka. The Germans attacked four times here, but each time encountered all types of organized fire.

The fiercest battles took place on Hill 257.0, which was 17th Guards Rifle Corps' key defensive sector. Three times, in groups of 60 to 100 tanks each, simultaneously from the northeast and north, the enemy attacked the hill; German infantry, despite fire from defending units, stubbornly attempted to advance behind tanks to the hill. By 1700 the enemy had successfully occupied it. His further advance was stopped. The enemy was completely unsuccessful in the remaining front sectors of 17th Guards Rifle Corps.

Thus, on 8 July, after fierce battles along this axis, German forces were unable to achieve significant success. The final attempt to penetrate Ol'khovatka failed.[92]

The commander of the 2d Destroyer Division's 3d Destroyer Brigade, sent the following report during the action:

The enemy has occupied Kashara, Kutyrka, Pogorelovtsy, and Samodurovka and, preparing for a second frontal attack, is moving up 200 tanks and motorized infantry in the direction of Teploe. Active operations are developing along the Nikolskoe axis. In spite of a series of attacks, conducted since 0730 hours, the offensive has been halted along the line of the northern outskirts of Teploe.

The 1st and 7th Batteries have perished, but they have not withdrawn a step. Forty tanks have been destroyed. There have been 70 percent losses in the first battalion of antitank rifles.

The 2d and 3d Batteries and the second battalion of antitank rifles have prepared to meet the enemy. I have communications with them. There will be a struggle. We will either stand or perish. There is no vehicular transport. I need all types of ammunition. I have committed all of my reserves. I await your orders. I am in communications with my neighbors.[93]

On 8 July the seesaw struggle also continued around Ponyri Station. At dawn the 307th Rifle Division counterattacked across terrain strewn with Soviet and German dead and the carcasses of tens of burned out tanks and smashed artillery pieces. Regaining a foothold in the town, the division once again faced renewed German counterattacks, which left part of the town in Soviet and part in German hands. Model stubbornly threw fresh troops into the struggle and Pukhov responded in kind.[94] Over the next two days, the German 10th Panzer Grenadier Division reinforced the shattered German front-line troops, only to be met by the Soviet 3d and 4th Guards Airborne Divisions, which Pukhov committed to combat at Ponyri from the second echelon Soviet 18th Guards Rifle Corps.[95] Tanks from the 3d Tank Corps, additional antitank guns from the 2d and 13th Antitank Brigade, and guns from tens of Soviet artillery regiments joined the battle to destroy and be destroyed as the front seesawed back and forth through the battered town. Through Herculean efforts and at immense cost, the Germans finally gained possession of most, but not all, of Ponyri. The largely Pyrrhic victory left the victorious attackers exhausted and utterly incapable of further offensive action.

Clearly, Model had almost shot his bolt. After four days of high-intensity combat, the troops of Ninth Army, particularly the infantry and tankers, were worn down and worn out. As in the south, the Luftwaffe had made a maximum effort and was now severely limited by its dwindling petroleum supply. On the evening of 8 July, Model reluctantly decided to regroup before resuming his assault on the ridge north of Ol'khovatka. Thus, while German forces continued their battle for Ponyri, on 9 July Model regrouped his forces for a final attempt to take the blood-soaked ground of Ol'khovatka (see Map 13). The assault by 300 tanks of the 2d, 4th, and 20th Panzer Divisions followed a devastating preparation by German Stuka dive-bombers and artillery. Despite the preparations and terrifying fire support, this attack too faltered against the stubborn Soviet defense, which had been reinforced in the interim by Major General S. Ia. Senchillo's fresh 162d Rifle Division from 70th Army.

Model's final failure epitomized German frustration in the Kursk operation. In six days Model's troops had advanced no more than fifteen kilometers (Map 13). Despite sacrificing about 50,000 men and 400 tanks to the god of war, they had utterly failed to penetrate even the Soviet tactical defenses.[96] Although they had horribly bloodied the defending Soviets, operational freedom remained but a dream. By 8 July any hope of German success at Kursk rested squarely on the shoulders of Hoth's armada struggling tens of kilometers to the south. Model's defeat, however, would make Hoth's task that much more difficult and challenging.

CRISIS IN THE SOUTH, 7–8 JULY

Secure in the knowledge that the 2d and 10th Tank Corps and Rotmistrov's powerful 5th Guards Tank Army were en route to his *front's* sector, early on 7 July Vatutin began implementing a plan that would permit his *front* to hold

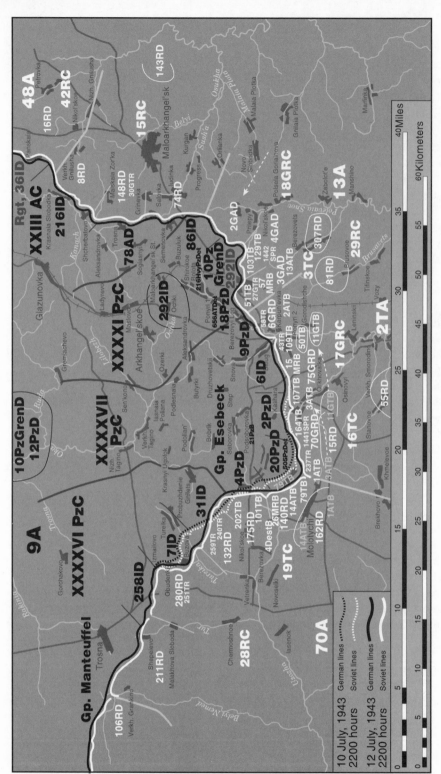

Map 13. Central Front, 10 July 1945

out the one to two days before these reinforcements arrived. Increasingly impatient over the previous days' frustrations, however, Hoth's two panzer corps would provide Vatutin with no respite. Early on 7 July, the II SS and XXXXVIII Panzer Corps resumed their attacks, this time against the second defensive belt of General Chistiakov's 6th Guards Army and the reinforcing mobile corps of General Katukov's 1st Tank Army, which were now arrayed in strong defensive positions along the Pena and Lukhanino Rivers and southeast of Pokrovka (see Map 14). As planned, Vatutin had reinforced these forces with all of his remaining armor, antitank, and fighter aviation units. However, the precipitous German assaults that materialized in the early morning hours preempted any hopes on Vatutin's part of launching an attack with Katukov's armor and, instead, produced immediate crisis.

Often-heated discussions between Vatutin and the *Stavka* had resulted in a reluctant decision by the latter to forgo the tank counterattacks and to permit Vatutin to dig in Katukov's armor, using it defensively rather than in costly assaults against the massed and deadly longer-range German antitank weapons. The harsh combat of the next few days would test the validity of that *Stavka* decision. The more than 600 tanks of Katukov's tank army would now conduct a strenuous defensive battle for the army's survival, side by side with Soviet infantrymen, artillerymen, and sappers.

General Hoth's carefully planned battle was also not developing according to his original plans. After two days of combat, Hausser's II SS Panzer Corps had discovered a weak point in Soviet defenses: the highway leading northeast from Pokrovka to the Prokhorovka area. Moreover, the vigorous Soviet defense around Pokrovka and Bol'shie Maiachki, on Hausser's left flank, also tended to canalize his corps' thrust toward Prokhorovka. The Prokhorovka highway, however, led away from the original objectives of Oboian' and Kursk. Therefore, on 7 July new combat realities required von Knobelsdorff's XXXXVIII Panzer Corps to fulfill two critical roles. While it shouldered the main responsibility for continuing the northward advance on Oboian', it was also charged with clearing and protecting the II SS Panzer Corps' left flank, a task it had to perform if it was to satisfy its principal offensive mission. Ironically, although von Knobelsdorff's powerful force could handle these two missions, it could not cope with the new dilemma that soon confronted it—that of protecting its own extended left flank as its armored spearheads lunged northward.

On the morning of 7 July, while Priess's SS Panzer Grenadier Division *Totenkopf* pressed Soviet forces eastward into the shallow valley of the Lipovyi Donets River along II SS Panzer Corps' long right flank, *Leibstandarte's* two panzer grenadier regiments assaulted Soviet positions around Pokrovka and Bol'shie Maiachki.[97] In fierce fighting the Soviet 49th and 100th Tank Brigades gave ground and by nightfall abandoned the pivotal positions. A Soviet account recorded:

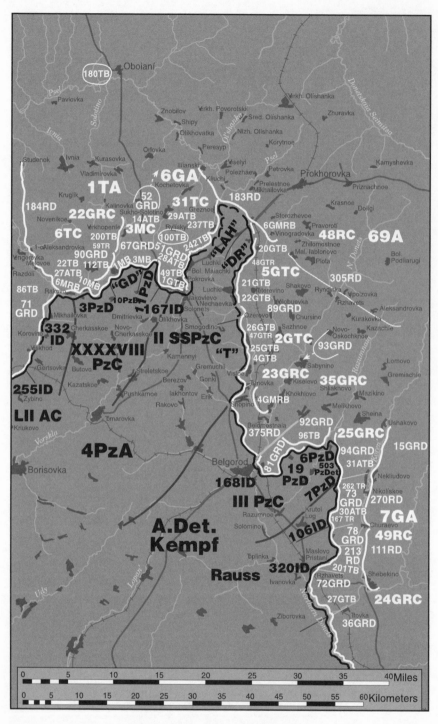

Map 14. Voronezh Front, 7 July 1943

In the Pogorelovka and Mikhailovka region, the enemy attacked the 1st Guards Tank Brigade. Up to 100 enemy combat aircraft bombed it from the skies. All enemy attempts to penetrate into the brigade's defenses failed. Simultaneously, the Hitlerite command threw up to 30 tanks and an infantry battalion against Pokrovka and captured it. This created a threat to the brigade's left flank. Lieutenant Colonel A. F. Burda's 49th Tank Brigade was rushed to the Pokrovka region to restore the situation. He drove the enemy from Pokrovka, but during the subsequent battles he fell back to the north and the enemy again occupied Pokrovka.[98]

Leibstandarte's history cryptically described the fighting around Pokrovka and confirmed the accuracy of the Soviet account:

At 06.15 [0815 Moscow time] hours, the enemy launched an attack against Lutschki [Luchki, four kilometers north of Pokrovka] with the support of seven tanks, which we initially repulsed. A second attack following a short time later, however, succeeded in breaking through into Lutschki. It came from about thirty tanks moving in from the northwest [the Soviet 100th Tank Brigade].

At 08.50 [1050 Moscow time] hours, this enemy force was pushed back in a counterattack by the II./2. The 1. Panzergrenadier-Regiment was able to improve its position considerably by capturing Pokrowka [Pokrovka] and Jakowlewo [Iakovlevo]. Two enemy tank forces with thirty and sixty tanks moving from the northwest out of Oboian [49th Tank Brigade] were beaten back by the Regiment, with excellent Luftwaffe support, in tough, but successful defensive fighting.[99]

Simultaneously, *Leibstandarte's* 1st SS Panzer Regiment and elements of 1st SS Panzer Grenadier Regiment drove up the Prokhorovka road in tandem with SS *Das Reich's* 2d SS Panzer Regiment, pushing back elements of General Kravchenko's 5th Guards Tank Corps through and past Teterevino. The forward momentum of II SS Panzer Corps' armored thrust was blunted, however, by the necessity of detaching the division's two panzer grenadier regiments to deal with Soviet forces along the corps' extended flanks. *Leibstandarte's* infantry struggled along an ever longer line northward from its newly seized prize of Pokrovka. As it advanced, the deploying armor from the 242d and 237th Tank Brigades of General Chernienko's 31st Tank Corps appeared along its left flank.[100] This caused *Brigadefuehrer* Wisch to detach additional forces to cover his threatened flank. Likewise, panzer grenadiers from *Gruppenfuehrer* Kruger's *Das Reich* Division also spread out along the II SS Panzer Corps' eastern flank to extend *Totenkopf's* thin defenses northward along the Lipovyi Donets River. These flank positions had to be held, since the next major threat to II SS Panzer Corps' advance would materialize along the shallow river valley.[101]

At day's end, the II SS Panzer Corps concentrated its two northernmost divisions in an attempt to complete the destruction of the pesky Soviet armored forces in its path. The corps' order for 8 July read, in part: "After assembling its attack forces by 06.00 hours with the main point of concentration on the right wing of its sector as far as the road from Belgorod to Obojan, the *LAH* is to move left of Panzergrenadierdivision *DR* and is to establish contact with the XXXXVIIII. Panzerkorps north of Nowosselowka. Elements should also be moved out of the Lutschki area, turned from the west to the south, and deployed to capture Bol. Majatschki. The completion of the preparations should be reported to the Korps [Corps]. The start of the attack will be given by order."[102]

As perilous as II SS Panzer Corps' advance was to the integrity of Vatutin's defenses, the most serious crisis arose in the sector defended by General Krivoshein's 3d Mechanized Corps of Katukov's 1st Tank Army. Krivoshein defended along the shallow Lukhanino River between Alekseevka and Pokrovka with four brigades—10th, 3d, and 1st Mechanized and 1st Guards Tank—abreast, reinforced by the dug-in tanks of the mechanized brigade's tank regiments, surviving antitank regiments, and infantry from General Chernov's 90th Guards Rifle Division. His front-line force of just under 200 tanks had few reserves, since Krivoshein's reserve 49th Tank Brigade had already been dispatched to reinforce Soviet defenses at Pokrovka. In addition, the corps' premier tank formation, Colonel V. M. Golelov's 1st Guards Tank Brigade, was already entangled in mortal combat against II SS Panzer Corps' forces around Pokrovka and General Getman's 6th Tank Corps was still occupying extended defenses farther west along the Pena River.[103]

Understanding the criticality of Krivoshein's sector and its inherent weaknesses, Vatutin desperately struggled to scrape together additional forces to thicken his defenses in front of and along the flank of the XXXXVIII Panzer Corps' likely advance route. The 38th and 40th Armies, holding the static front opposite the western flank of Fourth Panzer Army, released the 309th Rifle Division, three antitank brigades, and a variety of smaller units for this purpose.[104] The fact that the 52d Guards Rifle Division, severely mauled by the SS during the first two days of the battle, was now ordered to take up defensive positions along the axis of the German penetration indicates the shortage of forces that Vatutin was experiencing.

Vatutin's fears were borne out early on 7 July as the XXXXVIII Panzer Corps struck. Attacking in tandem along both sides of the Oboian' road, *Grossdeutschland* and 11th Panzer Division sliced through Krivoshein's defenses, threatening to rupture the 1st Tank Army's defensive front and, simultaneously, turn the flank of the 31st Tank Corps, which faced the II SS Panzer Corps' left flank.

More than 300 German tanks, including up to 40 Panthers, supported by waves of dive-bombers, ground through the 1st and 3d Mechanized Brigades' defensive front in an agonizingly slow, costly, but inexorable drive. In confused fighting that lasted all day, *Grossdeutschland* troopers pushed the Soviet defenders back to the outskirts of Syrtsevo and Gremiuchii, a distance of five kilometers, while the 11th Panzer rooted Soviet tanks from their dug-in positions for the same distance astride the Oboian' road. In the intense fighting, Soviet antitank units took a further toll on the attackers, claiming to have killed twenty-eight Tigers and seventy-six other tanks in one day.[105] Despite the losses, the XXXXVIII Panzer Corps stoically continued its advance.

A Soviet account captured the ferocity of the action:

> The Hitlerite attack began at 0300 hours. Especially ferocious battle developed in the sector of 1st and 3d Mechanized Brigades in the Syrtsevo region, where it raged on until 1500 hours. Separate groups of enemy tanks succeeded in reaching the artillery firing positions, but here they were destroyed by the accurate fire of the artillery.
>
> During the repeated attacks, by introducing fresh forces, the enemy penetrated the defensive front and began to spread in a northern and northwestward direction. The brigades withdrew in bitter fighting. A platoon of the 3d Battery, 35th Antitank Artillery Regiment occupied firing positions at a fork in the road at Hill 254.5. A group of enemy tanks, including "Tigers," advanced on the artillery's positions. Permitting the tanks to approach to within 200 to 300 meters, the artillery opened accurate fire and over the course of several minutes set fire to five heavy "Tiger" tanks. The remaining tanks turned back. . . .
>
> North of Syrtsevo, in the area of Hill 230.1, the tankists of Colonel M. T. Leonov's 112th Tank Brigade stood heroically in their defensive positions. Heavy battles raged here until late evening, during which the Hitlerites lost fifteen tanks, including six "Tigers." The brigade also suffered heavy losses, losing fifteen tanks.[106]

Once again German accounts confirm those of their opponents: *Grossdeutschland's* history described the day's fighting as follows:

> At dawn on 7 July the panzers and elements of II Battalion, Panzer Grenadier Regiment first took Dubrova, before veering northwest with I Battalion, Panzer-Grenadier Regiment GD. Unfortunately for the attackers, at this point the Panthers suffered enormous losses in tanks knocked out and the fully-deployed Strachwitz panzer group drove into a minefield which had not been identified, frustrating all further movement. An advance by I Battalion, Panzer-Grenadier Regiment GD was thus stopped for the time

being. The panzers and panzer-grenadiers tried to maintain their positions under very heavy fire, and the lack of mobility of the tanks cost them further losses. . . . Finally the remaining tanks of I Battalion, as well as the few remaining Panthers succeeded in crossing the minefield, in the course of which they became involved in a sharp tank-versus-tank engagement late in the morning. II Battalion, Panzer Regiment GD veered west and sought to escort I Battalion, Panzer-Grenadier Regiment to the scene of the fighting. The Remer Battalion finally arrived at about 11.30 and joined the battle. Meanwhile, farther to the north, II Battalion, Panzer-Grenadier Regiment GD launched an attack in the direction of Sirtsev [Syrtsevo] but progress was slow. By radio the battalion commander reported considerable losses to enemy fire from anti-tank guns, mortars and 102-mm canon.

The panzer-fusilier regiment in the meantime had gained a foothold in the Olkhovaya Gorge with its III Battalion on the right, while on the left I Battalion took up the assault on Point 1.2 north of Sirtsev. Very heavy attacks by enemy close-support aircraft disrupted these movements considerably; in some places the fighting in the system of positions entailed very heavy losses. The advance proved to be slow and laborious; heavy close-quarters fighting broke out over every single position.[107]

The same account also identifies the heavy fighting in the late afternoon, when elements of the Soviet 112th Tank Brigade arrived to reinforce Krivoshein's beleaguered mechanized brigades:

Finally the enemy withdrew from Sirtsev under the concentric attack by both GD regiments. Masses of Soviet troops streamed in a northwesterly direction toward Sirtsevo. By evening a small armoured group from the Armoured Reconnaissance Battalion GD and the Assault Gun Battalion GD, in cooperation with I Battalion, Panzer-Grenadier Regiment GD attacking from the east and aided by pressure exerted by the panzer-fusiliers from the south, succeeded in occupying the decisive Hill 230.1 against strong enemy armoured forces. The hill represented a favorable jumping-off point for further attacks to the north and against Sirtsevo. This was also the end of combat operations for that day; essentially it appeared that the Soviets' second system of positions had been successfully breached. Night fell and brought no rest. The sky was fire-red, heavy artillery shells shook the earth, rocket batteries fired at the last identified targets. Soon the Soviet "crows" were in the air, dropping large numbers of small bombs on the fires and other visible targets.[108]

Not only did the German advance threaten a German breakthrough to the north, but it also menaced the rear of Soviet forces defending to the east around Pokrovka. Consequently, Katukov and Vatutin ordered Krivoshein to withdraw his left flank back to the north, but to maintain links with the 31st Tank Corps' defense farther to the east.

General von Mellenthin, then Chief of Staff of the XXXXVIII Panzer Corps, later captured the atmosphere of his corps' confused battle:

On July 7, the fourth day of *Citadel*, we at last achieved some success. *Grossdeutschland* was able to break through on both sides of Ssyrzew [Syrtsevo], and the Russians withdrew to Gremutschy [Gremiuchii] and Ssyrzewo. The fleeing masses were caught by German artillery fire and suffered very heavy casualties; our tanks gained momentum and wheeled to the northwest. But at Ssyrzewo that afternoon they were halted by strong defensive fire, and the Russian armor counterattacked. However, on the right wing we seemed within reach of a big victory; the grenadier regiment of *Grossdeutschland* was reported to have reached Werhopenje [Verkhopen'e]. On the right flank of *Grossdeutschland* a battle-group was formed to exploit this success; it consisted of the reconnaissance detachment and the assault-gun detachment and was told to advance as far as Height 260.8 to the south of Nowosselowka [Novoselovka]. When this battle-group reached Gremutschy they found elements of the grenadier regiment in the village. The grenadiers were under the illusion that they were in Nowosselowka and could not believe that they were only in Gremutschy. Thus the report of the so-called success of the grenadiers was proved wrong; things like that happen in every war and particularly in Russia.[109]

Mellenthin's recollections were quite accurate as far as they went. What he did not know was that the force which *Grossdeutschland* ran into near Syrtsevo was a brigade of General Getman's 6th Tank Corps. When Krivoshein's defenses gave way, Katukov ordered Getman to shift his corps eastward, occupy new positions facing eastward across the Pena River south of Verkhopen'e, and counterattack into the flank of the advancing Germans in support of the withdrawing 3d Mechanized Corps. By nightfall the sixty tanks of Colonel M. T. Leonov's 112th Tank Brigade reached the river near Syrtsevo and attacked through the remnants of the 1st Mechanized Brigade. At the same time, Colonel N. V. Morganov's 200th Tank Brigade occupied positions farther north along the river's west bank opposite Verkhopen'e.[110]

The eastward shift of the 6th Tank Corps came none too soon, for on 8 July the XXXXVIII Panzer Corps continued its advance northward along the east bank of the Pena River and straight up the Oboian' road (see Map 15). Pressing the remnants of Krivoshein's now shattered 3d Mechanized Corps, the two German panzer divisions advanced abreast until halted by darkness

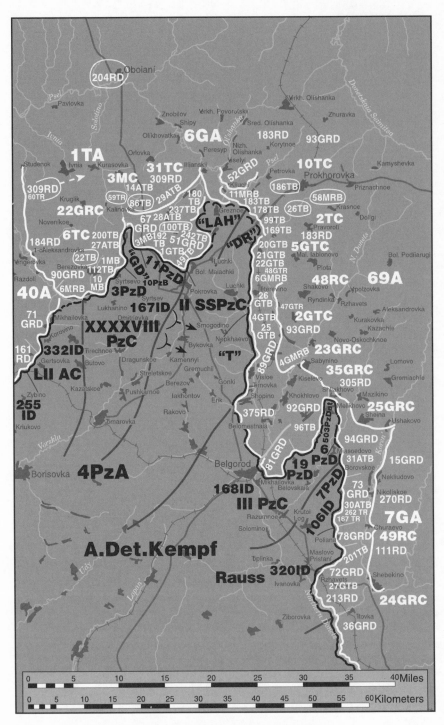

Map 15. Voronezh Front, 8 July 1943

and massed Soviet antitank fire from the high ground along the highway south of Il'inskii. *Grossdeutschland's* panzer grenadiers, flanked on the left by 3d Panzer Division forces that had sidestepped into *Grossdeutschland's* former sector, cleared Soviet troops from the east bank of the Pena under increasingly heavy tank and artillery fire, and *Grossdeutschland's* panzer regiment seized a portion of Verkhopen'e in a *coup de main*.[111]

According to German eyewitness accounts:

The sleepless night was followed by a sunny day. The first objective of 8 July was the capture of the well-defended village of Sirtsevo. Just as the attack was about to commence, however, the four panzers of II Battalion, Panzer Regiment's screening force under Leutnant Hausherr were knocked out of action. Leutnant Hausherr was killed along with his gunner and loader. It soon turned out that this tank-versus-tank duel was only the forerunner of a Soviet armoured advance by at least forty tanks.[112]

Confirming this action, Soviet sources recorded:

On 8 July the enemy decided to reach the Oboian' region at any cost. The main attack again developed along the Oboian' road. Here the Hitlerite command concentrated up to 500 tanks and a great quantity of infantry and artillery. An intense struggle developed along a thirty-kilometer front. The enemy tank assaults were supported by aviation operating over the battlefield in groups of forty to fifty aircraft. During the course of the day, 6th Tank Corps' 112th Tank Brigade and 3d Mechanized Corps' 10th and 1st Mechanized Brigades, which were subordinated to it, together with left-flank units of the 90th Guards Rifle Division, repulsed all of the attacks by the Germans, who were attempting to capture Syrtsevo, and clung to their defensive positions.[113]

German accounts, however, correctly qualify the overly optimistic Soviet description:

The [Soviet] assault, launched from Sirtsevo, also hit the Strachwitz group at Point 230.1. Strachwitz's crews destroyed 10 enemy tanks in short order, but this advance by the enemy also showed how strong were their forces in Sirtsevo. Nevertheless at about 10.30 [1230 Moscow time] the panzer-fusiliers moved out of the ravines south of the village and headed north, while I Battalion, Panzer-Grenadier Regiment GD together with the tanks advanced on Sirtsevo from the east. The attackers broke into the village at about 12.30 [1430] in the face of heavy anti-tank fire from the west bank, after which they mopped up the remaining Soviet defenders in

Sirtsevo. The 3d Panzer Division's 6th Panzer Regiment assisted in this attack from the west.[114]

Grossdeutschland's combat history then described the subsequent daring advance to Verkhopen'e and the confusion produced by the intense and fluid fighting:

> In the meantime the Armoured Reconnaissance Battalion, reinforced by the Assault Gun Battalion GD, had received orders to attack Verkhopenye from its previous positions. Since Sirtsevo was not yet in our hands at that point, the battalion commander decided to advance northeast through Gremiuchiy. There the battalion met III Battalion Panzer-Grenadier Regiment GD, which obviously thought it was in Verkhopenye and had caused some confusion in the command staff by reporting the same. An explanation of the true situation made it clear to the battalion command that they were in fact in Gremiuchiy. The load-bearing ability of the only available bridge held up the Armoured Reconnaissance Battalion advance for some time, and in the end the division decided to leave it where it was to guard the right flank. This measure quickly proved to be the right one. The enemy tank attack from the northeasterly direction followed soon after the battalion had formed a semi-circle north of Gremiuchiy. Scarcely an hour passed before waves of enemy tanks 20 to 40 attacked. The Assault Gun Battalion GD under Major Franz was able to destroy a total of 35 enemy tanks and 18 heavy anti-tank guns there in the course of a few hours. The positions, which extended in a semicircle across the road in the east across the M.T. [motor-tractor] station, were held. That evening the anti-tank battalion under Major Hacke . . . was sent to bolster the Armoured Reconnaissance Battalion. Meanwhile II Battalion, Panzer-Grenadier Regiment GD, together with I Battalion, Panzer Regiment GD . . . and the few surviving Panthers advanced past Point 230.1 to the north. That evening this force became involved in heavy fighting with fresh Soviet tank reserves at the eastern end of Verkhopenye. III Battalion, which had followed on the right, likewise became engaged in heavy fighting, but to the northeast of Verkhopenye. That evening, after refueling, the Gottberg Panzer Battalion (II Battalion) was pulled out of Sirtsevo and likewise sent in the direction of Verkhopenye. Stuka attacks had done effective preparatory work and the main body of the Panzer-Grenadier Regiment GD clawed its way into the town of Verkhopenye. Extending for a kilometer along the Penza in a north-south direction, it was a tough nut to crack. The effect of enemy fire from the west bank of the Penza on the mass of Panzer-grenadiers attacking from the south and east was especially uncomfortable and disruptive.[115]

Soviet classified sources confirm *Grossdeutschland's* description of the action, noting: "The 200th Tank Brigade did not succeed in entrenching itself along its designated lines and suffered considerable losses from enemy air attacks. During the course of the day the brigade held off twelve enemy attacks, but, by day's end, withdrew behind the Pena River, where it set about digging in its tanks."[116] It seemed as if the XXXXVIII Panzer Corps was on the verge of finally penetrating straight through the central sector of Vatutin's defense and racing on to Oboian'.

Vatutin, however, was aware of the danger and had taken the necessary precautions to deal with it. He ordered General Chernienko's 31st Tank Corps on his left flank, which, along with the remnants of the 3d Mechanized Corps, was now facing renewed pressure from the II SS Panzer Corps, to withdraw and occupy new prepared defenses extending from north of Verkhopen'e, across the Oboian' road, and along the Solotinka River forward of Sukho-Solotino and Kochetovka to the Psel River. There the two mobile corps would be joined by the 309th Rifle Division (from 40th Army), the 29th Antitank Brigade, two fresh tank brigades, and three antitank regiments.[117] Tied in with the defenses of General Getman's 6th Tank Corps to the west, Vatutin hoped Katukov's new defense line could hold, at least until he could realize the effects of the 2d, 10th Tank Corps', and 5th Guards Tank Corps' counterattacks, which were then under way at and south of Prokhorovka.[118]

As spectacular as the XXXXVIII Panzer Corps' advance had been on 7 and 8 July, the corps commander, von Knobelsdorff, now faced a new dilemma. Although he felt he could breach Soviet defenses along the Oboian' road and finally cross the Psel River and reach Kursk, he first had to deal with the threat to his left flank posed by the new Soviet armored force (6th Tank Corps). Ominously, intelligence reports also indicated a buildup of Soviet infantry in that sector. Therefore, on the night of 8 July, the XXXXVIII Panzer Corps commander ordered *Grossdeutschland* and 11th Panzer Division to advance five kilometers the next day to seize Hill 260.8, key high ground on the Oboian' road. Then, while the 11th Panzer continued forward along the road, *Grossdeutschland* was to wheel to the west to outflank and, in conjunction with the 3d Panzer and 332d Infantry Divisions, destroy the Soviet armored force defending west of Verkhopen'e. Specifically, *Grossdeutschland* was to seize key terrain on the 6th Tank Corps' flank and rear, in particular, Hill 243, which overlooked the flank of Soviet defenses along the Pena River, and Hill 247, which controlled Soviet reinforcement and withdrawal routes along the Berezovka-Ivnia road.[119] Once the threat to the XXXXVIII Panzer Corps' left flank had been eliminated, *Grossdeutschland*, trailed by the 3d Panzer Division, would rejoin the 11th Panzer Division for the final drive on Oboian' and Kursk.

This entire maneuver was timed to coincide with the reorientation of the II SS Panzer Corps' advance from the Prokhorovka axis to the Kursk axis. On

8 July, while the XXXXVIII Panzer Corps was punishing Katukov's armor along the Oboian' road, the II SS Panzer Corps began reorienting its northward drive away from Prokhorovka and toward Kursk. While the 2d SS Panzer Grenadier Division *Das Reich's Deutschland* and *Der Fuehrer* Panzer Grenadier Regiments held the front from Teterevino southward along the Lipovyi Donets River, the 1st SS Panzer Grenadier Division *Leibstandarte* thrust westward, followed by elements of the *Totenkopf* Division, which was just then in the process of turning its sector along the Donets to the 167th Infantry Division. Although the relief process was slow and the redeployment of *Totenkopf* took place in piecemeal fashion, the German advance was nothing short of spectacular, particularly since Vatutin had already ordered his forces to fall back to new defensive lines. German grenadiers from *Leibstandarte* cleared Soviet forces from Bol'shie Maiachki and adjacent villages and its panzer regiment advanced against the 31st Tank Corps' 242d Tank Brigade at Malye Maiachki. Shortly thereafter, *Totenkopf* went into action. Its two panzer grenadier regiments pressed the 31st Tank Corps 237th Tank Brigade back from Gresnoe and pushed on toward the Psel River, all the while covering its right flank near Teterevino with elements of the *Das Reich* Division.[120]

At this juncture, while the II SS Panzer Corps was in the midst of regrouping and was most vulnerable, Vatutin's supposedly coordinated armored counterattack occurred.[121] According to orders issued by Vatutin at 2300 hours the previous night, Major General V. G. Burkov's full-strength 10th Tank Corps (185 tanks and self-propelled guns) was to strike the II SS Panzer Corps directly "on the nose" by attacking southwestward along the road from Prokhorovka to Teterevino. Its right flank was protected by its 11th Motorized Rifle Brigade and the remnants of the 52d Guards Rifle Division, which were to attack along the banks of the Psel southward from Krasnyi Oktiabr'. On the 10th Tank Corps' left flank, General Kravchenko's already weakened 5th Guards Tank Corps (with about 100 tanks) was to strike westward across the Lipovyi Donets near Belenikhino, and Burdeiny's 2d Guards Tank Corps (with about 140 tanks) would do likewise farther south along the Lipovyi Donets near Nepkhaevo. Supposedly, this concerted armored assault against the right flank of German II SS Panzer Corps was timed to match the 6th Tank Corps' attack against the XXXXVIII Panzer Corps' left flank. A thirty-minute artillery preparation and most of the *front's* available aircraft would support the combined attacks.

When the appointed attack hour arrived on the morning of 8 July, the 10th Tank Corps' dawn attack was preempted by SS *Totenkopf's* and *Das Reich's* advance. Together with its supporting 183d Rifle Division, Burkov's brigades launched piecemeal attacks, which the Germans repelled with heavy losses, largely by means of devastating antitank fire.[122] Delayed in its movement forward, General Popov's 2d Tank Corps failed to support the afternoon attack by Burkov's armor. Instead, in late afternoon Popov's tank brigades also went into combat piecemeal and suffered the same rebuff as their predecessors. Kravchenko's 5th Guards went into action near Kalinin at 1000 hours and, after only minimal gains, was repulsed by the 1st and 2d Battalions of *Deutschland* Regiment, which were dug in around Iasnaia Poliana and Kalinin.

Burdeiny's 2d Guards Tank Corps fared little better. It jumped off at 1200 hours, and after limited progress suffered an unmerciful beating from German aircraft and *Totenkopf's* panzer regiment, losing fifty tanks in the process.[123] German aerial reconnaissance had detected Burdeiny's concentration of armor, and four squadrons of Henschel HS-109 aircraft, specially equipped with 30mm automatic cannon for antitank missions, broke up the Soviet attack, perforating the thin overhead armor of the tanks and leaving a hideous, burning wasteland. This unprecedented action, in which a tank attack was halted by air power alone, set a dangerous precedent. Indeed, throughout this battle, Soviet troop movements had to be conducted at night to minimize such losses. This in turn delayed the arrival of reserves to block the German penetration.

On that day alone, *Leibstandarte* reported destroying 82 enemy tanks, most by antitank fire, at a cost to the division of 66 dead, 178 wounded, and 6 missing.[124] The II SS Panzer Corps as a whole recorded 121 enemy tanks destroyed on 8 July. By this time SS Panzer Corps had irrevocably lost 17 tanks, and about 100 required repair.[125] This loss ratio of one German to eight Russian tanks persisted throughout much of the operation.

Despite the fierce Soviet attacks on his right flank, *Obergruppenfuehrer* Hausser of the II SS Panzer Corps ordered continuation of the attack northward to link up with the XXXXVIII Panzer Corps near Sukho-Solotino, to clear the south banks of the Psel, and to march on toward Oboian'. As a result of the intense combat on his right flank, he was forced to retain *Das Reich* in that sector until the III Panzer Corps could come up on his flank.

III PANZER CORPS' ADVANCE

Unfortunately for Hausser, that would not be soon, for Army Detachment Kempf and its critical armored force were still mired in the intense struggle raging southeast and east of Belgorod.

There, in the lowlands east of the Northern Donets River, Army Detachment Kempf continued its frustrating efforts to punch through an ever-strengthening Soviet 7th Guards Army.[126] On 7 July the armored spearheads of General Breith's III Panzer Corps planned to wheel northward in an attempt to outflank the Soviet 81st Guards Rifle Division defending across the river from Belgorod. Breith's ultimate goal was to reach and advance up the Northern Donets River valley to keep pace with and protect the right flank of Hausser's II SS Panzer Corps. Until he could do so, precious German forces would remain tied down in the Lipovyi Donets River valley.

Despite Kempf's best efforts, however, the going was tough. Soviet forces concentrated against his right flank forward of the Koren' River and were pouring fresh troops in to block his northward advance. Additionally, the Soviets clung to their positions opposite Belgorod and launched fierce counterattacks against the 106th and 320th Infantry Divisions, which were defending Army Detachment Kempf's right flank near Maslova Pristan'. These assaults by the newly committed Soviet 213th Rifle Division and the 72d Guards Rifle Division, with heavy armor support, inflicted severe casualties on the German 320th Infantry Division and prevented the 106th Infantry from relieving 7th Panzer Division forces so that they could shift their full strength to the critical drive to the north.[127]

Despite these frustrations, early on 7 July, General von Funck of 7th Panzer Division was able to extract part of his forces from the Batratskaia Dacha region and to commit them, in concert with the 6th Panzer Division, to a rapid advance against Soviet defenders at the key road junction of Miasoedovo. The 117 tanks of General von Hünersdorff's 6th Panzer Division, with the 45 Tiger tanks of the 503d Heavy Panzer Detachment in its vanguard, kept pace on the left by driving Soviet forces northward from Iastrebovo. Late in the day, the advanced guards of both panzer divisions clashed with advanced elements of the newly committed Soviet 92d and 94th Guards Rifle Divisions of 35th Guards Rifle Corps, which had been ordered forward to bolster sagging Soviet 25th Guards Rifle Corps' defenses east of Belgorod.[128]

Meanwhile, in extremely intense and grueling fighting, General Schmidt's 19th Panzer Division, on the III Panzer Corps' left flank, reached and secured Blizhniaia Igumenka, in the 81st Guards Rifle Division's rear. However, until Schmidt's division could pierce Soviet defenses across the Northern Donets River, the emerging Soviet salient east of Belgorod could not be eliminated. Nor was the 168th Infantry Division making spectacular progress against Soviet defenses anchored in the town of Staryi Gorod, east of the river and Belgorod.

The following day, while the 7th Panzer contended with a new threat to its flank and front between Miasoedovo and Batratskaia Dacha (the entire Soviet 94th Guards Rifle Division), the 6th Panzer's 11th Panzer and 4th Panzer Grenadier Regiments, with the 503d Panzer Detachment in the vanguard, lunged forward eight kilometers and captured the next key road junction and Soviet defensive strong point at the town of Melikhovo, east of the Lipovyi Donets. However, on the 6th Panzer's left flank, Schmidt's 19th Panzer had difficulty keeping up as it plowed through heavy Soviet defenses north of Blizhniaia Igumenka. More ominous, although the III Panzer Corps had irrevocably pierced the Soviet first defensive belt east of the Northern Donets, it was still thwarted in its attempts to cross the Lipovyi Donets River into the rear of Soviet forces defending east of Belgorod.

This was so due to the vigorous countermeasures taken by the Soviet 7th Guards Army commander General Shumilov. To counter the German northward thrust, throughout 7 and 8 July, Shumilov continued his attacks against Army Detachment Kempf's right flank with all of his defending divisions. Additionally, behind these attacking forces, Shumilov arrayed the 15th Guards, 270th, and 111th Rifle Divisions, which he could use to strengthen his flank defenses and, when appropriate, commit in expanded counterattacks.[129] The real and potential threat posed by these forces was the reason why the 7th Panzer Division remained tied down in defensive combat along Kempf's extended right flank.

To deal with the looming threat of a III Panzer Corps advance to the north, on 7 July Shumilov committed the 92d and 94th Guards Rifle Divisions of Major General S. G. Gorianov's 35th Guards Rifle Corps against the flanks and nose of the German penetration and reinforced them with tank and antitank units that had been defending west of the Lipovyi Donets River (the 96th Tank Brigade). When the 6th Panzer Division pierced this new defense on the 8th, Shumilov then committed Colonel A. F. Vasil'ev's reserve 305th Rifle Division from the 69th Army to erect a new defensive line extending east and west of Shliakhovo to block any further advance by 6th Panzer. As tense as the situation was, General Shumilov's 7th Guards Army was performing its role superbly on less than favorable terrain.

Throughout the bitter struggle on 7 and 8 July, Soviet aircraft sortie rates remained constant at between 1,100 and 1,500, while German rates continued to fall from 829 on 7 July to 652 on the 8th.[130] As before, the Germans concentrated their efforts in key sectors in support of their advancing armor and against looming Soviet armor threats. By concentrating quickly at certain key points, the Germans could gain local air superiority, but the dominance was only fleeting. Despite the growing Soviet overall air superiority, however, by Soviet admission, "[our aviation] still did not have air superiority over the enemy's main attack axis—along the Belgorod-Oboian' highway—until 10 July. Enemy aviation not only offered strong opposition to our assault aviation aircraft, it also gained air superiority over the battlefield relatively easily during the period necessary for his bomber operations."[131] This situation would sharply change in the Soviets' favor by 11 July.

FATEFUL DECISIONS, 9 JULY

Although they did not fully realize it at the time, on the night of 8–9 July and during combat the following day, Vatutin, Vasilevsky, the *Stavka,* and the German commands would make critical decisions that would ultimately decide the outcome of the Battle of Kursk. These decisions were based wholly on combat realities, which were, in turn, a product of decisions taken in earlier days and the outcome of battles already fought. As in all battles, therefore, the ultimate outcome would result from both the conscious actions of the contending commanders and a healthy dose of chance.

Given the challenges they faced, Vatutin, *Stavka* representative Vasilevsky, and the *Stavka* itself focused their efforts on shoring up Soviet defenses and preparing for the mighty Soviet counteroffensive, which they were convinced must follow. First and foremost, this meant that they had to defend the Oboian'-Kursk axis successfully. They could do so by two means: first, by erecting impenetrable defenses along the Oboian' road; and second, by continuing to weaken the German northward thrust with attacks against the flanks of the advancing panzer corps. In essence, this is what the Soviet commands had been doing since 5 July, and despite local setbacks and quite natural pessimism in some quarters, particularly at lower echelons where strategic realities were not always apparent, they had done so with a modicum of success. Soviet planners were also reassured by the knowledge that the offensive by Model's Ninth Army had essentially failed, that Western and Briansk Front forces would soon go over to the offensive north and east of Orel, and that General I. S. Konev's powerful Steppe Front forces were now poised to intervene decisively, if necessary, in the struggle.

Within this context, on the night of 8–9 July, the key Soviet players issued orders that would govern military actions over the ensuing climactic days.[132] The *Stavka,* on the advice of Vasilevsky and Vatutin, accelerated its assembly of strategic reserves by subordinating Lieutenant General P. A. Rotmistrov's 5th Guards Tank Army to Vatutin's Voronezh Front. Rotmistrov's army had closed into assembly areas in the Staryi Oskol region during the morning of 8 July, after moving over 200 kilometers from the Ostogozhsk region west of the Don River.[133] Now, the *Stavka* ordered Rotmistrov to hasten his march toward the Prokhorovka region. Moving at night to minimize the effects of German air attacks, the 593 tanks, 37 self-propelled guns, and thousands of artillery pieces, motor transports, and support vehicles of the 5th Guards Tank Army's three mobile corps were to close into new assembly areas by 2300 hours on 9 July. These areas extended over a vast expanse from east of Oboian' to northeast of Prokhorovka. On 10 July, Rotmistrov was to dispatch forward elements to the line of the Psel River and positions west of Prokhorovka.[134] The *Stavka* then transferred Lieutenant

General A. S. Zhadov's 5th Guards Army to Voronezh Front control, with orders to deploy its two guards rifle corps into positions along the Psel River from Oboian' to Prokhorovka.[135] Naturally, it would require several days for the 80,000 men of Zhadov's army to execute this order.

Later on 9 July, the *Stavka* directed Lieutenant General V. D. Kriuchenkin's 69th Army to take over responsibility for defense in the Prokhorovka-Lipovyi Donets River sector between the 6th Guards and 7th Guards Army. Kriuchenkin reinforced the Lipovyi Donets line with Major General V. V. Tikhomirov's 93d Guards Rifle Division of the 35th Guards Rifle Corps and prepared to defend the critical river sector with the 183d, 89th Guards, and 81st Guards Rifle Divisions, while his remaining 92d and 94th Guards and 305th Rifle Divisions contested the advance of German III Panzer Corps, east of the Northern Donets.[136]

Meanwhile, Vatutin conducted a general regrouping within the Voronezh Front to firm up his defenses along the Oboian' road and to generate forces necessary to launch a general counterattack against the advancing Germans' flanks. At 0035 hours on 9 July, he personally telephoned General Burkov, the 10th Tank Corps commander, and ordered him to turn over his defenses along the Prokhorovka road to General Popov's 2d Tank Corps. Now subordinated to Katukov's 1st Tank Army, Burkov was to move his corps westward, slow the advance of the II SS Panzer Corps toward the new Soviet defense lines around Kochetovka, and then occupy new defensive positions at Vladimirovka along the Oboian' road.[137] Vatutin then ordered General Kravchenko to prepare to redeploy his 5th Guards Tank Corps from its positions south of Prokhorovka. Moving westward late on 9 July, it too was to join Katukov's defense along the Oboian' road early on 10 July. Both tank corps, which were reinforced with new tanks en route, would then be in position either to support the 1st Tank Army's defense along the Oboian' road or to launch counterattacks against the German XXXXVIII Panzer Corps' left flank along the Pena River.

In addition to providing Katukov with two additional tank corps, Vatutin bolstered his infantry and antitank defenses along the Oboian' road. He had already ordered Colonel D. F. Dremin's 309th Rifle Division (from the 40th Army) to anchor the new 6th Guards Army defense from the Oboian' road to Peresyp on the Psel River. On 9 July, 31st Tank Corps and the remnants of the 3d Mechanized Corps were to fall back to these positions. He then ordered Colonel K. M. Baidak's 204th Rifle Division from the 38th Army to form as a new *front* reserve behind the 3d Mechanized Corps and prepare to bolster defenses along the Oboian' road. Vatutin also reinforced Katukov's 1st Tank Army with additional tank, antitank, and artillery regiments drawn from the 38th Army and *Stavka* reserve.[138]

Despite these reinforcements, General Katukov was becoming increasingly pessimistic about the outcome of the battle. The 1st Tank Army, his carefully forged weapon for offensive maneuver, had become a hodgepodge of units, many of them badly depleted, committed to a desperate defense against the determined German attacks. Katukov's tankers, gunners, and tank destroyers were unquestionably inflicting heavy casualties on the new German tanks, but nothing seemed to halt the steady penetration to the north. Katukov's army would remain the focal point of fighting on 9 July. Although this army was suffering major damage, its vigorous defense would once again deflect German attention to the west, this time with fatal consequences for the German offensive as a whole.

Meanwhile, Katukov's opponent, General Hoth, also sought to concentrate his remaining strength to continue the advance toward Oboian' and Kursk. To this end, Hoth requested, and later received, maximum air support for what he hoped would be the culminating drive on Kursk. But first, von Knobelsdorff's XXXXVIII Panzer Corps had to rid itself of the persistent threat to its left flank. While the *Grossdeutschland*, 3d Panzer, and trailing 332d Infantry Division dealt with this threat, the 11th Panzer Division and other elements of *Grossdeutschland* were to link up with the II SS Panzer Corps and continue the drive on Oboian' and Kursk. Von Knobelsdorff incorrectly assumed that *Grossdeutschland* could deal rather easily with the Russian armored force on its flank and then return quickly to participate in the critical drive on Oboian'.

Simultaneously, Hausser's II SS Panzer Corps was to attack northward on 9 July with *Leibstandarte* and *Totenkopf* Divisions, while protecting its flank between Prokhorovka and along the Lipovyi Donets River with *Das Reich* and the 167th Infantry Division. The bulk of the II SS Panzer Corps' remaining 283 tanks and assault guns would spearhead the thrust on Kursk.[139] For 9 July von Manstein assigned all available close air missions to support this attack. The intense combat which occurred that day, and in particular the fierce battle that developed on the XXXXVIII Panzer Corps' left flank, fundamentally altered these German plans.

At least initially on 9 July, operations unfolded according to German plan (see Map 16).[140] Attacking abreast, the II SS Panzer Corps' *Leibstandarte* and *Totenkopf* Panzer Grenadier Divisions rolled over the rear guards of General Krivoshein's already shattered 3d Mechanized Corps and drove General Chernienko's 31st Tank Corps back to Kochetovka. By day's end *Totenkopf* had reached the banks of the Psel River and, in a sharp fight, captured the village of Krasnyi Oktiabr' from remnants of the now regrouped Soviet 52d Guards Rifle Division and the 10th Tank Corps' 11th Motorized Rifle Brigade, which the corps had left behind to cover the 2d Tank Corps' extended right flank along the Psel. On the left flank, *Leibstandarte's* headlong advance propelled its forces across the Solotinka River, where division panzer grenadiers seized Sukho-Solotino, linked up with the 11th Panzer Division, and

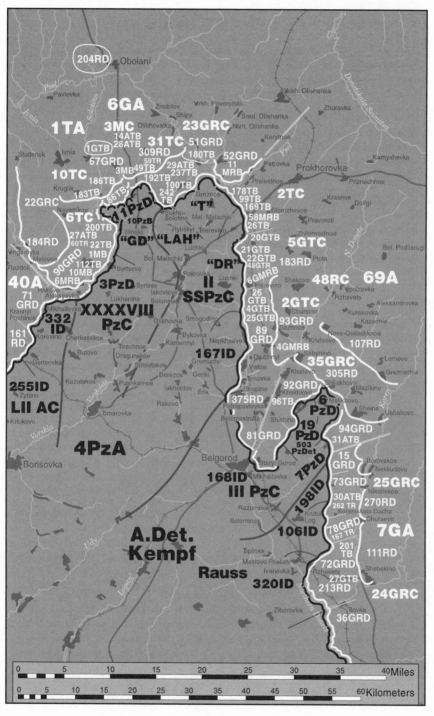

Map 16. Voronezh Front, 9 July 1943

were halted on the outskirts of Kochetovka only by the temporary intervention of the newly regrouped forces from the Soviet 10th Tank Corps.[141]

The II SS Panzer's northern thrust met less resistance than on previous
days but destroyed some Soviet tanks of the 31st Tank Corps as it withdrew
to the Solotinka River and of the 2d Tank Corps as it continued its attacks
against German troops along the approaches to Prokhorovka.[142] Throughout
the day along the Prokhorovka road, *Das Reich* had to contend with renewed
assaults by the Soviet 2d Tank and 5th Guards Corps. However, this fighting
tailed off late in the afternoon, when the 5th Guards Tank Corps disengaged
and began its westward march. Although the II SS Panzer Corps' losses had
been minimal, Soviet armor operations west of Prokhorovka were still disconcerting to Hausser at corps and Hoth at army. The reality of continued
intense combat along the Prokhorovka axis and the absence of major progress
by the III Panzer Corps to the south ultimately contributed to the fundamental
alteration in German plans that would be made later that afternoon.

Even more important in this crucial decision was the battle then unfolding in the XXXXVIII Panzer Corps' sector. There, on the morning of 9 July,
von Knobelsdorff unleashed the full force of his armor northward toward his
objective, Novoselovka, but to his utter consternation, by day's end the outskirts of the town were still in Soviet hands and his corps was advancing inexorably in two distinctly separate directions.[143] Major General Michl's 11th
Panzer Division attacked up the Oboian' road, penetrated the 3d Mechanized
Corps' defenses, seized Hill 260.8 (south of Novoselovka), and linked up with
Leibstandarte's panzer grenadiers north of Sukho-Solotino. The headlong
advance of 11th Panzer, which was supported on its left by elements of
Grossdeutschland, ground to a halt late in the day just south of Novoselovka
against the defenses of the 309th Rifle Division, backed up by intense Soviet
antitank and artillery fire. Nor could the 11th Panzer advance further until
joined by additional *Grossdeutschland* forces.

A Soviet source describes the strenuous defense in the Novoselovka
sector:

On 9 July the enemy delivered his main attack from the Krasnaia Dubrova
region toward Novoselovka against the units of General S. M. Krivoshein's
3d Mechanized Corps and Colonel A. I. Baksov's 67th Guards Rifle Division. . . . With the capture of Verkhopen'e, German tanks strengthened
their blows in the direction of Novoselovka. At mid-day the Hitlerites
penetrated 3d Mechanized Corps defensive front, and our units began
to withdraw in a northerly direction. Soldiers of Colonel V. S. Agafonov's
86th Tank Brigade were defending Novoselovka. The enemy attacked the
village from the south and the west. The battle took on an especially bitter character. The Hitlerites suffered great losses, but our forces were also

exhausted. Therefore, the 1st Tank Army commander decided to withdraw the 3d Mechanized Corps and 67th Guards Rifle Division behind
the combat formation of the 309th Rifle Division.[144]

Grossdeutschland's history describes the division's assault and explains
why the division was unable to throw its main weight northward along the
Oboian' road:

> The morning of 9 July saw the Panzer-Fusilier Regiment GD advancing
> beneath a cloudy sky past Verkhopenye to the east toward Novoselovka
> and Point 240.4 [just west of Novoselovka]. There, however, it was halted
> by a very strong defence of anti-tank guns and tanks. At about the same
> time—about 06.00 [0800 Moscow time]—the Armoured Reconnaissance
> Battalion, bolstered by the Assault Gun Battalion GD, was carrying out
> the division order for an advance toward Point 260.8 along the road to
> Oboyan. The attack was preceded by Stuka attacks on what appeared to
> be enemy armoured spearheads and troop concentrations farther to the
> north. Waves of dive-bombers dropped their loads with precision on the
> Russian tanks. A tall pillar of flame erupted each time a crew was sent to
> "commissar and Red Army heaven." Under cover of this really outstand-
> ing air support the battle group of the Armoured Reconnaissance Battal-
> ion GD approached Point 260.8. Observations revealed that to the east
> the 11th Panzer Division, which was still partially equipped with the Panzer
> III, was preparing to attack along the road to the north.
>   At about the same time, about 07.00, the panzer-grenadiers again set out
> against Verkhopenye with II and III Battalions in an effort to finally take
> possession of the town in spite of heavy flanking fire from the west. Battle
> Group von Strachwitz, supported the advance from the southern tip of
> Verkhopenye with about 19 Panzer IVs (long), 10 Tigers and about 10 of
> the surviving Panthers. At the same time, in a massed attack, Stuka wings
> dropped their bombs on recognized targets in the town and on the west
> bank of the Penza in order to soften up the objective. Finally, at about 08.35,
> the commandeer of II Battalion, Panzer-Grenadier Regiment GD reported
> that he was in the last houses in the northern part of Verkhopenye, which
> meant as much as the capture of the hotly contested town. The strong flank-
> ing fire from the west continued, an indication that our left neighbor had
> been unable to keep up with our advance; he was still farther to the south-
> west and was heavily engaged with enemy tank concentrations.
>   With the good progress of the panzer-fusiliers in the direction of
> Novoselovka and the reinforced Armoured Reconnaissance Battalion
> toward Point 260.8, the Strachwitz panzer group was pulled out of the
> area south of Verkhopenye as quickly as possible and sent to the north-

east. It soon reached Point 240.8. The panzer group then drove through the Armoured Reconnaissance Battalion battle group in the direction of Point 240.4. Our tanks soon ran into the enemy tank concentrations [86th Tank Brigade], however, which were sighted from a distance of 2,500–3,000 meters. A major tank-versus-tank battle developed, with the Stukas providing continuous support. Hill 243 was reached after heavy fighting and the panzers halted there initially. On the horizon were burning and smoking enemy tanks. Unfortunately three of 6th Company's tanks had been knocked out as well. . . . In the further course of the engagement Hauptmann von Wietersheim succeeded in carrying the attack as far as the anti-tank defenses at the village of Novoselovka and reached the hill. This in turn enabled the panzer-fusiliers to continue to advance and they arrived at the road fork due south of Point 244.8 on the road to Oboyan. They were called to an interim halt.

After reports of this success were received, the Panzer-Grenadier Regiment GD was withdrawn from the division's right attack lane at Verkhopenye and elements sent to Novoselovka. However, the difficult situation of the 3d Panzer Division on the left forced the division command to change its plans. The Panzer-Fusilier Regiment GD held farther north and northeast of Novoselovka and south of Point 244.8. I and II Battalions and the regimental command of the Panzer-Grenadier Regiment GD were now committed west and northwest of Novoselovka and screened the front to the north and northeast. Panzer Group Strachwitz had to turn almost ninety degrees in order to leave its former location on the road to Oboyan and head for Points 251.4 and 247.0 [northwest of Verkhopen'e]. Its orders were to make a frontal attack on the enemy tanks in that area which were holding up 3d Panzer Division's advance. The reinforced Armoured Reconnaissance Battalion followed this movement while screening the flanks to the southwest.

Our armoured spearheads encountered the first enemy tanks near Point 1.3 north of Verkhopenye, at about 22.00, in complete darkness. The panzers halted to refuel and rearm and then wait until morning. In the meantime the Armoured Reconnaissance Battalion and Assault Gun Battalion halted at a point south of 251.4 [northwest of Verkhopen'e].

These movements, the result of the difficult situation in which the 3d Panzer Division found itself, brought the division's units to Point 244.8 on the road to Oboyan, which was obviously the deepest penetration into the Kursk pocket by *Grossdeutschland*. It was possible only at the cost of extremely heavy fighting and in some cases considerable losses.[145]

The XXXXVIII Panzer Corps' chief of staff, von Mellenthin, played down the German success on 9 July and recognized the importance of *Gross-*

deutschland's turn to the west, writing, "Eleventh Panzer division was unable to advance very far, while the SS Panzer Corps operating on our eastern flank had to ward off strong armored counterattacks [by the 10th and 31st Tank Corps] all along the line; like ourselves it had gained little ground."[146]

Although the XXXXVIII Panzer Corps' gains were as extensive as those of previous days, German frustration was clearly showing. Writing after the war, von Mellenthin indicated that he had known that *Grossdeutschland* would never again join the critical drive toward Kursk.

Thus, as the 11th Panzer Division pushed north along the Oboian' road alone, General Walter Hoernlein's *Grossdeutschland* Division wheeled westward north of Verkhopen'e to outflank and destroy the stubborn Soviet armored force defending west of the Pena River. In so doing, it commenced a fierce battle that would last for days. Although *Grossdeutschland* ultimately mauled the Soviet 6th Tank Corps and the supporting infantry of the 90th Guards Rifle Division, the westward shift deprived the XXXXVIII Panzer Corps of the strength necessary to smash Soviet defenses along the Oboian'-Kursk axis and conditioned the subsequent fateful German decision to shift its main attack to the Prokhorovka axis.

Throughout 9 July, the Luftwaffe answered Hoth's summons for intensified air support by increasing its daily sortie rate to over 1,500, which was almost double the Soviet number. The Germans concentrated the bulk of their air effort along the Oboian'-Kursk axis. At the same time, given the increased German air activity, German aircraft losses, as recorded by the Soviets, fell from 106 planes on 8 July to only 71 on the 9th.[147]

Vatutin was quick to seize upon this opportunity afforded him by the Germans. Once the situation had stabilized along the Oboian' road, as it did late on 9 July, he shifted strong forces to his right flank. These would ensure that the *Grossdeutschland*, 3d Panzer Division, and the infantry divisions of Fourth Panzer Army's LII Army Corps (255th and 332d) would never again participate in the drive on Kursk. Simultaneously, the two powerful armies assigned to him from the Steppe Military District and the 69th Army could contend with whatever eventualities developed along his left flank near Prokhorovka.[148]

Vatutin well understood the potential threat to his plans posed by a continued advance by Army Detachment Kempf and its III Panzer Corps. Therefore, it was imperative that Kempf's armor be contained, at least until all German northward drives through Oboian' or elsewhere were blunted. Action on 9 July seemed to indicate that the III Panzer Corps could be stopped. During the day its forward progress was minimal. General von Hünersdorff's 6th Panzer Division regrouped around Melikhovo and dispatched armored feelers to the north, while the 19th and 7th Panzer Divisions struggled to defend or expand the flanks of the narrow German salient east of the Northern Donets River against stiffening Soviet resistance. All the while, General Kempf searched desperately for infantry forces that could free his panzers to continue their critical thrust to the north.

Field Marshal von Manstein's initial orders to Kempf, "to advance rapidly in the general direction of Korocha and to destroy the enemy forces expected from the east and north," still rang in Kempf's ears.[149] This meant that Kempf was "to intercept the Soviet Fifth Guards Tank Army, prevent it from linking up with Katukov's Army, and thereby keep Hoth's flank free."[150] Kempf had failed to do so, and the ugly consequences would soon be felt at Prokhorovka.

In the light of these stark realities, late in the afternoon of 9 July, Hoth fundamentally and, in retrospect, fatally altered his plans. Thwarted in the center and preoccupied with the threats to his flanks, he issued new orders to the II SS Panzer Corps to shift the axis of its advance northeastward toward Prokhorovka. At the same time, Hoth also requested the Luftwaffe to shift its efforts eastward. By attacking through Prokhorovka, Hoth was convinced that the still-powerful SS corps, with concentrated air support, could smash the armored threat to its east, unlock the advance of the III Panzer Corps, and open a new, albeit longer, approach route to the key city of Kursk. Perhaps then Model could finally break out of his confines along the northern flank of the Kursk Bulge.

The fateful order to the II SS Panzer Corps, which was passed on its subordinate divisions late on 9 July, read, in part (see Appendix E for full order):

1. *Enemy forces prepared for defense* are equipped with antitank weapons and tanks and are standing in a line from the western edge of the forest at Swch. Komssomolez [Komsomolets] to the railway line at Iwanowskij Wysselok [Ivanovskii Vyselok].

2. The II. SS-Panzerkorps [Panzer Corps] is to move out at 10 July 1943 with the *LSSAH* to the right and SS-Panzergrenadierdivision *Totenkopf* to the left on both sides of the Pssel and head northeast. *Attack objective*: Prochorowka [Prokhorovka]/East—Hill 252.4 (2.5 kilometers northeast of there)—Beregowoje [Beregovoe]—Hill 243.5 (2 kilometers northwest of Koritnje [Koritnoe])—Kartaschewka [Kartashevka].

3. The reinforced *LSSAH* is to move out at 06.00 hours on 10 July 1943 after the barrage by the entire Artillerie-Regiment/*LSSAH* and Werferregiment 55. After the Luftwaffe's preparation, the *LSSAH* is to move along the road from Teterewino [Teterevino] to Prochorowka, capture the latter town, and hold it. *First attack objective*: Prochorowka—Hill 252.4. SS-Panzergrenadierdivision *DR* is to set out with *LSSAH* and to capture the high ground 2 kilometers southeast of Iwanowskij Wysselok. SS-Panzergrenadierdivision *Totenkopf* is to move forward from the Kljutschi [Kliuchi] bridgehead to the northeast.[151]

With these changes in Hoth's plan, the German Kursk offensive was approaching its climax.

As the Germans altered their offensive plans, the *Stavka* was encouraged by the emerging strategic situation. By the end of 9 July, the battle in the north had gone largely as the *Stavka* and Rokossovsky had anticipated. Despite many anxious moments, the Central Front had effectively contained the Ninth German Army. More important, within a matter of days, the Soviet bombardment and counteroffensive would unfold along the Western and Briansk Fronts. Ninth Army might be preparing new attacks in the north, but these would be utterly futile unless von Manstein's forces succeeded in the south.

Vatutin, too, was confident that he had done all in his power to halt the German juggernaut. However, the battle-tested *front* commander knew better than to prejudge the outcome. A panoply of former military disasters and dashed expectations had bred an air of realism in Soviet command channels. As comforting as developments seemed to be, Vatutin grimly awaited the verdict of the fickle gods of war. He well understood that his forces still faced four superbly equipped elite divisions (the SS and *Grossdeutschland*), and that, despite the five days of heavy fighting, these forces were still a potent combat force. By its grinding defense, Katukov's 1st Tank Army had cheated the Fourth Panzer Army of its original objective, Kursk, and limited its advance to less than twenty-five kilometers. Despite reinforcement, the gallant 1st Tank Army was now a shell of its former self. Along with many other divisions of the 6th and 7th Guards Armies, it had completed its sacrificial role in the Kursk defense. Now the focus would turn to a new battlefield, and new forces would play key roles in the unfolding combat drama. The cream of von Manstein's panzer force was moving in a new direction, toward a head-to-head collision with the 5th Guards Tank Army at Prokhorovka.

PART III
STOPPING THE BLITZKRIEG

CHAPTER 5

Prokhorovka,
10–15 July

As Field Marshal von Manstein had predicted, the Kursk offensive had been delayed so long that it was now jeopardized by Allied action in the West. Half a continent away, on 10 July 1943, American and British forces landed on the southern coast of Sicily. Hitler had always been sensitive about the defense of the Mediterranean, and this new threat immediately forced him to consider redistributing his strategic reserves, in particular his vital II SS Panzer Corps. At first, Army Group South's progress on 10 July prompted Hitler to order, "Operation Citadel will be continued." Still, given Model's failure to penetrate the northern flank of the Kursk Bulge, the Sicilian invasion ultimately helped doom Operation Citadel.[1] Indeed, the battles of Kursk and Sicily posed a severe dilemma because Germany's strategic reserves were sufficient to meet only one of the two challenges.[2] While Hitler decided how to deal with the new threat in the West, however, the Battle of Kursk reached a crescendo. The struggle was most conspicuous in the vicinity of Prokhorovka.

The armored clashes around Prokhorovka have attained almost legendary status as the greatest armored combat of World War II, and perhaps the greatest of all time. While the nature and consequences of the Prokhorovka tank battles were no doubt momentous, hindsight has permitted myth to inform legend. After the titanic battle ended, the Soviet victors had every reason to inflate and elevate the grandeur of their feat, and they did so with abandon. On the other hand, shock and embarrassment conditioned the Germans, in particular, and historians, in general, to accept the inflated scope and consequences of the Prokhorovka battles. Hence, history has recorded that between 1,200 and 1,500 tanks clashed on the fields of Prokhorovka.[3]

The true number, however, while still impressive, was considerably lower. Given the attrition of the penetration battle, by 10 July the II SS Panzer Corps' strength had fallen to fewer than 300 tanks and assault guns, and Army Detachment Kempf's III Panzer Corps numbered fewer than 200.[4] On the Soviet side, General P. A. Rotmistrov's 5th Guards Tank Army eventually controlled five corps totaling 830 tanks and self-propelled guns. If the definition of this battle is broadened to include the nearby XXXXVIII Panzer Corps and 1st Tank Army, the total concentration of armor along the southern flank of the Kursk Bulge was probably fewer than 2,000 combat vehicles. Of these, around

1,250 (830 Soviet and 420 German) fought along the long eastern flank of the Kursk Bulge and about 572 met on the field of Prokhorovka itself.[5]

Moreover, Prokhorovka was not the single titanic struggle of legend. In reality, it was a confused and confusing series of meeting engagements and hasty attacks, with each side committing its forces piecemeal. The terrain around Prokhorovka, while relatively open to mechanized operations, was divided into compartments by the Psel and Lipovyi Donets Rivers and adjacent ridge lines. The II SS Panzer Corps' axis of advance led northeastward along both banks of the Psel River, with one division (*Totenkopf*, with 103 tanks and assault guns) advancing north of the river and two divisions (*Leibstandarte* and *Das Reich*, with 77 and 95 tanks and assault guns, respectively) advancing south of the river directly against Prokhorovka. Rotmistrov's tank army defended both approaches, and his corps also stretched far to the south to cover the advance of the III Panzer Corps from the Belgorod region. As a result, the fighting in the narrow plain adjacent to the rail line and main road immediately west and southwest of Prokhorovka involved elements of two German panzer grenadier divisions and three equivalent Soviet tank and mechanized corps.[6]

Even more important to the overall outcome of the Battle of Kursk was the vicious struggle that took place between 10 and 14 July along the XXXXVIII Panzer Corps' left flank. Overshadowed by the momentous events along the Prokhorovka axis and now almost wholly forgotten, the battle conducted along the flanks by Katukov's reinforced 1st Tank Army distracted the XXXXVIII Panzer Corps and prevented it from supporting the northeastward lunge of the II SS Panzer Corps, with fatal consequences for the Germans.

1ST TANK ARMY VERSUS XXXXVIII PANZER CORPS (10–11 JULY)

On the night of 9–10 July, General Katukov's hard-pressed 1st Tank Army tried to reorganize its defenses from the Psel River to the Oboian' road and southward along the Pena River in accordance with Vatutin's instructions. General Getman's 6th Tank Corps, with Colonel Chernov's weakened 90th Guards Rifle Division and the remnants of the 3d Mechanized Corps' 1st and 10th Mechanized Brigades, defended along the Pena River on the 1st Tank Army's right flank, with Getman's forces facing east and south. Although German forces had already penetrated menacingly westward into Katukov's defensive front just north of Verkhopen'e, Katukov took comfort from the fact that his defenses were now backed up by the fresh 184th and 204th Rifle Divisions, which were dug in to his rear. In addition, his corps, which had been reduced to a combined strength of roughly 100 tanks, was now backed up by the reinforcing armor of the 10th Tank Corps, also positioned to his rear (with about 120 tanks and self-propelled guns).[7]

In Katukov's center, General Krivoshein's shattered 3d Mechanized Corps now defended along the Oboian' road, backed up by elements of Colonel D. F. Dremin's fresh 309th Rifle Division, the newly redeployed armor of General Kravchenko's 5th Guards Tank Corps, survivors of the 67th Guards Rifle Division, and heavy antitank support provided by Vatutin. On the 1st Tank Army's left flank, General Chernienko's 31st Tank Corps clung grimly to defenses eastward to the banks of the Psel River, also backed up by riflemen of the 309th Division and remnants of the 51st Guards Rifle Division. Soviet armor in the sector from the Oboian' road to the banks of the Psel River numbered no more than 300 tanks and self-propelled guns.[8] By the evening of 9 July, Vatutin transferred control of the 5th Guards Tank Corps, 10th Tank Corps, and 204th Rifle Division from the Voronezh Front reserve to the 1st Tank Army. The stage was set for the bitter fighting that would follow.

General von Knobelsdorff of the XXXXVIII Panzer Corps had detected the weak junction between the Soviet 6th Tank and 3d Mechanized Corps, and during the night he concentrated his forces to exploit this weakness. His aim was to destroy the menacing Soviet force along his flank while continuing his northward drive along the Oboian' road. He assigned the flank task to the *Grossdeutschland* and 3d Panzer Divisions and the Oboian' thrust to the 11th Panzer. What von Knobelsdorff did not know, however, was that his forces could not do both. The combined armor strength of his corps had eroded to 173 tanks and assault guns (including 30 Panthers) and the *Grossdeutschland* Division and its attached 10th Panzer Brigade had fallen to 87 "runners."[9]

Beginning at 0330 hours on 10 July, *Grossdeutschland* Division fought a bitter battle through the groves and ravines northwest of Verkhopen'e (see Map 17). The attack smashed the defenses of the Soviet 200th Tank Brigade and forced General Getman frantically to shift his forces to his threatened left flank. In rapid succession he moved elements of his 112th Tank and 6th Motorized Rifle Brigades and 60th Heavy Tank Regiment into the threatened sector, and they were immediately sucked into the vortex of a confused meeting engagement with *Grossdeutschland's* advancing armor. Every advantage accrued to the Germans for, unlike their foes, they knew where they were going.

Grossdeutschland's reconnaissance battalion, with supporting assault gun and half-track battalions, lunged on through the gloom of dawn and seized Hill 247 along the Kruglik-Berezovka road. This severed Getman's communications with the rear and the supporting 10th Tank Corps and threatened the viability of his entire force. Simultaneously, the armor spearhead of

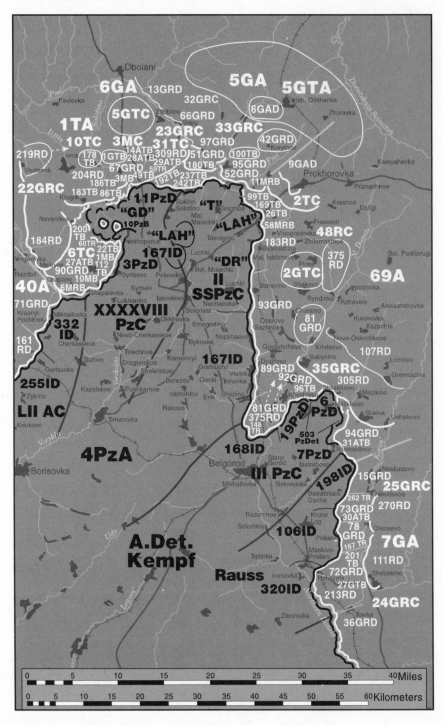

Map 17. Voronezh Front, 10 July 1943

Grossdeutschland, Panzer Group Strachwitz, supported by the division's Fusilier Regiment, captured Hill 243 after a vicious three-hour battle during which the Germans took heavy losses, including Colonel Graf von Strachwitz, who was wounded, from intense Soviet flanking fire.

Despite his frantic efforts to halt the German flank attack, Getman's tank corps was decimated in the heavy and confused fighting. When they went into combat along the corps' flank, the 200th Tank Brigade and the 6th Motorized and 112th Tank Brigades went into battle in piecemeal fashion and were cut into even smaller units and almost destroyed before darkness permitted their remnants to withdraw. By the evening of 10 July, the 3d Panzer Division joined the fray, sending its seventy-tank armored nucleus through Verkhopen'e and southward toward Berezovka into the midst of the 6th Tank Corps' defenses. As a result, the 6th Tank Corps had become virtually combat ineffective, with no more than thirty-five tanks and ten antitank guns surviving.[10]

A Soviet classified account graphically portrayed the 6th Tank Corps' fate on 10 July:

> Isolated and broken up tank groups of the 200th and 112th Tank Brigades were encircled in the region north of Berezovka, where, during the course of the day, they fought with enemy tanks and infantry. Only at night were they able to link up with the main force of the 6th Tank Corps. As a result of the combat on 10 July, the 6th Tank Corps suffered heavy losses and counted in its ranks only thirty-five tanks and ten antitank guns. Having withdrawn to the line Novoselovka 2-Noven'koe, the corps halved its defensive front (from twenty to ten kilometers) and again restored its smashed defenses.[11]

General Getman recounted in detail the heroic deeds of his defeated corps and summed up the action as follows:

> Many of our soldiers and commanders fell heroically in the five days of ferocious battle. Hundreds of corps' soldiers were wounded and evacuated to the rear. We suffered especially heavy losses in equipment. By the end of 10 July, not more than fifty tanks, more than one half light, remained operational and three batteries of antitank guns, two in the 6th Motorized Rifle Brigade and one in the 22d Tank Brigade. Reinforcing units—the 60th Tank, and the 270th and 79th Guards Mortar Regiments, and two batteries of self-propelled guns, as well as the subunits of the 1st and 10th Mechanized Brigades, which were operating with us, were also considerably weakened.
>
> Nevertheless, the corps continued to resist the enemy. Having littered the field of battle with hundreds of his burned and destroyed tanks and

guns and thousands of bodies, the enemy succeeded in pushing our lines
back several kilometers. His attempt to seize fully the village of Noven'koe
and advance further in a northern and western direction failed. Meeting
organized fire resistance, he ceased his attacks at nightfall. But, certainly,
only so that he could renew the attacks in the morning with new force.
Understanding this, we prepared for the new battle.[12]

General Katukov was more laconic about the day's events, writing in his
memoirs:

Finally, the Hitlerites succeeded in penetrating to the northwest and
reaching the population points of Noven'koe and Novoselovka 2. Clearly,
they were attempting to encircle the 6th Tank Corps and 90th Guards
Division, which were defending southwest of Verkhopen'e. On Shalin's
map [the army chief of staff] it was clear how the blue crayon line envel-
oped the positions of our forces from the northeast. I ordered the forces
to withdraw to the west and, together with the 10th Tank Corps and the
184th Rifle Division, to create a dense defense. As a result of these measures, the enemy attack misfired on the army's right flank.[13]

Unlike his corps commander, however, Katukov failed to mention his army's
grievous losses.

German accounts graphically underscore the severity of the struggle. A
history of the *Grossdeutschland* Division noted:

The dark of the night slowly passed over to the gray of the rising 10th of
July. At about 03.30, the tanks of Panzer Group Strachwitz at Point 1.8
southwest of Novoselovka spotted the enemy tanks they had heard during the night in the water-filled valley before them. Soon afterward the
first armour-piercing shells began falling: a battle between steel giants
began this day of fighting on the southern front of the Kursk bulge. By
04.00 the first enemy tanks could be seen burning on the battlefield; but
painful gaps had also been smashed in our own ranks. One of II Battalion's
command tanks took a direct hit in the turret which killed Unteroffizier
Konig. The rest of the crew, some of them wounded, were able to escape
from the tank. Oberst Graf von Strachwitz was also injured, by the recoil
of the breech, while destroying an enemy tank and had to hand command
of the Panzer Regiment GD to Hauptmann von Wietersheim.[14]

Major Franz, the commander of *Grossdeutschland's* assault gun battalion, related how, during the ferocious combat, in desperation the Soviets again
employed their Katiusha multiple rocket launchers in direct fire:

Widely separated, the assault guns of the two batteries drove at full speed toward the village [Kruglik]. At first there was no defense at all. At 300 meters from the village—I already had the impression that the enemy had left the field—I suddenly saw fiery arrows coming toward us from the outskirts of Kruglik. Before I could figure out what they were there were explosions directly in front of the mass of advancing assault guns. The vehicle next to me, I believe it was Wachtmeister Brauner of 1st Battery, began to stream smoke. Thank God it turned out to be one of the smoke candles that every assault gun carried. The vehicle had taken a direct hit in the bow plates but suffered no damage. The explosion and the effect of the projectile revealed that we were under direct fire from a Stalin Organ, the first time we experienced something like this in the campaign. Darkness slowly settled over the battlefield while the assault guns destroyed the Stalin Organ and the nests of resistance which repeatedly flared up at the outskirts of the village. The planned surprise attack misfired, nevertheless we—the armoured reconnaissance battalion and the assault gun battalion together—had once again achieved more than was expected of us.[15]

The XXXXVIII Panzer Corps Chief of Staff von Mellenthin cryptically summarized the action, later writing:

After a week of hard and almost uninterrupted fighting *Grossdeutschland* was showing signs of exhaustion and its ranks had been thinned out considerably. On 10 July this division was ordered to wheel to the southwest and clean up the enemy on the left flank. The panzer regiment, the reconnaissance detachment and the grenadier regiment were to advance towards Height 243.0 and to the north thereof; they were then to seize 247.0 to the south of Kruglik and move southward from there to the small forest north of Beresowka [Berezovka] where the Russians were holding up the 3d Panzer Division; strong formations of the Luftwaffe were to support this attack. . . .

Supported by the splendid efforts of the Luftwaffe, *Grossdeutschland* made a highly successful advance; heights 243.0 and 247.0 were taken, and Russian infantry and armor fled before the panzers and sought refuge in the wood north of Beresowka. Trapped between *Grossdeutschland* and the 3d Panzer, it seemed as if the enemy on the left flank had at last been liquidated, and the advance to the north could now be resumed. On 11 July the 48th Panzer Corps issued orders for the units of *Grossdeutschland* to be relieved by the 3d Panzer Division during the night; *Grossdeutschland* was to assemble astride the road south of Height 260.8 [along the Oboian' road], and to stand by for an advance to the north.[16]

Significantly, Mellenthin added, "In view of the breakdown of Model's attack, a successful advance in this quarter offered the only hope of victory."[17] Within twenty-four hours, von Mellenthin's hopes would be dashed, for, as Katukov had predicted, the battle on the flanks had not yet ended.

On 11 July the 3d Panzer Division and arriving infantry from the 332d Infantry Division cleared Soviet forces from the Berezovka region, forced the 71st Guards Rifle Division westward from Rakovo and Chapaev along the Pena River, and closed up to the Soviet 184th Rifle Division's defenses extending southward from Noven'koe to Melovoe on the Pena. The tattered remnants of the 6th Tank Corps filtered through the 184th's lines. Meanwhile Katukov, with Vatutin's approval, shifted his 10th Tank Corps into new assembly areas around Noven'koe to bolster the sagging defenses on the 1st Tank Army's right flank and to prepare for new counterattacks against the XXXXVIII Panzer Corps. The 219th Rifle Division, newly arrived from the *front* reserve, joined the 10th Tank Corps to round out Katukov's new shock force. To facilitate command and control, Vatutin subordinated all rifle forces from the Psel River to the Pena River (the 184th, 219th, 204th, and 309th Rifle Divisions) to General Chistiakov's 6th Guards Army and placed many of these forces under the operational control of Katukov's 1st Tank Army.

Meanwhile, *Grossdeutschland* tested Soviet defense lines around Kalinovka and regrouped its armor in preparation for the renewed northern thrust. The remnants of the 6th Tank Corps and the 90th Guards Rifle Division, the latter now down to less than 40 percent of its original strength, withdrew westward through defense lines manned by the 184th Rifle Division, while the Soviet 204th Rifle Division and supporting armor fended off German probes toward Kalinovka and Kruglik.

Late on 11 July, von Knobelsdorff began implementing his plan for a northern thrust in conjunction with the II SS Panzer Corps' drive on Prokhorovka. *Grossdeutschland's* history outlined von Knobelsdorff's intent:

The divisional orders issued during the night of 11/12 July 1943 were in keeping with this notion. Elements of the Panzer-Grenadier Division GD were relieved by units of 3d Panzer Division in their former positions and were transferred to the front of the attack lane in the area of Point 260.8 [along the Oboian' road] and to the north. The plan was for a continuation of the attack, primarily by the tanks and panzer-fusiliers, on 12 July in the direction of the Psel River, the last obstacle in front of Oboyan. It was learned from the division's neighbor on the right, II SS Panzer Corps, that its spearheads had already crossed the river.[18]

Thus, von Mellenthin's last hope was about to materialize.

Along the Oboian' road, on 10 and 11 July, the 11th Panzer Division, supported on its left by the *Grossdeutschland* Division's Fusilier Regiment, had inched forward against stiffened Soviet resistance. Count Schimmelmann's panzer group of the 11th Panzer Division seized Hill 260.8, and the Fusiliers took Hill 244.8 on the road itself. While bending, however, Soviet defenses failed to break, and by the end on 11 July, the 11th Panzer Division concentrated its efforts on consolidating its positions from the Oboian' road to Kochetovka and conducted reconnaissance forays forward to test Soviet defenses. All the while, the division extended its right flank and relieved elements of the *Leibstandarte* Division, which was regrouping its forces eastward for the decisive drive on Prokhorovka. By nightfall on 11 July, the 11th Panzer waited expectantly for *Grossdeutschland's* panzer group to concentrate on its left flank along the Oboian' road and for the successful lunge at Oboian', which it believed would follow.

A German account later poignantly recorded the opportunity at hand:

The highest point on the approaches to Oboyan had thereby been reached and, at the same time, the deepest penetration made into the Russian front. From the high ground one could see far into the valley of the Psel River, the last natural barrier this side of Kursk. With field-glasses the towers of Oboyan could be made out in the fine haze. Oboyan was the objective.

It seemed within arm's reach. Barely twelve miles away. No distance at all under normal circumstances for a fast formation. Would XLVIII Panzer Corps make this last leap?

According to Hoth's carefully worked out timetable the following should now have happened: XLVIII Panzer Corps to strike towards Oboyan and seize the crossings over the Pssel. Its bulk to wheel eastward and—before thrusting on Kursk—to defeat, jointly with Hausser's SS Panzer Corps, the enemy strategic armoured forces approaching across the strip of land of Prokhorovka. That was Hoth's plan.[19]

However, General Vatutin too was actively formulating new plans to thwart Hoth's and von Knobelsdorff's designs within the context of an even greater counterstroke ultimately designed to "encircle and destroy the main German grouping penetrating to Oboian' and Prokhorovka."[20] Specifically:

The main concept of this operation consisted of delivering concentric blows against the enemy grouping with the forces of the 5th Guards and 10th Tank Corps, together with the 6th Guards Army's 22d Guards Rifle Corps, in the general direction of Iakovlevo and with the 5th Guards Tank Army and the 5th Guards Army's 33d Guards Rifle Corps in the general direction of Gresnoe, Iakovlevo, and Bykovka. The left flank 23d Guards Rifle Corps of 6th Guards Army and the right flank 32d Guards Rifle Corps of 5th Guards Army were to deliver a secondary strike in the general direction of Pokrovka. With part of its forces, 7th Guards Army was to deliver a secondary blow on Razumnoe.[21]

Characteristically, these offensive plans, scheduled to be implemented on the morning of 12 July, reflected Vatutin's unremittingly offensive mindset. Despite the damage done in previous days to his once-mighty 6th Tank Corps and the remainder of his tank army, on 11 July Vatutin issued new orders to Katukov that mirrored his unrequited audacity:

> Having in your composition the 6th, 10th, and 31st Tank Corps, the 3d Mechanized Corps, the 5th Guards Stalingrad Tank Corps, the 204th and 309th Rifle Divisions, and reinforcing artillery units, using part of your forces prevent the enemy from penetrating northward of the Kruglik-Ol'khovatka line, and with your main forces, attack from the line Aleksandrovka 1-Noven'koe in a general southeastern direction in cooperation with the 6th Guards Army with the mission of seizing Iakovlevo and Pokrovka and, jointly with the 6th Guards and 5th Guards Tank Armies, encircle the penetrating [enemy] mobile group and subsequently exploit success to the south and southwest.[22]

This order prompted a massive regrouping of Voronezh Front forces to contain the German advance and to create the shock groups designated to launch Vatutin's two major counterstrokes. In the 1st Tank and 6th Guards Armies' sector, Kravchenko's 5th Guards Tank Corps relocated to assembly areas forward of Aleksandrovka 1 in the rear of the 184th Rifle Division. General Burkov's 10th Tank Corps shifted to its right into assembly areas near Noven'koe, where it formed up to attack with the 219th Rifle Division's infantry. The remnants of Getman's 6th Tank Corps remained in combat in support of the 184th Rifle Division and then reformed to the rear to support the 5th Guards' and 10th Tank Corps' attack. The shock group mustered just over 200 tanks. Vatutin's remaining forces, including about 150 tanks, were defending from the Psel River to west of the Oboian' road. These elements of the 204th and 309th Rifle Divisions and the 3d Mechanized and 31st Tank Corps) were to defend in place and then join the counterstroke when and if German forces attempted to withdraw southward. At the same time, the two corps of General Zhadov's 5th Guards Army moved forward from positions along the Psel River, which they had occupied the day before, and prepared to support Vatutin's counterstrokes.[23]

Thus, the most important and, subsequently, most apparent aim of Vatutin's counteroffensive was to halt the German advance on Prokhorovka and, hence,

German seizure of Oboian' and Kursk. However, the counterstroke Vatutin planned and carried out against the XXXXVIII Panzer Corps' left flank, although subsequently masked by the "noise" and furor of the Prokhorovka battle, was equally important, for it denied the Germans the opportunity of adding *Grossdeutschland* Division to their main attack on Oboian' and Kursk. This, in no small measure, conditioned the German setback at Prokhorovka and the overall failure of Operation Citadel.

No less critical to the success of the German offensive and the fate of Vatutin's counterattack plans was the situation east of the Northern Donets River, where General Breith's III Panzer Corps struggled to fulfill its offensive promise.

III PANZER CORPS VERSUS 7TH GUARDS ARMY (10–11 JULY)

The first six days of the German offensive had been expensive and frustrating for General Werner Kempf and his Army Detachment. Try as it might, Kempf's force seemed unable to penetrate deeply and rapidly through the dense fortifications of the Soviet 7th Guards Army. Its failure to do so deprived the II SS Panzer Corps of its flank support, disrupted its full concentration along the Prokhorovka axis, and threatened the viability of Hoth's offensive plans.

Kempf's problem was similar to, but more severe than, von Knobelsdorff's. While the XXXXVIII Panzer Corps' attention was constantly distracted by the endless battles along its left flank, Kempf's force had to contend with near-constant threats to both its flanks. On its left flank, Soviet forces held the salient anchored on the Northern Donets and Lipovyi Donets Rivers north and east of Belgorod, and the 19th Panzer Division had to divert significant forces to support the 168th Infantry Division, which was inching its way northward from the city along the banks of both rivers. Simultaneously, Kempf had to defend his increasingly long right flank southward to Maslovo Pristan' against ever more active Soviet forces. These twin flank threats denied Kempf the opportunity to concentrate Breith's critical armor for a decisive thrust to the north and Prokhorovka. Moreover, Kempf's slow northward progress required the II SS Panzer Corps to use its 167th Infantry and *Das Reich* SS Panzer Grenadier Divisions to protect its long and unprotected right flank along the Lipovyi Donets River, where Soviet armored forces were still most active.

Vatutin capitalized on this situation. He ordered Shumilov's 7th Guards Army to maintain pressure against Kempf's flank east of the Northern Donets and to prepare even stronger counterattacks for 12 July. General Kriuchenkin's 69th Army, now reinforced with the entire 35th Guards Rifle Corps, took over responsibility for defense between Prokhorovka and Miasoedovo, east of Belgorod. Kriuchenkin employed successive defense lines to block the III Panzer Corps' forward progress, while he orchestrated the tricky staged withdrawal of his forces from the Northern Donets salient north of Belgorod.

Accordingly, the 69th Army's 92d Guards, 94th Guards, and 305th Rifle Divisions, with modest armor and antitank support, contained the III Panzer Corps' spearhead 6th Panzer Division around Melikhovo. By the end of 10 July, Soviet defenders had used a mixture of antitank ditches, antitank guns, mines, and artillery to reduce the 6th Panzer's armored strength to only 47 functioning tanks, out of an original total of over 100.[24] Try as it might, the 6th Panzer could not break out northward until it received support from either the 7th or 19th Panzer Divisions or both, yet these divisions were tied down in fighting along Kempf's flanks.

To the south the 7th Panzer Division covered Kempf's long western flank to Miasoedovo and lent support to Corps Rauss's infantry divisions, which were under renewed pressure. This pressure, already heavy in the Rzhavets region, where the 72d Guards and 213th Rifle Divisions were launching nearly constant attacks, also materialized near Batratskaia Dacha, where Shumilov's 15th Guards Rifle Division went into action. Rauss's 320th and 106th Infantry Divisions had already suffered losses totaling over 40 percent of their original strength, and the newly arrived 198th Infantry had its hands full dealing with the threat posed by the Soviet 15th Guards' attacks. In combination, these actions kept the 7th Panzer tied down for days, helplessly out of supporting range of the 6th Panzer.

While the 6th and 7th Panzer Divisions were stalled at and south of Melikhovo, the 19th Panzer Division and the 168th Infantry cleared Soviet troops from the eastern bank of the Northern Donets River. They were assisted in this effort by Kriuchenkin's 10 July order to his 375th and 81st Guards Rifle Divisions. Kriuchenkin had instructed these two divisions to disengage, withdraw from the region south of the Lipovyi and Northern Donets Rivers, and turn over their defensive sector south of Gostishchevo to the 89th Guards Rifle Division. This shortening of lines permitted Kriuchenkin to create reserves to contend with a German advance northward from Melikhovo, which Kriuchenkin knew was inevitable.

Late on 10 July, at von Manstein's urging, Kempf finally orchestrated a rather desperate effort to break the stalemate east of the Northern Donets River. Slipping elements of the 7th Panzer Division northward to occupy 6th Panzer positions around Melikhovo, he concentrated the latter for a northward drive in concert with an advance along the eastern banks of the Northern Donets by 19th Panzer Division. At dawn on 11 July, the 6th Panzer struck, with the Tigers of the 503d Panzer Detachment in the vanguard. While the 19th Panzer lunged northward along the left bank of the Northern Donets through

Khokhlovo and Kiselevo to Sabynino, the 6th Panzer advanced twelve kilometers northward and seized Kazach'e. This headlong advance by massed Tiger tanks tore through the Soviet 305th Rifle Division's defenses and wedged into the prepared defense line of the 107th Rifle Division, ten kilometers to the rear.

In addition to unhinging Kriuchenkin's defenses, Kempf's audacious thrust rendered untenable the 89th Guards Rifle Division's defenses south of Gostishchevo. In desperation equal to that which propelled the Germans forward, Kriuchenkin threw his already battle-scarred 81st Guards Rifle Division into combat to block the German northward advance and ordered the 89th Guards to withdraw to new defenses just south of Gostishchevo. Kriuchenkin knew his situation was precarious. While he had held Kempf's force at bay for several days, and Kempf's armored spearheads were still twenty-five to thirty kilometers from Prokhorovka, he doubted that his remaining reserves (the threadbare 375th Rifle Division) could halt further German advances. Soviet records describe Kriuchenkin's subsequent decision:

To liquidate the existing penetration, the 69th Army commander made the decision to regroup his forces on the night of 12 July and to withdraw some formations to new defensive positions. After regrouping in accordance with this plan, by dawn on 12 July, the army formations occupied the following positions: the 93d Guards Rifle Division continued to defend its positions along the Rozhdestvenka-Druzhnyi line [southwest of Gostishchevo]; the 89th Guards Rifle Division, having left no more than two battalions with antitank guns on the front from Kalinin to Petropavlovka, occupied defenses along the front Kiselevo-Krivtsevo; the 81st Guards Rifle Division occupied defenses along the western bank of the Northern Donets from Krivtsevo to Rudinka; the 92d Guards Rifle Division with the 96th Tank Brigade occupied a prepared defense line along the front Vypolzovka-Novo-Alekseevskii Vyselok; the 107th and 305th Rifle Divisions occupied defenses along the line Razumnoe ravine-Gremiach'e; the 94th Guards Division with the 31st Antitank Brigade occupied defenses along the line Shliakhovtsevo-Mazikino-Sheina-Ushakovo, with one rifle regiment and a regiment of the 31st Antitank Brigade in second echelon along the line Ploskoe-Novoselovka, along the eastern bank of the Koren' River. To the left, 7th Guards Army's 15th Guards Rifle Division continued to defend along the line Sheina (excl.)-Solov'ev State Farm.[25]

Despite these elaborate defensive preparations, Kriuchenkin knew he could not successfully contain a renewed German assault. Therefore, late on 11 July, he appealed to Vatutin for help. The call for help came none too soon, for early on 12 July, the III Panzer Corps continued its desperate drive northward toward Prokhorovka.

PROKHOROVKA, 10–11 JULY

While the XXXXVIII Panzer Corps on Fourth Panzer Army's right flank struggled to destroy Soviet armor that thwarted its thrust on Oboian' and Kempf's III Panzer Corps finally broke out of the stifling grip of Soviet defenses east of Belgorod, Hausser's II SS Panzer Corps remained the star of von Manstein's drive. Ominously, however, Hausser too was facing increasing resistance and his forward progress was agonizingly slow.

After receiving Hausser's orders late on 9 July, II SS Panzer Corps' three divisions struggled through the humid darkness of night to fulfill their commander's wishes and reach new concentration areas from which they could launch a vigorous concerted assault on Prokhorovka. Night movement is always difficult, and this case was no exception. By dawn on the 10th, elements of *Leibstandarte* were still en route to the Teterevino region and it was clear the corps could not meet Hausser's ambitious timetable. Therefore, it launched the assault on Prokhorovka only with the forces it had at hand (Map 17, p. 154). The piecemeal attack immediately encountered difficulties and, once again, was forced off schedule. Just before dawn, *Totenkopf's* SS Panzer Grenadier Regiment *Eicke* attacked across the Psel River and attempted to seize Hill 226.6, the key high ground just east of the small fortified village of Kliuchi. However, this attack failed in the face of stout resistance by defending elements of the Soviet 52d Guards Rifle Division and 11th Motorized Rifle Brigade. Failure to capture Hill 226.6 meant that *Totenkopf* was unable to continue its critical drive northeast along the Psel and forced Hausser to delay his companion attack south of the river. Declaring, "*T* bridgehead not established, Postpone start of the attack," Hausser ordered his corps to attack at 1000 hours.[26] However, appallingly bad road conditions further complicated necessary artillery regrouping and ultimately delayed the attack another forty-five minutes.

Finally, at 1045 hours, the corps went into action. SS *Totenkopf* made up for its early morning failure when, by noon, its lead elements thrust across the Psel River and secured a foothold on the river's north bank (see Map 18). Heavy fighting raged all afternoon for possession of Hill 226.6, but when the fighting subsided at nightfall, *Totenkopf's* Regiment *Eicke* was in possession of the hill's southern slopes and a small bridgehead east of Kliuchi.

SS *Leibstandarte* made even more significant progress against equally heavy resistance. While its 1st SS Panzer Grenadier Regiment was regrouping from its previous day's action to the west near Sukho-Solotino, the 2d SS Panzer Grenadier Regiment's battalions, with supporting armor from the division's panzer regiment, advanced straight up the main road toward Prokhorovka. Repelling nearly constant Soviet tank attacks and under heavy fire from Soviet artillery north of the Psel, by 1300 hours the grenadiers had cleared Soviet forces from Komsomolets State Farm and began a bitter struggle for Hill 241.6, the

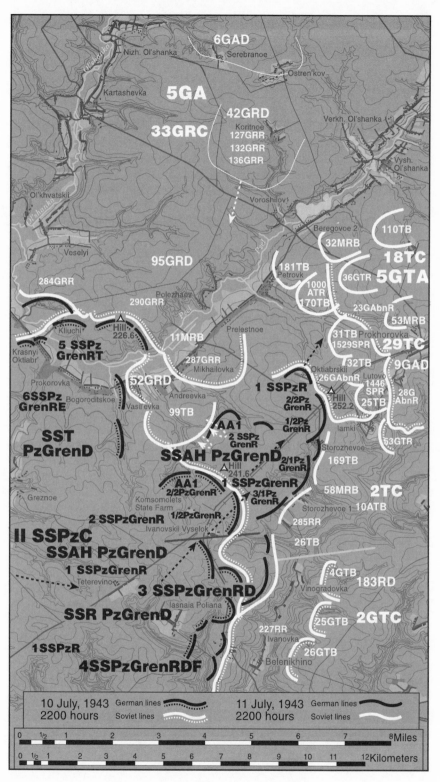

Map 18. Prokhorovka, 10–11 July

next dominant terrain feature along the road just east of the farm. Fierce Soviet resistance, in particular by dug-in Russian tanks, and scattered heavy mid-afternoon thunderstorms hindered *Leibstandarte's* advance until shortly after nightfall, when Hill 241.6 fell into German hands. The 2d SS Panzer Grenadier Regiment dug into new positions extending from the rail line to Hill 241.6, while the divisional reconnaissance battalion protected the panzer grenadiers' lengthening left flank and maintained contact with *Totenkopf* forces south of Mikhailovka. At a cost of 26 killed, 168 wounded, and 3 missing, *Leibstandarte* had taken 60 Russian prisoners and 130 deserters and had destroyed 53 Soviet tanks and 23 antitank guns.[27] Despite this impressive score, the division had failed to secure its day's objective.

SS *Das Reich* also made only limited gains on 10 July. Attacking at mid-morning with its Panzer Grenadier Regiment *Deutschland* and elements of the division's panzer regiment, *Gruppenfuehrer* Kruger's division thrust forward south of the Prokhorovka road from east of Teterevino across the rail line toward Storozhevoe 1. It too met heavy resistance, and after a grinding all-day advance, it seized a portion of Ivanovskii Vyselok, a small village lodged in a long ravine south of the Prokhorovka road and Storozhevoe 1. Deprived of support from its *Der Fuehrer* Regiment, which had to defend *Das Reich's* long right flank from Iasnaia Poliana to near Nechaevka, the best the division could do was to keep abreast of *Leibstandarte's* forward units.

Hausser was undeterred by his corps' slow progress, and late on 10 July he ordered the attack on Prokhorovka to continue the following day. He had every reason to remain optimistic, for by daybreak *Leibstandarte's* remaining regiment would be available to join the advance. Meanwhile, he urged both *Totenkopf* and *Das Reich* to shift more forces into the Prokhorovka sector. To facilitate that process, the remaining regiment of the 167th Infantry Division regrouped from the Pokrovka region to the Lipovyi Donets, where it relieved elements of *Das Reich* for use farther north.

Hausser's advance had caught Soviet defenders along the Prokhorovka axis at an awkward moment. During the hours of darkness before the German thrust began, Soviet forces frantically carried out Vatutin's regrouping orders, and their defenses suffered accordingly. On the morning of 9 July, General Burkov's 10th Tank Corps withdrew from its sector north of the Prokhorovka road and began the long march to join Katukov's 1st Tank Army defenses along the Oboian' road. It left behind its 11th Motorized Rifle Brigade, which defended along the Psel River from Krasnyi Oktiabr' to Mikhailovka, with the 52d Guards Rifle Division and its 178th Tank Brigade, which defended on the 2d Tank Corps' left flank north of the Prokhorovka road. It was the 11th Motorized that stoutly resisted *Totenkopf's* drive to gain a bridgehead over the Psel and continued to defend Hill 241.6 after the Germans finally achieved their foothold north of the river.

When the 10th Tank Corps withdrew, General Popov's 2d Tank Corps took over responsibility for defense of the Prokhorovka road. Popov deployed his brigades astride the road forward of Komsomolets State Farm and the rail line running south past Iasnaia Poliana. His 26th, 169th, and 99th Tank Brigades formed from left to right across the Prokhorovka road, and the 178th Tank Brigade concentrated along his right flank to the Psel valley. At dawn on 10 July, protected by infantry from the 183d Rifle Division, his brigades attacked down the road into the teeth of German antitank defenses and were soon enmeshed in a running battle with the two advancing regiments of *Leibstandarte* and *Das Reich*. Confused and costly fighting raged all day for possession of Komsomolets State Farm and Hill 241.6. Despite able support from the 1502d and 48th Antitank Regiments, by day's end Popov's forces had been driven from both points. Yet despite heavy losses Popov was still optimistic, for shortly after nightfall lead elements of General Zhadov's 5th Guards Army reached Prokhorovka to back up the flagging armor defense.

On Vatutin's orders, Colonel A. M. Sazonov's crack 9th Guards Airborne Division marched through the dusty streets of Prokhorovka and, by daybreak on 11 July, had dug into defensive positions anchored on the city's eastern suburbs to the rear of Popov's tired tankers. The sudden appearance of Sazonov's division marked the forward deployment of all of Zhadov's 33d Guards Rifle Corps into the II SS Panzer Corps' path. The rifle corps' 95th and 97th Guards Rifle Divisions occupied defenses along the Psel River to back up the depleted 51st and 52d Guards Rifle Divisions. All four divisions prepared to meet the II SS Panzer Corps' renewed advance north of the river. The 42d Guards Rifle Division remained in reserve, prepared to reinforce the 97th Guards or 9th Guards Airborne should the need arise. Once these forces were in place, late on 10 July, the 183d Rifle Division disengaged from combat and shifted its regiments southward by forced march to relieve 5th Guards Tank Corps forces, which, on Vatutin's orders, were also redeploying to join the 1st Tank Army.

The redeployment of the 5th Guards Tank Corps was also part of Vatutin's significant and tricky armored regroupment aimed at bolstering 1st Tank Army's defenses farther west. After days of intense combat against the II SS Panzer Corps' flank along the Lipovyi Donets south of Prokhorovka, late on 10 July, Kravchenko's corps began its long march to join the battle of Katukov's 1st Tank Army against the XXXXVIII Panzer Corps. At the same time, General Burdeiny's 2d Guards Tank Corps, which during previous days had repeatedly attacked the II SS Panzer Corps' right flank along the Lipovyi Donets south of Teterevino, itself regrouped. Replaced by the 93d Guards Rifle Division and now under 69th Army control, the corps withdrew late on 10 July into assembly areas around Maloe Iablonovo to rest and refit. Once it was rested, Vatutin planned to use the corps to support the future counterstroke of the 5th Guards Tank Army, which was then also closing into the Prokhorovka region.

The most significant aspect of Vatutin's extensive regrouping effort and his plans for a future decisive counterstroke was the movement of General P. A. Rotmistrov's powerful tank army into the Prokhorovka region. After receiving its alert order on 9 July, during the next twenty-four hours Rotmistrov's army moved by road 100 kilometers into designated assembly areas in the rear of Zhadov's 5th Guards Army.[28] Assigned to 69th Army control on 10 July, that day Rotmistrov met with Vatutin and *Stavka* representative Vasilevsky at *front* headquarters in Oboian' to review the situation. Rotmistrov recounted the conversation that ensued:

> The *front* commander invited me closer to the map and, pointing with a pencil at the Prokhorovka region, said:
>
> "Having failed to penetrate to Kursk through Oboian', clearly the Hitlerites have decided to shift the axis of their main blow farther east along the rail line to Prokhorovka. There, the forces of II SS Panzer Corps have assembled, which must attack along the Prokhorovka axis in cooperation with XXXXVIII Panzer Corps and tank formations of Group Kempf. N. F. Vatutin glanced at A. M. Vasilevsky and then, turning to me, he continued: "Thus, Pavel Alekseevich, we have decided to oppose the SS tank divisions with your tank guardsmen—to deliver a counterstroke against the enemy with 5th Guards Tank Army, reinforced by a further two tank corps."
>
> "Incidentally," said A. M. Vasilevsky, "the German tank divisions possess new heavy Tiger tanks and Ferdinand self-propelled guns. Katukov's tank army has suffered considerably from them. Do you know anything about this equipment and how do you feel about fighting with them?"
>
> "We know, Comrade Marshal. We received tactical-technical information about them from the Steppe Front staff. We have also thought about means for combating them."
>
> "Interesting!" added Vatutin, and nodding to me, said, "Continue."
>
> "The fact is that the Tigers and Ferdinands not only have strong frontal armor, but also a powerful 88mm gun with direct fire range. In that regard they are superior to our tanks, which are armed with 76mm guns. Successful struggle with them is possible only in circumstances of close-in combat, with exploitation of the T-34's greater maneuverability and by flanking fire against the side armor of the heavy German machines."
>
> "In other words, engage in hand-to-hand fight and board them," said the *front* commander, and again he turned to conversation about the forthcoming counterstroke, in which 1st Tank Army, 6th, 7th, and 5th Guards Armies were to take part.[29]

Vatutin reinforced Rotmistrov's army with the 2d Tank and 2d Guards Tank Corps, the 1529th Self-propelled, 522d and 148th Howitzer, and 148th and 93d Gun Artillery Regiments, and the 16th and 80th Guards Mortar (Katiusha) Regiments. After returning to his headquarters, later in the day Rotmistrov passed on to his forces Vatutin's order, which read, "On the morning of 12 July, together with the 1st Tank and 5th Guards Army, launch a decisive offensive to destroy the enemy southwest of Prokhorovka and, by the end of the day, reach the line Krasnaia Dubrova [northeast of Syrtsevo], Iakovlevo."[30]

With eighteen hours remaining before his attack, Rotmistrov made final adjustments in his force deployments, confident they could be completed before the appointed time. He chose for his jumping-off positions a fifteen-kilometer-wide swath through the broad rolling fields west and southwest of Prokhorovka from north of the Psel River south across the road and rail line to Storozhevoe. This offered more than ample space for deploying Major General B. S. Bakharov's 18th and Major General I. F. Kirichenko's 29th Tank Corps in first echelon, adjacent to the 2d Tank and 2d Guards Tank Corps, which were to attack abreast along his left flank in the Vinogradovka and Belenikhino sectors. Rotmistrov held Major General B. M. Skvortsov's 5th Guards Mechanized Corps in second echelon and a small task force commanded by his deputy army commander, Major General K. G. Trufanov, in army reserve.[31] During the final stages of the complex redeployment, on late 11 July, the 2d Tank Corps' 99th and 169th Tank Brigades, which were defending west of Prokhorovka along the road and rail line, were to withdraw and shift southward into their new attack sectors.

Hence, Rotmistrov planned to commit about 500 tanks and self-propelled guns in his initial assault. What he did not know was that the precipitous German advance the next day would severely disrupt his careful attack planning and the smooth regroupment of the 2d Tank Corps. His well-planned counteroffensive would quickly turn into a desperate and confused armored meeting engagement.

Early on 11 July, after the Soviets had completed their initial force regrouping but before Vatutin's counteroffensive preparations were complete, the II SS Panzer Corps resumed its headlong thrust on Prokhorovka, now supported by the bulk of Army Group South's aviation, which, as before, was able to achieve tenuous air superiority along the Prokhorovka axis, at least on 11 July (see Map 19). While *Totenkopf* struggled to expand its narrow bridgehead north of the Psel, anchored on the southern slopes of Hill 226.6, the now fully assembled *Leibstandarte* drove forward from Hill 241.6 along both sides of the road to Prokhorovka with *Das Reich's Deutschland* Regiment protecting its right flank.

At 0500 hours the 1st and 2d Battalions of *Leibstandarte's* 2d SS Panzer Grenadier Regiment advanced eastward astride the road, destroying or brush-

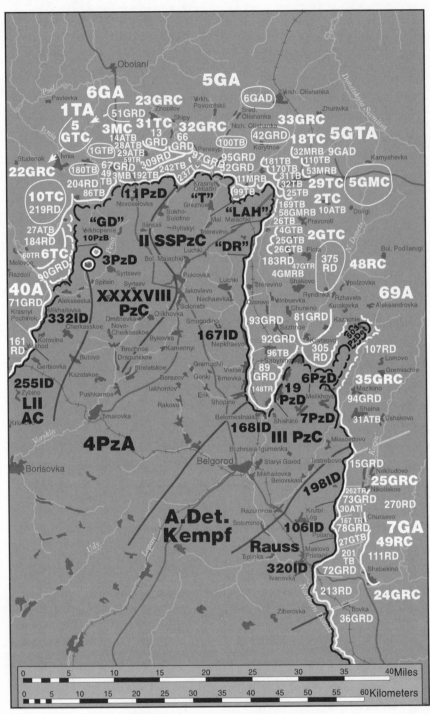

Map 19. Voronezh Front, 11 July 1943

ing by dug-in tanks and antitank guns of the Soviet 2d Tank Corps' 169th Tank Brigade. Although subjected to heavy flanking fire from Soviet forces on the northern bank of the Psel and from artillery firing from Prelestnoe and Petrovka, in less than two hours the panzer grenadier battalions traversed over two kilometers before being halted by heavy fire from Soviet troops dug in around Hill 252.4, just southeast of Oktiabr'skii State Farm. All the while, the two battalions fended off attacks by small groups of tanks against both of their flanks, launched by the Soviet 99th Tank Brigade from Andreevka in the Psel valley and the 169th Tank Brigade from Storozhevoe. These harassing attacks, the intense artillery and antitank fire, and an immense antitank ditch, which the Germans discovered covering the approaches to Oktiabr'skii State Farm, prompted the regiment to call for assistance.

Division headquarters responded promptly. At 0630 hours it ordered its 1st SS Panzer Grenadier Regiment, supported by the four Tiger tanks of its 13th Company, to join the attack and clear Soviet forces out of Storozhevoe on the 2d Regiment's right flank. Fifteen minutes later, it ordered the division's reconnaissance battalion into action to protect the division's left flank against Soviet attacks from Andreevka in the Psel valley. Meanwhile, the divisional artillery and Werfer regiments opened intense fire on Soviet artillery positions north of the Psel, and Stuka dive-bombers began hourly strikes against Soviet defenses to the front.

Up to now *Leibstandarte* had been contending only with elements of the already-depleted 2d Tank Corps and small infantry elements from the 183d Rifle Division. The initial German attack penetrated the 169th Tank Brigade's defense rather easily and forced the Soviet tankers to withdraw slowly up the Prokhorovka road and toward Storozhevoe. On the 169th's left, the 99th Tank Brigade wheeled back toward the Psel valley from which it began launching periodic forays against *Leibstandarte's* flank, supported by 52d Guards Rifle Division infantry. When the Germans resumed their assault, however, they ran straight into the dug-in troopers of the 9th Guards Airborne Division, which was now supported by the remaining tanks of the 169th Tank Brigade and the 57th Tank Regiment and 301st Antitank Artillery Regiment, provided by the 5th Guards Army. As the relative coolness of dawn gave way to the stifling heat and humidity of the full summer day, the fighting took on new ferocity.

The airborne troopers of Colonel A. M. Sazonov's division had occupied defenses forward of Prokhorovka only the night before to back up the 183d Rifle Division, which was supposed to be regrouping to the south, and to cover the forward deployment of Rotmistrov's tank army. Although they did not expect to go into combat until the next day, within hours they found themselves at the focal point of the II SS Panzer Corps' assault. Colonel Sazonov deployed his 26th and 28th Guards Airborne Regiments abreast, covering the southern approaches to Prokhorovka and Rotmistrov's projected tank assembly area. Guards Lieutenant Colonel G. M. Kashpersky's 26th Guards Airborne Regiment occupied the "place of honor" astride the Prokhorovka road. His 3d Battalion, commanded by Guards Major D. I. Boriskin, dug in around and south of Oktiabr'skii State Farm, protected, in part, by the imposing antitank ditch; his 2d Battalion defended from Hill 252.2 southward to Iamki; and his 1st Battalion was in second echelon, positioned north of Oktiabr'skii State Farm with a 76mm gun battalion of the regimental artillery regiment.

Sazonov's 28th Guards Airborne Regiment, commanded by Guards Major V. A. Ponomarov, occupied a strong defense due south of Prokhorovka, with two battalions forward and one in reserve in the city's suburbs. His third regiment, the 23d Guards, commanded by Lieutenant Colonel V. S. Savinov, together with the 10th Guards Separate Antitank Artillery Battalion, backed up the forward regiments from positions just northwest of Prokhorovka. The airborne division also had at its disposal the 57th Army Heavy Tank Regiment's twenty-one KV heavy tanks and twenty-four antitank guns of the 301st Army Antitank Artillery Regiment.

Sazonov and his expectant riflemen heard and even felt the early morning fighting to the south, which inched ever closer to their forward positions south of Oktiabr'skii and Hill 252.2. His artillery launched volley after volley in support of their Soviet comrades, but within a matter of hours the sounds of fighting had died out to be replaced only by the near-constant rumble of artillery fire. Within hours, Sazonov expected to see and hear the comforting rumbling steel monsters of Rotmistrov's tank army. Instead, the more menacing specter of massed German tanks soon emerged from the dust and the haze to the south.

At 0905 hours, after the artillery, Stukas, and Werfers had done their lethal work, *Leibstandarte* resumed its advance. Its 2d Battalion, 2d SS Panzer Grenadier Regiment, supported by Tiger tanks and assault guns, quickly pushed on toward Hill 252.2, where at 0950 hours it ran into intense fire from the 26th Guards Airborne Regiment's 2d Battalion and from Soviet positions covering Oktiabr'skii State Farm. Joined by the 1st Battalion, the two regiments fought an intense three-hour fight for the key hill but failed to dislodge the airborne defenders. At 1015 hours, the division's panzer group joined the attack, and finally, at 1310 hours, it captured the precious and now bloodsoaked crest of the hill.[32]

Leibstandarte's panzer group quickly exploited the opportunity and lunged down the hill's western slopes toward Oktiabr'skii State Farm, only to be struck by withering antitank fire and direct fire from artillery batteries. After an intense fight, the panzer group cleared Soviet defenders from the state farm. Throughout the remainder of the afternoon and into the early evening Soviet forces launched repeated counterattacks against the Panzer Regiment and its neighboring panzer grenadier regiments. At 1330 hours the 26th Guards Airborne Regiment and 169th Tank Brigade tanks struck the 1st Battalion, 2d SS Panzer Grenadier Regiment, on the southern slopes of Hill 252.4, and at 1440 hours the 99th Tank Brigade, then being forced out of the village of Vasil'evka by *Totenkopf's* troopers, again attacked the reconnaissance battalion protecting *Leibstandarte's* left flank. This threat became more serious when the Soviet 95th Guards Rifle Division, which by evening of 10 July had occupied positions along and south of the Psel on the 9th Guards Airborne's right flank, lent its weight to the 99th Tank Brigade's counterattacks.

A Soviet account captured the ferocity of the day's fighting in the 9th Guards Airborne Division's sector:

On the morning of 11 July, when the formations of 5th Guards Army had still not firmly occupied their positions, having completed their regrouping, the enemy renewed their offensive.

It was an overcast day. A fresh breeze disturbed the boundless sea of ripened grain between Prokhorovka, Prelestnoe, and Pravorot'.

Up to a battalion of infantry, supported by forty tanks and self-propelled guns, among them heavy Tigers and Panthers, and by hundreds of Ju-87 and Ju-88 aircraft, attacked the junction of the 9th Guards Airborne and 95th Guards Rifle Divisions. The main attack was against the 3d Battalion, 26th Guards Airborne Regiment, which was defending Oktiabr'skii State Farm. A short but powerful artillery preparation and strong bomber strikes preceded the enemy infantry and tank attack. Armored transporters carrying motorized infantry followed the tanks and self-propelled guns.

The commander of the 3d Battalion, Guards Major D. I. Boriskin, reported on the situation to his regimental commander, Guards Lieutenant Colonel G. M. Kashpersky, and ordered the commanders of his rifle companies and batteries to open massive fire as the tanks and infantry neared their positions.

Oktiabr'skii State Farm, Hill 252.2, and Lutovo [village] shuddered from exploding bombs, shells, and mines. The soldiers attentively observed the approaching enemy from the foxholes they had dug the night before.

When only several hundred meters remained to the edge of the state farm, infantry poured out of the armored transporters. Submachine gunners opened fire on the run, and concealing themselves behind the tanks, they began the assault. The distorted faces of the Fascists bore witness to the fact that their warlike ardor was roused by a fairly large dose of schnapps.

"Fire!" ordered the battery commander. A squall of 3d Battalion fire met the Fascists. The long bursts of I. V. Khoroshikh's and P. N. Lyznikov's heavy machine guns struck the infantry in the flanks and were echoed by the guardsmen's light machine guns and submachine guns. Divisional artillery and supporting artillery battalions of the *RGK* [Reserve of the High Command] 3d Artillery Penetration Division laid down an immovable defensive fire in front of Oktiabr'skii State Farm. The battalion and regimental artillery of Guards Lieutenants I. G. Samykin and A. F. Shestakov delivered fire over open sights.

The infantry were separated from the tanks, and facing a hurricane of fire from the state farm, they withdrew to the reverse slopes of Hill 215.4. The Fascists attacked the 3d Battalion two more times before 1400 hours. However, these were only reconnaissances in force.[33]

This account also captured the turn in fortunes in mid-afternoon:

At 1400 hours up to 100 enemy tanks and up to a regiment of infantry riding in armored transporters attacked Oktiabr'skii State Farm and Hill 252.2. Around forty tanks and up to a regiment of motorized infantry attacked the neighboring 287th Guards Rifle Regiment of 95th Guards Rifle Division. Discovering the junction between the 95th Guards and 9th Airborne Divisions, the Fascists tried to drive a wedge between them. One hundred and forty tanks were attacking along a front of three kilometers in the sector from Iamki Farm to Andreevka. A powerful fire raid and bombing strikes by fifty dive-bombers preceded the assault. Once again fierce battle raged, but the effort was unequal. The enemy possessed absolute numerical superiority and displayed special obstinacy at the junction of the 26th and 287th regiments. . . .

Having pressed back the 26th and 287th Regiments, up to forty enemy tanks concentrated against Prelestnoe and the southern edge of Petrovka and up to sixty tanks—across Hill 252.2 and along the rail line— toward Prokhorovka. The 26th Regiment withdrew to the positions of the 23d Guards Airborne Regiment, on the southwestern slopes of Hill 252.4 [one kilometer west of Prokhorovka].[34]

The day's bitter fighting ended in early evening. Although *Leibstandarte* had made considerable progress and taken Oktiabr'skii State Farm and Hill 252.2, its panzer group was unable to advance beyond the state farm and found itself in a precarious position with both of its flanks exposed and subject to heavy fire. The 2d SS Panzer Grenadier Regiment's 1st Battalion was able to secure the rail embankment southeast of Hill 252.2, and, jointly with the division's 1st Regiment's 2d Battalion, it cleared the small forest adjacent to the embankment. The remainder of the 1st Panzer Grenadier Regiment penetrated into the village of Storozhevoe, where by nightfall it was engaged in the nasty process of clearing the village house by house. However, the regiment was not able to seize Storozhevoe 1, and, since *Das Reich's* advance also lagged, this left the division's right flank still vulnerable.

Leibstandarte's day-long thrust had irreparably smashed the 2d Tank Corps' defenses, isolated the corps' 99th Tank Brigade in the Psel valley, driven a wedge between the 95th Guards and 9th Guards Airborne Divisions, and carved a deep salient in the 9th Guards Airborne Division's defenses forward of Prokhorovka. Most significantly, the German thrust had wholly preempted the 5th Guards Army's careful counterattack plans.

General Rotmistrov later provided his view of the day's surprising developments and vividly described the dilemma he faced:

At around 1900 hours on 11 July, Marshal A. M. Vasilevsky arrived at my CP [command post]. I reported to him about the army's combat formation and the missions assigned to the corps and the attached artillery. He approved my decisions and reported that he had had a conversation with I. V. Stalin, who ordered him to locate himself permanently with 5th Guards Tank and 5th Guards Armies, to coordinate their operations during the course of battle, and to render necessary assistance. I. V. Stalin ordered the *front* commander, N. F. Vatutin, to remain at his CP in Oboian'. The *front* chief of staff, Lieutenant General S. P. Ivanov, went to the Korocha axis.

Sufficient daylight still remained, and the marshal proposed an inspection of the jumping-off positions which I had selected for 29th and 18th Tank Corps. Our route passed through Prokhorovka to Belenikhino, and the quick-moving Willies, bobbing up and down over the potholes, skirted round vehicles with ammunition and fuel, which were heading to the front. Transports with wounded slowly went past us. Here and there destroyed trucks and smashed transports stood by the roadside.

The road passed through wide fields of yellowing wheat. Beyond them began a forest which adjoined the village of Storozhevoe.

"There, along the northern edge of the forest, were the jumping-off positions of the 29th Tank Corps. The 18th Tank Corps would attack to the right," I explained to A. M. Vasilevsky.

He intently peered into the distance and listened to the ever-growing rumble of battle. One could divine the front lines of our combined arms armies from the clouds of smoke and the explosions of aerial bombs and shells. The agricultural installations of Komsomolets State Farm could be seen two kilometers distant to the right.

Suddenly, Vasilevsky ordered the driver to stop. The vehicle turned off the road and abruptly halted amid the dust-covered roadside brush. We opened the doors and went several steps to the side. The rumble of tank engines could be clearly heard. Then the very same tanks came into sight.

Quickly turning to me, and with a touch of annoyance in his voice, Aleksandr Mikhailovich asked me, "General! What's going on? Were you not forewarned that the enemy must not know about the arrival of our tanks? And they stroll about in the light of day under the Germans' eyes. . . ."

Instantly, I raised my binoculars. Indeed, tens of tanks in combat formation, firing from the march from their short-barreled guns, were crossing the field and stirring up the ripened grain.

"However, Comrade General, they are not our tanks. They are German. . . ."

"So, the enemy has penetrated somewhere. He wants to preempt us and seize Prokhorovka."

"We cannot permit that," I said to A. M. Vasilevsky, and by radio I gave the command to General Kirichenko to move without delay two tank brigades to meet the German tanks and halt their advance.

Returning to my CP, we knew that the Germans had launched active operations against almost all of our armies.

Thus the situation suddenly became complicated. The jumping-off positions that we had earlier selected for the counterstroke were in the hands of the Hitlerites.[35]

What Rotmistrov did not know was that the advancing German tanks were from *Leibstandarte's* 1st SS Panzer Grenadier Regiment. He did, however, understand the grim and harrowing consequences: "In this regard, we had to prepare for the offensive anew, in particular, select artillery firing positions and deployment and attack lines. In the compressed time, we had to refine missions, organize cooperation between corps and units, revise the schedule for artillery support, and do all to facilitate the precise command and control of forces in combat."[36]

In short, within a matter of hours, the violent German assault had turned Rotmistrov's well-planned offensive into a hasty meeting engagement.

The day's developments along the flanks of *Leibstandarte's* drive on Prokhorovka did not help matters for Rotmistrov and Vasilevsky. SS Division *Totenkopf's* regiments fought to expand their bridgehead north of the Psel River, seize all of Hill 226.6, and clear Soviet forces from the southern bank of the Psel along *Leibstandarte's* left flank. Panzer Grenadier Regiment *Thule* managed to seize the village of Kliuchi but was halted by fresh troops from the 95th Guards Rifle Division's 284th Guards Rifle Regiment, backed up by 100th Tank Brigade tanks. The Soviet 290th Guards Rifle Regiment thwarted all German attempts to capture all of Hill 226.6. Meanwhile, Regiment *Eicke* drove into Vasil'evka on the south bank of the Psel, and although it forced the Soviet 99th Tank Brigade back through the village, it too was stopped by intervening 95th Guards Rifle Division troopers. Try as it might, it could not remove the threat to *Leibstandarte's* left flank.

On *Leibstandarte's* right flank, *Das Reich's Deutschland* Panzer Grenadier Regiment cleared Ivanovskii Vyselok of Soviet defenders but could not penetrate to Vinogradovka in the valley beyond. This failure, caused by stiff resistance of the 2d Tank Corps' 26th Tank Brigade and 183d Division riflemen, left a major portion of *Leibstandarte's* right flank uncovered and forced the latter to tie down the bulk of its 1st Panzer Grenadier Regiment in the role of flank security. The history of *Leibstandarte* captured the resulting difficult situation:

The line captured by this point [1700 11 July] ran Storozhevoe—western and eastern edges of the forest north of there (held by the 1st Regiment)—along the road as far as a point 500 meters northwest of Hill 252.2 (held by the 2d Regiment)—the hill just west of Swch. Oktjabrskij (held by the Panzergruppe)—eastern edge of Hill 252.2 (held by the reconnaissance battalion). That line's position was reported to the Korps, and it was not crossed again that day. The reason for stopping was the positions of the adjacent units on both sides. They were so far behind the Division's advance that we were outflanked on two sides. A frontal attack on Prochorowka would have resulted in heavy losses because of the strong enemy anti-tank and defensive artillery on the southeastern edge of Prochorowka and at the commanding position on Hill 252.4 northwest of the Pssel [should read: Prochorowka]. This situation was reported to the commanding general at about 17.00 hours at the Divisional headquarters in North Lutschki. A suggestion was made to him to concentrate all the Artillerie available to Korps and to focus on the *T*-Division's attack on Hill 226.2 on 12.7.1943. Only after the capture of this hill should the attack by Panzergrenadierdivision *DR* and Panzergrenadierdivision *LAH* on Prochorowka be continued. After conferring on the telephone with the Chief of the Generalstab, Standartenfuehrer Ostendorf, Obergruppen-fuehrer Hausser declared himself in agreement with that plan.[37]

Although Rotmistrov lost his army's jumping-off positions to the Germans, he did not have to commit any of his army to combat prematurely, thanks to *Leibstandarte's* decision to halt its attack.

Despite the problems the Germans faced, they had inflicted severe damage on Soviet forces on 11 July. Particularly vexing to Rotmistrov were the losses in the 2d Tank Corps, which was to have played a major role in the forthcoming Soviet counteroffensive, whose 99th Tank Brigade was now virtually isolated in the Psel valley and whose 169th and 26th Brigades had been mauled and numbered considerably fewer than 100 tanks. On 11 July the II SS Panzer Corps recorded 99 Soviet tanks and 26 assault guns destroyed (most by *Das Reich*), 245 POWs, and 114 deserters.[38] In a separate report, *Leibstandarte* claimed 21 enemy tanks, 36 antitank guns, and 9 artillery pieces destroyed, and 320 enemy prisoners and deserters, at a cost to themselves of 21 dead and 203 wounded.[39] More tellingly, *Leibstandarte's* panzer strength fell to 60 tanks, 10 assault guns, and 20 self-propelled tank destroyers.[40]

That evening Hausser issued orders for the next day's advance. *Totenkopf* was to complete the seizure of Hill 226.6 and then push northward along the ridge line north of the Psel to sever the Prokhorovka-Oboian' road and to protect *Leibstandarte's* left flank. *Leibstandarte* received the most critical mission. Its orders read:

> The reinforced 1. *Panzergrenadier-Regiment* with the Panzerabteilung subordinated to it is to set out at 04.50 hours and capture Swch. Stalinsk [Storozhevoe] and Jamki. It is to establish a position adjacent to the I./2. [1st Battalion, 2d SS Panzer Grenadier Regiment] at the road beside Hill 252.2.
>
> The reinforced 2. *Panzergrenadier-Regiment*, the *Panzergruppe*, and the reinforced *Aufklarungsabteilung* [reconnaissance battalion] are to stand ready to move in conjunction with elements of the *T*-Division as soon as that Division has neutralized the enemy attacks on our flank along the Pssel and to capture Prochorowka and Hill 252.4.
>
> The *Artillerie-Regiment LAH* is to send an Artillerie liaison Kommando [command] to the *T*-Division in order to support the attack by that Division on Hill 226.6.[41]

On *Leibstandarte's* right flank, Division *Das Reich* was to advance eastward with its Panzer Grenadier Regiment *Deutschland*, seize Storozhevoe 1 and Vinogradovka, clear Soviet forces from the southern approaches to Prokhorovka, and protect *Leibstandarte's* right flank. Its *Der Fuehrer* Regiment and elements of its Panzer Regiment were to support *Deutschland's* thrust (as they became available) and drive Soviet forces from Belenikhino.

Kempf's III Panzer Corps was to provide whatever support it could as the II SS Panzer advanced the final few kilometers to Prokhorovka. Ideally, von Manstein and Hoth wanted Kempf to link up quickly with Hausser's corps, but clearly, given the distances involved and previously demonstrated Soviet resistance, this would be a daunting task. At the least, von Manstein urged Kempf and his panzer corps commander, Breith, to drive northward, do as much damage as possible to the Soviets, and divert as many Soviet forces as possible from the decisive clash around Prokhorovka. The seizure of Prokhorovka by Hausser's armored armada was also timed to coincide with the XXXXVIII Panzer Corps' capture of the key Psel River crossings south of Oboian'. Once these critical river crossings and Prokhorovka were in German hands, the two panzer corps, with the III Panzer Corps not far behind, would complete their victorious drive on Oboian' and Kursk.

On the evening of 11–12 July, under the watchful eye of Vasilevsky, Vatutin and Rotmistrov did all in their power to deny the Germans their prize. Vatutin ordered Rotmistrov: "On 1000 hours 12 July, deliver a counterstroke in the direction of Komsomolets State Farm and Pokrovka and, in cooperation with 5th Guards Army and 1st Tank Army, destroy the enemy in the Kochetovka, Pokrovka, and Gresnoe regions and do not permit him to withdraw in a southern direction."[42] Colonel Sazonov's 9th Guards Airborne Division, which was to provide Rotmistrov with most of his infantry support, received an analogous order: "In cooperation with the 42d Guards Rifle Division on the right, which is being committed at the junction of 9th and 95th Divisions, and also with 5th Guards Tank Army's 29th Tank Corps, which is attacking in the division sector, destroy the opposing enemy and secure the line Komsomolets State Farm-Ivanovskii Vyselok. 2d Guards Tank Corps must attack on the division left."[43]

Although Vatutin dispatched orders to all of his attacking forces, the most critical seemed to be those that governed the operations and fate of Rotmistrov's five mobile corps and the two rifle corps of Zhadov's 5th Guards Army. Less apparent, but no less significant, were the orders that launched his counterstroke against the XXXXVIII Panzer Corps far to the west, for the seizure of Prokhorovka would mean little without near simultaneous seizure of the Psel River crossings on the road to Oboian'.

Later on the evening of 11 July, Rotmistrov finalized his attack planning and issued new orders to his corps. By this time the German advance on the previous day and the increased likelihood that the Germans would attack even earlier than predicted on the morning of the 12th prompted Rotmistrov to advance his H-hour to 0830 hours.

Rotmistrov also adjusted his plan to Vatutin's new order and to accommodate harsh and unpleasant combat realities. It was now clear that General Popov's 2d Tank Corps was in no condition to participate in the counterstroke. In fact, his few remaining tanks were still locked in desperate combat for Storozhevoe and Storozhevoe 1 or in the Psel valley, out of contact with their parent headquarters. In addition Rotmistrov had to designate new jumping-off positions, which, because of the German advance, were now in the very suburbs of Prokhorovka. His decision was as follows:

To strike a blow with the forces of 18th, 29th, and 2d Guards Tatsinskaia Tank Corps in the sector: to the right—Beregovoe, Andreevka, and Iasnaia

Poliana; to the left—Pravorot', Belenikhino, Marker 232.0 and, by the end of the day, reach the line Krasnaia Dubrova-Iakovlevo. The 5th Guards Zimovnikovskii Mechanized Corps, located in army second echelon, received the mission of being prepared to exploit the success of 29th Tank Corps and 2d Guards Tatsinskaia Tank Corps in the general direction of Luchki and Pogorelovka. The tank corps had to occupy jumping-off positions from Prelestnoe through Storozhevoe to Mal. Iablonovo by 2400 hours on 11 July and be ready to attack by 0300 on 12 July.[44]

To accomplish this daunting mission, Rotmistrov placed his two full-strength tank corps and the still strong 2d Guards Tank Corps in first echelon to maximize the force of his initial blow. General Bakharov's 18th Tank Corps formed up on the army right flank in a two-kilometer sector east of Petrovka in the Psel valley just to the rear of the 9th Guards Airborne Division's dug-in 23d and 26th Regiments. Bakharov placed his 181st and 170th Tank Brigades in first echelon, supported by the 1000th Antitank Regiment, with orders to attack southeast along the narrow plain between the Psel River and German defenses at Oktriabr'skii State Farm to reach Andreevka and Komsomolets State Farm. This force of over 100 tanks would be followed by the 32d Motorized Rifle Brigade, 36th Guards Tank Regiment, and the 110th Tank Brigade in second and third echelon. Bakharov's full force of about 190 tanks would strike *Leibstandarte's* 2d Panzer Grenadier Regiment and the right flank of *Totenkopf's* Regiment *Eicke* and, he hoped, link up with the remnants of the 99th Tank Brigade en route. Overnight, Rotmistrov reinforced Bakharov's corps with a regiment of 57mm antitank guns from the 10th Antitank Artillery Brigade.

General Kirichenko's 29th Tank Corps occupied a dubious place of honor in the center of Rotmistrov's formation astride the Prokhorovka road. Deprived of its intended jumping-off positions in the open fields south of Prokhorovka, instead his corps formed for the attack in the city's southern suburbs. Kirichenko's 31st, 32d, and 25th Tank Brigades and the 1446th Self-propelled Artillery Regiment, with 191 tanks and self-propelled guns, supported by 21 additional self-propelled guns of the 1529th Self-propelled Artillery Regiment, were to lead the assault against German forces dug in between Oktiabr'skii State Farm and Storozhevoe. They would be accompanied by the 9th Guards Airborne Division's 28th Regiment, and the corps' 53d Motorized Rifle Brigade would follow in second echelon.

During the night of 11–12 July, General A. S. Burdeiny's 2d Guards Tank Corps regrouped its 120 surviving tanks into new assembly areas east of Belenikhino. This corps would attack with its 4th, 25th, and 26th Tank Brigades arrayed in single echelon against German forces of *Das Reich* occupying positions from west of Vinogradovka along the rail line to Belenikhino. In the gap between the 29th and 2d Guards Tank Corps, Popov's two weakened brigades of the 2d Tank Corps would attempt to join the effort. By attaching the remaining regiments of 10th Antitank Artillery Brigade (forty-eight 57mm guns), Rotmistrov hoped Popov could at least protect the flanks of his main shock groups between Storozhevoe and Ivanovskii Vyselok. For insurance he deployed the army's reserve 53d Guards Tank Regiment (with 21 KV heavy tanks) near Iamki in Popov's rear area and kept the 228 tanks and self-propelled guns of General Skvortsov's 5th Guards Mechanized Corps in reserve east of Prokhorovka, ready to respond to any eventuality. General Trufanov's small reserve group assembled near Pravorot' to await further orders.

In addition, Vatutin provided Rotmistrov with five artillery or mortar regiments, the 17th Artillery Brigade, and the 26th Antiaircraft Artillery Division. All told, Rotmistrov was to commit about 430 tanks and self-propelled guns in his initial assault, followed by another 70 from second echelon. Except for the 261 lightly armored T-70 tanks in his army, most of his tanks were reasonably effective weapons. However, the superior armor and armament of the newest German tanks and assault guns made it imperative that Rotmistrov's tankers fight at ranges of 500 meters or less, where the German technical advantage would be almost neutralized. Engaging at such close ranges would also make it more difficult for the Germans to use artillery or air support against the Soviet tanks. Accordingly, Rotmistrov ordered all of his commanders to close with German armored formations at high speed and "gang up" on each German target, in particular, the heavy Tigers.

By 0200 hours on 12 July, Rotmistrov's forces had completed most of their combat preparations, and the army commander was relatively satisfied with his day's labors. By pure dint of will and superb *Stavka* support, his tank force had maintained its imposing strength despite the many long days of near constant movement. Rotmistrov also knew that his troops were already dead tired, and he hoped that the inevitable and obligatory last-minute political meetings in the combat battalions would inspire the troops. If not, perhaps the vodka ration would.

Rotmistrov himself and his staff had little sleep that fateful night. No sooner had attack preparations been completed than at 0400 hours Vatutin called and ordered him to dispatch his reserve southward. Disturbing word had arrived that Kempf's armored spearhead had broken through in the south and was already on the outskirts of the Northern Donets River town of Rzhavets, less than twenty kilometers from Prokhorovka. Without reflection, Rotmistrov radioed his deputy General Trufanov and ordered him to march south with all haste and throw his group in the advancing Germans' path.[45] This incident prompted Rotmistrov, and probably Vatutin and Vasilevsky as well, to reflect that, while the upcoming engagement around Prokhorovka was critical, it was not the only critical battle the next day.

PROKHOROVKA, 12 JULY

The morning of 12 July dawned warm, humid, and cloudy. Light rain showers would develop in the afternoon, but these were not intense enough to hinder operations during most of the day. Toward evening, however, heavier showers turned many of the roads into muddy quagmires, particularly in the valleys in *Das Reich's* sector, where the rain crippled the Soviet 2d Guards Tank Corps' operations.

Just after dawn Hausser's three divisions began their assault according to plan, but within hours, all across the front, his panzers and panzer grenadiers ran into the teeth of the Soviet counterstroke (see Maps 20 and 21). *Leibstandarte* initiated the attack at 0650 hours when its 1st SS Panzer Grenadier Regiment inched eastward south of the rail line, completed clearing Russian infantry from Storozhevoe, and prepared to continue its advance to Iamki two kilometers southwest of Prokhorovka. Less than an hour later, the 2d SS Panzer Grenadier Regiment began its advance along a line from Hill 252.2 on the rail line to Oktiabr'skii State Farm. Shortly before 0815 hours, after the panzer grenadiers had reached the ridge line north of Oktiabr'skii and headed down into the valley beyond, Leibstandarte's Panzer Regiment, with sixty-seven tanks, prepared to roll forward to spearhead the advance.[46] The panzer grenadiers had already reported enemy infantry in regimental strength defending the ridge, but as they mounted the undulating heights and headed into the valley, they detected enemy tanks massed on the next ridge line. Before these reports could reach them, however, the 1st SS Panzer Regiment had formed to support and exploit their advance. As a Tiger tank company commander from the panzer regiment, Rudolf von Ribbentrop, later wrote:

> A purple wall of smoke rose into the air, produced by smoke shells. It meant: "Tank warning!"
>
> The same signals were to be seen all along the crest of the slope. The threatening violet danger signals also appeared farther to the right at the railroad embankment.
>
> Everything immediately became clear: beyond the hill, still out of sight of those in the valley, a major Soviet armoured attack was under way. . . .
>
> On reaching the rest of the slope we saw another low rise about 200 meters away on the other side of a small valley, on which our infantry positions were obviously located. . . .

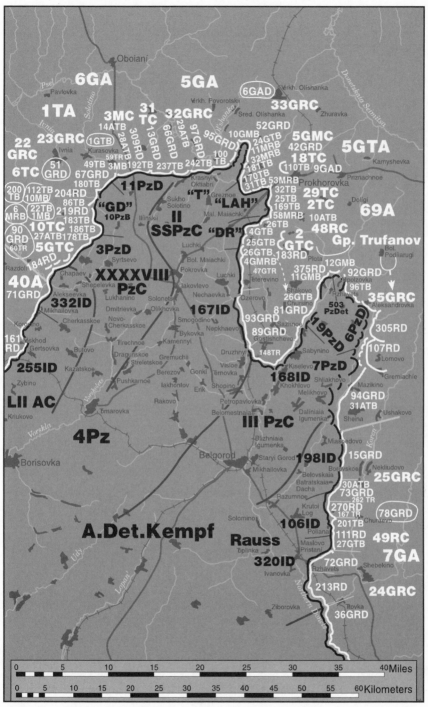

Map 20. Voronezh Front, 12 July 1943

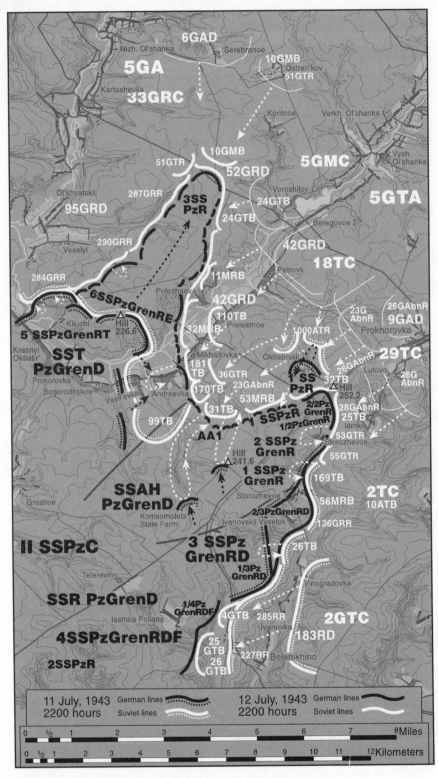

Map 21. Prokhorovka, 11–12 July 1943

The small valley extended to our left, and as we drove down the forward slope we spotted the first T-34s, which were apparently attempting to outflank us from the left.

We halted on the slope and opened fire, hitting several of the enemy. A number of Russian tanks were left burning. For a good gunner 800 meters was the ideal range.

As we waited to see if further enemy tanks were going to appear, I looked around, as was my habit. What I saw left me speechless. From beyond the shallow rise about 150–200 metres in front of me appeared fifteen, then thirty, then forty tanks. Finally there were too many to count. The T-34s were rolling toward us at high speed, carrying mounted infantry.[47]

Unbeknownst to von Ribbentrop, his Tiger company had run directly into the Soviet 29th Tank Corps' 31st and 32d Tank Brigades.

Simultaneously, on the 1st SS Panzer Regiment's left flank north of Oktiabr'skii, its 13th Company ran into a force of sixty Soviet tanks, which it engaged at a range of 600 to 1,000 meters. As the ranges rapidly closed, another Russian force of like strength descended on the 13th Company of the panzer regiment's 2d Battalion. A swirling, deadly, three-hour battle ensued, during which the Soviet tanks suffered appalling losses as they closed within killing range of the German armor to even the odds. *Leibstandarte's* division history captured the ferocity of the fighting:

At 06.00 hours [0800 Moscow time], there was an attack by a force of regimental size across the line Prochorowka-Petrovka. About fifty enemy tanks ran into Panzergruppe *LAH*, which was just beginning its advance. The fighting lasted two hours. *Untersturmfuehrer Guehrs.*, the *Zugfuehrer* of a *Kraftwagenkanonenzug* [armoured gun platoon] in the III.(armoured)/2. [2d Panzer Grenadier Regiment], reported as follows: "They attacked us in the morning. They were around us, on top of us, and between us. We fought man-to-man, jumping out of our foxholes to lob our magnetic hollow-charge grenades at the enemy tanks, leaping on our Schuetzenpanzerwagens to take on any enemy vehicle or man we spotted. It was hell! At 09.00 hours [1100 Moscow time], the battlefield was once again firmly in our hands. Our Panzers had helped us mightily. My Kompanie alone had destroyed fifteen Russian tanks."[48]

Similar scenes of vicious fighting engulfed the II SS Panzer Corps' entire front, but particularly in *Leibstandarte's* sector. Everywhere, the attackers became desperate defenders, and the battlefield carnage mounted. The division's 1st SS Panzer Grenadier Regiment had no sooner seized Storozhevoe than it too was struck repeatedly by waves of Soviet tanks and mounted infantry. A crew member of the regiment's 3d Tank Destroyer Battalion later recorded his vivid impressions of the heated action:

It was about 04.00 hours in the early morning when a motorcycle messenger brought us a new order. We were to provide defense at the collective farm in Stalinsk [Storozhevoe]. We should pay particular attention to the right in the direction of the forest and toward the railroad embankment. It was not much longer before we saw about twenty-five or thirty T-34s moving along to our right six or seven kilometers away, heading straight for Division *DR*'s battle line. They were too far away for us, but the Artillerie trained its sights on them and made sure that they did not pass our right flank unscathed. Then there was a silence. But at 08.00 hours, the magic began with a bang. Salvo after salvo from "Stalin organs" rained down on our positions, with artillery and mortar shells in between. All in all, it looked like a preparation for a real attack, and it lasted almost one and a half hours. A German reconnaissance plane fairly deep over Russian territory signaled to us with his wings, dropped a message canister, and released two violet smoke flares. That meant tanks. Left of the railroad embankment, there were also violet smoke signals going off, so there must be tanks there, too. The enemy fire stopped at the same moment, and over the hill to the left of the embankment came three . . . five . . . ten . . . But what was the use of counting? Racing at full speed and firing from all barrels, T-34 after T-34 rolled over the hill, right into the middle of our Infantrie positions. We opened fire with our five guns as soon as we saw the first tank, and it was only seconds before the first T-34s stood shrouded in black smoke. Sometimes we had to take care of the Russian infantry riding on top of the tank in hand-to-hand fighting.

Then, suddenly, there were forty or fifty T-34's coming at us from the right. We had to turn and open fire on them. All of a sudden, three bold giants among them raced off across the basin toward the collective farm. They captured the road leading to it. I did not have a chance to fire. The gun on the right wing had a jammed loading mechanism, and we could not seem to get it fixed. So we had to shift positions through the farm buildings. I had barely taken aim when I had to fire at my first T-34. My shell went past it, and the shell case got stuck in the gun. I ducked between the houses once again, and I was in front of one when I got the mechanism unjammed. A T-34 appeared right in front of me when my assistant gunner yelled so loud that I could hear him without the headphones. "Last shell in the barrel." On top of everything else! I swiveled around to face the T-34 racing toward us a distance of about 150 meters when the next tragedy struck. The rear support for the gun collapsed, and the barrel swung up to point at the sky. I used the force of swiveling the turret to bring the barrel of my 7.5cm gun down, managed to get the T-34's turret in my sights, and fired. A hit! The hatch opened and two men jumped out. One stayed put while the other hopped across the road between the houses. About thirty meters in front of me, I hit the T-34 again.

After the shooting match with the Russian infantrymen and the tank crews who had jumped out of their damaged vehicles, in which our Infantrie provided magnificent help, we took off at full speed to get our gun out of the hole we were in. We raced to the forest between burning T-34s. With that the Russian tank attack, supported by three or four waves of infantry, was broken and pushed back.

Everywhere, there were the shells of burning tanks, standing in a sector about 1,500 meters wide; about ten or twelve artillery pieces were smoldering there, too. One hundred twenty were supposed to have been in the attack, but there could well have been more. Who counted![49]

These frantic assaults were by the Soviet 29th Tank Corps' 25th Tank Brigade, supported by tanks from the 2d Tank Corps' 169th Tank Brigade and, soon, from the 53d Guards Tank Regiment. The fighting along the entire front intensified throughout late morning and into early afternoon, as wave after wave of Soviet armor washed around the II SS Panzer Corps' lead elements.

Quite obviously, Rotmistrov's counterattack had begun on schedule. At 0600 hours Rotmistrov himself, with a small operational group of staff officers, joined his 29th Tank Corps commander, General Kirichenko, at the corps' forward command post. He used the CP, which was located on a small hillock southwest of Prokhorovka and afforded an excellent view of the battlefield, as his army observation post during the assault. German Messerschmitt aircraft appeared at 0630 to sweep the skies clear of Soviet aircraft, and waves of German bombers followed a half hour later. As Rotmistrov gazed skyward, swarms of Soviet fighters and then bombers began an air battle that swirled overhead as the two ground armadas embraced each other in mortal combat, undeterred by the falling bombs and carnage overhead.

At 0815 hours Soviet artillery roared and for fifteen minutes pounded German positions until giving way to fiery sheets of Katiusha multiple rocket fire, which announced the end of the artillery preparation. Soviet gunners then shifted their thousands of tubes from fire on preplanned concentrations to creeping barrage fire, which inched forward toward German advanced positions. From his OP (observation post) Rotmistrov could already see German forces on the march, forward into the teeth of his anxious host. "Indeed," he later recorded, "it turned out that both we and the Germans went over to the offensive simultaneously."[50] At precisely 0830 hours, Rotmistrov's radioman shouted the signal, *"Stal', Stal', Stal'"* (Steel, Steel, Steel), into his radio transmitter, and the ether resounded with Rotmistrov's command to attack as it passed to his assembled corps, brigades, regiments, and battalions. Shortly thereafter, his 500 tanks and self-propelled guns carrying mounted riflemen from the 9th Guards Airborne Division lurched forward into action. Rotmistrov later described the imposing scene and the ferocious combat that ensued:

> The tanks were moving across the steppe in small packs, under cover of patches of woodland and hedges. The bursts of gunfire merged into one continuous mighty roar. The Soviet tanks thrust into the German advanced formation at full speed and penetrated the German tank screen. The T-34s were knocking out Tigers at extremely close range, since their powerful guns and massive armor no longer gave them an advantage in close combat. The tanks of both sides were in the closest possible contact. There was neither time nor room to disengage from the enemy and reform in battle order or operate in formation. The shells fired at close range pierced not only the side armor but also the frontal armor of the fighting vehicles. At such range there was no protection in armor, and the length of the gun barrels was no longer decisive. Frequently, when a tank was hit, its ammunition and fuel blew up, and torn-off turrets were flung through the air over dozens of yards. At the same time, furious aerial combats developed over the battlefield. Soviet as well as German airmen tried to help their ground forces to win the battle. The bombers, ground support aircraft, and fighters seemed to be permanently suspended in the sky over Prokhorovka. One aerial combat followed another. Soon the whole sky was shrouded by the thick smoke of the burning wrecks. On the black, scorched earth the gutted tanks burnt like torches. It was difficult to establish which side was attacking and which defending.[51]

As evocative and accurate as Rotmistrov's dramatic description of the battlefield was, he failed to mention that the bulk of the burning tank hulks were Soviet.

On Rotmistrov's right flank, the 181st and 170th Tank Brigades of General Bakharov's 18th Tank Corps advanced abreast across a small valley south of Petrovka, with riflemen from the 23d Guards Airborne Regiment riding on the decks of the tanks. North of Oktiabr'skii, Lieutenant Colonel V. D. Tarasov's 170th Tank Brigade smashed through the left flank of *Leibstandarte's* advancing panzer grenadiers but soon encountered its deploying panzer regiment. An intense and costly struggle followed until at 1000 hours the supporting 1000th Antitank Artillery Regiment erected blocking positions in front of the German armor, which permitted the 170th to wheel to the right and to catch the German armor in the flank. By this time the German panzer regiment was under assault by the 29th Tank Corps' 31st and 32d Tank Brigades, and although it took a terrible toll on Soviet armor, the panzers were forced to give way and slowly withdraw, with guns blazing, back toward the relative safety of Oktiabr'skii.

Although the 170th Tank Brigade lost its commander and as many as thirty of its sixty tanks in the fighting near Oktiabr'skii, by early afternoon it pushed southward, grappling with *Leibstandarte's* armored reconnaissance battalion, which struggled to defend the SS division's left flank and rear. This battle intensified in the afternoon, when Bakharov's second echelon 36th Guards Tank Regiment arrived to support the 170th. By this time the 170th Tank Brigade, now commanded by Lieutenant Colonel A. I. Kazakov, had joined its neighboring 181st Brigade in an assault on *Totenkopf* positions east of Andreevka.

Lieutenant Colonel V. A. Puzyrev's 181st Tank Brigade, attacking along the southern banks of the Psel, drove *Totenkopf's* panzer grenadiers, which had themselves just begun an attack eastward, back toward the west. By 1800 hours, assisted by the 170th Brigade, Puzyrev's tankers penetrated into the village of Vasil'evka, thereby threatening to sever *Totenkopf's* communications with *Leibstandarte*. However, within an hour *Totenkopf* dispatched a relief column consisting of a Tiger tank company from Hill 226.2, and, with deadly artillery support from Gresnoe, these tanks forced both the 181st and 170th Brigades to withdraw to Andreevka. Although Bakharov's tank corps had made spectacular progress, it could advance no further until the 29th Tank Corps closed up on its left flank. In the meantime, Bakharov brought his second echelon 110th Tank Brigade and 36th Guards Tank Regiment forward and placed them in defensive positions to the rear, where they could either defend or exploit on 13 July. During the day's fighting, Bakharov's 32d Motorized Rifle Brigade was drawn into heavy combat north of the Psel, where the planned assault by *Totenkopf's* Panzer Regiment had made striking gains.

Bakharov's success clashed vividly with General Kirichenko's frustration. The latter's 29th Tank Corps also attacked at 0830 hours, but since it struck *Leibstandarte's* main strength deployed between Oktiabr'skii State Farm and Storozhevoe, its gains were more limited and the price it paid was far higher. Attacking on the corps' right flank toward Oktiabr'skii, Colonel S. F. Moiseev's 31st Tank Brigade struck *Leibstandarte's* panzer regiment directly on the nose, while the neighboring 170th Tank Brigade hit the German left flank. Although Colonel A. A. Linev's 32d Tank Brigade attempted to support the 31st, Linev's tanks were also attacking the spearhead of the German penetration along the rail line. Moiseev's brigade fought a prolonged and costly battle, losing fully half of its tanks while driving *Leibstandarte's* panzer regiment back to Oktiabr'skii.

With Lieutenant Colonel N. P. Lipichev's second echelon 53d Motorized Rifle Brigade in support, Moiseev's remaining tanks raced southward and tore through *Leibstandarte's* reconnaissance screen south of Oktiabr'skii and north of Komsomolets State Farm. Soviet classified accounts stated: "Exploiting the success of 18th Tank Corps, the 53d Motorized Rifle Brigade advanced forward in a decisive bound and at 1730 hours penetrated into Komsomolets State Farm. Having smashed the enemy defending that point, the brigade, seeking to reestablish contact with remaining corps units and also under pressure from superior enemy forces, withdrew to the region of Hill 252, where it went over the defense with 25th Tank Brigade."[52]

In actuality, the 31st Tank and 53d Motorized Rifle Brigades penetrated *Leibstandarte's* reconnaissance battalion in two places as they lunged for their immediate objective of Komsomolets. In so doing they threatened the SS division's command post and key lines of communications with the rear. The exploiting Soviet tanks were repulsed only by rapid action by *Leibstandarte's* Panzer Regiment and, farther south, only by *Leibstandarte's* Artillery Regiment after the Soviet tanks had penetrated into the very heart of its firing positions. *Leibstandarte's* history recorded this action, and the events that preceded it:

> At 09.20 hours [1120 Moscow time], there was a renewed tank attack from Prochorowka. Thirty-five tanks attacked Panzergruppe *LAH*, while forty tanks moved out of Petrovka against the fork in the road one kilometer south-southeast of Swch. Oktjabrskij. These enemy tanks received very strong artillery support and were engaged at high speed.
>
> In this attack, four of the seven Panzers used by the 6./Panzerregiment *LAH* . . . were put out of commission at a distance of only about 220 meters. The remaining three Panzers joined the ranks of the advancing Russian tanks and moved with the pack of them into the fire range of the II./Panzerregiment *LAH* . . . , located about 800 yards to the rear. These three could fire at the Russians from a distance of 10 to 30 meters and make every shell a direct hit because the Russians could not see through the dust and smoke that there were German tanks rolling along with them in the same direction. There were already nineteen Russian tanks standing burning on the battlefield when the Abteilung opened fire for the first time . . . [II./ Panzerregiment] destroyed about sixty-two T-70s and T-34s in a three-hour-long battle that could almost be termed hand-to-hand tank combat. . . .
>
> After this heavy attack had been repulsed, which the divisional commander and the Ia [operations officer] had observed from their advanced command post on Hill 241.6, a small enemy tank force managed to penetrate the Aufklarungsabteilung's [reconnaissance battalion's] thin flank defense and make it through into the Artillerie's positions. There, the enemy force was destroyed, either in the direct fire from the Artillerie or in close-range fighting with the infantry.[53]

The sharp struggle for Hill 241.6 and Komsomolets State Farm gave way to desultory fighting as the 31st Tank Brigade tried in vain to find a weak point in *Leibstandarte's* left flank.

The most intense fighting on 12 July took place along the 29th Tank Corps' front. While joining the 31st Tank Brigade's assault on Oktiabr'skii, Lieutenant Colonel Linev's 32d Tank Brigade also repeatedly attacked German positions on the northern slopes of Hill 252.2. By noon Major P. S. Ivanov's 1st Battalion was encircled and nearly destroyed in a counterattack by *Leibstandarte's* Panzer Regiment, while Captain A. E. Vakuletsko's 2d Battalion struggled with the 2d SS Panzer Grenadier Regiment along both sides of the rail line. At 1300 hours Vakuletsko's tankers, with infantry from the 9th Guards Airborne Division's 23d Airborne Regiment and assisted by a battalion from the neighboring 25th Tank Brigade and 9th Guards Airborne's 28th Regiment, recaptured Hill 252.2. However, incessant German counterattacks and heavy air strikes halted the drive and forced the Soviets to dig in. German reports laconically recorded, "At 11.30 hours [1330 Moscow time], there was a localized breakthrough near Hill 252.2, but it was cleared away by 13.15 [1515]."[54] In the meantime, after heavy resistance and with their left flank threatened, *Leibstandarte's* Panzer Regiment and 2d Battalion, 1st SS Panzer Grenadier Regiment abandoned their positions around Oktiabr'skii and withdrew one kilometer to the rear to regroup and reestablish firmer defense lines.

On Kirichenko's left flank, Colonel N. K. Volodin's 25th Tank Brigade, supported by Captain M. S. Lunev's 1446th Self-propelled Artillery Regiment and cooperating with Major V. A. Ponomarov's 28th Guards Airborne Regiment, struck hard at German positions from south of the rail line to Storozhevoe, supported on the left by the 55th Guards Tank Regiment and remnants from the 2d Tank Corps' 169th Tank Brigade.[55] Major G. A. Miasnikov's tank battalion of the 25th penetrated into and through German defenses at Storozhevoe, and his lead tanks reached the Prokhorovka road before the 1st Battalion, 2d SS Panzer Grenadier Regiment, counterattacked and drove them back into the village. Ferocious fighting raged in Storozhevoe, along the southern slopes of Hill 252.2, and in the fields west of Iamki as Soviet and German troops and tanks attacked and counterattacked through falling shells and devastating antitank fire. At day's end the best Kirichenko could claim was a stalemate, although his corps had certainly halted the German attack on Prokhorovka.

Fighting in the 18th and 29th Tank Corps' sectors died down by midafternoon. The troops on both sides were exhausted and emotionally drained. While both sides had suffered heavy losses, the two Soviet tank corps paid a dear price for their headlong attack. At a cost of 48 killed, 321 wounded, and 5 missing, *Leibstandarte* claimed to have destroyed 192 Soviet tanks and 19 antitank guns and captured 253 prisoners. In the process, the Germans reported losing fewer than half of their own tanks. These figures were not far from the truth.[56] Even allowing for some German inflation of Soviet casualties and double counting of Soviet tank kills, the two Soviet tank corps had lost nearly half of their initial strength. The 29th Tank Corps was particularly hard hit because it had already committed virtually its entire combat strength to battle and lost over half of its tanks in the process. In the 18th Tank Corps the 170th and 181st Tank Brigades were relatively intact, and Bakharov still retained the fresh 110th Tank Brigade and 36th Guards Tank Regiment in second echelon defensive positions. The position of both corps was made even more precarious by the failure of the 2d Guards Tank Corps' attack on their right flank and by the progress made by *Totenkopf* Division north of the Psel River.

The three tank brigades of General Burdeiny's 2d Guards Tank Corps, along with riflemen from the 183d Rifle Division, went into action at 0830 hours. Although the corps could field just over 120 tanks, Burdeiny's small force attacked with offensive abandon. The ferocity of this effort disrupted II SS Panzer Corps' careful plans by preventing Das Reich with its approximately 95 tanks and assault guns from joining the eastward thrust of *Leibstandarte*.[57] Even worse, when the Soviet counterstroke began, *Das Reich* was in no position to defend *Leibstandarte's* right flank.

Das Reich's Deutschland Regiment had no sooner begun its advance from the eastern end of Ivanovskii Vyselok than it was struck in its front by the Soviet 26th Tank Brigade, with heavy antitank support. While *Deutschland's* 3d Panzer Grenadier Battalion recoiled from the shock, its 1st Battalion confronted a strong armored thrust against its right flank. This force, spearheaded by Colonel A. K. Brazhnikov's 4th Guards Tank Brigade, swept past the SS battalion, through the forward defenses of neighboring *Der Fuehrer* Regiment's 1st Battalion, across the rail line north of Belenikhino, and into the eastern edge of the village of Iasnaia Poliana. Simultaneously, *Der Fuehrer's* 1st and 4th Battalions, under attack by Lieutenant Colonel S. M. Bulygin's 25th Guards and Colonel S. K. Nesterov's 26th Guards Tank Brigades at and south of Belenikhino, were themselves forced back to the outskirts of Iasnaia Poliana and Kalinin. A history of *Das Reich* described the action as follows:

> *Deutschland* Regiment continued to protect the flank of the advancing *Leibstandarte,* while the rest of *Das Reich,* still on the defensive, flung back a succession of infantry and tank attacks. One interesting incident was the employment against the Russians of T-34s, which *Das Reich* had seized from a factory in Khar'kov. During the day a column of fifty Russian vehicles was seen driving along one of the *balkas* or valleys. . . . The direction of the column's advance showed that it was moving to attack *Der Fuehrer.* On the high ground above the Russian column stood the

division's group of T-34s, which opened a destructive fire upon the Russian tanks. The panzermen's tactic was one which they had learned early in the war with Russia; kill the enemy's command tank first. It was the only machine fitted with both a radio receiver and transmitter. The other vehicles had only receivers and could not communicate by wireless with one another. This was yet another weakness in Red Army tactics. Russian tanks carried on their rear decks a metal drum containing reserve fuel supplies. A hit on the drum ignited the fuel and caused the tank to "brew up."[58]

Another account captured the frustration in German ranks and, at the same time, underscored the source of that frustration: "Heavy fighting developed on the right flank of *Das Reich* Division. There the Soviet II Guards Tank Corps attacked repeatedly from the gap between Hausser's corps and Breith's divisions, which had not yet arrived. That accursed gap! 'The Russian attacks on our flanks are tying down half of our effectives and taking the steam out of our operation against the enemy at Prokhorovka,' growled the regimental commander, Sylvester Stadler."[59]

The assault by Burdeiny's tank brigades ended by 1430 hours, when *Das Reich* dispatched forces from other sectors to reinforce its beleaguered right flank. Ostensibly, stiffened German resistance and heavy tank losses had brought Burdeiny's force to a halt. In fact, other circumstances had intervened to stop Burdeiny. First, heavy thunderstorms rolled through the region, turning the roads to glue and ruling out further attacks.[60] Even more critical, the deteriorating situation to the south, where Kempf's III Panzer Corps was accelerating its northward attack along the Northern Donets, forced Vatutin to appeal to Burdeiny for help. Late in the day, Burdeiny responded by dispatching his 26th Guards Tank Brigade southward to help counter the new German threat. With his corps' main force reduced to a strength of about fifty tanks, Burdeiny had no choice but to give up his hard-earned gains and withdraw to his jumping-off positions, where he went over to the defense.

While Rotmistrov's army halted the direct German thrust on Prokhorovka and kept a weary eye on German armor to the south, it confronted a dangerous deteriorating situation north of the Psel River. There, *Totenkopf* assembled 121 tanks and assault guns from its 3d SS Panzer Regiment and grenadiers from its 6th SS Panzer Grenadier Regiment *Eicke* and attacked to break through Soviet defenses on Hill 226.6 and drive northward along the ridge line north of the Psel.[61] As described in formerly classified Soviet accounts:

By 1200 hours, when it had became clear to the German command that its attempt to penetrate to Prokhorovka had failed, it decided to assist its main grouping, which was advancing in the direction of Oboian'; and, to achieve this, part of the force was to penetrate along the northern bank of the Psel to envelop the flanks of 6th Guards Army and 1st Tank Army and then to reach the region north of Prokhorovka in the rear of 5th Guards Tank Army.

With this aim, the Germans concentrated a shock group consisting of 100 tanks, 1 motorized infantry regiment, up to 200 motorcycles, and several self-propelled guns in the Krasnyi Oktiabr', Kozlovka region. At 1200 hours the shock group, supported by aviation, shifted to the offensive, penetrated 52d Guards Rifle Division's defense, and by 1300 captured Hill 226. On the northern slopes of this hill, the attacking enemy encountered strong resistance from 95th Guards Rifle Division units, which had prepared defenses in this region. All attempts by German tanks, infantry, and motorcyclists to penetrate the defense were repelled successfully by fire and counterattacks from this division's units. At 1800 hours the enemy ceased his attacks and began to regroup.

After a massive air raid, at 2000 hours the Germans once again attacked 95th Guards Rifle Division's combat formation, and by the time darkness fell they had pushed our units back and captured Polezhaev but were unable to advance further along this axis.[62]

The German thrust rendered the depleted 52d Guards Rifle Division *hors de combat* and severely shook the stability of the 95th's defenses. Even Rotmistrov's early evening commitment of his second echelon 42d Guards Rifle Division did not seem to mitigate the situation. In his memoirs, Rotmistrov recalled the seriousness of the situation and the remedies he adopted to stem the tide of *Totenkopf's* advance:

By 1300 hours enemy tanks succeeded in penetrating the combat formation of the 95th and 42d Guards Rifle Divisions in the Krasnyi Oktiabr', Kochetovka [should read: Kozlovka] sector and advanced in a northeastern and eastern direction to the line Veselyi-Polezhaev. It was necessary to eliminate quickly the threat to the army's right flank and rear and also assist our neighbor, Lieutenant General A. S. Zhadov's 5th Guards Army. This army completely lacked tanks and did not dispose of sufficient artillery support. Furthermore, it had entered battle essentially from the march, deploying its main force in the face of the attacking enemy.

Inasmuch as my reserve was already committed to combat and moving to the south, I had to assign forces from my main grouping to help Zhadov. I ordered that the 24th Guards Tank Brigade [from 5th Guards Mechanized Corps] of Guards Colonel V. P. Karpov be sent to the region of K. E. Voroshilov State Farm, where, in cooperation with the right flank units of 18th Tank Corps and the infantry of 5th Guards Army, it was to destroy the enemy at Polezhaev. Simultaneously, Colonel I. B. Mikhailov's 10th Guards Mechanized Brigade successfully moved to Ostren'kov (nine kilometers northwest of Prokhorovka) with the mission of preventing enemy movement in a northeastern direction. The decisive movement of these brigades into these regions and the decisiveness of their meeting blow against penetrating Hitlerite tanks stabilized the situation at the adjacent flanks of 5th Guards Tank and 5th Guards Army. The enemy here was forced to withdraw and then shift to the defense.[63]

Although basically correct, Rotmistrov's recollections were a bit premature. It took most of the evening for his two fresh brigades to reach their appointed jumping-off positions. Only at dawn of 13 July did they go into action along with the supporting riflemen of the 95th and 42d Guards Rifle Divisions. In the meantime, *Totenkopf* dug in to its advanced positions and forced the 18th Tank Corps to divert part of its force to the Psel River's northern bank to assist the worn and beleaguered 11th Motorized Rifle Brigade.[64]

Overall, Rotmistrov had diverted but not halted the German advance on 12 July. After-action reports cryptically recorded: "Thus, during the course of 12 July, the mission assigned to 5th Guards Tank Army had not been fulfilled. As a result of the frontal blow, the army's corps conducted heavy combat with large enemy tank forces, during the course of which they were forced to shift to the defense. During the night of 13 July, the army's corps were ordered to fortify themselves along existing lines and to regroup their units in order to be ready to continue the offensive on the morning of 13 July."[65]

Rotmistrov well understood the effect the day's fighting had had on his army's combat capabilities. Popov's 2d Tank Corps was a shell of its former self and virtually combat ineffective. Burdeiny's 2d Guards was likewise finished, and the bulk of its remaining combat strength had marched south with its 26th Tank Brigade. Rotmistrov's army reserve had also marched south, and the bulk of Skvortsov's 5th Guards Mechanized Corps had also marched or was marching in opposite directions to meet the threat on the flanks. This left Rotmistrov with but two shaken corps, the 18th and 29th, with perhaps 200 tanks between them, with which to resume the attack in the morning.

During the evening, according to Rotmistrov's instructions, Bakharov and Kirichenko erected strong defenses, withdrew units shattered in the day's fighting into second echelon, and resupplied existing vehicles with fuel and ammunition. Vatutin at *front* did all in his power to speed tank replacements forward. In the meantime Bakharov formed his 170th and 181st Tank Brigades into a shock group, with orders to once again attack Vasil'evka in the morning. His 110th Brigade prepared to support. Kirichenko pulled back his shattered 31st and 32d Tank Brigades, replaced them with infantry from the

53d Motorized Rifle Brigade and 9th Guards Airborne Division, and placed them in second echelon defenses around Oktiabr'skii. All the while he worried about how his depleted forces could resume the attack in the morning, particularly since the 5th Guards Mechanized Corps was no longer able to support him.

What Kirichenko did not know was that Rotmistrov was increasingly preoccupied by developments along his flanks, specifically the threat posed by *Totenkopf* north of the Psel and the III Panzer Corps to the south. By nightfall Rotmistrov was satisfied he had met the first threat. "In the morning," he thought, "the two fresh mobile brigades and combined infantry of the 42d and 95th Guards Divisions will be able to eradicate *Totenkopf's* threat." To make sure, he issued orders for the 6th Guards Airborne Division to march at night to join the counterattack. Rotmistrov, however, was less certain he could deal with the second threat. He had already dispatched the army reserve to deal with it, and now bad news forced him to send other precious forces southward. Preoccupied with these problems, Rotmistrov had neither the time nor the inclination to think about yet another threat, the planned northward thrust of the XXXXVIII Panzer Corps. Fortunately, Vatutin had both the time and inclination, and on 12 July he removed that threat, once and for all.

The principal tank of the Red Army during the Kursk fighting, the T-34 Model 1943. Because Soviet policy maximized production at the expense of modernization, the Red tank force at Kursk lacked the firepower and armor necessary to withstand the new German heavy tanks.

The crews of a T-34 Model 1943 of the 5th Guards Tank Corps enjoy a musical interlude prior to the outbreak of fighting in the Kursk area in July 1943.

The Red Army made some use of Lend-Lease tanks in the 1943 fighting. Here, a Lend-Lease American M3 Lee medium tank burns after having been hit by German fire. The M3 medium tank earned the grim sobriquet "grave for seven brothers" due to its archaic layout and poor armor.

At least one Red Army heavy tank regiment used the Churchill infantry tank in combat at Kursk in 1943. Although well armored, the Churchill was slow and poorly armed by Soviet standards and so was relegated to infantry support units.

The standard Soviet heavy tank in 1943 was the KV-1S, which had a smaller turret than previous models to reduce the overall vehicle weight. Because the KV compared very poorly to the German Tiger, the Red Army ceased its production in 1943 in favor of the completely redesigned IS-2 heavy tank.

The standard Red Army light tank in 1943 was the T-70. Based on the earlier T-60, it had a larger turret armed with the 45mm tank gun, which was too light to seriously threaten German tanks and was only kept in production because the automotive plants producing it could not manage medium or heavy tanks.

The SU-152 assault gun was nicknamed *Zvierboi* (animal hunter) by Soviet troops to acknowledge that it could handle the new German Panther, Elephant, and Tiger tanks. It was a crude improvisation mounting a 152mm gun-howitzer on a KV-1S tank chassis and small numbers were in service during the Kursk battle.

Although the Tiger and Panther tanks are more commonly associated with the Kursk battle, the Pz.Kpfw. III (background) and Pz.Kpfw. IV (foreground) made up the bulk of the German tank forces in 1943. Both have been refitted with armored side skirts to minimize the effects of Soviet antitank rifles.

German Pz.Kpfw. IV tanks move into the attack at Kursk in 1943. The added armor around the turret frequently caused Soviet tankers to mistake the Pz.Kpfw. IV for a Tiger, with the result that historical accounts tend to exaggerate the numbers and importance of the Tiger during the Kursk fighting.

Red Army prisoners sit near a platoon of German Panther tanks during the Kursk fighting. Eventually one of the most feared weapons in the German arsenal, the Panther's performance at Kursk was disappointing because of its automotive immaturity.

A Tiger I heavy tank is followed by the much lighter Pz.Kpfw. III. On the battlefield, the Tiger I's 88mm gun could destroy any Soviet tank, and its thick frontal armor made it virtually invincible to Soviet tank fire. Its high cost meant those Tigers available were assigned to special missions, such as leading spearhead formations during the Kursk offensives.

The Elephant tank destroyer is the armored vehicle most closely associated with the Battle of Kursk. The Elephant, also known as the Ferdinand, was an improvisation created by adding an 88mm gun in a fixed superstructure on the surplus hulls of a failed Porsche heavy tank design. Although quite lethal when employed in the overwatch role at long ranges, the Elephant was quite vulnerable to infantry at close ranges.

The workhorse of the *Wehrmacht,* the StuG III assault gun mated the hull of the obsolete Pz.Kpfw. III medium tank with the long 75mm gun of the Pz.Kpfw. IV tank. Although lacking the flexibility of a tank due to its lack of a traversable turret, the assault gun proved an invaluable weapon for infantry support both in the direct artillery fire role and in antitank defense.

During the Kursk fighting, the Germans employed special armored engineer units using a B IV remote control demolition vehicle (the small tank-like vehicle in front) commanded from a StuG III assault gun. The remote control vehicle was intended to attack heavily defended bunkers, but like many German schemes, this technically ingenious weapon proved impractical in battle.

The standard German mechanized infantry vehicle (seen here passing a Soviet ZIS-3 76mm divisional gun) was the Hanomog SdKfz 251 half-track, which Panzer grenadier units used to transport their infantry.

Artillery attached to panzer divisions was often mechanized. The standard type was the *Wespe* (wasp), which consisted of an obsolete Pz.Kpfw. II light tank chassis refitted with a 105mm howitzer. To the left is a Soviet ZIS-3 76mm divisional gun.

Because of Soviet *Shturmovik* attack aircraft, German armored units were provided with mobile antiaircraft guns, a standard type consisting of a 20mm FlaK 30 automatic cannon mounted on a Demag one and one-half ton half-track.

Here Soviet infantry armed with the widely used PPSh submachine gun advance through a ruined town. By the summer of 1943, the Red Army placed greater emphasis on sub-machine guns than other armies did. Among the PPSh's advantages were its ease of operation and inexpensive manufacture and ammunition.

The Red Army's principal infantry antitank weapon was the PTRD 14.5mm antitank rifle. Marginally effective in 1941 against lightly armored German tanks, by 1943 they were obsolete. In the later years of the war, the Red Army's lack of a modern infantry antitank weapon proved a serious shortcoming.

The Red Army still relied on large numbers of the obsolete 45mm Model 1932 antitank gun even as late as 1943. An improved version with a lengthened barrel was introduced in 1943, but was inadequate against the newer, more heavily armored German tanks.

Among the most effective antitank weapons available to the Red Army were antitank mines, which were used in large numbers in the defensive belts of the Kursk Bulge.

The standard Red Army heavy machine gun was the World War I 7.62mm Maxim on its cumbersome, heavy PM 1910 wheeled carriage, which compared poorly to German machine guns.

The counteroffensives following in the wake of Operation Citadel showed a growing maturity in Soviet offensive operations, witness the increasing use of specialized *razvedchik* advance reconnaissance units, the forerunners of the contemporary *Spetsnaz* (reconnaissance-diversionary) forces.

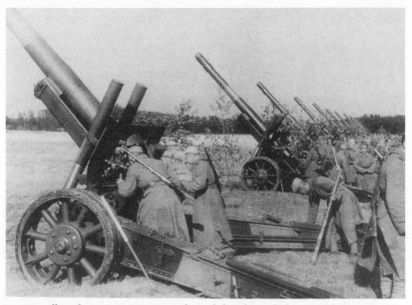

Soviet artillery forces grew in size and capability through the war. This unit is equipped with the 152mm ML-20 Model 1937 gun-howitzer, which had an effective range of 17 km and were typically deployed in the heavy artillery brigades subordinate to the armies and fronts.

CHAPTER 6

The Germans Halt

THE BATTLE ON THE FLANKS, 12 JULY

When on 11 July General Vatutin planned his counterstroke for the 12th, he had placed primary emphasis on the attacks by Katukov's 1st Tank, Chistiakov's 6th Guards, Rotmistrov's 5th Guards Tank, and Zhadov's 5th Guards Armies against the principal German threats posed by the II SS Panzer and XXXXVIII Panzer Corps (Map 20, p. 183). At the same time, however, he had demonstrated continuing concern for his *front's* left flank along the Northern Donets River by ordering General Shumilov, the 7th Guards Army commander, to mount an attack with his second echelon 49th Rifle Corps against Army Detachment Kempf's right flank east of Razumnoe. This blow was designed to foment crisis in this German sector, attract and tie down III Panzer Corps forces, and prevent them from continuing their advance toward Prokhorovka.

Although Shumilov carried out Vatutin's orders, the attack failed to achieve its ultimate goal. A Soviet critique cryptically recorded: "In accordance with the *front* commander's plan, at 0900 hours on 12 July, the 7th Guards Army's 49th Rifle Corps (73d Guards, 270th, and 111th Rifle Divisions) went over to the attack from the Solov'ev Collective Farm and Poliana State Farm regions. As a result of heavy combat, by day's end the corps reached the line of Hills 207.9 and 191.2 [less than two kilometers forward]. Further attempts to attack achieved little success."[1] It added, somewhat disingenuously and much less accurately: "As a result of the battles on 12 July, the enemy was forced to turn away from further attempts to continue his offensive in a northern direction to penetrate to Prokhorovka. The day of 12 July was a day of final crisis for the German offensive and a day of full renunciation by the enemy of fulfilling the assigned mission of securing Kursk from the south."[2]

In reality, even though Shumilov's 7th Guards and Kriuchenkin's 69th Armies had seriously delayed Kempf's advance and prevented him from linking up on 12 July with the II SS Panzer Corps at Prokhorovka, it had been a close call. For on the morning of 12 July, the III Panzer Corps resumed its northward drive in spectacular fashion and by day's end was slightly over fifteen kilometers from Prokhorovka. If Kempf's force was unable to participate in a final drive on Kursk, it was not because it never linked up with II SS

Panzer. Rather it was because it linked up too late, and by that time Adolf Hitler had ordered von Manstein to abort his Citadel offensive.

On the morning of 12 July, Kempf and his III Panzer Corps commander, Breith, could think of little else than the necessity of reaching Prokhorovka, and fast. To that end Breith had orchestrated a bold armored thrust to capitalize on the 6th Panzer Division's advance to Kazach'e the previous day. Leaving its 4th Panzer Grenadier Regiment in Kazach'e with orders to push on to Aleksandrovka, Breith ordered Major Baeke's 11th Panzer Regiment of General Hünersdorff's 6th Panzer Division, supported by the Tiger tanks of the 503d Panzer Detachment, to race northward and prepare to seize Rzhavets and key crossing sites over the Northern Donets the next morning. Exploiting the shock of 6th Panzer's northward lunge, General Schmidt's 19th Panzer would simultaneously leapfrog along the southern bank of the Northern Donets, seize the key town of Krivtsevo, and join the 6th Panzer at Rzhavets after nightfall, in time to assist it in making the vital river crossing operation early on 13 July.

German intelligence believed that primarily infantry forces faced Breith, including elements of the 81st, 89th, 92d, 93d Guards and 305th Rifle Divisions, with a scattering of infantry support tank and antitank guns from understrength Russian tank brigades.[3] Essentially they were correct, for Vatutin was relying on Rotmistrov's and Shumilov's thrusts to distract and contain the III Panzer Corps. A superb German account captured the drama of Breith's race to Rzhavets:

> Breith could be relied upon. He was one of the most experienced and most successful tank commanders in the army. . . . The crucial point . . . was that General Breith's III Panzer Corps must get across the Donets.
>
> Rzhavets was twelve miles away from the main battlefield. The roar of the guns at Prokhorovka could be heard from there. The commanders and chiefs of staff of the reinforced 11th Panzer Regiment were sitting beside the command tank of their combat-group leader.
>
> Colonel von Oppeln-Bronikowski was listening to a suggestion by Major Dr. Franz Baeke. Kazachye, eight miles short of the river and the objective of the day's attack, had been reached after a daring raid and much hard fighting. Baeke now suggested that the strongly fortified town of Rzhavets should be taken by a surprise coup during the night of 11/12 July, the Donets River crossed, and a bridgehead established.
>
> Oppeln had misgivings. Divisional orders were that the crossing was to be forced on the following day, after artillery bombardment. Baeke objected that the Russians were there in strength and that a daytime attack was bound to be very costly. A coup under darkness might be easier.
>
> Might! But there was no certainty. However, Oppeln was an experienced tank commander and accepted Baeke's reasoning. He agreed.

Baeke organized the coup in the traditional manner. With his 2d Battalion, 11th Panzer Regiment, and the 2d (armoured infantry carrier) Battalion, 114th Panzer Grenadier Regiment, under Lieutenant Roembke, the small force pushed on towards the river after nightfall. A captured T-34 was placed at the head of the column to deceive the enemy. True, the German cross had been painted on it—but not very large. And at night all cats are gray. What mattered was the silhouette.

Radio silence. No fire to be opened. No talking. But smoking permitted. In fact, the men were encouraged to ride on top of the tanks, relaxed and smoking, as if this was a normal movement by a unit. "But not a single word in German," the company commanders had impressed on their men.

The ghost column moved on. It was led by Baeke in person, then came a troop of tanks and a few armoured infantry carriers with grenadiers and engineers, then the command tanks. There was only the rumble of the engines and the clank of the chains. Enemy columns passed shoulder to shoulder. The silhouette of the T-34 at the head of the German unit deceived the Russians.

They moved past manned and well-established emplacements of anti-tank guns and multiple rockets. The moon shed a dim light. The Russians did not budge. Sleepily they were leaning in their positions along the road. They were used to such columns. All day long Soviet formations had been rumbling past them. Baeke overtook an enemy infantry column. Fortunately no Soviet soldier thought of hitching a ride on the tanks.[4]

In this manner, Breith and Baeke stealthily penetrated the infantry defenses of the Soviet 107th and 81st Guards Rifle Divisions. The frenetic regrouping movements mandated by Vatutin and Kriuchenkin masked their march. The dramatic account continued:

After about six miles [Dr. Baeke records], our T-34 went on strike. Moved no doubt by national sentiments, it stopped and blocked the road. So our men had to climb out of their tanks and in spite of the Russians standing all round them, watching curiously, they had to haul the T-34 off the road and push it into the ditch in order to clear the way for the rest of the formation. In spite of the order that not a word of German was to be spoken, a few German curses were heard. Never before had I winced so much under a curse as at Rzhavets. But the Russians did not notice anything. The crew of our T-34 was picked up, and on we moved.

The first houses of Rzhavets appeared in front of them. And the first Soviet tanks. They were T-34s lined up along the road. Their hatches stood open. The crews were lying in the grass. But worse was to come. Lieutenant Huchtmann, riding in the lead tank, excitedly reported by radio telephone: "Russian tanks coming up to meet us. What am I to do?" Baeke replied: "Take a deep breath so that I can hear it in my earphones, and start counting them."

Huchtmann counted into his microphone: "one—two—three—four—five . . . ten . . . fifteen . . . twenty—twenty-one—twenty-two."

Twenty-two enemy tanks. They moved past the German column, within arm's reach.

Everybody heaved a sigh of relief. But suddenly the Soviet column showed signs of uneasiness. Half a dozen T-34s wheeled out of line and drove back. Had they noticed anything?

Baeke ordered his combat group to move on, in the direction of Rzhavets and in his command tank III, which carried only a wooden dummy gun, he halted across the road. Seven T-34s moved up and placed themselves around Baeke's tank in a semi-circle at roughly twenty yards' distance. They leveled their guns. But evidently they were not quite sure what to do. They were foxed by the darkness. Things were looking bad for Baeke. A wooden gun was not much use. But something had to be done to prevent the whole enterprise from being jeopardized at the last moment. It was too late to bring back the combat group. Baeke therefore decided upon a piece of bravado. With his orderly officer, Lieutenant Zumpel, he jumped out of his command tank. Each of them carried an explosive charge, a "sticky bomb," in each hand. They dashed by the armoured infantry carrier of Sergeant-Cadet Dehen, who was all set, waiting for permission to open fire.

Five leaps. Demolition charge attached to the first enemy tank. A few Soviet infantrymen were sitting on top of it and turned their heads in alarm. One of them raised his rifle, but Baeke snatched it from his hands. He leapt in the ditch for cover. He found himself chest-deep in water. There were two dull explosions. Lieutenant Zumpel, for his part, had attached his demolition charge to the other tank.

Up again. The next two. Back under cover. But this time there was only one bang. The other charge did not go off.

One of the T-34s menacingly traversed its cannon.

Baeke jumped up on one of his own tanks, which was coming up, ducked behind the turret, and yelled: "Open fire!"

The German gun-aimer was quicker than his Russian opponent. One shot and the Soviet tank was knocked out.

But now all hell was let loose. The ghost journey was over. The Russians fired flares. Machine-gun fire rattled wildly from all sides.

Baeke's tanks and armoured infantry carriers raced into the village. Anti-tank gun positions were overrun. Engineers captured a troop of multiple mortars.

From the direction of the river came several dull thuds. "The bridge!" Baeke thought in alarm.

A moment later his tank stood at the bridge over the Donets. The bridge had been blown. The combat group had missed the turn in the village which led to it.

However, engineers and grenadiers managed to reach the far bank by a foot bridge. And the surprise among the Russians was such that the Germans succeeded in forming a bridgehead. At daybreak Baeke's vanguard detachment of 6th Panzer Division was firmly established on the northern bank of the Donets. General von Hünersdorff immediately sent across the 1st Battalion, 114th Panzer Grenadier Regiment, under Captain Oekel. By late afternoon on 12th July the Combat-Group Horst of 19th Panzer Division had also been brought up. The panzer divisions of Breith's corps were able to move across the speedily repaired bridge and to extend the narrow bridgehead. Parts of the overrun Soviet formations, which were trying to fall back to the north, were intercepted.[5]

Baeke's thrust into Rzhavets caught the Soviets by surprise. At the time the 92d Guards Rifle Division and 96th Tank Brigade were regrouping eastward through the town, and it was these forces that Baeke's column met and dispersed. After the sharp fight in the town, the Soviet units continued their march to the east (to block the German thrust on Aleksandrovka), leaving hastily deployed elements of the now-reserve 375th Rifle Division to contest their forward progress. Since these forces were clearly inadequate to the task, a frantic call for help resounded up the Soviet chain of command through the 69th Army to Vatutin at *front.*

The bold night raid by 6th Panzer did not pass without misfortune. Early on 12 July, Luftwaffe He-III bomber aircraft mistakenly attacked the 11th Panzer's command group on the north bank of the Northern Donets, thinking them to be Russians. General von Hünersdorff and fourteen of his officers and men were wounded in this ghastly error.[6] While Hünersdorff chose to remain with his division, Major Bieberstein, commander of the 114th Panzer Grenadier Regiment, and Captain Oekel died of their wounds. Two days later Hünersdorff's military career ended, as he fell victim to a Soviet sniper.[7]

As dramatic as Breith's and Baeke's raid was, by nightfall the III Panzer Corps was still fifteen kilometers from Prokhorovka, and Soviet resistance was stiffening. According to the same candid German source: "But Baeke was unable to exploit his advantage. While he carried out his coup against Rzhavets, the bulk of 6th Panzer Division had been attacking the important high ground of Aleksandrovka, six miles farther east. However, the Soviets vigorously defended this key point of their Donets position in the flank of the German advance. The battalions of the reinforced 4th Panzer Grenadier Regiment were pinned down by heavy enemy fire outside Aleksandrovka."[8] As a result, late on 12 July, Baeke's 11th Panzer Regiment and most of the accompanying 114th Panzer Grenadier Regiment had to halt, turn their positions over to the 19th Panzer, and return to support the 4th Panzer Grenadier Regiment at Aleksandrovka. This deprived Kempf of most of the benefits of 6th Panzer's raid.

The stiffened Soviet resistance was not coincidental, for when he received news of the fall of Rzhavets, Vatutin too had acted decisively. His staff had notified him shortly before 0400 hours about the III Panzer Corps' raid on Rzhavets. Although he had few details of the size and configuration of the German force and the report said that Rzhavets had not yet fallen, Vatutin realized the significance of the German action. Given the short distances involved and the lack of Soviet armor in the area, it was conceivable that the German III Panzer Corps could take a chance, ignore the impending Soviet attacks against their flanks, and thrust directly northward toward Prokhorovka. Conditioned to expect the worst, Vatutin immediately contacted Rotmistrov and ordered him to dispatch his reserves to the Northern Donets.

Rotmistrov acted quickly. Based on initial reports, which did not indicate the size of the attacking German force, he alerted his deputy, General K. G. Trufanov, to prepare his group for movement south. An hour later, after Rotmistrov learned that the German force consisted of around seventy tanks and motorized infantry and that Rzhavets had fallen, he refined Trufanov's orders. According to classified accounts:

At 0500 hours 12 July, the *front* commander ordered the 5th Tank Army commander to throw strong forward detachments rapidly into the Rydinka, Avdeevka, Bol. Pod'iarugi region to halt the German attack and drive him back from Rydinka and Rzhavets. The army commander ordered two detachments be formed under the overall command of his deputy, General Trufanov. The right [flank] detachment consisted of the 11th and 12th Guards Mechanized Brigades of 5th Guards Mechanized Corps and the 26th Guards Tank Brigade of 2d Guards Tank Corps. After the detachment's arrival in Rydinka, Avdeevka region, the 92d Guards Rifle Division and one regiment of the 375th Rifle Division were included in it. The left detachment (the former army forward detachment) consisted of the 1st Separate Motorcycle Regiment, the 53d Guards Tank Regiment, and the 689th and 678th Howitzer Regiments.[9]

Trufanov's force was to cooperate with the 81st, 375th, and 92d Guards Rifle Divisions, which were already in contact with the Germans. Finally, General Popov of the 2d Tank Corps was also ordered to dispatch a brigade southward, but events of 12 July prevented this from occurring.[10] Instead, during the course of 12 July, Major N. A. Kurnosov's 53d Guards Tank Regiment joined Trufanov's force. The combined forces of Group Trufanov and Kriuchenkin's rifle division were to "destroy the enemy in the Rydinka, Rzhavets region and reach the line Shakhovo-Shchelokovo by the end of the first day."[11]

The strongest elements of Trufanov's detachments were the two mechanized brigades. Each had a tank regiment equipped with thirty-two T-34 and sixteen to seventeen T-70 tanks.[12] Late on 11 July, these forces had been in the 5th Guards Mechanized Corps' second echelon and reserve, with orders to exploit the attack of the 29th and 2d Guards Tank Corps on the 12th. In fact, the 12th Brigade's 55th Guards Tank Regiment was already formed and ready to support their attack. This sudden change in plans required wholesale regrouping and the extraction of the 55th Tank Regiment from combat.

Despite these regrouping difficulties, Trufanov acted quickly. He dispatched three reconnaissance detachments from Captain V. P. Kuz'min's 2d Guards Motorcycle Battalion to establish contact with the 26th Guards Tank Brigade and the 81st, 375th, and 92d Guards Rifle Divisions and to determine actual combat conditions. Based on their initial reports, he issued the following orders to his two detachments:

> While delivering a strong flank attack with the forces of the 26th Guards Tank Brigade along the axis Shakhovo-Shchelokovo and with the 11th Guards Mechanized Brigade and 104th Guards Antitank Artillery Regiment on Plota and Rydinka, in cooperation with the 81st Guards Rifle Division, strike a blow against the 19th Panzer Division, halt its attack, and throw it back to the eastern bank of the Northern Donets. . . . The 12th Guards Mechanized Brigade, reinforced by the 1447th Self-propelled Artillery Regiment will strike a blow along the axis Vypolzovka-Rzhavets, Novo-Oskochnoe to destroy the Hitlerite 6th Panzer Division in a meeting battle in the Avdeevka, Bol. Pod'iarugi region, and seize the line Krasnoe Znamia-Vypolzovka-Rzhavets.[13]

The lead elements of Trufanov's two detachments went into action late on 12 July after their strenuous march south. Before the left column reached the Vypolzovka-Aleksandrovka region, the 92d Guards Rifle Division and 96th Tank Brigade, still smarting over their reverse at Rzhavets, struck hard at the 6th Panzer's 4th Panzer Grenadier Regiment on the outskirts of Aleksandrovka, prompting Hünersdorff's decision to move the bulk of his division back across the Northern Donets. By evening Trufanov's left detachment reinforced this Soviet effort. Meanwhile, at 1800 hours the forward elements of Trufanov's right detachment struck German positions at Rydinka and south of Avdeevka. Colonel V. Piskarev's 26th Guards Tank Brigade attacked the southern portion of the 19th Panzer's bridgehead at Shchelokovo, while Colonel N. V. Grishchenko's 11th Guards Mechanized Brigade and Colonel G. Ia. Borisenko's 12th Guards Mechanized Brigade attacked German positions covering Rydinka and Vypolzovka. Not only did these attacks prevent the 19th Panzer from expanding their tenuous bridgehead across the Northern Donets, but they also forced German forces out of Rydinka. The swirling fight ended at nightfall, when Soviet forces dug in and regrouped for a coordinated attack the next morning.

Vatutin's and Rotmistrov's quick action temporarily restored Soviet defenses along the Northern Donets and, most important, prevented the III Panzer Corps from marching northward to Prokhorovka on 12 July. By the time Kempf could react, the critical day had passed. Kempf did react after nightfall to restore his forces' forward momentum. He ordered the 6th Panzer to clear Soviet forces from the Vypolzovka and Aleksandrovka region the following day, while he shifted the 7th Panzer Division northward to join the 19th Panzer in the precious bridgehead. His decision would pay dividends, but too late to affect the outcome of the battle of Prokhorovka to the north or the overall outcome of Citadel.

From the standpoint of the outcome of the critical 12 July struggle at Prokhorovka, far more important developments were unfolding to the west, along the left flank of Hoth's Fourth Panzer Army. There, at the very moment when the XXXXVIII Panzer Corps was poised to thrust across the Psel River and join the II SS Panzer Corps' victorious advance on Oboian', Vatutin struck once again. A violent attack by Katukov's massed armor and infantry of the 22d Guards Rifle Corps forced von Knobelsdorff of the XXXXVIII Panzer Corps to revise his plans. Although, as before, he ultimately defeated Vatutin's riposte, by that time the critical point had passed and the XXXXVIII Panzer Corps' role in Citadel had ended.

Both von Knobelsdorff and Vatutin worked frantically to prepare their forces for crucial action on 12 July. As recorded by the history of the *Gross-deutschland* Division, during the night of 11 and 12 July:

> Elements of the Panzer-Grenadier Division GD were relieved by units of 3d Panzer Division in their former positions and were transferred to the front of the attack lane in the area near Point 260.8 and to the north. The plan was for a continuation of the attack, primarily by the tanks and panzer-fusiliers on 12 July in the direction of the Psel River, the last obstacle in front of Oboyan. It was learned from the division's neighbor on the right, II SS Panzer Corps, that its spearheads had already crossed the river.
>
> The artillery, antitank units and other heavy weapons were the first to be withdrawn from their positions in this reorganization and sent

northeast. The Armoured Reconnaissance Battalion GD had no special role in the new plan. Like the Panzer-Grenadier Regiment GD it remained in the previous combat area at the disposal of the division. The panzer-grenadiers remained in their positions east and southeast of Kalinovka and waited for relief by the 3d Panzer Division. The first of this division's units to arrive, at Point 247.0 south of Kruglik, was the reconnaissance battalion. It relieved the Armored Reconnaissance Battalion GD early the next morning. The Assault Gun Battalion GD was placed under the command of the Panzer-Grenadier Regiment GD in its sector. Sadly, before its departure for the new sector it lost the commander of 2d Battery, Oberleutnant Bremer, who was killed by a sudden enemy artillery barrage.[14]

While the *Grossdeutschland* Division concentrated along and west of the Oboian' road, the 3d Panzer took over responsibility for defense of the Berezovka-Verkhopen'e sector, and the 332d Infantry Division filled in 3d Panzer's former lines north of the Pena River forward of Rakovo. In turn, the 255th Infantry Division itself stretched its lines northward to Mikhailovka. While this "castling" of forces northward by the XXXXVIII Panzer Corps provided the forces needed for its critical assault, inevitably it left its flanks weaker than ever.

Unbeknownst to the *Grossdeutschland* soldiers, the artillery barrage that killed Lieutenant Bremer also announced the opening of Vatutin's and Katukov's new offensive. Soon, renewed fighting would inexorably suck these Germans into the vortex of a new struggle and away from the 11th Panzer Division and Oboian'. By early morning on 12 July, Katukov's forces had completed their somewhat hasty preparations for the new assault. General Burkov's 10th Tank Corps, now lacking only its 11th Motorized Rifle Brigade and numbering about 100 tanks, was poised in jumping-off positions on the western outskirts of Noven'koe with the massed riflemen of Major General V. P. Kotel'nikov's 219th Rifle Division. The combined force had orders to advance at daybreak toward Berezovka and Syrtsevo. To the south, forward of Melovoe, General Kravchenko's 5th Guards Tank Corps, with about 70 tanks, deployed with Colonel S. I. Tsukarev's 184th Rifle Division with orders to attack toward Shepelovka and Lukhanino. Getman's shattered 6th Tank Corps, now refitting in army reserve and numbering fewer than 50 tanks, received orders to deploy a mixed brigade into second echelon behind Popov's and Kravchenko's advancing corps and assist when and where required.[15]

In addition, Vatutin ordered his forces along and east of the Oboian' road, specifically the 6th Guards Army's 23d Rifle and the 3d Mechanized and 31st Tank Corps, to first defend and then, when and if the Germans gave way, to join in a general counterthrust all along their front. The same orders went to the 5th Guards Army's 32d Guards Rifle Corps, whose fresh 13th, 66th, and 97th Guards Rifle Divisions now filled in the Soviet line from just east of the Oboian' road eastward to the bank of the Psel River.

Katukov's cobbled force struck at 0900 hours on 12 July. Kravchenko's tank corps smashed through the 332d Infantry Division's defenses near Chapaev and produced hours of bitter fighting, which did not die down until 1700 hours, when Kravchenko's tankers were on the outskirts of Rakovo. Only Kravchenko's reduced tank strength prevented his force from driving the 332d Division into the Pena River. To the north, Burkov's 10th Tank Corps made even more spectacular progress. The 10th Tank Corps history described the corps' initial assault: "After a strong artillery and aviation preparation, at 0800 hours 12 July, the corps went over to the offensive while operating on the left flank of 1st Tank Army's shock group. The 183d and 178th Tank Brigades attacked in first echelon, reinforced, accordingly, by the 727th Antitank Artillery and 287th Mortar Regiments. The 186th Tank Brigade and the 1450th Self-propelled Artillery Regiment made up the corps second echelon."[16]

After clearing German forward outposts from Noven'koe, Colonel G. I. Andrushchenko's 183d Brigade struck out for Verkhopen'e. A tank platoon commanded by Lieutenant M. Kadiev, which was reconnoitering Andrushchenko's way, lunged through Urochishche Tol'stoe (Tol'stoy Woods), severed the Berezovka-Kruglik road, and dispersed a small German force defending along the road. By 1700 hours, after a running fight with small tank elements of the 3d Panzer Division, its parent brigade advanced twelve to fifteen kilometers and approached Verkhopen'e from the west. By this time, the neighboring 178th and 186th Tank Brigades, together with riflemen from the 219th Rifle Division, drove 3d Panzer Division forces back to the outskirts of Verkhopen'e and Berezovka.

Although the 3d Panzer Division mounted heavy counterattacks in late afternoon, it was unable to restore its positions. By day's end its strength had dwindled to fewer than forty tanks. Help was needed to forestall collapse of the XXXXVIII Panzer Corps' flank defenses. General von Mellenthin summarized the grim events:

> The last stages of the [Grossdeutschland's] relief were carried out under heavy enemy shelling, and the men of Grossdeutschland left their trenches to the accompaniment of the battle noises of a Russian counterattack. Their fears, alas, came true, for that very night the 3d Panzer Division was thrown out of its forward positions. . . . On the morning of 12 July . . . heavy firing was heard from the west, and the news from 3d Panzer was not encouraging. . . . On the afternoon of 13 July, the corps commander . . . gave orders which left no hope for any advance to the north; in fact, the division was again to attack westward. . . . Indeed

the situation on the left flank had deteriorated to such a degree that an attack northwards was no longer possible. On 12 and 13 July the 3d Panzer Division had lost Beresowka, had been driven off the Rakowa-Kruglik road and had been compelled to give up Height 247.0 under stubborn onslaughts by Russian armor. The enemy was being reinforced, and the 3d Panzer Division was now too weak to stem the Russian advance from the west.[17]

To make matters worse for *Grossdeutschland,* at the same time its own elements defending west of Kalinovka also came under strong attack by the Soviet 204th Rifle Division and 86th Tank Brigade. *Grossdeutschland's* history described the resulting dilemma:

Scarcely had the Armoured Reconnaissance Battalion GD been relieved at Point 247.0, when at 06.20 [0820 Moscow time] the enemy attacked east with strong tank and infantry forces from the area west of Kruglik—Point 254.5 and against Point 247.0. The latter position was soon lost, and the Armoured Reconnaissance Battalion GD withdrew to the south. At the same time, enemy armour and infantry attacked from Kalinovka against the positions of II and II Battalions, Panzer Grenadier Regiment GD. The situation quickly became critical. II Battalion under Major Bethke, which was tied up by the enemy coming out of Kalinovka, found itself in a particularly precarious situation, which temporarily forced the battalion to withdraw from its positions. . . . The battalion retook its former positions at about 18.00. Only then did the enemy attacks subside. . . .

As a result of these heavy defensive battles, the division's plans for a further advance to the north were initially overtaken. The units already on the move were recalled and placed in positions behind especially threatened points. The panzers stood ready to counterattack, everything was organized for defense. The danger now lay on the left, west flank, especially since the 3d Panzer Division was apparently too weak to win through there. The villages of Gertzovka and Berezovka were back in enemy hands, and the danger that Soviet forces were advancing into the rear of the German attack divisions was increasing.[18]

Deprived of its opportunity to join the triumphal march on Oboian' and Kursk, *Grossdeutschland* Division reluctantly deployed to meet the new, all too familiar threat. To the north along the Oboian' road, the 11th Panzer, now about fifty tanks strong, probed along its front but was unable to advance further. Throughout the day, its troops listened in fascination and expectation to the rumble of firing to the east and the west. But the order to advance never came. Instead, late in the afternoon, massed Soviet troops supported by tanks struck their positions. Heavy fighting produced local Soviet gains, but no major dent in the 11th Panzer's defenses. The bloodletting ended shortly after darkness as thunderstorms wet down the field of battle and Vatutin called off the attacks along and east of the Oboian' road.

Vatutin's main counterstroke by his 5th Guards and 10th Tank Corps had achieved its purpose. The remaining attacks by the 6th Guards Army's 23d Guards Rifle Corps and the 5th Guards Army's 32d Guards Rifle Corps were simply designed to add insult to injury, for by afternoon Vatutin knew that von Knobelsdorff's beleaguered 11th Panzer Division would not be able to respond. What von Knobelsdorff did or did not do in coming days mattered little to Vatutin, because whatever he did would be anticlimactic.

Late on 12 July, commanders on both sides assessed the grim consequences of the battle and decided what to do next. *Stavka* representative Vasilevsky, still with Rotmistrov at the 5th Guards Tank Army command post, coordinated with Vatutin at *front,* and the two agreed that the situation was still serious enough to warrant continuation of the pressure on German forces across the entire front. This was particularly important since the shock groups of the Western and Briansk Fronts had commenced Operation Kutuzov, the first phase of the Soviet offensive on that very morning (see Chapter 7). This major operation and the Allied landings in Italy were bound to have a negative effect on the German High Command. Based on these discussions, Vatutin issued orders to all *front* forces to "prevent further enemy movement on Prokhorovka from the west and the south; liquidate the enemy grouping that had penetrated to the north bank of the Psel River by the joint operations of part of the forces of the 5th Guards Army and two brigades of the 5th Guards Mechanized Corps (5th Guards Tank Army); liquidate units of the German III Panzer Corps that had penetrated to the Rzhavets region; and continue the offensive of the 1st Tank, 6th Guards, and the right flank of 5th Guards Army."[19]

Finally, he assigned the 2d Air Army the task of destroying enemy forces penetrating from the Kurasovka, Novo-Oskochnoe, and Kazach'e regions in front of Group Trufanov.[20] After planning was complete for operations on 13 July, the *Stavka* ordered Vasilevsky to join the Southwestern Front to coordinate its upcoming counteroffensive operations. Late in the evening, Marshal G. K. Zhukov flew to Vatutin's headquarters to assume the task of coordinating the Voronezh and Steppe Fronts' operations and preparing them for a decisive counteroffensive. It was a clear indication that *Stavka* thoughts were already turning from defensive to offensive operations.[21]

Meanwhile, Rotmistrov ordered all of his corps to fortify themselves in positions they had seized that day and to organize strong artillery and anti-tank defenses against the German attacks he was convinced would material-ize the following morning.[22] Throughout the night his forces worked feverishly to replenish fuel and ammunition, resupply all other necessities, and evacuate the many wounded. The dead were buried, most in unmarked graves. All eyes were still on the south. There, in the critical Rzhavets sector, General Trufanov refined his attack plans for an assault the following morning designed, once and for all, to halt the forward progress of the German III Panzer Corps.

Despite the local successes of Army Detachment Kempf on 12 July, the surprises, setbacks, and disappointments experienced by Hoth's Fourth Panzer Army posed major questions and challenges to every German level of command. Moreover, the situation had to be judged within the depressing context of what was happening in Italy and elsewhere along the Eastern Front, particularly opposite Orel. Despite the complexity of the situation and the doubts in many quarters that further attack was useful, inertia ruled for one more day. Hoth issued orders that scaled down significantly the offensive aims of the previous day. All the while, von Manstein at Army Group South remained confident that something positive could still be gleaned from the heavy fighting.

Hoth's orders, as well as those of Kempf, continued the offensive in key sectors. Transmitted through army and corps level, *Leibstandarte's* order reflected that cautious optimism:

The *Oberbefehlshaber* of *Heeresgruppe Sud* [Army Group South], Generalfeldmarschall von Manstein, wishes to express his thanks to and admiration for the Division of the II. SS-Panzerkorps for their outstanding success and exemplary behavior in this fighting.

The II. SS-Panzerkorps is to orchestrate cooperative action between the *LAH* and the SS *T*-Division in order to destroy the enemy forces which have moved across the eastern and western banks of the Pssel in the area southeast and southwest of Petrowka. It is to hold the line captured by its outer wing against enemy flank attacks.

The *DR* [Division] is to expand the line it has captured to a full-fledged main battle line. . . .

The *LAH* is to hold the line it has captured. On its right wing and its front, it should be fortified to a full-fledged battle line. The Division is to stand ready to move out as soon as the *T*-Division's attack from the northeast becomes effective to destroy the enemy on its left flank in cooperation with the *T*-Division.

The *T*-Division is to continue its right wing attack in the Pssel valley to the northeast and is to move forces as strong as possible (at least one armoured force) onto the ridge of hill north of the Pssel as far as the road from Beregowoje to Kartschewka. It is to force a crossing over the Pssel to the southeast and to destroy the enemy forces southeast and southwest of Petrovka in cooperation with the *LAH*.

New boundary line: between the *DR* on the right and the *LAH* on the left: northern edge of Iwanowskij Wysselok—northern edge of Storoshewoje—southern edge of Jamki.[23]

This order and similar orders to Army Detachment Kempf indicated that von Manstein and Hoth, at the least, intended to encircle and destroy Soviet forces still remaining within the grasp of the II SS and III Panzer Corps. What more could be accomplished depended entirely on Soviet actions the next day and, more important, on decisions made in ensuing days within the German High Command.

STALEMATE, 13 JULY

While the German High Command agonized over the fate of Operation Citadel, fighting raged on across the breadth of Army Group South's front, as if the struggling armies were addicted to the sounds and horrors they had experienced during the previous week's fighting. The tone of official orders, some strident, others resigned, seemed to indicate that all understood that resolution was near at hand. Pride, stubbornness, mind-numbing exhaustion, and often sheer fatalism alone drove the soldiers on, into the meat grinder that was Kursk.

Despite the orders and the lofty aims they reflected, combat itself on 13 July clearly demonstrated that a turning point was at hand (see Map 22). Along the Prokhorovka axis, combat degenerated into virtual stalemate, as both Soviet and German forces utterly failed to achieve their desired ends. To the south, along the Northern Donets River, the III Panzer Corps' dramatic advance of 12 July was reduced into a slugfest with defending Group Trufanov. In the west the XXXXVIII Panzer Corps almost mechanically mustered its forces for yet another counterattack to the west, as if to exact revenge against the Soviet armored force that had denied the German corps its glory at Kursk. Against this almost surreal combat mosaic, both High Commands reached decisions that would inexorably alter the course of the war.

On the morning of 13 July, remaining German hopes rested on the progress of the II SS Panzer Corps' *Totenkopf* Division and III Panzer Corps. The former had seized a narrow but tenuous salient that extended deep into Soviet defenses north of the Psel River. Hausser still felt that if his *Leibstandarte* and *Das Reich* Divisions could muster enough strength to reach the outskirts of Prokhorovka, *Totenkopf's* threat to their flank would compel the Russians to withdraw from the city. Then, reasoned Hausser, a linkup between his corps and Kempf's III Panzer Corps might restore energy and some momentum to the German attack.

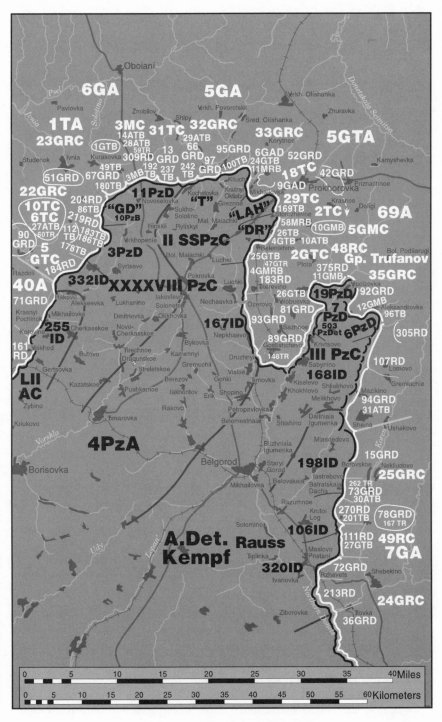

Map 22. Voronezh Front, 13 July 1943

Although the attrition caused by the previous day's ferocious battle had taken a severe toll on the three SS divisions, repaired tanks made up much of the difference. While the corps lost between 60 and 70 of its armored vehicles in combat on 12 July, it now counted just under 250 tanks and assault guns (including 4 Tigers and about 11 T-34s).[24] *Leibstandarte* had fallen in strength to 50 tanks and 20 assault guns, *Das Reich* had repaired enough vehicles to rise to 83 tanks and 24 assault guns, and *Totenkopf* had 54 tanks and 20 assault guns.[25] Clearly, however, the panzer corps had also exacted a terrible toll on Soviet armor. Therefore, with both Hoth's and von Manstein's agreement, Hausser made arrangements to continue his attacks. Ominously, however, that morning Hitler summoned von Manstein to the *Wolfsschanze* (Wolf's Lair), Hitler's headquarters in East Prussia, for consultations regarding future strategic options.

After a relatively quiet night in the Prokhorovka sector, at 0730 hours Soviet forces conducted reconnaissances-in-force across their front to feel out German dispositions and to determine their intentions (see Map 23). However, Vatutin and Rotmistrov had no intention of resuming their assaults across the bloody fields south of the Psel River. Now their attention was riveted on dealing with *Totenkopf*'s salient north of the river and the approach of the III Panzer Corps from the south. To that end, they had split General Skvortsov's 5th Guards Mechanized Corps in two and had ordered each half to spearhead one of the two critical operations. His 10th Guards Mechanized and 24th Guards Tank Brigade joined with rifle forces to eradicate *Totenkopf*'s threat in the north. To the south his 11th and 12th Guards Mechanized Brigades, which with the 2d Guards Tank Corps' 26th Guards Tank Brigade formed the nucleus of Group Trufanov, were to deal with the threat posed by the III Panzer Corps.

Rotmistrov's forces north of the Psel River had gone into action against *Totenkopf* in piecemeal fashion the previous evening, but the uncoordinated night attacks had failed to prevent the Germans from cutting the Beregovoe-Kartashevka road.[26] By morning, however, the Soviet assaults intensified as the Germans felt the full weight of the Soviet 10th Guards Mechanized and 24th Guards Tank Brigades and the former's 51st Guards Tank Regiment. A Soviet account noted the ferocity of the fighting:

> To cooperate in restoring the situation of the left flank of 5th Guards Army, the [5th Guards Tank] army commander directed 5th Guards Mechanized Corps' 10th Guards Mechanized Brigade to move forward to the region of Ostren'kov village (ten kilometers north of Prokhorovka) with the mission of cooperating with 33d Guards Rifle Corps in halting the German advance in a northeastern direction.
>
> The brigade, under the command of Colonel I. B. Mikhailov and his chief of staff, Lieutenant Colonel I. T. Noskov, reached Ostren'kov and,

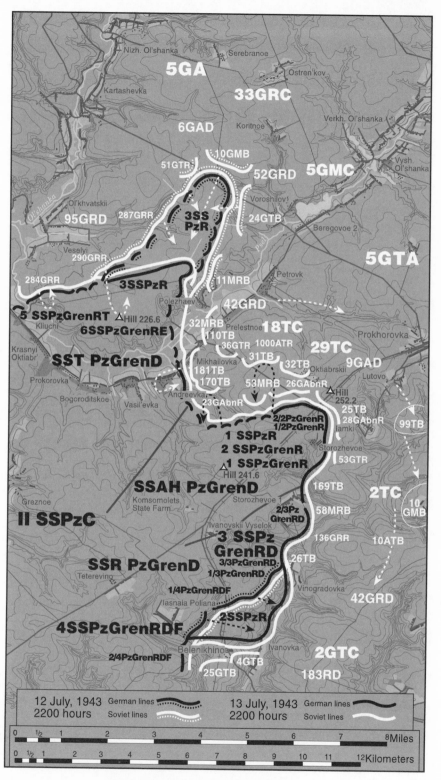

Map 23. Prokhorovka, 12–13 July 1943

in cooperation with the 95th and 52d Guards Rifle Divisions, which were engaged in heavy fighting with elements of 11th Panzer Division and SS Division "Death's Head," by a decisive meeting blow, halted the attack by the Hitlerites, who were forced back on the defense. Tankmen of the 51st Guards Tank Regiment, commanded by Colonel D. Ia. Klinfel'd, conducted fierce combat with the enemy tanks. While skillfully maneuvering on the field of battle and delivering flank blows, their fire inflicted heavy losses on the enemy. . . . By the end of 13 July, they were ordered into 5th Guards Tank Army's reserve at Zhilomest'e (nine kilometers southeast of Prokhorovka).[27]

The Soviet counterattacks north of the Psel raised concern in the II SS Panzer Corps and forced Hausser to refine his day's objectives. At 1130 hours the Ia (operations officer) of *Leibstandarte* was briefed by his counterpart from *Totenkopf*. The latter reported that *Totenkopf*'s panzer group had managed to reach the road from Prokhorovka to Kartashevka as ordered, but that he had to decide whether to pull them back from that position because the enemy had been attacking its left wing since dawn with numerically superior forces moving in from the north. "A concentrated attack on Prochorowka," he added, "could not be expected, as far as the *T*-Division was considered."[28]

Fifteen minutes later, after a short conference at corps headquarters, Hausser ordered the *Leibstandarte* to employ its reformed panzer group in an attack on Soviet positions northeast of Oktiabr'skii State Farm. At the same time, the division's reconnaissance battalion was to attack on the panzer group's left flank along the south bank of the Psel from Andreevka toward Mikhailovka "with the intent of solidifying the loose contact it [*Leibstandarte*] had with the *T*-Division in Andrejewka [Andreevka]."[29] The panzer group and reconnaissance battalion attacked at 1200 hours, but after encountering a hail of Soviet fire and strong resistance, both attacks soon faltered. During a sharp thirty-minute engagement the panzer group seized a single hill along the ridge northwest of Oktiabr'skii State Farm but then ran smack into a solid antitank front reinforced by dug-in tanks on the far side of the ridge. Simultaneously, the reconnaissance battalion penetrated into Mikhailovka but was forced to withdraw to Hill 241.6 by heavy Soviet counterattacks and devastating artillery and antitank fire from the northern bank of the Psel. Two hours later the Soviets compounded German consternation by commencing heavy armored counterattacks in both sectors.[30]

Hausser's assault tactics had played right into Vatutin's and Rotmistrov's hands. Both of the Soviet commanders had planned to open the day on the defensive in the critical sector between the Psel River and the Prokhorovka road and then to counterattack as required. To that end, during the night they formed the 18th and 29th Tank Corps into several distinctive defensive belts, with infantry, motorized riflemen, and dug-in tanks forward, backed up by strong dug-in armor and antitank strong points formed in solid ranks to the rear. Farther to the rear, they placed the corps' remaining armor, poised in assembly areas from which they could counterattack.

In this fashion the remnants of the 29th Tank Corps' 31st and 32d Tank Brigades took some measure of revenge on the Germans who had ravished them the previous day. When *Leibstandarte's* panzer group ground its way through the infantry of the 9th Guards Airborne Division and the 53d Motorized Rifle Brigade, it ran into the two Soviet tank brigades backed up by the remaining guns of the 1000th Antitank Artillery Regiment. Within hours after repelling *Leibstandarte's* final offensive effort, the two Soviet brigades again went over to the attack with supporting infantry, only to be halted and thrown back just north of Komsomolets State Farm. *Leibstandarte* reported, "At 12.40 hours [1440 Moscow Time], this enemy attack collapsed at our main battle line. Our defensive success is to be ascribed primarily to the Artillerie-Regiment *LAH,* the Werferregiment [rocket-launcher regiment] 55, and the concentrated fire of our heavy infantry weapons."[31]

To the north the Soviet 33d Guards Rifle Corps' 42d Guards Rifle Division infantry, which had been committed along the banks of the Psel early in the morning, absorbed the initial attack by the *Leibstandarte's* reconnaissance battalion. Then the 18th Tank Corps' 170th and 181st Tank Brigades launched counterattacks that drove the Germans back to Andreevka. General Rotmistrov later recorded the action:

> That morning, while I was at 29th Tank Corps' CP, the Hitlerites first attacked 18th Tank Corps after a short artillery preparation. More than fifty enemy tanks firing from the march or from short halts, followed by ranks of motorized infantry, advanced on our positions. Allowing the Germans to approach to a distance of 500 to 600 meters, our antitank artillery and tanks opened direct fire on them. Several enemy machines froze in place with broken tracks or began to rush about the fields engulfed in flames. Those which still moved forward exploded on mines. However, the Fascist motorized infantry still came forward. But, then a volley of Lieutenant Colonel A. I. Semchenko's 80th Guards Mortar Regiment followed. The fire of our Katiushas always instilled terror in the Fascists. Suffering great losses, the enemy was forced to fall back, abandoning the burning tanks and the bodies of his dead soldiers and officers.
>
> While covering its right flank with part of its force because of the withdrawal of 5th Guards Army's left flank, using its main force, 18th Tank Corps developed the attack on Andreevka and, after a short battle, penetrated into the village. Its 181st Tank Brigade, commanded by Lieutenant Colonel V. A. Puzyrev, suddenly attacked a column of enemy tanks, which

was advancing toward Mikhailovka, and, pursuing the withdrawing enemy, captured Vasil'evka.[32]

The failure of the *Leibstandarte* to crack Soviet defenses near Oktiabr'skii State Farm condemned the *Totenkopf* advance north of the river to failure. With its southern flank unsecured and Soviet attacks raging along its flanks and to its front, the division had no choice but to withdraw its panzer regiment to its starting positions. Accordingly, Soviet classified accounts recorded: "By its active operations, the 5th Guards Zimovnikovskii Mechanized Corps improved its position on the right flank of the army. Its 10th Guards Mechanized and 24th Guards Tank Brigades, having exploited the embarrassment of the enemy in its battles with units of our 18th Tank Corps, went over to the offensive, drove the Germans from Polezhaev, captured Hill 226, and, after regrouping, began to attack in the direction of Krasnyi Oktiabr'. However, meeting organized enemy opposition, they were unable to capture this point."[33]

Farther south, in accordance with Hausser's orders, the SS Division *Das Reich* improved its defenses throughout the day and reconfigured its depleted armor for a thrust south of Prokhorovka to link up with the III Panzer Corps. During the day it attacked locally north of Belenikhino to drive back Soviet armor from the 2d Guards Tank Corps and to improve its jumping-off positions for the new assault planned for 14 July. The 2d Guards Tank Corps, which had dispatched its 26th Guards Tank Brigade to the south, could do little to prevent the German gains, especially since the 2d Tank Corps on its right flank had already been decimated. By 1500 hours lead elements of *Das Reich* captured the village of Storozhevoe 1 and reached the western outskirts of Vinogradovka.

The subsequent movement of the 10th Guards Mechanized Brigade into army reserve signaled the end of the German threat north of the Psel and in the immediate vicinity of Prokhorovka. By nightfall on 13 July, the II SS Panzer Corps' *Leibstandarte* and *Totenkopf* Divisions had shot their bolt. At the same time, however, Rotmistrov's hasty movement of the 5th Guards Mechanized Corps' 10th Guards Mechanized Brigade into reserve south of Prokhorovka also evidenced his and Vatutin's increasing concern over the deteriorating situation to the south. Although they were worried primarily about the III Panzer Corps' future movements, *Das Reich's* activity also bothered them. To assuage those growing concerns, late on 13 July, Vatutin also ordered that the 42d Guards Rifle Division be shifted from the Psel valley southward to confront *Das Reich*.

Along the banks of the Northern Donets River, twelve kilometers south of Kursk, combat grew in intensity as General Breith regrouped his III Panzer Corps into the bridgehead across the river. The swirling fight on 13 July in this region was initiated by General Trufanov's left column. This column, which contained the 53d Guards Tank Regiment, reinforced the 92d Guards Rifle Division and 96th Tank Brigade near Aleksandrovka and attempted to exploit Breith's concentration of both his 19th and 7th Panzer Divisions in the Northern Donets bridgeheads. While Trufanov's left column attacked German forces on the outskirts of Aleksandrovka, his 12th Guards Mechanized Brigade (of his right column) drove into the 6th Panzer Division's lines between Vypolzovka and Aleksandrovka. To add confusion to the affair, both the 26th Guards Tank Brigade and the 11th Guards Mechanized Brigades of Trufanov's right column assaulted German positions at Rydinka just as the 19th Panzer Division was attacking to expand the bridgehead. Although the 19th Panzer's thrust was ultimately contained, the heavy fighting inflicted heavy losses on Trufanov's force. Even worse, by day's end the 7th Panzer Division had fully concentrated in the bridgehead and prepared to join 19th Panzer in a concerted drive to the north at dawn the next day.

As promising as these developments seemed for those German commands participating in them, by this time they were irrelevant to the outcome of Operation Citadel. Far more telling actions had already been made hundreds of kilometers to the west at Hitler's headquarters in East Prussia.

DECISION

On 13 July, in response to Adolf Hitler's summons, his two army group commanders, Marshals von Manstein and von Kluge, flew to *Fuehrer* Headquarters at the *Wolfsschanze*. Although concerned by the state of operations in the East, Hitler remained preoccupied with the American and British invasion of Sicily. He was convinced the Italians had no intention of defending the island and, in turn, that all of Italy was in danger. In order to defend Italy and the Balkans, the dictator announced his intention to cancel Citadel and withdraw reserves for use in the West. He had no choice but to defend Italy with reliable German troops, and the best of these were in the East. In addition, Hitler was concerned about the situation on the Eastern Front, in particular about the Soviet Orel offensive, which had begun the day before, and the apparent buildup for an offensive against Army Group South in the Donbas south of Khar'kov (see Chapter 7). Citadel had cost Model's Ninth Army 20,000 casualties, and now most of Model's and the army group's already severely worn mobile forces were being sucked into operations north and east of Orel.

Faced with the failure of Ninth Army north of Kursk and the threat posed by new and apparently successful Soviet Orel offensives, von Kluge was only too willing to agree with Hitler. Any other course might jeopardize his army group as well as the entire German field army. Von Manstein, however, discounted the threat of Soviet attack south of Khar'kov and protested that a renewed effort by the Ninth and Fourth Panzer Armies might yet achieve victory. So convinced was von Manstein that he could prevail at Kursk, he was prepared to commit his operational reserve, the XXIV Panzer Corps (the SS *Wiking* Panzer Grenadier and 23d Panzer Divisions), against the tired Soviet defenders. In fact, he had already moved the corps northward into assembly areas around Khar'kov.[34] Von Manstein also knew that he argued in the name of his army commanders, Hoth and Kempf, both of whom remained bellicose and confident that victory could be achieved. At the least, von Manstein was convinced his forces could complete the task of destroying Soviet strategic reserves.

Hitler categorically rejected von Manstein's counsel. The most that Hitler would concede was that Army Group South might continue its offensive for several days in hopes of destroying the Soviet operational reserves and thereby preventing any Red attack for the rest of the summer.[35] The next day Hitler placed the final seal on the fate of Operation Citadel. He appointed Model commander of both the Ninth and Second Panzer Armies and ordered him to contain the Soviet offensive near Orel and to restore the original front. Four days later, on 17 July, OKH ordered the II SS Panzer Corps to be withdrawn from combat and prepared for movement to the West. A day later two other divisions, including *Grossdeutschland*, were transferred from Army Group South to Army Group Center. What von Manstein, Model, and even Hitler did not know, however, and probably could not comprehend, was that the German Army in the East now faced the most ambitious Soviet strategic offensive of the war, one that would forever end major German offensive operations in the East. Mollified to a degree, von Manstein immediately flew back to his army group to fulfill at least the promise to savage Soviet reserves where he could.

Von Manstein was a man of his word. As disappointed as he was, he was determined to do what he had promised Hitler he would do. He would destroy as many Soviet forces as possible along Hoth's and Kempf's front. Translated into operational terms, he would strike back at Katukov's forces and eradicate Soviet forces lodged in the salient between the Fourth Panzer Army and Army Detachment Kempf. From 14 through 15 July von Manstein set about fulfilling his promise in what became a fitting conclusion to the frustrating Citadel phase of the Battle of Kursk.

DENOUEMENT, 14–17 JULY

On 14 July the *Grossdeutschland* Division, regrouped from its jumping-off positions astride the Oboian' road, joined the 3d Panzer Division in a counterattack against the Soviet 5th Guards and 10th Tank Corps. The two-day attack savaged the two Soviet corps, as well as the remnants of Getman's 6th Tank Corps, which had reinforced them on 13 July, and cooperating Soviet rifle divisions, and drove them back to their start point of 12 July. Soviet classified accounts laconically recorded: "As a result of an enemy offensive on 14 July from the Rakovo, Berezovka region against the right flank of 6th Guards Army, after a heavy resistance, our units withdrew 1.5 to 2 kilometers. . . . 1st Tank Army formations continued the offensive, but had no success. On 15 July the army was ordered on the defense and prepared to hand over its sector to forces of 6th and 5th Guards Armies. On the night of 16 July the 1st Tank Army entered *front* second echelon."[36] Von Mellenthin, who also provided an account of the action during this stage of the operation in the XXXXVIII Panzer Corps' sector, astutely remarked: "All of this was certainly a success of some sorts; the dangerous situation on the left wing had been rectified, and the 3d Panzer Division had been given some support. But *Grossdeutschland* was dangerously weak after heavy fighting lasting for ten days, while the Russian striking power had not appreciably diminished. In fact, it seemed to have increased. . . . By the evening of 14 July it was obvious that the timetable of the German attack had been completely upset. Of the eighty Panthers available when battle was joined only a few were left on 14 July."[37] On the Soviet side, Zhukov and Vatutin simply understood that Katukov had done what was required of him. He had denied the *Grossdeutschland* Division and its parent XXXXVIII Panzer Corps the opportunity of participating in a triumphal German entrance into Kursk.

From von Manstein's perspective, it was essential for his forces to establish a continuous front somewhere near Prokhorovka before operations ground to a halt. While this would help elevate German morale after the failure of Citadel, it would also enable him to inflict maximum damage on Soviet reserves. Orders issued by the army group on the evening of 13 July reflected von Manstein's intent. The II SS Panzer Corps' order for the new operation, code-named Roland, read:

1. Division-*DR* is to continue the attack started on 13.7.1943 across the line Iwanovka-Winogradowka. It is to capture the enemy positions on the eastern bank of this sector and is to attack Praworot [Pravorot'] as soon as the Panzerregiment has moved up. . . .

2. The *LAH* is to hold its current line at first and prepare itself to move its right wing via Jamki on Prochorowka as soon as the attack by Division-DR on Praworot and Prochorowka becomes effective.

3. The *T*-Division is to hold its current position against any and all attacks.[38]

At the same time, Kempf ordered General Breith to complete the concentration of the III Panzer Corps' 7th and 19th Panzer Divisions in the

Rydinka bridgehead and attack northward and northwestward to link up with *Das Reich*, to clear Soviet forces from the region between the Lipovyi Donets and Northern Donets Rivers, to destroy as many of these Soviet forces as possible, and, if feasible, to capture Prokhorovka. As the panzer divisions completed their deadly work, the 168th and 167th Infantry Divisions, operating along the Fourth Panzer Army's and Army Detachment Kempf's inner flanks, would "clean up" encircled Soviet forces and consolidate the panzer corps' gains. Simultaneously, the 6th Panzer Division would attack Soviet positions at Aleksandrovka and north of Vypolzovka, east of the Northern Donets, to protect the III Panzer Corps' right flank.

Vatutin and Zhukov anticipated the German assaults and did all in their power to halt them. They dispatched all available armored reserves southward to assist Group Trufanov, including the remainder of General Skvortsov's 5th Guards Mechanized Corps. At the same time, however, their concern over the Prokhorovka sector required that they leave Rotmistrov's 18th and 29th Tank Corps there, with orders to hold firm and deny the II SS Panzer Corps any offensive success. Subsequent combat on 14 July indicated that the salient between the two branches of the Donets River could not be held. As described by classified Soviet accounts:

> During the course of 14 and 15 July concentrated enemy blows from the Iasnaia Poliana and Shchelakovo regions in the general direction of Shakhovo attempted to encircle the right wing of 69th Army. Given the threat of encirclement posed to five of 69th Army's divisions, on the night of 15 July the decision was made about their withdrawal from the developing sack.
>
> On 15 July, in fierce battle and under the cover of rear guards, the divisions withdrew to the line Storozhevoe, Zhilomest'e, Novoselovka, Shipy. Thus, the persistent and long-standing enemy attempts to encircle the army's right wing were unsuccessful.[39]

There is no doubt but that the fighting during these final two days of Citadel was as bitter as it had been in previous days, particularly in *Das Reich's* and the III Panzer Corps' sector. *Das Reich's* history recorded:

> At 0400 hours on the 14th, *Das Reich* opened Corps' new drive with an artillery and Nebelwerfer barrage followed by an infantry assault spearheaded by the panzer grenadiers of the 1st and 2d Battalions of *Der Fuehrer*. Stolidly they accepted casualties from the extensive minefields across which they marched to gain the high ground south-west of Pravorot. The first houses in Belenichino, a village at the foot of the high ground, were taken by midday, when the fighting was from house to house and

hand to hand. Twelve of the Russian tanks which intervened in the battle were destroyed by grenadiers using hollow-charge grenades, while overhead Stukas dive-bombed the Russians, destroying their resistance inside and outside the village. With Belenichino at last in German hands the grenadier battalions regrouped under the protection of the panzer regiment whose counterattacks threw the Russians back in confusion. Panzer regiment then led the division's attack for what remained of the day and continued this throughout. But the attack which began with good success during the night of the 15th lost momentum as heavy rain washed away the road surfaces. Corps' other order, to gain touch with III Corps, was accomplished when the Panzer Regiment met the leading elements of 7th Panzer. That junction surrounded the enemy forces in the Gostischevo-Leski area and destroyed them.[40]

The account then qualified the apparent success, noting, "Despite this successful operation it was clear that Citadel could not succeed, for on both the northern and southern flanks the German advances had not gained the ground expected of them and there was still more than 130 kilometers between the pincers of Kempf's and Hoth's armies—130 kilometers of trenches, minefields, and Russian armor."[41] What this account might have but did not add was that the bulk of Soviet forces in the Donets salient survived to fight another day and that on 15 July Soviet resolve to win had not flagged.

The III Panzer Corps' headlong attack from the Northern Donets River bridgehead did succeed. Group Trufanov, now reinforced with massive new antitank forces, bent and gave way but not until the 69th Army's divisions had executed their withdrawal orders.[42] Supported by the 5th Guards Mechanized Corps' armor, Trufanov's group and the half-encircled rifle divisions conducted a fighting withdrawal back to new defensive lines from southwest of Prokhorovka to the banks of the Northern Donets River. The final vicious fighting even denied the Germans their limited objective of Pravorot'. All the while, Soviet armored forces west of Prokhorovka and north of the Psel River probed and pressured German defense lines in repeated local assaults. By the evening of 15 July, *Leibstandarte's* armored strength had fallen to 57 tanks, 28 assault guns, and 18 tank destroyers; II SS Panzer Corps' remaining two panzer grenadier divisions were in scarcely better shape. Although the *Leibstandarte* Division counted 501 enemy tanks destroyed through the evening of 14 July and Hausser's corps 1,149, *Leibstandarte* and *Totenkopf* Divisions still faced the over 200 remaining tanks of Soviet 18th and 29th Tank Corps.[43]

Even more ominous, if unbeknownst to the German command, on the night of 15 July, the 27th and 53d Armies of General I. S. Konev's Steppe Front, accompanied by the fresh 4th Guards Tank and 1st Mechanized Corps

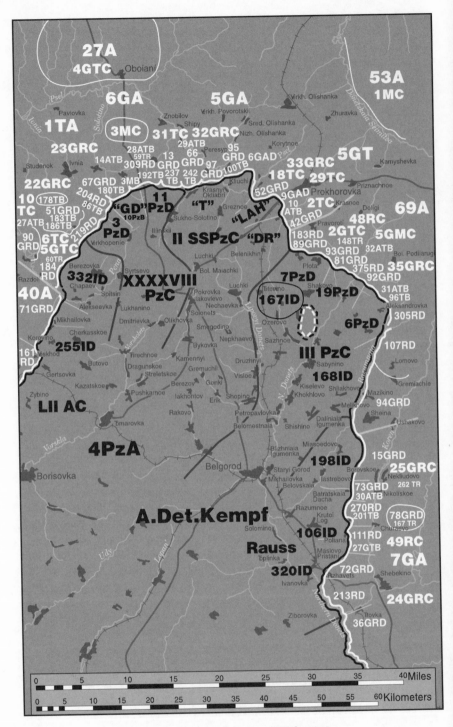

Map 24. Voronezh Front, 15 July 1943

(with almost 400 tanks), began closing into assembly areas around Oboian'
and northeast of Prokhorovka, while lead elements of 47th Army closed up
behind Shumilov's 7th Guards and Kriuchenkin's 69th Armies (see Map 24).[44]
Although these armies had orders to join with Voronezh Front on 17 July in
a general offensive designed to push German forces back to their starting
positions, the Soviet offensive never fully materialized.[45] It did not have to,
for shortly after 1300 hours on 17 July, the II Panzer Corps was ordered to
halt Operation Roland and withdraw its divisions into assembly areas around
Belgorod.

Ironically, however, in the end, the fears that Hitler had voiced on 13 July
proved to be well founded. Two days after von Manstein's forces linked up
south of Prokhorovka to create the continuous front that had eluded them
for so long, on 17 July, the forces of the Soviet Southwestern and Southern
Fronts struck hard at German defenses along the Northern Donets River near
Izium and along the Mius River. The bulk of the II SS Panzer Corps, which
had been ordered out of the front that very day, soon found itself racing to
the south. Less than three weeks later, while the corps itself was en route to
Italy, two of its divisions would hastily return to Khar'kov in altogether different circumstances. This time, rather than reaping honors as the spearhead
of victorious Operation Citadel, they would have the gruesome task of helping stave off utter German disaster near Khar'kov.

PART IV
COUNTEROFFENSIVE
AND CONCLUSIONS

CHAPTER 7

Soviet Counteroffensives

Just as they had been prepared for a preemptive Soviet offensive prior to Operation Citadel, from the moment that Citadel began, German commanders were aware of the possibility of a Soviet counteroffensive at any time after 5 July. This was particularly true in Army Group Center's Orel salient, which was the reciprocal, eastward bulge just north of the Kursk Bulge and, to a lesser extent, in Army Group South's gentle Donbas salient, which extended southeastward from Khar'kov along the Northern Donets and Mius Rivers to the Sea of Azov. The vulnerability of German defenses in these regions had only been increased as German forces gravitated toward the flanks of the Kursk Bulge prior to and during Citadel. In fact, so grave were these concerns that the OKH planned to follow their victorious entry into Kursk by implementing variants of older plans Panther and Habicht to clear Soviet forces from the region east of Khar'kov. The failure of Citadel not only frustrated these plans but also increased the vulnerability of German defenses both around Orel and in the Donbas.

In mid-May 1943, when it approved the concept of a premeditated defense at Kursk, the *Stavka* had also mandated the preparation of a series of major counteroffensives, which, taken together, formed an impressive Soviet summer strategic offensive (see Map 25). The *Stavka* ordered the Western, Briansk, and Central Fronts to prepare an offensive against German forces defending the Orel salient, code-named Operation Kutuzov, which was to commence as soon as the German attack on Kursk was halted. Thus, when Model's assault stalled by 10 July, the *Stavka* ordered the Briansk and left wing of the Western Front to attack on 12 July, while the Central Front, although exhausted after repelling Model's attack, was to join the assault on 15 July. In fact, the counterstroke by Vatutin's Voronezh Front on 12 July, which culminated in the Battle of Prokhorovka, was but a part of this larger Soviet offensive mosaic. Soviet classified studies emphasize the premeditated nature of these *Stavka* offensives: "The offensive plan of the Western Front's left wing was worked out in timely fashion. All readiness measures took shape by 25 May 1943. Therefore, when the German command undertook its large-scale offensive along the Orel-Kursk axis, it was not unexpected; forces of the Western Front's left wing were prepared not only for stubborn defense but also to deliver powerful answering strikes against the enemy."[1]

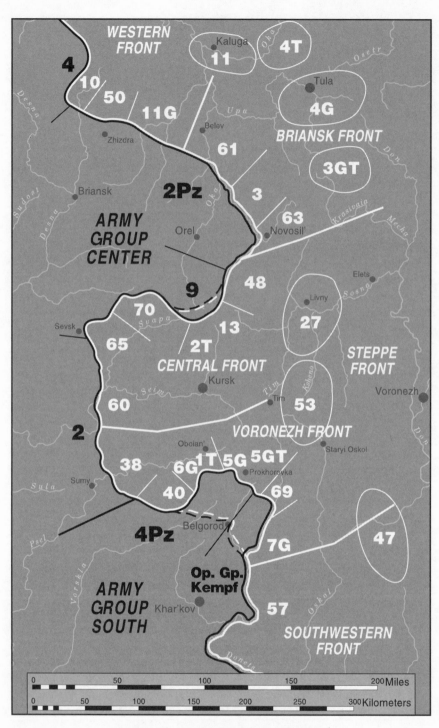

Map 25. The Battle of Kursk, 12 July 1943

To cover this and subsequent offensives, the Southwestern and Southern Fronts were ordered to conduct diversionary attacks in the Donbas and along the Mius River in mid-July to draw German operational reserves away from the flanks of the Kursk Bulge and to facilitate the two principal Soviet thrusts against Orel and Belgorod. Zhukov later described Soviet motives; "In order to tie down enemy forces and forestall maneuver of his reserves, separate offensive operations were envisioned on a number of axes in the south of the country, and also in the northwestern direction."[2]

Within weeks after the Orel blow, the Voronezh and Steppe Fronts would conduct a second and even larger offensive along the Belgorod-Khar'kov axis, code-named Operation Rumiantsev, designed to complete the demolition of von Manstein's Kursk shock force, now denuded of its powerful II SS Panzer Corps. The *Stavka* correctly assumed that, by that time, the II SS Panzer Corps and other key German operational reserves would have moved to counter the massive Soviet Orel offensive, diversionary attacks to the south, or the growing Allied threat in Western Europe. Thereafter, the Soviet strategic blow would expand to encompass forces of the Kalinin, Southwestern, and Southern Fronts. By mid-August, the entire front from Velikie Luki to the Sea of Azov would be set ablaze in a titanic struggle that the *Stavka* hoped would break the back of the *Wehrmacht* in the East.[3]

Although they had no knowledge of these ambitious Soviet plans, German field commanders were not particularly surprised when the Red Army attacked the Orel salient on 12 July 1943. Nor were they surprised when Soviet forces poured over the Northern Donets and Mius Rivers five days later. While the OKH and German field commands had detected clear indicators that a Soviet Donbas thrust was imminent, they were probably startled by the force and speed of these attacks and by the appearance of numerous fresh Soviet armored and mechanized formations there and around Orel, forces that were supposed to have been consumed in the flames of the Kursk struggle. Yet what astonished the Germans most about these massive and numerous Soviet offensives was the fact that the defenders of Kursk were able to go from a desperate defensive to a full-fledged offensive in a matter of days. The ability of the Red Army to do this after absorbing the best that the *Wehrmacht* could offer was the ultimate proof that Citadel had accomplished nothing for the Germans. Soon German frustration would turn to utter consternation.

OPERATION KUTUZOV: ASSAULT ON THE OREL SALIENT

As early as April 1943, Soviet commanders had contemplated the offensive against Orel, an offensive ultimately named Operation Kutuzov. They had completed planning for the operation in early June and refined force missions while Operation Citadel raged north and south of Kursk. Under the watchful supervision of *Stavka* representatives Zhukov and General N. N. Voronov, Chief of Red Army Artillery, the Western Front commander, General V. D. Sokolovsky, and the Briansk Front commander, General M. M. Popov, prepared to launch three powerful thrusts against the flanks and nose of the Orel salient (see Maps 25 and 26).

The most powerful of these forces was the Western Front contingent, which consisted of Lieutenant General I. Kh. Bagramian's 11th Guards Army, Lieutenant General I. V. Boldin's 50th Army, and Major Generals V. V. Butkov's and M. S. Sakhno's supporting 1st and 5th Tank Corps. This force of 211,458 men, 745 tanks and self-propelled guns, and 4,285 guns and mortars was supposed to strike southward east of Zhizdra to sever the Briansk-Orel rail line near Karachev and isolate and destroy German forces around Orel in conjunction with the Briansk and, later, the Central Fronts' attacks from the east and south. Bagramian's 11th Guards Army, with three full rifle corps, a total of twelve rifle divisions, two tank corps, and a host of supporting artillery, would spearhead Sokolovsky's offensive.[4] In reserve, the *Stavka* retained Lieutenant General I. I. Fediuninsky's 11th Army and Lieutenant General V. M. Badanov's newly formed 4th Tank Army, the latter equipped with another 652 tanks and self-propelled guns. Both were earmarked to support Bagramian's thrust.[5]

From the east, General Popov's Briansk Front prepared to launch two separate attacks against the nose of the Orel salient, the main attack by the 3d and 63d Armies and a secondary attack by the 61st Army. Lieutenant General A. V. Gorbatov's 3d Army and Lieutenant General V. Ia. Kolpakchi's 63d Army, supported by Major General M. F. Pankov's 1st Guards Tank Corps and the 25th Rifle Corps, were to advance from the Novosil' region directly westward through the nose of the German salient toward the key transportation hub of Orel.[6] The full striking power of these two armies, over 170,000 men and more than 350 tanks and self-propelled guns, was focused at the common boundary between the two. In addition, the *Stavka* kept General Rybalko's newly formed 3d Guards Tank Army, with 731 tanks and self-propelled guns, in reserve behind Popov's *front* to exploit along the Novosil'-Orel axis.[7]

To increase the pressure on German defenses forward of Orel, Popov ordered Lieutenant General P. A. Belov's 61st Army, supported by Major General I. G. Lazarov's 20th Separate Tank Corps, to deliver a secondary attack against German defenses east of the critical communications center of Bolkhov and to roll up German Orel defenses from the north.[8] Ultimately, the Briansk Front would commit 433,616 personnel to combat during the Orel operation.[9]

Finally, on 15 July the Central Front's right wing 70th, 13th, and 48th Armies would attack northward out of the Kursk Bulge, to link up with the thrust by Bagramian's 11th Guards Army and assist in cutting off the German Orel

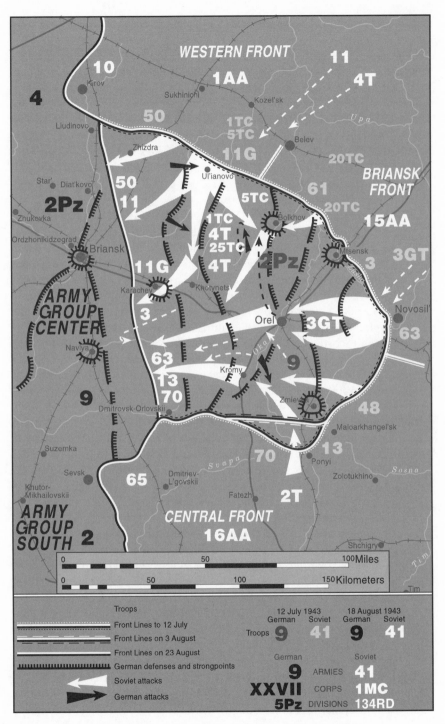

WESTERN FRONT

10

1AA

4

50

Kirov

Sukhinichi

Kozel'sk

Liudinovo

1TC
5TC
11G

Belev

Zhizdra

20TC

**BRIANSK
FRONT**

Star' Diat'kovo

50
11

Ul'ianovo

5TC

61

20TC

15AA

2Pz

Zhukovka

1TC
4T
25TC

Bolkhov

Ordzhonikidzegrad

Brlansk

11G

4T

2Pz

Mtsensk

3

3GT

**ARMY
GROUP
CENTER**

Karachev

3

Khotynets

Orel

3GT

Novosil'

63

Naviya

63
13
70

Kromy

9

Dmitrovsk-Orlovskii

Zmiev

48

Suzemka

70

13

Maloarkhangel'sk

Ponyi

Sosna

Sevsk

65

Dmitriev-
L'govskii

Zolotukhino

Khutor-
Mikhailovskii

Fatezh

2T

**ARMY
GROUP
SOUTH** 2

CENTRAL FRONT

16AA

Shchigry

| 0 | | 50 | | 100 | Miles |
| 0 | 50 | | 100 | | 150 | Kilometers |

Tim

Tim

Troops

Front Lines to 12 July
Front Lines on 3 August
Front Lines on 23 August
German defenses and strongpoints
Soviet attacks
German attacks

	12 July 1943		18 August 1943	
	German	Soviet	German	Soviet
Troops	9	41	9	41

German		Soviet	
9	ARMIES	41	
XXVII	CORPS	1MC	
5Pz	DIVISIONS	134RD	

Map 26. The Orel Operation, 12 July to 18 August 1943

defenders. This last phase of the Orel assault was the most challenging and least realistic, since the very troops that had fought the Ninth German Army to a standstill in Citadel would have to be resupplied and reequipped for offensive operations in a matter of only days. Like their German counterparts, these forces had suffered heavy losses.[10] This was particularly true in the case of General Rodin's 2d Tank Army, which was now designated to exploit the Central Front's offensive. During Operation Citadel proper, Rodin's tank army had lost well over 50 percent of the armor in its three committed tank corps (3d, 9th, and 16th); now it was supposed to conduct a new attack with the hastily refitted but still tired 3d and 16th Tank Corps.[11]

The German defense of the Orel salient fell to the LV, LIII, and XXXV Army Corps of Lieutenant General Rudolf Schmidt's Second Panzer Army, whose fourteen infantry divisions, with the 5th Panzer Division in reserve, were far too weak to halt the mass of forces arrayed against them.[12] To compound their problems, the soldiers of the Second Panzer Army lost their experienced commander only two days before the impending offensive. On 10 July the Gestapo arrested General Schmidt for his continued criticism of the Nazi regime. General Model, the Ninth Army commander, temporarily assumed control over the Second Panzer Army as well. There were few operational reserves to back up Second Panzer Army. The OKH had the 8th Panzer Division in reserve within striking distance of the salient and two security divisions to watch the partisans and defend communications routes and supply bases in the rear. Citadel, however, had denuded the front of combat troops and riveted German attention to the south.[13]

Popov, Bagramian, and other Soviet commanders had made extensive efforts to conceal the strength and intentions of their attacks from the north and east, and few, if any, Germans could imagine a threat from Kursk toward Orel. German intelligence seriously underestimated the strength of the attack against the northern flank of the Orel salient, in particular in the sectors east of Zhizdra and east of Bolkhov. It failed to detect the forward deployment of the 1st and 5th Tank Corps and the immense concentration in the 11th Guards Army's sector. In fact, intelligence still identified Bagramian's army under its older designation of 16th Army and failed to detect fully half of the new Guards army's strength. Nor did German analysts detect the concentration of the 9th Guards Rifle Corps and the 20th Tank Corps in the 61st Army's Bolkhov sector.[14] Meanwhile, in the days prior to 12 July, Soviet partisan and reconnaissance units identified most of the German defensive positions as well as the extensive supply depots concentrated around Orel.

Soviet deception efforts were less effective on the eastern flank of the Orel salient, where Major General Lothar Rendulic, commander of the XXXV Army Corps, became aware of the preparations by the 3d and 63d Army to attack at the junction of his 56th and 262d Infantry Divisions. Radio intercept and aerial reconnaissance allowed Rendulic to identify the main Soviet effort up to a week prior to the offensive. From his limited resources, Rendulic concentrated six of his twenty-four infantry battalions, eighteen of his forty-two artillery batteries, and twenty-four of his forty-eight heavy antitank guns opposite the narrow attack sector.[15] Such careful preparation would seriously disrupt the Soviet timetable in this sector and force the *Stavka* to commit its operational armored force prematurely.

Timing the Soviet counteroffensive was critical. If the Soviets counterattacked too early, the Ninth Army would still have sufficient strength and freedom of action to wheel about and shatter the attacking forces. If the counterattack came too late, however, the Germans might no longer be preoccupied with Kursk. As the pressure built up against the Central and Voronezh Fronts, Stalin and his advisors concluded that it was time to launch Kutuzov. During the early morning of 11–12 July, after a short but violent artillery preparation, reinforced reconnaissance battalions from the Western and Briansk Fronts probed the German defenses in the Orel salient and seized forward German combat outposts. Based on the results of the reconnaissance, assault rifle forces adjusted their attack formations and supporting tank corps moved into jumping-off positions. That same night long-range Red bombers raided the German bases in the salient.[16]

Dawn comes early to Russia in mid-summer. At 0300 hours on the morning of 12 July 1943, fresh battalions relieved the exhausted reconnaissance battalions that had been fighting continuously for the previous twenty-four hours. Thirty minutes later, Soviet artillery opened an intense artillery bombardment that plowed up German tactical defenses for two hours and forty minutes. During the last ten minutes of the preparation, forward rifle battalions of first echelon rifle divisions moved into assault positions accompanied by tank platoons and companies from army tank brigades and regiments and covered by swarms of Soviet bomber and assault aircraft. Finally, at 0605 hours, all of the Western and Briansk Fronts' first echelon forces joined the assault as the entire front exploded in a crescendo of smoke and flame.

In the north, the 11th Guards Army achieved an early success against the thin German defenses. Six Guards rifle divisions, concentrated on a sixteen-kilometer sector at the junction of the 211th and 293d Infantry Divisions, brushed aside the German defenders with ease, shattering two German infantry regiments. By the afternoon of the 12th, Bagramian began committing his second echelon rifle divisions to broaden the penetration, and his 1st and 5th Tank Corps entered the breach and prepared to exploit to the south. The 5th Panzer Division, stationed nearby in anticipation of such an emergency, began piecemeal counterattacks late on the 12th, slowing the Soviet advance. In response, Bagramian ordered General Sakhno's 5th Tank Corps into combat. By nightfall Sakhno's concentrated armored spearhead plunged ten kilometers deep into the German defenses and reached Ul'ianov in the German second defensive belt. However, fresh 5th Panzer Division forces thwarted Sakhno's attempt to rip through the second defensive belt from the march. Once again, Bagramian had to halt and prepare a deliberate assault the next morning.

On the morning of 13 July, the Soviet assault resumed, this time joined by General Boldin's 50th Army on Bagramian's left flank. At 1430 hours Bagramian committed General Butkov's 1st Tank Corps into the penetration along with Major General N. A. Kropotin's 1st Guards Rifle Division. Although Boldin's initial attack faltered, the 1st and 5th Tank Corps finally smashed the German second defensive belt and began a more rapid advance. By day's end, in intense fighting, Soviet forces had penetrated German defenses to a depth of fifteen kilometers along a front of twenty-three kilometers. Although both sides suffered heavy casualties, the German defenders could not halt Bagramian's offensive. Try as it might, the 5th Panzer Division could not prevent the ultimate disintegration of the German northern flank. Only the arrival of fresh German forces from the Ninth Army could stave off wholesale German disaster.[17]

To the east of Orel, however, Rendulic's careful preparations took a heavier toll on the Briansk Front's forces. Although Soviet engineers completed a bridge over the Susha River under heavy fire, the ensuing attack by 3d and 63d Army forces on the XXXV Army Corps' 56th and 262d Infantry Division was a near disaster. Generals Gorbatov and Kolpakchi initially attacked with six rifle divisions concentrated along a fourteen-kilometer front supported by army tank regiments. Three more divisions were poised in second echelon to develop the attack.[18] However, during the initial assault, KV-1 heavy tanks, unsupported by Red infantry, blundered into German mines and heavy antitank guns. By the end of 12 July, the defenders had surrendered their first defensive line and had lost three antitank guns, but sixty Soviet tanks were left disabled on the field of battle.[19] Soviet gains were minimal, and the two Soviet army commanders had to organize an even heavier assault for the following day. Lieutenant General L. M. Sandalov, the Briansk Front Chief of Staff, later recorded the action:

> The first day of the offensive did not produce appreciable success in the Briansk Front. In spite of the powerful artillery and aviation support of the attacking forces, on 12 July the *front* shock groups penetrated only five to eight kilometers into the depths. The almost two years of enemy preparation of the Orel salient had a telling effect. Behind the first captured trench was a second, after each occupied position there was another, and beyond each line another appeared. We did not succeed in introducing the tank corps to battle on 12 July.[20]

By day's end Rendulic committed his corps reserve, the 36th Infantry Division, to contain the limited penetration, and, soon after, the 8th and 2d Panzer Divisions arrived to block the Soviets' further progress. Gorbatov and Kolpakchi responded by committing their second echelon rifle divisions to combat and by ordering the 207 tanks of General Pankov's 1st Guards Tank Corps into the small breach at midday on the 13th. The fresh Soviet corps was almost immediately enmeshed in heavy combat with arriving German armor, and the Soviet advance remained agonizingly slow. In the ensuing days, the XXXV Army Corps put up a stubborn defense that eventually earned Rendulic promotion to command Second Panzer Army.[21]

Despite Rendulic's initial success, Model was acutely aware of the threat posed by the new Soviet offensive. Within hours of the start of Operation Kutuzov, four divisions of the Ninth Army were ordered to disengage from the Kursk Bulge and to redeploy to meet the new threat. The 2d and 8th Panzer Divisions, the latter from OKH reserve, arrived to reinforce Rendulic's XXXV Corps on the night of 13–14 July, while the 12th, 18th, and 20th Panzer Divisions moved quickly to plug the gap created by Bagramian's assault. East of Orel the 1st Guards Tank Corps ran head-on into these two panzer divisions on the 14th and was unable to make significant progress thereafter.[22]

Meanwhile, to the north, just east of Bolkhov, General Belov's forces went into action at the junction between two units of the German LIII Army Corps, the 208th and 34th Infantry Divisions. The assault by the 9th Guards Rifle Corps' 12th, 76th, and 77th Guards Rifle Divisions encountered heavy resistance similar to that in Rendulic's sector, and despite an advance of from three to seven kilometers, Soviet troops failed to penetrate the first German tactical defense line. The following day Belov ordered General Lazarov's 20th Tank Corps into action, but the tanks became enmeshed with the infantry in a grueling and costly battle of attrition for possession of the dense German defensive positions. Confronted by German reinforcements, first the 112th Infantry Division and then elements of the 12th Panzer Division, Soviet forward progress remained agonizingly slow. So heavy and costly was the fighting that Belov soon withdrew the 20th Tank Corps for refitting.[23]

Despite, or perhaps because of, his initial failure against Rendulic, the Briansk Front commander, Popov, again tried to convince the *Stavka* to give him control of General Rybalko's powerful 3d Guards Tank Army.[24] Late on the night of the 13th, the tank army was finally transferred to Popov's control, but it required two days of exhausting night marches, lying under camouflage in the daytime, for Rybalko to concentrate his three corps near the eastern end of the Orel salient. By that time the 3d and 63d Armies had effectively lost any chance of achieving a rapid breakthrough and the Germans had further reinforced their defenses. Furthermore, under pressure from the *Stavka,* Popov altered the tank army's objective at the last minute. Instead of attacking to envelop Orel from the north and west, in light of the Central Front's inability to make progress in its 15 July assault northward toward Orel, Rybalko's army was to wheel south of Orel and envelop the city from the southwest.

The impatient Rybalko determined to force his way through the German defenders, committing his tankers to attempt a fresh penetration instead of exploiting the earlier efforts of the 3d and 63d Armies. Rybalko's force had 698 serviceable tanks and 32 self-propelled guns, included 473 T-34s, but most of the remainder were light T-70s or Lend-Lease British vehicles. The Soviet crews regarded these obsolescent Matildas and Valentines as unreliable and highly flammable, derisively calling them "field crematoriums." Moreover, Rybalko lacked the artillery and engineers for such a deliberate assault. To make matters worse, he was facing two fully alert panzer divisions, including a handful of Tigers and Ferdinands, and most of two infantry divisions.

Nevertheless, Rybalko's 12th and 15th Tank Corps attacked, almost from the march, at 1030 hours on the morning of 19 July. Coordinated artillery fire and fighter-bomber strikes allowed the tank corps to cross the Oleshen River and to advance twelve kilometers by nightfall. Fierce German tank and air resistance slowed but could not halt Rybalko until that evening, when Major General F. N. Rudkin's 15th Tank Corps was held up by stiffening resistance from the 8th Panzer Division. Major General M. I. Zinkovich's 12th Tank Corps continued to advance on the northern flank. The next morning, 20 July, the *front* commander, Popov, ordered Rybalko to exploit this success by attacking to the northwest in order to seize the town of Otrada, astride a railroad line into Orel. Popov smoothly committed Major General I. M. Korchagin's 2d Mechanized Corps, hitherto following behind the two tank corps, to conduct this attack but was unable to cross the Oka River, a major water obstacle. A disgruntled Stalin interfered personally, hectoring Popov's chief of staff, Sandalov, over the telephone, but to no avail.

At 0300 hours on 21 July, Popov abruptly assigned Rybalko a new mission, in effect splitting the tank army in half. While 15th Tank and 2d Mechanized Corps were still committed around Otrada, northeast of Orel, the rest of 3d Guards Tank Army was to shift to the south and punch through the southern shoulder of the penetration. Rybalko immediately drove to Major General I. I. Iakobovsky's 91st Tank Brigade, 3d Guards Tank Army reserve, to relay this order. En route his jeep was strafed by German fighters, killing his driver and wounding his adjutant. Rybalko arrived at the tank brigade headquarters on foot and urged both it and the 12th Tank Corps forward across swampy ground that impeded the advance. By 25 July this advance had cut the rail line between Kursk and Orel. In the ensuing days, Rybalko's army would alter its path repeatedly in an attempt to find a weak point in German defenses. No such weak point existed, however, and Rybalko's intended daring exploitation turned into a grinding battle of armored attrition.

For their flexible and tenacious efforts in Operation Kutuzov, the 3d Guards Tank Army's component 12th and 15th Tank Corps and 2d Mechanized Corps received the "Guards" honorific, despite their inability to achieve decisive results.[25] Rybalko was certainly a daring and resourceful commander, but his impatient efforts to break through prepared enemy defenses had seriously depleted his force, which ultimately had to be withdrawn from combat to refit. The more audacious Soviet commanders made similar mistakes in the misuse of tank armies throughout the war. Despite these problems the sheer weight of Soviet steel in the Orel slugfest took its toll on the German defenses, which inexorably caved in under the unremitting Soviet pressure.

GERMAN WITHDRAWAL FROM OREL

Time was running out for the Germans in the Orel salient. On 13 July, after the conference that terminated Citadel, Hitler had ordered Model to seal off the penetrations and to restore the original front north and east of Orel.[26] Within days, however, this goal proved illusory. On 15 July Rokossovsky's Central Front launched its own offensive from the southern side of the salient. Predictably, this attack by forces that had only recently defended against the Ninth Army accomplished little. Still, the need to contain this new offensive further complicated Model's task in reshuffling the Ninth Army's dwindling resources to fill the other gaps torn in the Second Panzer Army. In particular, the 11th Guards Army and 1st and 5th Tank Corps had broken into open ground west of Bolkhov. Bagramian threw Major General F. G. Anikushkin's fresh 25th Tank Corps into combat on 17 July, attempting to threaten the rear of German forces defending Bolkhov. The Germans countered by shifting the 9th Panzer, the 10th Panzer Grenadier, and the 253d Infantry Divisions northward in a futile attempt to seal the gaping breach.[27] It also dispatched the 26th Infantry to reinforce sagging defenses east of Bolkhov. At times, the only defenders opposing the Soviet advance detachments were scratch elements of the 441st and 707th Security Divisions, none of which were equipped to face tanks. The German defenders, already strained by weeks of combat at Kursk, were close to the breaking point. On 21 July, for example, Model relieved Lieutenant General Walter Scheller, veteran commander of the 9th Panzer Division, for refusing to make a suicidal counterattack against Bagramian's eastern flank west near Krasnikov.[28]

To relieve the unrelenting pressure on sagging German defenses, the fighter-bombers of Lieutenant General Deichmann's 1st Air Division threw themselves into the defense with great daring and claimed to have destroyed a Soviet tank brigade without any ground support. Yet the Luftwaffe was so short of fuel and spare parts that Deichmann often had to refuse desperate requests for air support. In any event, the German pilots could only control the main roads in daylight. Soviet units moving forward at night or in the vast woodland were almost impossible to detect. Motorized FlaK guns were also pressed into service to give the lightly equipped German defenders some capability against Red armor. The FlaK gunners claimed to have destroyed 229 tanks and 383 Soviet aircraft in late July, but the Soviet advance continued.[29]

Model recognized the real danger of losing the entire Orel salient. As a precaution, on 16 July he ordered work to begin on the Hagen position, a line of defenses along the Desna River, across the base of the Orel salient covering the critical city of Briansk. Four days later Hitler issued a *Fuehrer* order forbidding further withdrawals by the Ninth and Second Panzer Armies, but Model appealed to von Kluge to dissuade the dictator from this course. Model could do so with greater force, for on 21 July General Fediuninsky's 11th Army joined Bagramian's assault, occupying positions between the 50th and 11th Guards Armies (see Map 27).[30]

Bowing to the inevitable, on 22 July Hitler agreed that Model could conduct an "elastic defense." Then, on the 25th, the king of Italy dismissed and arrested Mussolini, and Hitler was galvanized into action to shore up his Italian ally. He summoned the Army Group Center commander, von Kluge, to a meeting at *Fuehrer* headquarters at noon on 26 July. Hitler abruptly announced that the II SS Panzer Corps would leave Russia immediately for Italy, with numerous other divisions to follow. (In practice, only the 1st SS Panzer Grenadier Division *Leibstandarte Adolf Hitler* actually reached Italy, while the remainder of the SS Corps was redeployed elsewhere in the east.) To free such a large force, the Orel Bulge had to be evacuated as quickly as possible. Kluge protested that the Hagen line was hardly begun, but Hitler was adamant, and preparations for evacuation began. On the 28th, OKH issued the formal order for Operation Herbstreise (Autumn Journey), the withdrawal from Orel.[31]

Intensified combat north of Orel indicated the wisdom of this decision. By late July Soviet forces were introducing major new forces to combat and threatened, simultaneously, to collapse German defense around Bolkhov and lunge southward toward the key rail line at Karachev. Seizure of Karachev would sever all German communications with Orel. On 26 July the three tank corps of General Badanov's 496-tank 4th Tank Army struck west of Bolkhov, and Bagramian committed the 2d Guards Cavalry Corps and a corps of the 11th Guards Army in a thrust on Karachev.[32] Although the German XXIII and XXXXI Panzer Corps stubbornly resisted, the immense pressure forced the Germans to abandon Bolkhov and to withdraw to new defense lines northwest of Orel and less than ten kilometers from the vital Briansk-Orel rail line. Only the timely arrival of the Panzer Grenadier Division *Grossdeutschland* contained the southward drive of Bagramian's 11th Guards Army and 2d

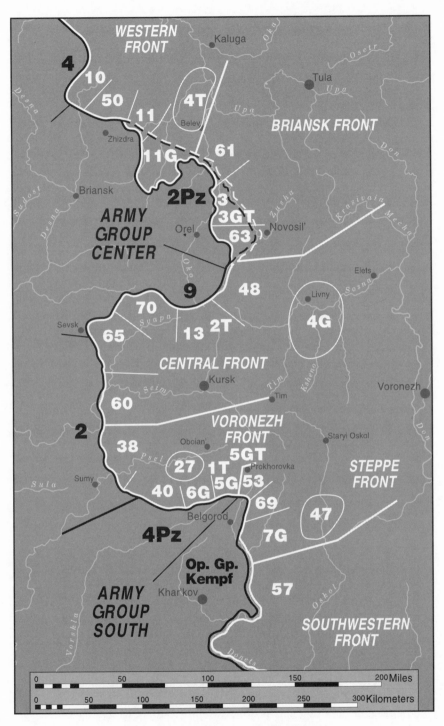

Map 27. The Battle of Kursk, 21 July 1943

Guards Cavalry Corps. A frustrated Bagramian threw division after division against German forces defending Karachev as Model shifted his bedraggled panzer divisions westward from the Bolkhov sector to contain Soviet forces short of the critical rail line.

The German withdrawal to the Hagen line finally began on the night of 31 July, and the Soviets soon became aware that their opponents were slipping away. The Central Partisan Bureau ordered massive sabotage to delay the German withdrawal. Halting the movement of combat units was difficult, but the huge German supply depots around Orel were another matter. On the night of 2 August, partisans detonated almost 5,000 demolition charges, destroying thirty miles of rail and interrupting rail traffic for twenty-four to forty-eight hours. Another 1,700 demolitions were set off the following night, followed by 4,100 attacks on the night of the 4th.[33]

By early August the *Stavka* had reorganized its force around the Orel salient to improve command and control and to mount a final drive to liberate Orel. It transferred the 11th Guards and 4th Tank Armies to Briansk Front control and ordered Popov to make a concerted attempt to collapse German defenses once and for all. At the same time, it transferred Rybalko's tank army to Central Front control and ordered Rokossovsky to use the combined weight of the 3d Guards and 2d Tank Armies in a renewed northwestward thrust south of Orel. On 5 August Popov's and Rokossovsky's forces resumed their attacks against the northern and southeastern faces of the rapidly deflating German salient. That same day, however, the Second Panzer Army completed the evacuation of 53,000 tons of supplies and 20,000 wounded soldiers from Orel and demolished the last bridges and other military installations in the sector. Subsequently, while heavy fighting raged, the Germans executed a scorched earth policy throughout the salient, burning the rye harvest and forcing 250,000 civilians, with their cattle and possessions, toward the west.[34]

By 16 August the German withdrawal to the Hagen line was virtually complete, and further Soviet efforts to outflank Army Group Center proved vain. The fighting exacted a frightening toll on Germans and Soviets alike. Despite Bagramian's spectacular early progress, the Orel battle had degenerated into a bloody frontal assault that consumed immense resources. The Soviet Orel offensive bore all of the characteristics of the ferocious defensive fighting in Citadel. Skillful German defense against overwhelming odds succeeded in denying Soviet commanders the rapid and dramatic offensive success they so ardently sought and, in the process, cost the Red Army almost a half million casualties.[35] While saving the Second Panzer Army from envelopment and destruction, however, the Germans could not save their Orel salient. The German High Command had no time to savor the salvation of the Second Panzer Army, for by early August it was contending with yet another looming operational disaster, this time south of Kursk.

OPERATION RUMIANTSEV: THE BELGOROD-KHAR'KOV OFFENSIVE OPERATION

For all its power, Operation Kutuzov was a subsidiary operation, intended to take the pressure off the Central Front in the defense of Kursk and to initiate Soviet counteroffensive action. The main Soviet counterstroke, Operation Rumiantsev, was yet to come. Its objective was nothing less than the destruction of the Fourth Panzer Army and Army Detachment Kempf, already weakened by the long struggle on the road to Prokhorovka. Indeed, Stalin and Antonov, Chief of the General Staff's Operations Directorate, hoped to cut off the other two elements of Army Group South, the First Panzer and Sixth Armies, by advancing 180 kilometers through Khar'kov to Dnepropetrovsk and then on to the Black Sea coast.

Although Rumiantsev had been a key component of Soviet strategic planning since April, detailed planning had to wait upon the exact outcome of the Kursk defensive battle. Initially, Stalin had wished to launch the offensive on 23 July, as soon as German forces had been forced back to their jumping-off positions for Citadel. Zhukov, however, had protested vigorously that the Voronezh and Steppe Fronts were in no condition to conduct a major offensive and required a minimum of eight days for requisite preparations.[36] Stalin relented, and on 24 July the *Stavka* notified Vatutin and Konev, the two *front* commanders involved, to begin their final offensive preparations. Vatutin, Konev, and *Stavka* representative Zhukov refined their concept for the operation, which Stalin approved on 1 August. The operation was assigned the code-name "Great Captain [*Polkovodets*] Rumiantsev."[37]

The ensuing plan was vintage Zhukov in that it called for a simple, massive assault by concentrated armies of the Voronezh and Steppe Fronts (see Maps 28 and 29).[38] Two Voronezh Front armies—General Zhadov's 5th Guards and General Chistiakov's 6th Guards—and three Steppe Front armies—Lieutenant General I. M. Managarov's 53d, General Kriuchenkin's 69th, and elements of General Shumilov's 7th Guards—were to attack north and northwest of Belgorod on 3 August. To complicate matters, four of these seven armies had been severely depleted by von Manstein's offensive. The same could be said for General Katukov's 1st Tank and General Rotmistrov's 5th Guards Tank Armies, which were assigned to pass through the rifle forces and advance southwestward as rapidly as possible. The immediate goal of these tank armies was the rail and logistical center of Bogodukhov, moving parallel to the rivers in the area along a large ridge line. Once there, the two tank armies would encircle Khar'kov, with Katukov forming the outer encirclement line, facing westward, and Rotmistrov forming the inner encirclement line, facing the city.[39]

Vatutin arrayed Lieutenant General S. G. Trofimenko's 27th, Lieutenant General K. S. Moskalenko's 40th, and Lieutenant General N. E. Chibisov's

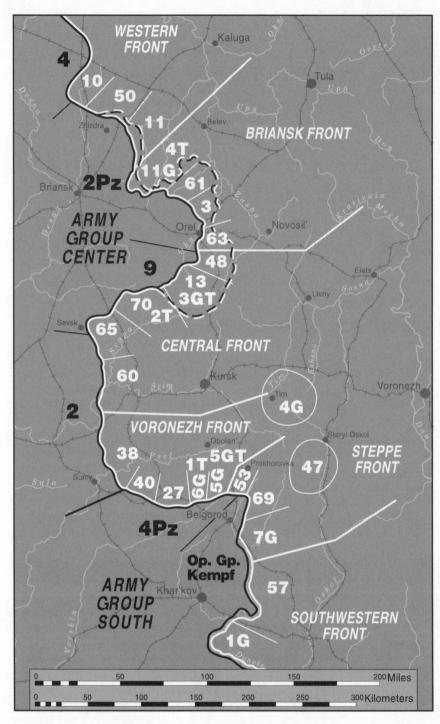

Map 28. The Battle of Kursk, 4 August 1943

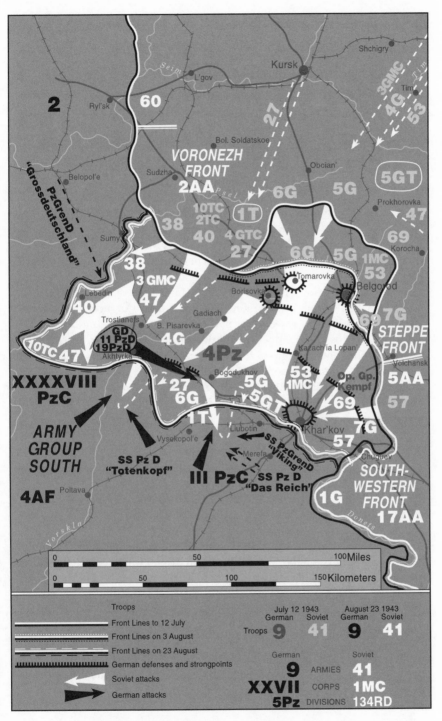

Map 29. The Belgorod-Khar'kov Operation, 3–23 August 1943

38th Armies along his shock group's right flank with orders to join the offensive while in progress.[40] The remainder of Shumilov's 7th Guards Army would perform the same function on Konev's left flank. *Stavka* retained Major General P. M. Kozlov's 47th Army and Lieutenant General G. I. Kulik's 4th Guards Army, together with Major General I. A. Vovchenko's 3d Guards Tank Corps, in reserve with the mission of developing the Voronezh Front assault, while Lieutenant General S. A. Krasovsky's 2d and Lieutenant General S. K. Goriunov's 5th Air Armies would provide air support for the offensive.

Stalin wisely rejected the possibility of a double envelopment of Khar'kov as too difficult for his tired troops to accomplish.[41] Yet, in fact, the final plan was remarkably complex. First, the *Stavka* chose to strike the strongest portion of von Manstein's defense head-on, to engage and defeat the German force and avoid the problems with flank threats that the *Stavka* had experienced in February and March 1943.[42] Second, the focus of the offensive was precisely at the boundary between the Voronezh and Steppe Fronts, causing increased coordination problems from the start of the operation. Third, in addition to the two tank armies, there were separate tank or mechanized corps attached to most of the rifle armies participating in the penetration to serve as mobile groups and conduct operational maneuver.[43] Thus the 2d Tank Corps was the mobile group of the 40th Army, the 4th Guards Tank Corps performed the same function for the 27th Army, while the 5th Guards Tank Corps was subordinate to the 6th Guards Army and the 1st Mechanized Corps to the 53d Army. This fully accorded with the emerging Soviet concept for operational maneuver, by which these separate corps conducted shallower, tactical penetrations and the tank armies developed and exploited deeper, operational-level penetrations. In this case both the tank armies and the separate corps were supposed to enter battle on the first day of the offensive, as soon as the infantry forces had achieved an initial penetration.[44]

Fourth, the offensive was planned as a series of sequential attacks, beginning in the Soviet main attack sector northwest of Belgorod and rippling outward toward the Soviet flanks. The 5th Guards, 6th Guards, 53d, and 69th Armies, plus one corps of the 7th Guards Army, would attack on 3 August. Two days later the neighboring 40th and 27th Armies would launch their own attacks to the west, followed on 6 August by the remainder of 7th Guards Army. As the operation developed, on 8 August the Southwestern Front's 57th and 1st Guards Armies were to attack from the east toward Khar'kov. This ripple of offensives was intended to achieve two goals simultaneously. First, it allowed the *front* commanders, Vatutin and Konev, to economize on artillery and other support assets, shifting them laterally from army to army over the course of several days. Second, the Soviets hoped that this spreading offensive would pin down German forces, making it more difficult for von Manstein to redistribute his forces in response to the main attack.

Once Citadel ended, von Manstein's battered forces had withdrawn from their penetration at Prokhorovka and had begun to reorganize for other missions. The SS Panzer Grenadier Division *Leibstandarte Adolf Hitler* and the headquarters of the II SS Panzer Corps entrained for redeployment to Italy, although this headquarters was later diverted into the Donbas along with its *Totenkopf* and *Das Reich* Divisions. The Panzer Grenadier Division *Grossdeutschland* raced northward to fend off disaster around Orel, and the 3d Panzer Division joined German forces in the south. Thus Rumiantsev had enormous potential to succeed against the weakened and battle-weary Germans, provided that surprise could be achieved.

As a first step in achieving surprise, on 17 July the Southwestern and Southern Fronts launched offensive operations against the easternmost bulge of Army Group South's defenses in the Donbas along the Northern Donets and Mius Rivers. These assaults had the desired effect of distracting the Germans, since Hitler and von Manstein had anticipated both attacks and the Soviets did little to conceal their offensive preparations in these regions. The presence of one separate tank corps and three mechanized corps, the hallmarks of major offensive action, helped convince the German leaders that their southern flank was in danger.[45] As early as 14 July, Hitler had directed that the XXIV Panzer Corps be moved into reserve behind the First Panzer Army along the Northern Donets River near Izium. Eventually, the SS Divisions *Das Reich* and *Totenkopf*, under the II SS Panzer Corps headquarters, moved south to the Mius Front, where they inflicted a terrible beating on the Red attackers. For the remainder of July, the Soviet offensive in the south continued to draw German attention and reserves away from Khar'kov.[46] The Izium offensive terminated on 27 July and the Mius offensive on 3 August, long after they had failed and the very day that Soviet forces commenced Rumiantsev.

More locally, the *Stavka* directed an elaborate deception effort by the Voronezh Front to portray a major Soviet attack from the southwestern end of the Kursk Bulge (the region recommended by General Moskalenko, the 40th Army commander), rather than in the southeast. In the area around Sudzha in the southwestern extremities of the Kursk Bulge, dummy positions and radio transmissions simulated the concentration of two rifle corps, a tank army, and several tank corps. Under the supervision of deputy *front* commander General I. F. Nefterev, large portions of the 38th Army maintained this fiction brilliantly from 26 July to 4 August. Elsewhere, false defensive positions were constructed to conceal the attack preparations of the main Soviet forces. In order to facilitate the forward movement of armored forces, Soviet engineers constructed twenty-two secret underwater bridges across the Northern Donets River and its tributaries.[47]

This deception was particularly necessary because of the extreme weakness of the attacking units, most of which had just finished the bitter defensive battles of Kursk. The rifle regiments of the Red Army were asked to launch an offensive with only a skeleton of their authorized troops and equipment. For example, the 7th Guards Army had only 50,000 of an authorized 80,000 troops when it re-entered battle. Although each of the tank armies was rapidly restored to a strength of more than 500 tanks each, the new tanks and crews had not been fully integrated into their units when Rumiantsev began.[48] Konev in particular repeatedly asked Stalin for more men, more tanks, and more time before the attack. Yet Stalin and Vatutin had taken a calculated risk, arguing that a rapid offensive would find the Germans even weaker than the Soviets.

Despite the haste, the resulting offensive was generally well prepared. The three rifle armies launching the main attack—the 6th Guards, 5th Guards, and 53d—all attacked on extremely narrow frontages, usually 1.5 to 3 kilometers per rifle division, in order to achieve overwhelming local superiority despite their depleted ranks. The divisions of these armies were generally concentrated three deep.[49]

On 31 July Vatutin and Zhukov held a meeting of the army commanders involved in the operation. Afterward, the two tank army commanders, Katukov and Rotmistrov, met at the headquarters of the 5th Guards Army, through which they were to advance. Like the assaulting infantry forces, the two tank armies were echeloned to pass through the infantry on narrow fronts—three kilometers wide for the 1st Tank Army, and five for the 5th Guards Tank Army. These two sectors were adjacent to each other to preclude the Germans from sealing off a narrow penetration after the first assault. Katukov and Rotmistrov negotiated every detail of the operation so that each of their leading tank corps would have two routes of advance. Zhadov, the commander of the 5th Guards Army, arranged for his army artillery and multiple rocket launchers to support the advance of the two tank armies. In accordance with the developing Soviet doctrine, each tank army was preceded by a reinforced tank brigade acting as a forward detachment to bypass and preempt German defenses.[50]

In truth, the German defenses were rudimentary at best. Although several defensive belts existed at the point where the Fourth Panzer Army had launched its offensive a month before, only the first belt was held in any strength. With the exception of the 11th Panzer Division, the forward defenses were manned by understrength infantry divisions, backed up by combat groups from the 19th and 6th Panzer Divisions. By the time Rumiantsev commenced, the *Stavka* had concentrated 980,588 men, 12,627 guns and mortars, and 2,439 tanks and self-propelled guns for the attack. The German defenders could muster scarcely 210,000 men and approximately 250 tanks and assault guns. Soviet force superiority in main attack sectors was even more pronounced.[51]

At 0500 hours on 3 August, the Soviets opened an intense artillery barrage. At 0755 the Soviet guns shifted to targets in the German rear, while tailored assault units of infantry and sappers, supported by individual tanks, moved forward against the German defenses. By 1000 the first German defensive positions were disrupted, and the second echelon Soviet regiments passed through the attackers to continue the advance. At 1300, General Vatutin decided to authorize the forward detachments of the four tank corps—two brigades each from the 1st and 5th Guards Tank Armies—to advance, and within two hours these detachments had cleared the German first defensive belt.[52]

The penetration was not uniformly successful, however. The 200th Tank Brigade, acting as the forward detachment of the 1st Tank Army's 6th Tank Corps, pushed the German infantry back but was unable to punch through into the undefended German rear. To the west the 6th Guards Army experienced difficulty penetrating the German defenses, and Kravchenko's separate 5th Guards Tank Corps became involved in supporting the infantry rather than exploiting into the depth of the battlefield. Similarly, the weak 53d Army encountered determined resistance along the Erik River, and its 1st Mechanized Corps was broken down into brigades to support the slow penetration effort. Nevertheless, by the end of the first day, the leading elements of the two tank armies had advanced as much as twenty-five kilometers and had severed the Belgorod-Tomarovka road, while the rifle forces behind them had reached a depth of eight to ten kilometers.

Despite their usual determined efforts, the front-line defenders of the Fourth Panzer Army and Army Detachment Kempf were obviously surprised and outclassed. For the weary German infantry, it was as if their beaten opponent had risen from the grave with renewed strength. In one day the attackers had torn a ten-kilometer gap between the two German armies. A regiment of the 167th Infantry Division almost ceased to exist on 3 August, and neighboring divisions were also heavily damaged.

Right up to the eve of the Rumiantsev offensive, von Manstein had been confident that his opponents would require time-consuming refitting before they could attack. Now he had to reshuffle forces from his other armies, which were already engaged against the attacking South and Southwestern Fronts. The well-equipped SS divisions remained his strongest force to meet the new threat. The SS Panzer Grenadier Divisions *Das Reich* and *Totenkopf* were shifted north by rail within days. Von Manstein put these divisions, together with the veteran but depleted 3d Panzer Division, under the headquarters of the III Panzer Corps to strike against the Soviet armored advance northwest of Khar'kov. Meanwhile the 5th SS Panzer Grenadier Division *Wiking* was assigned to reinforce beleaguered Army Detachment Kempf.[53]

While these frantic redeployments continued, the Fourth Panzer Army fought desperately to survive. Late on 3 August, combat groups of the 19th and 6th Panzer Divisions established blocking positions just northeast of Tomarovka and provided the first serious resistance to the two attacking tank armies. General Chernienko's 31st Tank Corps of the 1st Tank Army became tied down fighting at Tomarovka, but on 4 August the other two corps, General Getman's 6th Tank and General Krivoshein's 3d Mechanized, continued to exploit to the southwest toward the town of Borisovka, with 6th Guards Army infantry riding on the backs of the tanks. This was a recurring pattern during the Belgorod-Khar'kov operation; because of the overall weakness of the Soviet forces, commanders could not accept the risk of leaving a bypassed German strong point to be dealt with by follow-on forces.

To the east Konev's Steppe Front continued to encounter serious resistance, complicated by the difficulty of crossing the Northern Donets River. At Konev's request Vatutin detached the second echelon corps of 5th Guards Tank Army to assist the 7th Guards Army in breaking the cohesion of the German defense. General Skvortsov's 5th Guards Mechanized Corps pivoted to the east, toward the village of Krasnoe, while Rotmistrov's 18th and 29th Tank Corps continued toward the south, roughly parallel with the 1st Tank Army. This diversion undoubtedly hastened the German withdrawal from Belgorod but in the process weakened the offensive force of the two tank armies.

In the ensuing days, the 1st Tank Army continued to plunge toward the southwest. Yet the stubborn German resistance in strong points such as Borisovka meant that supporting Red rifle units, as well as various brigades of the tank corps, were falling farther and farther behind the armored spearheads. The 27th and 6th Guards Armies were tied up for days attempting to destroy elements of five German divisions encircled in the towns of Graivoron and Borisovka. From 7 through 9 August, the 11th Panzer Division and the Panzer Grenadier Division *Grossdeutschland,* the latter hastily deploying into battle piecemeal after an arduous redeployment from the Orel region, fought a skillful operation to extricate these partially encircled divisions.

Without infantry and artillery support, the combat power of the two tank armies declined steadily.[54] By 6 August, however, the 6th Guards Army had finally broken through in the west, and its battered 5th Guards Tank Corps passed under the control of Katukov's 1st Tank Army. Meanwhile the planned rippling offensive was gradually widening the Soviet effort. These flanking attacks undoubtedly prevented some lateral redistribution of defending forces, but they were generally weaker than the initial assault and, therefore, rarely penetrated the German defenses. One exception was Major General P. P. Poluboiarov's 4th Guards Tank Corps of the 27th Army, which pushed back a combat group of the 11th Panzer Division and advanced steadily to the south, providing the 1st Tank Army with protection on its western flank.

MEETING ENGAGEMENT AT BOGODUKHOV

By the evening of 7 August, the gap between the two defending German armies had widened to more than fifty kilometers.[55] Only scratch units, composed principally of German rear service troops, opposed the Red advance. The leading elements of the German SS divisions were arriving south of the road junction and German supply base at Bogodukhov, but these divisions would not be ready for combat until late on the 9th. Meanwhile General Kravchenko's 5th Guards Tank Corps, attached to the 1st Tank Army, pushed to the southwest of Bogodukhov.

At this point, however, the overextended tank armies finally encountered von Manstein's assembling counterattack forces. Each side's mechanized forces arrived over a period of three days. The result was a remarkable series of complex, vicious, seesawing, mobile battles first around Bogodukhov and then to the west around the key road junction at Akhtyrka (see Map 30).

On 12–13 August, three combat groups of *Totenkopf* were finally able to conduct a concerted attack against the by now overextended forward detachments of the 1st Tank Army, which had severed German rail communications with Khar'kov. Katukov lost 100 tanks when three of his forward detachments were surrounded, although some of the Soviet troops escaped on foot. Yet unlike previous German counterattacks, this success did not cause the Red units to collapse and withdraw. Instead, the 6th Guards Army, reinforced by the 5th Guards Mechanized Corps of 5th Tank Army, counterattacked *Totenkopf* on the 13th, penetrating to Vysokopol'e, another small village located on the key Khar'kov-Poltava rail line, along which vital German reserves were moving to reinforce the Khar'kov defenses. At the same time, elements of *Das Reich* and *Wiking* launched a concerted attack on the weakened elements of the 1st Tank Army south of Bogodukhov, reaching almost to the town itself. Rotmistrov committed the remaining two tank corps of his 5th Guards Tank Army to extricate Katukov. For three days the opposing forces maneuvered around Bogodukhov, while the tank strength of both Katukov and Rotmistrov declined alarmingly.[56] Finally, on 16–17 August, the III Panzer Corps succeeded in pushing the 6th Guards Army and the remnants of the 1st Tank Army back to the Merchik River, stabilizing the front line and destroying the offensive power of both Red armies.

While burning German and Soviet tanks littered the landscape around Bogodukhov, the Soviet advance on Khar'kov continued inexorably. The

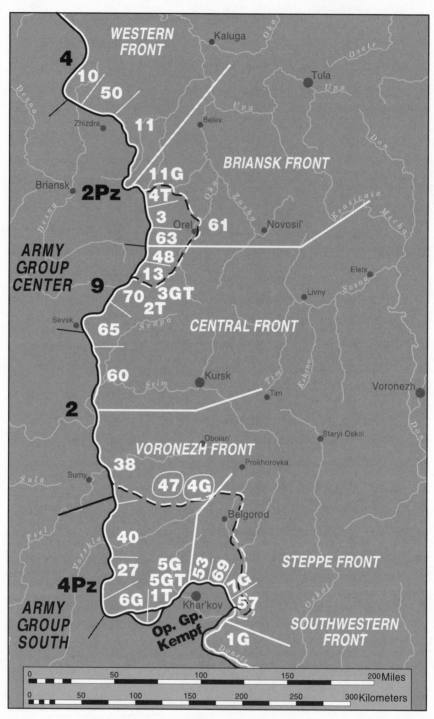

Map 30. The Battle of Kursk, 11 August 1943

German defenses were not broken but had to retreat steadily under the weight of Konev's advance. Rather than assaulting the city directly, Konev attempted to cut the rail lines around the city, forcing the Germans to withdraw. General Kempf planned to evacuate the city, and von Manstein acquiesced in this decision. When Hitler heard of this on 12 August, however, he issued one of his characteristic orders to hold at all costs. Two days later von Manstein relieved the unfortunate Kempf, replacing him with General Otto Woehler.[57]

Meanwhile Hoth's Fourth Panzer Army gathered its forces for yet another counterattack, one intended to cut off the Soviet 27th and 6th Guards Armies. The remaining elements of the 7th Panzer, 19th Panzer, and *Grossdeutschland* Divisions prepared to attack to the southeast from Akhtyrka to link up with the III Panzer Corps and to encircle and destroy Soviet forces that had penetrated between Akhtyrka and Bogodukhov. After six weeks of combat, these three divisions could muster only about 100 tanks and assault guns between them. Nevertheless, this attack, launched on 17 August, succeeded in making tenuous contact with the III Panzer Corps' *Totenkopf* and 223d Infantry Divisions. The resulting encirclement was too weak to actually destroy Soviet units, but it disrupted and split the Soviet 4th and 5th Guards Tank Corps and severely damaged the 27th and 6th Guards Armies. The result was a further reduction in the tank and personnel strength of the Red units in the area. Vatutin requested and was given permission by the *Stavka* to commit Lieutenant General G. I. Kulik's 4th Guards Army and its associated 3d Guards Tank Corps to restore the situation. Kulik's subsequent clumsy use of his army earned later censure by Vatutin and the *Stavka*.[58]

Just prior to the German attack on Akhtyrka, on 16 August, Major General P. M. Kozlov's 47th Army, consisting of two Guards rifle corps and Major General V. T. Obukhov's 3d Guards Mechanized Corps, launched an attack by passing through a ten-kilometer sector of the 40th Army near Boromlia, north of Akhtyrka.[59] The 57th German Infantry Division was shattered by sustained artillery fire on the 18th. With most of its junior officers and sergeants killed, the 57th simply ran away.[60] This rare breakdown of discipline was a clear indication of how close the Germans were to collapse. By 19 August the 47th Army was threatening the rear of the German Akhtyrka group. This, in connection with a renewed Soviet effort from the north, forced the *Grossdeutschland* Division back from Akhtyrka on 19 August.

KHAR'KOV

All this maneuvering to the west of Khar'kov did not change the city's fate. The German infantry forces were steadily depleted, and the defending artillery ran short of ammunition. By 18 August General Otto Woehler, the new commander of Army Detachment Kempf (now redesignated as the Eighth German Army), repeated his predecessor's request to withdraw. If the Germans were to have enough forces to conduct an orderly retreat to the Dnepr River, they could not afford to lose major forces defending a doomed city. Hitler finally saw the necessity for retreat, although he asked Woehler to delay the action to minimize the political impact on Germany's remaining allies.

The savage battles west of Khar'kov did have one positive benefit for the Germans; they prevented Soviet encirclement of the city. Desperate attacks by the 5th Guards and 5th Guards Tank Armies on 22 August failed to close off the evacuation routes. Finally, on the night of 23–24 August, Konev ordered an all-out assault on Khar'kov, but the assault fell on air—only a few German stragglers remained in the city (see Map 31).

Although Soviet forces failed to destroy the German Fourth Panzer Army and Army Detachment Kempf in the Belgorod-Khar'kov operation, they added insult to German Citadel injuries and subjected the *Wehrmacht* to a bloodletting that it could no longer withstand. German infantry divisions eroded to mere shadows of their former selves. The 255th and 57th Infantry Divisions emerged from the operation with 3,336 and 1,791 men, respectively. The 332d, which had already suffered heavily in Citadel, was reduced to a strength of 342 men. One regiment of the 112th Infantry Division had but 1 officer and 45 men. Panzer divisions fared little better. By 23 August the 11th Panzer's strength stood at 820 panzer grenadiers, 15 tanks, and 4 assault guns, while the 19th Panzer Division, minus its commander, General Schmidt, who was killed in the Borisovka encirclement, had only 760 panzer grenadiers and 7 tanks.[61] The SS panzer grenadier divisions fared somewhat better but were still heavily damaged. By 25 August *Das Reich* and *Totenkopf* fielded 55 and 61 tanks and assault guns, respectively, and all of their remaining armor had to be consolidated into a single combat group to parry Rotmistrov's final drive on Khar'kov.[62]

The Soviet Voronezh and Steppe Fronts paid dearly for their victory. The frontal hammer blows, so characteristic of an operation planned by Zhukov, produced over 250,000 Soviet casualties, more than one quarter of the initial Soviet force. By the time the operation had ended, rifle divisions had fallen to an average strength of between 3,000 and 4,000 men each, and tank forces suffered equally appalling losses. Katukov's 1st Tank Army, which had lost upwards of 80 percent of its initial strength of 646 tanks and self-propelled guns in Citadel, lost an additional 1,042 tanks in the Belgorod-Khar'kov operation, while falling in strength from 542 to 120 during the course of the operation. Rotmistrov's 5th Guards Tank Army had 50 of its original 503 tanks and self-propelled guns serviceable on 25 August. During the operation his army lost 60 to 65 percent of its staff officers, 85 percent of its company and battalion commanders, and 75 percent of its radios. Two months would pass before the tank army would again be fit for field combat duty.[63]

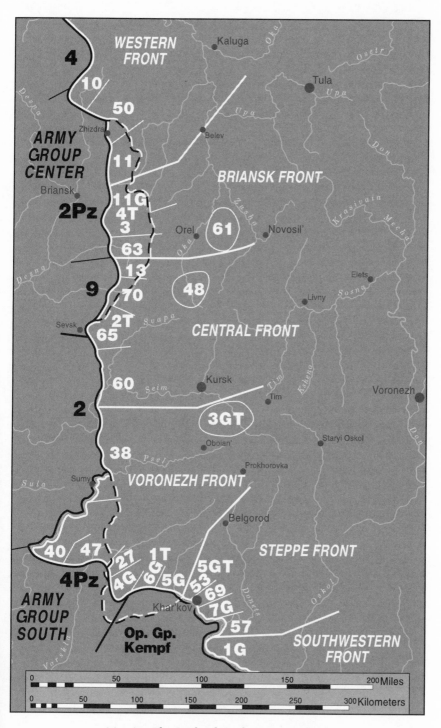

Map 31. The Battle of Kursk, 23 August 1943

Weighing the relative costs, the *Stavka* was well satisfied with what Zhukov, Vatutin, and Konev had achieved. German Army Group South's left flank could no longer hold, even if Vatutin and Konev's forces were too weak to capitalize on their advantage. Within days, the adjacent Central Front would strike at the vulnerable junction between Army Group Center and Army Group South. Von Manstein's beleaguered forces would have no choice but to withdraw rather precipitously to the Dnepr River line.

While the bitter fighting raged along the Belgorod-Khar'kov axis, the entire Soviet-German front erupted in flames as the Soviet summer offensive took shape. *Front* after Soviet *front* joined the concerted assault. The Western and Kalinin Fronts kicked off Operation Suvorov on 7 August by launching a major drive on Smolensk via Dukhovshchina and Roslavl'. The Southwestern and Southern Fronts once again thrust across the Northern Donets and Mius Rivers on 13 August, this time with a force that the Germans could not endure. The unremitting pressure of the incessant Soviet hammer blows left the German High Command with no alternative but to do the unthinkable and to begin a major strategic withdrawal.

By the end of August, the German hopes of Citadel were but a bitter memory. The German and Red Armies were engaged in a race to the Dnepr River, the next logical defensive line for Army Group South. In three weeks the Red Army had succeeded where the *Wehrmacht* had failed, and the battlefields of Kursk were soon left far behind. Hitler was reluctant to accept the strategic consequences of this defeat, but German professional soldiers recognized the decisive turn of events. At OKH, General Zeitzler told Army Group A to begin evacuation of its bridgehead east of the Black Sea, since there was little likelihood that Germany would ever again be able to launch a major offensive in southern Russia.[64] Blitzkrieg was at an end.

CHAPTER 8

Conclusions

GERMAN EXPECTATIONS AND REALITIES

German operations in 1943 were based on a number of important assumptions:

1. A well-prepared blitzkrieg would be able to achieve penetration and exploitation through any Soviet defense.
2. Superior German staff work, tactics, and weaponry would more than compensate for any Soviet numerical superiority; the Red Army was too inept to conduct the complex coordination necessary on the modern battlefield.
3. In particular, the Red Army was incapable of launching an effective offensive except under winter or other adverse weather conditions.
4. Even if the Soviets generated a major offensive, the German mastery of mobile counterattacks would always be able to derail and halt such an offensive.

In retrospect, all of these assumptions, which had generally held true in the period 1941–1942 and even as late as March 1943, proved to be wishful thinking four months later. The fault did not lie primarily with the German armed forces of 1943, which in some ways were superior to those of previous years. German commanders, particularly those of the Waffen SS, had matured under the stress of previous battles. Tiger and Panther tanks were indeed formidable weapons, if not the invincible war-winners that Hitler had hoped. Even the poorly designed Ferdinand could be used effectively in an overwatching role, where it was not exposed to Soviet infantry attacks. Only the Luftwaffe had severe limitations, due primarily to logistical constraints. Even here, the advent of tank-killer aircraft gave Germans a valuable new weapon. Moreover, the Red Air Force of 1943 more closely resembled the German stereotype of Soviet incompetence than did its counterpart on the ground.

German critics of Operation Citadel, in particular high-ranking participants and most historians who have since analyzed the operation, universally agree that the German strategic and operational aims in Citadel were excessively ambitious. With equal unanimity they place blame for this at the feet of Hitler and his principal General Staff advisers. Army Group South commander, Erich von Manstein, explained the rationale for the operation:

> Our minds now turned to the idea of a "forehand stroke." An attempt must be made to strike the enemy a blow of limited scope before he could recover from his losses in the winter campaign and resuscitate his beaten forces.
>
> A suitable target was presented by the Soviet salient which protruded far into our own front line around the city of Kursk. The Russians facing the boundary between Central and Southern Army Groups had been able to retain this when the muddy season set in, and now it formed a jumping-off position for any attacks they might be contemplating against the flanks of the two German army groups. The appreciable Soviet forces inside the salient would be cut off if our attack were successful, and provided that we launched it early enough we could hope to catch them in a state of unpreparedness. In particular, the enemy would have to commit the armoured units which had been so severely battered towards the end of the winter campaign, thereby giving us a chance to punish them wholesale.[1]

Von Manstein then blamed Hitler for the operation's failure, stating that, "as a result of the delivery of our own new tanks, the Army Group was not ultimately able to move off on Citadel until the beginning of July, by which time the essential advantage of a *forehand* blow was lost."[2] Ironically, von Manstein then bitterly criticized Hitler's 13 July decision to call off the operation: "Speaking for my own Army Group, I pointed out that the battle was now at its culminating point and that to break it off at this moment would be tantamount to throwing victory away. On no account should we let go of the enemy until the mobile reserves he had committed were completely beaten." Von Manstein ruefully added, "And so the last German offensive in the east ended in a fiasco, even though the enemy opposite the two attacking armies of the Southern Army Group had suffered four times their losses in prisoners, dead and wounded."[3]

The Inspector of Armored Troops for the *Wehrmacht*, General Heinz Guderian, who was responsible for creating the impressive armored armada the Germans employed in Citadel, attributed the idea for the Citadel offensive to Chief of the Army General Staff, Kurt Zeitzler: "This [the concept of the offensive] had arisen as a result of a proposed operation by the Chief of the Army General Staff, General Zeitzler, which envisaged a double enveloping attack against the big Russian salient west of Kursk; such an operation, if successful, would destroy a large number of Russian divisions, would decisively weaken the offensive strength of the Russian Army, and would place the German High Command in a more favorable position for continuing the war in the east."[4] Guderian added that "despite the fact that we [von Manstein and he] were the only two men . . . who were prepared bluntly to oppose Zeitzler's plan. . . . It is not yet clear why Hitler was eventually persuaded to launch this attack. It seems likely that pressure from the Chief of the Army General Staff was the deciding factor."[5]

The experienced armored commander and Chief of Staff of XXXXVIII Panzer Corps, von Mellenthin, agreed that the credit for the concept of Operation Citadel belonged to General Zeitzler:

> Zeitzler's object was a limited one; he wished to bite out the great Russian bulge which closed Kursk and projected for seventy-five miles into our front. A successful attack in this area would destroy a number of Soviet divisions and weaken the offensive power of the Red Army to a very considerable degree. As part of Fourth Panzer Army, the 48th Panzer Corps was to be the spearhead of the main drive from the south. I welcomed the idea, for our hardened and experienced panzer divisions had suffered little in the recent thrust on Kharkov, and were fit and ready for another battle as soon as the state of the ground would permit us to move. Moreover, at this stage the Russian defenses around Kursk were by no means adequate to resist a determined attack.[6]

He too then described his reservations associated with the delay of the operation: "Zeitzler then said that Hitler wanted to make the results still more decisive and wished to postpone the offensive until the arrival of a Panther Brigade. I listened to this with misgiving, and reported that according to the latest intelligence appreciations the Russians were still smarting under our recent blows and the losses incurred in the rapid and costly withdrawal from Kharkov had not been made good. A delay of one or two months would make our task far more formidable."[7] Von Mellenthin indicated, "When the attack was originally proposed, Field Marshal von Manstein was strongly in favor and believed that if we struck soon a notable victory could be won."[8] However, in von Mellenthin's words, "the repeated postponements made von Manstein 'dubious' and prompted Guderian to term the operation 'pointless.'"[9] Once approved, von Mellenthin described what he termed as the "greatest armoured onslaught in the history of the war," a "veritable death ride, for virtually the whole of the operational reserve was to be flung into this supreme offensive."[10]

General Gottfried Heinrici, then commander of the German Fourth Army and later a preeminent German defensive specialist, agreed with these assessments:

> Hitler stuck fast to his decision to preempt the Soviets with his own attack. This required an attack against their defensive front. . . . The intent

was to destroy the forces in the Kursk salient by an envelopment attack and then defeat the strong enemy reserves east of Kursk that were being assembled for the later Russian offensive. The elimination of the Kursk salient would shorten the German front by 240 kilometers and, therefore, make it possible to free up additional reserves. Above all, this attack would eliminate the Soviet departure positions for an attack into the deep flank of Army Group South in the direction of the Dnepr or an outflanking of Army Group Center's Orel salient. The Kursk salient also formed a particularly weak point on the German Eastern Front.[11]

Heinrici then joined the chorus of criticism over Hitler's postponement of the operation:

If the conditions for the execution of Hitler's operation plan *Zitadelle*— regardless of its expediency—were no longer favorable at the end of April, then the delay of the operation and the insufficient concentration of forces proved to be the main reasons for its failure. The troops and their leaders had made extreme efforts to see that the attack had a chance of succeeding. However, the strength of the three Russian fronts . . . and their defensive readiness insured that the attack must fail unless the Russian troop leadership or the morale of the Russian troops had completely collapsed.[12]

In retrospect, Heinrici then outlined the stark implications of the Citadel defeat:

The departure point for the planning of the summer campaign was the idea that the elimination of the Kursk salient and the destruction of Russian reserves would make the holding of the Donets region and the Orel salient possible. Neither of these things was achieved. Under these circumstances maintaining the requirement of defending these areas no longer made any sense. If during the next few weeks the majority of the Eastern Front was thrown into flux and setbacks piled onto setbacks it can be ascribed to Hitler's inflexibility, and to his continued aversion to transitioning to a mobile defense, which was the only chance the Eastern Army had left.[13]

In short, like his counterparts, Heinrici concluded, "it can be said of the outcome of *Zitadelle*: its failure had its basis in Hitler's operational planning."[14] Specifically:

The missions assigned to the Eastern Army, which were to hold the present front and prevent the far superior enemy from launching an offensive by conducting a partial offensive, overtaxed their capabilities after the losses suffered during the winter. The setting of objectives for Eastern Army operations, which were so important for the outcome of the entire war, should not have been founded upon political, economic or prestige factors, which were used by Hitler as the basis of his order to hold on to the existing front, in light of the threatening developments in the strategic situation. The holding of the existing defensive front—strategically speaking—was unnecessary in order to protect the rear of the Western Army from an invasion and to give the High Command operational freedom in the use of its own forces. In order to secure both of these factors it was necessary to weaken the Soviets in the limited time still available, and this would not be achieved by tying oneself down, but by creating more favorable combat conditions.

Hitler's ideas of taking the unprepared enemy by surprise and, when this proved to be impossible, to make up for the German inferiority by committing stronger technical combat equipment were, as experience showed, an unstable foundation to build a basis for an operation as important as *Zitadelle*. Only a change in the conduct of operations would have been able to secure success against a superior enemy who was prepared for all eventualities. It was also necessary to abandon the inflexible defense and make the transition to mobile operations in which the attacks of the superior enemy forces could be parried by withdrawals until the opportunity for an operational counterstroke offered itself. At the same time, the Eastern Army would have freer use of its available forces in a mobile defense than when tied to the defense of fixed positions.[15]

Unlike other German officers, when assessing the strategic wisdom of Citadel Heinrici emphasized the oft-ignored link between operations in the East and West and touched upon possible Soviet and Allied strategic cooperation. He concluded:

Such combat operations, nevertheless, stood in stark contrast to those of the enemy, who made it clear during May that they would not attack until the Western Powers landed in the Mediterranean Sea area. By making the decision for mobile combat operations and voluntarily withdrawing, the enemy would be forced to pursue and also take up mobile combat operations. Since the coordination of the Soviet offensive with the invasion of the Western powers could not have been prevented by German countermeasures, the chances of the Eastern Army successfully conducting a mobile combat operation against their enemy were greater than being tied to their fixed positions.[16]

Thus, to a greater or lesser degree, during the postwar years all four German commanders questioned the wisdom of launching Operation Citadel in the first place. While some admitted to the marginal value of the operation had it been launched in May, they categorically criticized delay of the operation to early July. Furthermore, they maintained that the delay condemned Citadel to failure, and this failure, in turn, threatened the viability of the entire German war effort. In short, in their view, Hitler's irrational and arbitrary decisionmaking conditioned the subsequent defeat at Kursk and severely undercut the German war effort.

Understandably, but unfortunately, most postwar historians have accepted these judgments on Citadel, in particular, and the war, in general, as representing historical truths. There are now compelling reasons for questioning, qualifying, or categorically rejecting these "historical truths." These reasons fall into two general but distinct categories. First, at least in part, these judgments were a product of their time and circumstances. In other words, they reflect their historical context. Second, and even more important, many of the authors' assumptions were patently incorrect, although often through no fault of their own, since they were writing from memory and archival materials were either scarce (German) or nonexistent (Soviet).

Regarding historical context, the senior German officers who wrote these critiques did so after the war had ended and after both they and Germany had tasted defeat. Moreover, they wrote during the height of the Cold War, when the Soviet Union was the *bête noir* of the West. It was only natural that they should seek and find a single and simple cause for the German defeat that had propelled the Soviet Union into a premier world power and the Red Army into the dreaded instrument of Soviet world expansion. They found such a scapegoat in Hitler, and since the scapegoat was dead and thoroughly discredited, no one was inclined to question their judgments. It is not coincidental that these memoirs reek with self-pity and regret over the failure of the German Army to defeat what would become the premier instrument of postwar Soviet power. At the least, these works subtly imply that, under a "nicer" German leader or a German leader who deferred to professional military advice, the German Army and state might have done the world a favor. At times, the word "could" can even be substituted for the weaker "might."

Closely related to the issue of historical context is the subject of historical reality. While the 1950s and 1960s provided a unique, powerful, and compromising context for these judgments, it also tended to cloud historic perspective and to pervert reality. This kind of *ex post facto* analysis permitted the authors to judge the war after it had already been lost. Quite naturally, therefore, the authors accepted the premise that the German defeat, both at Kursk and overall, was inevitable. Having surrendered to what they knew had happened, they focused their attention on assessing blame for that defeat and for their nation's ensuing misery.

The historical realities of 1943, some new and some not so new, compel us to challenge several key aspects of the most important and vulnerable of these traditional interpretations associated with German defeat in Citadel:

- Citadel would have succeeded had it been launched according to original plans (in spring 1943).
- When it was launched in July, Citadel was destined to fail.
- German adoption of a mobile defensive strategy at Kursk and thereafter would have produced either German victory or stalemate, or, at least, delayed German defeat.
- Hitler, and Hitler alone, was responsible for the failure of Citadel.

There is absolutely no basis for assuming that Citadel would have succeeded had it been launched in spring 1943. This assumption is based on the false premise that von Manstein was prevented by higher authorities from fully exploiting his March 1943 victory around Khar'kov and that Soviet military weakness in spring would have permitted von Manstein's counterstroke to be continued in March or resumed in May. One cannot deny the brilliance of von Manstein's operation. In fact, it can now be argued that his winter counterstroke was, in reality, a counteroffensive, since it had strategic rather than just operational significance. This is so because, rather than forestalling a Soviet drive into the Donbas, von Manstein's operations actually thwarted a larger and more ambitious Soviet effort to split the entire German front.

To accept this reality, however, requires acceptance of an even greater reality, namely, that the Soviets concentrated a strategic-size force to conduct operations in spring 1943 and that this force was far larger than either von Manstein or German intelligence knew at that time or that historians have since known. After mid-March 1943, von Manstein faced not only the threadbare armies he defeated in the Donbas and Khar'kov regions but also faced General Rokossovsky's newly formed and reinforced Central Front, several powerful armies dispatched into the Kursk region (the 1st Tank, 21st, 62d, and 64th), and a growing Soviet strategic reserve deploying along the Don River (the 24th, 63d, and 66th Armies). In late March, these armies began preparing heavy defenses within the Kursk Bulge.[17]

German forces, in particular the critical panzer divisions, had also suffered severely from attrition during the desperate fighting in late winter and spring. The panzer divisions of the XXXXVIII Panzer Corps, for example, often counted fewer than twenty tanks each, and the SS Panzer Corps suffered 12,000 casualties in the February and March battles. Extensive refitting was required before these formations could resume offensive operations with any prospect for success. In short, from March through July, the relative strength of Soviet and German forces in and adjacent to the Kursk Bulge developed apace. While the Soviets firmed up their Kursk defenses, they assembled the seven armies and over 500,000 men of the Steppe Military District in the region east of Kursk and Khar'kov. At the same time, however, the Germans reinforced their forces around the Kursk Bulge significantly. Soviet classified records indicate that, between 27 March and 4 July 1943, the Germans nearly doubled their strength along the flanks of the Kursk Bulge by redeploying an additional 234,000 men and 2,485 tanks and assault guns into the region.[18]

Most important, the extended period from March through early July permitted the Germans to rest and refit all of their forces, in particular, their panzer forces. In July they would go into combat near full strength and equipped as well as they ever had been. There was every reason to assume that the new German weaponry, in particular, the Tigers, Panthers, and Ferdinands, would tip the scales in the *Wehrmacht's* favor. Soviet reactions to these new weapons clearly indicate that these German assumptions were correct. While in hindsight it seems easy to criticize the performance of these new weapons in combat, in early July few anticipated the technical problems these weapons would experience. Ironically, these problems alone argued for further postponement rather than acceleration of the German offensive timetable.

The nearly universal postwar judgment that Citadel was destined to fail utterly ignores 1943 realities and is also the product of hindsight. Before July 1943 the German High Command had launched two carefully prepared strategic offensives: the Barbarossa drive of 22 June 1941 and the Blau offensive of 28 June 1942. With relative ease these offensives propelled German forces into the Soviet strategic depths. German forces smashed Soviet tactical defenses in a matter of hours and operational defenses within several days. German defeats ensued only after their forces had penetrated up to 800 kilometers deep into Soviet strategic defenses over the course of months of operations (five months at Moscow and four months at Stalingrad). In short, even the most pessimistic German general presumed German forces could easily penetrate Soviet tactical and operational defenses. What worried them at Kursk was what they would do once they reached the strategic depths. How could they avoid overextension and ultimate strategic defeat?

To a greater degree than before, Hitler's plan addressed these concerns by incorporating more modest strategic objectives. Thus, tactically and operationally, the leadership on both sides accepted the inevitability of initial German success, for anything less would be unprecedented. It was for this reason that Soviet defense lines at Kursk extended to a depth of about 200 kilometers. It was also for this reason that the Soviets backed up their forces in the Kursk Bulge with Konev's strong Steppe Military District. As unprecedented as it would be, for the first time in the war, the Soviets hoped to halt the German drive in the operational depths, in the Kursk Bulge itself. Their Herculean efforts to do so underscored how seriously they addressed the German threat.

In 1943 the concept of mobile defense was still in its infancy and had not gained the credence that the remainder of the war would accord it. Certainly there had been occasions earlier in the war when Hitler's insistence on defending terrain had, in the opinion of some commanders, contributed to German defeat and excessive German losses. By summer 1943 the classic instance was Stalingrad, where Hitler had overruled von Manstein's request to permit the German Sixth Army to break out of its deadly trap. Hitler refused, and von Manstein and others bitterly criticized the decision after war's end. What von Manstein did not know then or after the war, however, was that strong Soviet strategic reserves in the Stalingrad region would have thwarted the breakout effort. Later in the war, when the instances of Hitler's defensive stubbornness increased with ever more catastrophic consequences, arguments for the utility of a mobile defense gained greater credence. After the war it became a German shibboleth, a virtual explanation of how the war might have been won, or at least how catastrophic and total defeat might have been avoided.

These critiques of Hitler's strategy and the utility of a mobile defense overlook several marked instances where Hitler's stand-fast mentality succeeded. Specifically, his insistence on holding strategic hedgehog positions outside Moscow in the horrible winter 1941–1942 battles spelled doom for the Soviet counteroffensive and perhaps staved off German collapse and even costlier defeats in that sector. Likewise, Hitler's insistence upon holding the Rzhev salient in November and December 1942 inflicted a severe rebuff to Soviet strategic plans for achieving victory along the entire front in winter 1942–1943. While retrospective analysis of the ultimate German defeat on the Eastern Front rendered these cases superfluous, they were not superfluous in July 1943. Mobile defense seemed prudent and wise to postwar military analysts, but the generals of 1943 knew that it could not produce victory in a war that most thought could still be won.

Finally, it is disingenuous at best to blame Hitler alone for the defeat in Citadel. This judgment, however, rests within a broader context. The traditional scapegoat for all German failures in World War II is, of course, Adolf Hitler. In many instances this argument has been justified; Hitler's arbitrary interference and stubbornness were legendary. Yet, in the case of Kursk, Hitler almost always followed the best advice of his professional soldiers and, in at least one instance, grasped the situation more clearly than did they. In deciding to attack in 1943, Hitler reflected not only his political priorities but also the prevailing German military belief, noted above, that their forces would always be able to triumph in a well-prepared offensive. In delaying Citadel for two months, Hitler was responding to the tactical warnings of Model and the production promises of Guderian and Speer. In deciding to halt the offensive after the Allied invasion of Sicily, Hitler made the correct decision for the wrong reason, and even then he permitted von Manstein to continue the doomed attack on Prokhorovka because the field marshal overestimated the degree of damage he was inflicting on his opponents. It is true that the dictator's initial reaction to both of the Soviet counteroffensives was to defend every inch of ground, but in each instance he soon authorized the necessary withdrawals. Indeed, the decision to re-create a strategic reserve by evacuating the Orel salient was undoubtedly the best precaution to deal with threats both in Italy and at Khar'kov.

In a broader context, the German General Staff and senior officer corps willingly shared Hitler's and the grateful nation's enthusiasm for the unbroken string of German victories in Poland, Norway, the Low Countries, and Russia. They too relished the plaudits of a grateful nation and planned for even greater victories. While disputes between the *Wehrmacht* leadership and their political masters had occasionally flared, in 1943 these disputes and tensions were still minor. It would take many more defeats to produce the level of criticism and officer corps' disgust so apparent in 1944. Even Guderian, in retrospect a self-described harsh critic of Hitler, could willingly accept the post of Chief of the General Staff in July 1944.

In short, the German Army enthusiastically undertook Operation Citadel. It was an opportunity to achieve revenge for the embarrassing defeats at Moscow in 1941 and at Stalingrad in 1942. More importantly, success at Kursk might solve the German dilemma of coping with a war that no longer promised outright strategic victory. With the more realistic strategic goals, prior experience clearly indicated that the Kursk Bulge could be smashed and the Red Army could be made to bleed. If this bloodletting occurred, subsequent similar operations just might, in the judgment of the German political and military leadership, permit Germany to escape her strategic dilemma. Rather than strategic victory, Germany might achieve stalemate and perhaps even a political solution on the Eastern Front. This took on even greater importance given increasing German concerns about her vulnerable Western Front.

SOVIET EXPECTATIONS AND REALITIES

Citadel notwithstanding, Soviet strategic planning in the summer of 1943 was inherently offensive in nature. *Stavka* strategic objectives for the summer campaign replicated those which it had failed to achieve during the waning stages of the winter campaign, namely, collapse of German defenses and an advance to the line of the Dnepr River from Smolensk in the north southward to the Black Sea.

Stavka representative Vasilevsky later described the ambitious plan:

> The Soviet High Command, putting into effect the earlier worked out and accepted plan for a summer–fall strategic offensive and taking advantage of the favorable conditions resulting from Kursk, decided without delay to widen the offensive front of our forces in the southwestern direction. The Central, Voronezh, Steppe, Southwestern, and Southern Fronts were given the mission of destroying the main enemy forces on one of the central sectors and all of the southern wing of the Soviet-German front, of liberating the Donbas, the left bank of the Ukraine and Crimea, of reaching the Dnepr, and of securing bridgeheads on its right bank. . . .
>
> Simultaneously, operations were prepared to the north and south. The main forces of the Western Front and the left wing of the Kalinin Front planned to inflict defeat on 3d Panzer and 4th Field Armies of German Army Group Center and reach Dukhovshchina, Smolensk, and Roslavl', in order to drive his front lines a greater distance from Moscow, to create better conditions for the liberation of Belorussia, and to deprive the fascists of the ability to transfer forces from there to the south, where the main objective of the campaign would be decided. The North Caucasus Front, in cooperation with the Black Sea Fleet and Azov Flotilla, was to clear the Taman Peninsula and secure a bridgehead at Kerch. Thus, the *Stavka* planned to conduct a general offensive on a front from Velikie Luki to the Black Sea.[19]

Plans for the summer campaign, however, differed in several critical respects from those which had governed the course and outcome of the winter campaign. These differences demonstrated a sharp "learning curve" among Soviet planners and a willingness to profit from previous experiences and mistakes.

First, Soviet spring plans reflected and exploited harsh lessons that the *Stavka* had learned in February and March 1943. The most important of these lessons was the Soviet realization that sufficient forces had to be assembled to conduct and sustain the strategic effort throughout its entire duration and to the full depth of Soviet strategic objectives. Hence, the *Stavka* regrouped and concentrated forces that it deemed necessary to execute every phase of the strategic operation. In addition, *Stavka* planners exploited geographical and terrain lessons derived from the earlier failed offensive. They defended where defense was most important, and they planned subsequent offensive action so as to deny the Germans the advantages they had exploited in February and March, namely, the ability to strike the vulnerable flanks of advancing Soviet forces.

Second, the *Stavka* understood the unprecedented nature of the planned Soviet offensive. For the first time in the war, Soviet forces would attack in summer, a season that German forces had previously "owned." The *Stavka* was acutely aware of the fact that Soviet offensive operations in summer had never before succeeded. This, in part, conditioned the Soviets to first defend and then attack. This reality, too, prompted the careful and painstaking Soviet preparations for both the defensive and the offensive phases of the campaign.

Third, and perhaps most important, for the first time in the war the *Stavka*, in general, and Stalin, in particular, were able to control their hitherto unbridled optimism and establish more realistic and achievable strategic objectives. Despite Stalin's nearly uncontrollable urge to strike first, for the first time in the war, he deferred to the wise counsel of his military advisors. He accepted the necessity of the initial defensive phase of the operation and acquiesced in the more limited aims of subsequent offensive actions. Only during the waning stages of the campaign (in October and November), when the summer campaign had become the summer–fall campaign, did Stalin assign his forces excessively unrealistic objectives. Even then his advisors acquiesced in his opinions, since only by such offensive action could the limits of German power be tested.

In retrospect, Soviet successes during the defensive phase of the campaign (Citadel) exceeded their expectations. Despite nagging doubts as to whether a German offensive could be stopped, halted it was, and short of the operational depths. Careful Soviet preparations paid off, and the defeat of German forces along the flanks of the Kursk Bulge paved the way for further successes in Operations Kutuzov and Rumiantsev. In the classified words of a Red Army General Staff analysis of the operation:

> Our command adequately discovered the plan for the German 1943 summer offensive; as early as March 1943 the *Stavka* of the Supreme High Command had not only already made a completely accurate prognosis with respect to the overall nature of forthcoming enemy operations, but also had determined the deployment regions of his principal groupings and the probable attack directions.
>
> Accurate and correct analysis of the situation made it possible to make an absolutely correct decision that was appropriate for the circumstances: *to meet the enemy attack on a well-prepared defensive bridgehead, to bleed attacking German groupings dry, and then to shift to a general offensive.* The defeat of the enemy shock groups created favorable prerequisites for

developing new, extensive offensive operations. Thus, *our defense was prepared with the objective of a subsequent shift to the offensive.*[20]

The initial phases of the Soviet offensive, which took the form of a strategic counteroffensive, while often crude, messy, and costly in a tactical and operational sense, achieved their general strategic and operational objectives. Operational regroupings, deception plans, and diversionary operations worked well, and the Germans reacted as the *Stavka* anticipated they would. Whatever difficulties ensued resulted from the tactical and operational skill of German forces rather than from faulty Soviet plans.

The crude success the Soviets achieved in Operations Kutuzov and Rumiantsev was assisted by and, in turn, conditioned Soviet successes in the other operations that subsequently rippled along the front. The Western and Kalinin Fronts' Operation Suvorov, that began on 7 August against German Army Group Center forces forward of Smolensk, and the Southwestern and Southern Fronts' Donbas offensive, which commenced on 13 August against the already-beleaguered forces of Army Group South, exploited German preoccupation with their defense of Orel and Khar'kov. Then, by increasing the unremitting pressure on the German front as a whole, successive Soviet blows rendered German defense of Orel and Khar'kov utterly futile. With the Smolensk and Donbas fronts aflame and Orel and Khar'kov abandoned, on 26 August the Central, Voronezh, and Steppe Fronts began the Chernigov-Poltava strategic operation, which was designed to exploit the gains of Rumiantsev. Less than a week later, on 1 September, the Briansk Front exploited the successes of Kutuzov by launching an offensive toward its namesake city. As difficult as these operations were for Soviet forces, the German Army could no longer withstand the pressure. The ensuing "Race to the Dnepr" propelled Soviet forces to the banks of that long-sought-after Soviet objective in late September 1943.

Only then did *Stavka* expectations exceed Soviet capabilities. It was realistic for the Soviets to attempt to exploit their successes and to continue the offensive beyond the Dnepr River. However, it was unrealistic to do so on a broad front. Nevertheless, in early November 1943, Stalin and the *Stavka* established new strategic objectives that encompassed a simultaneous advance into both Ukraine and Belorussia (see Map 32). This decision proved to be overly ambitious. Consequently, while the Soviets lunged across the Dnepr River at Kiev in early November and began a successful operation to form a strategic bridgehead in Ukraine, they failed to replicate this feat in Belorussia. It would take six more months to mount a proper effort into Belorussia.

The spectacular Soviet performance during the summer–fall campaign was a direct result of the Soviet defeat of Operation Citadel. For the first time in the war, the *Stavka* and the Red Army met and, at times, exceeded their

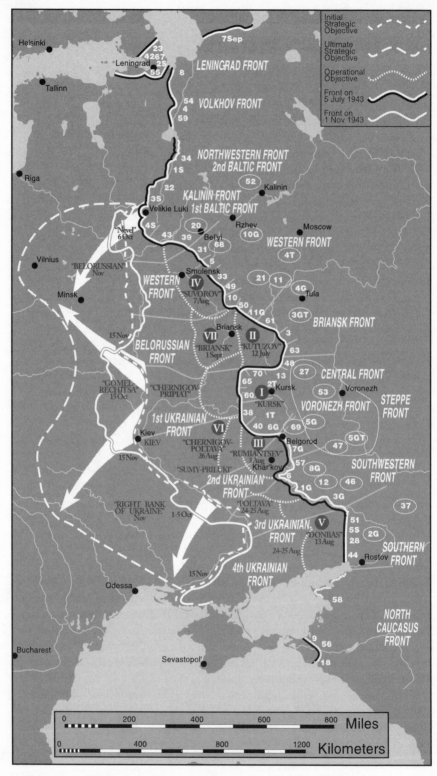

Map 32. Strategic Offensive Plan, Summer–Fall 1943

strategic expectations. The defeat of blitzkrieg at Kursk opened a new phase of the war, a phase in which, strategically at least, future Soviet offensive action would always exceed expectations.

CITADEL

Armies are frequently accused of preparing to fight the previous war. While this is often a base canard, it is true that the vanquished are more likely to question their assumptions and revise their military procedures than are the victors. In the context of the German-Soviet struggle, the Germans, flush with frequent successes from June 1941 through March 1943, naturally clung to outmoded assumptions about their own superiority over their opponents. By contrast, the Red Army systematically reviewed its performance after every failure. By 1943 Soviet doctrine, organization, and expectations were much closer to battlefield reality than were those of the senior German leadership.

Indeed, in both a defensive and an offensive sense the battles of July and August 1943 were the first modern Soviet operations of the war. Although it lacked technological superiority in terms of individual weapons systems, for the first time in the war, the Soviet Union learned to integrate combined arms forces into a mix that proved lethal for the attacking Germans. This was, however, only a beginning, for the integration was often crude and entailed great losses in manpower and weaponry. For the remainder of the war, the Soviets were essentially elaborating upon the doctrine, force structure, and procedures first tested at Kursk, Orel, and Khar'kov.

The hallmarks of the new Red Army were evident throughout the defensive operation.[21] The Red Army's concealed defensive regroupment and force concentration at the strategic and operational levels denied the Germans force superiority both in the Kursk sector overall and in the two German main attack sectors. Tactically, similar force concentration, the echelonment of defenses to depths of up to sixty kilometers, and the establishment of row after row of antitank obstacles, regions, and strong points deprived the Germans of even tactical superiority, negated the impact of massed armor, and produced a tremendous erosion of German offensive power throughout their offensive. The hallmarks of this defense were the density, redundancy, and thorough integration of Soviet defensive weapons systems and the forces that manned them.

Even more important was the constant Soviet strengthening of their defenses through reinforcement, or what the Soviets have since termed *narashchivanie* (augmentation, or strengthening). Skillful Soviet deployment of strategic, operational, and tactical reserves, in particular, mobile armor and antitank reserves, compensated for high initial losses, countered every German tactical gain, immediately threw the German offensive timetable off schedule, forced the Germans to alter their plans constantly, and ultimately frustrated the Germans' realization of their operational objectives. The presence of strategic reserves enabled the Red Army to both contain the German offensive and launch powerful counteroffensives on and adjacent to the initial field of battle. Finally, as was their custom, the Germans placed full faith in the success of a single blow. This, coupled with their lack of operational reserves, made defeat, when it occurred, final and irrevocable.

At Kursk, for the first time in the war, the Soviets contested with the Germans in the air on an almost equal footing. They began the battle with an audacious preemptory strike against German air installations, but this strike failed to achieve its intended effect and, in fact, hindered Soviet air operations during the initial stages of the German assault. The ferocity of the subsequent German blow forced Soviet aviation "off plan" during the bulk of the first day of the defensive battle, but thereafter Soviet fighters slowly whittled away at German tactical air dominance in both the north and south. By the end of the second day of operations, the 16th Air Army had achieved "equilibrium" in the north. But although it was able to deny German fighters air superiority, German bombers could still operate effectively against ground targets. From 7 July onward, however, the scales of battle tipped in the Soviets' favor as the 16th Air Army plan came into full effect. Thereafter, while the Germans could mass aircraft in particular sectors, its effectiveness faded and Soviet air took a heavier toll on German ground forces.

In the south, German aviation dominated the skies on the first two days of the German attack. By late 6 July, however, the 2d Air Army had reached parity with German air, and thereafter the Germans were able to achieve only temporary local air superiority. By "surging" their aircraft and shifting the focus of their efforts the Germans were able to inflict sizable damage on particular Soviet targets (the 2d Guards Tank Corps, for example) and maintain cover for their ground forces along key axes (for example, along the Oboian' axis on 9 July and along the Prokhorovka axis on 11 July). All the while, attrition took its toll and German sortie rates fell steadily after 7 July and precipitously after 14 July. All of this was achieved, however, at great cost in Soviet aircraft.

Soviet critiques of their air effort noted that despite their numerical superiority they did not achieve air superiority until 7–8 July on the northern axis and 11 July on the southern axis. This was because of better German aircraft concentration and individual and group tactics and command and control problems experienced by Soviet aviation units (mostly associated with a shortage of radios). Therefore, the Soviets required a sortie rate twice that of the Germans to achieve ultimate air dominance.

The Soviets noted other particular features of the air operation that had a significant impact on the outcome of the battle. For example, aside from the early Soviet preemptive blow, neither side employed air forces against targets deeper in the rear area. Although circumstances such as shortages in aircraft and the desire to maintain operational secrecy before the assault prevented them from doing so, the German failure to attack Soviet rear targets permitted the Soviet High Command to move great quantities of operational and tactical reserves to key sectors throughout the operation. On the other hand, poor fighter operations hindered the employment of Soviet assault aviation and facilitated the dangerous German advance along the southern axis. In the end, Soviet air power, by Soviet calculation, produced only between 2 and 6.5 percent of overall German tank losses.[22]

Given these circumstances, it is not surprising that the fortunes of forces struggling on the ground closely coincided with the ebb and flow of air combat. Although air did not play a decisive active role in the Soviet victory on the ground, Soviet denial to the Germans of their accustomed air superiority did.

General Heinrici later echoed many of these Soviet judgments on Kursk. He pinpointed the delay in launching the operation and insufficient concentration of forces as the main reason for German failure in Citadel. "The strength of the three Russian fronts . . . and their defensive readiness insured that the attack [would] fail unless the Russian troops had completely collapsed."[23] That collapse never occurred. Echoing Soviet critiques, Heinrici claimed that the loss of surprise and the Russians' deeply constructed defensive system enabled the defenders to hold out "long enough so that Soviet reserves could arrive on time and parry the offensive." More important from a strategic standpoint, the skillful defense provided time to "allow the Soviets to prepare for their counterstroke against the neighboring fronts."[24]

Heinrici also lamented the lack of infantry forces available to the attacking Germans, and he claimed this factor had a markedly deleterious effect on the offensive:

The infantry forces available to the army groups were too weak to drive a screening front to the east along the intended line. Above all, infantry divisions—especially in the Army Group South area of operations—were lacking to screen the flanks of the attack groups; therefore, this mission had to be taken over by panzer divisions, which were then missing from the attack in the main direction. The planned "panzer raid" very soon turned into a gradual forward battle. The perception that the strength of the German attack was ebbing, together with the news of the landing of the Western Powers, compelled the Soviets to make the decision to launch their counterattack in the region of the Orel salient and south of Kharkov. The inferior German defenses there made it easy for the attackers to bring an immediate end to *Zitadelle* by breaking into the operational rear and threatening the flanks.[25]

This perceptive comment unwittingly highlights the primary reason for the defeat of Army Group South in Citadel. Rather than the climactic battle at Prokhorovka, it was the incessant Soviet pressure against the flanks of the XXXXVIII and II SS Panzer Corps, together with Soviet denial of air superiority to the Germans, that conditioned ultimate German defeat. The numerous flank attacks orchestrated by Vatutin using Katukov's 1st Tank Army and various separate tank corps sapped German strength, prevented full concentration of German panzer forces along the Oboian'-Kursk axis, delayed the German advance, permitted the timely arrival of Soviet operational and strategic reserves, and led directly to Soviet victory at Prokhorovka, in particular, and in Citadel as a whole.

The elaborate, deeply echeloned defenses around Kursk and artful Soviet deployment and commitment of mobile reserves had made the Soviets the first force to halt a blitzkrieg offensive. It is true that the Germans played into Soviet hands by attacking at such an obvious location, yet it still required remarkable self-confidence for Vatutin, Rokossovsky, and the other Soviet commanders to wait calmly while the German juggernaut prepared to do its worst. When the worst came, Soviet numerical superiority, the stubborn tenacity of the Soviet soldier, the improved combat skill of his commanders, and the Soviets' ability to sustain staggering losses spelled doom for Citadel.

THE COUNTEROFFENSIVES

On the offensive, the pattern of Soviet success in 1944 and 1945 was already evident in Operations Rumiantsev and Kutuzov. Prior to an attack, reconnaissance forces carefully scouted the enemy and then eliminated key strong points. Concealment of actual troop formations and elaborate deception measures misled the Germans as to the location of the coming attack. Specially configured teams of infantry, sappers, and infantry support tanks made the main assault after a massive, carefully targeted artillery barrage. As quickly as possible, tank corps and armies passed through the attacking infantry to complete the penetration and then exploit hundreds of kilometers into the German rear area. The tank armies struck deep at operational objectives, while the separate tank and mechanized corps aimed at closer, tactical targets. These mechanized exploitation forces were preceded by swiftly moving, combined arms forward detachments that bypassed centers of resistance in order to encircle the defenders or seize crossings over the next major river line. Although German Panzer forces often counterattacked with great effect, after Kursk they were rarely able to derail the Soviet offensive completely.

For the Soviets neither Operation Kutuzov nor Rumiantsev was an offensive work of art. Succeed they did, however, and with tragic consequences for the Germans. But they did so at immense cost, with nagging difficulties, and in far more time than anticipated. The two concentric blows of Kutuzov developed at an unequal pace, and the third scarcely materialized at all against skillful and desperate German resistance. Because of his imposing force and successful secret concentration, the assault by Bagramian's 11th Guards Army achieved spectacular immediate success. It tore through German defenses along the northern face of the Orel salient, and German reserves could not repair the breach. On the other hand, the assaults by the 3d and 63d Armies bogged down very quickly and became brutal slugfests. These attacks, however, played a significant role in the operation by attracting German forces and preventing the repair or containment of Bagramian's breach.

Throughout the remainder of the operation, the *Stavka* constantly threw reserves into both sectors and maintained unremitting pressure on the defending Germans. The ensuing meatgrinder produced heavy Soviet casualties and a staggering toll in armor. Although neither 3d Guards Tank nor 4th Tank Army nor the multiple tank corps committed by the Western and Briansk Fronts achieved the clean penetration they sought, their mere presence on the battlefield and the sheer weight of armor spelled doom for the German defense. After weeks of grinding battle that consumed what was left of the Ninth Army's armored strength, German forces fell back to the Hagen line.

Unlike the case in Kutuzov, in Rumiantsev the Soviet command achieved its clean deep penetration, even through Zhukov had chosen to assault the very nose of the German defense. Within two days the 1st and 5th Guards Tank Armies were in the operational open, and it seemed that complete and rapid victory was at hand. Then, however, the same circumstances that had plagued the Germans in Citadel denied the Soviets rapid success in Rumiantsev. The separate tank and mechanized corps that were subordinate to rifle armies could not replicate at a tactical level the tank armies' success on the broader stage of deep operations. Instead, most of these separate mobile corps were forced to join in costly penetration battles along the two tank armies' flanks. Subsequently, the tenacious defense by semi-encircled German forces along the flanks eroded the strength of the advancing tank armies, delayed their exploitation southward, and permitted German mobile reserves to intervene short of the Soviet final objectives. This resulted in the climactic meeting battles around Akhtyrka and Bogodukhov, which ultimately blunted and slowed the Soviet drive.

Although the exploiting Soviet mobile force could validly claim that for the first time in the war they fought German mobile forces to a standstill, the cost was a delay in the capture of Khar'kov and an irrevocable loss rate in tanks almost eight times that of the Germans. Ultimately, the sheer weight of Soviet strength and the vicious combat along an ever extending front forced the Germans to abandon the key city.

Thus, a new Red Army with a markedly improved force structure and vastly enhanced offensive capabilities made its presence felt in Operations Kutuzov and Rumiantsev. Yet the new mobile force structure equipped with new offensive regulations and procedures still lacked combat experience, and it showed. It would take many such operations and considerable learning for the mature armored force of 1944 to emerge. Kutuzov and Rumiantsev were critical and costly first steps in that education process.

COSTS

For years debate has raged over German and Soviet combat losses in the various phases of the Battle of Kursk. No comprehensive tally has been made on the German side, in part due to problems in defining the operation's parameters and in part to the lack of a comprehensive, archival-based account of the operation. At the same time, until recently Soviet authorities have studiously avoided the topic entirely, preferring to talk about losses only in the context of medical support to Soviet forces and, even then, only in terms of percentages and daily casualty rates. Soviet accounts, including the memoirs of participating figures such as Zhukov and Vasilevsky, routinely inflated German strength and losses, apparently to portray Soviet combat performance in a better light.

After the fall of the Soviet Union, many, but not all, of the restrictions over Russian archival materials were loosened, and official and unofficial historians began addressing this hitherto forbidden topic. Although several books and articles have appeared on Soviet wartime losses, these cannot be considered as definitive, for the circumstances of Soviet wartime recordkeeping were so chaotic that actual loss figures may never be fully known. Thus the debate rages on, with official accounts contending with a host of unofficial estimates, many of which reflect the reformist zeal and hatred of the Communist regime of their authors.

The most authoritative official account of wartime losses, edited by Colonel General G. F. Krivosheev, considers Soviet Kursk losses within the context of overall Soviet combat strength in each major phase of the Kursk Strategic Operation. According to Krivosheev, Soviet forces suffered 177,847 casualties out of a total committed strength of 1,272,700 personnel in Citadel.[26] These losses were broken down as follows:

Front	Strength	Irrevocable	Medical	Total
Central	738,000	15,336	18,561	33,897
Voronezh	534,700	27,542	46,350	73,892
Steppe	—	27,452	42,606	70,058
Total	1,272,700	70,330	107,517	177,847

It must be borne in mind that these figures include the strength of the entire Central and Voronezh Fronts, about one quarter of whose formations were not engaged directly in the battle (for example, much of the 48th Army and all of the 60th, 65th, and 38th Armies). Therefore, the percentage of losses indicated above (about 14 percent) rises sharply if only committed forces are included.[27]

If combat support and rear service elements are stripped from the equation (because their losses were significantly lower than losses in tactical formations), the loss percentages rise precipitously. On a division-by-division and corps-by-corps basis, formation losses ranged from a low of 20 percent to losses as high as 70 percent, depending on the role and function of each formation in combat.[28]

According to German records, between 5 and 11 July, German Ninth Army's losses totaled 20,720 killed, wounded, and missing. Other records indicate that from 5 through 20 July, Army Group South lost 29,102 killed, wounded, and missing. Thus, the Germans lost a total of 49,822 men in Citadel, somewhat less than a third of the admitted Soviet troop losses.[29] Once again, precise losses depended on the intensity of combat individual divisions experienced, but in no case did German losses reach Soviet proportions.[30]

The same official Soviet source indicated that during Citadel the Soviets lost 1,614 tanks and self-propelled guns out of the 5,035 tanks and self-propelled guns committed to action.[31] (See Appendix C for available data on the losses of the Soviet tank armies in the various phases of the Battle of Kursk.)

German armor losses in Citadel are more difficult to pin down. The II SS Panzer Corps' records indicate that, on 13 July, the corps had 251 operational tanks and assault guns, including 4 Tigers and 11 captured T-34s as opposed to an initial strength of 494 tanks and assault guns and a strength of 293 on 11 July. Considering repaired armored vehicles, these figures indicate that the corps lost between 60 and 70 tanks on 12 July (at Prokhorovka) and 243 tanks and assault guns since the operation commenced. By 13 July the XXXXVIII Panzer Corps' strength had fallen from 601 to 173 tanks and assault guns and Fourth Panzer Army's as a whole from 1,095 to 466. Army Detachment Kempf had 83 operational tanks on 13 July, including 9 Tigers, or 37 fewer tanks than on 11 July and 243 tanks fewer than on 5 July.

Although his figures differ slightly, Heinrici agrees that Fourth Panzer Army lost up to 60 percent of its tank and assault gun strength during the entire operation. Of this total, Heinrici points out that between 15 and 20 percent were irreparably destroyed. This would equate to roughly 629 tanks and assault guns damaged and up to 126 destroyed in Fourth Panzer Army. Similar losses in Army Detachment Kempf would have resulted in the damage of as many as 336 tanks and assault guns and the outright destruction of 67. In Model's Ninth Army similar loss rates would have produced figures of 647 damaged and 130 destroyed. Thus, total German armor losses in Citadel would have amounted to up to 1,612 tanks and assault guns damaged and 323 destroyed. On the basis of these figures, admitted Soviet tank losses (1,614 destroyed) were at least five times higher than German losses and probably even higher.[32]

Calculation of absolute and comparative losses in the Orel operation is more difficult due to the absence of definitive sources on the Soviet side and the less attention paid to the operation on the German side. Official Soviet sources indicate the following overall losses:[33]

Front	Strength	Irrevocable	Medical	Total
Western (left wing)	233,300	25,585	76,856	102,441
Briansk	409,000	39,173	123,234	162,407
Central	645,300	47,771	117,271	165,042
Total	1,287,600	112,529	317,361	429,890

The high Soviet losses are indicative of Soviet difficulties in the operation, in particular their inability to achieve a clean penetration and the grinding combat that ensued. The same source indicates that Soviet forces lost 2,586 tanks and self-propelled guns in the operation out of at least 3,925 committed to combat (well over 50 percent).[34] Precise German armor losses are not available but were certainly less than those incurred during Citadel, probably amounting to about 500 of the committed tanks and assault guns. Thus, armor loss ratios probably amounted to at least five to one in the Germans' favor. Once again, this favorable ratio was due, in part, to German repair and evacuation capabilities as well as to their still-superior tactical skills.

Soviet official sources indicate the following losses in the Belgorod-Khar'kov operation:[35]

Front	Strength	Irrevocable	Medical	Total
Voronezh	739,400	48,339	108,954	157,293
Steppe	404,600	23,272	75,001	98,273
Total	1,144,000	71,611	183,955	255,566

These figures are also indicative of the intense fighting.[36] Soviet losses were considerably fewer than in the Orel offensive because of the successful Soviet penetration operation. Krivosheev also indicates that in the operation Soviet forces lost 1,864 tanks and self-propelled guns out of 2,439 engaged, or well over 50 percent of the Voronezh and Steppe Fronts' initial armored strength.

Fragmentary data indicate that the Germans lost as many as 327 of the 600 tanks and assault guns they committed in the operation. Hence, the resulting loss ratio of roughly five Soviet armored vehicles to one German would accord with losses the Soviets experienced in the Orel operation and Citadel.

Although the three phases of the Kursk strategic operation proved costly to both sides, the Soviets could afford the losses and the Germans could not.

CONSEQUENCES

Virtually all participants in the Kursk operation and historians writing after the war have agreed on the catastrophic consequences of the German Kursk defeat for the German war effort. Marshal von Manstein cataloged the grim consequences in his memoirs:

> When "Citadel" was called off, the initiative in the Eastern theatre of war finally passed to the Russians. . . . Henceforth Southern Army Group found itself waging a defensive struggle which could not be anything more than a system of improvisations and stopgaps. . . . To maintain ourselves in the field, and in doing so to wear down the enemy's offensive capability to the utmost, became the whole essence of this struggle.[37]

In his final judgment on Citadel, Guderian echoed von Manstein's view:

> By the failure of Citadel we had suffered a decisive defeat. The armoured formations, reformed and re-equipped with so much effort, had lost heavily both in men and equipment and would now be unemployable for a long time to come. It was problematical whether they could be rehabilitated in time to defend the Eastern Front; as for being able to use them in defense of the Western Front against Allied landings that threatened for next spring, this was even more questionable. Needless to say the Russians exploited their victory to the full. There were to be no more periods of quiet on the Eastern Front. From now on the enemy was in undisputed possession of the initiative.[38]

In retrospect, von Mellenthin also judged Citadel to have been "a complete and most regrettable failure." He explained:

> It is true that Russian losses were much heavier than German; indeed tactically the fighting had been indecisive. Fourth Panzer Army took thirty-two thousand prisoners, and captured or destroyed more than two thousand tanks and nearly two thousand guns. But our panzer divisions—in such splendid shape at the beginning of the battle—had been bled white, and with Anglo-American assistance the Russians could afford losses on

this colossal scale. With the failure of our supreme effort, the strategic initiative passed to the Russians.[39]

Heinrici too sketched out the tragic consequences of the failure of Citadel, once again emphasizing the broader strategic implications:

The failure of *Zitadelle* had momentous results, in the political as well as the military realm. The ratio of forces of the Eastern Army to its enemy was now more unfavorable than it was before. While only a portion of the Soviet operational reserves were reduced in their combat effectiveness, all of the troops available to the Eastern Army had suffered considerably. The initiative, which thanks to Hitler's plans had now fallen into the hands of the enemy, would never again be seized because of the requirement to defend an over-extended front with insufficient forces. Therefore, having the Eastern Army render effective support to any of the OKW theaters of war was now out of the question. Germany's allies recognized that the outcome of *Zitadelle,* combined with the successful landing of the Western Powers in Sicily, meant that they could no longer anticipate a final victory by the Axis Powers. Therefore, there emerged efforts in all of these countries to oppose their own leadership so that their countries would avoid the effects of the coming defeat.[40]

Soviet assessments of the consequences of Kursk generally agree with German perceptions. In his memoirs Zhukov emphasized the obvious while underscoring the psychological impact of German defeat:

The battle fought in the Kursk, Orel, and Belgorod area was one of the most important engagements of the Great Patriotic War and the Second World War as a whole. Not only were the picked and most powerful groupings of the Germans destroyed here, but the faith of the German Army and the German people in the Nazi leadership and Germany's ability to withstand the growing might of the Soviet Union was irrevocably shattered.

The defeat of the main grouping of German troops in the Kursk area paved the way for the subsequent wide-scale offensive operations by the Soviet forces to expel the Germans from our soil completely, and then from the territories of Poland, Czechoslovakia, Hungary, Yugoslavia, Romania, and Bulgaria and ultimately to crush Nazi Germany.[41]

Vasilevsky later echoed Zhukov's assessment:

We were unable then [in late August] to analyze thoroughly the results of the Battle of the Kursk Bulge. Yet one thing was clear: we had not only won a great battle, we had matured in it. Our positions in working out the plan of the summer campaign had been justified: we had learned how to assess the enemy's intentions better than we had done in the past. We had had enough willpower, character, sheer stamina and nerve to avoid a miscalculation, a premature battle engagement or presenting the enemy with a chance to retrieve the situation. Elaboration of the operational and strategic assignments had been done successfully. Troop control had grown in skill at all levels. In a word, our leadership qualities had displayed both a creative skill and a superiority over the military skill of the Nazi command.

As a result of the Kursk Battle, the Soviet Armed Forces had dealt the enemy a buffeting from which Nazi Germany was never to recover. It lost 30 of its divisions, including 7 Panzer divisions. Losses of German land forces amounted to over 500,000 men, 1,500 tanks, 3,000 guns and over 3,500 warplanes. These losses and the failure of the offensive which had been so widely acclaimed in Nazi propaganda forced the Germans to go over to a strategic defense along the entire Soviet-German front. The big defeat at the Kursk Bulge was the beginning of a fatal crisis for the German Army.[42]

Vasilevsky then added a word about the international significance of the operation, evidencing Soviet bitterness over the perceived lack of Western appreciation of the Soviet war effort:

In reading works by several bourgeois writers on World War II, I have frequently noticed their inclination to play down the Red Army victory in the summer of 1943. They try to instill in their readers the idea that the Kursk Battle was just an ordinary, insignificant episode in the war; to these ends they either barely mention it or just skip it. Very rarely have I come across in such books any real assessment of the Nazi plan of revenge for the summer of 1943 as an adventurous or a bankrupt end to the strategy of the fascist generals. But, as the saying has it, deeds speak louder than words. I would mention just one elementary fact: at the height of the Kursk Battle our Allies landed in Sicily and, on 17 August, crossed over into Italy. Could they have possibly done so with even half the forces against them that we had to contend with in the summer of 1943? I think not.[43]

All of this is not to deny that the Red Army made costly mistakes, both at Kursk and throughout the remainder of the war. Although the Central Front halted the Ninth German Army more or less according to plan, the entire Soviet leadership underestimated the power of the Fourth Panzer Army opposite the Voronezh Front. This failure is even more surprising considering the extensive Red knowledge of the powerful SS and *Wehrmacht* forces assembled in the south. In addition, throughout the defensive battle, Soviet counterattacks and counterstrokes tended to be launched prematurely, before the force of the German assault had been absorbed by the antitank defenses. The four tank armies and numerous separate mobile corps employed in the Kursk campaign were frequently mishandled, as a result their combat power was blunted against prepared defenses or they were forced to attack in two different directions. Yet these errors, costly as they were, were errors of execution, not conception.

The Battle of Kursk meant an end to blitzkrieg in a strategic and operational sense. For the first time in the war, a German offensive was contained in the tactical or shallow operational depths. This was surprising and, ultimately, catastrophic for an army whose past strategic successes had been predicated on the delivery of successful deep operational thrusts that paralyzed its foes militarily and psychologically. Kursk proved that massed German armor covered by swift fighter escort could no longer range deep into the Soviet rear with abandon as it had in 1941 and 1942.

Even more striking, Kursk also spelled doom for German blitzkrieg in a tactical sense. Since the start of the war, and in fact since 1939, the Germans had successfully employed panzer divisions and carefully organized combat groups *(kampfgruppen)* of tanks and motorized infantry, supported by the vaunted Stuka dive-bomber, to smash through enemy tactical defenses and commence deep exploitations. To the utter consternation of the German command, they were unable to do so at Kursk even though they maintained clear technological superiority in tanks and antitank weapons. This was so because the Soviets had learned, albeit painfully, some fundamental and critical lessons from their numerous past failures. The most important of these lessons was that the only effective defense was one that exploited all arms and possessed both depth and flexibility. At Kursk the Soviets clearly demonstrated that only such a defense had the resilience to withstand traditional German tank assault. As a result, the Soviets proved that a determined and properly constructed infantry-based defense could defeat the tactics of blitzkrieg.

Hence, Kursk marked a turning point in the war strategically, operationally, and tactically. Building on the lessons of Kursk, the Soviets also applied their new combined-arms techniques to offensive situations, at first tentatively and later with greater effect. At Orel and Belgorod-Khar'kov, the Soviets led their assaults with infantry supported by massive artillery preparations that softened up German front-line defenses. The infantry was accompanied by infantry support tanks and self-propelled guns, which overcame the most stubborn German tactical resistance. They then committed, first, their tank and mechanized corps and, then, their tank armies to complete the penetration and commence the operational exploitation. Despite early problems, this cascading torrent of properly supported armor became an ever more effective means for subsequent Soviet operational and strategic advances.[44]

Beset by growing political constraints imposed by a frustrated and increasingly irrational Hitler, unable to match Soviet weapons production, and bled white by the attrition among younger experienced combat commanders, German tactics stagnated. Confronted with the death of blitzkrieg and unable to develop defensive tactics necessary to halt the Soviet juggernaut, German defeat simply became a matter of blood and time.

The battles of July and August 1943 associated with the German Operation Citadel and the Soviet Kursk Strategic Offensive Operation not only ended the myth of German invincibility but clearly demonstrated that the Red Army was rapidly developing the skills to match its enormous numbers. The resulting combination proved fatal to blitzkrieg and, ultimately, lethal to Germany.

German Order of Battle, 1 July 1943

The Orel Axis

ARMY GROUP CENTER—Field Marshal Guenther von Kluge

Second Panzer Army—Lieutenant General Rudolf Schmidt
  LV Army Corps
    321st Infantry Division
    339th Infantry Division
    110th Infantry Division
    296th Infantry Division
    134th Infantry Division
  LIII Army Corps
    211th Infantry Division
    293d Infantry Division
    25th Panzer Grenadier Division
    208th Infantry Division
    112th Infantry Division (reserve)
  XXXV Army Corps—General Lothar Rendulic
    34th Infantry Division
    56th Infantry Division
    262d Infantry Division
    299th Infantry Division
    36th Infantry Division (2 regiments) (reserve)
    5th Panzer Division (army reserve in LV Army Corps' sector) (strength: 102 tanks)
    8th Panzer Division (OKH reserve, arrive on 12 July) (strength: 101 tanks)
    305th Security Division
    707th Security Division

  ARMY STRENGTH: 160,000 men, 325 tanks and assault guns

The Orel-Kursk Axis

Ninth Army—Colonel General Walter Model
  XXIII Army Corps—General Johannes Freissner
    383d Infantry Division—Major General Edmund Hoffmeister

Note: All figures denote on-hand tank and assault gun strengths. Operational (serviceable) strengths were somewhat less. See Appendix D for specific day-to-day operational variations.

216th Infantry Division—Major General Schack
78th Assault Division—Lieutenant General Hans Traut
36th Infantry Division (1 regiment) (reserve)
185th Assault Gun Detachment (strength: 36 assault guns)
189th Assault Gun Detachment (strength: 36 assault guns)
Corps strength: 72 assault guns
XXXXI Panzer Corps: General Joseph Harpe
86th Infantry Division—Lieutenant General Helmuth Weidling
292d Infantry Division—Lieutenant General Guenther von Kluge
18th Panzer Division—Major General Karl Wilhelm von Schlieben (strength: 72 tanks)
656th Antitank Detachment
653d Antitank Detachment (Ferdinand) (strength: 55 self-propelled antitank guns)
654th Antitank Detachment (Ferdinand) (strength: 5 tanks and 50 self-propelled antitank guns)
177th Assault Gun Detachment (strength: 36 assault guns)
244th Assault Gun Detachment (strength: 36 assault guns)
216th Heavy Panzer Detachment (Grizzly Bear)
313d Panzer Company (strength: 23 assault guns)
314th Panzer Company (strength: 22 assault guns)
21st Panzer Brigade
909th Assault Gun Detachment (strength: 36 assault guns)
505th Panzer Detachment (Tiger) (strength: 46 tanks [31 Tigers])
Corps strength: 123 tanks and 258 self-propelled and assault guns
XXXXVII Panzer Corps—General Joachim Lemelsen
6th Infantry Division—Lieutenant General Horst Grossmann
20th Panzer Division—Major General von Kessel (strength: 82 tanks)
9th Panzer Division—Lieutenant General Walter Scheller (strength: 83 tanks)
2d Panzer Division—Lieutenant General Vollrath Lubbe (strength: 118 tanks)
245th Assault Gun Detachment (strength: 36 assault guns)
904th Assault Gun Detachment (strength: 36 assault guns)
312d Panzer Company (216th Heavy Panzer Detachment) (strength: 22 assault guns)
Corps strength: 283 tanks and 94 assault guns
XXXXVI Panzer Corps—General Hans Zorn
31st Infantry Division—Lieutenant General Friedrich Hossbach
7th Infantry Division—Lieutenant General Fritz-Georg von Rappard
258th Infantry Division—Lieutenant General Hans-Kurt Hocker
102d Infantry Division—Major General Otto Hitzfeld
XX Army Corps—General Freiherr von Roman
72d Infantry Division—Lieutenant General Albert Muller-Gebhard
45th Infantry Division—Major General Freiherr Hans von Falkenstein
137th Infantry Division—Lieutenant General Kamecke
251st Infantry Division—Major General Felzmann

VIII Army Corps (Hungarian)
  102d Infantry Division (Hungarian)
  105th Infantry Division (Hungarian)
  108th Infantry Division (Hungarian)
10th Panzer Grenadier Division (army reserve in XXXXVII Panzer Corps'
  sector)
12th Panzer Division (army reserve in XXXXVII Panzer Corps' sector)
  (strength: 83 tanks)
4th Panzer Division (army reserve, committed 9 July) (strength: 101 tanks)
203d Security Division
221st Security Division

ARMY STRENGTH: 335,000 men, 590 tanks, and 424 assault guns

Second Army—Colonel General Walter Weiss
  XIII Army Corps
    82d Infantry Division
    340th Infantry Division
    327th Infantry Division
  VII Army Corps
    88th Infantry Division
    75th Infantry Division
    68th Infantry Division   ·
    26th Infantry Division (reserve)
    323d Infantry Division (under the 26th Infantry Division)

    ◦   ◦   ◦

    202d Antitank Detachment
    559th Antitank Detachment
    616th Antitank Detachment

ARMY STRENGTH: 96,000 men and 100 assault and antitank guns

Sixth Air Fleet—Colonel General Ritter von Greim
  First Air Division—Lieutenant General Deichmann

The Belgorod-Oboian'-Kursk Axis

ARMY GROUP SOUTH—Field Marshal Erich von Manstein

Fourth Panzer Army—Colonel General Hermann Hoth
  LII Army Corps: General Eugen Ott
    57th Infantry Division—Major General Maxmillian Fretter-Pico: 179th
      Infantry Regiment, 199th Infantry Regiment, 217th Infantry Regiment,
      157th Artillery Regiment, 57th Reconnaissance Battalion, 157th Antitank
      Battalion
    255th Infantry Division—Lieutenant General Poppe: 455th Infantry
      Regiment, 465th Infantry Regiment, 475th Infantry Regiment, 255th
      Artillery Regiment, 255th Reconnaissance Battalion, 255th Antitank
      Battalion

332d Infantry Division—Lieutenant General Schaefer: 676th Infantry
  Regiment, 677th Infantry Regiment, 678th Infantry Regiment, 332d
  Artillery Regiment, 332d Reconnaisance Battalion, 332d Antitank
  Battalion
137th Artillery Command (Arko): 1st Field Howitzer Detachment, 1st
  Battalion, 108th Artillery Regiment (motorized); Cannon Battery, 3d
  Battalion, 731st Artillery Regiment (150mm); 1st Werfer (Engineer
  Mortar) Regiment (Heavy)
677th Pioneer (Engineer) Regiment (74th Pioneer Battalion)
226th Motorcycle Battalion (–1 company)
XXXXVIII Panzer Corps—General Otto von Knobelsdorff
  3d Panzer Division—Lieutenant General Franz Westhoven: 6th Panzer
    Regiment, 3d Panzer Grenadier Regiment, 394th Panzer Grenadier
    Regiment, 75th Panzer Artillery Battalion, 3d Motorcycle Battalion, 3d
    Panzer Reconnaissance Battalion, 39th Panzer Engineer Battalion, 543d
    Antitank Battalion, 314th Antiaircraft (Flak) Detachment
    Strength: 90 tanks
  11th Panzer Division—Major General Mickl: 15th Panzer Regiment, 110th
    Panzer Grenadier Regiment, 111th Panzer Grenadier Regiment, 119th
    Panzer Artillery Regiment, 61st Motorcycle Battalion, 61st Panzer
    Reconnaissance Battalion, 231st Panzer Engineer Battalion, 61st Antitank
    Battalion, 277th Antiaircraft Detachment
    Strength: 113 tanks
  167th Infantry Division—Lieutenant General Wolf Trierenberg: 315th
    Infantry Regiment, 331st Infantry Regiment, 339th Infantry Regiment,
    167th Artillery Regiment, 167th Reconnaissance Battalion, 167th Antitank
    Battalion
  Panzer Grenadier Division *Grossdeutschland*—Lieutenant General Walter
    Hoernlein: *Grossdeutschland* Panzer Regiment, *Grossdeutschland* Panzer
    Grenadier Regiment, *Grossdeutschland* Fusilier Regiment,
    Grossdeutschland Artillery Regiment, *Grossdeutschland* Panzer
    Reconnaissance Battalion, *Grossdeutschland* Antitank Battalion,
    Grossdeutschland Panzer Engineer Battalion, *Grossdeutschland* Panzer
    Antiaircraft Battalion, *Grossdeutschland* Assault Gun Battalion
    Strength: 132 tanks and 35 assault guns
  10th Panzer Brigade (Panther), 39th Panzer Regiment: 51st Panzer
    Detachment (strength: 100 tanks), 52d Panzer Detachment (strength: 100
    tanks)
  132d Artillery Command (Arko)
  144th Artillery Command (Arko)
  70th Artillery Regiment: Mortar Detachment, 3d Battalion, 109th Mortar
    Regiment; 101st Heavy Howitzer Detachment; 842d Cannon Detachment
    (100mm)
  911th Assault Gun Detachment (strength: 31 assault guns)
  515th Pioneer Regiment: 48th Pioneer Battalion (motorized), 1st Pioneer
    Lehr (Training) Battalion (motorized)

616th Army Antiaircraft (Flak) Battalion
Corps strength: 535 tanks and 66 assault guns
II SS Panzer Corps—SS *Obergruppenfuehrer* Paul Hausser
   1st SS Panzer Grenadier Division *Leibstandarte Adolf Hitler*—SS
    Brigadefuehrer Wisch: 1st SS Panzer Regiment, 1st SS Panzer
    Grenadier Regiment, 2d SS Panzer Grenadier Regiment, 1st SS Panzer
    Artillery Regiment, 1st SS Panzer Reconnaissance Battalion, 1st SS
    Antitank Battalion, 1st SS Panzer Engineer Battalion, 1st SS Antiaircraft
    Battalion
    Strength: 106 tanks and 35 assault guns
   2d SS Panzer Grenadier Division *Das Reich*—SS *Gruppenfuehrer* Kruger: 2d
    SS Panzer Regiment, 3d SS Panzer Grenadier Regiment *Deutschland,* 4th
    SS Panzer Grenadier Regiment *Der Fuehrer,* 2d SS Panzer Artillery
    Regiment, 2d SS Panzer Reconnaissance Battalion, 2d SS Antitank
    Battalion, 2d SS Panzer Engineer Battalion, 2d SS Antiaircraft Battalion
    Strength: 145 tanks and 34 assault guns
   3d SS Panzer Grenadier Division *Totenkopf*—SS *Brigadefuehrer* Priess: 3d
    SS Panzer Regiment, 5th SS Panzer Grenadier Regiment *Thule,* 6th SS
    Panzer Grenadier Regiment *Theodor Eicke,* 3d SS Panzer Artillery
    Regiment, 3d SS Panzer Reconnaissance Battalion, 3d SS Antitank
    Battalion, 3d SS Panzer Engineer Battalion, 3d SS Antiaircraft Battalion
    Strength: 139 tanks and 35 assault guns
   122d Artillery Command (Arko): 1st Field Howitzer Detachment, 861
    Artillery Regiment (motorized); 1st Field Howitzer Detachment, 3d
    Battalion, 818th Artillery Regiment (motorized); 3d Smoke Troop; 55th
    Werfer (Engineer Mortar) Regiment; 1st Werfer Lehr (Training)
    Regiment
   680th Pioneer Regiment: 627th Pioneer Battalion (motorized), 666th
    Pioneer Battalion (motorized)
   Corps strength: 390 tanks and 104 assault guns
   VIII Air Corps

ARMY STRENGTH: 223,907 men, 925 tanks, AND 170 assault guns

Army Detachment Kempf—General Werner Kempf
  XI Army Corps (Corps Rauss)—General Erhard Rauss
    106th Infantry Division—Lieutenant General Werner Forst: 239th Infantry
     Regiment, 240th Infantry Regiment, 241st Infantry Regiment, 106th
     Artillery Regiment, 106th Reconnaissance Battalion, 106th Antitank
     Battalion
    320th Infantry Division—Major General Georg Postel: 585th Infantry
     Regiment, 586th Infantry Regiment, 587th Infantry Regiment, 320th
     Artillery Regiment, 320th Reconnaissance Battalion, 320th Antitank
     Battalion
    52d Werfer (Engineer Mortar) Regiment
    2d Battalion, 1st Werfer (Engineer Mortar) Regiment (Heavy)
    4th Antiaircraft (Flak) Regiment

7th Antiaircraft (Flak) Regiment

48th Antiaircraft (Flak) Regiment

18th Pioneer Regiment: 52d Pioneer Battalion, 923d Pioneer Bridge Battalion

153d Artillery Command: 1st Battalion, 77th Light Artillery Regiment (105mm), 2d Battalion, 54th Light Artillery Regiment (105mm), 51st Light Detachment, 1st Battalion, 213th Artillery Regiment (105mm)

905th Assault Gun Detachment (strength: 25 assault guns)

393d Assault Gun Company (strength: 25 assault guns)

Corps strength: 50 assault guns

XXXXII Army Corps—General Franz Mattenklott

39th Infantry Division—Lieutenant General Loenweneck: 113th Infantry Regiment, 114th Infantry Regiment, 139th Artillery Regiment, 39th Reconnaissance Battalion, 139th Antitank Battalion

161st Infantry Division—Lieutenant General Recke: 336th Infantry Regiment, 364th Infantry Regiment, 371st Infantry Regiment, 241st Artillery Regiment, 161st Reconnaissance Battalion, 241st Antitank Battalion

282d Infantry Division—Major General Kohler: 848th Infantry Regiment, 849th Infantry Regiment, 850th Infantry Regiment, 282d Artillery Regiment, 282d Fusilier Battalion, 282d Antitank Battalion

77th Antiaircraft (Flak) Regiment

560th Heavy Panzer Destroyer Detachment "Hornet" (strength: approximately 40 assault guns)

Heavy Panzer Destroyer Detachment C (strength: approximately 40 assault guns)

107th Artillery Command: 2d Battalion, 800th Heavy Artillery Detachment (150mm); 13th Light Detachment

Corps strength: approximately 80 assault guns

III Panzer Corps—General Hermann Breith

6th Panzer Division—Major General von Hünersdorff: 11th Panzer Regiment, 4th Panzer Grenadier Regiment, 114th Panzer Grenadier Regiment, 76th Panzer Artillery Regiment, 82d Motorcycle Battalion, 6th Panzer Reconnaissance Battalion, 41st Antitank Battalion, 57th Panzer Engineer Battalion, 298th Antiaircraft Detachment

Strength: 117 tanks

7th Panzer Division—Lieutenant General Freiherr Hans von Funck: 25th Panzer Regiment, 6th Panzer Grenadier Regiment, 7th Panzer Grenadier Regiment, 78th Panzer Artillery Battalion, 58th Motorcycle Battalion, 7th Panzer Reconnaissance Battalion, 42d Antitank Battalion, 58th Panzer Engineer Battalion, 296th Antiaircraft Detachment

Strength: 112 tanks

19th Panzer Division—Lieutenant General Rudolf Schmidt: 27th Panzer Regiment, 73d Panzer Grenadier Regiment, 74th Panzer Grenadier Regiment, 19th Panzer Artillery Regiment, 19th Motorcycle Battalion, 19th Panzer Reconnaissance Battalion, 19th Antitank Battalion, 19th

Panzer Engineer Battalion, 272d Antiaircraft Detachment
Strength: 70 tanks
168th Infantry Division—Major General Charles de Beaulieu: 417th Infantry
  Regiment, 429th Infantry Regiment, 442d Infantry Regiment, 248th
  Artillery Regiment, 168th Reconnaissance Battalion, 248th Antitank
  Battalion
54th Werfer (Engineer Mortar) Regiment
503d Heavy Panzer Detachment (Tiger) (strength: 45 tanks)
99th Antiaircraft (Flak) Regiment
153d Antiaircraft (Flak) Regiment
674th Pioneer Regiment: 70th Pioneer Battalion, 651st Pioneer Battalion
601st Pioneer Regiment: 127th Pioneer Battalion (–1 company), 531st
  Pioneer Bridge Battalion
3d Artillery Command: 612th Artillery Regiment, 228th Assault Gun
  Detachment (strength: 25 assault guns), 2d Battalion, 71st Artillery
  Regiment (150mm), 857th Heavy Artillery Detachment (210mm), 2d
  Battalion, 62d Artillery Regiment (105mm)
Corps strength: 344 tanks and 25 assault guns

DETACHMENT STRENGTH: 126,000 men, 344 tanks, and 155 antitank and
assault guns

Fourth Air Fleet—Commander, General Otto Dessloch

Red Army Order of Battle, 1 July 1943

Stavka coordinators—Marshal of the Soviet Union G. K. Zhukov (to 12 July for Western, Briansk, and Central Fronts; after 12 July for Voronezh and Steppe Fronts) and Marshal of the Soviet Union A. M. Vasilevsky (to 12 July for Voronezh Front; after 12 July for Southwestern Front)

The Orel Axis

WESTERN FRONT—Commander, Colonel General V. D. Sokolovsky; Commissar, Lieutenant General N. A. Bulganin; Chief of Staff, Lieutenant General A. P. Pokrovsky

50th Army—Commander, Lieutenant General I. V. Boldin; Commissar, Major General L. M. Chumakov; Chief of Staff, Major General N. G. Brilev
    38th Rifle Corps—Major General A. D. Tereshkov
        17th Rifle Division—Major General I. L. Radulia
        326th Rifle Division—Major General V. G. Terent'ev (to 30 July), Colonel Ia.
          V. Karpov (1 to 20 August), Colonel V. A. Gusev (from 21 August)
        413th Rifle Division—Colonel I. S. Khokhlov
    49th Rifle Division—Colonel A. V. Chuzhov
    64th Rifle Division—Colonel I. I. Iaremenko
    212th Rifle Division—Colonel A. P. Mal'tsev
    324th Rifle Division—Colonel E. Zh. Sedulin
    196th Tank Brigade—Lieutenant Colonel E. E. Dukhovny
    1536th Self-propelled Artillery Regiment (152mm)
    21st Separate Armored Train Battalion
    43d Separate Armored Train Battalion
    447th Gun Artillery Regiment
    523d Gun Artillery Regiment
    1091st Gun Artillery Regiment
    600th Antitank Artillery Regiment
    541st Mortar Regiment
    542d Mortar Regiment
    54th Guards Mortar Regiment
    1275th Antiaircraft Artillery Regiment
    1482d Antiaircraft Artillery Regiment

Note: Denotes on-hand tank and self-propelled gun strengths. Operational (serviceable) strengths were somewhat less. See Appendix D for specific operational variations.

1483d Antiaircraft Artillery Regiment
307th Separate Engineer Battalion
309th Separate Engineer Battalion

ARMY STRENGTH: 54,062 men, 236 guns (over 76mm), 241 antitank guns, 50 antiaircraft guns, 594 mortars (82mm, 120mm), and 87 tanks and self-propelled guns.)

11th Guards Army—Commander, Lieutenant General I. Kh. Bagramian; Commissar, Major General P. N. Kulikov; Chief of Staff, Major General N. P. Ivanov
    8th Guards Rifle Corps—Major General P. F. Malyshev
        11th Guards Rifle Division—Major General I. F. Fediun'kin (to 22 July), Major General A. I. Maksimov (from 23 July)
        26th Guards Rifle Division—Major General N. N. Korzhenevsky
        83d Guards Rifle Division—Major General Ia. S. Vorob'ev
    16th Guards Rifle Corps—Major General A. V. Lapshov (KIA on 13 July), Major General I. F. Fediun'kin (from 22 July)
        1st Guards Rifle Division—Major General N. A. Kropotin
        16th Guards Rifle Division—Major General P. G. Shafranov
        31st Guards Rifle Division—Colonel I. K. Shcherbin
        169th Rifle Division—Major General Ia. F. Eremenko
    36th Guards Rifle Corps—Major General A. S. Ksenefontov
        5th Guards Rifle Division—Colonel N. L. Soldatov
        18th Guards Rifle Division—Colonel M. N. Zavodovsky
        84th Guards Rifle Division—Major General G. B. Peters
    108th Rifle Division—Colonel P. A. Teremov
    217th Rifle Division—Colonel E. V. Ryzhikov
    10th Guards Tank Brigade—Colonel A. R. Burlyga
    29th Guards Tank Brigade—Colonel S. I. Tokerov (to 29 July), Colonel G. L. Iudin (from 30 July)
    43d Guards Tank Brigade—Lieutenant Colonel (Colonel on 11 July) M. P. Lukashev
    213th Tank Brigade—Lieutenant Colonel V. S. Gaev
    2d Guards Separate Heavy Tank Regiment—Colonel M. F. Kutuzov
    4th Guards Separate Tank Regiment
    1453d Self-propelled Artillery Regiment (152mm)
    8th Artillery Penetration Corps—Lieutenant General N. F. Salichko
        3d Artillery Penetration Division—Colonel I. F. San'ko: 15th Light Artillery Brigade, 5th Gun Artillery Brigade, 1st Howitzer Artillery Brigade, 117th High-power Howitzer Artillery Brigade, 7th Mortar Brigade
        6th Artillery Penetration Division—Major General A. S. Bitiutsky: 21st Light Artillery Brigade, 10th Gun Artillery Brigade, 18th Howitzer Artillery Brigade, 119th High-power Howitzer Artillery Brigade, 3d Mortar Brigade
    14th Artillery Division—Colonel L. I. Kozhukhov
    54th Light Artillery Brigade
    48th Gun Artillery Brigade

43d Howitzer Artillery Brigade
9th Mortar Brigade
56th Guards Corps Artillery Regiment
1st Guards Gun Artillery Regiment
17th Guards Gun Artillery Regiment
74th Guards Gun Artillery Regiment
75th Guards Gun Artillery Regiment
39th Gun Artillery Regiment
403d Gun Artillery Regiment
537th Gun Artillery Regiment
761st Gun Artillery Regiment
995th Gun Artillery Regiment
1093d Gun Artillery Regiment
1165th Gun Artillery Regiment
15th Guards Howitzer Artillery Regiment
16th Guards Howitzer Artillery Regiment
128th Howitzer Artillery Regiment
360th Howitzer Artillery Regiment
364th Howitzer Artillery Regiment
5th Guards Antitank Artillery Regiment
545th Mortar Regiment
546th Mortar Regiment
24th Guards Mortar Brigade
25th Guards Mortar Brigade
40th Guards Mortar Regiment
59th Guards Mortar Regiment—Lieutenant Colonel G. T. Frich
60th Guards Mortar Regiment
74th Guards Mortar Regiment
325th Guards Mortar Regiment—Lieutenant Colonel A. N. Kovalevich
14th Antiaircraft Artillery Division—Colonel (Major General on 9 July) A. I.
    Vasiuta
    525th Antiaircraft Artillery Regiment
    715th Antiaircraft Artillery Regiment
    718th Antiaircraft Artillery Regiment
    721st Antiaircraft Artillery Regiment
17th Antiaircraft Artillery Division—Colonel A. M. Shumikhin
    500th Antiaircraft Artillery Regiment
    1267th Antiaircraft Artillery Regiment
    1276th Antiaircaft Artillery Regiment
    1279th Antiaircraft Artillery Regiment
48th Antiaircraft Artillery Division—Colonel P. M. Barsky
    231st Guards Antiaircraft Artillery Regiment
    50th Antiaircraft Artillery Regiment
    1277th Antiaircraft Artillery Regiment
    1278th Antiaircraft Artillery Regiment

716th Antiaircraft Artillery Regiment
739th Antiaircraft Artillery Regiment
1280th Antiaircraft Artillery Regiment
1484th Antiaircraft Artillery Regiment
4th Separate Antiaircraft Artillery Battalion
614th Separate Antiaircraft Artillery Battalion
6th Guards Separate Engineer Battalion
84th Separate Engineer Battalion
226th Separate Engineer Battalion
243d Separate Engineer Battalion
367th Separate Engineer Battalion
61st Pontoon-Bridge Battalion

ARMY STRENGTH: 135,000 men, 280 tanks and self-propelled guns, 2,652 guns and mortars, 468 antitank guns, 255 antiaircraft guns, 89 multiple rocket launchers (BM-8, BM-13), and 55 multiple rocket launchers (M-30, M-31)

1st Air Army—Commander, Lieutenant General M. M. Gromov; Commissar, Major General I. G. Livinenko; Chief of Staff, Major General A. S. Pronin
   2d Assault Aviation Corps—Major General V. V. Stepichev
      231st Assault Aviation Division—Colonel L. A. Chizikov
      232d Assault Aviation Division—Colonel A. G. Val'kov
   2d Fighter Aviation Corps—Lieutenant General A. S. Blagoveshchensky
      7th Guards Fighter Aviation Division—Major General V. M. Zabaluev
   8th Fighter Aviation Corps—Major General F. F. Zherebchenko
      215th Fighter Aviation Division—Colonel N. M. Iakushin
      323d Fighter Aviation Division—Colonel P. P. Rubakov
   204th Bomber Aviation Division—Colonel S. P. Andreev
   224th Assault Aviation Division—Colonel M. V. Kotel'nikov
   233d Assault Aviation Division—Colonel V. V. Smirnov (to 27 July), Colonel V. V. Vasil'ev (from 28 July)
   311th Assault Aviation Division—Colonel V. V. Vasil'ev
   303d Fighter Aviation Division—Major General G. N. Zakhorov
   309th Fighter Aviation Division: Colonel I. I. Gribo (to 15 July), Lieutenant Colonel V. N. Buss (from 16 July)
   213th Fighter Bomber Aviation Division—Major General V. S. Molokov
   10th Reconnnaissance Aviation Regiment
   1st Medical Aviation Regiment
   713th Transport Aviation Regiment
   65th Corrective Aviation Squadron
Front subordination
   371st Rifle Division—Colonel V. L. Alekseenko
   36th Rifle Brigade
   1st Tank Corps—Major General V. V. Butkov
      89th Tank Brigade—Colonel K. N. Bannikov
      117th Tank Brigade—Lieutenant Colonel A. S. Voronkov

159th Tank Brigade—Colonel S. P. Khaidukov
44th Motorized Rifle Brigade
1437th Self-propelled Artillery Regiment (85mm)
    Strength: 184 tanks and self-propelled guns
5th Tank Corps—Major General M. S. Sakhno
    24th Tank Brigade—Colonel V. S. Sytnik (KIA on 17 July), Colonel V. K.
        Borodovsky (from 18 July)
    41st Tank Brigade—Colonel S. I. Alaev (to 6 August), Lieutenant Colonel
        V. M. Tarakanov (from 7 August)
    70th Tank Brigade—Colonel S. V. Kuznetsov (KIA on 15 July), Lieutenant
        Colonel V. E. Noda (16 July to 15 August), Lieutenant Colonel S. I.
        Nikitin (from 16 August)
    5th Motorized Rifle Brigade
    1435th Self-propelled Artillery Regiment (85mm)
    731st Separate Antitank Artillery Battalion
    277th Mortar Regiment
        Strength: 184 tanks and self-propelled guns
2d Guards Tank Brigade—Colonel N. A. Obdalenko
94th Tank Brigade—Colonel E. A. Novikov
120th Tank Brigade—Colonel n. I. Bukov
187th Tank Brigade—Major General M. V. Kolosov (converted to the 187th
    Separate Tank Regiment on 15 July)
56th Guards Separate Tank Regiment
161st Separate Tank Regiment
233d Separate Tank Regiment
248th Separate Tank Regiment
7th Separate Aero-sleigh Battalion
37th Separate Aero-sleigh Battalion
38th Separate Aero-sleigh Battalion
40th Aero-sleigh Battalion
758th Antitank Artillery Regiment
307th Guards Mortar Regiment
11th Guards Mortar Battalion (59th Guards Mortar Regiment)
1272d Antiaircraft Artillery Regiment (49th Antiaircraft Artillery Division)
1281st Antiaircraft Artillery Regiment
324th Separate Antiaircraft Artillery Battalion
11th Engineer Miner Brigade
12th Engineer Miner Brigade
33d Special Designation Engineer Brigade
11th Guards Battalion of Miners
6th Separate Engineer Battalion
113th Separate Engineer Battalion
122d Separate Engineer Battalion
129th Separate Engineer Battalion
133d Separate Engineer Battalion
229th Separate Engineer Battalion

230th Separate Engineer Battalion
537th Separate Mine Sapper Battalion
738th Separate Mine Sapper Battalion
9th Pontoon Bridge Battalion
51st Pontoon Bridge Battalion
62d Pontoon Bridge Battalion
87th Pontoon Bridge Battalion
88th Pontoon Bridge Battalion
89th Pontoon Bridge Battalion
90th Pontoon Bridge Battalion
91st Pontoon Bridge Battalion
99th Pontoon Bridge Battalion

FRONT STRENGTH: 211,458 men, 4,285 guns and mortars, 144 multiple rocket launchers, 745 tanks and self-propelled guns, and 1,300 aircraft

BRIANSK FRONT—Commander, Colonel General M. M. Popov; Commissar, Lieutenant General L. Z. Mekhlis; Chief of Staff, Lieutenant General L. M. Sandalov

3d Army—Commander, Lieutenant General A. V. Gorbatov; Commissar, Major General I. P. Konnov; Chief of Staff, Major General M. V. Ivashechkin
    41st Rifle Corps (headquarters only by 22 July)—Major General V. K. Urbanovich
        235th Rifle Division—Colonel F. N. Romashin (KIA on 13 July), Colonel A. F. Kubasov (14 to 28 July 7), Colonel L. G. Basenets (from 29 July)
        308th Rifle Division—Major General L. N. Gurt'ev (KIA on 3 August), Colonel N. K. Maslennikov (from 4 August)
        380th Rifle Division—Colonel A. F. Kustov
    269th Rifle Division—Major General P. S. Merzhakov (to 28 July), Colonel A. F. Kubasov (from 29 July)
    283d Rifle Division—Colonel V. A. Konovalov (to 21 July), Lieutenant Colonel S. F. Bazanov (22 to 30 July), Colonel S. K. Reznichenko (31 July to 5 August), Colonel V. I. Kuvshinnikov (from 5 August)
    342d Rifle Division—Major General L. D. Chervony
    82d Separate Tank Regiment
    114th Separate Tank Regiment
    1538th Self-propelled Artillery Regiment (152mm)
    10th Separate Armored Train Battalion
    55th Separate Armored Train Battalion
    20th Artillery Penetration Division—Colonel N. V. Bogdanov
        34th Light Artillery Brigade
        53d Gun Artillery Brigade
        60th Howitzer Artillery Brigade
        93d Heavy Howitzer Artillery Brigade
        102d High-power Howitzer Artillery Brigade
        20th Mortar Brigade

420th Gun Artillery Regiment
584th Antitank Artillery Regiment
475th Mortar Regiment
24th Antiaircraft Artillery Division—Colonel I. G. Liarsky
    1045th Antiaircraft Artillery Regiment
    1337th Antiaicraft Artillery Regiment
    1343d Antiaircraft Artillery Regiment
    1349th Antiaircraft Artillery Regiment
1284th Antiaircraft Artillery Regiment
348th Separate Engineer Battalion

ARMY STRENGTH: 60,000 men and 100 tanks and self-propelled guns

61st Army—Commander, Lieutenant General P. A. Belov; Commissar, Major
General D. G. Dubrovsky; Chief of Staff, Colonel M. N. Salnikov
    9th Guards Rifle Corps—Major General A. A. Boreiko
        12th Guards Rifle Division—Major General K. M. Erastov (to 9 July),
            Colonel D. K. Mal'kov (from 10 July)
        76th Guards Rifle Division—Major General A. V. Kirsanov
        77th Guards Rifle Division—Major General V. S. Askalepov
    97th Rifle Division—Major General P. M. Davydov
    110th Rifle Division—Colonel S. K. Artem'ev
    336th Rifle Division—Major General V. S. Kuznetsov (to 1 July), Colonel M. A.
        Ignachev (2 July to 4 August), Colonel I. I. Petykov (5 to 22 August), Colonel
        L. V. Grinval'd-Mukho (from 23 August)
    356th Rifle Division—Colonel M. G. Makarov
    415th Rifle Division—Colonel N. K. Maslennikov (to 30 July), Colonel P. I.
        Moshchalkov (from 1 August)
    12th Separate Destroyer Brigade
    68th Tank Brigade—Colonel P. F. Iurchenko (to 13 August), Lieutenant
        Colonel G. A. Timchenko (from 14 August)
    36th Separate Tank Regiment
    1539th Self-propelled Artillery Regiment (85mm)
    31st Separate Armored Train Battalion
    45th Separate Armored Train Battalion
    60th Guards Gun Artillery Regiment
    67th Guards Gun Artillery Regiment
    554th Gun Artillery Regiment
    533d Antitank Artillery Regiment
    547th Mortar Regiment
    13th Antiaircraft Artillery Division—Colonel V. M. Kochubei
        1065th Antiaircraft Artillery Regiment
        1173d Antiaircraft Artillery Regiment
        1175th Antiaircraft Artillery Regiment
        1218th Antiaircraft Artillery Regiment
    1282d Antiaircraft Artillery Regiment

310th Separate Engineer Battalion
344th Separate Engineer Battalion

ARMY STRENGTH: 80,000 men and 110 tanks and self-propelled guns

63d Army—Commander, Lieutenant General V. Ia. Kolpakchi; Commissar, Major
General K. K. Abramov; Chief of Staff, Colonel N. V. Eriomin
   35th Rifle Corps (headquarters only)—Major General V. G. Zholudev
   40th Rifle Corps (headquarters only)—Major General V. S. Kuznetsov
   5th Rifle Division—Lieutenant Colonel F. Ia. Volkovitsky (to 9 July), Colonel
      P. T. Mikhalitsyn (from 10 July)
   41st Rifle Division—Colonel A. I. Surchenko
   129th Rifle Division—Colonel I. V. Panchuk
   250th Rifle Division—Colonel V. M. Muzitsky (to 5 July), Colonel I. V. Mokhin
      (from 6 July)
   287th Rifle Division—Major General I. N. Pankratov
   348th Rifle Division—Colonel I. F. Grigor'evsky
   397th Rifle Division—Colonel N. F. Andron'ev
   231st Separate Tank Regiment
   1452d Self-propelled Artillery Regiment (85mm)
   1071st Antitank Artillery Regiment
   1311st Antitank Artillery Regiment
   286th Mortar Regiment
   28th Antiaircraft Artillery Division—Colonel G. E. Drabkov
      1355th Antiaircraft Artillery Regiment
      1359th Antiaircraft Artillery Regiment
      1365th Antiaircraft Artillery Regiment
      1371st Antiaircraft Artillery Regiment
   356th Separate Engineer Battalion

ARMY STRENGTH: 70,000 men and 60 tanks and self-propelled guns

15th Air Army—Commander, Lieutenant General N. F. Naumenko; Commissar,
Colonel M. N. Sukhachev; Chief of Staff, Colonel A. A. Sakovnin
   1st Guards Fighter Aviation Corps—Lieutenant General E. M. Beletsky: 3d
      Guards Fighter Aviation Division—Colonel V. P. Ukhov, 4th Guards Fighter
      Aviation Division—Colonel V. A. Kitaev
   3d Assault Aviation Corps—Major General Gorlachenko
      307th Assault Aviation Division—Colonel A. V. Kozhemiakin
      308th Assault Aviation Division—Colonel G. P. Turykin
   113th Bomber Aviation Division—Lieutenant Colonel F. G. Michugin
   225th Assault Aviation Division—Colonel A. F. Obukhov
   284th Night Bomber Aviation Division—Major G. P. Pokoevoi (to 22 July),
      Lieutenant Colonel I. A. Trushkin (from 23 July)
   234th Fighter Aviation Division—Colonel E. Z. Tatanashvili
   315th Fighter Aviation Division—Colonel V. Ia. Litvinov
   99th Guards Reconnaissance Aviation Regiment

Front subordination

    25th Rifle Corps—Major General P. V. Pererva

        186th Rifle Division—Colonel N. P. Iatskevich (to 26 July), Colonel G. V. Revunenkov (from 27 July)

        283d Rifle Division—Colonel I. D. Krasnoshtanov

        362d Rifle Division—Major General D. M. Dalmatov

    1st Guards Tank Corps—Major General M. F. Pankov

        15th Guards Tank Brigade—Lieutenant Colonel V. S. Belousov (to 18 July), Colonel K. G. Kozhanov (from 19 July)

        16th Guards Tank Brigade—Colonel M. N. Filippenko

        17th Guards Tank Brigade—Colonel B. V. Shul'gin

        1st Guards Motorized Rifle Brigade

        34th Guards Tank Regiment

        65th Motorcycle Battalion

        1001st Antitank Artillery Regiment

        732d Separate Antitank Artillery Battalion

        455th Mortar Regiment

        80th Guards Antiaircraft Artillery Regiment

        Strength: 207 tanks and self-propelled guns

    11th Guards Separate Tank Regiment

    12th Guards Separate Tank Regiment

    13th Guards Separate Tank Regiment

    26th Guards Separate Tank Regiment

    253d Separate Tank Regiment

    1444th Self-propelled Artillery Regiment (152mm)

    1445th Self-propelled Artillery Regiment (152mm)

    1535th Self-propelled Artillery Regiment (152mm)

    55th Separate Motorcycle Battalion

    54th Separate Armored Train Battalion

    2d Artillery Penetration Corps (to the 63d Army): Lieutenant General M. M. Barsukov

        13th Artillery Penetration Division—Colonel D. M. Krasnokutsky: 42d Light Artillery Brigade, 47th Howitzer Artillery Brigade, 88th Heavy Howitzer Artillery Brigade, 91st Heavy Howitzer Artillery Brigade, 101st High-power Howitzer Artillery Brigade, 17th Mortar Brigade

        15th Artillery Penetration Division—Colonel A. A. Korochkin: 69th Light Artillery Brigade, 35th Howitzer Artillery Brigade, 85th Heavy Howitzer Artillery Brigade, 87th Heavy Howitzer Artillery Brigade, 106th High-power Howitzer Artillery Brigade, 18th Mortar Brigade

        3d Heavy Guards Mortar Division—Colonel P. V. Kolesnikov: 15th Guards Mortar Brigade, 18th Guards Mortar Brigade, 19th Guards Mortar Brigade

    7th Artillery Penetration Corps (the 61st Army)—Major General P. M. Korol'kov

        16th Artillery Penetration Division—Colonel P. S. Ivanov (to 29 August), Colonel F. V. Fedoseev (from 30 August): 49th Light Artillery Brigade, 61st Gun Artillery Brigade, 52d Howitzer Artillery Brigade, 90th Heavy

Howitzer Artillery Brigade, 109th High-power Howitzer Artillery Brigade, 14th Mortar Brigade

17th Artillery Penetration Division—Major General S. S. Volkenshtein: 37th Light Artillery Brigade, 39th Gun Artillery Brigade, 50th Howitzer Artillery Brigade, 92d Heavy Howitzer Artillery Brigade, 108th High-power Howitzer Artillery Brigade, 22d Mortar Brigade

2d Heavy Guards Mortar Division—Major General A. F. Tveretsky: 3d Guards Mortar Brigade, 17th Guards Mortar Brigade, 26th Guards Mortar Brigade

44th Gun Artillery Brigade

12th Antitank Artillery Brigade

13th Mortar Brigade

8th Guards Mortar Brigade—Colonel A. O. Sheinin

85th Guards Mortar Regiment

93d Guards Mortar Regiment

310th Guards Mortar Regiment

311th Guards Mortar Regiment—Lieutenant Colonel G. Zhuravlev

312th Guards Mortar Regiment

313th Guards Mortar Regiment

10th Separate Guards Mortar Battalion

1477th Antiaircraft Artillery Regiment

386th Separate Antiaircraft Artillery Battalion

8th Special Designation Engineer Brigade

57th Engineer Sapper Brigade

3d Guards Battalion of Miners

131st Separate Sapper Battalion

231st Separate Engineer Battalion

740th Separate Engineer Battalion

48th Pontoon Bridge Battalion

53d Pontoon Bridge Battalion

131st Pontoon Bridge Battalion

136th Pontoon Bridge Battalion

FRONT STRENGTH: 433,616 men, 7,642 guns and mortars, 160 multiple rocket launchers, 794 tanks and self-propelled guns (1.578 on 15 July), and 1,000 aircraft

The Orel-Kursk Axis

CENTRAL FRONT—Commander, Army General K. K. Rokossovsky; Commissar, Major General K. F. Telegin; Chief of Staff, Lieutenant General M. S. Malinin

13th Army—Commander, Lieutenant General N. P. Pukhov; Commissar, Major General M. A. Kozlov; Chief of Staff, Major General A. V. Petrushevsky

17th Guards Rifle Corps—Lieutenant General A. L. Bondarev

6th Guards Rifle Division—Major General D. P. Onuprienko

70th Guards Rifle Division—Colonel I. A. Gusev
75th Guards Rifle Division—Major General V. A. Goroshny
18th Guards Rifle Corps—Major General I. M. Afonin
2d Guards Airborne Division—Major General I. F. Dudarev
3d Guards Airborne Division—Colonel I. N. Konev
4th Guards Airborne Division—Major General A. D. Rumiantsev
15th Rifle Corps—Major General I. I. Liudnikov
8th Rifle Division—Colonel P. M. Gudz'
74th Rifle Division—Major General A. A. Kazarian
148th Rifle Division—Major General A. A. Mishchenko
29th Rifle Corps—Major General A. N. Slyshkin
15th Rifle Division—Colonel V. N. Dzhandzhgava (KIA on 14 July), Colonel
V. I. Bulakov (15 July to 7 August), Colonel K. E. Grebonnik (from 8
August)
81st Rifle Division—Major General A. B. Barinov
307th Rifle Division—Major General M. A. Enshin
129th Tank Brigade—Colonel N. V. Petrushin
27th Guards Separate Tank Regiment
30th Guards Separate Tank Regiment
43d Separate Tank Regiment
58th Separate Tank Regiment—Lieutenant Colonel I. P. Priakhin
237th Separate Tank Regiment
1442d Self-propelled Artillery Regiment (152mm)
49th Separate Armored Train
4th Artillery Penetration Corps—Major General N. V. Ignatov
5th Artillery Penetration Division—Colonel A. I. Snegirov: 16th Light
Artillery Brigade, 24th Gun Artillery Brigade, 9th Howitzer Artillery
Brigade—Colonel T. N. Vishnevsky, 86th Heavy Howitzer Artillery
Brigade, 100th High-power Howitzer Artillery Brigade, 1st Mortar Brigade
12th Artillery Penetration Division—Colonel M. N. Kurkovsky: 46th Light
Artillery Brigade, 41st Gun Artillery Brigade, 32d Howitzer Artillery
Brigade, 89th Heavy Howitzer Artillery Brigade, 104th High-power
Howitzer Artillery Brigade, 11th Mortar Brigade
5th Guards Mortar Division—Colonel E. A. Firsov (to 15 July), Colonel
G. M. Fantalov (from 16 August): 16th Guards Mortar Brigade—Colonel
P. I. Val'chenko, 22d Guards Mortar Brigade—Colonel V. V. Rusanov, 23d
Guards Mortar Brigade—Colonel N. N. Koryt'ko
19th Guards Gun Artillery Regiment
874th Antitank Artillery Regiment
476th Mortar Regiment—Major V. G. Gladky
477th Mortar Regiment
6th Guards Mortar Regiment—Major N. I. Murzaev
37th Guards Mortar Regiment—Lieutenant Colonel K. N. Osteiko
65th Guards Mortar Regiment—Major N. V. Soklakov
86th Guards Mortar Regiment—Lieutenant Colonel P. A. Zazirny
324th Guards Mortar Regiment—Lieutenant Colonel B. I. Orlov

1st Antiaircraft Artillery Division—Major General R. A. Dzivin
    1042d Antiaircraft Artillery Regiment—Lieutenant Colonel A. S. Peshakov
      (ill on 3 July), Major N. P. Khusid (from 3 July)
    1068th Antiaircraft Artillery Regiment—Lieutenant Colonel V. I. Zhukov
    1085th Antiaircraft Artillery Regiment—Major V. E. Kalitsky
    1090th Antiaircraft Artillery Regiment—Lieutenant Colonel I. I. Lozitsky
25th Antiaircraft Artillery Division—Colonel K. M. Andreev
    1067th Antiaircraft Artillery Regiment
    1356th Antiaircraft Artillery Regiment
    1362d Antiaircraft Artillery Regiment
    1368th Antiaircraft Artillery Regiment
1287th Antiaircraft Artillery Regiment
275th Separate Engineer Battalion

ARMY STRENGTH: 114,000 men, 2,934 guns and mortars, 105 multiple
rocket launchers, and 270 tanks and self-propelled guns

48th Army—Commander, Lieutenant General P. L. Romanenko; Commissar,
Major General N. A. Istomin; Chief of Staff, Major General M. V. Bobkov
    42d Rifle Corps—Major General K. S. Kolganov
      16th Rifle Division (Lithuanian)—Major General V. A. Karvialis
      202d Rifle Division—Colonel Z. S. Revenko
      399th Rifle Division—Colonel D. M. Ponomarov (to 9 July), Colonel P. I.
        Skachkov (from 10 July)
    73d Rifle Division—Major General D. I. Smirnov
    137th Rifle Division—Colonel M. G. Volovich (to 29 August), Colonel A. I.
      Alferov (from 30 August)
    143d Rifle Division—Colonel D. I. Lukin
    170th Rifle Division—Colonel A. M. Cheriakh
    45th Separate Tank Regiment
    193d Separate Tank Regiment
    299th Separate Tank Regiment
    1454th Self-propelled Artillery Regiment (76mm)
    1455th Self-propelled Artillery Regiment (of 9th Tank Corps) (76mm)
    1540th Self-propelled Artillery Regiment (152mm)
    37th Separate Armored Train
    1168th Gun Artillery Regiment
    2d Antitank Artillery Brigade
    220th Guards Antitank Artillery Regiment
    479th Mortar Regiment
    16th Antiaircraft Artillery Division—Colonel (Major General on 7 August) I. M.
      Seredin
      728th Antiaircraft Artillery Regiment
      1283d Antiaircraft Artillery Regiment
      1285th Antiaircraft Artillery Regiment
      1286th Antiaircraft Artillery Regiment
    461st Antiaircraft Artillery Regiment

615th Separate Antiaircraft Artillery Battalion
313th Separate Engineer Battalion

ARMY STRENGTH: 84,000 men, 1,454 guns and mortars, and 178 tanks and self-propelled guns

60th Army—Commander, Lieutenant General I. D. Cherniakhovsky; Commissar, Colonel V. M. Olenin; Chief of Staff, Major General G. A. Ter-Gasparian
   24th Rifle Corps—Major General N. I. Kiriukhin
      112th Rifle Division—Colonel P. S. Poliakov (to 23 August), Colonel A. V. Gladkov (from 24 August)
      42d Rifle Division—Major General N. N. Mul'tan
      129th Rifle Brigade
   30th Rifle Corps—Major General G. S. Laz'ko
      121st Rifle Division—Major General I. I. Ladygin
      141st Rifle Division—Colonel S. S. Rassadnikov
      322d Rifle Division—Colonel N. I. Ivanov (to 22 August), Colonel P. N. Lashchenko (from 26 August)
      55th Rifle Division—Colonel N. N. Zaiiulev
      248th Rifle Brigade
      150th Tank Brigade—Lieutenant Colonel I. V. Safronov (to 15 August), Lieutenant Colonel S. I. Ugriumov (from 16 August)
      58th Separate Armored Train
      1156th Gun Artillery Regiment
      1178th Antitank Artillery Regiment
      128th Mortar Regiment
      138th Mortar Regiment
      497th Mortar Regiment
      98th Guards Mortar Regiment
      286th Separate Guards Mortar Battalion
      221st Guards Antiaircraft Artillery Regiment
      217th Antiaircraft Artillery Regiment
      59th Engineer Sapper Brigade
      317th Separate Engineer Battalion

ARMY STRENGTH: 96,000 men, 1,376 guns and mortars, and 67 tanks and self-propelled guns

65th Army—Commander, Lieutenant General P. I. Batov; Commissar, Colonel N. A. Radetsky; Chief of Staff, Major General I. S. Glebov
   18th Rifle Corps—Major General I. I. Ivanov
      69th Rifle Division—Colonel I. A. Kuzovkov
      149th Rifle Division—Colonel A. A. Orlov
      246th Rifle Division—Lieutenant Colonel M. G. Fedosenko
   27th Rifle Corps—Major General F. M. Cherokmanov
      60th Rifle Division—Major General I. V. Kliaro (to 27 August), Colonel A. V. Boroiavlensky (from 29 August)

193d Rifle Division—Major General F. N. Zhobrev (to 26 August), Colonel
A. G. Frolenkov (from 28 August)
115th Rifle Brigade—Colonel I. I. Sankovsky
37th Guards Rifle Division—Colonel E. G. Ushakov
181st Rifle Division—Major General A. A. Saraev
194th Rifle Division—Colonel P. P. Opiakin
354th Rifle Division—Major General D. F. Alekseev
29th Guards Separate Tank Regiment
40th Separate Tank Regiment
84th Separate Tank Regiment
255th Separate Tank Regiment—Lieutenant Colonel V. I. Mukhin
120th Antitank Artillery Regiment
543d Antitank Artillery Regiment
143d Guards Mortar Regiment
218th Mortar Regiment
478th Mortar Regiment
94th Guards Mortar Regiment
235th Antiaircraft Artillery Regiment
14th Engineer Miner Brigade
321st Separate Engineer Battalion

ARMY STRENGTH: 100,000 men, 1,837 guns and mortars, and 124 tanks
and self-propelled guns

70th Army—Commander, Lieutenant General I. V. Galanin; Commissar, Major
General N. N. Savkov; Chief of Staff, Major General V. M. Shaparov
  28th Rifle Corps—Major General A. N. Nechaev
    132d Rifle Division—Major General T. K. Shkrylev
    211th Rifle Division—Major General V. L. Makhlinovsky
    280th Rifle Division—Major General D. N. Golosov
  19th Rifle Corps (added by 20 July)
  102d Rifle Division—Major General A. N. Andreev
  106th Rifle Division—Major General F. N. Smekhotvorov (to 1 August),
    Colonel M. M. Vlasov (from 2 August)
  140th Rifle Division—Major General A. Ia. Kiselev
  162d Rifle Division—Major General S. Ia. Senchillo
  175th Rifle Division—Colonel V. A. Borisov
  3d Destroyer Brigade (2d Destroyer Division)—Colonel V. N. Rukosuev
  240th Separate Tank Regiment
  251st Separate Tank Regiment
  259th Separate Tank Regiment
  1st Guards Artillery Division—Colonel G. V. Godin
    3d Guards Light Artillery Brigade—Colonel M. A. Grekhov
    1st Guards Gun Artillery Brigade—Colonel V. M. Kerp
    2d Guards Howitzer Artillery Brigade—Colonel A. I. Telegin
  378th Antitank Artillery Regiment
  136th Mortar Regiment

12th Antiaircraft Artillery Division—Lieutenant Colonel (Colonel on 11 July)
P. I. Korchagin
836th Antiaircraft Artillery Regiment
977th Antiaircraft Artillery Regiment
990th Antiaircraft Artillery Regiment
581st Antiaircraft Artillery Regiment
169th Separate Engineer Battalion
371st Separate Engineer Battalion
386th Separate Engineer Battalion

ARMY STRENGTH: 96,000 men, 1,658 guns and mortars, and 125 tanks and
self-propelled guns

2d Tank Army—Commander, Lieutenant General A. G. Rodin (ill on 2 August),
Lieutenant General S. I. Bogdanov (from 2 August); Commissar, Major General
P. M. Latyshev; Chief of Staff, Colonel G. Ia. Preisman
3d Tank Corps—Major General M. D. Sinenko
50th Tank Brigade—Colonel F. I. Konovalov (to 27 July), Lieutenant Colonel
V. A. Bzyrin (from 28 July)
51st Tank Brigade—Lieutenant Colonel G. A. Kokurin (KIA on 14 July),
Lieutenant Colonel P. K. Borisov (from 14 July)
103d Tank Brigade—Colonel G. M. Maksimov (to 27 July), Lieutenant
Colonel A. I. Khalaev (from 28 July)
57th Motorized Rifle Brigade
74th Motorcycle Battallion
881st Antitank Artillery Regiment
728th Separate Antitank Artillery Battalion
234th Mortar Regiment
121st Antiaircraft Artillery Regiment
Strength: 204 tanks
16th Tank Corps—Major General V. E. Grigor'ev
107th Tank Brigade—Lieutenant Colonel N. M. Teliakov
109th Tank Brigade—Lieutenant Colonel P. D. Babkovsky
164th Tank Brigade—Lieutenant Colonel N. V. Kopylov
15th Motorized Rifle Brigade—Colonel P. M. Akimochkin
51st Motorcycle Battalion
1441st Self-propelled Artillery Regiment (76mm)
614th Antitank Artillery Regiment
729th Separate Antitank Artillery Battalion
226th Mortar Regiment
Strength: 220 tanks and self-propelled guns
11th Guards Tank Brigade—Colonel N. M. Bubnov (KIA on 2 August),
Lieutenant Colonel N. M. Koshaev (from 3 August)
87th Separate Motorcycle Battalion
357th Separate Engineer Battalion

ARMY STRENGTH: 37,000 men, 338 guns and mortars, and 456 tanks and
self-propelled guns

16th Air Army—Commander, Lieutenant General S. I. Rudenko; Commissar,
Major General A. S. Vinogradov; Chief of Staff, Major General P. I. Braiko
  3d Bomber Aviation Corps—Major General A. Z. Karavatsky
    241st Bomber Aviation Division—Colonel I. G. Kurilenko
    301st Bomber Aviation Division—Colonel F. M. Fedorenko
  6th Mixed Aviation Corps—Major General I. D. Antoshkin
    221st Bomber Aviation Division—Colonel S. F. Buzylev
    282d Fighter Aviation Division—Colonel A. M. Riazanov (to 16 July),
      Lieutenant Colonel Iu. M. Berkel' (from 17 July)
  6th Fighter Aviation Corps—Major General E. E. Erlykin
    273d Fighter Aviation Division—Colonel I. F. Federov
    279th Fighter Aviation Division—Colonel F. N. Dement'ev
  2d Guards Assault Aviation Division—Colonel G. I. Komarov
  299th Assault Aviation Division—Colonel I. V. Krupsky
  1st Guards Fighter Aviation Division—Lieutenant Colonel I. V. Krupenin (to
    2 August), Colonel V. V. Sukhoriakov (from 3 August)
  283d Fighter Aviation Division—Colonel S. P. Denisov
  286th Fighter Aviation Division—Colonel I. I. Ivanov
  271st Night Bomber Aviation Division—Lieutenant Colonel K. I. Rasskazov (to
    18 July), Colonel M. Kh. Borisenko (from 19 July)
  16th Reconnaissance Aviation Regiment
  6th Medical Aviation Regiment
  14th Corrective Aviation Squadron
Front subordination
  4th Destroyer Brigade (2d Destroyer Division)
  115th Fortified Region
  119th Fortified Region
  161st Fortified Region
  14th Separate Destroyer Brigade
  9th Tank Corps—Major General S. I. Bogdanov
    23d Tank Brigade—Colonel M. S. Demidov
    95th Tank Brigade—Colonel I. E. Galushko (to 25 August), Colonel A. I.
      Kuznetsov (from 26 August)
    108th Tank Brigade—Colonel R. A. Liberman (to 2 August), Lieutenant
      Colonel M. K. Elenko (from 3 August)
    8th Motorized Rifle Brigade
    730th Separate Antitank Artillery Battalion
    Strength: 168 tanks
  19th Tank Corps—Major General I. D. Vasil'ev
    79th Tank Brigade—Lieutenant Colonel F. P. Vasetsky
    101st Tank Brigade—Colonel I. M. Kurdupov (to 15 August), Colonel A. N.
      Pavliuk-Moroz (from 16 August)
    202d Tank Brigade—Colonel N. V. Kostelev
    26th Motorized Rifle Brigade
    Strength: 168 tanks
  1541st Self-propelled Artillery Regiment (152mm)
  40th Separate Armored Train

68th Gun Artillery Brigade
1st Antitank Artillery Brigade—Colonel A. S. Rybkin
13th Antitank Artillery Brigade—Colonel N. P. Sazonov
130th Antitank Artillery Regiment
563d Antitank Artillery Regiment
21st Mortar Brigade
84th Guards Mortar Regiment (to the 70th Army)—Lieutenant Colonel M. M. Kolomiets
92d Guards Mortar Regiment
323d Guards Mortar Regiment (to the 13th Army)—Lieutenant Colonel A. F. Artiushenko
10th Antiaircraft Artillery Division—Lieutenant Colonel (Colonel on 9 July) S. Ia. Sussky
  802d Antiaircraft Artillery Regiment
  975th Antiaircraft Artillery Regiment
  984th Antiaircraft Artillery Regiment
  994th Antiaircraft Artillery Regiment
997th Antiaircraft Artillery Regiment (12th Antiaircraft Artillery Division)
  325th Antiaircraft Artillery Regiment
  1259th Antiaircraft Artillery Regiment
  1263d Antiaircraft Artillery Regiment
13th Guards Separate Antiaircraft Artillery Battalion
27th Separate Antiaircraft Artillery Battalion
31st Separate Antiaircraft Artillery Battalion
1st Guards Special Designation Engineer Brigade—Colonel M. F. Ioffe
6th Engineer Miner Brigade
12th Guards Battalion of Miners
120th Separate Engineer Battalion
257th Separate Engineer Battalion
9th Pontoon Bridge Battalion
49th Pontoon Bridge Battalion
50th Pontoon Bridge Battalion
104th Pontoon Bridge Battalion

FRONT STRENGTH: 711,575 men, 11,076 guns and mortars, 246 multiple rocket launchers, 1,785 tanks and self-propelled guns, and 1,000 aircraft

The Belgorod-Oboian'-Kursk Axis

VORONEZH FRONT—Commander, Army General N. F. Vatutin; Commissar, Lieutenant General N. S. Khrushchev; Chief of Staff, Lieutenant General S. P. Ivanov

6th Guards Army—Commander, Lieutenant General I. M. Chistiakov; Commissar, Major General P. I. Krainov; Chief of Staff, Major General V. A. Penkovsky

22d Guards Rifle Corps—Major General N. B. Ibiansky
  67th Guards Rifle Division—Major General A. I. Baksov: 196th Guards Rifle
    Regiment, 199th Guards Rifle Regiment, 201st Guards Rifle Regiment,
    138th Guards Artillery Regiment—Lieutenant Colonel M. I. Kidrianov,
    73d Guards Separate Antitank Artillery Battalion
  71st Guard Rifle Division—Colonel I. P. Sivakov: 210th Guards Rifle
    Regiment, 213th Guards Rifle Regiment, 219th Guards Rifle Regiment,
    151st Guards Artillery Regiment, 76th Guards Separate Antitank Artillery
    Battalion, 134th Separate Antitank Rifle Battalion (attached), 136th
    Separate Antitank Rifle Battalion (attached)
  90th Guards Rifle Division—Colonel V. G. Chernov: 268th Guards Rifle
    Regiment, 272d Guards Rifle Regiment, 274th Guards Rifle Regiment,
    193d Guards Artillery Regiment
23d Guard Rifle Corps—Major General P. P. Vakhrameev (to 21 July), Major
  General N. T. Tavartkiladze (from 22 July)
  51st Guards Rifle Division—Major General N. T. Tavartkiladze (to 20 July),
    Colonel I. M. Sukhov (from 21 July): 154th Guards Rifle Regiment, 156th
    Guards Rifle Regiment, 158th Guards Rifle Regiment, 122d Guards
    Artillery Regiment—Major M. N. Uglovsky
  52d Guards Rifle Division—Major General. I. M. Nekrasov: 151st Guards
    Rifle Regiment—Lieutenant Colonel I. F. Iudich, 153d Guards Rifle
    Regiment, 155th Guards Rifle Regiment, 124th Guards Artillery
    Regiment, 57th Guards Separate Antitank Artillery Battalion
  375th Rifle Division—Colonel P. D. Govorunenko (to 35th Guards Rifle
    Corps on 8 July) (to 69th Army on 10 July): 1241st Rifle Regiment, 1243d
    Rifle Regiment, 1245th Rifle Regiment, 193d Artillery Regiment:
    Lieutenant Colonel P. T. Gubarev
  89th Guards Rifle Division—Colonel I. A. Pigin (to 69th Army on 10 July)
    267th Guards Rifle Regiment
    270th Guards Rifle Regiment
    273d Guards Rifle Regiment
    196th Guards Artillery Regiment
  96th Tank Brigade—Major General V. G. Lebedev (to 15 July), Colonel A. M.
    Popov (from 16 July) (attached to 52 Guards Rifle Division) (to 69th Army on
    10 July)
    228th Tank Battalion
    331st Tank Battalion
  230th Separate Tank Regiment (attached to 52d Guards Rifle Division)
  245th Separate Tank Regiment (attached to 67th Guards Rifle Division)
  1440th Self-propelled Artillery Regiment (76mm) (attached to 67th Guards
    Rifle Division)
  60th Separate Armored Train Battalion
  27th Gun Artillery Brigade (to 69th Army on 10 July and 5th Guards Tank
    Army on 11 July)
    93d Gun Artillery Regiment (122mm) (attached to 375th Rifle Division)
    142d Gun Artillery Regiment (152mm) (attached to 52d Guards Rifle Division)

33d Gun Artillery Brigade (to 1st Tank Army on 8 July)
  163d Gun Artillery Regiment (attached to 67th and 71st Guards Rifle
    Divisions)
  159th Gun Artillery Regiment (attached to 67th Guards Rifle Division)
  628th Separate Gun Artillery Regiment (spt 71st Guards Rifle Division)
27th Antitank Artillery Brigade—Lieutenant Colonel N. D. Chevola (attached
  to 71st Guards Rifle Division on 6 July)
  1837th Antitank Artillery Regiment—Major N. E. Plysiuk
  1839th Antitank Artillery Regiment—Major Ia. E. Kuvshinov
  1841st Antitank Artillery Regiment—Major V. G. Gashkov
28th Antitank Gun Artillery Brigade (attached to 52d Guards Rifle Division on
  6 July)
  1838th Antitank Artillery Regiment
  1840th Antitank Artillery Regiment
  1842d Antitank Artillery Regiment
493d Antitank Artillery Regiment (attached to 71st Guards Rifle Division on
  5 July)
496th Antitank Artillery Regiment (attached to 71st and 67th Guards Rifle
  Divisions on 6 July)
538th Antitank Artillery Regiment (from 1st Tank Army in April) (attached to
  52d Guards Rifle Division on 6 July)
611th Antitank Artillery Regiment (attached to 67th Guards Rifle Division)
694th Antitank Artillery Regiment (attached to 375th Rifle Division)
868th Antitank Artillery Regiment (attached to 71st Guards Rifle Division)
1008th Antitank Artillery Regiment—Lieutenant Colonel Kotenko (from 1st
  Tank Army in April) (attached to 52d Guards Rifle Division on 6 July)
1240th Antitank Artillery Regiment (attached to 375th Rifle Division)
1666th Antitank Artillery Regiment (attached to 71st Guards Rifle Division)
1667th Antitank Artillery Regiment (attached to 375th Rifle Division)
263d Mortar Regiment (attached to 375th Rifle Division) (to 69th Army on 13
  July)
295th Mortar Regiment (attached to 71st Guards Rifle Division)
5th Guards Mortar Regiment—Lieutenant Colonel L. Z. Parnovsky (two
  battalions to 67th Guards Rifle Division and one to 52d Guards Rifle
  Division)
16th Guards Mortar Regiment—Lieutenant Colonel Ia. T. Petrakovsky
  (attached to 375th Rifle Division) (to the 5th Guards Tank Army on 11 July)
79th Guards Mortar Regiment (two battalions to 375th Rifle Division and one
  to 67th Guards Rifle Division) (to 6th Tanks Corps, 1st Tank Army on 6 July)
314th Guards Mortar Regiment (attached to 22d Guards Rifle Corps)
316th Guards Mortar Regiment (from 1st Tank Army in April)
26th Antiaircraft Artillery Division—Colonel A. E. Florenko
  1352d Antiaircraft Artillery Regiment
  1357th Antiaircraft Artillery Regiment
  1363d Antiaircraft Artillery Regiment
  1369th Antiaircraft Artillery Regiment

1487th Antiaircraft Artillery Regiment
205th Separate Engineer Battalion
540th Separate Engineer Battalion

ARMY STRENGTH: 79,900 men, 1,682 guns and mortars, 92 multiple rocket launchers, and 155 tanks and self-propelled guns

o   o   o

31st Antitank Artillery Brigade (from 7th Guards Army on 8 July) (to 69th Army on 13 July)
184th Rifle Division (from 40th Army on 12 July)
219th Rifle Division (from 40th Army on 12 July)
7th Guards Army—Commander, Lieutenant General M. S. Shumilov; Commissar, Major General Z. T. Serdiuk; Chief of Staff, Major General G. S. Lukin
   24th Guards Rifle Corps—Major General N. A. Vasil'ev:
      15th Guards Rifle Division—Major General E. I. Vasilenko: 44th Guards Rifle Regiment—Major I. A. Usikov: 47th Guards Rifle Regiment—Major I. I. Bat'ianov, 50th Guards Rifle Regiment, 43d Guards Artillery Regiment
      36th Guards Rifle Division—Major General M. I. Denisenko: 104th Guards Rifle Regiment—Major P. A. Il'ichev, 106th Guards Rifle Regiment—Major I. A. Zaitsev, 108th Guards Rifle Regiment—Major I. P. Moiseev, 65th Guards Artillery Regiment, 39th Guards Separate Antitank Artillery Battalion—Captain N. A. Borisov
      Strength: 8,013 men
      72d Guards Rifle Division—Major General A. I. Losev: 222d Guards Rifle Regiment, 224th Guards Rifle Regiment, 229th Guards Rifle Regiment, 155th Guards Artillery Regiment—Major Resenuk
   25th Guards Rifle Corps—Major General G. B. Safiullin
      73d Guards Rifle Division—Colonel S. A. Kozak: 209th Guards Rifle Regiment—Lieutenant Colonel G. P. Slatov, 211th Guards Rifle Regiment—Major P. N. Petrov, 214th Guards Rifle Regiment—Major V. I. Davidenko, 153d Guards Artillery Regiment—Major A. A. Nikolaev
      78th Guards Rifle Division—Major General A. V. Skvortsov: 223d Guards Rifle Regiment—Major S. A. Arshinov, 225th Guards Rifle Regiment—Major D. S. Khorolenko, 228th Guards Rifle Regiment: Major I. A. Khitsov, 158th Guards Artillery Regiment, 81st Guards Antitank Artillery Battalion
      Strength: 7,854 men
      81st Guards Rifle Division—Colonel I. K. Morozov (to 35th Guards Rifle Corps on 8 July) (to 69th Army on 10 July): 233d Guards Rifle Regiment, 235th Guards Rifle Regiment, 238th Guards Rifle Regiment, 173d Guards Artillery Regiment
   213th Rifle Division—Colonel I. E. Buslaev
      585th Rifle Regiment
      702d Rifle Regiment
      793d Rifle Regiment
      671st Artillery Regiment

27th Guards Tank Brigade—Colonel M. V. Nevzhinsky (to 18 August), Colonel N. M. Brizhinov (from 19 August) (attached to 24th Guards Rifle Corps)

201st Tank Brigade—Colonel (Major General on 16 July) A. I. Taranov (attached to 24th Guards Rifle Corps) (to 78th Guards Rifle Division on 6 July)

295th Tank Battalion

296th Tank Battalion

148th Separate Tank Regiment (attached to 24th Guards Rifle Corps) (to 69th Army on 10 July)

167th Separate Tank Regiment (attached to 25th Guards Rifle Corps) (to 73d Guards Rifle Division on 6 July)

262d Separate Tank Regiment (attached to 25th Guards Rifle Corps)

1438th Self-propelled Artillery Regiment (122mm) (attached to 25th Guards Rifle Corps) (to 73d Guards Rifle Division on 6 July)

1529th Self-propelled Artillery Regiment (152mm) (attached to 24th Guards Rifle Corps)

34th Separate Armored Train Battalion

38th Separate Armored Train Battalion

109th Guards Gun Artillery Regiment (attached to 24th Guards Rifle Corps)

161st Guards Gun Artillery Regiment (attached to 25th Guards Rifle Corps)

265th Guards Gun Artillery Regiment (attached to 25th Guards Rifle Corps) (to 73d Guards Rifle Division on 6 July)

30th Antitank Artillery Brigade (army reserve, attached to 78th Guards Rifle Division, 25th Guards Rifle Corps on 6 July) (to 69th Army on 10 July)

1844th Antitank Artillery Regiment

1846th Antitank Artillery Regiment

1848th Antitank Artillery Regiment

114th Guards Antitank Artillery Regiment—Lieutenant Colonel N. Shubin (attached to 25th Guards Rifle Corps)

115th Guards Antitank Artillery Regiment—Lieutenant Colonel N. Koziarenko (attached to 36th Guards Rifle Division, 24th Guards Rifle Corps) (to 69th Army on 13 July)

1669th Antitank Artillery Regiment (attached to 36th Guards Rifle Division on 5 July and 78th Guards Rifle Division on 6 July)

1670th Antitank Artillery Regiment

1st Antitank Rifle Battalion (attached to 24th Guards Rifle Corps)

2d Antitank Rifle Battalion (attached to 81th Guards Rifle Division)

3d Antitank Rifle Battalion

4th Antitank Rifle Battalion (attached to 78th Guards Rifle Division)

5th Antitank Rifle Battalion (attached to 24th Guards Rifle Corps)

290th Mortar Regiment (attached to 25th Guards Rifle Corps) (to 69th Army on 13 July)

5th Antiaircraft Artillery Division—Colonel M. A. Kudriasov

670th Antiaircraft Artillery Regiment

743d Antiaircraft Artillery Regiment

1119th Antiaircraft Artillery Regiment

1181st Antiaircraft Artillery Regiment

162d Guards Antiaircraft Artillery Regiment
258th Guards Antiaircraft Artillery Regiment
60th Engineer Sapper Brigade—Colonel D. Sh. Tsepeniuk
175th Separate Engineer Battalion
329th Separate Engineer Battalion—Major A. I. Sychev (to 73d Guards Rifle
  Division on 6 July)

ARMY STRENGTH: 76,800 men, 1,573 guns and mortars, 47 multiple rocket
launchers, and 246 tanks and self-propelled guns

o   o   o

97th Guards Mortar Regiment (from *front* on 4 July) (attached to 81st Guards Rifle
  Division, 25th Guards Rifle Corps) (to 72d Guards Rifle Division on 6 July)
309th Guards Mortar Regiment (from *front* on 5 July) (to 78th Guards Rifle
  Division on 6 July)
315th Guard Mortar Regiment (from *front* on 4 July) (attached to 25th Guards
  Rifle Corps) (to 69th Army on 13 July); 443d Guards Mortar Battalion (to
  81st Guards Rifle Division on 5 July), 477th Guards Mortar Battalion (to 81st
  Guards Rifle Division on 5 July)
31st Antitank Artillery Brigade (from *front* on 6 July) (to 73d Guards Rifle
  Division on 6 July) (to 6th Guards Army on 8 July)
38th Army—Commander, Lieutenant General N. E. Chibisov; Commissar, Major
General I. D. Rybinsky; Chief of Staff, Major General A. P. Pilipenko
  50th Rifle Corps—Major General S. S. Martirosian
    167th Rifle Division—Major General I. I. Mel'nikov: 465th Rifle Regiment,
      520th Rifle Regiment, 615th Rifle Regiment, 576th Artillery Regiment
    232th Rifle Division—Colonel N. P. Ulitin: 712th Rifle Regiment, 605th
      Rifle Regiment, 498th Rifle Regiment, 676th Artillery Regiment
    340th Rifle Division—Colonel M. I. Shadrin (to 12 August), Colonel I. E.
      Zubarev (from 12 August): 1140th Rifle Regiment, 1141st Rifle Regiment,
      1144d Rifle Regiment, 911st Artillery Regiment
  51st Rifle Corps—Major General P. P. Andreenko
    180th Rifle Division—Major General F. P. Shmelev: 21st Rifle Regiment,
      42d Rifle Regiment, 86th Rifle Regiment, 627th Artillery Regiment
    240th Rifle Division—Major General T. F. Umansky: 836th Rifle Regiment,
      842d Rifle Regiment, 931st Rifle Regiment, 692d Artillery Regiment
  204th Rifle Division—Colonel K. M. Baidak (to *front* reserve on 8 July)
    700th Rifle Regiment
    706th Rifle Regiment
    730th Rifle Regiment
    657th Artillery Regiment
  180th Separate Tank Brigade—Colonel M. Z. Kiselev (attached to 51st Rifle
    Corps) (to 1st Tank Army on 7 July)
    392d Tank Battalion
    393d Tank Battalion
  192d Separate Tank Brigade—Colonel A. F. Karavan (to 21 August),
    Lieutenant Colonel N. N. Kitvin (from 22 August) (attached to 50 Rifle
    Corps) (to 40th Army on 6 July and 1st Tank Army on 7 July)

416th Tank Battalion
417th Tank Battalion
112th Guards Gun Artillery Regiment
111th Guards Howitzer Artillery Regiment (to 40th Army on 6 July and 1st
Tank Army on 7 July)
29th Antitank Artillery Brigade (to 6th Guards Army and 1st Tank Army on 7 July)
1843d Antitank Artillery Regiment
1845th Antitank Artillery Regiment
1847th Antitank Artillery Regiment
222d Antitank Artillery Regiment (to 1st Tank Army and 69th Army on 7 July)
483d Antitank Artillery Regiment (to 1st Tank Army on 8 July)
1658th Antitank Artillery Regiment (to 69th Army on 13 July)
1660th Antitank Artillery Regiment
491st Mortar Regiment
492d Mortar Regiment
66th Guards Mortar Regiment (to 1st Tank Army on 7 July)
441st Guards Mortar Battalion, 314th Guards Mortar Regiment (to 69th Army
on 7 July)
981st Antiaircraft Artillery Regiment, 9th Antiaircraft Artillery Division
1288th Antiaircraft Artillery Regiment
235th Separate Engineer Battalion
268th Separate Engineer Battalion
108th Pontoon Bridge Battalion
1505th Separate Mine Sapper Battalion

ARMY STRENGTH: 60,000 men, 1,168 guns and mortars, 32 multiple rocket
launchers, and 150 tanks and self-propelled guns

40th Army—Commander, Lieutenant General. K. S. Moskalenko; Commissar,
Major General K. V. Krainiukov; Chief of Staff, Major General A. G. Batiunia
47th Rifle Corps—Major General A. S. Griaznov
161st Rifle Division—Major General P. V. Tertyshny (to 52d Rifle Corps on
6 July): 565th Rifle Regiment—Major A. A. Ermolaev, 569th Rifle
Regiment—Major V. Ia. Nagin, 575th Rifle Regiment—Lieutenant
Colonel M. I. Sipovich, 1036th Artillery Regiment—Major N. V. Platonov,
413th Separate Antitank Battalion—Lieutenant I. M. Lysenko
206th Rifle Division—Colonel V. I. Rut'ko (to 11 August), Major General
S. P. Merkulov (from 12 August): 722d Rifle Regiment, 737th Rifle
Regiment, 748th Rifle Regiment, 661st Artillery Regiment
237th Rifle Division—Colonel P. A. D'iakonov (to 26 August), Colonel V. I.
Novozhilov (from 27 August): 835th Rifle Regiment, 838th Rifle
Regiment, 841st Rifle Regiment, 691st Artillery Regiment
52d Rifle Corps—Lieutenant General F. I. Perkhorovich
100th Rifle Division—Colonel N. A. Bezzubov (to 17 July), Colonel P. T.
Tsygankov (from 23 July): 454th Rifle Regiment, 460th Rifle Regiment,
472d Rifle Regiment, 1031st Artillery Regiment, one antitank rifle
battalion (attached)

219th Rifle Division—Major General V. P. Kotel'nikov (to 29 August), Colonel A. S. Pypyrev (from 30 August) (to 6th Guards Army on 12 July): 375th Rifle Regiment, 710th Rifle Regiment, 727th Rifle Regiment, 673d Artillery Regiment, one antitank rifle battalion (attached)

309th Rifle Division—Colonel D. F. Dremin (to 1st Tank Army on 8 July) (returned on 12 July): 955th Rifle Regiment, 957th Rifle Regiment, 959th Rifle Regiment, 842d Artillery Regiment

184th Rifle Division—Colonel S. I. Tsukarev (to 6th Guards Army on 12 July)
    262d Rifle Regiment
    294th Rifle Regiment
    297th Rifle Regiment
    616th Artillery Regiment

86th Separate Tank Brigade—Colonel V. S. Agafonov (to 1st Tank Army on 8 July)
    232d Tank Battalion—Captain N. G. Guba
    233d Tank Battalion

59th Separate Tank Regiment (to 1st Tank Army on 8 July)

60th Separate Heavy Tank Regiment (to 1st Tank Army on 8 July)

36th Gun Artillery Brigade

29th Howitzer Artillery Brigade
    805th Howitzer Artillery Regiment
    839th Howitzer Artillery Regiment

76th Guards Gun Artillery Regiment

32d Antitank Artillery Brigade (to 69th Army on 13 July)
    1850th Antitank Artillery Regiment
    1852d Antitank Artillery Regiment
    1854th Antitank Artillery Regiment

4th Guards Antitank Artillery Regiment (to 1st Tank Army on 8 July)

12th Antitank Artillery Regiment (to 1st Tank Army on 8 July)

869th Antitank Artillery Regiment (to 1st Tank Army on 8 July)

1244th Antitank Artillery Regiment (to 1st Tank Army on 7 July)

1663d Antitank Artillery Regiment

1664th Antitank Artillery Regiment

493d Mortar Regiment

494th Mortar Regiment

9th Mountain Mortar Regiment

10th Mountain Mortar Regiment

9th Antiaircraft Artillery Division—Lieutenant Colonel (Colonel on 9 July) N. A. Roshchitsky (to 1st Tank Army on 8 July)
    800th Antiaircraft Artillery Regiment
    974th Antiairctaft Artillery Regiment
    993d Antiaircraft Artillery Regiment

1488th Antiaircraft Artillery Regiment

14th Separate Engineer Battalion

ARMY STRENGTH: 77,000 men, 1,636 guns and mortars, and 237 tanks

∘   ∘   ∘

1461st Self-propelled Artillery Regiment (76mm) (from 1st Tank Army on 5 July)

1689th Antitank Artillery Regiment (from *front* on 5 July)

111th Guards Howitzer Artillery Regiment (from 40th Army on 7 July) (to 1st Tank Army on 8 July)

204th Rifle Division (from *front* reserve on 12 July)

69th Army—Commander, Lieutenant General V. D. Kriuchenkin; Commissar, Major General A. V. Shchelakovsky; Chief of Staff, Colonel S. M. Protas

  48th Rifle Corps—Major General Z. Z. Rogozny

    107th Rifle Division—Major General P. M. Bezhko (to 35th Guards Rifle Corps on 10 July): 504th Rifle Regiment, 516th Rifle Regiment, 522d Rifle Regiment, 1032d Artillery Regiment

    183d Rifle Division—Major General A. S. Kostitsyn (to 24 July), Colonel I. D. Vasilevsky (from 25 July): 227th Rifle Regiment, 285th Rifle Regiment, 296th Rifle Regiment, 623d Artillery Regiment—Major I. N. Sadovnikov

    305th Rifle Division—Colonel A. F. Vasil'ev (to 35th Guards Rifle Corps on 10 July): 1000th Rifle Regiment, 1002d Rifle Regiment, 1004th Rifle Regiment, 830th Artillery Regiment

  49th Rifle Corps—Major General G. P. Terent'ev (to 7th Guards Army on 7 July)

    111th Rifle Division—Lieutenant Colonel A. N. Petrushin: 399th Rifle Regiment, 468th Rifle Regiment, 532d Rifle Regiment, 286th Artillery Regiment

    270th Rifle Division—Colonel I. P. Beliaev: 973d Rifle Regiment, 975th Rifle Regiment, 977th Rifle Regiment, 810th Artillery Regiment

  1661st Antitank Artillery Regiment

  496th Mortar Regiment

  225th Guards Antiaircraft Artillery Regiment

  322d Separate Antiaircraft Artillery Battalion

  328th Separate Engineer Battalion

ARMY STRENGTH: 52,000 men and 889 guns and mortars

    o   o   o

35th Guards Rifle Corps (from *front* on 5 July): 92d Guards Rifle Division, 94th Guards Rifle Division

93d Guards Rifle Division (from *front* on 7 July)

81st Guards Rifle Division (from 7th Guards Army on 10 July)

89th Guards Rifle Division (from 6th Guards Army on 10 July)

10th Antitank Artillery Brigade (from Southwestern Front on 10 July) (to 5th Guards Tank Army on 11 July) (from 5th Guards Tank Army on 13 July)

375th Rifle Division (from 6 Guards Army on 10 July)

2d Guards Tank Corps (from 1st Tank Army on 10 July)

96th Tank Brigade (from 6th Guards Army on 10 July)

148th Separate Regiment (from 7th Guards Army on 10 July)

30th Antitank Artillery Brigade (from 7th Guards Army on 10 July)

27th Gun Artillery Brigade (from 6th Guards Army on 10 July) (to 5th Guards Tank Army on 11 July) (returned on 13 July)

32d Antitank Artillery Brigade (from 40th Army on 13 July)
36th Antiaircraft Artillery Division (from *front* reserve on 13 July)
    1385th Antiaircraft Artillery Regiment
    1391st Antiaircraft Artillery Regiment
    1397th Antiaircraft Artillery Regiment
    1399th Antiaircraft Artillery Regiment
80th Guards Mortar Regiment (from 5th Guards Tank Army on 13 July)
1076th Antitank Artillery Regiment (from 2d Guards Tank Corps on 13 July)
31st Antitank Artillery Brigade (from 6th Guards Army on 13 July)
115th Guards Mortar Regiment (from 7th Guards Army on 13 July)
1658th Antitank Artillery Regiment (from 38th Army on 13 July)
315th Guards Mortar Regiment (from 7th Guards Army on 13 July)
293d Mortar Regiment (from 6th Guards Army on 13 July)
290th Mortar Regiment (from 7th Guards Army on 13 July)
48th Antitank Artillery Regiment (from 2d Tank Corps on 13 July)
638th Antitank Artillery Regiment (on 13 July) (from another antitank brigade)
1510th Antitank Artillery Regiment (on 13 July) (from another antitank
    brigade)
1st Tank Army—Commander, Lieutenant General M. E. Katukov; Commissar,
Major General N. K. Popel'; Chief of Staff, Major General M. A. Shalin
    3d Mechanized Corps—Major General S. M. Krivoshein
        1st Mechanized Brigade—Colonel F. P. Lipatenkov: 14th Tank Regiment
        3d Mechanized Brigade—Colonel A. Kh. Babadzhanian: 16th Tank
            Regiment
        10th Mechanized Brigade—Colonel I. I. Iakovlev: 17th Tank Regiment—
            Major I. N. Boiko
        1st Guards Tank Brigade—Colonel V. M. Gorelov
        49th Tank Brigade—Lieutenant Colonel A. F. Burda
        58th Motorcycle Battalion
        35th Antitank Artillery Regiment
        265th Mortar Regiment
        405th Separate Guards Mortar Battalion
        34th Separate Armored Car (Reconnaissance) Battalion
        Corps strength: 250 tanks
    6th Tank Corps—Major General A. L. Getman
        22d Tank Brigade—Colonel N. G. Vedenichev: 1st Tank Battalion, one tank
            battalion
        112th Tank Brigade—Colonel M. T. Leonov: 124th Tank Battalion—Major
            F. P. Borid'ko, 125th Tank Battalion—Major P. I. Orekhov
        200th Tank Brigade—Colonel N. V. Morgunov: 191st Tank Battalion, 192d
            Tank Battalion
        6th Motorized Rifle Brigade—Colonel I. P. Elin
        85th Motorcycle Battalion
        1461st Self-propelled Artillery Regiment (76mm) (to 40th Army on 5 July)
        538th Antitank Artillery Regiment—Major V. I. Barkovsky (to 6th Guards
            Army in April)

1008th Antitank Artillery Regiment—Major I. K. Kotenko (to 6th Guards
  Army in April)
270th Mortar Regiment
40th Separate Armored Car (Reconnaissance) Battalion
Corps strength: 179 tanks on 6 July and 52 tanks on 18 July)

o   o   o

79th Guards Mortar Regiment (from 6th Guards Army on 6 July)
31st Tank Corps—Major General D. Kh. Chernienko
  100th Tank Brigade—Colonel N. M. Ivanov (to 21 July), Major V. M.
    Potapov (from 22 July): 1st Tank Battalion—Captain P. F. Kunchenko, 2d
    Tank Battalion—Captain M. G. Marilov
  237th Tank Brigade—Major N. P. Protsenko: 1st Tank Battalion—Captain
    N. M. Godin, 2d Tank Battalion
  242d Tank Brigade—Lieutenant Colonel V. P. Sokolov: 1st Tank Battalion,
    2d Tank Battalion
  31st Separate Armored Car (Reconnaissance) Battalion
  210th Antitank Rifle Battalion
  Corps strength: 43 T-34 and 12–17 T-60 and T-70 tanks per brigade for a
    total of 196 (155 T-34 and 41 T-60 and T-70) tanks

o   o   o

753d Antitank Artillery Battalion (on 10 July)
316th Guards Mortar Regiment (attached to 6th Guards Army in April)
8th Antiaircraft Artillery Division—Colonel I. G. Kamen'sky: 797th Antiaircraft
  Artillery Regiment, 848th Antiaircraft Artillery Regiment, 978th Antiaircraft
  Artillery Regiment, 1063d Antiaircraft Artillery Regiment
71st Separate Motorized Engineer Battalion
267th Separate Motorized Engineer Battalion
385th Signal Aviation Regiment (19 PO-2)
83d Signal Regiment
35th Auto Transport Regiment
6th Repair-Reconstruction Battalion
7th Repair-Reconstruction Battalion

ARMY STRENGTH: 40,000 men, 419 guns and mortars, 56 multiple rocket
launchers, 646 tanks and self-propelled guns, and several thousand vehicles)

o   o   o

2d Guards Tank Corps (from front on 5 July)
5th Guards Tank Corps (from front on 5 July)
29th Antitank Artillery Brigade (from 38th Army on 7 July) (attached to 31st
  Tank Corps)
180th Separate Tank Brigade (from 38th Army on 7 July)
192d Separate Tank Brigade (from 38th Army on 7 July)
111th Guards Howitzer Artillery Regiment (from 38th Army on 7 July)
222d Antitank Artillery Regiment (from 38th Army on 7 July)
1244th Antitank Artillery Regiment (from 40th Army on 7 July) (attached to
  31st Tank Corps)

66th Guards Mortar Regiment (from 38th Army on 7 July)
754th Antitank Artillery Battalion (from 38th Army or 40th Army on 8 July)
756th Antitank Artillery Battalion (from 38th Army or 40th Army on 8 July)
138th Antitank Rifle Battalion (from 38th Army or 40th Army on 8 July)
139th Antitank Rifle Battalion (from 38th Army or 40th Army on 8 July)
86th Separate Tank Brigade (from 40th Army on 8 July)
33d Gun Artillery Brigade (from 6th Guards Army on 8 July)
4th Guards Antitank Artillery Regiment (from 40th Army on 8 July)
12th Antitank Artillery Regiment (from 40th Army on 8 July)
36th Guards Mortar Regiment (from *front* on 8 July)
10th Tank Corps (from Steppe Front on 8 July)
309th Rifle Division (from 40th Army on 8 July) (to 40th Army on 12 July)
59th Separate Tank Regiment (from 40th Army on 8 July)
60th Separate Heavy Tank Regiment (from 40th Army on 8 July)
203d Separate Tank Regiment (from *front* on 8 July)
483d Antitank Artillery Regiment (from 38th Army on 8 July)
869th Antitank Artillery Regiment (from 40th Army on 8 July)
14th Antitank Artillery Brigade (from *front* on 8 July)
9th Antiaircraft Artillery Division (from 40th Army on 8 July)
204th Rifle Division (from *front* on 10 July)
2d Air Army—Commander, Lieutenant General S. A. Krasovsky; Commissar, Major General S. N. Romanazov; Chief of Staff, Colonel A. I. Asaulenko
1st Bomber Aviation Corps—Colonel I. S. Polbin
1st Guards Bomber Aviation Division—Colonel F. I. Dobysh
293d Bomber Aviation Division—Colonel G. V. Gribakin
1st Assault Aviation Corps—Lieutenant General V. G. Riazanov
266th Assault Aviation Division—Colonel F. G. Podiakin
292d Assault Aviation Division—Major General F. A. Agal'tsov
4th Fighter Aviation Corps—Major General I. D. Podgorny
294th Fighter Aviation Division—Colonel V. V. Sukhoriakov (to 27 July), Lieutenant Colonel I. A. Taranenko (from 28 July)
302d Fighter Aviation Division—Colonel B. I. Litvinov
5th Fighter Aviation Corps—Major General D. P. Galunov
8th Guards Fighter Aviation Division—Colonel I. P. Lariushkin
205th Fighter Aviation Division—Colonel Iu. A. Nemtsevich
291st Assault Aviation Division—Major General A. N. Vitruk
203d Fighter Aviation Division—Major General K. G. Baranchuk
208th Night Bomber Aviation Division—Colonel L. N. Iuseev
385th Light Bomber Aviation Regiment
454th Light Bomber Aviation Regiment
50th Reconnaissance Aviation Regiment
331st Corrective Aviation Squadron
1554th Antiaircraft Artillery Regiment
1555th Antiaircraft Artillery Regiment
1605th Antiaircraft Artillery Regiment

Front subordination

35th Guards Rifle Corps—Major General S. G. Goriachev (to 69th Army on 5 July)

92d Guards Rifle Division—Colonel V. F. Trunin (to 10 August), Colonel A. N. Petrushin (from 11 August) (to 69th Army on 5 July): 276th Guards Rifle Regiment, 280th Guards Rifle Regiment, 282d Guards Rifle Regiment, 197th Guards Artillery Regiment—Colonel S. I. Shapovalov

93d Guards Rifle Division—Major General V. V. Tikhomirov (to 48th Rifle Corps on 7 July): 278th Guards Rifle Regiment, 281st Guards Rifle Regiment, 285th Guards Rifle Regiment, 198th Guards Artillery Regiment

94th Guards Rifle Division—Colonel I. G. Russkikh (to 69th Army on 5 July, returned to 35th Guards Rifle Corps on 8 July): 283d Guards Rifle Regiment, 286th Guards Rifle Regiment, 288th Guards Rifle Regiment, 199th Guards Artillery Regiment

Corps strength: 35,000 men and 620 guns and mortars

o   o   o

81st Guards Rifle Division (from 7th Guards Army on 8 July, returned to 48th Rifle Corps, 69th Army on 10 July)

375th Rifle Division (from 6th Guards Army on 8 July, returned to 48th Rifle Corps, 69th Army on 10 July)

305th Rifle Division (from 69th Army on 10 July)

107th Rifle Division (from 69th Army on 10 July)

1510th Antitank Artillery Regiment (45mm) (corps reserve on 13 July)

2d Guards Tank Corps—Major General A. S. Burdeiny (to 1st Tank Army on 5 July, 69th Army on 10 July, and 5th Guards Tank Army on 11 July)

4th Guards Tank Brigade—Colonel A. K. Brazhnikov

25th Guards Tank Brigade—Lieutenant Colonel S. M. Bulygin

26th Guards Tank Brigade—Colonel S. K. Nesterov

4th Guards Motorized Rifle Brigade

47th Guards Tank Regiment

1500th Antitank Artillery Regiment

755th Separate Antitank Artillery Battalion

273d Mortar Regiment

1695th Antiaircraft Artillery Regiment

19th Separate Armored Car (Reconnaissance) Battalion

79th Separate Motorcycle Battalion

Strength: 200 tanks on 5 July and 100 tanks on 11 July

o   o   o

1076th Antitank Artillery Regiment (from *front* on 7 July) (to 69th Army on 13 July)

5th Guards Tank Corps—Major General A. G. Kravchenko (to 1st Tank Army on 5 July)

20th Guards Tank Brigade—Lieutenant Colonel P. F. Okhrimenko

21st Guards Tank Brigade—Colonel K. I. Ovcharenko

22d Guards Tank Brigade—Colonel F. A. Zhilin

6th Guards Motorized Rifle Brigade
48th Guards Tank Regiment
1499th Antitank Artillery Regiment
454th Mortar Regiment
1696th Antiaircraft Artillery Regiment
23d Separate Armored Car (Reconnaissance) Battalion
80th Separate Motorcycle Battalion
    Strength: 200 tanks
One battalion, 203d Separate Heavy Tank Regiment
1528th Howitzer Artillery Regiment (29th Howitzer Artillery Brigade)
522d High-powered Howitzer Artillery Regiment (to 5th Guards Tank Army on 11 July)
1148th High-powered Howitzer Artillery Regiment (to 5th Guards Tank Army on 11 July)
14th Antitank Artillery Brigade (to 1st Tank Army on 8 July)
    1177th Antitank Artillery Regiment
    1207th Antitank Artillery Regiment
    1212th Antitank Artillery Regiment
31st Antitank Artillery Brigade (to 7th Guards Army on 6 July and 6th Guards Army on 8 July)
    1849th Antitank Artillery Regiment
    1851st Antitank Artillery Regiment
    1853d Antitank Artillery Regiment
1076th Antitank Artillery Regiment—Lieutenant Colonel Kalinin (to 2d Guards Tank Corps on 7 July)
1689th Antitank Artillery Regiment (to 40th Army on 5 July)
12th Mortar Brigade
469th Mortar Regiment
36th Guards Mortar Regiment (to 1st Tank Army on 8 July)
80th Guards Mortar Regiment—Lieutenant Colonel Samchenko (to 5th Guards Tank Army on 11 July)
97th Guards Mortar Regiment—Lieutenant Colonel M. M. Chumak (to 7th Guards Army on 4 July)
309th Guards Mortar Regiment (to 7th Guards Army on 5 July)
315th Guards Mortar Regiment—Lieutenant Colonel A. F. Ganiushkin (to 7th Guards Army on 4 July)
22d Guards Separate Antiaircraft Battalion
4th Engineer Mine Brigade
5th Engineer Mine Brigade
42d Engineer Brigade (Spetznaz)
6th Pontoon Bridge Brigade
13th Guards Miners Battalion
6th Pontoon Bridge Battalion
20th Pontoon Bridge Battalion

o   o   o

1529th Self-propelled Artillery Regiment (from RVK in July)
36th Antiaircraft Artillery Division (from RGK in July)
    1385th Antiaircraft Artillery Regiment
    1391st Antiaircraft Artillery Regiment
    1397th Antiaircraft Artillery Regiment
    1399th Antiaircraft Artillery Regiment
204th Rifle Division (from 38th Army on 8 July)
13th Artillery Penetration Division—Major General D. M. Krasnokutsky (from
    Briansk Front after 20 July) (to 5th Guards Army by 1 August)
    42d Light Artillery Brigade
    47th Howitzer Artillery Brigade
    88th Heavy Howitzer Artillery Brigade
    91st Heavy Howitzer Artillery Brigade (to 27th Army by 1 August)
    101st High-powered Howitzer Artillery Brigade
    17th Mortar Brigade
17th Artillery Penetration Division (7th Artillery Penetration Corps) (from
    Briansk Front after 20 July)
    37th Light Artillery Brigade
    39th Gun Artillery Brigade
    50th Gun Artillery Brigade
    92d Heavy Gun Artillery Brigade
    108th Gun Artillery Brigade
    22d Mortar Brigade

FRONT STRENGTH: 625,591 men, 8,718 guns and mortars, 272 multiple
rocket launchers, 1,704 tanks and self-propelled guns, and 900 aircraft

The Khar'kov Axis

SOUTHWESTERN FRONT—Commander, Army General R. Ia. Malinovsky;
Commissar, Lieutenant General A. S. Zheltov; Chief of Staff, Major General
F. K. Korzhenevich

57th Army (to Steppe Front on 8 August)—Commander, Lieutenant General
N. A. Gagen; Commissar, Major General L. P. Bocharev; Chief of Staff, Major
General V. D. Karpukhin
    27th Guards Rifle Corps—Lieutenant General F. E. Sheverdin (to 22 August),
        Major General E. S. Alekhin (from 23 August)
        14th Guards Rifle Division—Colonel V. V. Rusakov
        48th Guards Rifle Division—Colonel G. N. Korchikov
        58th Guards Rifle Division—Colonel P. I. Kazatkin
    19th Rifle Division—Colonel P. E. Lazarov
    24th Rifle Division—Major General F. A. Prokhorov
    52d Rifle Division—Lieutenant Colonel P. D. Fadeev (to 11 August), Colonel
        A. Ia. Maksimov (from 12 August)
    113th Rifle Division—Major General E. S. Alekhin (to 22 August), Lieutenant
        Colonel M. I. Pogorelov (from 23 August)

303d Rifle Division—Colonel K. S. Fedorovsky
1st Separate Destroyer Brigade
173d Tank Brigade—Colonel V. P. Korotkov
179th Tank Brigade—Lieutenant Colonel V. I. Tutushkin
26th Light Artillery Brigade (9th Artillery Division)
9th Guards Gun Artillery Brigade
1110th Gun Artillery Regiment
374th Antitank Artillery Regiment
595th Antitank Artillery Regiment
523d Mortar Regiment
45th Guards Mortar Regiment
303d Guards Mortar Regiment
71st Antiaircraft Artillery Regiment
227th Separate Antiaircraft Artillery Battalion

ARMY STRENGTH: 65,000 men and 80 tanks

2d Tank Corps—Major General A. F. Popov (to Southwestern Front on 8 July and
5th Guards Tank Army on 11 July)
26th Tank Brigade
99th Tank Brigade—Lieutenant Colonel S. Malov (KIA on 11 July)
169th Tank Brigade
58th Motorized Rifle Brigade
83d Motorcycle Battalion
48th Antitank Artillery Regiment (to 69th Army on 13 July)
1502d Antitank Regiment
269th Mortar Regiment
1698th Antiaircraft Regiment
307th Guards Mortar Battalion
    Corps Strength: 168 tanks on 8 July and 100 tanks on 12 July
17th Air Army—Commander, Lieutenant General V. A. Sudets; Commissar,
Major General V. N. Tolmachev; Chief of Staff, Major General N. M. Korsakov
    1st Mixed Aviation Corps—Major General V. I. Shevchenko
        5th Guards Assault Aviation Division—Colonel L. V. Kolomeistev
        288th Fighter Aviation Division—Colonel B. A. Smirnov
    3d Mixed Aviation Corps—Major General V. I. Aladinsky
        290th Assault Aviation Division—Major General P. I. Mironenko
        207th Fighter Aviation Division—Colonel A. P. Osadchy
    9th Mixed Aviation Corps—Major General O. V. Tolstikov
        305th Assault Aviation Division—Lieutenant Colonel N. G. Mikhevichev
        295th Fighter Aviation Corps
    244th Bomber Aviation Division—Major General V. I. Klebtsov
    306th Assault Aviation Division—Lieutenant Colonel A. V. Ivanov
    262d Night Bomber Aviation Division—Colonel G. I. Belitsky
    39th Reconnaissance Aviation Regiment
    3d Medical Aviation Regiment

SOUTHERN FRONT

8th Air Army—Commander, Lieutenant General T. T. Khriukin; Commissar, Major General A. I. Vikhorev; Chief of Staff, Colonel I. M. Belov

    289th Assault Aviation Division (10th Mixed Aviation Corps)—Colonel I. P. Putsykin

    270th Bomber Aviation Division—Colonel G. A. Chuchev

    1st Guards Assault Aviation Division—Major General B. K. Tokarev

    6th Guards Fighter Aviation Division—Colonel B. A. Sidnev

    2d Guards Night Bomber Aviation Division—Major General P. O. Kuznetsov

    8th Reconnaissance Aviation Regiment

    406th Light Bomber Aviation Regiment

    678th Transport Aviation Regiment

    5th Medical Aviation Regiment

    87th Guards Aviation Regiment (Civil Air Fleet)

Stavka Reserves

STEPPE MILITARY DISTRICT (STEPPE FRONT ON 9 JULY)—Commander, Colonel General I. S. Konev; Commissar, Lieutenant General I. Z. Susaikov; Chief of Staff, Lieutenant General M. V. Zakharov

4th Guards Army—Commander, Lieutenant General G. I. Kulik; Commissar, Colonel I. A. Gavrilov; Chief of Staff, Major General P. M. Verkholovich

    20th Guards Rifle Corps—Major General N. I. Biriukov

        5th Guards Airborne Division—Major General M. A. Bogdanov (to 16 July), Major General V. I. Kalinin (from 20 July)

        7th Guards Airborne Division—Major General M. G. Mikeladze

        8th Guards Airborne Division—Major General V. F. Stenin (to 25 August), Major General M. A. Bogdanov (from 25 August)

    21st Guards Rifle Corps—Major General P. I. Fomenko

        68th Guards Rifle Division—Major General G. P. Isakov

        69th Guards Rifle Division—Major General K. K. Dzhakhua

        80th Guards Rifle Division—Colonel A. E. Iakovlev

    3d Guards Tank Corps—Major General I. A. Vovchenko

        3d Guards Tank Brigade—Colonel G. A. Pokhodzeev

        18th Guards Tank Brigade—Colonel D. K. Gumeniuk

        19th Guards Tank Brigade—Colonel T. S. Pozolotin

        2d Guards Motorized Rifle Brigade—Colonel A. D. Pavlenko

        1436th Self-propelled Artillery Regiment

        76th Motorcycle Battalion

        1496th Antitank Artillery Regiment

        266th Mortar Regiment

        1701st Antiaircraft Artillery Regiment

        749th Separate Antiaircraft Artillery Battalion

        324th Guards Mortar Battalion

        Corps strength: approximately 178 tanks and self-propelled guns

    452d Antitank Artillery Regiment

1317th Antitank Artillery Regiment
466th Mortar Regiment
96th Guards Mortar Regiment
27th Antiaircraft Artillery Division—Colonel N. A. Bogun
    1354th Antiaircraft Artillery Regiment
    1358th Antiaircraft Artillery Regiment
    1364th Antiaircraft Artillery Regiment
    1370th Antiaircraft Artillery Regiment
48th Separate Engineer Battalion

ARMY STRENGTH: 70,000 men and 178 tanks and self-propelled guns

5th Guards Army (to Voronezh Front on 8 July)—Commander, Lieutenant
General A. S. Zhadov; Commissar, Major General A. M. Krivulin; Chief of Staff,
Major General N. I. Liamin
    32d Guards Rifle Corps—Major General A. I. Rodimtsev
        13th Guards Rifle Division—Major General G. V. Baklanov: 34th Guards
            Rifle Regiment—Lieutenant Colonel D. I. Panikhin, 39th Guards Rifle
            Regiment—Lieutenant Colonel A. K. Shchur, 42d Guards Rifle
            Regiment—Lieutenant Colonel A. V. Kolesnik, 32d Guards Artillery
            Regiment—Lieutenant Colonel A. V. Klebanovsky
        66th Guards Rifle Division—Major General A. V. Iakushin: 145th Guards
            Rifle Regiment, 193d Guards Rifle Regiment, 195th Guards Rifle
            Regiment, 135th Guards Artillery Regiment
        6th Guards Airborne Division—Colonel M. N. Smirnov: 14th Guards
            Airborne Regiment, 17th Guards Airborne Regiment, 20th Guards
            Airborne Regiment, 8th Guards Airborne Artillery Regiment
    33d Guards Rifle Corps—Major General I. I. Popov (to 30 August), Major
        General M. I. Kozlov (from 31 August)
        95th Guards Rifle Division—Colonel A. N. Liakhov: 284th Guards Rifle
            Regiment—Lieutenant Colonel V. S. Nakaidze, 287th Guards Rifle
            Regiment—Lieutenant Colonel F. M. Zaiarny, 290th Guards Rifle
            Regiment, 233d Guards Artillery Regiment—Lieutenant Colonel A. P.
            Revin, 103d Guards Separate Antitank Battalion
        97th Guards Rifle Division—Colonel I. I. Antsiferov: 289th Guards Rifle
            Regiment—Lieutenant Colonel P. R. Pansky, 292d Guards Rifle
            Regiment—Lieutenant Colonel V. S. Savinov, 294th Guards Rifle
            Regiment, 232d Guards Artillery Regiment, 104th Guards Separate
            Antitank Artillery Battalion—Major I. D. Rudenko
        9th Guards Airborne Division—Colonel A. M. Sazonov: 23d Guards Airborne
            Regiment—Lieutenant Colonel N. M. Nazarov, 26th Guards Airborne
            Regiment—Lieutenant Colonel G. M. Kashpersky, 28th Guards Airborne
            Regiment—Major V. A. Ponomarev, 7th Guards Artillery Regiment—
            Major V. K. Valuev, 10th Guards Antitank Artillery Battalion
        42d Guards Rifle Division—Major General F. A. Bobrov: 127th Guards Rifle
            Regiment, 132d Guards Rifle Regiment, 136th Guards Rifle Regiment,
            75th Guards Artillery Regiment

10th Tank Corps—Major General V. G. Burkov (to *front* on 7 July and 1st Tank
Army on 8 July)
178th Tank Brigade—Major K. M. Pivorarov
183d Tank Brigade—Colonel G. Ia. Andriushchenko (to 15 August),
Lieutenant Colonel M. K. Akopov (from 15 August)
186th Tank Brigade—Lieutenant Colonel A. V. Ovsiannikov
11th Motorized Rifle Brigade—Colonel P. G. Borodkin
1450th Self-propelled Artillery Regiment (122m/76mm)—Lieutenant
Colonel L. M. Lebedev
30th Separate Armored Car (Reconnaissance) Battalion
77th Motorcycle Battalion
727th Antitank Regiment—Lieutenant Colonel V. S. Shonichev (20 76mm guns)
287th Mortar Regiment—Lieutenant Colonel V. F. Druzhinin (36 120mm
mortars)
1693d Antiaircraft Regiment—Major N. A. Shumilov (16 37mm antiaircraft guns)
Corps strength: 9, 612 men, 164 tanks (99 T-34, 64 T-70, 1 KV), 21 self-
propelled guns (12 SU-122, 9 SU-76), 77 guns (28 76mm, 32 45mm, 17
37mm), 123 mortars, 983 vehicles, 14 tractors, 70 motorcycles, 52 armored
transporters, 44 armored cars, 4,613 rifles, 2,917 auto weapons, 209
submachine guns, 58 heavy machine guns, 57 antiaircraft machine guns,
and 202 antitank rifles
301st Antitank Artillery Regiment (attached to 33d Guards Rifle Corps) (to
95th Guards Rifle Division on 12 July)
1322d Antitank Artillery Regiment
308th Guards Mortar Regiment
29th Antiaircraft Artillery Division—Colonel Ia. M. Liubimov (to 23 July),
Colonel M. A. Vialov (from 24 July): 1360th Antiaircraft Artillery Regiment,
1366th Antiaircraft Artillery Regiment, 1372d Antiaircraft Artillery
Regiment, 1374th Antiaircraft Artillery Regiment
256th Separate Engineer Battalion
431st Separate Engineer Battalion

ARMY STRENGTH: 80,000 men, 1,953 guns and mortars, 133 multiple rocket
launchers, and 185 tanks and self-propelled guns

27th Army (to Voronezh Front on 14 July)—Commander, Lieutenant General
S. G. Trofimenko; Commissar, Major General I. P. Shevchenko; Chief of Staff,
Colonel G. S. Lukianchenko
71st Rifle Division—Major General N. M. Zamirovsky
147th Rifle Division—Major General M. P. Iakimov
155th Rifle Division—Colonel I. V. Kaprov
163d Rifle Division—Colonel F. V. Karlov
166th Rifle Division—Colonel B. I. Poltorzhitsky (to 19 August), Colonel A. I.
Svetlaikov (from 20 August)
241st Rifle Division—Colonel P. G. Arabei
93d Tank Brigade—Major S. K. Doropei or Major A. A. Dement'ev
39th Separate Tank Regiment
680th Antitank Artillery Regiment

1070th Antitank Artillery Regiment
480th Mortar Regiment
47th Guards Mortar Regiment
23d Antiaircraft Artillery Division—Colonel N. S. Sitnikov
  1064th Antiaircraft Artillery Regiment
  1336th Antiaircraft Artillery Regiment
  1342d Antiaircraft Artillery Regiment
  1348th Antitank Artillery Regiment
25th Separate Engineer Battalion
38th Separate Engineer Battalion

ARMY STRENGTH: 70,000 men and 92 tanks

47th Army—Commander, Major General P. M. Kozlov; Commissar, Major
General I. N. Korolev; Chief of Staff, Colonel E. V. Ivanov
  21st Rifle Corps—Major General V. L. Abramov
    23d Rifle Division—Colonel A. I. Korolev
    218th Rifle Division—Colonel P. T. Kliushnikov (to 14 August), Colonel D. N.
      Dolganov (15 August–26 August), Colonel S. F. Skliarov (from 26 August)
    337th Rifle Division—Major General G. O. Liaskin
  23d Rifle Corps—Major General N. E. Chuvakov
    29th Rifle Division—Colonel N. M. Ivanovsky
    30th Rifle Division—Colonel M. E. Savchenko
    38th Rifle Division—Colonel S. F. Skliarov (to 10 August), Lieutenant
      Colonel F. S. Esipov (from 11 August)
  269th Antitank Artillery Regiment
  1593d Antitank Artillery Regiment
  460th Mortar Regiment
  83d Guards Mortar Regiment
  21st Antiaircraft Artillery Division—Colonel G. V. Kasatkin
    1044th Antiaircraft Artillery Regiment
    1334th Antiaircraft Artillery Regiment
    1340th Antiaircraft Artillery Regiment
    1346th Antitaircraft Artillery Regiment
  91st Separate Engineer Battalion

ARMY STRENGTH: 65,000 men

53d Army (to Voronezh Front on 14 July)—Commander, Lieutenant General
I. M. Managarov; Commissar, Major General P. I. Gorokhov; Chief of Staff,
Major General K. N. Derevianko
  28th Guards Rifle Division—Major General G. I. Churmaev
  84th Rifle Division—Colonel P. I. Buniashin
  116th Rifle Division—Major General I. M. Makarov
  214th Rifle Division—Major General P. P. Dremin (to 1 August), Colonel Ia. I.
    Brovchenko
  233d Rifle Division—Colonel Ia. N. Bransky (to 26 July), Colonel Iu. I. Sokolov
    (from 27 July)
  252d Rifle Division—Major General G. I. Anisimov

299th Rifle Division—Colonel A. Ia. Klimenko (to 12 August), Major General
N. G. Travnikov (from 12 August)
34th Separate Tank Regiment
35th Separate Tank Regiment
232d Antitank Artilllery Regiment
1316th Antitank Artillery Regiment
461st Mortar Regiment
89th Guards Mortar Regiment
30th Antiaircraft Artillery Division—Colonel N. V. Popov
   1361st Antiaircraft Artillery Regiment
   1367th Antiaircraft Artillery Regiment
   1373d Antiaircraft Artillery Regiment
   1375th Antiaircraft Artillery Regiment
11th Separate Engineer Battalion
17th Separate Engineer Battalion

ARMY STRENGTH: 65,000 men and 78 tanks

5th Guards Tank Army (to Voronezh Front on 11 July)—Commander, Lieutenant
General P. A. Rotmistrov; Commissar, Major General P. G. Grishin; Chief of
Staff, Major General V. N. Baskakov
  5th Guards Mechanized Corps—Major General B. M. Skvortsov
    10th Guards Mechanized Brigade—Colonel I. B. Mikhailov: 51st Guards
      Tank Regiment—Colonel D. Ia. Klinfel'd
    11th Guards Mechanized Brigade—Colonel N. V. Grishchenko: 54th Guards
      Tank Regiment—Lieutenant Colonel V. Riazantsev
    12th Guards Mechanized Brigade—Colonel G. Ia. Borisenko: 55th Guards
      Tank Regiment—Lieutenant Colonel M. Gol'dberg
    24th Guards Tank Brigade—Lieutenant Colonel V. P. Karpov (to 29 July),
      Colonel T. A. Akulovich (30 July–11 August), Lieutenant Colonel V. P.
      Karpov (from 12 August)
    4th Guards Separate Armored Car (Reconnaissance) Battalion—Captain
      N. A. Shtykoi
    2d Guards Motorcycle Battalion—Captain V. P. Kuz'min
    1447th Self-propelled Artillery Regiment (85mm)—Major V. F. Gaidash
    104th Guards Antitank Artillery Regiment (57mm)—Major F. Z. Babachenko
    285th Mortar Regiment—Major S. S. Belen'kovo
    737th Separate Antitank Artillery Battalion
    409th Separate Guards Mortar Battalion—Captain N. A. Kolupaev
      Strength: 212 tanks and 16 self-propelled guns; tank regiment strength 32
        T-34, 16–17 T-70 each; and tank brigade strength 63 T-34 each
  29th Tank Corps—Major General I. F. Kirichenko
    25th Tank Brigade—Colonel N. K. Volodin
    31st Tank Brigade—Colonel S. F. Moiseev (to 8 August), Colonel A. A.
      Novikov (from 9 August)
    32d Tank Brigade—Colonel A. A. Linev (KIA on 25 August), Colonel K. K.
      Vorob'ev (from 26 August)

53d Motorized Rifle Battalion—Lieutenant Colonel N. P. Lipichev
1446th Self-propelled Artillery Regiment 85mm)—Captain M. S. Lunev
38th Separate Armored Car (Reconnaissance) Battalion
75th Motorcycle Battalion
108th Antitank Artillery Regiment
271st Mortar Battalion
747th Separate Antitank Battalion
  Strength: 170 tanks and 21 self-propelled guns

o   o   o

76th Guards Mortar Regiment: (attached on 5 July)
53d Guards Separate Tank Regiment—Major N. A. Kurnosov (to Group
  Trufanov on 11 July) (strength: 21 tanks)
1549th Self-propelled Artillery Regiment (152mm)
1st Separate Guards Motorcycle Regiment—Lieutenant Colonel V. A.
  Dokudovsky (to Group Trufanov on 11 July)
678th Howitzer Artillery Regiment (to Group Trufanov on 11 July)
689th Antitank Artillery Regiment—Major I. S. Guzhvy (to Group Trufanov on
  11 July)
76th Guards Mortar Regiment
6th Antiaircraft Artillery Division—Colonel G. P. Mezhinsky
  146th Antiaircraft Artillery Regiment (attached to 5th Guards Motor Corps)
  366th Antiaircraft Artillery Regiment (attached to 29 Tank Corps)
  516th Antiaircraft Artillery Regiment
  1062d Antiaircraft Artillery Regiment
4th Separate Signal Regiment—Lieutenant Colonel A. M. Gorbachev
994th Light Bomber Aviation Regiment
377th Separate Engineer Battalion
18th Tank Corps—Major General B. S. Bakharov (from RVK on 7 July)
  110th Tank Brigade—Lieutenant Colonel M. G. Khliupin
  170th Tank Brigade—Lieutenant Colonel V. D. Tarasov (to 13 July),
    Lieutenant Colonel A. I. Kazakov (14 July–7 August), Colonel N. P.
    Chunikin (from 8 August)
  181st Tank Brigade—Lieutenant Colonel V. A. Puzyrev (to 15 August),
    Lieutenant Colonel A. F. Shevchenko (from 16 August)
  32d Motorized Rifle Brigade—Lieutenant Colonel I. A. Stukov (KIA on 13
    July), Colonel M. E. Khvatov (from 13 July)
  36th Guards Separate Tank Regiment (Heavy)
  1000th Antitank Artillery Regiment
  736th Separate Antitank Artillery Battalion
  292d Mortar Regiment
  1694th Antiaircraft Artillery Regiment
  29th Separate Armored Car (Reconnaissance) Company
  78th Separate Motorcycle Battalion
    Strength: 190 tanks

ARMY STRENGTH: 37,000 men, 593 tanks, and 37 self-propelled guns on 6 July) o   o   o

2d Tank Corps—Major General A. F. Popov (from Southwestern Front on 8 July, to 5th Guards Tank Army on 11 July)
1529th Self-propelled Artillery Regiment (from RVK and Voronezh Front on 11 July) (attached to 29th Tank Corps)
522d High-power Howitzer Artillery Regiment (from Voronezh Front on 11 July)
148th High-power Howitzer Artillery Regiment (from Voronezh Front on 11 July)
148th Gun Artillery Regiment (from Voronezh Front on 11 July)
93d Gun Artillery Regiment (from Voronezh Front on 11 July)
16th Guards Mortar Regiment—Lieutenant Colonel Ia. T. Tsetrakovsky (from 6th Guards Army, Voronezh Front on 11 July)
80th Guards Mortar Regiment—Lieutenant Colonel I. Samchenko (from Voronezh Front on 11 July) (to 69th Army on 13 July)
10th Antitank Artillery Brigade (57mm) (from 69th Army on 11 July) (1 regiment to 18th Tank Corps, remainder to 2d Guards Tank Corps) (to 69th Army on 13 July)
  532d Antitank Artillery Regiment
  1243d Antitank Artillery Regiment
  1245th Antitank Artillery Regiment
27th Gun Artillery Brigade (from 6th Guards Army on 11 July) (to 69th Army on 13 July)
  5th Guards Tank Army strength on 11 July, with 2d Guards Tank Corps and 2d Tank Corps: 793 tanks and 37 self-propelled guns, including 501 T-34, 261 T-70, and 31 Mk. IV Churchill tanks
5th Air Army—Commander, Lieutenant General S. K. Goriunov; Commissar, Major General V. I. Alekseev; Chief of Staff, Major General N. G. Seleznev
  7th Mixed Aviation Corps—Major General P. P. Arkhangel'sky
    202d Bomber Aviation Division—Colonel S. I. Nechiporenko
    287th Fighter Aviation Division—Major General S. P. Danilov
  8th Mixed Aviation Corps—Major General N. P. Kamanin
    4th Guards Assault Aviation Division—Major General G. F. Baidukov
    264th Assault Aviation Division—Colonel N. I. Olenev
    256th Fighter Aviation Division—Colonel N. S. Gerasimov
  3d Fighter Aviation Corps—Major General E. Ia. Savitsky
    265th Fighter Aviation Division—Lieutenant Colonel A. A. Kariagin
    278th Fighter Aviation Division—Colonel V. T. Lisin
  7th Fighter Aviation Corps—Major General A. V. Utin
    259th Fighter Aviation Division—Colonel S. S. Iachmenev (to 13 August), Lieutenant Colonel Ia. A. Kurbatov (from 14 August)
    304th Fighter Aviation Division—Colonel I. K. Pechenko
  69th Guards Fighter Aviation Regiment
  511th Reconnaissance Aviation Regiment
Steppe Military District Subordination
  35th Rifle Corps (headquarters only)

3d Guards Cavalry Corps—Major General N. S. Oslikovsky
  5th Guards Cavalry Division—Major General N. S. Chepurkin
  6th Guards Cavalry Division—Colonel P. P. Brikel'
  32d Cavalry Division—Colonel G. F. Maliukov
  144th Guards Antitank Artillery Regiment
  3d Guards Separate Antitank Artillery Battalion
  64th Guards Mortar Battalion
  1731st Antiaircraft Artillery Regiment
5th Guards Cavalry Corps—Major General A. G. Selivanov
  11th Guards Cavalry Division—Colonel L. A. Slanov
  12th Guards Cavalry Division—Colonel V. I. Grigorovich
  63d Cavalry Division—Major General K. P. Beloshnichenko
  —Self-propelled Artillery Battalion
  150th Guards Antitank Artillery Regiment
  5th Guards Separate Antitank Artillery Battalion
  72d Guards Mortar Battalion
  585th Antiaircraft Artillery Regiment
7th Guards Cavalry Corps—Major General M. F. Maleev
  14th Guards Cavalry Division—Colonel Kh. V. Fiksel'
  15th Guards Cavalry Division—Major General I. T. Chalenko
  16th Guards Cavalry Division—Colonel G. A. Belov
  145th Guards Antitank Artillery Regiment
  7th Guards Separate Antitank Artillery Battalion
  57th Guards Mortar Battalion
  1733d Antiaircraft Artillery Regiment
4th Guards Tank Corp—Major General P. P. Poluboiarov
  12th Guards Tank Brigade—Lieutenant Colonel (Colonel on 11 July) N. G.
    Dushak
  13th Guards Tank Brigade—Colonel L. I. Baukov
  14th Guards Tank Brigade—Colonel I. P. Mikhailov (to 15 August), Major
    V. M. Pechkovsky (from 16 August)
  3d Guards Motorized Rifle Brigade—Colonel M. P. Leonov
  1451st Self-propelled Artillery Regiment (76mm)—Major S. I. Sytnikov
  76th Motorcycle Battalion—Major P. I. Tanachakov
  756th Antitank Artillery Regiment—Major A. A. Chertov
  264th Mortar Regiment—Major S. S. Osipov
  752d Separate Antitank Artillery Battalion
  120th Guards Antiaircraft Artillery Regiment—Major A. I. Bragin
    Strength: 189 tanks and self-propelled guns
3d Guards Mechanized Corps—Major General V. T. Obukhov
  7th Guards Mechanized Brigade—Colonel M. I. Rodionov: 43d Guards Tank
    Regiment—Lieutenant Colonel L. P. Oguzh
  8th Guards Mechanized Brigade—Colonel D. N. Bely: 44th Guards Tank
    Regiment—Lieutenant Colonel F. F. Kornienko
  9th Guards Mechanized Brigade—Colonel P. I. Goriachev: 45th Guards
    Tank Regiment—Lieutenant Colonel Ia. A. Burtsev

35th Guards Tank Brigade—Colonel A. A. Aslanov
1st Guards Motorcycle Battalion—Major A. A. Sviatodukh
1510th Antitank Artillery Regiment—Major G. G. Shukakidze
1831st Self-propelled Artillery Regiment (152mm)—Lieutenant Colonel
    A. K. Kulikov
129th Mortar Regiment—Major S. S. Barvinsky
743d Separate Antitank Artillery Battalion—Captain Bezverkhy
334th Guards Mortar Battalion—Major A. A. Toruzaev
1705th Antiaircraft Artillery Regiment—Major V. K. Skopenko
1st Mechanized Corps—Major General M. D. Solomatin
    19th Mechanized Brigade—Lieutenant Colonel V. V. Ershov: 9th Tank Regiment
    35th Mechanized Brigade: 4th Tank Regiment
    37th Mechanized Brigade—Lieutenant Colonel P. V. Tsyganenko: 3d Tank
        Regiment
    219th Tank Brigade—Lieutenant Colonel S. T. Khilobok
    57th Motorcycle Battalion—Major A. N. Lediok
    75th Antitank Artillery Regiment
    294th Mortar Regiment
    Strength: 204 tanks
78th Separate Motorcycle Battalion
11th Antiaircraft Artillery Division—Colonel K. Ia. Pavlov
    804th Antiaircraft Artillery Regiment
    976th Antiaircraft Artillery Regiment
    987th Antiaircraft Artillery Regiment
    996th Antiaircraft Artillery Regiment
8th Engineer Sapper Brigade
27th Special Designation Engineer Brigade
7th Pontoon Bridge Battalion
19th Pontoon Bridge Battalion
40th Pontoon Bridge Battalion
246th Separate Engineer Battalion
247th Separate Engineer Battalion
248th Separate Engineer Battalion
250th Separate Engineer Battalion
284th Separate Engineer Battalion

STEPPE FRONT STRENGTH: 573,195 men, 8,510 guns and mortars, and
1,639 tanks and self-propelled guns

11th Army (to Western Front by 12 July)—Commander, Lieutenant General I. I.
Fediuninsky; Commissar, Major General S. I. Pankov; Chief of Staff, Major
General N. V. Korneev
    53d Rifle Corps (from 26 July)—Major General I. A. Gartsev
        135th Rifle Division—Colonel A. N. Sosnov (to 15 August), Colonel F. N.
            Romashin (from 21 August)
        197th Rifle Division—Colonel B. N. Popov (to 10 August), Colonel F. S.
            Danilovsky (from 10 August)
        369th Rifle Division—Major General I. V. Khazov

4th Rifle Division—Colonel D. D. Vorob'ev

96th Rifle Division—Colonel F. G. Bulatov

260th Rifle Division—Colonel G. K. Miroshnichenko (to 27 August), Colonel
S. V. Maksimovsky (from 28 August)

273d Rifle Division—Colonel A. I. Baliugin

323d Rifle Division—Major General I. A. Gartsev (to 13 August), Colonel I. O.
Naryshkin (14–16 August), Colonel A. M. Bakhtizin (16 August), Colonel
S. F. Ukrainets (from 16 August)

225th Separate Tank Regiment

1179th Antiank Regiment

1321st Antitank Regiment

481st Mortar Regiment

90th Guards Mortar Regiment

31st Antiaircraft Artillery Division—Colonel I. S. Shilin

    1376th Antiaircraft Artillery Regiment

    1380th Antitank Artillery Regiment

    1386th Antitank Artillery Regiment

    1392d Antitank Artillery Regiment

202d Separate Engineer Battalion

277th Separate Engineer Battalion

ARMY STRENGTH: 65,000 men and 30 tanks

3d Guards Tank Army (to Briansk Front on 13 July) (to Central Front on
26 July)—Commander, Lieutenant General P. S. Rybalko; Commissar,
Major General S. I. Mel'nikov; Chief of Staff, Major General V. A.
Mitrofanov

    12th (6th Guards°) Tank Corps—Major General M. I. Zin'kovich

        30th (51st Guards) Tank Brigade—Lieutenant Colonel M. S. Novokhat'ko

        97th (52d Guards) Tank Brigade—Colonel I. T. Potapov (to 15 August),
Colonel A. S. Borodin (from 16 August)

        106th (53d Guards) Tank Brigade—Colonel G. G. Kuznetsov (WIA on 23
July), Major S. V. Tashkin (KIA on 29 July), Lieutenant Colonel V. A.
Bzyrin (3–15 August), Colonel V. S. Arkhipov (from 16 August)

        13th (22d Guards) Motorized Rifle Brigade—Colonel N. L. Mikhailov (to 20
August), Colonel Kh. S. Bogdanov (from 20 August)

        1417th (292d Guards) Self-propelled Artillery Regiment (85mm)

        66th Motorcycle Battalion

        1498th (289th Guards) Antitank Artillery Regiment

        757th Separate Antitank Artillery Battalion

        272d Mortar Regiment

        1703d (286th Guards) Antiaircraft Artillery Regiment

        Strength: 209 tanks and 16 self-propelled guns

    15th (7th Guards°) Tank Corps—Major General F. N. Rudkin

        88th (54th Guards) Tank Brigade—Colonel I. I. Sergeev

°Received Guards designation on 26 July.

113th (55th Guards) Tank Brigade—Colonel L. S. Chigin (KIA on 19 July),
Lieutenant Colonel V. S. Belousov (from 20 July)
195th (56th Guards) Tank Brigade—Colonel V. A. Lomakin (KIA on 19
July), Lieutenant Colonel T. F. Malik (from 19 July)
52d (23d Guards) Motorized Rifle Brigade—Colonel A. A. Golovachev (WIA
on 19 July)
1418th (293d Guards) Self-propelled Artillery Regiment (85mm)
89th Separate Armored Car Battalion
1503d (290th Guards) Antitank Artillery Regiment
733d Separate Antitank Artillery Battalion
467th Mortar Regiment
1704th (287th Guards) Antiaircraft Artillery Regiment
Strength: 209 tanks and 16 self-propelled guns
91st Separate Tank Brigade—Colonel I. I. Iakobovsky
50th Motorcycle Regiment
2d (7th Guards) Mechanized Corps (from RVK reserves to 3d Tank Army on 14
July)—Major General I. M. Korchagin
18th (24th Guards) Mechanized Brigade: one tank regiment
34th (25th Guards) Mechanized Brigade: 12th Tank Regiment
43d (26th) Mechanized Brigade—Major General D. M. Barinov: 215th Tank
Regiment
33d (57th Guards) Tank Brigade—Colonel I. P. Silaev
68th Motorcycle Battalion
79th (291st Guards) Antitank Artillery Regiment
468th Mortar Regiment
734th Separate Antitank Artillery Battalion
410th Guards Mortar Battalion
1706th (288th Guards) Antiaircraft Artillery Regiment
Strength: 204 tanks

ARMY STRENGTH—ON 18 JULY: 37,266 men, 492 guns and mortars, and 731
tanks and self-propelled guns (475 T-34s, 224 T-70s, and 32 self-propelled
guns

4th Tank Army (Moscow Military District on 1 July and to Western Front on 18
July)—Commander, Lieutenant General V. M. Badanov; Commissar, Major
General V. G. Guliaev
6th Guards Mechanized Corps—Major General A. I. Aksimov
16th Guards Mechanized Brigade: 28th Tank Regiment
17th Guards Mechanized Brigade: 126th Tank Regiment
49th Guards Mechanized Brigade: Tank Regiment
29th Separate Tank Regiment
56th Separate Tank Regiment
1st Guards Self-propelled Artillery Regiment (152mm)
95th Motorcycle Battalion
51st Guards Antitank Artillery Regiment
740th Separate Antitank Artillery Battalion

240th Mortar Regiment
31st Guards Separate Antiaircraft Artillery Battalion
   Strength: 216 tanks and self-propelled guns
11th Tank Corps—Major General N. N. Radkevich
   20th Tank Brigade—Colonel B. M. Konstantinov
   36th Tank Brigade—Colonel T. I. Tanaschishin (to 15 July), Colonel A. Ia.
      Eremin (from 16 July)
   65th Tank Brigade—Colonel A. I. Shevchenko
   12th Motorized Rifle Brigade
   1493d Antitank Artillery Regiment
   93d Motorcycle Battalion
   1507th Antitank Artillery Regiment
   738th Separate Antitank Artillery Battalion
   243d Mortar Regiment
   1388th Antiaircraft Artillery Regiment
      Strength: 204 tanks
30th Tank Corps—Colonel G. S. Rodin
   197th Tank Brigade—Colonel Ia. I. Trotsenko (to 14 August), Lieutenant
      Colonel N. G. Zhukov (from 15 August)
   243d Tank Brigade: Lieutenant Colonel V. I. Prikhod'ko (to 22 August),
      Lieutenant Colonel S. A. Denisov (from 23 August)
   244th Tank Brigade: Colonel V. I. Konovalov (to 15 July), Lieutenant Colonel
      M. G. Fomichev (from 16 July)
   30th Motorized Rifle Brigade—Colonel M. S. Smirnov
   1621st Self-propelled Artillery Regiment (85mm)
   88th Motorcycle Battalion
   1513th Antitank Artillery Regiment
   742d Separate Antitank Artillery Battalion
   299th Mortar Regiment
   248th Separate Guards Mortar Battalion
   219th Antiaircraft Artillery Regiment
      Strength: 216 tanks and self-propelled guns
1545th Self-propelled Artillery Regiment
51st Motorcycle Regiment

ARMY STRENGTH: 37,000 men and 652 tanks and self-propelled guns

20th Tank Corps—Major General I. G. Lazarov (to 61st Army by 13 July)
   8th Guards Tank Brigade: Colonel I. M. Morus (to 15 July), Colonel V. F. Orlov
      (from 16 July)
   80th Tank Brigade: Colonel V. N. Busaev (to 14 July), Colonel V. I. Evsiukov
      (from 15 July)
   155th Tank Brigade: Colonel N. V. Belochkin (to 9 August), Lieutenant Colonel
      I. I. Proshin (from 10 August)
   7th Guards Motorized Rifle Brigade
   1419th Self-propelled Artillery Regiment (85mm)
   1505th Antitank Artillery Regiment

291st Mortar Regiment

1711st Antiaircraft Artillery Regiment

735th Antitank Artillery Battalion

Corps strength: 184 tanks and self-propelled guns

25th Tank Corps—Major General F. G. Anikushkin (to 11th Guards Army on 17 July)

111th Tank Brigade—Lieutenant Colonel I. N. Granovsky

162d Tank Brigade—Colonel I. A. Volynets (WIA on 19 July), Lieutenant Colonel N.I. Syropiatov (19 July–15 August), Colonel I. P. Mikhailov (from 15 August)

175th Tank Brigade—Lieutenant Colonel A. N. Petushkov (to 15 July), Lieutenant Colonel S. I. Drilenok (16–22 July), Lieutenant Colonel A. N. Petushkov (23 July to 10 August), Lieutenant Colonel V. I. Zemliakov (from 11 August)

20th Motorized Rifle Brigade—Major General P. S. Il'in

53d Motorcycle Battalion—Captain I. V. Volkov

1497th Antitank Artillery Regiment—Major V. A. Zaletov

459th Mortar Regiment

746th Antitank Artillery Battalion

1702d Antiaircraft Artillery Regiment—Major G. S. Turov

1829th Heavy Self-propelled Artillery Regiment (152mm)—Major M. S. Korolev

41st Self-propelled Artillery Regiment (85mm)—Lieutenant Colonel V. N. Sedov

Corps strength: 196 tanks and self-propelled guns

2d Guards Cavalry Corps—Lieutenant General V. V. Kriukov (to 11th Guards Army on 25 July)

3d Guards Cavalry Division—Major General M. D. Iagodin

4th Guards Cavalry Division—Major General G. I. Pankratov

20th Cavalry Division—Major General P. T. Kursakov

149th Guards Antitank Artillery Regiment

2d Guards Separate Antitank Artillery Battalion

60th Guards Mortar Battalion

1730th Antiaircraft Artillery Regiment

Long-range Aviation

1st Guards Aviation Corps (Orel axis)—Major General D. P. Iukhanov

1st Guards Long-range Aviation Division—Colonel S. S. Lebedev

6th Guards Long-range Aviation Division—Colonel S. I. Chemodanov

2d Guards Aviation Corps (Orel axis)—Major General E. F. Loginov

2d Guards Long-range Aviation Division—Major General A. I. Shcherakov

8th Guards Long-range Aviation Division—Colonel V. G. Tikhonov

3d Guards Long-range Aviation Corps (Orel axis)—Major General N. A. Volkov

3d Guards Long-range Aviation Division—Colonel I. K. Brobko

7th Guards Long-range Aviation Division—Colonel F. S. Shiroky

4th Guards Aviation Corps (Poltava axis)—Colonel S. P. Kovalev

4th Guards Long-range Aviation Division—Colonel I. I. Kozhemaikin

5th Guards Long-range Aviation Division—Lieutenant Colonel P. E. Timashev

5th Long-range Aviation Corps (Orel axis)—Major General I. V. Georgiev

    53d Long-range Aviation Division—Colonel V. I. Labudev

    54th Long-range Aviation Division—Colonel V. A. Shchelkin

6th Long-range Aviation Corps (Poltava axis)—Major General G. N. Tupikov

    50th Long-range Aviation Division—Colonel F. I. Men'shikov

    62d Long-range Aviation Division—Colonel G. S. Schetchikov

7th Long-range Aviation Corps (Orel Axis)—Major General V. E. Nestertsev

    1st Long-range Aviation Division—Colonel I. V. Filippov

    12th Long-range Aviation Division—Colonel G. D. Bozhko

    45th Long-range Aviation Division—Colonel V. I. Lebedev

5th Assault Aviation Corps (to Voronezh Front's 2d Air Army by 3 August)—Major General N. P. Kamanin

    4th Guards Assault Aviation Division—Major General G. F. Baidukov

    264th Assault Aviation Division—Colonel N. I. Olenev

10th Fighter Aviation Corps (to Voronezh Front's 2d Air Army by 3 August)—Major General M. M. Golovnia

    201st Fighter Aviation Division—Lieutenant Colonel R. P. Zhukov (to 17 July), Lieutenant Colonel I. V. Vladimirov (18 July to 15 August), Colonel V. A. Sryvkin (from 15 August)

    235th Fighter Aviation Division—Major General I. A. Lakeev

202d Bomber Aviation Division (to Voronezh Front's 2d Air Army by 3 August)—Colonel S. I. Nechiporenko

Comparative Strengths and Losses in the Battle of Kursk

The Kursk Defensive Operation (1 July 1943)

Red Army Strengths

	Men	Guns and Mortars	MRLs	Tanks and SP Guns	
Central Front					
48th Army	84,000	1,454		178	(134 and 44)
13th Army	114,000	2,934	105	270	(223 and 47)
		(3,369)†			
70th Army	96,000	1,658		125	(125 and 0)
65th Army	100,000	1,837		124	(124 and 0)
60th Army	96,000	1,376		67	(67 and 0)
2d Tank Army	37,000	338		456	(456 and 0)
Front Reserves	184,575	1,128		387	(387 and 0)
Total	711,575	11,076	246	1,785	(1,694 and 91)
	(738,000)°				
	(667,500)†	14,163†		1,745†	
Combat	510,983	10,725	246	1,607	(1,516 and 91)
Voronezh Front					
38th Army	60,000	1,168	32	150	(150 and 0)
40th Army	77,000	1,636		237	(237 and 0)
6th Gds Army	79,700	1,682	92	155	(135 and 20)
7th Gds Army	76,800	1,573	47	246	(224 and 22)
69th Army	52,000	889		—	
1st Tank Army	40,000	419	56	646	(631 and 17)
35th Gds RC	35,000	620		—	
Front Reserve	204,591	579		265	(265 and 0)
Total	625,591	8,718	272	1,704	(1,662 and 42)
	(534,700)°				
	(420,000)†	10,850†		1,530†	
Combat	466,236	8,584	272	1,699	(1,657 and 42)
Central and Voronezh					
Total	1,337,166	19,794	518	3,489	(3,356 and 133)
	(1,272,700)°				
	(1,087,500)†	25,013†		3,275†	
Combat	977,219	19,306	518	3,306	(3,173 and 133)
Steppe Front					
Total	573,195	8,510	—	1,639	(1,513 and 126)
Combat	449,133	8,357	—	1,632	(1,506 and 126)
Engaged‡	295,000	5,300	—	1,500	

Red Army Strengths, *Continued*

	Men	Guns and Mortars	MRLs	Tanks and SP Guns	
Central, Voronezh, and Steppe Fronts					
Grand Total	1,910,361	28,304	518	5,128	(4,869 and 259)
Combat	1,426,352	27,663	518	4,938	(4,679 and 259)

Sources: G. Koltunov, "Kurskaia bitva v tsifrakh" [The Battle of Kursk in numbers], *VIZh* 6 (June 1968); 58–68; and G. Koltunov, *Kurskaia bitva* [The Battle of Kursk] (Moscow: Voenizdat, 1970), 50, 53, 55.

Note: Many Soviet army strengths are rough estimates based on division slices.

*See G. F. Krivosheev, *Grif sekretnosti sniat: poteri vooruzhennykh sil SSSR v voinakh, boevykh deistviiakh i voennykh konfliktakh* [The classification secret removed: The losses of the USSR's armed forces in wars, combat operations, and military conflicts] (Moscow: Voenizdat, 1993), 188.

[1]See V. N. Simvodikov, *Bitva pod Kurskom, 1943 goda* [The Battle of Kursk, 1943] (Moscow: Voroshilov General Staff Academy, 1950), 20; and *Armeiskaia operatsii* [Army operations] (Moscow: Voroshilov General Staff Academy, 1989), appendix 4. Both classified secret.

[1]See I. Parotkin, ed., *The Battle of Kursk* (Moscow: Progress, 1974), supplement 6. Includes 5th Guards Tank Army, and 5th Guards, 53d, and 27th Armies. By 12 July, however only the 150,000 troops of 5th Guards Tank and 5th Guards Armies were engaged.

Red Army Personnel Losses

	Irrevocable	Medical	Total
Central Front (5–11 July)	15,336	18,561	33,897
Voronezh Front (5–23 July)	27,542	46,350	73,892
Steppe Front (9–23 July)	27,452	46,606	70,058
Total	70,330	107,517	177,847

Note: B. Sokolov, "The Battle for Kursk, Orel, and Char'kov," in *Gezeitenwechsel im Zweiten Weltkrieg* (Hamburg: Mittler, 1996), 79–81, challenges these official figures. He places Central Front losses at 90,000 and Voronezh and Steppe Front losses at 227,000, including 60,000 killed, 133,000 wounded and ill, and 34,000 prisoners, for total losses at Kursk of 317,000 out of the 1.9 million engaged.

German Army Strengths

	Men	Tanks and Assault Guns	
Army Group Center			
Ninth Army	335,000	1,081	(658 and 423)
XXIII Army Corps		72	(0 and 72)
XXXXI Panzer Corps		390	(133 and 257)
XXXXVII Panzer Corps		426	(332 and 94)
XXXXVI Panzer Corps			
XX Army Corps			
Reserve		193	(193 and 0)
Second Army	96,000	approximately 100	(0 and 100)
Army Group South			
Fourth Panzer Army	223,907	1,235	(1,063 and 172)
LII Army Corps			
XXXXVIII Panzer Corps		637	(569 and 68)
II SS Panzer Corps		598	(494 and 104)
Army Detachment Kempf	126,000	512	(357 and 155)
Grand Total	780,900	2,928	(2,078 and 850)

Sources: N. Zetterling, "Loss Rates on the Eastern Front during WWII," *Journal of Slavic Military Studies* 9 (4) (December 1996):895–907; M. Healy, *Kursk 1943* (London: Osprey, 1992); and Gotthard Heinrici and Fredrick Wilhelm Hauck, *Citadel* (U.S. National Archives).
Note: According to Heinrici, Army Group South's total tank strength on 5 July was 1,352, of which 1,183 were operational. Of the 1,150 tanks available for the Citadel force, 997 were operational. This included 192 Panthers and 100 Tigers. In addition, 376 assault guns were available. The slightly higher tank figures indicated above account for Soviet models and German undercounting. Heinrici states that Ninth Army tank and assault gun strength was just short of 1,000, vice the 1,081 listed above.

German Army Losses

	Killed	Wounded	Missing	Total
Ninth Army (5–11 July)	—	—	—	20,720
Fourth Panzer Army	2,309	10,874	278	13,461
Army Detachment Kempf	2,450	12,482	709	15,641
Total	4,759	23,356	987	49,822

Source: N. Zetterling, "Loss Rates on the Eastern Front during WWII," *Journal of Slavic Military Studies* 9 (4) (December 1996): 895–907.

ed Army Tank Losses

aily Tank Losses of the 2d Tank Army in Defensive Combat, 6–14 July 1943

	2D TANK CORPS		16TH TANK CORPS		11TH GUARDS TANK BRIGADE		TOTAL	
	Total	Irrecoverable	Total	Irrecoverable	Total	Irrecoverable	Total	Irrecoverable
July	3	—	88	69	—	—	91	69
July	14	7	35	20	—	—	49	27
July	45	32	3	1	1	—	49	33
July	8	5	—	—	—	—	8	5
) July	8	4	1	—	—	—	9	4
(July	—	—	1	—	—	—	1	—
2 July	—	—	2	—	—	—	2	—
(July	—	—	4	—	—	—	4	—
Total	78	48	134	90	1	—	213	138

urce: M. Kolomiets and M. Spirin, *Kurshkaia duga* [The Kursk bulge] (Moscow: EksPrinte NB, 1998), 22, portions of
hich are confirmed by documents contained in V. A. Zolotarev et al., eds., *Russkii arkhiv: Velikaia Otechestvennai:
urskaia bitva: Dokumenty i materialy, 27 marta–23 avgusta 1943 g.," T-15 (4-4)* [Russian archive: The Great Patriotic:
he Battle of Kursk: Documents and materials, 27 March to 23 August 1943, vol. 15 (4-4)] (Moscow: Terra, 1997).
ote: Figures do not include three tank regiments with Lend-Lease tanks (90–110).
mmary: Total armored strength on 6 July, 607 tanks (367 T-34s and 240 T-70s and T-60s) (including the 19th Tank
orps); operable tanks on 6 July, 456; total losses, 6–14 July, 213 tanks; irrecoverable tanks, 6–14 July, 138.

MATERIAL LOSSES OF THE VORONEZH FRONT IN DEFENSIVE COMBAT,
4–23 JULY 1943

During the period of defensive combat from 4 through 22 July 1943, the forces of
the Voronezh Front suffered the following losses:

1. For the period of the enemy offensive from 4 through 16 July 1943:
    a. Personnel: killed—18,097, wounded—47,272, missing in action—24,851,
    captured—29, total—90,249.
    b. Horses: killed—1,295, wounded—333, total—1,628.
    c. Armored and mechanized equipment: tanks irrevocably lost—1,204, dam-
    aged—655, total—1,859. Irrevocably lost self-propelled guns—29.
    d. Guards-mortar [multiple rocket launcher] equipment: damaged vehicles—16.
    e. Aircraft: shot down and damaged—347.
    f. Artillery weaponry: guns of all caliber—1,605, mortars—1,734, sub-machine
    guns—4,381, heavy machine guns—1,634, PPSh [machine pistols]—35,026,
    rifles—40,520, antitank rifles—3,247.
    g. Vehicles—137.
2. For the period of our forces' counteroffensive from 16 through 22 July:
    a. Personnel: killed—2,481, wounded—7,155, missing—1,047, total—10,683.
    b. Horses: killed—550, wounded—107, total—657.
    c. Armored and mechanized equipment: tanks irrevocably lost—367, dam-
    aged—179, total—516. D. Irrevocably lost self-propelled guns—28, dam-
    aged—15, total—43.
    d. Guards-mortar [multiple rocket launcher] equipment: damaged vehicles—4.
    e. Aircraft: shot down and damaged—40.

f. Artillery weaponry: guns of all caliber—108, mortars—162, sub-machine guns—399, heavy machine guns—161, PPSh—872, rifles—1,612, antitank rifles—212.

g. Vehicles—41.

Signed: Chief of Staff of the Voronezh Front, Lieutenant General Ivanov; Chief of the Operations Department (Voronezh Front headquarters), Major General Teteshkin[1]

[Revised Material Losses:]

The *front's* forces also suffered considerable losses as a result of the fierce combat, chiefly from the fire of enemy tank and aircraft. This can be seen from the following table:

Killed, wounded, and missing in action	74,500 men
Damaged and destroyed tanks	1,397
Vehicles	145
Aircraft (irrevocably lost)	387
Gun systems of all types	672
Mortars of all caliber	622
Heavy machine guns	588
Sub-machine guns	2,152
Automatic rifles	12,434
Rifles	27,800

In spite of the losses suffered, the *front's* forces remain fully combat capable and are rapidly beginning to restore the most victimized of its formations and units. By 25 July the most victimized rifle divisions of the 6th Guards Army already had up to 5,500 soldiers and command cadre and had considerably replenished their weaponry and transport.

To replenish their losses, the tank formations have received new tanks from the country's deep rear, as well as weapons and transport.

The aviation formations and other types of forces are also filling out and, to a considerable degree, have restored their combat equipment and transport.

In summary, by the end of the July defensive operation the Voronezh Front's forces were fully combat ready to fulfill active offensive missions to destroy the enemy who had been shattered in previous battles. . . .

Signed: Senior General Staff Officer in the Voronezh Front, Colonel Kostin[2]

Notes

1. From Voronezh Front combat report no. 01398, dated 24 July 1943, to the General Staff concerning losses, in *Russkii arkhiv: Velikaia Otechestvennaia: Kurskaia bitva: Dokumenty i materialy, 27 marta–23 avgusta 1943 g.," T-15 (4-4)* [The Russian archive: The Great Patriotic: The Battle of Kursk: Documents and materials, 27 March to 23 August 1943, vol. 15 (4-4)] (Moscow: Terra, 1997), 272–273.

2. From a report by the Senior General Staff Officer in the Voronezh Front to the Chief of the General Staff concerning the defensive operations of the *front's* forces from 4 through 23 July 1943, dated 23 August 1943, in *Russkii arkhiv: Velikaia Otechestvennaia: Kurskaia bitva: Dokumenty i materialy, 27 marta–23 avgusta 1943 g.," T-15 (4-4)* [The Russian archive: The Great Patriotic: The Battle of Kursk: Documents and materials, 27 March to 23 August 1943, vol. 15 (4-4) (Moscow: Terra, 1997), 387.

Material Losses of the 5th Guards Tank Army in Combat, 11–14 July 1943

	TO&E	On-hand	Survived	LOSSES	
				Irrecoverable	Evacuated
18th Tank Corps					
"Churchill"	21	21	9	7	0
T-34	131	103	45	23	10
T-70, T-60	70	63	44	—	11
BA-64	51	58	46	—	1
BTR	39	29	10	—	—
Total	222	187	98	30	21
29th Tank Corps°					
KV	21	1	—	—	—
T-34	131	130	153	99	???
T-70	70	85	86	55	???
"Praga"	—	1	—	—	—
BA-10	—	12	—	—	—
BA-64	51	56	4	4	—
SU-76	—	9	9	6	3
SU-122	—	12	10	8	2
Total	222	216	239	154	???
Group Trufanov†					
T-34	???	71	20	18	???
T-70, T-60	???	29	17	11	???
Total	???	100	37	29	???
5th Guards Tank Army					
Total‡	about 680	about 615	374	113	???

Source: M. Kolomiets and M. Spirin, *Kurskaia duga* [The Kursk bulge] (Moscow: EksPrinte NB, 1998), 48.
Summary: Total armored strength on 10 July: 680–720 tanks and self-propelled guns; operable armor on 15 July: 272–288 tanks and self-propelled guns; total losses, 10–14 July: 408–432 tanks and self-propelled guns; irrecoverable tanks, 6–14 July: 138.
°29th Tank Corps figures includes as reinforcements the 5th Guards Mechanized Corps' 53d Guards Tank Regiment (10th Guards Mechanized Brigade) and the 24th Guards Tank Brigade.
†Group Trufanov's figures includes the 11th and 12th Guards Tank Brigades (54th and 55th Guards Tank Regiments).
‡These TO&E and on-hand figures include the 5th Guards Mechanized Corps strength of about 212 tanks.

Overall Losses of the Tank Armies in Combat Operations, July–August 1943

Tanks at the Beginning of the operation	Losses for the Period	From Combat Damage	For Technical Disrepair	For Other Reasons
1st Tank Army, 3–31 August 1943 (Belgorod-Khar'kov) 542 (418)	1,049 (889)	706 (646)	334 (283)	—
2d Tank Army, 15 July through 3 August 1943 (Orel) 358	unavailable	189	unavailable	unavailabl
3d Guards Tank Army, 19–30 July 1943 (Orel) 799 (574)	669 (471)	606 (???)	35 (???)	28 (???)
4th Tank Army, 15 July through 31 August 1943 (Orel) 767 (571)	1,283 (859)	1,189 (786)	80 (61)	14 (12)
5th Guards Tank Army, 3–31 August 1943 (Belgorod-Khar'kov) 503°	445 (361)	445 (361)	unavailable	unavailabl

Source: M. Kolomiets and M. Spirin, *Kurskaia duga* [The Kursk bulge] (Moscow: EksPrinte NB, 1998), 78.
Note: The first figure denotes all tanks and self-propelled guns. The figure in parentheses denotes T-34 tanks. Of the irrecoverable figures, 31 percent are T-34 tanks and 43 percent are T-70 tanks.
°This figure is from other sources.

The Orel Offensive Operation (10 July 1943)

Red Army Strengths

	Men	Guns and Mortars	MRLs	Tanks and SP Guns
Western Front				
50th Army	54,062 (62,800)°	1,071		87 (87 and 0)
11th Guards Army	135,000 (170,500)°	3,120	144	648 (615 and 33)
Total	211,458 (233,300)°	4,285	144	745 (712 and 33)
Combat Reinforcements	189,043	4,194	144	735 (702 and 33)
Front Reserves				300
4th Tank Army	37,000			652
Briansk Front				
3d Army	60,000			100
61st Army	80,000			110
63d Army	70,000			60
1st Guards Tank Corps	13,000			200
20th Tank Corps	12,000			180
Front Reserves	198,616			144
Total	433,616 (409,000)°	7,642	160	1,087 (952 and 135)
Combat Reinforcements	298,068	7,144	160	794 (661 and 133)
3d Guards Tank Army	37,000	492	—	731 (699 and 32)

Red Army Strengths, *Continued*

	Men	Guns and Mortars	MRLs	Tanks and SP Guns
Central Front				
48th Army	80,000			
13th Army	120,000			
70th Army	90,000			
65th Army	120,000			
60th Army	96,000			
2d Tank Army	30,000			
Front Reserve	103,000			
Total	640,975 (645,300)°	10,144	200	1,492 (1,429 and 63)
Combat	440,383	9,939	200	1,311 (1,248 and 63)
Western, Briansk and Central				
Grand Total	1,286,049	22,075	496	3,324 (3,093 and 231)
Combat	927,494	21,259	496	2,840 (2,611 and 229)

See G. F. Krivosheev, ed., *Grif sekretnosti sniat* [The seal of secrecy removed] (Moscow: Voerizdat, 1993), 189.

Red Army Losses

	Irrevocable	Medical	Total
Western Front (left wing)	25,585	76,856	102,441
11th Guards Army (12–30 July)	12,768	38,513	51,281
50th Army (12 July to 18 August)	5,395	17,767	23,162
11th Army (20 July to 18 August)	4,979	15,580	20,559
4th Tank Army (20 July to 18 August)	2,443	4,996	7,439
Briansk Front (12 July to 18 August)	39,173	123,234	162,407
Central Front (12 July to 18 August)	47,771	117,271	165,042
Total	112,529	317,361	429,890

Note: Boris Sokolov, *Tsera pobedy* [The price of Victory] (Moscow: Moskovskii rabachii, 1991), 82, places total Soviet losses at 860,000 of the 1.29 million engaged.

German Army Strengths

	Men	Tanks and Assault Guns
Army Group Center		
Second Panzer Army	160,000 (est.)	325 (175 and 150) (est.)
Ninth Army	315,000	500 (est.)
Grand Total	475,000	825

Note: These figures do not count reinforcements dispatched by Army Group South into the Orel region (for example, *Grossdeutschland* Panzer Grenadier Division).

German Army losses are unavailable.

The Belgorod-Khar'kov Offensive Operation (3 August 1943)

Red Army Strength

	Men	Guns and Mortars	MRLs	Tanks and SP Guns
Voronezh Front				
38th Army	60,000			
40th Army	80,000			200
27th Army	80,000			200
5th Guards Army	80,000	1,953	133	120
6th Guards Army	80,000			270
1st Tank Army	37,000			542
5th Guards Tank Army	37,000			503
47th Army	80,000			200
Front Reserves	159,554			
Total	693,554 (739,400)°	8,177 (6,968)°	269	1,972 (1,859 and 113) (2,171)°
Combat	458,167	7,783	269	1,957 (1,845 and 112)
Steppe Front				
53d Army	77,000	2,088	48	302 (291 and 11)
69th Army	70,000			40
7th Guards Army	50,000			105
Front Reserves	90,000			20
Total	287,034 (404,600)°	4,459	66	467 (454 and 13)
Combat	198,034	4,230	66	461 (448 and 13)
Voronezh and Steppe Fronts				
Grand Total	980,588 (1,144,000)°	12,627	335	2,439 (2,313 and 126)
Combat	656,201	12,013	335	2,418 (2,293 and 125)

°According to G. F. Krivosheev, ed., *Grif sekretnasti sniat* [The seal of secrecy removed] (Moscow: Voerizdat, 1993), and classified documents.

Red Army Losses

	Irrevocable	Medical	Total
Voronezh Front (3–23 August)	48,339	108,954	157,293
Steppe Front	23,272	75,001	98,273
Total	71,611	183,955	255,566

Note: Boris Sokolov, *Tsera pobedy* [The price of victory] (Moscow: Moskovski rabochii, 1991), 81–82, estimates total Soviet losses at 500,000 men of the total of 1.14 million troops engaged in the operation.

German Army Strength

	Men (estimated)	Tanks and Assault Guns
Army Group South		
Fourth Panzer Army	120,000	150
Army Detachment Kempf	90,000	100
Reinforcements (5–23 August)	120,000	280
Grand Total	330,000	530

German Army losses are unavailable.

Summary of the Kursk Operation

Soviet and German Strengths and Losses

	MEN		TANKS AND SP GUNS	
	Committed	Lost	Committed	Lost
Soviet				
Kursk defensive operation	1,910,361	177,847	5,128	1,614
Orel offensive operation	1,286,049	429,890	3,324	2,586
Belgorod-Khar'kov offensive operation	980,588	255,566	2,439	1,864
Total	2,500,000°	863,303	7,360°	6,064
German				
Kursk defensive operation	780,900	49,822	2,928	
Orel offensive operation	475,000	NA	825	
Belgorod-Khar'kov offensive operation	330,000	NA	530	
Total	940,900	NA	3,253	

Note: Boris Sokolov, *Tsera pobedy* [The price of victory] (Moscow: Maskovskii rabochii, 1991), claims losses of 1,677,000 troops.
°Without double counting Central, Voronezh, and Steppe Front forces.

Correlation of Forces

	Soviet	Correlation	German
Kursk defensive operation			
Men	1,910,361	2.4 : 1	780,900
Tanks and self-propelled guns	5,128	1.8 : 1	2,928
Orel offensive operation			
Men	1,286,049	2.7 : 1	475,000
Tanks and self-propelled guns	3,324	4 : 1	825
Belgorod-Khar'kov offensive operation			
Men	980,588	3 : 1	330,000
Tanks and self-propelled guns	2,439	4.6 : 1	530
Kursk operation			
Men	2,500,000	2.7 : 1	940,900
Tanks and self-propelled guns	7,360	2.3 : 1	3,253

Note: These calculations are based on on-hand tank, assault gun, and self-propelled gun strengths. Where available (as with the case of German formations), data indicate somewhat lower operational strengths at any given stage of the operation. Nevertheless, the ratios are still roughly applicable, since Soviet operational figures were also lower (and demonstrably more so) due to their more severe maintenance and logistical problems.

Comparative Armor Strengths at Kursk

Soviet Armor Strength (on-hand strength returns)

	TANKS					
	T-60s, 70s	T-34s	KVs	Subtotal	SP guns	Total
Orel Axis						
Western Front				1,653	84	1,737
50th Army				75	12	87
11th Guards Army				268	12	280
1st Tank Corps				168	16	184
5th Tank Corps				168	16	184
Reserves				350	—	350
4th Tank Army				624	28	652
Briansk Front				1,458	120	1,578
3d Army				88	12	100
61st Army				98	12	110
63d Army				48	12	60
1st Guards Tank Corps				207	—	207
20th Tank Corps				168	16	184
Reserves				150	36	186
3d Guards Tank Army	224	475	—	699	32	731
Total				3,111	204	3,315
Orel-Kursk Axis						
Central Front				1,677	108	1,785
13th Army				258	12	270
48th Army				124	54	178
60th Army				67	—	67
65th Army				124	—	124
70th Army				125	—	125
2d Tank Army				456	21	477
9th Tank Corps				168	—	168
19th Tank Corps				168	—	168
Reserves				187	21	208
Kursk-Oboian' Axis						
Voronezh Front				1,634	70	1,704
6th Guards Army				134	21	155
7th Guards Army				218	28	246
38th Army				106	—	106
40th Army				113	—	113
69th Army				—	—	—
1st Tank Army				625	21	646
2d Guards Tank Corps				200	—	200
5th Guards Tank Corps				200	—	200
Reserves				38	—	38

Soviet Armor Strength (on-hand strength returns), *Continued*

	TANKS					
	T-60s, 70s	T-34s	KVs	Subtotal	SP guns	Total
Reinforcements (by 12 July)				925	58	983
2d Tank Corps				168	—	168
10th Tank Corps	64	99	1	164	21	185
5th Guards Tank Army				593	37	630
From Steppe Front (by 15 July)				542	21	563
27th Army				92	—	92
53d Army				78	—	78
4th Guards Tank Corps				168	21	189
1st Mechanized Corps				204	—	204
Total				3,101	149	3,250
Total: Orel-Kursk and Kursk-Oboian' axes				4,778	257	5,035

German Armor Strength (on-hand strength returns on 1 July 1943)

	TANKS										Assault guns	Total
	Mk II	Mk III s	Mk III l	Mk IV s	Mk IV l	Mk V	Mk VI	T-34	Command	Subtotal		
Orel Axis												
Second Panzer Army	14	25	51	8	90	—	—	—	15	203	—	203
5th Panzer	—	—	17	—	76	—	—	—	9	102	—	102
8th Panzer (OKH)	14	25	34	8	14	—	—	—	6	101	—	101
Orel-Kursk Axis												
XXIII Army Corps	—	—	—	—	—	—	—	—	—	—	72	72
185th Assault Gun Detachment	—	—	—	—	—	—	—	—	—	—	36	36
189th Assault Gun Detachment	—	—	—	—	—	—	—	—	—	—	36	36
XXXI Panzer Corps	5	18	27	5	29	—	31	—	3	123	258	381
18th Panzer	5	10	20	5	29	—	—	—	3	72	—	72
653d Antitank Detachment	—	—	—	—	—	—	—	—	—	—	55	55
654th Antitank Detachment	—	—	—	—	—	—	—	—	—	5	50	55
177th Assault Gun Detachment	—	—	—	—	—	—	—	—	—	—	36	36
244th Assault Gun Detachment	—	—	—	—	—	—	—	—	—	—	36	36
216th Heavy tank [Panzer] Detachment	—	—	—	—	—	—	—	—	—	—	45	45
21st Panzer Brigade	—	8	7	—	—	—	31	—	—	46	36	82
XXXXVII Panzer Corps	22	18	77	18	129	—	—	—	19	283	94	377
20th Panzer	9	2	15	9	40	—	—	—	7	82	—	82
9th Panzer	1	8	30	8	30	—	—	—	6	83	—	83
2d Panzer	12	8	32	1	59	—	—	—	6	118	—	118
245th Assault Gun Detachment	—	—	—	—	—	—	—	—	—	—	36	36
904th Assault Gun Detachment	—	—	—	—	—	—	—	—	—	—	36	36
312th Panzer Company	—	—	—	—	—	—	—	—	—	—	22	22
4th Panzer	—	—	15	1	79	—	—	—	6	101	—	101
12th Panzer	6	15	21	1	36	—	—	—	4	83	—	83
Ninth Army	33	51	140	25	273	—	31	—	32	590	424	1,014

German Armor Strength (on-hand strength returns on 1 July 1943), *Continued*

| | TANKS | | | | | | | | | | Assault | |
	Mk II	Mk III s	Mk III l	Mk IV s	Mk IV l	Mk V	Mk VI	T-34	Command	Subtotal	guns	Total
Kursk-Oboian' Axis												
XXXXVIII Panzer Corps	19	20	124	8	109	200	15	—	40	535	66	601
3d Panzer	7	8	51	2	21	—	—	—	1	90	—	90
11th Panzer	8	11	51	1	25	—	15	—	17	113	—	113
Grossdeutschland	4	1	22	5	63	—	15	—	22	132	35	167
51st Panzer Detachment	—	—	—	—	—	100	—	—	—	100	—	100
52d Panzer Detachment	—	—	—	—	—	100	—	—	—	100	—	100
911th Assault Gun Detachment	—	—	—	—	—	—	—	—	—	—	31	31
II SS Panzer Corps	5	3	135	8	144	—	42	25	28	390	104	494
SS *Leibstandarte Adolf Hitler*	4	3	10	—	67	—	13	—	9	106	35	141
SS *Das Reich*	1	—	62	—	33	—	14	25	10	145	34	179
SS *Totenkopf*	—	—	63	8	44	—	15	—	9	139	35	174
Fourth Panzer Army	24	23	259	16	253	200	57	25	68	925	170	1,095
Corps Raus	—	—	—	—	—	—	—	—	—	—	50	50
905th Assault Gun Detachment	—	—	—	—	—	—	—	—	—	—	25	25
393d Assault Gun Detachment	—	—	—	—	—	—	—	—	—	—	25	25
III Panzer Corps	27	5	129	3	105	—	45	—	30	344	25	369
6th Panzer	13	—	52	1	32	—	—	—	20	117	—	117
7th Panzer	12	5	55	2	37	—	—	—	7	112	—	112
19th Panzer	2	—	22	—	36	—	—	—	3	70	—	70
503d Heavy Tank Panzer Detachment	—	—	—	—	—	—	45	—	—	45	—	45
228th Assault Gun Detachment	—	—	—	—	—	—	—	—	—	—	25	25
Army Detachment Kempf	27	5	129	3	105	—	45	—	30	344	75	419
Total	51	28	388	19	358	200	102	25	98	1,269	245	1,514
Total Orel-Kursk and Kursk-Oboian' axes										1,859	669	2,528

Note: 38T tanks included in Panzer II figures, 75mm III in Panzer III long, and flame tanks in command catagory.
Source: Thomas L. Jentz, ed. *Panzertruppen: The Complete Guide to the Creation and Combat Employment of Germany's Tank Force, 1943–1945*, vol. 2 (Atglen, Pa.: Schiffer Military History, 1996), 78–82.

German Armor Strength (operational strength returns)

	TANKS										Assault guns	Total
	Mk II	Mk III s	Mk III l	Mk IV s	Mk IV l	Mk V	Mk VI	T-34	Command	Subtotal		
4 July 1943												
SS Panzer Corps	4	1	117	5	151	—	35	18	25	356	95	451
SS *Leibstandarte Adolf Hitler*	4	—	11	—	79	—	12	—	9	115	34	149
SS *Das Reich*	—	1	47	—	30	—	12	18	8	116	33	149
SS *Totenkopf*	—	—	59	5	42	—	11	—	8	125	28	153
XXXXVII Panzer Corps	—	13	89	24	98	204	14	—	22(f)	464	89	553
3d Panzer	—	3	27	17	21	—	—	—	—	68	2	70
11th Panzer	—	8	42	—	22	—	—	—	8(f)	80	22	102
Grossdeutschland	—	2	20	7	55	—	14	—	14(f)	112	34	146
51st Panzer Detachment	—	—	—	—	—	104	—	—	—	104	—	104
52d Panzer Detachment	—	—	—	—	—	100	—	—	—	100	—	100
911th Assault Gun Detachment	—	—	—	—	—	—	—	—	—	—	31	31
Fourth Panzer Army	4	14	206	29	249	204	49	18	47	820	184	1,004
Corps Rauss	—	—	—	—	—	—	—	—	—	—	50	50
905th Assault Gun Detachment	—	—	—	—	—	—	—	—	—	—	25	25
393d Assault Gun Detachment	—	—	—	—	—	—	—	—	—	—	25	25
III Panzer Corps	—	—	—	—	—	—	48	—	—	—	—	382
6th Panzer (est.)	—	—	—	—	—	—	—	—	—	—	—	124
11th Panzer (est.)	—	—	—	—	—	—	—	—	—	—	—	103
19th Panzer (est.)	—	—	—	—	—	—	—	—	—	—	—	82
503d Panzer Detachment	—	—	—	—	—	—	48	—	—	—	—	48
228th Assault Gun Detachment	—	—	—	—	—	—	—	—	—	—	—	25
Army Detachment Kempf	—	—	—	—	—	—	48	—	—	—	—	432
Grand Total	—	—	—	—	—	204	97	—	—	—	—	1,436
8 July 1943												
SS Panzer Corps												283
SS *Leibstandarte Adolf Hitler*	4	—	10	—	40	—	1	—	6	61	20	81
SS *Das Reich* (est.)												90
SS *Totenkopf*	—	—	52	7	28	—	5	—	7	99	13	112

German Armor Strength (operational strength returns), *Continued*

| | | | | TANKS | | | | | | | | Assault | |
	Mk II	Mk III s	Mk III l	Mk IV s	Mk IV l	Mk V	Mk VI	T-34	Command	Subtotal	guns	Total
9 July 1943												
SS Panzer Corps	4	—	82	7	65	—	7	8	17	190	59	249
SS *Leibstandarte Adolf Hitler*	4	—	4	—	32	—	4	1	5	50	21	71
SS *Das Reich*	—	—	31	—	13	—	1	7	7	59	26	85
SS *Totenkopf*	—	—	47	7	20	—	2	—	5	81	12	93
10 July 1943												
SS Panzer Corps	4	—	85	7	77	—	7	7	18	205	67	272
SS *Leibstandarte Adolf Hitler*	4	—	4	—	41	—	4	—	6	59	20	79
SS *Das Reich*	—	—	33	—	15	—	1	7	7	63	26	89
SS *Totenkopf*	—	—	48	7	21	—	2	—	5	83	21	104
11 July 1943												
SS Panzer Corps	4	—	93	4	91	—	15	8	21	236	57	293
SS *Leibstandarte Adolf Hitler*	4	—	5	—	47	—	4	—	7	67	10	77
SS *Das Reich*	—	—	34	—	18	—	1	8	7	68	27	95
SS *Totenkopf*	—	—	54	4	26	—	10	—	7	101	@20	121
XXXXVII Panzer Corps	—	5	31	10	50	30	—	—	5(f)	131	42	173
3d Panzer	—	3	3	10	7	—	—	—	—	23	—	23
11th Panzer	—	2	28	—	13	—	—	—	5(f)	48	—	48
Grossdeutschland with 51st and												
52d Panzer Detachment	—	—	—	—	30	30	—	—	—	60	27	87
911th Assault Gun Detachment	—	—	—	—	—	—	—	—	—	—	@15	@15
Fourth Panzer Army	4	5	124	14	141	30	15	8	26	367	99	466
13 July 1943												
SS Panzer Corps	4	—	80	3	65	—	4	11	20	187	64	251
SS *Leibestandarte Adolf Hitler*	4	—	5	—	31	—	3	—	7	50	20	70
SS *Das Reich*	—	—	43	—	20	—	1	11	8	83	24	107
SS *Totenkopf*	—	—	32	3	14	—	—	—	5	54	20	74

German Armor Strength (operational strength returns), *Continued*

						TANKS						Assault guns	Total
	Mk II	Mk III s	Mk III l	Mk IV s	Mk IV l	Mk V	Mk VI	T-34	Command	Subtotal		
XXXXVII Panzer Corps	—	4	43	16	43	43	6	—	17	172	55	227
3d Panzer	—	3	13	13	11	—	—	—	—	40	1	41
11th Panzer	—	1	22	—	13	—	—	—	5 (f)	41	14	55
Grossdeutschland with 51st and 52d Panzer Detachment	—	—	8	3	19	43	6	—	12 (f)	91	25	116
911th Assault Gun Detachment	—	—	—	—	—	—	—	—	—	—	@15	@15
Fourth Panzer Army	4	4	123	19	108	43	10	11	37	359	119	478
15 July 1943												
SS Panzer Corps	4	4	71	3	66	—	17	13	20	194	71	265
SS *Leibstandarte Adolf Hitler*	4	—	6	—	32	—	8	—	7	57	28	85
SS *Das Reich*	—	—	37	—	17	—	2	13	7	76	23	99
SS *Totenkopf*	—	—	28	3	17	—	7	—	6	61	@20	81
16 July 1943												
SS Panzer Corps	4	—	72	4	83	—	23	11	20	217	75	292
SS *Leibstandarte Adolf Hitler*	4	—	5	—	42	—	9	—	6	66	30	96
SS *Das Reich*	—	—	37	—	18	—	5	11	7	78	25	103
SS *Totenkopf*	—	—	30	4	23	—	9	—	7	73	20	93

Sources. For 4 July 1943: "Tagesmeldungen vom 4.7.43," *4.Panzerarmee*, in NAM T-354, roll 605; and "Tagesmeldung XXXXVII.Pz.Korps vom 4.7.1943," *4.Panzerarmee*, in NAM T-313, roll 368.

For 8 July 1943: "Tagesmeldungen der Pz.Gren.Div. 'Totenkopf' v.8.7.43.," *Generalkommando II. SS-Pz.Korps, 4.7.43, 1845*, in NAM T-354, roll 605; and "Tagesmeldungen der 'ISSAH''-Pz.Gren.Div. v.8.7.43.," *Generalkommando II. SS-Pz.Korps, 4.7.43, 1845*, in NAM T-354, roll 605.

For 9 July 1943: "'ISSLAH,' Tagesmeldungen vom 9.7.43," *Generalkommando II. SS-Pz.Korps, 4.7.43, 1845*, in NAM T-354, roll 605; "SS 'T,' Tagesmeldungen vom 9.7.43," *Generalkommando II. SS-Pz.Korps, 4.7.43, 1845*, in NAM T-354, roll 605; and "Ta—Tagesmeldungen, SS-Panzer-Grenadier-Division 'Das Reich,' Div.Gef.St., 9.7.43," *Generalkommando II. SS-Pz.Korps, 4.7.43, 1845*, in NAM T-354, roll 605.

For 10 July 1943: "Ia—Tagesmeldungen, SS-Panzer-Grenadier-Division 'Das Reich,' Div. gef. St., 10.7.43," *Generalkommando II. SS-Pz.Korps, 4.7.43, 1845*, in NAM T-354, roll 605; and "Tagesmeldung vom 10.7.43," *Gen.Kdo. II.SS-Pz.Korps*, in NAM T-354, roll 605.

For 11 July 1943: "Tagesmeldung vom 11.7.43," *Gen.Kdo. II.SS-Panzer-Korps*, in NAM T-354, roll 605; "Tagesmeldung II. SS Pz.Korps. 11.7.43. 18.35 Uhr," *4. Panzerarmee*, in NAM T-313, roll 368; and "Tagesmeldung XXXXVIII. Pz.K. vom 11.7.43. 20.45 Uhr.," *4. Panzerarmee*, in NAM T-313, roll 368.

For 13 July 1943: "Tagesmeldungen vom 13.7.43," *Gen.Kdo.II.SS-Pz.Korps*, in NAM T-354, roll 605; "Tagesmeldung II.SS-Pz.Korps vom 13.7.43. 19.35 Uhr," *4. Panzerarmee*, in NAM T-313, roll 368; and "Tagesmeldung XXXXVIII.Pz.Korps vom 13.7.43. 20.00 Uhr.," *4. Panzerarmee*, in NAM T-313, roll 368.

For 15 July 1943: "Tagesmeldung vom 15.7.43, SS-Pz.Gren.Div. 'Das Reich;" *Gen.Kdo.II.SS-Pz.Korps*, in NAM T-354, roll 605; "Tagesmeldung vom 15.7.43 vom SS-Panzer-Gren. Div. 'Totenkopf'," 17.05 Uhr," *Gen.Kdo.II.SS-Pz.Korps*, in NAM T-354, roll 605; and "Tagesmeldung 'ISSAH'-Pz.Gren.Div. vom 15.7.1943," *Gen.Kdo.II.SS-Pz.Korps*, in NAM T-354, roll 605.

For 16 July 1943: "Tagesmeldung vom 16.7.1943," *Gen.Kdo.II.SS-Pz.Korps*, in NAM T-354, roll 605.

Key German Orders

Operation Order No. 5

OKH/GenSt d H/OpAbt (vorg-St)   13 March 1943
Nr. 430 163/43 g. Kdos.Chefs
Secret, Commanders' Eyes Only   5 copies

Operation Order Nr. 5 (instructions for the conduct of combat during the next months).

It can be anticipated that the Russians will resume their attack after the end of the winter and the mud period and after a period of refitting and reconstitution.

Therefore, the time has come for us to attack in as many sectors of the front as possible before he does—at least in one sector of the front, for example, in the Army Group South area of operations.

We must let them crash against the other sectors of the front and bloody them. Here, we must strengthen our defenses by committing heavy defensive weapons and by constructing positions, laying mines, establishing rear area positions, maintaining mobile reserves, etc.

In addition, the preparations must be made immediately in all army group areas of operations. The attack formations must be refitted with personnel, equipment, and they must conduct training. Since the mud period is expected to end earlier than usual this year, each day must be used properly for the preparations. The army groups must report each week (every Monday) on the status of their preparations. The OKH will deploy the necessary equipment and heavy defensive weapons. In detail, I order:

1. Army Group A:

As soon as the weather permits, conduct the planned shortening of the Gotenkopf [Kuban bridgehead] in order to free up forces for Army Group South.

Army Group A must realize that its main mission is to make forces available. The quicker they are provided, the better and more effective they will be.

All ways and means will be used for their transport.

Nevertheless, the mission of the army group remains the defense of the Gotenkopf and the Crimea. The construction of the Crimean coastal defense must be accomplished with all means available so that—as in the West—the best possible defense against enemy landings will be provided.

2. Army Group South:

The entire Mius front and the remaining eastern front, as well as the Donets front, must be brought to the highest degree of defensive readiness. The regions threatened by armor must be reinforced with antitank weapons.

The HKL [front line] has to be held in the sector's front. The enemy must not be allowed to establish any bridgeheads on the far side of the river.

A strong panzer army has to be formed on the northern flank of the army group immediately and no later than mid-April so that it will be ready for commitment at the end of the mud period, before the Russian offensive. The objective of this offensive is the destruction of enemy forces in front of 2d Army by attacking to the north out of the Kharkov area in conjunction with an attack group from 2d Panzer Army. Details on this attack and the command structure and force deployments will follow in a special supplement.

3. Army Group Center:

First, the situation between 2d and 2d Panzer Armies must be straightened out; then the defensive *fronts* are to be strengthened and equipped with antitank weapons as planned. This is especially important near Kirov, in the region north and northwest of Smolensk, as well as at Velikie Luki. Then an attack group is to be formed to attack in conjunction with the northern flank of Army Group South. The forces are to be obtained by the Beuffelbewegung [the operation to abandon the Rzhev salient]. Special instructions will follow. Also, establish what forces will be made available to the OKH Reserve from the Beuffelbewegung.

4. Army Group North:

Since there is no plan for a major offensive operation during the first half of the summer in the Army Group North area of operations, the main effort will be applied to defense. The entire *front* must be brought to the highest degree of defensive readiness. The construction of necessary defensive positions must be carried out at the highest tempo. Divisions freed up by the evacuation of the Demyansk pocket are to be used for reinforcement of the defensive front and as an attack reserve. The formations are to be reorganized. Strong artillery groups are to be reformed and supplied with ammunition. Mobile artillery groups are to be held back for rapid commitment. Reinforcement of the southern flank of the army group near Staraya Russa and the entire region to the south and southeast is particularly important. An enemy offensive is anticipated toward Pleskau [Pskov] in the south of the army group to cut off the army group and near Leningrad to relieve the threat to Leningrad.

An operation against Leningrad is planned for the second half of the summer (after the beginning of July). It will be conducted with the close cooperation of all available artillery and with the commitment of the most modern weapons. Artillery deployments and resupply with ammunition will be initiated at the earliest time. Additional details will follow.

Document Annexes: Details on the deployment of personnel, weapons, and equipment, and on the deployment of individual divisions and *Heeres* [OKH] troops will be specially sent to the army groups. For the construction of rear area positions [fallback positions], refer to my Order Nr. 8. Maps with the designated rear area positions will be forwarded to the army groups.

The army groups will report their intentions on 25 March. Reports on the current status of preparations will be forwarded each Monday.

Signed: Adolf Hilter[1]

Operation Order No. 6 (the Citadel order)

OKH, GenStdH, Op.Abt (I)   Fuehrer Headquarters, 15 April 1943
Nr. 430246/43 g.Kdos.Chefs.
SECRET   13 copies

OPERATION ORDER NR. 6.

I have decided to conduct Citadel, the first offensive of the year, as soon as the weather permits.

This attack is of the utmost importance. It must be executed quickly. It must seize the initiative for us in the spring and summer. Therefore, all preparations must be conducted with great circumspection and enterprise. The best formations, the best weapons, the best commanders, and great stocks of ammunition must be committed in the main efforts. Each commander and each man must be impressed with the decisive significance of this offensive. The victory at Kursk must be a signal to all the world. I hereby order:

1. The objective of this offensive is to encircle enemy forces located in the Kursk area by means of rapid and concentrated attacks of shock armies from the Belgorod area and south of Orel and to annihilate the enemy in concentrated attacks. During the offensive a new abbreviated *front*, which will save strength, will be established along the line: Nezhegol-Korocha sector—Skorodnoye—Tim-east of Shchigry-Sosna sector.

2. We must insure that
   a. The element of surprise is preserved and the enemy be kept in the dark as to when the attack will begin.
   b. The attack forces are concentrated on a narrow axis, in order to provide local overwhelming superiority of all attack means (tanks, assault guns, artillery, rocket launchers, etc.) to insure contact between the two attacking armies and closure of the pocket.
   c. The attack wedge is followed by forces from the depths to protect the flanks, so that the attack wedge itself will only have to be concerned with advancing.
   d. By prompt compression of the pocket, the enemy will be given no respite and will be destroyed.
   e. The attack is conducted so quickly that the enemy will be denied the opportunity of either breaking out of encirclement or of deploying strong reserves from other *fronts*.
   f. Additional forces, particularly mobile formations, are freed up by quickly constructing a new *front*.

3. Army Group South will jump off with strongly concentrated forces from the Belgorod-Tomarovka line, break through the Prilepy-Oboyan line, and link up with the attacking armies of Army Group Center at east of Kursk. The line Nezhegol-Korocha sector—Skorodnoye-Tim must be reached as soon as possible to protect the attack from the east without jeopardizing the concentration of forces on the main effort in the direction of Prilepy-Oboyan. Forces will be committed to protect the attack in the west; they will later be used to attack into the pocket.

4. Army Group Center will launch a concentrated attack from the line Trossna-north of Maloarkhangelsk with the main effort on the eastern flank, break through the line Fatezh-Veretenovo, and establish contact with the attacking army from Army Group South near and east of Kursk. . . . The line Tim-east of Shchigry—Sosna sector is to be reached as soon as possible. To protect the attack from the east, however, the concentration of forces on the main effort is not to be disturbed. Secondary forces will be employed to cover [the attack] from the west.

At the beginning of the attack, Army Group Center forces operating west of Trosna to the boundary with Army Group South are to fix the enemy with local attacks of specially concentrated attack groups and then attack promptly into the forming pocket. Continuous ground reconnaissance and air observation is to insure that the enemy does not withdraw unnoticed. If this occurs, there is to be an immediate attack along the entire front.

5. The preparation of both army groups' forces is to be conducted under the best deception measures possible and far removed from jumping-off positions. The earliest date for the attack will be 3 May. The march to jumping-off positions will be conducted only at night under as much cover as possible.

6. Preparations for Panther will continue in the Army Group South area of operations to deceive the enemy. This is to be reinforced by all means available (conspicuous reconnaissance, deployment of tanks, assembly of crossing equipment, radios, agents, rumors, commitment of the Luftwaffe, etc.) and be kept up for as long as possible. These deception operations will also be supported by measures necessary to strengthen defensive forces along the Donets front (see paragraph 11). Deception operations of this scale are not to be conducted in the Army Group Center area of operations, however, all means are to be employed to blur the enemy's picture of the situation (false and retrograde movements as well as marches during the day, distribution of incorrect intelligence data concerning a start date in early June, etc.).

The two army groups will maintain radio silence between the attack armies and the newly deployed formations.

7. To ensure secrecy only those persons who absolutely need to know will be informed of the plan. These instructions will be passed down to lower echelons as late as possible. In any case, these plans must not be betrayed by carelessness or neglect. Furthermore, enemy espionage will be combated by reinforced Abwehr agencies.

8. The attack map will be limited to previous operations and will not indicate the attack objectives.

9. Orders for supply and the immediate registration of prisoners, residents, and captured material, as well as enemy propaganda, will be treated in Annexes 1–3.

10. The Luftwaffe will likewise commit all of its available forces on the main effort. Coordination with Luftwaffe commands will begin immediately. Special attention will be afforded in order to maintain secrecy (see paragraph 7).

11. For the success of the attack it is mandatory that the enemy does not succeed in forcing the transfer of attack formations from Citadel by attacking other Army Group South and Army Group Centers sectors.

Therefore, just as they are preparing for the Citadel offensive battle, until the end of the month, both army groups must systematically prepare for defensive battle in remaining threatened *front* sectors. Therefore, the construction of defensive positions is to be hastened, the sectors threatened by tanks must be equipped with sufficient antitank weapons, local reserves have to be prepared, enemy's main axes have to be determined early through brisk reconnaissance, etc.

12. The final objectives of the operation are:

    a. The shifting of the boundary line between Army Groups South and Center to the general line Konotop (South)—Kursk (South)—Dolgoe (Center).

    b. The transfer of the 2d Army with three corps and nine infantry divisions, as well as the attached *Heeres* troops, from Army Group Center to Army Group South.

    c. The assembly of three additional infantry divisions from Army Group Center to be made available to the OKH in the area northwest of Kursk.

    d. The removal of all mobile formations from the front for use elsewhere.

Movement, especially that of 2d Army formations, must be adapted to these plans.

As planned, during the operation I will initiate the movement to the southeast (Panther) as quickly as possible in order to take advantage of the enemy's confusion.

13. The army groups will report offensive and defensive measures they have taken based on this operational order on 1:300,000 maps, showing dispositions, distribution of *Heeres* troops, coordination with Luftflotte 4 or Luftwaffenkommando Ost in support of the attack, and all diversionary measures.

SUSPENSE 24/4

Signed: Adolf Hitler; Heusinger, Generalleutnant[2]

II SS Panzer Corps Order (the Prokhorovka order)

22.15 hours, 9 July 1943   Divisionbefehl No. 17

1. *Enemy forces prepared for defense* are equipped with antitank weapons and tanks and are standing in a line from the western edge of the forest at Swch. Komssomolez to the railway line at Iwanowskij Wysselok.

2. The II. SS-Panzerkorps is to move out at 10 July 1943 with the LSSAH to the right and SS-Panzergrenadierdivision *Totenkopf* to the left on both sides of the Pssel and head northeast. *Attack objective:* Prochorowka/East—Hill 252.4 (2.5 kilometers northeast of there)—Beregowoje—Hill 243.5 (2 kilometers northwest of Koritnje)—Kartaschewka.

3. The reinforced *LSSAH* is to move out at 06.00 hours on 10 July 1943 after the barrage by the entire Artillerie-Regiment/*LSSAH* and Werferregiment 55. After the Luftwaffe's preparation, the *LSSAH* is to move along the road from Teterewino to Prochorowka, capture the latter town, and hold it. *First attack objective:* Prochorowka—Hill 242.4. SS-Panzergrenadierdivision *DR* is to set out with the *LSSAH* and to capture the high ground 2 kilometers southeast of Iwanowskij Wysselok. SS-Panzergrenadierdivision *Totenkopf* is to move forward from the Kljutschi bridgehead to the northeast.

4. Dividing lines: *To the right* between the *LSSAH* and Division *DR:* Teterewino (held by the *LSSAH*—forest east of Iwanowskij Wysselok (held by the *LSSAH*)—Storoshewoje (held by the *LSSAH*)—Jamki (held by the *LSSAH*)—Hill 230.5 (south of Prochorowka and held by the *LSSAH*)—road from Prochorowka to Prisnatschnoje (held by the *LSSAH*). *To the left* between the *LSSAH* and Panzergrenadierdivision

T: Hill 254.5 (500 meters north of Teterewino and held by the *LSSAH*)—Wassilewka (held by *T*)—the towns in the Pssel basin (held by *T*)—railway line to the northwest (held by the *LSSAH*). *Between the reinforced* 2. Panzergrenadier-Regiment and the reinforced Aufklarungsabteilung [reconnaissance detachment] *LSSAH:* northern tip of the forest at Swch. Komssomolez—Swch. Oktabrskij (held by the Aufklarungsabteilung)—Dumnoje (held by the Aufklarungsabteilung).

5. To accomplish this, I order the following:

a. The reinforced 2. Panzergrenadier-Regiment *LSSAH* (the Sturmgeschutzabteilung [assault gun detachment], the Tigerkompanie, one Kompanie of the Pionier-Bataillon [engineer battalion], and the 5. Flakabteilung [antiaircraft detachment]) is to attack at 06.00 hours on 10 July 1943 after the barrage from the entire Artillerie-Regiment *LSSAH* and Werferregiment 55 (minus one Abteilung). It is to attack the enemy installations, penetrate them, and then continue the attack immediately on Prochorowka. *Attack objective:* eastern edge of Prochorowka.

b. The reinforced Aufklarungsabteilung *LSSAH* (one Kompanie of the Panzerjagerabteilung [panzer hunter—tank destroyer—detachment] deployed to cover the left flank) is to start out on 10 July 1943 after the 2. Panzergrenadier-Regiment's successful breakthrough. It is to move around the northern tip of Swch. Komssomolez forest and is then to move through Swch. Oktabrskij to Hill 252.4. There it is to stop.

c. The Panzerregiment *LSSAH* (minus the Tigerkompanie) is to stand ready in the area south of the road from Teterewino to Lutschki (excluding the towns) in order to be moved up behind the reinforced 2. Panzergrenadier-Regiment *LSSAH*.

The subordination of the Tigerkompanie is to end after the successful breakthrough. The 6. Flakabteilung *LSSAH* is to be moved up to the Artillerie-Regiment *LSSAH* and subordinated to it.

d. The reinforced 1. Panzergrenadier-Regiment *LSSAH* (the Panzerjagerabteilung minus one Kompanie and the 4. Flakabteilung) is to stand ready in the eastern part of Bol. Majatschki so that it can be moved up. It should prepare itself to capture and hold the southern edges of the towns Storoshewoje, Jamki, and Prochorowka.

e. The reinforced Artillerie-Regiment *LSSAH* is to launch a barrage of five minutes' duration to support the attack. Its use in the continuing course of the fighting will be in cooperation with the reinforced 2. Panzergrenadier-Regiment.

Firing should begin as soon as there is daylight. It should arrange itself so as to support the breakthrough into Prochorowka with at least two Abteilung. The 12. (10 cm) Batterie is not to take part in the barrage because of insufficient ammunition supplies.

f. The Werferregiment (minus the III. Abteilung) is to support the attack on the first position if its ammunition supply allows it. It is to use one Abteilung to support the breakthrough into Prochorowka. Smoke will probably be used in the forests southeast and northwest of the point of breakthrough.

Firing should begin as soon as there is daylight.

g. The Pionier-Bataillon *LSSAH* is to subordinate one Kompanie to the reinforced 2. Panzergrenadier-Regiment and to stand ready in the area east of Lutschki for expanding the paths through the minefields.

The commander of the Pionier-Bataillon *LSSAH* is ordered to cooperate closely with the 2. Panzergrenadier-Regiment *LSSAH* in clearing mines and expanding the paths through the minefields.

h. The Flakabteilung *LSSAH* (minus the light and medium Batterie) is to remain initially in its previous area. The 6. Flakabteilung is to be subordinated to the Artillerie-Regiment *LSSAH* .

6. Reconnaissance:

a. *Ground reconnaissance:* by the reinforced 2. Panzergrenadier-Regiment *LSSAH* as far as the line Prisnatschnoje—Skorowka, by the Aufklarungsabteilung *LSSAH* as far as the line Dumnoje—Werchn. Olschanke.

b. *Aerial reconnaissance:* as far as the line Don—Seimiza river.

7. Luftwaffe action has been promised at the point of concentration in front of the *LSSAH*.

8. Traffic along the march route should be regulated with particular emphasis on the Lutschki—Teterewino sector.

The *LSSAH* has the right-of-way at intersections over the march of Panzergrenadier-division *Totenkopf.*

9. The main medical clearing station will be ready to accept patients in northern Bol. Majatschki starting at 10.00 hours.

10. The distribution point for ammunition for the Infantrie, Artillerie, and Panzers will be five kilometers southeast of Jakowlewo.

11. Fuel distribution point: Imkerei, five kilometers south of Bykowka.

12. The combat support section of the maintenance Abteilung is in Bykowka.

13. Prisoner assembly point: Bykowka.

14. Communications as follows: The *Nachrichtenabteilung* [signal detachment] *LSSAH* is to secure radio communications between the 2. Panzergrenadier-Regiment *LSSAH* and Panzergrenadier-Regiment *Deutschland.* The trunk link is to be along the march route.

15. The divisional headquarters are to be in Lutschki starting at 12.00 hours on 10 July 1943.

16. The regulations for keeping information secret are to be observed according to content and distributor.

Signed: Commander of the *Leibstandarte SS Adolf Hitler;* Wisch SS-Oberfuhrer[3]

Sources

1. Gotthard Heinrici and Friedrick Wilhelm Hauck, *Citadel* (U.S. National Archives), appendixes.

2. Ibid.

3. Rudolf Lehmann, *The Leibstandarte III* (Winnipeg: J. Fedorowicz, 1993), 224–226.

Key Soviet Documents

Zhukov's Strategic Assessment

TOP SECRET.
8 April 1943. 0530 hours.
To Comrade Vasil'ev [Stalin's code-name].

I hereby state my opinion about the possible movements of the enemy in the spring and summer of 1943 and my thoughts about our defensive actions in the immediate future:

1. Having suffered serious losses in the winter campaign of 1942–43, evidently the enemy would not appear to be able to build up big reserves by the spring to resume the offensive on the Caucasus and to push forward to the Volga to make a wide enveloping movement around Moscow.

Owing to the inadequacy of large reserves, in the spring and first half of the summer of 1943, the enemy will be forced to launch offensive operations on a narrower front and resolve the task facing him strictly in stages, his main aim being the seizure of Moscow.

Proceeding from the fact that, at the given moment, there are groupings deployed against our Central, Voronezh and Southwestern Fronts, I believe that the enemy's main offensive operations will develop against these three *fronts*, in order to rout our forces along this axis and to gain freedom of maneuver to envelop Moscow along the shortest axis.

2. Having assembled as many of his forces as possible, including at least thirteen to fifteen tank divisions and the greatest quantity of air support, evidently, during the first stage the enemy will deliver a blow with his Orel-Kromy grouping to envelop Kursk from the northeast and with his Belgorod-Khar'kov grouping to envelop Kursk from the southeast.

An additional attack on Kursk from the southwest aimed at dividing our *front* must be expected from the west, from the area around Vorozhba between the rivers Seim and Psel. By means of this offensive, the enemy will strive to defeat and surround our 13th, 70th, 65th, 38th, 40th, and 21st Armies.

His ultimate aim at this stage can be to reach the line Korocha River, Korocha, Tim, Tim River, and Droskovo.

3. During the second stage, the enemy will attempt to reach the flank and the rear of the Southwestern Front along the general axis through Valuiki-Urazovo. The enemy may strike a blow from the Lisichansk region in a northern direction to Svatovo-Urazova to link up with this attack.

In the remaining sectors, the enemy will strive to reach the Livny-Kastornoe-Staryi and Novyi Oskol line.

4. During the third stage, after the corresponding regrouping, the enemy will possibly try to reach the Liski, Voronezh, Elets front and, protecting himself in the southeastern direction, can organize a blow to envelop Moscow from the southeast via Ranenburg, Riazhsk, and Riazan'.

5. In his offensive operations this year, the enemy may be expected to count chiefly on his panzer divisions and air force, since his infantry is at present considerably less well prepared for offensive action than it was last year.

At the present time, the enemy has as many as twelve panzer divisions opposite the Central and Voronezh Fronts, and, by bringing up three or four panzer divisions from other sectors, the enemy can throw as many as fifteen or sixteen panzer divisions with some 2,500 tanks against our Kursk grouping.

6. If the enemy is to be defeated by our defense, besides measures to build up the antitank defenses on the Central and Voronezh Fronts, we must gather thirty antitank artillery regiments from the passive sectors as rapidly as possible and redeploy them as part of the Supreme Command's reserve [RGK] in the areas threatened: all the regiments of self-propelled artillery must be concentrated in the Livny, Kastornoe, Staryi Oskol sector. Even now it would be desirable for some of the regiments to be placed under Rokossovsky and Vatutin as reinforcements and for as many aircraft as possible to be transferred to the Supreme Command's reserve to smash the shock groupings with massed attacks from the air, coordinated with action by tank and rifle formations, and to frustrate the plan for the enemy's offensive.

I am not familiar with the final dispositions of our operational reserves; therefore I believe it expedient to propose their deployment in the Efremov, Livny, Kastornoe, Novyi Oskol, Valuiki, Rossosh', Liski, Voronezh, and Elets region.

Then, the main mass of reserves will be located in the Elets, Voronezh region. Deeper reserves will be located in the Riazhsk, Ranenburg, Michurinsk, and Tambov regions.

There should be one reserve army in the Tula-Stalinogorsk area.

I consider it inexpedient for our forces to mount a preventive offensive in the near future. It will be better if we wear out the enemy in our defense, destroy his tanks, and then, having introduced fresh reserves, by going over to an all-out offensive, we will finish off the enemy's main grouping.

Signed: Konstantinov [Zhukov's code-name]; Colonel Zimin[1]

Central Front Strategic Assessment

From the Central Front, 10 April 1943.
To the Chief of the Operations Directorate, General Staff of the Red Army, Colonel General Antonov.

I am reporting information on the state of enemy forces in front of the Central Front as of 10 April 1943 and the probable nature of their actions during the spring–summer period of 1943.

1. The grouping of enemy forces on 10 April 1943 has taken shape as a result of the concentration of large forces along the line—Ponyri, Kursk—and the March offensive of our forces from that line in the general direction of Dmitriev-L'govsk, Sevsk, Seredina Buda, and Zhikhov.

Subsequent events have indicated that the enemy expected the development of our powerful blow on Konotop, Romny, Mirgorod—in the rear of his southern grouping. In order to halt our offensive and, by doing so, to stave off the impending threat to all of his forces in the south, the enemy quickly began to transfer large forces from the Western and Kalinin Fronts to the Central Front. . . .

2. As of 10 March 1943, formations of the following groupings of the German 2d Tank Army and 2d Army are operating against the Central Front's forces . . .

In all, more than eighteen divisions are in the first line opposite the Central Front. . . . In all, up to nineteen divisions are in the second line, in reserve, and on the march, including up to thirteen infantry divisions (two Hungarian, one Italian, and one Spanish), up to two motorized [panzer grenadier] divisions, three panzer divisions, and one cavalry division.

3. The greatest density of enemy forces and reinforcing means continues to remain opposite the 65th Army's front (more than seven divisions in the first line). The main mass of reserves is in the Lokot', Trubchevsk, Novgorod-Severskii, and Seradina Buda region (up to eight divisions). Rather than being concentrated for active operations, all of these enemy forces are concentrated passively to prevent an offensive by our forces along the Sevsk, Krolevets, Konotop, Romny axis.

The spring *razputitsa* [thaw] and spring floods have severely hindered enemy regrouping of forces and the concentration of necessary forces and equipment on probable offensive axes.

As a result, one can assume that, during the *rasputitsa* period, the enemy will remain in his existing grouping and, after its end, will set about regrouping his forces and means [weapons] for active operations.

4. The objective and most probable axes of the enemy offensive in the spring and summer period of 1943:

    a. Taking into account the forces and means and, what is most important, the outcome of offensive operations in 1941 and 1942, in the spring and summer period of 1943, an enemy offensive is to be expected only along the Kursk-Voronezh operational axis. There is hardly any likelihood of an enemy offensive along other axes.

    The general strategic situation being as it is at this stage of the war, it would be to the Germans' benefit to ensure a firm hold on the Crimea, the Donbas, and the Ukraine and, for that purpose, to advance the front to the Shterovka, Starobel'sk, Roven'ki, Liski, Voronezh, Livny, Novosil' line. To achieve this the enemy will require no fewer than sixty infantry divisions with the corresponding air, tank, and artillery support. The enemy can concentrate such a quantity of forces and means along the given axis.

    This is why the Kursk-Voronezh operational axis is acquiring paramount importance.

    b. Proceeding from these operational suppositions, the enemy is expected to direct his main efforts simultaneously along inner and outer radii of action: along the inner radius—from the Orel region via Kromy to Kursk and from the Belgorod area via Oboian' to Kursk; [and] along the outer radius—from the Orel area through Livny to Kastornoe and from the Belgorod region through St. Oskol to Kastornoe.

c. In the absence of measures on our side to counter this enemy intention, his successful operations along these axes could lead to the rout of Central and Voronezh Front forces, to the capture by the enemy of the vital Orel, Kursk, Khar'kov railway line, and to the attainment by his forces of an advantageous line, which would secure his firm hold on the Crimea, the Donbas, and the Ukraine.

d. The enemy cannot set about regrouping and concentrating his forces along the probable offensive axes and also build up necessary reserves until the end of the spring *rasputitsa* and the spring floods. Consequently, the enemy may be expected to go over to a decisive offensive tentatively in the second half of May 1943.

5. Under the circumstances of the existing operational situation, the following measures would be considered expedient:

a. Destroy the enemy Orel grouping by the joint efforts of the Western, Briansk, and Central Fronts' forces, thereby depriving him of the opportunity of delivering a blow from the Orel region through Livny against Kastornoe; to seize the Mtsensk, Orel, Kursk railway, which is vital to us; and to deprive the enemy of the possibility of using the Briansk network of railroads and dirt roads.

b. To disrupt the enemy's offensive operations, it is necessary to reinforce the Central and Voronezh Fronts' forces with aircraft, particularly fighter type, and not fewer than ten regiments of antitank artillery per front.

c. It is desirable to have strong *Stavka* reserves in the Livny, Kastornoe, Liski Voronezh, and Elets regions.

Signed: Central Front Chief of Staff, Lieutenant General Malinin[2]

Voronezh Front Strategic Assessment

From the Voronezh Front, 12 April 1943.
To the Chief of the Operations Directorate, General Staff of the Red Army, Colonel General Antonov.

At the present time, it has been established that the Voronezh Front is confronted by:

1. Nine infantry divisions in the first line (the 26th, 68th, 323d, 75th, 255th, 57th, 332d, 167th, and one unidentified). These divisions are positioned along the Krasnyi Oktiabr', Bol'shaia Chernetchina, Krasnopol'e, Kazatskoe front. According to information provided by prisoners, the unidentified division is advancing toward the Soldatskoe region and is to replace the 332d Infantry Division.

These data are being verified. Information is available but has not been verified that there are six infantry divisions in the second echelon. Their position has not yet been established, and these data are also being verified.

According to signal intelligence, the headquarters of a Hungarian division that may be moved forward along a secondary axis has been located in the Khar'kov region.

2. In all, there are now six panzer divisions (*Velikaia Germaniia [Grossdeutschland]*, Adolf Hitler, *Mertvaia golova [Totenkopf]*, *Reich [Das Reich]*, the 6th, and the 11th). Of these, three are in the first line, and three divisions (*Velikaia Germaniia*, 6th, and 11th) are in the second line. According to signal intelligence, the headquarters of the

17th Panzer Division has moved from Alekseevskoe to Tarnovka, which indicates that this division is moving northward. With his present forces, the enemy can bring as many as three more panzer divisions into the Belgorod area from the Southwestern Front sector.

3. Thus, the enemy is likely to create a shock group of up to ten panzer divisions and not fewer than six infantry divisions, all in all as many as 1,500 tanks to counter the Voronezh Front; this concentration of forces may be expected in the Borisovka, Belgorod, Murom, Kazach'ia Lopan' region. This shock group can be supported by aircraft numbering approximately 500 bombers and no fewer than 300 fighters.

The enemy's intention is to deliver concentric blows from the Belgorod region to the northeast and from the Orel region to the southeast in order to surround our forces located west of the Belgorod, Kursk line.

Subsequently an enemy attack is expected in a southeastern direction into the flank and rear of the Southwestern Front with the objective of eventually pushing northward.

It is not out of the question, however, that the enemy will decide not to launch an offensive to the southeast this year and will put another plan into effect, namely, after the attacks made concentrically from the Belgorod and Orel regions, he will pursue an offensive to the northeast for the purpose of a wide envelopment movement around Moscow.

This possibility must be taken into account and the resources prepared accordingly.

Thus, opposite the Voronezh Front, the enemy will probably spearhead his main offensive from the Borisovka, Belgorod region in the direction of Staryi Oskol, with part of his forces moving on Oboian' and Kursk. Secondary attacks are to be expected along the Volchansk, Novyi Oskol and Sudzha, Oboian', Kursk axes.

The enemy is still not ready for a large-scale offensive. The offensive is not expected to begin earlier than 20 April of this year, but most likely in early May.

However, local attacks can be expected at any time. Therefore, I am demanding a constant state of full combat readiness on the part of our forces.

Signed: Fedorov Nikitin; Fedotov Korzhenevich[3]

Voronezh Front Report

A report from the Voronezh Front command to Comrade Stalin concerning the grouping of enemy forces before the *front* and considerations on the preparation of an offensive operation.

TOP SECRET: SPECIAL IMPORTANCE.
Only personal, 21 April 1943.
To the Supreme High Commander, Marshal of the Soviet Union—
Comrade Stalin.

I report:

1. At the present time [the following forces] have been identified opposite the Voronezh Front:

   a. Eight infantry divisions in the first line on the front Krasnooktiabr'skoe, Bol. Chernetchina, Krasnopol'e, Kazatskoe (the 26th, 68th, 323d, 75th, 255th, 57th, 332d, 167th, and one division with an unknown designation).

According to information that requires confirmation, there are six German infantry divisions in the second line, and, furthermore, based on radio intelligence one Hungarian division is in Khar'kov region, and a Hungarian army corps, which, in the beginning of an offensive, the Germans can employ on a secondary axis and at whose expense the German shock group can be reinforced, is in the Konotop region.

According to a personal report of Major General Cherniakhovsky, the commander of the Central Front's 60th Army, the enemy withdrew the 340th and 377th Infantry Divisions from the 60th Army front and moved them to the south.

b. We must assess that there are now up to eight panzer divisions, including three in the first line and up to five refitting in the second line.

Second echelon panzer divisions are grouped with up to two panzer divisions in the Trostianets and Akhtyrka region and in the forests to the east, and up to three panzer divisions are at and north of Khar'kov.

In addition, based on the presence of his forces, for an offensive the enemy can bring two to three panzer divisions forward to the Belgorod region from the Southwestern Front sector.

Thus, for an offensive the enemy can assemble up to twenty infantry and up to eleven panzer divisions (around 1,600 tanks) opposite the Voronezh Front, and, of these, he can employ up to ten infantry and up to ten panzer divisions (1,500 tanks) on the main axis.

This enemy shock group can be supported by strong aviation numbering up to 500 bombers and not fewer than 300 fighters.

We lack documentary information concerning enemy intentions. However, the following enemy plan is most probable: The enemy will prepare for an offensive and will deliver concentric blows northeast from the Belgorod-Borisovka region and southeast from the Orel region to encircle our forces located west of the Belgorod-Kursk line.

Subsequently, the enemy will attempt either to repeat his attack to the southeast into the rear of the Southwestern Front with a subsequent turn to the north, or he will give up the notion of an attack to the southeast this year and will adopt another plan, namely, after concentric attacks from the Belgorod and Orel regions, he will launch an attack to the northeast to envelop Moscow.

Given this possibility, it is essential to consider and, accordingly, prepare reserves.

Consequently, it is most likely that the enemy opposite the Voronezh Front will deliver his main attack from the Borisovka, Belgorod region along the Staryi Oskol axis and, with part of his forces, on Oboian' and Kursk.

Supporting attacks can be expected along the Volchansk, Novyi Oskol and Sudzha, Oboian', and Kursk axes.

The enemy is not ready for a large-scale offensive, and we must expect the beginning of his offensive in the first days of May.

As experience has shown, as before, the enemy will attack mainly with aircraft, tanks, and motorized infantry. Therefore, it is now necessary to work out a plan for a large-scale air operation to destroy enemy aircraft at their airfields and, simultaneously, to begin carrying out that plan, as well as the most careful measures to prepare to repel the massive enemy tank attack and to destroy his tanks.

During spring of this year, the enemy employed the following new methods: tank-destroying aircraft armed with 37mm guns; and the heavy T-6 tank, which has strong frontal armor and is armed with an 88mm gun. As far back as the winter period, the enemy introduced a machine gun that, according to prisoners, could fire up to 1,400 bullets per minute.

2. The Voronezh Front's forces are continuing to rearm and refit.

In connection with some tardiness in the arrival of weapons and uniforms, the rearming and refitting of first echelon armies will be completed by 25 April 1943 and of the 69th Army by 5 May 1943. By this period divisions will be raised in strength to 7,000 to 8,000 men each.

Tanks for the 2d and 5th Guards Tank Corps have been partially received, and full refitting will be completed roughly by 25 April 1943.

It is projected that all remaining *front* tank units will be refitted by 1 May 1943, mainly by means of repairs.

In addition, the 7th Separate Rifle Corps, which has been included in the *front*, will arrive in its newly designated region. Its refitting will be complete by 25 April 1943.

Thus, full reestablishment of the combat readiness of *front* forces and their rearmament and refitting will be completed by 5 May 1943. The *front* will then include:

31 rifle divisions
7 rifle brigades
2 cavalry divisions
2 tank corps
6 separate tank brigades
7 separate tank regiments
6 antitank artillery brigades
24 antitank artillery regiments, including 12 regiments in the stage of formation
3 self-propelled artillery regiments
9 RGK gun artillery regiments and 1 RGK gun artillery division, including 5 regiments in transit along the railways
3 RGK howitzer artillery regiments
12 mortar regiments, including 7 regiments in the stage of formation and en route along the railway
2 M-8 multiple rocket launcher regiments
5 M-13 multiple rocket launcher regiments
2 M-30 multiple rocket launcher brigades
27 antitank rifle battalions all in the process of rearming and refitting

In all, [there are] a total of 540 tanks, 101 fighter aircraft, 173 assault aircraft, 170 daylight bombers, and 43 night bombers, for a total of 487 aircraft on 17 April 1943.

The correlation of forces is at Enclosure No. 1.

3. During the period of rearming and refitting, the *front's* armies have the mission of firmly holding occupied positions and preventing any sort of penetration by enemy forces.

In the event of an enemy offensive, to defeat the enemy in a defensive battle and, then, having selected a favorable moment, to go over to the offensive and destroy him.

The concrete decision regarding defense is set forth in my Order No. 0093 and on the attached map, a copy of which has been presented to you.

I have enclosed with this report a verified map of the organization of *front* defenses.

ENCLOSURE NO. 2

The proposed basis of the defense:

a. The construction of a deep defense, for which not only have a series of lines been prepared, but they have also been occupied by forces. These should not permit the enemy to execute an operational penetration.

b. The organization of a dense antitank defense in great depth, especially on important tank axes, to which end [we] have worked out a careful plan for antitank defense, created antitank regions echeloned in depth, erected engineer antitank obstacles and minefields both in front of the forward edge and in the depth, employed flamethrowers, and prepared artillery and multiple rocket launcher fire and aviation strikes along possible axes for the movement of enemy tanks.

Operational obstacles have been prepared at great depth. There are mobile antitank reserves in all units and formations.

c. The organization of a reliable antitank defense by means of the creation of cover for combat formations, *maskirovka,* and massive use of antiaircraft means on important axes.

However, the most effective means of antiaircraft defense is the destruction of enemy aircraft at their airfields and the destruction of fuel reserves, for which it is necessary to employ in timely fashion the aviation of all *fronts,* as well as long-range aviation.

d. The preparation and implementation of maneuver as the basis for success in the defense.

The undertaking of measures to protect maneuver by antitank means, artillery, multiple rocket launcher units, and second echelons and reserves, to create quickly great density and a deep defense on enemy attack axes, to accumulate forces rapidly to conduct counterattacks, and to achieve force superiority necessary to launch a counteroffensive.

Specifically, I report about measures to repulse large-scale tank attacks. I have decided at all cost to achieve that aim:

a. To arm all units and formations fully with antitank rifles and antitank artillery as determined by establishment [table of organization] and equip sapper and engineer units above required levels with antitank rifles.

b. By 25 April 1943 to equip all antitank artillery brigades and all antitank artillery regiments, having allocated them to armies on the following basis: 38th and 40th Armies—one antitank artillery brigade and three antitank artillery regiments each; 21st [6th Guards] Army—six antitank and self-propelled artillery and two antitank artillery brigades; 64th [7th Guards] Army—six antitank and self-propelled artillery regiments and one antitank artillery brigade; and 69th Army—one antitank artillery brigade. Additionally, on 25 April 1943 six antitank artillery regiments and three light artillery regiments will be arrayed in *front* reserve.

c. By 25 April 1943 form and equip three antitank rifle battalions each in the 38th and 40th Armies, five antitank rifle battalions each in the 21st and 64th Armies, three antitank rifle battalions in the 69th Army, and five antitank rifle battalions in the *front* reserve. Moreover, three antitank rifle battalions are arriving from the *Stavka* reserve. Thus, in all, there will be twenty-seven antitank rifle battalions.

d. The task has been given to lay 150,000 antitank mines during the course of April.

e. Implement practical measures in accordance with my enciphered telegram No. 52/k of 12 April 1943, a copy of which has been forwarded to the Chief of the Red Army General Staff.

4. At the same time, I am reporting my thoughts on the preparation of offensive operations. Since the offensive operations have to be conducted in close cooperation with other *fronts*, I am obliged to report consideration regarding not only the Voronezh Front but relating to other *fronts* as well. During the 1943 summer campaign, the aim of offensive operations in the south should be the destruction of enemy armed forces in the Ukraine, the full cleansing of them from the left bank of the Ukraine, and the seizure of a large-scale bridgehead on the right bank of the Dnepr River, reaching the front Kremenchug, Krivoi Rog, Kherson, and, in favorable circumstances, the front Cherkassy, Nikolaev. The achievement of this large-scale aim will deprive the enemy of the richest foodstuffs bases and large industrial regions and centers such as the Donbas, Krivoi Rog, Khar'kov, and Dnepropetrovsk. It will put out of commission the most active part of the German Army and bring us nearer to her southern ally, and this will speed up their exit from the war.

Therefore, in the event this projected operation succeeds, it will be expedient to throw in large *Stavka* reserves to exploit the success to the maximum and to achieve results here that will be decisive for the outcome of the war. The fulfillment of these offensive operations requires the conduct of the following three stages:

a. The first and most essential stage of these operations must be combined offensive operations by the Voronezh and Southwestern Fronts with the aim of encircling and destroying the enemy Khar'kov-Belgorod grouping, the capture of Khar'kov, and the arrival at the line Sumy, Akhtyrka and farther, along the Vorskla River to Poltava, Karlovka, Zachepilivka, Pereshchino, Orel'ko, Krasnopavlovka, and Petrovskaia.

The crushing defeat of the enemy Khar'kov-Belgorod grouping will inflict a large-scale defeat on him and put out of action the most active of his units. The seizure of the indicated region is not a simple pursuit of territory, but rather it isolates the enemy Donbas grouping from its central grouping, leads to the deep envelopment of the enemy Donbas grouping, and creates favorable conditions for its subsequent encirclement. The depth of the first stage of the operation is 200 kilometers. Its fulfillment will require up to fifteen days.

b. The second stage of the operation must be a combined offensive operation by the Voronezh, Southwestern, and Southern Fronts with the aim of encircling and destroying the entire enemy grouping located east of the line Poltava,

Dnepropetrovsk, Dnepr River, with the arrival on the front Sumy, Mirgorod, Psel River, Kremenchug, Dnepr River, Melitopol' (see map at Enclosure No. 3). In this operation the left wing of the Voronezh Front must deliver a blow on Dnepropetrovsk and, with part of its forces, on Kremenchug. The Southwestern Front must make its main attack by its right flank in a southeastern and southern direction in order that the eastern part of the front will reach the line Mariupol, Volnovakha, Stalino, Kantinirovskaia, Slaviansk, and firmly block the enemy Donas group from the rear. The other part of Southwestern Front forces must reach a *front* to the west along the line Dnepropetrovsk, Dnepr River, Melitopol' and prevent any enemy forces from coming to the assistance of the encircled enemy Donbas group. It would be expedient for the Southern Front to launch its attack by its right flank along the axis Slavianoserbsk, Delbal'tsevo, and Stalino. The Southwestern and Southern Front operations must lead to the solid encirclement of the enemy in the Donbas. While doing so it is not excluded that it may be expedient to leave the subsequent destruction of the encircled enemy to the Southern Front, while the Southwestern Front will operate facing west. The depth of the second stage of the operation for the Voronezh Front is 200 kilometers and for the Southwestern Front 300 kilometers. With necessary preparations, it will require up to thirty days to complete it.

    c. The third stage must be a general offensive by the Voronezh, Southwestern, Southern, and Central Fronts with the aim of reaching the line Dnepr River, Kremenchug, Krivoi Rog, Kherson and, in favorable circumstances, the line Dnepr River, Cherkassy, and Nikolaev. For rough axes of advance, see Enclosure No. 5. Obviously, the third stage will also lead to realization of the destruction of the encircled enemy grouping in the Donbas. The depth of the third stage of the operation is 300 kilometers. Its fulfillment will require up to thirty days. Thus, the overall depth of the operation is up to 700 kilometers. Its fulfillment will require two and a half months. It is difficult to envision the start of the operation. For this it is necessary to select a favorable moment in the process of the defensive battle. In approximate terms, it can occur in the month of June.

5. The Voronezh Front can begin fulfillment of the initial offensive operation with the aim of destroying the enemy Khar'kov-Belgorod grouping in various circumstances, namely:

    a. When the enemy anticipates us and goes over to the offensive against our defense; this is the most probable and, in the existing conditions, the most acceptable for us.

    b. When we are first to go over to the offensive against the defending enemy.

In the first instance (see map at Enclosure No. 3), the Voronezh Front must conduct a defensive battle as a preliminary, in the process of which it must exhaust the enemy, prevent him from penetrating the front, defeat him, and, in a favorable moment, go over to a counteroffensive with the aim of encircling and definitively destroying the enemy main force.

In this case, in the event of some enemy progress, strong counterstrokes must be delivered against him north of Belgorod. For that purpose, the front main attack will be delivered roughly by the forces of the 6th Guards Army (the 1st Tank Army, two tank armies, etc.) and the 2d Guards Tank Corps with reinforcements and support by *front* aviation to envelop Khar'kov from the west along the axis Tomarovka, Malaia Pisarevka and farther along the front Krasnograd, Merefa.

A secondary attack will be conducted along the Belgorod-Khar'kov axis by the 7th Guards Army, reinforced by three tank brigades and three tank regiments and, simultaneously, the enemy front will be rolled up along the Northern Donets River. I consider the linkup of these attacks to be expedient and essential.

a. The Southwestern Front will launch its main attack with the forces of two armies and one tank army from the bridgehead that is south of Savintsy in the direction of Alekseevskoe and, farther along the front, Nov. Vodolaga, Krasnograd, and, simultaneously, construct a strong front along the line Zachepilovka, Pereshchepino, Orel'ka, Krasnopavlovka, Petrovskaia.

b. The Southwestern Front will conduct a secondary attack with the forces of 6th Army from the front Mokhnachi, Cherk. Bishkin to the front Khar'kov, Nov. Vodolaga.

The axes of advance of the two fronts will lead to the encirclement and destruction of the greatest quantity of enemy forces and, in the final analysis, to a huge penetration of his front in a more than 300-kilometer sector.

To protect the Voronezh Front's main attack from the west in this operation:

a. The 38th Army with two tank brigades will perform the mission of firm defense and will attack with limited aims only on its left flank.

b. The 40th Army with the 5th Guards Tank Corps, one tank brigade, and two tank regiments must deliver an attack with its left flank in a western direction with the mission of rolling up the enemy front in the Krasnopol'e, Soldatskoe sector and reaching the front Sumy (inclusive), Trostianets.

c. During the operation, it will be necessary to commit 69th Army with tanks in the interval between the 40th and 6th Guards Armies with the mission of delivering an attack along the Graivoron, Kotel'va axis and reaching the front Akhtyrka, Oposhnia.

d. Subsequently during the operation, one more army, in cooperation with one of the tank armies, must be committed into the interval between the 69th and 6th Guards Armies to develop success along the Bogodukhov, Poltava axis with the mission of seizing the Poltava region and reaching the front Oposhnia, Poltava, Mashevka.

The Voronezh Front does not have this army or the one more tank army necessary for use on the main axis in its composition, and, in addition, it is essential that they be attached to the front. Moreover, while delivering the main attack along the southern and southwestern axes, it is essential to consider the constant threat of a possible enemy flanking counterattack from the Sumy, Akhtyrka, and Lebedin region. To parry that attack the *front* must have strong reserves echeloned to the right in the Miropol'e, Beloe, and Sudzha region. I believe that it is necessary for this reserve to include the 35th Guards Rifle Corps, the 6th Guards Cavalry Corps, and one tank army, which, in addition, must also be attached to the Voronezh Front. During the second stage of the operation, this reserve will be used for active aims. In its stead a new reserve in the strength of one tank army and one combined-arms army must be created from *Stavka* reserves. Thus, in summary, the initial operation of Voronezh Front forces must reach the front Bol. Chernetchina, Nizh. Syrovatka, Akhtyrka, Poltava, Karlovka, including Zachepilovka. At that time, the 35th Guards Rifle Corps, the 6th Guards Cavalry Corps, and one tank army will be in reserve in the Miropol'e, Beloe, Sudzha regions, and the 7th Guards Army will be in reserve in the Khar'kov region. This will provide the *front* with the capability of quickly continuing the subsequent operation. In summary, it will be expedient during the initial operation for Southwestern Front forces to reach the front Zachepilovka, Pereshchipino, Orel'ka, Krasnopalovka, Petrovskaia so that, subsequently, an attack can be launched from this front into the rear of the enemy Donbas grouping.

The [following] boundary lines are advisable between

a. The Voronezh and Southwestern Fronts: Volokonovka, Volchansk, Khar'kov, Merefa, Krasnograd, Buzovka, Dnepropetrovsk. All points inclusive for the Voronezh Front.

b. The Voronezh and Central Fronts: Staryi Oskol, Verkh. Reutets, Soldatskoe, Krasryi Oktiabr', Seim River, Putovl', Nezhalovka, Seim River, Chernigov. All points besides Staryi Oskol and Chernogov are exclusive.

In the event the Voronezh Front begins the initial offensive operation against a defending enemy, I propose that the formation for such an operation be in accordance with the map at Enclosure No. 4.

The calculation of forces according to this variant remains the same as in the first instance, and the presence of strong reserves on the right flank will have even greater significance.

In both instances close cooperation and purposeful use of the Voronezh, Southwestern, Southern, and Central Fronts' aviation, as well as long-range aviation, must be envisioned to destroy enemy aviation and combat personnel, particularly his main grouping.

It is necessary to begin the joint work of the aviation of the several *fronts* while the enemy is still preparing for his offensive in order to destroy enemy aircraft on their airfields and troop concentrations and also to disrupt rail transport.

Thus, by the beginning of the offensive operation, the Voronezh Front must be reinforced by (a) one army consisting of six rifle divisions; [and] (b) three tank armies (including attachment of Katukov's 1st Tank Army). During the operation and before the beginning of the second stage I foresee the allocation of one tank army and one combined-arms army to the Voronezh Front. Moreover, the withdrawal from the *front* of Savitsky's fighter aviation corps requires reinforcement with fighter aviation.

I request:

1. Approval of the proposals expounded above.

2. Reinforcement of the Voronezh Front before the beginning of the offensive operation with: (a) one army of six rifle divisions, (b) three tank armies, and (c) three separate tank brigades; [and] (d) one fighter aviation corps to replace Savitsky's withdrawn fighter aviation corps. Furthermore, fill *front* aviation formations with aircraft and increase the overall quantity of aircraft to no fewer than 1,000, including up to 600 fighters.

3. During the operation and before the second stage, allocate the *front* one additional tank army and one combined-arms army.

4. By the beginning of the operation provide *front* ground forces and aviation with ammunition and fuel in acordance with additional requirements.

Enclosures:
1. Table of correlation of forces.
2. Map with the *front's* defensive organization.
3. Map—stages of the operation in the 1943 summer campaign and planning of the initial and second operation.
4. Map—planning for the initial operation in the event we go over to the offensive first.

Signed: Voronezh Front Commander, Army General Vatutin; Member of the Voronezh Front, Military Council, Lieutenant General Khrushchev
Front Chief of Staff, Major General Korshenevich[4]

Stavka Order

The *Stavka* decision of 25 April 1943 on the Voronezh Front plan [is as follows]:
The initial stage of the Voronezh Front's operational plan is deemed correct.
From 28 April Katukov's tank army is allocated to the Voronezh Front. The *front* must be fully prepared for defense not later than 10 May.
The *front* must be prepared for an offensive no later than 1 June. The final decision on the first point will be made after discussions with the commander of the Southwestern Front.
The commander of the Voronezh Front will place the 7th Guards Rifle Corps [should read: army] in *front* reserve by 20 May.
Signed: A. Vasilevsky[5]

Stavka Directive

From a 5 May 1943 *Stavka* Directive to the commanders of the Briansk, Central, Voronezh, and Southwestern Fronts.

In recent days considerable movement of enemy forces and transports in the Orel, Belgorod, and Khar'kov regions and the approach of troops to the front lines has been noticed. This prompts us to expect active operations on the part of the enemy in the near future.
The *Stavka* of the Supreme High Command requires you pay attention to the following:
1. Complete fulfillment of the plan for using frontal aviation for the destruction of enemy aircraft and the disruption of work on railways and dirt roads. . . .
2. Devote maximum attention to all types of intelligence in order to discover the enemy's grouping and his intentions. At this time it is obligatory to take daily prisoners, especially in the most important *front* sectors.
3. Once again, check the state of your defenses, the vigilance of your security, and the readiness of all forces and weapons, including force, army, and *front* reserves, to meet the enemy's prepared attack. Use every hour to strengthen the

defenses. Organize the checks personally are through responsible representatives of your headquarters.
Signed: A. Vasilevsky; Antonov[6]

Stavka VGK Directive

Front Directive No. 12248, 8 May 1943. 0420 hours.
To the commander of the Steppe Front concerning the regrouping of the 27th and 5th Guards Armies.

The *Stavka* of the Supreme High Command orders:

1. The 27th Army (without the 126th Rifle Brigade) will move into the Elets, Izmalkovo, Livny, Dolgorukovo region with the mission of firmly covering the Elets railway junction and the Elets, Dolgorukovo railway sector, having prepared a defensive line roughly along the Izmalkovo, Livny, Kshen' River line.

Be prepared to deliver a counterstroke from the Livny region along the Maloarkhangel'sk and Shchigry axes.

The army is reinforced with one tank brigade and one line tank regiment, which is bound for Elets Station along the railway.

Leave the 126th Rifle Brigade in place, having resubordinated it to the commander of the 52d Army, which is arriving in that region.

2. The 53d Army will firmly hold the Kastornoe railway junction and the Dolgorukovo, Gorshechnoe railroad sector, having prepared defenses along the Kshen' River.

Be prepared to deliver a counterstroke from the Kastornoe region along the Kursk and Oboian' axes.

The army is reinforced with two line tank regiments, which are bound for Kastornoe Station along the railway.

3. The 5th Guards Army will move into the St. Oskol, Iastrebovka, Bol'sh. Khoprn', Chernianka region with the mission of firmly protecting the sector (inclusive) Gorshechnoe, St. Oskol, Chernianka, having prepared defenses roughly along the line Iastrebovka, Istobnoe, Belyi Kolodez'. Deploy three understrength rifle divisions along the line St. Oskol, Chernianka. Be prepared to deliver a counterstroke from the St. Oskol region along the Oboian' and Belgorod axes.

4. Complete the regrouping of the armies by 15 May, while making the march without the 155th Rifle Division, which is being transferred by railroad to Stanovaia Station and Telegino Station (near Elets).

Begin movement from morning on 9 May and carry it out exclusively at night time. Pay special attention to *maskirovka* [deception].

Quickly dispatch command groups from these armies to reconnoiter defensive lines and new force deployment regions. . . .

On the instructions of the Stavka of the Supreme High Command.
Signed: A. Vasilevsky; Antonov[7]

Voronezh Front Defenses

A *short* tactical-technical description of the Voronezh Front defensive sector as of 12 May 1943.

The Voronezh Front's defensive system consists of the following belts:

1. A main defensive belt 244 kilometers [long]
2. A second defensive belt 235 kilometers [long]
3. A rear army defensive belt 258 kilometers [long]
4. Cutoff and intermediate positions 94 kilometers [long]
5. A first front rear line [positions] 150 kilometers [long]
6. A second *front* rear line with St. Oskol and Nov. Oskol 175 kilometers [long]
7. A front cutoff line 140 kilometers [long]

In all, the *front* defensive system totals 1,288 kilometers of defensive belts.

The construction of the main defensive belt has been carried out exclusively with the forces of troop units, the second defensive belt and army rear defensive belt has been constructed by troop units and the local population, and the front lines are being erected by *front* defensive construction directorates (UOS-38 and UOS-27).

The most important axes for the *front* are:

1. Sumy, Sudzha, Soldatskoe
2. Krasnopol'e, Miropol'e, Sudzha
3. Kr. Iaruga, Belaia
4. Tomarovka, Ivnia, Oboian'
5. Belgorod, Prokhorovka, Marino
7. Belgorod, Korocha
6. [*sic*] Volchansk, Veliko-Mikhailovka . . .
10. Volchansk-Volokonovka.

The most likely axes for possible enemy attack are the Belgorod, Oboian' and Belgorod, Korocha axes. Accordingly, the 6th Guards Army belt is the best prepared with defensive works. A description of the defensive belts within the confines of each army is provided below.

38TH ARMY

1. The forward edge of the main army defensive belt is 80 kilometers long, consists of thirty-four battalion regions, and proceeds across broken terrain, which is open in the Snagost', Pisarevka sector and forested in the Pisarevka, Krasnopol'e sector. On average, each battalion region occupies a front of 2.5 kilometers. Battalion regions are deeply echeloned at the junction with the Central Front, that is, at Snagost', Liubimovka, and Kasach'ia Loknia on the right flank.

Likely tank axes, such as Snagost', Liubimovka, Troitskoe, Uspenskoe, Vladimirovka, Vodolagi, and Belovody; Khoten, Iunakovka; B. Chernotchina, Birilovka; Glybnaia, Timofeevka; and Krasnopol'e, Ugroedy are protected by a system of antitank obstacles, including mines, obstructions, stakes, and escarpments. Troop units and establishment firing means have been provided with basic fortified works.

The average saturation of the main defensive belt, per kilometer of front, is:

Antitank mines	122
Antipersonnel mines	64
Antitank obstacles	.22 km
Antipersonnel obstacles	.5 km
Machine-gun areas	11
Bomb shelters and pillboxes	3.2
Mortar positions	4
Antitank rifle positions	2.6
Artillery dugouts	3.3
Communications trenches	1.25

On principal likely tank axes, the density of emplaced mines is: right flank—1,800 to 2,000 antitank and antipersonnel mines per kilometer of front; and left flank—700 to 900 antitank and antipersonnel mines per kilometer of front.

2. The second defensive belt also traverses broken terrain and, by occupying the commanding heights, permits observation of terrain situated four to six kilometers forward. The second defensive belt extends along a front of sixty kilometers and consists of twenty-five battalion regions. In some sectors, as near Sverlikoshchina "Gornaia" and M. Rybnitsa, battalion regions are echeloned to the depth of the regimental sectors. All battalion regions are functioning.

The average saturation of the second defensive belt, per kilometer of front, is:

Antitank mines	10
Antipersonnel mines	4
Antitank obstacles	.23 km
Machine-gun areas	6.5
Bomb shelters and pillboxes	3
Mortar positions	5
Antitank rifle positions	6
Artillery dugouts	2.2
Communications trenches	1.8

3. The army rear defensive belt extends along a front of fifty kilometers and consists of thirty-five battalion regions. The forward edge of the army rear defensive belt extends along the Ivnitsa, Sudzha, and Psel rivers. At crossing sites battalion regions exploit heights and population points close to the rivers, which they have prepared for defense.

The average saturation of the third defensive belt, per kilometer of front, is:

Antitank obstacles	.1 km
Machine-gun areas	7
Bomb shelters and pillboxes	6.1 km
Mortar positions	6
Antitank rifle positions	5
Artillery dugouts	2.6
Communications trenches	1.4

The following cutoff positions are found in the army defensive belt: Makhnovka, Miropol'e—twenty kilometers and nine battalion regions; and Soldatskoe, N. Makhnovka —twenty-four kilometers and six battalion regions.

All battalion regions are functioning.

40TH ARMY

1. The main defensive belt extends along a front of fifty kilometers and consists of thirty battalion regions. On the right and left flanks, the battalion regions are echeloned to the depth of the regimental sectors. The defensive belt is equipped with a system of primary firing positions interconnected by communications trenches in such quantity as to provide defense for available personnel of the division that occupies the belt.

Likely tank approaches are Aleksandrovka, Uspenskoe; Pushkarnoe, Pokrovskoe, Viazovoe; and Berezovka, Kr. Iaruga, in a sector of around twenty-four kilometers. This sector is covered chiefly by antitank obstacles.

The average saturation of the main defensive belt, per kilometer of front, is:

Antitank mines	140
Antipersonnel mines	75
Antitank obstacles	.18 km
Antipersonnel obstacles	.16 km
Machine-gun areas	11
Bomb shelters and pillboxes	10
Mortar positions	7.5
Antitank rifle positions	7.5
Artillery dugouts	6
Communications trenches	2.3

2. The second defensive belt traverses open terrain and is equipped mainly with open firing positions. The belt extends along a front of fifty kilometers and consists of twenty battalion regions.

The average saturation of the second defensive belt, per kilometer of front, is:

Antitank obstacles	.08 km
Antipersonnel obstacles	.01 km
Machine-gun areas	26
Bomb shelters and pillboxes	5
Mortar positions	13
Antitank rifle positions	9
Artillery dugouts	6.6
Communications trenches	3.3

3. The army rear defensive belt is situated along the Psel River, extends along a front of forty kilometers, and consists of eighteen battalion regions. The belt is equipped chiefly with open firing positions.

The average saturation of the army rear defensive belt, per kilometer of front, is:

Machine-gun positions	7.5
Mortar positions	1.5
Antitank rifle positions	2
Artillery dugouts	1.5
Communications trenches	1.55

6TH GUARDS ARMY

1. The main defensive belt extends along a front of sixty-four kilometers and consists of thirty-one battalion regions. On the right and left flank and also at Dragunskoe,

the battalion regions are echeloned to the depth of the regimental sectors. A reserve line, which extends along a front of fifteen kilometers and consists of six battalion regions, has been erected on the right flank along the line Kovylevka, Zavidovka. The junction with the 40th Army is protected by four antitank regions.

Likely tank approaches, which are Tomarovka, Sumovskaia; Tomarovka, Butovo, Zavidovka; Tomarovka, Dmitrievka; Tomarovka, Bykovka; Belgorod, Iakovlevo; and Belgorod, Petropavlovka, are protected by antitank regions, which have been reinforced with engineer obstacles. Troop units and establishment firing means have been provided with basic fortified works.

The average saturation of the main defensive belt, per kilometer of front, is:

Antitank mines	375
Antipersonnel mines	182
Antitank obstacles	.28 km
Antipersonnel obstacles	1 km
Machine-gun areas	14
Bomb shelters and pillboxes	3.2
Mortar positions	5
Antitank rifle positions	5.5
Artillery dugouts	7.7
Communications trenches	2.2

2. The second defensive belt extends along a front of seventy kilometers and consists of thirty battalion regions. All battalion regions are functioning. On the right flank, a sector twelve kilometers wide is inaccessible to tanks.

The most important and dangerous tank approach is in the Lukhanevo, Iakovlevo sector, through which pass roads leading to the main Belgorod, Oboian' road. Likely dangerous tank axes are covered by antitank obstacles. Population points located within the limits of the defensive belt are adapted to a long defense.

The average saturation of the second defensive belt, per kilometer of front, is:

Antitank mines	25
Antitank obstacles	.15 km
Antipersonnel obstacles	.3 km
Machine-gun areas	4.5
Bomb shelters and pillboxes	1
Mortar positions	14
Antitank rifle positions	5
Artillery dugouts	3
Communications trenches	2.6

3. The army rear defensive belt extends along a front of forty kilometers and consists of twenty-two battalion regions, of which eighteen are functioning. The belt proceeds along the right bank of the Psel River. The 6th Guards Army is carrying out work in the Uslanka, Bogorditskoe sector. Forward of the army rear defensive belt is the intermediate line (the outer Oboian' defensive line) Peschanoe, Ivnia, Kruglik, Shipy, which extends thirty-two kilometers and consists of eleven battalion regions, all of which are functioning.

7TH GUARDS ARMY

1. The main defensive belt extends for fifty kilometers along the left bank of the Northern Donets River and consists of twenty-eight battalion regions. On the right flank, battalion regions are echeloned to the depth of regimental sectors. On the left flank, at the junction with the Southwestern Front, the battalion regions are echeloned to the depth of the divisional belt.

Important axes are Belgorod, Dal'naia Igumenka; Belgorod, Iastrebovo, Nikol'skoe; Belgorod, Razumnoe, Miasoedovo; Murom, Maslovo Pristan', Nuraevo; Murom, Staraia Tavolzhanka, Nevezhino; and Murom, Volchansk, Baikova. Dangerous tank axes are covered by antitank obstacles, mines, and wooden obstructions. All battalion regions are functioning. The available number of force units that occupy the defense and the establishment quantity of weapons are protected by fortifications.

The average saturation of the main defensive belt, per kilometer of front, is:

Antitank mines	170
Antipersonnel mines	280
Antitank obstacles	.1 km
Antipersonnel obstacles	.3 km
Machine-gun areas	12
Bomb shelters and pillboxes	10.5
Mortar positions	10
Antitank rifle positions	12
Artillery dugouts	8.3
Communications trenches	1.6

2. The second defensive belt traverses forested terrain from the right flank to Shchebe-kino and open terrain from Shchebekino to the left flank. The belt extends along a front of fifty-five kilometers and consists of twenty-two battalion regions. All battalion regions are functioning and fortified. Population points within the limits of the belt have been prepared for defense. Important axes are covered by engineer obstacles.

The average saturation of the second defensive belt, per kilometer of front, is:

Antitank mines	11
Antipersonnel obstacles	.33 km
Machine-gun areas	12.5
Bomb shelters and pillboxes	4
Mortar positions	8.3
Antitank rifle positions	8.5
Artillery dugouts	4.5
Communications trenches	.55

69TH ARMY

1. The army rear defensive belt in the sector Boroditskoe (incl.), Nechaeva (incl.), within the sector of the 6th Guards Army, and in the sector Nechaevo, Efremovka, within the sector of the 7th Guards Army, is manned by the 69th Army. The belt extends along a front of 120 kilometers and consists of fifty-eight battalion regions, eight company strong points, and one battalion strong point. The terrain that the defensive belt traverses generally predominates over the approaches to the belt and the terrain lying forward of it. Most of the defensive belt is covered by its own natu-

ral obstacles, ravines, branches of the Northern Donets River, forested masses (individual forest paths, and paths covered with wooden barriers), and, on the left flank, the Nezhegol' River.

The most important approaches are Iakovlevo, Prokhorovska; Petropavlovsk, Sabinino, Prokhorovka; Shliakhovo, Korocha; Repnoe, Bekhteevka; Repnoe, Khoroshchevatoe; Voznesenovka, Popovka; and Staraia Tavolzhka, Terezovka.

The average saturation of the army rear defensive belt, per kilometer of front, is:

Antitank mines	36
Antitank obstacles	.05
Antipersonnel obstacles	.08 km
Machine-gun areas	20
Bomb shelters and pillboxes	2
Mortar positions	3.5
Antitank rifle positions	5
Artillery dugouts	7
Communications trenches	2

THE FIRST *FRONT* REAR DEFENSIVE LINE extends from Vyshniaia Kotova, Marbino, Donetskaia Seimitsa River, Skorodnoe, Korocha River, Korotkoe, Pskovo-Mikhailovka, Bogdanovka, to Pltovianka. The overall extent of the line is 150 kilometers. The construction of sixty-three battalion regions and two company strong points are planned. At Vyshniaia Kotovo, on the right flank, the line joins with the Central Front's front line, which extends farther through Paniki to Gostomlia. On the left flank, at Plotvianka, Borisovka and, farther, to St. Khutor, it links up with the Southwestern Front's front line, which is being erected by the 26th Defensive Construction Directorate.

The line traverses open treeless terrain throughout its entire length, both on our side and the side of the enemy. In the sector from Vyshniaia Kotovo to Skorodnoe, the terrain through which the line extends dominates the territory in front of the forward edge. In the sector along the Korocha River and farther to the left flank, it is otherwise; the terrain on the enemy's side is much higher than that along which the line passes. On average, individual heights on the enemy side exceed our side by five to ten meters.

The most important axes are Marino, Solntsevo; Skorodnoe, St. Oskol; Skorodnoe, Chernianka; Iablonovo, Chernianka; Veliko-Mikhailovka, Nov. Oskol; Sidorovka, Slonovka; Volchansk, Slonovka; and Volchansk, Volokonovka.

Work on constructing this line is being accomplished by the 38th Defensive Construction Directorate. Of the sixty-eight intended battalion regions, sixty have been reconnoitered, eight are being reconnoitered, sixty battalion regions are functioning, and work has been completed on the first and second lines of five battalion regions (three on the right flank at Vyshniaia Kotovo and two at Skorodnoe).

The average saturation of the line (per kilometer of front) with engineer fortification is as follows:

Rifle trenches	6.4
Firing positions for heavy machine guns (areas, nests, etc.)	12
Trenches for antitank rifles	4.3
Trenches for mortars	3.3
Communications trenches	.95

35TH GUARDS RIFLE CORPS

As a part of the first *front* rear defensive belt, on 20 April 1943 the 35th Guards Rifle Corps set about constructing the additional line Krivosheevka, Andreevskii, Plotavets, Zhigailovka, Bogdanovka, Nemtsev, Bubikovo, which extended along an eighty-six-kilometer front and consisted of twenty-six battalion regions.

The terrain in front of the forward edge of the corps' defensive belt had a great quantity of hollows, ravines, and population points, which permit the enemy to conceal the concentration of his forces and position his artillery observation posts not far from the forward edge. A number of heights located in front of the corps' front provide for excellent observation of individual sectors of the defensive line. The most probable axes are Korocha, St. Oskol; and Volchansk, Nov. Oskol. The terrain within the corps' defensive belt commands the terrain of the enemy. The presence of population points and heights located in the forward edge of the defensive lines supports the creation of strong points and centers of resistance.

On 10 May 1943 work has been completed on the lines' first line. Work continues on the second line.

The average density of the defensive line, per kilometer of front, is:

Trenches for rifle squads	10
Heavy machine gun areas	8.2
Trenches for antitank rifles	9
Trenches for artillery	3.4
Trenches for mortars	10.5
Command and observation points	3.8
Communications trenches	.8
Dugouts	13

THE SECOND *FRONT* REAR DEFENSIVE LINE (forty-three battalion regions) extends along the left bank of the Oskol River, and, from Okumi through Chernianka, Nov. Oskol (with its defensive line), and Volokonovka, it is a natural antitank obstacle. Furthermore, with its eighteen battalion regions, the Staryi Oskol defensive line forms a separate sort of defensive line within this line. Of the forty-three battalion regions, eighteen have been reconnoitered, and construction has begun on thirteen along the most important Chernianka, Nov. Oskol, and Volokonovka axes.

The average saturation of the line with erected engineer fortifications per kilometer of front in the sector where construction has begun (Chernianka-Volokonovka) is as follows:

Rifle trenches	3
Firing positions for heavy machine guns	9
Trenches for antitank rifles	2
Trenches for mortars	.4
Communications trenches	.5

The line is being constructed by the 38th Defensive Construction Directorate and the Staryi Oskol defensive line by the 27th Defensive Construction Directorate.

The fortifications at St. Oskol consist of an external defensive line (fourteen battalion regions and one company strong point) and city fortifications (four battalion regions and one company strong point). The external defensive line forms a half-circle with a radius of about fifteen kilometers. Its frontage is forty kilometers. Reconnoitering has been completed on nine battalion regions, three battalion regions are being reconnoitered, and construction has begun on eight battalion regions.

THE FRONT CUTOFF LINE extends along a frontage of sixty kilometers through Gushchino, Iushkovo, Gneloe, and Poserednoe, where the construction of forty-three battalion regions and three company strong points is planned. The 38th Defensive Construction Directorate is constructing the Gushchino, Gniloe sector, and the 27th Defensive Construction Directorate the Gniloe, Alekseevka sector. In the Gushchino, Gniloe sector, reconnoitering has been completed on thirteen of twenty-three battalion regions and one of one company strong points, ten battalion regions are being reconnoitered, and construction has begun on thirteen battalion regions at Gushchino (on the left flank) and at Iuskovo, Myshinka, Volkovo, Orlik, and Okuni.

The average saturation of the line with erected engineer fortifications per kilometer of front in the Gushchino, Gniloe sector is as follows:

Rifle trenches	15
Firing positions for heavy machine guns	15
Trenches for antitank rifles	4
Trenches for mortars	4.2
Communications trenches	.7

The Gniloe, Poserednoe sector (27th Defensive Construction Directorate) has an overall length of sixty-five kilometers. Of the planned twenty-one battalion regions and two company strong points, work has begun on nine battalion regions.

The average saturation of firing positions per kilometer of front in sectors where construction has begun is:

Rifle trenches	3.1
Firing positions for heavy machine guns	4
Trenches for antitank rifles	1
Trenches for mortars	3

DESCRIPTION OF DEFENSIVE POSITIONS. Troops lines are being outfitted with fortified firing positions, the majority of which meet the requirements of BUP-42 [1942 Infantry Combat Regulations], which provide for the creation in front of the forward edge of two to three layers of flanking fire or oblique cross-fire, in addition to frontal fire from the depth. The type of position selected depends on terrain conditions (and the requirements for camouflaging the position) and on the presence of construction materials. On the whole, the following types of positions are being constructed:

1. For machine guns:
   a. Machine-gun areas in accordance with the 1942 Infantry Combat Regulations. The areas are forward of the main trenches or immediately adjacent to the trenches. Open areas often form reserve firing positions for the main pillbox.
   b. Antifragmentary nests [bomb shelters] consist of four rows of eighteen to twenty-centimeter diameter beams, which are felled above ground. They are

covered by two layers [of beams] with a diameter of twenty centimeters and with fifty to sixty centimeters of earthen facing. Thus, they are earthen, fortified by woven brush fencing. The nests have single and double embrasures.

c. The overwhelming majority of pillboxes consist of felled timber, emplaced fully in a trench. Their cover consists of two series of log beams covered with up to sixty centimeters of sprinkled earth. The wooden pillboxes have both single and double embrasures. The internal dimensions of a pillbox is a height of 1.9 meters. The opening of the embrasure is sixty centimeters, and by plan 2.2 by 2.2 meters. In 38th Army the pillboxes are constructed with double partial walls.

2. Trenches for mortars and antitank rifles are being constructed in accordance with the requirements of part 1 of the 1942 Infantry Combat Regulations. See Enclosure 7.

3. The majority of artillery positions consist of open areas with cover for the crews, recesses for shells (for 45mm and 76mm guns), and protection for equipment—for 45mm guns.

4. Communications trenches are open and full-profile. Thought is being given to their subsequent development for use as trenches with foxholes. Communications trenches are being fitted with recesses for ammunition, and drainage ditches, steps, cul-de-sacs, parapet covers, and blindages are being made. Communications trenches (external and internal) are being accommodated for defense.

5. Command-observation points for company and battalion commanders are being prepared in accordance with 1939 Engineer Instructions and have one to two layers of overhead cover. Each command-observation point has been provided with a dugout or a blindage, and the majority of command-observation points of regimental and division commanders have defensive thickness sufficient to protect against 76mm shells and all calibers of mortars.

6. As a rule, dugouts are situated on reverse slopes and are exposed to daylight. They have antifragmentary type overhead cover. . . .

Maskirovka measures such as the creation of a system of false positions and regions, as well as *maskirovka* of the positions themselves, have still not been sufficiently developed.

According to this description, further refinement is required of the defensive system, while improving *maskirovka*, both from the land and from air observation.

Chief of the Section of Fortified Regions of the Voronezh Front staff, Colonel Naumov[8]

Stavka Directive

VGK Directive No. 46196, 9 July 1943.
To the commander of the Steppe Military District.

The *Stavka* of the Supreme High Command orders:

1. Effective 24.00 9 July, the Steppe Military District is redesignated the Steppe Front.

2. The Steppe Front will include the 27th Army with the 4th Guards Tank Corps, the 53d Army with the 1st Mechanized Corps, the 47th Army with the 3d Guards Mechanized Corps, the 4th Guards Army with the 3d Guards Tank Corps, the 52d

Army, the 3d, 5th, and 7th Guards Cavalry Corps, the 5th Air Army, and all reinforcing and rear service units and installations of the Steppe Military District.

3. The *front's* armies will deploy in accordance with verbal orders given by the
General Staff.

4. Complete force movements exclusively at night.

5. From 12 July the Steppe Front command post will be in the Goriainovo
region.

Signed: *Stavka* of the Supreme High Command, I. Stalin Antonov[9]

Vasilevsky Message to the Stavka of the Supreme High Command

14 July 1943. 02.47 hours.
From the 5th Guards Tank Army.

In accordance with your personal order of the evening of 9 July 1943, I have been
continuously located with Rotmistrov's and Zhadov's forces on the Prokhorovka and
southern axes. Inclusively, up to today, the enemy has continued massive tank attacks
and counterattacks against our attacking tank units on Zhadov's and Rotmistrov's
fronts. The liquidation of the penetration of Kriuchenkin's army, which on 11 July
created a serious threat to the rear of the main forces of Rotmistrov's army and a
corps of Zhadov, required the assignment of two of the 5th Mechanized Corps'
mechanized brigades and individual units of Rotmistrov to the Shakhovo, Avdeevka,
and Aleksandrovskaia region. The liquidation of the penetration in Zhadov's army in
the Veselyi, Vasil'evka, and Petrovka regions on 12 July 1943 forced us to dispatch
the remaining units of the 5th Mechanized Corps there. To a considerable extent,
this weakened the strength of Rotmistrov's main blow from Prokhorovka to the
southwest. Based on observation of the course of the ongoing battle and prisoner
reports, I have concluded that, in spite of huge losses both in personnel and especially
in tanks and aircraft, the enemy still has not abandoned his notion of penetrating to
Oboian' and further to Kursk, while achieving that at whatever cost. Yesterday I myself
observed the tank battle southwest of Prokhorovka between our 18th and 29th Tank
Corps and more than 200 counterattacking enemy tanks. Simultaneously, hundreds
of guns and all of our available multiple rocket launchers took part in the battle. As
a result, within an hour, the entire field of battle was littered with burning German
tanks and our tanks.

During the two days of battle, Rotmistrov's 29th Tank Corps irreparably and temporarily lost 60 percent of its tanks, and the 18th Tank Corps up to 30 percent of its
tanks. Losses in the 5th Mechanized Corps are insignificant. The following day the
threat of the penetration of enemy tanks from the south in the Shakhovo, Avdeevka,
and Aleksandrovka region continued to remain serious. During the night I took all
possible measures to transfer there all of the 5th Mechanized Corps, the 32d Motorized Brigade, and four antitank artillery regiments. Considering the large-scale enemy tank forces on the Prokhorovka axis, on 14 July Rotmistrov's main forces, together
with Zhadov's rifle corps, have been assigned the limited mission of destroying the
enemy in Storozhevoe region, north of Storozhevoe, and in the region of Komsomolets
State Farm, reaching the line Griaznoe–Iasnaia Poliana, and, especially, covering the
Prokhorovka axis.

Here the possiblity of a tank meeting engagement tomorrow cannot be excluded. In all, no fewer than eleven panzer divisions, which have been systematically reinforced with tanks, are continuing to operate against the Voronezh Front. Prisoners interrogated today have indicated that the 19th Panzer Division has around 70 serviceable tanks, and division "Reich" up to 100 tanks, although the latter was already replenished twice since 5 July 1943. Report delayed in connection with late arrival from the front.[10]

Sources

1. *Dokumenty sovetskogo komandovaniia v period Velikoi Otechestvennoi voiny (aprel'–mai 1943 g.)* [Documents of the Soviet Command during the Great Patriotic War (April–May 1943) (Podol'sk: Arkhiv Ministerstva oborony SSSR, undated), with notation inv. no. 0110.

2. *TsAMO,* f. 233, op. 2307, d. 3, ll. 29–33, as published in V. Gurkin, "Podgotovka k Kurskoi bitve" [Preparation for the Battle of Kursk], *VIZh* 6 (June 1983); 64–65.

3. *TsAMO,* f. 203, op. 2777, d. 75, ll. 116–121, as published in Gurkin, "Podgotovka," 65–66.

4. *Dokumenty sovetskogo komandovaniia.*

5. Ibid.

6. *TsAMO,* f.3, op. 11556, d. 13, ll. 30–31, as published in Gurkin, "Podgotovka," 67–68.

7. Ibid., ll. 40–42, as published in Gurkin, "Podgotovka," 68.

8. *Dokumenty sovetskogo komandovaniia.*

9. *TsAMO,* f. 3, op. 11556, d. 13, l. 160, as published in Gurkin, "Podgotovka," 71.

10. A. M. Vasilevsky, *Delo vsei zhizni* [A lifelong cause] (Minsk: Belarus, 1984), 309.

Prologue

1. This account is based primarily on Heinz Guderian, *Panzer Leader* (Washington, D.C.: Ballantine, 1979), 241–247; see also Janusz Piekalkiewicz, *Operation "Citadel": Kursk and Orel: The Greatest Tank Battle of the Second World War*, Michaela Nierhaus, trans. (Novato, Ca.: Presidio Press, 1987), 91–93.

2. Erich von Manstein, *Lost Victories*, Anthony C. Powell, ed. and trans. (Chicago: Henry Regnery, 1958), 447–448.

3. Guderian, *Panzer Leader*, 308–309.

1. Barbarossa to Donbas

1. O. F. Suvenirov, "Vsearmeiskaia tragediia" [An Army-Wide Tragedy], *Voenno-istoricheskii zhurnal* [Military-historical journal, hereafter abbreviated as *VIZh*] 3 (March 1989): 42. See also "Attache Assessments of the Impact of the 1930's Purges on the Red Army," *Journal of Soviet Military Studies* (hereafter abbreviated as *JSMS*) 2, 3 (September 1989): 417–436.

2. David M. Glantz, "Soviet Mobilization in Peace and War, 1924–62: A Survey," *JSMS* 5, 3 (September 1992): 345–352. See also A. I. Evseev, "Manevr strategicheskimi rezer-vami v pervom periode Velikoi Otechestvennoi voiny" [Maneuver of strategic reserves during the first period of the Great Patriotic War], *VIZh* 3 (March 1986): 11–13; and V. Golubovich, "Sozdanie strategicheskikh reservov" [The creation of strategic reserves], *VIZh* 4 (April 1977): 12–19. Complete mobilization figures are contained in David M. Glantz, *Stumbling Colossus: The Red Army on the Eve of World War* (Lawrence: University Press of Kansas, 1998), which incorporates formerly classified information from the recently released Soviet study, *Boevoi sostav Sovetskoi armii, chast' 1 (iun'–dekabr' 1941)* [The combat composition of the Soviet Army, part 1 (June–December 1941)] (Moscow: Voroshilov Academy of the General Staff, 1963); hereafter cited as *Boevoi sostav*. According to this volume, between 22 June and 31 December 1941, the Red Army mobilized 285 rifle divisions, 12 re-formed tank divisions, 88 cavalry divisions (most light), 174 rifle brigades, and 93 tank brigades. For accounting purposes, 2 brigades are equivalent to 1 division. During the same period the Red Army lost 147 rifle divisions, 40 tank divisions, 11 mechanized divisions, 10 cavalry divisions, and 21 rifle and tank brigades.

3. O. A. Losik, ed., *Stroitel'stvo i boevoe primenenie sovetskikh tankovykh voisk v gody Velikoi Otechestvennoi voiny* [Formation and combat use of Soviet tank forces in the Great Patriotic War] (Moscow: Voenizdat, 1979). See also Iu. P. Babich and A. G. Baier, *Razvitie vooruzheniia i organizatsii sovetskikh sukhoputnykh voisk v gody Velikoi Otechestvennoi voiny* [Development of the armament and organization of

Soviet ground forces in the Great Patriotic War] (Moscow: Izdanie Akademii, 1990), 42–45. Precise Red Army order of battle is found in *Boevoi sostav, part 2 (January–December 1942)* (Moscow: Voroshilov Academy of the General Staff, 1963).

4. For details on the Khar'kov defeat, see David M. Glantz, *Kharkov 1942: Anatomy of a Military Disaster* (New York: Sarpedon, 1998).

5. See David M. Glantz, *Marshal Zhukov's Greatest Defeat: Operation Mars, November–December, 1942* (Lawrence: University Press of Kansas, 1999).

6. This discussion is based upon David M. Glantz, "Prelude to Kursk: Soviet Strategic Operations, February–March 1943," *JSMS* 8, 1 (March 1995): 1–35. See also A. M. Vasilevsky, *A Lifelong Cause* (Moscow: Progress, 1976), 273–279.

7. For details on these and other operations in the winter campaign, see David M. Glantz, *From the Don to the Dnepr: Soviet Offensive Operations, December 1942 to August 1943* (London: Frank Cass, 1991).

8. Erich von Manstein, *Lost Victories* (Chicago: Henry Regnery, 1958), 436.

9. Earl Ziemke, *Stalingrad to Berlin: The German Defeat in the East* (Washington, D.C.: Office of the Chief of Military History, United States Army, 1968), 120.

10. Walter S. Dunn, Jr. *Kursk: Hitler's Gamble, 1943* (Westport, Ct.: Praeger, 1997), 38–47.

11. Heinz Guderian, *Panzer Leader* (Washington, D.C.: Zerger, 1979), 284–299.

12. Technically, the Waffen SS divisions were not designated as panzer divisions until October 1943, after the Battle of Kursk. See Bryan Perrett, *Knights of the Black Cross: Hitler's Panzerwaffe and Its Leaders* (New York: St. Martin's Press, 1986), 159, 242; and F. W. von Senger under Etterlin, *Die Panzergrenadiere: Geschichte und Gestalte der mechanisierten Infanterie 1930–1960* [Panzergrenadiers: The history and organization of mechanized infantry 1930–1960] (Munich: J. F. Lehmanns, 1961), 88–91.

13. Timothy A. Wray, *Standing Fast: German Defensive Doctrine on the Eastern Front During World War II: Prewar to March 1943* (Ft. Leavenworth, Kans.: Combat Studies Institute, 1986), 113.

14. This discussion of tank design is based upon the following sources: Albert Speer, *Inside the Third Reich,* Richard and Clara Winston, trans. (New York: Macmillan, 1970), 234; Perrett, *Knights of the Black Cross,* 103–106; Guderian, *Panzer Leader,* 276–283; Dunn, *Kursk: Hitler's Gamble,* 88–94; Jonathan M. House, "Waiting for the Panther: Kursk, 1943," in Andrew J. Bacevich and Brian R. Sullivan, eds., *The Limits of Technology in Modern Warfare* (Cambridge: Cambridge University Press, forthcoming); Richard L. DiNardo, *Germany's Panzer Arm* (Westport, Ct.: Greenwood Press, 1997), 11–20. In addition, the authors are indebted to Steven Zaloga for his generous assistance on these technical matters.

15. Steven J. Zaloga and James Grandsen, *Soviet Tanks and Combat Vehicles of World War II* (London: Arms and Armour Press, 1984), 156–166.

16. Denoted in German as Panzer Detachment *(Abteilung)* 505. Henceforth, all German unit designations are rendered in standard U.S. parlance (e.g., 505th Panzer Detachment). Thomas J. Lentz, ed., *Panzertruppen: The Complete Guide to the Creation and Combat Employment of Germany's Tank Force,* vol. II: *1943–45* (Atglen, Pa.: Schiffer Military History, n.d.), 78–82, gives slightly different figures in a unit-by-unit breakdown of German tanks at Kursk.

17. Janusz Piekalkiewicz, *Operation "Citadel": Kursk and Orel: The Greatest Tank Battle of the Second World War,* trans. Michaela Nierhaus (Novato, Ca.: Presidio Press, 1987), 114.

18. Thomas Jentz, *Germany's Panther Tank: The Quest for Combat Supremacy* (Chester, Pa.: Schiffer, 1995). See also DiNardo, *Germany's Panzer Arm,* 17–18; and Dunn, *Kursk: Hitler's Gamble,* 88.

19. Perrett, *Knights of the Black Cross,* 104–105; Guderian, *Panzer Leader,* 299; DiNardo, *Germany's Panzer Arm,* 18.

20. This discussion of German strategy is based primarily on Ziemke, *Stalingrad to Berlin,* 121–132.

21. Piekalkiewicz, *Operation "Citadel,"* 32; Ziemke, *Stalingrad to Berlin,* 121.

22. See annex 2 of Gotthard Heinrici and Friederick Wilhelm Hauck, "Citadel: The Attack on the Russian Kursk Salient," Joseph Welch, trans. Manuscript, U.S. National Archives.

23. Ibid.

24. Ibid., annex 3, with notation OKH, GenStdH, Op.Abt(I), 15.4.43, Nr. 430246/ 43 g. Kdos/Chefs, classified Secret Officers Only!

2. The Red Army in 1943

1. After Zhukov's defeat in Operation Mars, the *Stavka* assigned him to oversee operations in the Leningrad region. From 10 through 24 January, he coordinated Volkhov and Leningrad Front operations at Siniavino just east of Leningrad, which opened a narrow but vulnerable relief corridor to the beleaguered city. Then, between 6 February and 16 March, he coordinated planning for a more ambitious operation well south of the city. The new plan, code-named Operation Polar Star, called for the Northwestern Front's 1st Shock Army, made up primarily of elite airborne divisions and ski brigades, to penetrate German defenses south of Lake Il'men' and to advance via Dno to Pskov deep in the German rear. Then, specially formed Group Zhozin, consisting of General M. E. Katukov's newly formed 1st Tank Army and General F. I. Tolbukhin's 68th Army, would exploit through Luga to the Baltic Sea to cut off and encircle German Eighteenth Army in the Leningrad region. This ambitious operation, designed to encircle the encirclers and raise the Leningrad siege, was timed to coincide with the destruction of German Army Groups Center and South. However, it was canceled by 16 March, ostensibly due to poor weather and terrain conditions in the region, which made large-scale armored operations impossible. In actuality, von Manstein's success forced the *Stavka* to cancel the operation and to redeploy Katukov's tank army southward to Kursk to bolster the sagging Voronezh Front. Tolbukhin's army soon followed Katukov's army southward, as the *Stavka's* focus shifted to the central sector of the Eastern Front. For details, see Zhukov's wartime schedule in S. I. Isaev, "Vekhi frontovogo puti" [Landmarks of a *front* path], *VIZh* 10 (October 1991): 26; and details of the Soviet plan in M. E. Katukov, *Na ostrie glavnogo udara* [At the point of the main attack] (Moscow: Voenizdat, 1976), 193–195.

2. G. K. Zhukov, *Reminiscences and Reflections,* vol. 2 (Moscow: Progress, 1985), 145–148.

3. For more details on the debate, see David M. Glantz, *Soviet Military Intelligence in War* (London: Frank Cass, 1990), 185–198.

4. "Iz direktivy nachal'nika general'nogo shtaba ot 2 aprelia 1943 goda komand-uiushchim voiskami frontov i otdel'nykh armii" [From a 2 April 1943 directive of the chief of the General Staff to the commanders of *fronts* and separate armies], *Dokumenty sovetskogo komandovaniia v period Velikoi Otechestvennoi voiny (aprel'– mai 1943 g.)* [Documents of the Soviet commands during the Great Patriotic War (April–May 1943)] (Podol'sk: Archives of the USSR Ministry of Defense, n.d.), classified top secret. General Staff document no. 11916, archival citation *Tsentral'nyi Arkhiv Ministerstva Oborony SSSR*, f. 3, op. 11556, d. 12, l. 333. Hereafter cited as *TsAMO* with appropriate reference.

5. "Iz direktivy nachal'nika general'nogo shtaba ot 3 aprelia 1943 goda komand-uiushchim voiskami frontov i 7-i otdel'noi armii" [From a 3 April 1943 directive of the chief of the General Staff to the commanders of *fronts* and 7th Separate Army], Gurkin, *Dokumenty i materialy: podgotovka k kurskoi bitve* [Documents and materials: Preparations for the Battle of Kursk], *VIZh* 6 (June 1983): 64, archival document *TsAMO*, f. 3, op. 11556, d. 12, l. 343.

6. "Direktiva general'nogo shtaba ot 10 aprelia 1943 goda komanduiushchim voiskami frontov" [General Staff directive, dated 10 April 1943, to *front* commanders], in Gurkin, *Dokumenty i materialy*, 64, archival citation *TsAMO*, f. 48–A, op. 1691, d. 14, l. 132.

7. Zhukov, *Reminiscences*, 2: 152.

8. "Iz doklada shtaba tsentral'nogo fronta ot 10 aprelia 1943 goda nachal'niku operativnogo upravleniia general'nogo shtaba s otsenkoi protivnika i kharaktera ego vozmozhnykh deistvii" [From a 10 April 1943 report of the Central Front headquarters to the chief of the General Staff's Operational Directorate with an evaluation of the enemy and his possible actions], in Gurkin, *Dokumenty i materialy*, 64–65, archival citation *TsAMO*, f. 233, op. 2307, d. 3, ll. 29–33.

9. "Iz doklada voennogo soveta voronezhskogo fronta nachal'niku general'nogo shtaba ot 12 aprelia 1943 goda s otsenkoi protivnika i kharaktera ego vozmozhnykh deistvii" [From a 12 April 1943 report of the Voronezh Front Military Council to the chief of the General Staff with an evaluation of the enemy and his possible actions], in Gurkin, *Dokumenty i materialy*, 65–66, archival citation *TsAMO*, f. 203, op. 2777, d. 75, ll. 116–121.

10. S. M. Shtemenko, *The Soviet General Staff at War 1941–1945* (Moscow: Progress, 1970), 218–219.

11. Zhukov, *Reminiscences*, 2: 160–161.

12. Shtemenko, *The Soviet General Staff at War*, 221.

13. "Iz direktivy Stavki VGK ot 21 aprelia 1943 goda komanduiushchemy voiskami tsentral'nogo fronta" [From a *Stavka* VGK directive of 21 April 1943 to the commander of the Central Front], in Gurkin, *Dokumenty i materialy*, 66, archival citation *TsAMO*, f. 3, op. 11556, d. 12, ll. 413–414.

14. Formed on 15 April 1943 on the basis of field headquarters of the Reserve Front, the Steppe Military District, headquartered in Voronezh, embraced the territory of Voronezh, Kursk, Tambov, and Rostov *oblasts* (regions). The military district possessed the establishment (TOE) of a wartime *front* and was filled out with *Stavka* reserves. By 1 May it consisted of 24th, 27th, 46th, 47th, 53d, and 66th Armies, 5th Guards Tank Army, 5th Air Army, 1st Guards, 3d Guards, and 4th Guards Tank Corps, and other separate units and formations. See *Boevoi sostav Sovetskoi armii,*

[The combat composition of the Soviet Army], part 3 (1972) (Moscow: Voroshilov Academy of the General Staff, 1963), 121.

15. "Iz direktivy Stavki VGK ot 23 aprelia 1943 goda komanduiushchemy voiskami stepnogo voennogo okruga" [From a *Stavka VGK* directive of 23 April 1943 to the commander of the Steppe Military District], in Gurkin, *Dokumenty i materialy*, 67, archival citation *TsAMO*, f. 3, op. 11556, d. 12, ll. 426–428.

16. Major General V. M. Badanov had led his 24th Tank Corps in a deep exploitation operation to Tatsinskaia during the December 1942 Middle Don operation (Operation Little Saturn). Although his corps was encircled and almost totally destroyed by counterattacking German armor, his effort ruined German plans to employ XXXXVIII Panzer Corps in the relief of encircled German Sixth Army at Stalingrad and helped condemn that army to destruction. Stalin concluded from this operation that Badanov's corps should have operated more closely with other tank corps advancing along the same general axis. Therefore, in the February 1943 Operation Gallop, Stalin assigned Major General M. M. Popov a force of several tank corps, operating as a "mobile group," which was, in essence, a new type of tank army. However, since all of Popov's corps were understrength, his group was destroyed during its raid to Krasnoarmeiskaia. Soviet study of these tank operations and the performance of earlier tank armies of mixed composition led in January 1943 to the formation of new tank armies that would receive their baptism by fire at Kursk.

17. For initial and subsequent changes in tank army organization, see O. A. Losik, ed., *Stroitel'stvo i boevoe primenenie sovetskikh tankovykh voisk v gody Velikoi Otechestvennoi voiny* [The formation and combat use of Soviet tank forces in the Great Patriotic War] (Moscow: Voenizdat, 1979), 59–78 and I. M. Anan'ev, *Tankovye armii v nastuplenii* [Tank armies in the offensive] (Moscow: Voenizdat, 1988).

18. For superb sketches of the careers and personalities of these tank army commanders, see Richard N. Armstrong, *Red Army Tank Commanders: The Armored Guards* (Atglen, Pa.: Schiffer Military/Aviation History, 1994).

19. The 1941 reorganization is discussed in Iu. P. Babich and A. G. Baier, *Razvitie vooruzheniia i organizatsii sovetskikh sukhoputnykh voisk v gody Velikoi Otechest-vennoi voiny* [Development of the armament and organization of Soviet ground forces in the Great Patriotic War] (Moscow: Izdanie akademii, 1990).

20. For this process, see the appropriate monthly Orders of Battle in *Boevoi sostav*, part 3.

21. Steven J. Zaloga and James Grandsen, *Soviet Tanks and Combat Vehicles of World War II* (London: Arms and Armour, 1984); Steven Zaloga and Jim Kinnear, *T-34/76 Medium Tank 1941–1945* (London: Osprey, 1994); Steven Zaloga and Jim Kinnear, *KV-1&2 Heavy Tanks 1941–1945* (London: Osprey, 1995).

22. Whereas a regular tank regiment had thirty-nine tanks. Tank brigades varied from fifty-three to sixty-five tanks.

23. The Soviets fielded their new self-propelled guns in a variety of regimental configurations. The heavy SP artillery regiments contained twelve 152mm SU-152s, the medium regiment sixteen SU-122s and one T-34 tank, the light regiment twenty-one SU-76s or sixteen SU-85s and one T-34, and the older composite regiment seventeen SU-76s and eight SU-122s. The 152mm regiments were normally assigned to armies conducting penetration operations and to selected tank armies. The 76mm

and 85mm self-propelled regiments were assigned to tank corps and the composite regiments to mechanized corps. However, this assignment pattern was not consistent in July 1943.

24. Dunn suggests that the Soviets up-gunned some British tanks to carry 76mm weapons and concentrated most foreign tanks to the less-important separate tank units, while the tank armies were equipped almost exclusively with domestically produced tanks. See Walter S. Dunn, Jr., *Kursk: Hitler's Gamble, 1943* (Westport, Ct.: Praeger, 1997), 91–92, 167.

25. Most of these antitank regiments and brigade were formally named "destroyer antitank artillery" regiments and brigades. A few were termed "destroyer" brigades, and these formed "destroyer" divisions. The antitank brigades were artillery units, while the destroyer divisions were rifle formations.

26. This section is based upon Von Hardesty, *The Red Phoenix: The Rise of Soviet Air Power 1941–1945* (Washington, D.C.: Smithsonian Institution Press, 1982), 121–179. For comparative aircraft data, see Janusz Piekalkiewicz, *Operation "Citadel": Kursk and Orel*, Michaela Nierhaus, trans. (Novato, Ca.: Presidio, 1987), 278–279.

27. K. Yu. Kominkov, "Les chasseurs Lavotchkine a moteur pistons-Lavotchkine, de 5-7." *Le fana de l'aviation* (February 1995): 40–51.

28. Williamson Murray, *Luftwaffe* (Baltimore, Md: Nautical and Aviation, 1985), 144, table 31.

29. Hermann Plocher, *The German Air Force Versus Russia, 1943*, USAF Historical Studies, no. 155 (New York: Arno Press, 1967), 83.

30. For example, see the role of Mekhlis and other Stalin cronies in Dmitri Volkogonov, *Triumf i tragediia: politicheskii portret I. V. Stalina v dvukh knigakh, kniga II, chast' 1* [Triumph and tragedy: A political portrait of I. V. Stalin in 2 books, book II, part 1] (Moscow: Novosti, 1989).

31. See G. Zhukov, *Reminiscences and Reflections*, 2 vols. (Moscow: Progress, 1985), and a number of Western biographies based largely on his memoirs. All contain the same errors and distortions, such as the coverup of his role in Operation Mars and certain of his more negative character traits.

32. See his modest memoirs, A. M. Vasilevsky, *Delo vsei zhizni* [Life's work] (Moscow: Politizdat, 1983); and Geoffrey Jukes, "Aleksander Mikhailovich Vasilevsky," in *Stalin's Generals*, Harold Shukman, ed. (London: Weidenfeld and Nicolson, 1993), 275–285.

33. Based upon his Civil War service, Stalin developed a close association with the then commander of the famed Soviet 1st Cavalry Army, S. I. Budenny, and his subordinates, which matured in the postwar years. This circle, often termed the "cavalry clique," included Budenny, Voroshilov, Timoshenko, Zhukov, and other favorites of Stalin.

34. Among the many biographies of Antonov, see I. I. Gaglov, *General Antonov* (Moscow: Voenizdat, 1978); and Richard Woff, "Alexei Innokentievich Antonov," in *Stalin's Generals*, 11–23.

35. "Vasili Danilovich Sokolovsky," in *Sovetskaia Voennaia entsiklopediia* [Soviet military encyclopedia], vol. 7, (Moscow: Voenizdat, 1970), 436–437. Hereafter abbreviated as *SVE*.

36. For the censoring of Sokolovsky, see M. A. Gareev, "O neudachnykh nastupatel'nykh operatsiiakh sovetskikh voisk v Velikoi Otechestvennoi voine: po neopublikovannym dokumentam *GKO*" [Concerning unsuccessful offensive operations of

Soviet forces in the Great Patriotic War: based on unpublished GKO documents],
Novaia i noveishaia istoriia [New and recent history] 1 (January 1994): 3–27. Gareev
is the first to detail hidden aspects of the failed Belorussian operation of fall and winter
1943–1944.

37. "Markian Mikhailovich Popov," in *SVE*, vol. 6 (1978), 453–454.

38. Petro G. Grigorenko, *Memoirs* (New York: Norton, 1982), 113.

39. See V. S. Golubovich, *Marshal Malinovsky* (Moscow: Voenizdat, 1984); and
John Erickson, "Rodion Yakovlevich Malinovsky," in *Stalin's Generals*, 117–124.

40. Richard Woff, "Rokossovsky," in *Stalin's Generals*, 187.

41. K. Rokossovsky, *A Soldier's Duty* (Moscow: Progress, 1985).

42. Woff, "Rokossovsky," 177.

43. Iu. D. Zakharov, *General armii Vatutin* [Army General Vatutin] (Moscow:
Voenizdat, 1985); and David M. Glantz, "Nikolai Fedorovich Vatutin," in *Stalin's
Generals*, 287–298.

44. The General Staff Academy's 1937 course was truncated as a direct result of
the ongoing purges. Graduating officers replaced key purged commanders and senior
staff officers.

45. W. F. von Mellenthin, *Panzer Battles* (Norman: University of Oklahoma Press,
1968), 295.

46. Unfortunately, Konev's memoirs begin in January 1943 [see I. S. Konev, *Zapiski
komanduiushchego frontom* [Notes of a *front* commander] (Moscow: Voenizdat,
1981). See also P. M. Portugal'sky, *Marshal I. S. Konev* (Moscow: Voenizdat, 1985).
Both these works and others ignore Konev's role in Operation Mars and provide scant
information on Konev's activities in 1941 and 1942.

47. See Oleg Rzheshevsky, "Konev," in *Stalin's Generals*, 91–107, for these positive
and negative comments on Konev's personality. Rzheshevsky is the first to surface
Konev's problems during the purges.

48. Grigorenko, *Memoirs*, 112–113.

3. Preparations

1. For details on German abandonment of the Rzhev-Viaz'ma salient, see Earl F.
Ziemke, *Stalingrad to Berlin: The German Defeat in the East* (Washington, D.C.:
Office of the Chief of Military History, United States Army, 1968), 116–117. Details
of the fierce fighting around the salient in November and December 1942 are in David
M. Glantz, *Operation Mars: Marshal Zhukov's Greatest Defeat* (Lawrence: University
Press of Kansas, 1999).

2. The 8th Panzer Division was in OKH reserve. The combined strength of 5th
and 8th Panzer totaled just over 200 tanks. Second Panzer Army's changing order of
battle in July is found in "Sommerschlacht um den Orelbogen vom 5. Juli–12 Aug
1943, in *Pz A. O. K. 2., Ia 1375/4*, in National Archives Microfilm (hereafter NAM)
T-313, roll 171.

3. Albert Seaton, *The Russo-German War, 1941–1945* (New York: Praeger, 1971),
360n.

4. For Ninth Army's order of battle, see "Lagenkarten. Anlage zu KTB Nr. 8,"
AOK 9.Ia. AOK 9.35939/7, 26 Mar–18 Aug 1943, in NAM T-312, roll 320. Ninth

Army participation in the Battle of Kursk is particularly difficult to reconstruct because the Red Army captured Ninth Army's records for this period. Although the author has seen the appropriate *Tagebuchen*, the Russians have not yet returned them to the German archives.

5. For the roles performed by these commanders in the Rzhev battles (Operation Mars), see Horst Grossman, "Rzhev: Cornerstone of the Eastern Front," unpublished translation by Joseph G. Welsh.

6. For Second Army's order of battle, see "K.T.B. Feindlagenkarten (1:300,000) vom 1.7 1943 bis 30.9.1943," *AOK 2, Ic/AO*, in NAM T-312, roll 1253, and other Second Army Ia documents in the same series.

7. "Chefkarten, 23 Anlagen, Anlagenband 36 zum KTB Pz AOK 2, Ia.," *Pz AOK 2*, 37075/49 1 Jun–13 Aug 1943, in NAM T-313, roll 171, and other Ia documents in the same series. See accurate Soviet commentary on this and other German orders of battle in P. P. Vechnyi, et al., eds., *Sbornik materialov po izucheniiu opyta voiny, no. 11 mart–aprel' 1944 g.* [Collection of materials for the study of war experience, no. 11, March–April 1944] (Moscow: Voenizdat, 1944), 39–42. Classified secret, this study prepared by the Red Army General Staff's Directorate for the Use of War Experience covers all aspects of the Battle of Kursk. Hereafter cited as *Sbornik*, no. 11.

8. Fourth Panzer Army's order of battle is found in many documents, including "Lagenkarte 4. Pz Armee, Stand 2–4.7.43 2200," *PzAOK 4, Ia*, in NAM T-313, roll 369. English sources that cover German order of battle and strengths include Seaton, *The Russo-German War;* Bryan Perrett, *Knights of the Black Cross: Hitler's Panzerwaffe and its Leaders* (New York: St. Martin's Press, 1986); and Mark Healy, *Kursk 1943: The Tide Turns in the East* (London: Osprey, 1992).

9. For details on II SS Panzer Corps' strength and role in the battle, see the archival documents cited in Appendix D and the superb study by Silvester Stadler, *Die Offensive gegen Kursk 1943: II. SS-Panzerkorps als Stosskeil im Grosskampf* (Osnabruck: Munin Verlag GmbH, 1980), which contains direct reproductions of the daily reports, operational maps, and combat strengths of II SS Panzer Corps and its subordinate divisions. It also contains periodic data on Soviet losses. The names of the three SS panzer grenadier divisions are variously abbreviated as *LAH* or *AH, DR*, and *T*, respectively. *Grossdeutschland* also had a company of 15 Tiger tanks. II SS Panzer Corps reports in Stadler, *Die offensive gegen Kursk*, 34, places the corps' operational strength on 4 July at 356 tanks and 95 assault guns, while Heinrici states the corps had 352 tanks and 91 assault guns on 5 July; see Gotthard Heinrici and Friedrich Wilhelm Hauck, *Citadel: The Attack on the Russian Kursk Salient*, trans. Joseph Welch, U.S. National Archives, note 92. See Appendix D for archival reports of divisional strengths.

10. For Army Detachment Kempf organization, see "Tagliche Lagenkarten vom 1.7.43– 31.12.43," *Kriegstagebuch No. 2, AOK 8, Ia*, AOK 8, 44701/14, in NAM T-312, roll 56, and other AOK 8 reports in the T-312 series. An excellent and accurate survey of German armored organization and strength is found in Healy, *Kursk*, 22. Heinrici and Hauck, *Citadel*, note 92, credits Army Detachment Kempf with 311 tanks (48 Tigers) and 150 assault guns on 5 July, of which 281 tanks (40 Tigers) were operational. Thomas L. Jentz's exhaustive study, *Panzertruppen* (Atglen, Pa.: Schiffer

Military History, 1996), places Detachment strength at 344 tanks (45 Tigers) and 75 assault guns, but these are on-hand rather than operational figures.

11. This strength figure also excludes the eighty assault guns of Group Kempf's XXXXII Army Corps, which did not participate directly in the battle. See Appendix D for full details of German armored strength.

12. Hermann Plocher, *The German Air Force Versus Russia, 1943* (New York: Arno Press, 1967), 78, 81.

13. Ibid., 78, 83.

14. Janusz Piekalkiewicz, *Operation "Citadel": Kursk and Orel: The Greatest Tank Battle of the Second World War*, Michaela Nierhaus, trans. (Novato, Ca.: Presidio Press, 1987), 18–19.

15. Plocher, *The German Air Force Versus Russia*, 75–77.

16. German decisionmaking prior to the Battle of Kursk is thoroughly covered in Ziemke, *Stalingrad to Berlin*, 130–133, and in Heinrici and Hauck, *Citadel*.

17. For these global strategic considerations, see Heinrici, "Citadel," 1–20.

18. While most German memoir writers claim to have voiced their reservations about the attack to Hitler, it is difficult to ascertain how much of this criticism was retrospective in nature. Certainly much of it was.

19. Data on the Soviet buildup and order of battle on 1 July and 1 August is found in *Sbornik*, no. 11, 10–19, and *Boevoi sostav Sovetskoi armii, chest' 3 (ianvar–dekabr' 1943 goda)* [Combat composition of the Soviet Army, part 3 (January–December 1943)] Moscow: Voenizdat, 1972), 155–210. Classified secret, this survey of order of battle was prepared by the Military-Scientific Directorate of the Soviet General Staff. Hereafter cited as *Boevoi sostav* with appropriate page. The names of all commanders of Soviet corps, divisions, and tank brigades are found in the companion document, entitled *Komandovanie korpusnogo i divizionnogo zvena Sovetskikh Vooruzhennykh sil perioda VOV 1941–1945* [Commanders at the corps and divisional level of the Soviet Armed Forces in the Great Patriotic War, 1941–1945] (Moscow: Frunze Academy, 1964). Also classified secret.

20. G. Koltunov, "Kurskaia bitva v tsifrak (period oborony)." [The Battle of Kursk in numbers (the period of the defense)], *Voenno-istoricheskii zhurnal* [Military-historical journal] 6 (June 1968); 62. Hereafter cited as *VIZh* with appropriate article and date.

21. For details on Bagramian's career, see I. Kh. Bagramian, *Tak shli my k pobede* [As we went on to victory] (Moscow: Voenizdat, 1988). Details on 11th Guards Army's order of battle and participation in the Battle of Kursk are found in P. P. Vechnyi, ed., "Proryv oborony na flange orlovskoi gruppirovki nemtsev" [Penetration of the defense on the flank of the German Orel grouping], in *Sbornik materialov po izucheniiu opyta voiny, no. 10, ianvar–fevral' 1944 g.* [Collection of materials for the study of war experience, no. 10, January–February 1944 (Moscow: Voenizdat, 1944), 3–45. Prepared by the Red Army General Staff Directorate for the use of war experience and classifed secret. Hereafter abbreviated as *Sbornik* with appropriate volume.

22. According to G. Koltunov, "Kurskaia bitva v tsifrakh (Period kontrnastupleniia)" [The Battle of Kursk in figures (The period of the counteroffensive)], *VIZh* 7 (July 1968); 80, Bagramian's army and 50th Army totaled 211,458 men, with 188,043 of

these in combat forces. *Sbornik*, no. 10, p. 8, states that 11th Guards Army concentrated nearly 60,000 men in its penetration sector.

23. For details on 50th Army's organization, strength, and role in the operation, see F. D. Pankov, *Ognennye rubezhi* [Firing lines] (Moscow: Voenizdat, 1984), 140–169. Details of Boldin's career are found in I. V. Boldin, *Stranitsy zhizni* [Life's pages], (Moscow: Voenizdat, 1961).

24. For details on 3d Army's history and Gorbatov's wartime career, see A. V. Gorbatov, *Gody i voiny* [Years and wars] (Moscow: Voenizdat, 1980). Briansk Front's role in the operation is covered in L. Sandalov, "Brianskii front v Orlovskoi operatsii" [The Briansk Front in the Orel operation], *VIZh*, 8 (August 1963); 62–72. Sandalov was the *front* chief of staff.

25. See V. A. Beliavsky, *Strely skrestilis' na Shpree* [Arrows crisscrossed along the Spree] (Moscow: Voenizdat, 1973), 76–113, for 63d Army's role in the operation. Kolpakchi's biography is found in *Sovetslcaia voennaia entsiklopediia* [Soviet military encyclopedia] vol. 4 (Moscow: Voenizdat, 1977), 244–245. Hereafter cited as *SVE* with appropriate volume and page.

26. For details on 61st Army's combat path, see "Shest'desiat pervaia armiia" [61st Army], in *SVE*, vol. 8 (1980), 512–513, and in Sandalov, "Brianskii front."

27. See the memoirs, P. A. Belov, *Za nami Moskva* [Behind us Moscow] (Moscow: Voenizdat, 1963). For details on his deep raid, see David M. Glantz, *A History of Soviet Airborne Forces* (London: Frank Cass, 1994), 104–228.

28. Koltunov, "Kurskaia bitva, kontrnastuplenIia," 80. Of the over 400,000 troops, 298,068 were in combat forces.

29. For details of 13th Army's organization, strength, and role in the operation, see M. A. Kozlov, ed., *V plameni srazhenii: boevoi put' 13-i armii* [In the flame of battle: the combat path of 13th Army] (Moscow: Voenizdat, 1973), 89–128; *Sbornik*, no. 11; and the classified study, V. T. Iminov, *Organizatsiia i vedenie oborony v bitve pod Kurskom na primere 13-i armii tsentral'nogo fronta (iiul' 1943 g.)* [The organization and conduct of the defense in the Battle of Kursk based on the example of Central Front's 13th Army (July 1943)] (Moscow: Voroshilov General Staff Academy, 1979).

30. For details on Pukhov's career, see *SVE*, vol. 6 (1978), 640–641.

31. See "Semidesiataia armiia " [70th Army], *SVE*, vol. 7 (1979), 317–318.

32. Galanin's biography is in *SVE*, vol. 2 (1976), 464.

33. See "Sorok vos'maia armiia" [48th Army], *SVE*, vol. 7 (1979), 447–448.

34. Data on Romanenko's career is in *SVE*, vol. 7 (1979), 141; and I. Grebov, "General-polkovnik P. I. Romanenko" [Colonel General P. I. Romanenko], *VIZH*, no. 3 (March 1977); 125–126.

35. *Boevoi sostav*, part 3, 162.

36. According to *Sbornik*, no. 11, the armored strength of Central Front was 1,150 tanks and self-propelled guns. G. Koltunov and B. G. Solov'ev, *Kurskaia bitva* [The Battle of Kursk] (Moscow: Voenizdat, 1970), cite Central Front armored strength at 1,607, including 91 self-propelled guns. The former probably counts only serviceable weapons.

37. See biographical summary in *SVE*, vol. 7 (1979), 137–138.

38. Details on the order of battle and the roles of 38th and 40th Armies in the Kursk operation are also found in I. Ia. Vyrodov, ed., *V srazheniiakh za pobedu: boevoi*

put' 38-i armii v gody Velikoi Otechestvennoi voiny 1941–1945 g. [In battles for victory: the combat path of 38th Army in the Great Patriotic War 1941–1945] (Moscow: "Nauka," 1974); and K. S. Moskalenko, *Na iugo-zapadnom napravlenii 1943–1945.* [On the Southwestern Direction, 1943–1945] (Moscow: "Nauka," 1972), 12–80.

39. For additional details on the strength and composition of 6th and 7th Guards Armies, see *Boevoi sostav*, 163; and Koltunov and Solov'ev, *Kurskaia bitva*, 61–62. Antitank artillery units were also termed "tank destroyer."

40. For details on Chistiakov's career, see I. M. Chistiakov, *Sluzhim otchizne* [We serve the Fatherland] (Moscow: Voenizdat, 1975).

41. Shumilov's biography is in *SVE*, vol. 8 (1980), 545–546. 7th Guards Army's record is found in D. A. Dragunsky, ed., *Ot Volgi do Pragi* [From the Volga to Prague] (Moscow: Voenizdat, 1966).

42. See *SVE*, vol. 5 (1978), 408–409.

43. See *SVE*, vol. 4 (1979), 498.

44. See Katukov's excellent memoirs, M. E. Katukov, *Na ostrie glavnogo udara* [At the point of the main attack] (Moscow: Voenizdat, 1976).

45. Koltunov and Solov'ev, *Kurskaia bitva*, 62–63. Only a portion of these forces would be committed in the defensive phase of the Battle of Kursk.

46. Ibid., 63.

47. *Boevoi sostav*, 169.

48. *Sbornik*, no. 11, p. 21.

49. Koltunov and Solov'ev, *Kurskaia bitva*, 63.

50. *Sbornik*, no. 11, p. 27.

51. Ibid., 28.

52. Ibid. For details on engineer forces and engineer defensive measures at Kursk, see S. Kh. Aganov, *Inzhenernye voiska Sovetskoi armii 1918–1945* [Engineer forces of the Soviet Army 1918–1945] (Moscow: Voenizdat, 1985), 318–375; and A. D. Tsirlin, ed., *Inzhenernye voiska v boiakh za sovetskuiu rodinu* [Engineer forces in battles for the Soviet fatherland] (Moscow: Voenizdat, 1970), 153–176.

53. *Sbornik*, no. 11, p. 27. For details on the strength, composition, and employment of antitank forces at Kursk, see A. N. Iachinsky, *Boevoe ispol'zovanie istrebitel'no-protivotankovoi artillerii RVGK v Velikoi Otechestvennoi voine* [The combat employment of antitank artillery of the Reserve of the High Command in the Great Patriotic War] (Moscow: Voroshilov General Staff Academy, 1951). This academy dissertation is classified secret.

54. See L. Kozlov, "Sovershenstvovanie protivotankovoi oborony strelkovykh soedinenii" [Perfection of the antitank defense of rifle formations], *VIZh* 3 (March 1971); 32. For other sources, see David M. Glantz, "Soviet Defensive Tactics at Kursk, July 1943," CSI Report no. 11 (Fort Leavenworth, Kans.: Combat Studies Institute, 1986).

55. Glantz, "Soviet Defensive Tactics," 20–21.

56. For details on 52d Guards Rifle Division's defense, see V. A. Vostrov, ed., *Tematicheskii sbornik boevykh primerov iz opyta Velikoi Otechestvennoi voiny i lokal'nykh voin (polk-armiia)* [A thematic collection of combat examples from the experience of the Great Patriotic War and local wars (regiment-army)] (Moscow: Voenizdat, 1989), 54–55; A. I. Radzievsky, ed., *Taktika v boevykh primerov: polk* [Tactics by combat example: regiment] (Moscow: Voenizdat, 1974), 231–232; K. S.

Kolganov, ed., *Razvitie taktiki Sovetskoi armii v gody Velikoi Otechestvennoi voiny (1941–1945 gg.)* [The development of Soviet Army tactics during the Great Patriotic War (1941–1945)] (Moscow: Voenizdat, 1958), 281–282, 294–295, 353, 374; and A. I. Radzievsky, *Taktika v boevykh primerov (diviziia)* [Tactics by combat example (division)] (Moscow: Voenizdat, 1976), 184–185, 215–216, 228, 235–236. The map reconstructs the details of 52d Guards Rifle Division defenses on a current Russian 1:50,000 scale map, which has been corrected to match 1943 specifications.

57. For the organization and employment of the 1008th Antitank Artillery Regiment, see R. B. Braginsky, N. S. Popel'nitsky, and M. G. Usenkov, *Taktika artillerii v boevykh primerakh (podrazdeleniia i chasti)* [Artillery tactics by combat example (subunit and unit)] (Moscow: Voenizdat, 1977), 228–231.

58. See *Oborona v gody Velikoi Otechestvennoi voiny: sbornik boevykh primerov* [Defense in the Great Patriotic War: A collection of combat examples] (Moscow: Frunze Academy, 1989), 64–80; Vostrov, *Tematicheskii sbornik*, 22–23, 56–58; Kolganov, *Razvitie taktiki*, 281–282, 294–295, 374–375.

59. Vostrov, *Tematicheskii sbornik*, 56.

60. Details on the elaborate Soviet deception plan are found in David M. Glantz, *Soviet Military Deception in the Second World War* (London: Frank Cass, 1989), 149–153.

61. For details on the operations, successes, and failures of Soviet intelligence organs at Kursk, see David M. Glantz, *Soviet Military Intelligence in War* (London: Frank Cass, 1990), 172–283.

62. Glantz, *Soviet Deception*, 146–181.

63. See, for example, German intelligence appreciations on the eve of Kursk, including Fremde Heere Ost (Ic), *Ubersicht uber Streitkrafte, Fronten, Armeen und Korps der Roten Armee*, Gleiderung am 4.4.43, 14.4.43, 24.4.43, 4.5.43, 14.5.43, 24.5.43, 3.6.43, 13.6.43, 23.6.43, 3.7.43, 13.7.43, in NAM T-78, roll 588. The intelligence maps of Fourth Panzer Army and Army Detachment Kempf accord with Fremde Heere Ost assessments.

64. *Sbornik*, no. 11, pp. 33–35.

65. Details on Soviet intelligence collection and the role of agents in these activities is thoroughly covered in Glantz, *Soviet Military Intelligence*, 172–283; and David M. Glantz, "Soviet Operational Intelligence in the Kursk Operation, July 1943," *Intelligence and National Security* 5, 1 (January 1990); 5–49. See also F. H. Hinsley et al., *British Intelligence in the Second World War: Its Influence on Strategy and Operations*, vol. 2 (New York: Cambridge University Press, 1981), 620–627. However, such intelligence sharing declined during 1943.

66. Details of these warnings and alerts are found in Glantz, *Soviet Military Intelligence*, 192–198.

67. G. K. Zhukov, *Reminiscences and Reflections*, vol. 2, (Moscow: Progress, 1985), 166–169.

68. Piekalkiewicz, Operation "Citadel," 94, 100.

69. Ibid., 115; and Glantz, *Soviet Military Intelligence*, 201–243.

4. Frontal Assault

1. Terrain descriptions in this and other chapters are based on written accounts in P. P. Vechnyi et al., eds., *Sbornik materialov po izucheniiu opyta voiny* [Collection

of materials for the study of war experience], no. 11, March–April 1944 (Moscow: Voenizdat, 1944), German operational and tactical maps found in the appropriate records of German Second Panzer, Ninth, and Fourth Panzer Armies and Army Detachment Kempf, and study of Soviet 1:50,000 scale maps in the General Staff series M-37. Prepared and updated in 1988 on the basis of 1955 surveys, these newly released Russian maps were published by VTU Gsh (Military Topographical Directorate of the General Staff) from originals prepared by the GUGK SSSR (Main Directorate of Geographical Maps of the USSR). These 1:50,000 maps also provide the base for maps prepared for this volume and for an atlas and guidebook on the Battle of Kursk that is being prepared for separate publication.

2. *Geschichte der 3. Panzer-Division: Berlin-Brandenburg 1935–1945* (Berlin: Verlag der Buchhandlung Gunter Richter, 1967), 372–373, and Paul Carell, *Hitler's War on Russia 1941–1943*, Ewald Osers, trans., vol. 2 (London: George G. Harrap, 1970), 29–32. Helmut Spaeter, *The History of the Panzercorps Grossdeutschland*, vol. 2 (Winnipeg, Canada: J. J. Fedorowicz, 1995), 114–115, wrote:

> At about 15.00 [1700 Moscow time] on 4 July 1943, with III Battalion, Panzer-Grenadier Regiment, led by 11th Company, on the right and III Battalion Panzer-Fusilier Regiment farther to the left, launched a surprise attack in driving rain. The attack had a limited objective, namely the line of hills. However, with its excellent observation sites on the hills the Soviet artillery quickly saw through the plan and inflicted the first painful losses. . . .
>
> In the course of the briefings all of the commanders had been warned of the possibility of mines. We were soon proved correct. The damned things were everywhere. . . . The bad news poured in. Everyone moved through the terrain with extreme caution. What had happened to our planned tempo? I had serious doubts that we would be able to make it at all by dawn of the day of the attack. . . .
>
> The attack on the afternoon of 4 July 1943, which was led off by a Stuka attack at 14.50 [1650 Moscow time], proved to be a difficult affair, contrary to expectations. Resistance and other obstacles were stronger than expected. Losses mounted, but by 16.00 the right section of the lines of hills due west of Butovo was taken. . . . At precisely 16.45 the new positions were firmly in German hands and the view to the north was clear. Farther left, with III Battalion, Panzer-Fusilier Regiment GD, things did not go quite so well. The battalion commander, Hermann Bolk, lost a leg to a mine and had to be evacuated to the rear. There too the troops moved toward the slope in driving rain, however, it was hours before it was reached. Very well-aimed enemy artillery and mortar fire repeatedly forced the attackers to halt and start again. The hill due southeast of Gerzovka was finally taken after darkness fell and the position nearest the Russian forward outposts was occupied. The attack's objective was finally reached, but at the cost of very painful losses.

3. *Po prikazu rodiny: boevoi put' 6-i gvardeiskoi armii v Velikoi Otechestvennoi voiny 1941–1945 gg.* [By order of the fatherland: The combat path of 6th Guards Army in the Great Patriotic War 1941–1945] (Moscow: Voenizdat, 1971), 83–84; and V. F. Egorov et al., *Rozhdennaia v boiakh: boevoi put' 71-i gvardeiskoi strelkovoi vitebskoi ordena Lenina, krasnoznamennoi divizii* [Born in battles: The combat path of the 71st Guards Vitebsk Order of Lenin, Red Banner Rifle Division] (Moscow: Voenizdat, 1986), 103–106.

4. G. A. Koltunov and B. G. Solov'ev, *Kurskaia bitva* [The Battle of Kursk] (Moscow: Voenizdat, 1970), 136.

5. Carell, *Scorched Earth*, 32.

6. More details are found in Silvester Stadler, *Die Offensive gegen Kursk 1943: II SS-Panzerkorps als Stosskeil im Grosskampf* (Osnabrueck: Munin Verlag GmbH,

1980), 34–36. This invaluable volume contains the daily reports of II SS Panzer Corps and its subordinate divisions throughout the Kursk operation and the daily situation maps of II SS Panzer Corps. These maps have been compared with and verified by the daily operational and intelligence maps of Fourth Panzer Army (series NAM T-313) and Army Detachment Kempf (series NAM T-12).

7. For further details on Soviet intelligence collection and assessments on the eve of the battle, see *Sbornik*, no. 11, pp. 43–46; and David M. Glantz, *Soviet Military Intelligence in War* (London: Frank Cass, 1989), 185–199, 231–235, 243–244.

8. Details on the distribution and employment of Soviet artillery, including a detailed assessment of the strength and effectiveness of the counterpreparation, are found in *Sbornik*, no. 11, pp. 109–132. See appendixes for details concerning the allocation of artillery to Central and Voronezh Fronts and their component armies.

9. Janusz Piekalkiewicz, *Operation "Citadel"; Kursk and Orel*, Michaela Nierhaus, trans. (Novato, Ca.: Presidio Press, 1987), 137–138. Other German sources disagree with Soviet sources regarding the importance of the counter-preparation. For example, citing German divisional reports, Gotthard Heinrici and Friedrich Wilhelm Hauck, in *Citadel, The Attack on the Russian Kursk Salient*, Jospeh Welch, trans., U.S. National Archives, note 72, terms the counter-preparation as "harassment fire, without causing serious casualties." He adds, "It appears that the effect of the fire was overrated." On the other hand, Paul Carell, in *Scorched Earth: Hitler's War on Russia 1941–1943*, Ewald Osers, trans., vol. 2 (London: Harrap, 1970), 34, states, "At 0100 hours, all of a sudden, an infernal roar came from the Soviet side. Artillery of all calibres, heavy mortars, multiple rocket launchers, and other heavy weapons were hurling their shells and rockets at the German assembly positions, their rearward lines, and their approach roads. . . . The Russian bombardment lasted for over an hour and caused heavy losses." Carell, however, does not define what he means by heavy losses. Examination of German sources does not indicate any significant German armor losses from the Soviet artillery fire.

10. For a thorough, English-language account of Soviet employment of air power at Kursk, see Von Hardesty, *Red Phoenix: The Rise of Soviet Air Power 1941–1945* (Washington, D.C.: Smithsonian Institution Press, 1982), 149–179. For the German view, see Hermann Plocher, *The German Air Force Versus Russia, 1943* (New York: Arno Press, 1967), 83–84. The official authoritative Soviet account is found in *Sbornik*, no. 11, pp. 160–189. According to this source, the Soviets concentrated 80 percent of their entire air fleet on the Eastern Front for use at Kursk (p. 160). The Soviet assaults on German air bases were conducted at 0430 hours on 5 July by 417 aircraft from 2d and 17th Air Armies. Each of five German bases was struck by a group of from eighteen to twenty-four assault aircraft with accompanying fighter cover. According to this source (p. 168), "In spite of the well-organized actions against enemy airdromes, the strikes did not produce expected results because, at the time of the attacks, the main mass of enemy aircraft had already taken off for operations against our defending force. As a result of the actions up to sixty German aircraft were destroyed or damaged." See appendixes for aircraft engagements, sorties, and losses throughout the operation.

11. *Sbornik*, no. 11, p. 175 states:

Aviation began active combat operations at 0425 5 July; at that time enemy aviation carried out their first raid against our artillery firing positions, centers of resistance, and infantry and tank combat formations in the Maloarkhangel'sk Station region. More than 150 bombers under cover of 50 to 60 fighters took part in the raid, the greater part of which, when the attack began, subdivided into groups of 4 to 6 aircraft, flew forward 10 to 15 kilometers, and created screens to intercept our aircraft approaching the battlefield. Subsequently, every 10 to 15 minutes, after the enemy bombers left the battlefield, a new group of aircraft approached and subjected our forces in the first line of defense to attack. During the period from 0425 through 1100 hours alone, our forces registered up to 1,000 enemy aircraft sorties, of which around 800 were carried out by bombers.

Aircraft of the Soviet 6th Fighter Aviation Corps and 2d Guards Fighter Aviation Division (2d Air Army) responded, but rather than planned, their actions were "episodic." In essence, the intense German air attacks disrupted the Soviet aviation support plan, Soviet fighters concentrated on engaging the enemy aircraft. Later in the day, the 2d and 17th Air Armies began operating according to plan.

12. *Sbornik*, no. 11, p. 73. For details of 13th Army's defense throughout the operation, see M. A. Kozlov, ed., *V plameni srazhenii: Boevoi put' 13-i armii* [In the flame of battle: The combat path of 13th Army] (Moscow: Voenizdat, 1973), 89–127; and the formerly classified study, V. T. Iminov, *Organizatsiia i vedenie oborony v bitve pod Kurskom na primer 13-i armii tsentral'nogo fronta (iiul' 1943 g.)* [The organization and conduct of the defense in the Battle of Kursk based on the example of Central Front's 13th Army (July 1943)] (Moscow: Voroshilov General Staff Academy, 1979), 26–43. See also the generally accurate and detailed open-source account, Koltunov and Solov'ev, *Kurskaia bitva*, 101–134.

13. *Sbornik*, no. 11, p. 73. For a detailed account of the 8th Rifle Division's participation in the battle, see Kolganov, *Razvitie taktiki*, 45, 62, 281, 381; and Sbornik boevykh primerov iz opyta Velikoi Otechestvennoi voiny [Collection of combat examples from the experience of the Great Patriotic War] (Moscow: Voenizdat, 1982), 130–134, prepared by the Main Staff of the Ground Forces, Ministry of Defense of the USSR.

14. Carell, *Scorched Earth*, 36–37; and *Sbornik*, no. 11, p. 74.

15. Koltunov and Solov'ev, *Kurskaia bitva*, 107.

16. Details on the defensive struggle of the 15th Rifle Division are found in Kozlov, *V plameni*, 102–104; and A. Bazhanov, "Razvitie taktiki oboronitel'nogo boia po opytu kurskoi bitvy" [The development of defensive combat tactics based on the experience of the Battle of Kursk], *Voenno-istoricheskii zhurnal* [Military-historical journal; hereafter cited as *VIZh*] 6 (June 1983); 34–42. See also Mark Healy, *Kursk 1943* (London: Osprey, 1993), 35–36, for a summary of the German attack.

17. *Sbornik*, no. 11, pp. 73–74; and Carell, *Scorched Earth*, 38–42.

18. *Sbornik*, no. 11, p. 75; and "Manevr podvizhnymi protivotankovymi rezervami v oboronitel'noi operatsii" [The maneuver of mobile antitank reserves in defensive operations] *Sbornik*, no. 10 [January–February 1944] (Moscow: Voenizdat, 1944), 112–125. This formerly classified source details antitank operations at Kursk.

19. A. Bazhenov, "Razvitiia taktiki," 42.

20. *Sbornik*, no. 11, pp. 174–175.

21. Ibid., 175.

22. Carell, *Scorched Earth*, 41.

23. *Sbornik*, no. 11, pp. 176–177; and Piekalkiewicz, *Operation "Citadel,"* 139–142.

24. *Sbornik*, no. 11, pp. 75–76. General Rokossovsky's order to Rodin read, "Advance into action quickly. Move forward in groups of companies and battalions. The 19th Tank Corps will be under your operational subordination." See Koltunov and Solov'ev, *Kurskaia bitva*, 115–116, for further details of the deployment of 2d Tank Army.

25. For details on the commitment of the 16th Tank Corps and the battles of the 107th and 164th Tank Brigades, see *Sbornik*, no. 11, pp. 76–77, 136; and A. Vitruk, "Bronia protiv broni" [Armor versus armor], *VIZh* 6 (June 1983); 72–79. According to these sources, the two tank brigades destroyed thirty German tanks, including four Tigers.

26. For details on the 2d Tank Army's role in the battle, see F. I. Vysotsky et al., *Gvardeiskaia tankovaia* [Guards Tank] (Moscow: Voenizdat, 1963), 29–54.

27. In its defense forward of Ponyri, the 81st Rifle Division lost 2,518 of its original 8,000 men. In the process, it claimed to have destroyed or disabled seventy German tanks and assault guns. See Kozlov, *V plameni*, 110–112. For details on the 307th Rifle Division's subsequent fight around Ponyri, see M. A. Enshin, "Na oborone Ponyrei" [In the defense of Ponyri], in *Kurskaia bitva* [The Battle of Kursk] (Moscow: Voenizdat, 1970), 141–148. An English-language account of this and other examples of Soviet tactical defense at Kursk is found in David M. Glantz, "Soviet Defensive Tactics at Kursk, July 1943," CSI Report no. 11 (Fort Leavenworth, Kans.: Combat Studies Institute, 1986).

28. *Sbornik*, no. 11, p. 176.

29. The most vivid and accurate account of the XXXXVIII Panzer Corps' assault is found in Carell, *Scorched Earth*, 51–56. With the notable exception of German armored strength, Carell's data and blow-by-blow combat accounts closely match the information in formerly classified Soviet archival materials. According to Carell, the Germans committed 1,300 tanks and assault guns against the Voronezh Front. Heinrici, in *Citadel*, records 443 tanks and assault guns in the II SS Panzer Corps, 311 in the III Panzer Corps, and almost 600 in the XXXXVIII Panzer Corps. Archival records place German strength at 1,436 tanks and assault guns (see Appendix D). See also *Sbornik*, no. 11, p. 54; and *Po prikazu*, 86–94. According to these Soviet sources, the Germans lost 200 tanks, 10,000 men, and 154 aircraft during the first day of combat against Voronezh Front forces. German accounts cite heavy, but somewhat smaller, losses.

30. Spaeter, *Grossdeutschland*, 116.

31. Ibid., 116–117, quoting from an account by *Oberstleutnant* Albrecht.

32. Carell, *Scorched Earth*, 55–56; and Spaeter, *Grossdeutschland*, 118–120. Colonel Kassnitz was evacuated to Germany, where he died on 29 July. Major Graf Saurma, commander of Panzer Regiment GD's 2d Battalion, was also severely wounded in the aborted assault.

33. For details about the 67th Guards Rifle Division's fight, see *Oborona v gody Velikoi Otechestvennoi voiny* [Defense during the Great Patriotic War] (Moscow: Izdanie Akademii, 1989), 64–81; V. A. Vostrov, *Tematicheskii sbornik boevykh primerov iz opyta Velikoi Otechestvennoi voiny i lokal'nykh voin (polk-armiia)* [Thematic collection of combat examples from the experience of the Great Patriotic War and local wars (regiment-army)] (Moscow: Voenizdat, 1989), 22–23, 56–58; and Kolganov, *Razvitie taktiki*, 281–283, 294–297, 374–375.

34. *Po prikazu*, 87.

35. For details of combat in the 71st Guards Rifle Division's sector, see Egorov, *Rozhdennaia v boiakh*, 107–112; and *Geschichte der 3. Panzer-Division*, 372–375.

36. See Stadler, *Die offensive*, 34–36; and Carell, *Scorched Earth*, 59–62. Carell claims the II SS Panzer Corps had 300 operational tanks and 120 assault guns, while Heinrici places the number of serviceable weapons at 352 tanks and 91 assault guns. See also Appendix D.

37. Carell, *Scorched Earth*, 60.

38. For details on the 52d Guards Rifle Division's defense and the role of the 1008th Antitank Artillery Regiment, see *Oborona v gody Velikoi Otechestvennoi voiny*, 64–80; *Tematicheskii sbornik*, 54–56; and R. B. Bragunsky, N. S. Popel'nitsky, and M. G. Userkov, *Taktika artillerii v boevykh primerakh (podrazdeleniia i chasti)* [Artillery tactics in combat examples (subunits and units)] (Moscow: Voenizdat, 1977), 228–231.

39. Bragunsky, Popel'nitsky, and Userkov, *Taktika artillerii*, 230.

40. Rudolf Lehmann, *The Leibstandarte III*, Nick Olcott, trans. (Winnipeg, Canada: J. J. Fedorowicz, 1993), 215.

41. Lehmann, *Leibstandarte*, 214–215, records Soviet losses as 15 tanks, 3 aircraft, and 88 prisoners. These losses are indicative of the Soviet intent to hold back their armor during the initial fighting and to rely instead on antitank weaponry to blunt and produce attrition among the German armored assault forces. Stadler, *Die offensive gegen Kursk*, 55, records Soviet losses on 5 July throughout the II SS Panzer Corps sector as 7 tanks, 1 assault gun, 27 antitank guns, 30 antitank rifles, and 552 prisoners, but does not record losses for 6 July.

42. *Das Reich's* participation in the operation is detailed in James Lucas, *Das Reich: The Military Role of 2d SS Division* (London: Arms and Armour, 1991), 101–113.

43. SS Panzer Division *Totenkopf's* role in the Kursk operation is summarized in Charles W. Sydnor, Jr., *Soldiers of Destruction: The SS Death's Head Division, 1933–1945* (Princeton: Princeton University Press, 1977), 281–294. Sydnor relies heavily on the Heinrici and Hauck manuscript, as later published in three articles, entitled "Zitadelle," in *Wehrwissenschaftliche Rundshau* 15 (August–October 1965); 463–482, 529–544, 582–604. These three articles are hereinafter referred to as Heinrici and Hauck, *Citadel*.

44. *Sbornik*, no. 11, pp. 54–55; and *Po prikazu*, 96–102.

45. For details on the 1st Tank Army's operations at Kursk, see "Boevye deistviia 1-i tankovoi armii" [Combat operations of 1st Tank Army], in *Sbornik*, no. 11, pp. 139–147; A. Kh. Babadzhanian et al., *Liuki otkryli v Berline: boevoi put' 1-i gvardeiskoi tankovoi armii* [They opened the hatchways to Berlin: The combat path of 1st Guards Tank Army] (Moscow: Voenizdat, 1973), 27–55; and M. E. Katukov, *Na ostrie glavnogo udara* [At the point of the main attack] (Moscow: Voenizdat, 1976), 198–240. The latter is the memoirs of the tank army commander. For details on the 6th Tank Corps' operations, see the memoirs of its commander, A. L. Getman, *Tanki idut na Berlin (1941–1945)* [Tanks advance on Berlin (1941–1945)] (Moscow: Nauka, 1973), 78–114; and the history of the corps' 112th Tank Brigade, A. V. Karavaev, *Serdtsa i bronia: boevoi put' 44-i gvardeiskoi tankovoi brigady* [Hearts and armor: The combat path of the 44th Guards [112th] Tank Brigade] (Moscow: Voenizdat, 1971), 20–47.

46. See the memoirs of the 3d Mechanized Corps commander, S. Krivoshein, *Ratnaia byl': Zapiski komandira mekhanizirovannogo korpusa* [It was warlike: The notes of a mechanized corps commander] (Moscow: Molodaia Gvardiia, 1962), 158–175, and those of two of his subordinate mechanized brigade commanders, A. Kh. Babadzhanian, *Dorogi pobedy* [Highways to victory] (Moscow: Voenizdat, 1981), 108–135; and D. A. Dragunsky, *Gody v brone* [Years in armor] (Moscow: Voenizdat, 1973), 94–111. Babadzhanian commanded the 3d Mechanized Brigade and Dragunsky the 1st.

47. See A. F. Smirnov and K. S. Ogloblin, *Tanki za Visloi: Boevoi put' 31-go tankovogo vislenskogo korpusa* [Tanks across the Vistula: The combat path of the 31st Vistula Tank Corps] (Moscow: Voenizdat, 1991), 6–35.

48. No unit histories exist for the 2d and 5th Guards Tank Corps. For additional information on the 5th Guards Tank Corps, see Anna Stroeva, *Komandarm Kravchenko* [Army commander Kravchenko] (Kiev: Politicheskoi literatury Ukrainy, 1984), 50–57.

49. See Ia. Zimin, "Boevye deistviia 1-i tankovoi armii v oboronitel'nom srazhenii pod Kurskom" [The combat actions of 1st Tank Army in the defensive battle at Kursk], *Voennaia mysl'* [Military thought], no. 3 (March 1957): 45–46. According to Zimin, Katukov told him that, during the day on 5 July, he received a telephonic order from the Voronezh Front commander, Colonel General N. F. Vatutin, to deliver a counterattack with the forces of the 1st Tank Army against the enemy grouping that had penetrated the main defensive belt of the 6th Guards Army. Forward tank brigades, which had been urgently dispatched to the main defensive belt, engaged in battle with enemy tank formations, which had in their composition a great number of T-IV and T-V type tanks, heavy self-propelled guns, and mobile antitank artillery. Katukov's tanks began to suffer losses from the fire of the heavy enemy tanks, and his artillery and aviation. The enemy tank formations preserved almost their entire strength and, in these circumstances, it was considered inexpedient to attempt to destroy them in a head-on tank battle. General M. E. Katukov reported on this to the *front* commander and proposed to use his 1st Tank Army for defense in the second defensive belt of 6th Guards Army in order to exhaust the attacking enemy in defensive battles and then deliver a counterstroke. The Voronezh Front commander agreed with that proposal and at 1600 hours on 5 July issued the appropriate order to the 1st Tank Army.

Katukov's army order read, in part: "3d Mechanized Corps, located in the Kurasovka region, must by 2400 5 July move to the line (inclusive) Shepelovka, Iakovlevo and once there organize a firm defense in a 19-kilometer sector; 6th Tank Corps, having begun its march an hour later, must move from the Oboian' region along the march route of 3d Mechanized Corps and, by the same time, reach the line Melovoe, Chapaev, Shepelovka, where it will go over to the defense in a 16-kilometer sector of 90th Guards Rifle Division's combat formation."

Simultaneously, together with the 5th and 2d Guards Tank Corps, these corps were given the mission to prepare a joint counterstroke in the general direction of Dmitrievka, Tomarovka, and Belgorod. The mission of the 3d Mechanized Corps also included the organization of defenses at the junction with the 5th Guards Tank Corps and the maintenance of cooperative communications with that corps. The 5th Guards Tank Corps would reach the line Iakovlevo, Teterevino and the 2d Guards Tank Corps the line Rozhdestvenka, Druzhnyi. Both these corps fell under the operational control of the 6th Guards Army. Note that since the 31st Tank Corps was newly formed, unlike other tank corps, it had no organic motorized rifle brigade.

When fully deployed, the 1st Tank Army's first echelon (6th Tank and 3d Mechanized Corps) numbered 419 tanks, 158 guns, 243 mortars, 56 M-13 multiple rocket launchers, and 533 antitank rifles. The 31st Tank Corps in second echelon had 196 tanks, 16 guns, and 13 mortars. Katukov's reserve was the 180th Tank Brigade, attached from the 38th Army. His army's mobile obstacle detachment, which consisted of two engineer battalions with a supply of antitank mines and explosive materials, was deployed in the Gremiuchii region behind the 3d Mechanized Corps. All army artillery was attached down to corps.

50. For the details of the failed counterattack, see *Sbornik*, no. 11, pp. 141–143.

51. Heinrici, *Citadel*, note 73, states, "The 6th Panzer Division, which was committed near Belgorod, attacked into strong resistance. Therefore, they were removed during the night of 5–6 July and directed across the Donets on 6 July, 7 kilometers south of Belgorod behind the 7th Panzer Division, which had made good progress on 5 July."

52. For details on the 19th Panzer Division's operations and the 81st and 78th Guards Rifle Divisions' defense, see *Sbornik*, no. 11, pp. 54–56; Otto von Knobelsdorff, *Geschichte der niedersachsischen 19. Panzer-Division* (Bad Neuheim: Verlag Hans-Henning Podzun, 1958), 207–217; Albert Krull, *Das Hannoversche Regiment 73*, Regimentskameradschaft 73 (undated), 290–315; the divisional history of the 78th Guards Rifle Division, B. I. Mutovin, *Cherez vse ispytaniia* [Throughout all the trials] (Moscow: Voenizdat, 1986), 80–103; and the memoirs of the 81st Guards Rifle Division commander, I. K. Morozov, *Ot Stalingrada do Pragi: zapiski komandira divizii* [From Stalingrad to Prague: The notes of a division commander] (Volgograd: Nizhne-Volzhskoe, 1976), 100–119.

53. For additional details on Skvortsev's struggle, see Glantz, *Soviet Defensive Tactics*, 35–42.

54. See *Sbornik*, no. 11, pp. 55–56, for Vatutin's regrouping on the night of 5–6 July.

55. Ibid., 168.

56. For example, air sorties were said to decrease by 55 percent after 5 July. For details of day-to-day sorties, see *Sbornik*, no. 11, p. 169. The Soviets claim to have shot down 173 German aircraft on 5 July.

57. Ibid., 55–56; and *Po prikazu*, 96–100.

58. *Geschichte der 3. Panzer-Division*, 375.

59. F. W. von Mellenthin, *Panzer Battles* (Norman; University of Oklahoma Press, 1956), 220. See also *Sbornik*, no. 11, 55–56.

60. Spaeter, *Grossdeutschland*, 121–122. *Grossdeutschland* was fighting the dug-in 1st and 3d Mechanized Brigades of Krivoshein's 3d Mechanized Corps, reinforced by a regiment of the 90th Guards Rifle Division and the remnants of the 67th Guards Rifle Division.

61. Koltunov and Solov'ev, *Kurskaia bitva*, 147–148. Zimin, "Boevye deistviia 1-i tankovoi armii," 48, records that the Germans lost seventy-four tanks by 1700 hours 6 July in combat along the Pena River.

62. For details on the sharp fight for Iakhevlevo, see *Sbornik*, no. 11, 57; Stadler, *Die offensive gegen Kursk*, 57–64; Lehmann, *The Leibstandarte*, 217–219; and S. M. Krivoshein, "V boiakh pod Iakovlevo" [In battles at Iakovlevo], in *Kurskaia bitva* [The Battle of Kursk] (Voronezh: Tsentral'no-Chernozemnoe, 1982), 230–237. Indicative of the intensified fighting, on 7 July *Leibstandarte* reported 75 enemy tanks, 12 aircraft, and 23 artillery pieces destroyed, 13 Soviet deserters and 244 prisoners, at a cost to themselves of 24 dead, 164 wounded, and 2 missing. The II SS Panzer Corps as a whole reported destroying 90 Soviet tanks, 28 aircraft, 83 antitank guns, and 140 antitank rifles and taking 1,609 prisoners of war.

63. *Sbornik*, no. 11, p. 57.

64. The Soviet defenders of the Iakovlevo-Pokrovka and Bol'shie Maiachki sector included the 52d Guards Rifle Division's 151st and 153d Guards Rifle Regiments, the 51st Guards Rifle Division's 154th and 156th Guards Rifle Regiments, the 3d Mechanized Corps' 1st Guards (at Iakovlevo) and 49th Tank Brigades (at Pokrovka), the 31st Tank Corps' 100th Tank Brigade (at Bol'shie Maiachki), the 230th Tank Regiment, and elements of the 28th Antitank Brigade and the 496th and 1008th Antitank Regiments.

65. Lehmann, *Leibstandarte*, 216–217.

66. *Leibstandarte* quickly detected the new threat from the 2d Guards Tank Corps. In response, the corps headquarters called for air attacks and *Leibstandarte* moved a reinforced battalion to firm up its links with *Totenkopf* forces defending along the Lipovyi Donets. The air attacks took a heavy toll on 2d Guards Tank Corps armor.

67. Ibid., 217. The Soviet armored force was Kravchenko's regrouping 5th Guards Tank Corps and Burdeiny's 2d Guards Tank Corps.

68. *Totenkopf* was supposed to be relieved along the Lipovyi Donets River by infantry from the 167th Rifle Division. However, after the German seizure of Iakovlevo and the linkup of the II Panzer Corps with the 11th Panzer Division, the 167th spent days clearing Soviet forces out of the salient between the two panzer corps.

69. See *Sbornik*, no. 11, pp. 57, 142; and Babadzhanian, *Liuki otkryli*, 37–38.

70. Koltunov and Solov'ev, *Kurskaia bitva*, 150.

71. For details of the 6th Panzer Division's operations, see Wolfgang Paul, *Brennpunkte: Die Geschichhte der 6. Panzerdivision, 1937–1945* (Krefeld: Hontges, 1977), 300–322; and *Sbornik*, no. 11, 57–58.

72. Von Knobelsdorff, *Geschichte 19. Panzerdivision*, 207; Krull, *Das Hannoversche Regiment 73*, 294–296; and Morozov, *Ot Stalingrada*, 103–108.

73. For details on the 73d Guards Rifle Division's defense, see *Sbornik*, no. 11, 57–58; V. I. Davidenko, "Pod Belgorodom v sorok tret'em" [At Belgorod in 1943], in *73-ia gvardeiskaia: sbornik vospominaniii dokumentov i materialov o boevom puti 73-i gvardeiskoi strelkovoi stalingradsko-dunaiskoi krasnoznamennoi divizii* [The 73d Guards: A collection of recollections, documents, and materials about the combat path of the 73d Guards Stalingrad-Danube Red Banner Rifle Division] (Alma-Ata: Kazakhstan, 1986), 96–104; and V. Nazarov, "Muzhestvo i masterstvo v oborone" [Courage and skill in the defense], *VIZh*, no. 6 (June 1963); 47–52.

74. Ziemke, *Stalingrad to Berlin*, 136.

75. Piekalkiewicz, *Operation "Citadel,"* 151–152. Indicative of the lessening effectiveness of Luftwaffe support was the steady decrease in German air sorties from 4,298 on the first day of the operation to 2,100 on 6 July. Although confirming the same pattern, Soviet sources credit the Germans with fewer sorties. See Hardesty, *Red Phoenix*, 163. Heinrici, in *Citadel*, confirms Hardesty's and Soviet conclusions:

The development of the air situation appeared satisfactory—at least at the beginning. The German pilots dominated the battlefield. During the following days Russian aircraft arrived in increasing numbers, which ultimately exceeded the Germans, and allowed the enemy to inflict greater casualties. On the German side, on the other hand, the losses and the shortage of fuel began to make themselves felt. Air support more and more had to be limited to climaxes and crises in the battle. Moreover, the Luftwaffe could only support the attack tactically. They lacked sufficient forces to affect the battle operationally by engaging the Russian deployments by intensively bombing the rail traffic or blocking the railroad network. Therefore, the German leadership was denied an important trump card, with which they could have influenced the course of the battle decisively.

76. *Sbornik,* no. 11, p. 58.

77. Ibid., 59.

78. Ibid.

79. For details on the 5th Guards Tank Army's movement forward, see *Sbornik,* no. 11, pp. 148–149; P. Ia. Egorov, I. V. Krivoborsky, N. K. Ivlev, and A. I. Rogalevich, *Dorogami pobed: boevoi put' 5-i gvardeiskoi tankovoi armii* [On the roads to victory: The combat path of 5th Guards Tank Army] (Moscow: Voenizdat, 1969), 23–25; and P. A. Rotmistrov, *Stal'naia gvardiia* [Steel guard] (Moscow: Voenizdat, 1984), 172–178.

80. For details on the 2d and 10th Tank Corps' participation in the operation, see E. F. Ivanovsky, *Ataku nachinali tankisty* [Tankers began the attack] (Moscow: Voenizdat, 1984), 121–134; and I. M. Kravchenko and V. V. Burkov, *Desiatyi tankovyi dneprovskii: boevoi put' 10-go tankovogo dneprovskogo ordena Suvorova korpusa* [The 10th Dnepr Tank: The combat path of the Dnepr, Order of Suvorov 10th Tank Corps] (Moscow: Voenizdat, 1986), 59–102. The 2d Tank Corps had just refitted in the Valiuki region east of Khar'kov. Although it had its full complement of tanks and other weapons, it lacked transport for its motorized rifle brigades and the motorized rifle battalions in its tank brigades. Therefore, its infantry had to deploy forward on foot. The 10th Tank Corps assembled near Staryi Oskol and was initially subordinate to the 5th Guards Army. Its strength on the eve of battle was 9,612 men, 164 tanks (99 T-34, 64 T-70, and 1 KV), 21 self-propelled guns (12 SU-122 and 9 SU-76), 77 guns (28 76mm, 32 45mm, and 17 37mm), 123 mortars (82mm and 120mm), 938 vehicles (trucks and "Willies"), 14 tractors, 70 motorcycles, 52 armored transporters, 44 armored cars, 4,613 rifles, 2,917 sub-machine guns, 209 light machine guns, 58 heavy machine guns (on wheels), 57 antiaircraft machine guns, and 202 antitank rifles. Its armament was typical for a full-strength Soviet tank corps.

81. *Sbornik,* no. 11, p. 59.

82. Carell, *Scorched Earth,* 47.

83. *Sbornik,* no. 11, 77–79; Kozlov, *V plameni,* 113–117; Glantz, *Soviet Defensive Tactics,* 53–61. Initially, the 307th Rifle Division was supported by the 5th Artillery Penetration Division, 13th Antitank Artillery Brigade, 11th and 22d Guards Mortar Brigades, and elements of the 1st Guards Engineer Brigade (Special Designation).

84. Carell, *Scorched Earth*, 45. See also *Sbornik*, no. 11, p. 77.

85. The 70th Guards Rifle Division's participation in the ferocious fighting around Ol'khovatka is described in B. S. Venkov and P. P. Dudinov, *Gvardeiskia doblest': boevoi put' 70-i gvardeiskoi strelkovoi glukhovskoi ordena Lenina, dvazhdy krasnoznamennoi ordenov Suvorova, Kutuzova i Bogdana Khmel'nitskogo divizii* [Guards valor: The combat path of the Glukhov, Order of Lenin, twice Red Banner, Orders of Suvorov, Kutuzov, and Bogdan Khmel'nitsky 70th Guards Rifle Division] (Moscow: Voenizdat, 1979), 60–73. In his memoirs, *A Soldier's Duty* (Moscow: Progress, 1985), 199, the *front* commander, K. K. Rokossovsky, wrote: "Although the counterattack undertaken by the 17th Guards Rifle Corps had not lived up to expectations, it had prevented the enemy from advancing in the Ol'khovatka direction. It was this that decided the fate of the German Orel group's offensive. We had gained time to concentrate the necessary forces and materiel in the most threatened sector."

86. Carell, *Scorched Earth*, 45–46. 2d Panzer's strength included reinforcing armor and assault guns.

87. For details, see *Sbornik*, no. 11, pp. 176–179.

88. Carell, *Scorched Earth*, 46–48.

89. Ibid., 46. See also *Sbornik*, no. 11, pp. 79–80; and Koltunov and Solov'ev, *Kurskaia bitva*, 124–125.

90. The 1st Battery, 3d Antitank Artillery Brigade, took part in the heavy fighting around Teploe. Signifying the intensity of the fight, before being itself destroyed, the battery destroyed nineteen German tanks and an estimated 150 German soldiers. See "Podvig batarei kapitana Igusheva" [The feat of Captain Igushev's battery], in Bragunsky, Popel'nitsky, and Usenkov, *Taktika artillerii*, 221–223.

91. Carell, *Scorched Earth*, 47.

92. *Sbornik*, no. 11, pp. 79–80.

93. Koltunov and Solov'ev, *Kurskaia bitva*, 128.

94. The 307th Rifle Division was supported by the 129th Tank Brigade, the 51st Tank Brigade of 2d Tank Army's 3d Tank Corps, and the 27th Guards Tank Regiment, which had a combined initial strength of approximately 140 tanks. See ibid., 129.

95. The 4th Guards Airborne Division's role in the Battle for Ponyri is covered in M. Goncharov, *Golubaia pekhota* [Sky blue infantry] (Kishinev: Karta Moldoveniaske, 1979), 20–29.

96. Healy, *Kursk 1943*, 72. Albert Seaton, *The Russo-German War* (New York: Praeger, 1971), 358, places Model's losses in the first two days alone at 10,000 men.

97. *Sbornik*, no. 11, pp. 59–60, 144; Stadler, *Die offensive gegen Kursk*, 57–64; and Lehmann, *Leibstandarte*, 217–221.

98. Koltunov and Solov'ev, *Kurskaia bitva*, 153.

99. Lehmann, *Leibstandarte*, 218.

100. Smirnov, *Tanki za Visloi*, 20–22.

101. Lehmann, *Leibstandarte*, 220–221, records Soviet losses of 41 tanks (later raised to 75), 12 aircraft, 23 artillery pieces, 13 deserters, and 244 prisoners on 7 July. This raised the total Soviet loss count since the beginning of the operation in *Leibstandarte's* sector to 123 tanks, 37 artillery pieces, 13 deserters, and 259 prisoners.

102. Ibid., 221.

103. *Sbornik*, no. 11, pp. 59–60, 143–144; and Babadzhanian, *Liuki otkryli*, 39–44.

104. The reinforcements Vatutin provided Katukov included the 29th Antitank Artillery Brigade, 180th and 192d Tank Brigades, 222d and 1244th Antitank Artillery Regiments, 66th Guards Mortar Regiment, 753d, 754th, and 756th Antitank Artillery Battalions, and the 138th and 139th Antitank Rifle Battalions. In addition, the remnants of the 52d and 67th Guards Rifle Divisions (heavily damaged during the initial defense) reinforced the 3d Mechanized Corps. See Babadzhanian, *Liuki otkryli*, 39.

105. Carell, *Scorched Earth*, 69, confirms the intensity and costliness of the fighting:

> On the left of Hausser's Waffen SS, at XLVIII Panzer Corps, progress continued to be good on 7th July. . . . At dawn the grenadiers of "Grossdeutschland" took Dubrovo. But the misfortunes which had been dogging the Panthers of "Grossdeutschland" Division since the first day of the offensive were not yet at an end. Lauchert's Panther Brigade again blundered into a minefield and suffered very heavy losses. Captain von Gottberg's 2d Battalion, Panzer Regiment "Grossdeutschland," saved the situation. It swept the grenadiers of Remer's battalion with it. The attack got moving again. From the ravines on the left wing of the division, the battalion of the Panzer Fusilier Regiment also burst forward. In a bold, concerted action the main defensive line of Krivoshein's mechanized corps was torn open.

106. Koltunov and Solov'ev, *Kurskaia bitva*, 153.

107. Spaeter, *Grossdeutschland*, 122–123. This account describes action against the Soviet 1st and 3d Mechanized Brigades.

108. Ibid., 123. The "crows" were small Soviet PO-2 night bombers, which were often flown by female pilots. The heavy artillery fire was understandable, since Vatutin had reinforced Katukov's tank army with the 33d Artillery Brigade (from the 6th Guard Army), a total of 144 guns. In addition, 116 guns and 72 multiple rocket launchers from the 6th Guards Army's army artillery group supported the 1st Tank Army. See Zimin, "Boevye deistviia 1-i tankovoi armii," 49.

109. Von Mellenthin, *Panzer Battles*, 220–223.

110. Getman, *Tanki idut*, 93–94. Getman also reinforced his 112th Tank Brigade with the 79th and 270th Guards Mortar Regiments.

111. About the heavy fighting along the Pena, Carell, *Scorched Earth*, 70, states:

> Meanwhile, the Armored Reconnaissance Battalion of "Grossdeutschland" . . . had thrust further to the north. Strong packs of tanks of the Soviet VI Tank Corps, with ten, twenty, or even forty, steel monsters were approaching from the north-east. Since the Reconnaissance Battalion could not get across the weak bridge quickly enough, division instead placed in a semi-circle to cover its right flank in front of Verkhopenye. There, [the battalion] awaited the enemy's armoured thrusts. Fortunately he had a battalion of assault guns with him. . . . After three hours [of heavy combat], thirty-five wrecked tanks littered the battle-field. Only five T-34s, all of them badly damaged, limped away from the smoking arena to seek shelter in a small wood. The road to Verkhopenye was clear.

Conversely, Getman, *Tanki idut*, 92, states: "During the course of battle [throughout the corps' sector], which lasted up to sixteen hours, corps units repelled four attacks and destroyed around seventy enemy tanks." About fighting near Verkhopen'e, he quotes archival documents, which stated, "On that day [7 July], the 124th Tank Battalion destroyed six enemy tanks, two artillery pieces, and an armored transporter. The brigade [112th] as a whole destroyed and burned twenty-one enemy tanks, including six Tigers."

112. Lehmann, *Grossdeutschland*, 123.

113. Koltunov and Solov'ev, *Kurskaia bitva*, 156.

114. Lehmann, *Grossdeutschland,* 123. Classified Soviet accounts confirm German seizure of Syrtsevo: "Up until 1300 hours, the 10th Mechanized Brigade, the remains of 1st Mechanized Brigade and the 112th Tank Brigade held off the German attack by a force of up to two infantry regiments and seventy tanks, while suffering heavy losses from aviation and artillery fire. In light of the great losses, at 1300 hours the 6th Tank Corps commander gave permission to his brigades to withdraw across the Pena River [from Syrtsevo] and dig in. "See *Sbornik,* no. 11, pp. 144.

115. Lehmann, *Grossdeutschland,* 123–124.

116. *Sbornik,* no. 11, p. 144. For more detailed accounts of the Soviet defense of Verkhopen'e, see Getman, *Tank idyt,* 98–101, Babadzhanian, *Liuki otkryli,* 47–50; and Katukov, *Na ostrie,* 231–232. Katukov and Getman, who spent the day with the 200th Tank Brigade, insisted that the brigade still held at Verkhopen'e at day's end, but this is incorrect.

117. Vatutin ordered the 309th Rifle Division with the 86th Tank Brigade and 36th Guards Mortar Regiment: to occupy defenses along the line Hills 251.4, 240.0, 235.9, and 207.8 [from Novenkoe eastward through Kalinovka to the Oboian' road] with the mission of preventing an enemy penetration along the Belgorod-Oboian' road." At the same time, on 6th Guards Army's right flank, the 71st Guards and 161st Rifle Divisions, now under 40th Army control, were to launch a counterattack toward Gertsovka.

118. *Sbornik,* no. 11, pp. 60–61.

119. Von Mellenthin, *Panzer Battles,* 221–223; and Carell, *Scorched Earth,* 71–73.

120. Stadler, *Die offensive gegen Kursk,* 65–73. Koltunov and Solov'ev, *Kurskaia bitva,* 156–157, noted, "The soldiers of the 29th Antitank Brigade distinguished themselves in the battles for Gresnoe. During the course of the first half of the day, they repulsed several German tank attacks and covered the withdrawal of [31st Tank] corps units to Kochetovka. The 2d Battalion, 184th Antitank Regiment, which was surrounded by the enemy, struggled to their last shell."

121. For details on the counterattack, see *Sbornik,* no. 11, pp. 61–62; Kravchenko, *Desiatyi tankovyi,* 76–78; and Ivanovsky, *Ataku nachinali,* 125–127.

122. Lehmann, *Leibstandarte,* 222, recorded that eighty-two enemy tanks were destroyed, adding, "Most of the tanks were destroyed by our close-range antitank weapons."

123. The most vivid account of the repulse of 2d Guards Tank Corps is found in Carell, *Scorched Earth,* 75–76.

124. Lehmann, *Leibstandarte,* 122.

125. Stadler, *Die offensive gegen Kursk,* 73. Archival data record the SS Panzer Corps strength at nightfall on 8 July as being 283 tanks and assault guns. See Appendix D for details.

126. For action on 7 and 8 July in Army Detachment Kempf's sector, see *Sbornik,* no. 11, pp. 60–61; Morozov, *Ot Stalingrada,* 108–113; Carell, *Scorched Earth,* 73–74; and Krull, *Das Hannoversche Regiment 73,* 298–300.

127. Army Detachment Kempf's losses were indicative of the heavy fighting in its sector, a fact that has often been overlooked in previous histories of the battle. For example, Heinrici, *Citadel,* states, "In the 320th ID by 7/7 there were 1,600 wounded.

Four battalions of the division now had only 200 men. On 10/7 the combat strength of the 73d Panzergrenadier Regiment [19th Panzer Division] had dropped to 250, and the 74th Panzergrenadier Regiment to 85 men."

128. Carell, *Scorched Earth,* 74. Details about the 92d Guards Rifle Division's meeting engagement with the III Panzer Corps are in A. I. Radzievsky, ed., *Taktika v boevykh primerakh, polk* [Tactics by combat example, regiment] (Moscow: Voenizdat, 1974), 143–144, 155–163, 173–180.

129. In addition to *Sbornik,* no. 11, p. 62, see S. I. Vasil'ev and A. P. Dikan, *Gvardeitsy piatnadtsatoi: boevoi put' Piatnadtsatoi gvardeiskoi strelkovoi divizii* [15th Guards: The combat path of the 15th Guards Rifle Division] (Moscow: Voenizdat, 1960), 81–84.

130. *Sbornik,* no. 11, p. 170.

131. Ibid., 171.

132. Key Soviet command decisions are detailed in *Sbornik,* no. 11, pp. 62–63.

133. *Sbornik,* no. 11, p. 148, describes the details of the 5th Guards Tank Army's movement:

On 5 July, that is, on the first day of the German offensive, the 5th Guards Tank Army received a combat order in which the military district commander [Konev] demanded full combat readiness on the part of all army units and, simultaneously, indicated that the 18th Tank Corps, located in the Rossosh' region, would become part of the army. At 2300 hours 6 July, an order by the commander of the Steppe Military District assigned the army the following mission: "By forced march army units are to concentrate on the western bank of the Oskol River in the Saltykovo, Melovoe, and Orlik regions, in readiness to operate along the Oboian'-Kursk axis."

Having been brought up to combat readiness two hours and thirty minutes after receipt of the order, the units of the 5th Guards Tank Army left the dispersal area and, by the morning of 8 July, completed concentrating along the western banks of the Oskol River, having completed a 200- to 220-kilometer march in a little longer than a day.

During the day of 8 July, the army put its material base in order and the staff reconnoitered the prospective region of combat operations.

At 0100 9 July, the 5th Guards Tank Army headquarters received an order that required [it] "to reach the Bobryshevo, Bol. Psinka, Prelestnoe, Aleksandrovka, and Bol. Seti region by day's end on 9 July with the mission to be prepared to repel attacks of the advancing enemy." Thus, army forces once again completed a march and, having traversed 100 kilometers in one day, concentrated in the rear of the 5th Guards Army, which, at that time, was already conducting combat operations.

134. See also Rotmistrov, *Stal'naia gvardiia,* 178–179; and Egorov, Krivoborsky, Ivlev, and Rogalevich, *Dorogami pobed,* 24–26.

135. For details on the 5th Guards Army's participation in the battle, see the memoirs of the army commander, A. S. Zhadov, *Chetyre goda voiny* [Four years of war] (Moscow: Voenizdat, 1978), 75–118; and the history of the army, I. A. Samchuk, P. G. Skachko, Iu. N. Babikov, and I. L. Gnedoi, *Ot Volgi do El'by i Pragi (Kratkii ocherk o boevom puti 5-i gvardeiskoi armii)* [From the Volga to the Elbe and Prague (A short survey about the combat path of the 5th Guards Army]) (Moscow: Voenizdat, 1970), 45–72.

136. *Sbornik,* no. 11, p. 63.

137. Ibid., 62; and Kravchenko, *Desiatyi tankovyi,* 78–80.

138. *Sbornik,* no. 11, p. 63; and Babadzhanian, *Liuki otkryli,* 50–51. The 1st Tank Army's reinforcements included the 59th, 60th, and 203d Tank Regiments from 40th

Army, the 483d and 869th Antitank Artillery Regiments, the 14th Antitank Artillery Brigade, the 9th Antiaircraft Artillery Division, and for transport of the 309th Rifle Division, the 35th Army Automobile Regiment. The 1st Tank Army dispositions on the evening of 8 July were as follows: the 6th Tank Corps with the 3d Mechanized Corps' 10th and 1st Mechanized Brigades, the 60th Heavy Tank Regiment and the 90th Guards Rifle Division, defended from Chapaev, through Shepelovka, and along the right bank of the Pena to Verkhopen'e with its main forces on its left flank; the 3d Mechanized Corps, reinforced by the 86th and 180th Tank Brigades, the 203d Heavy Tank Regiment, and the 67th Guards Rifle Division defended from Ver-khopen'e through Hill 261, to Sukho-Solotino; and the 31st Tank Corps, with the 192d Tank Brigade, the 59th Tank Regiment, and the 51st Guards Rifle Division, defended the left bank of the Solotinka River, while holding on to the western outskirts of Sukho-Solotino and Kochetovka.

139. The II SS Panzer Corps' combat order for 9 July (see Lehmann, *Leibstandarte*, 223) read:

The *LAH* is to move forces into the gap between the left wing of *DR* (one kilometer southwest of Teterewino) and its own former right wing. This gap must be secure before the attack can begin.

The Panzergruppe is to pull back behind the main line of battle. The Panzers should be repaired and made fit for battle. The subordination of the III. (armoured)/2. and the II./ Artillerie-Regiment is suspended.

The Division is to move a Grenadierregiment out of the area north of Lutschki and pull it up into Ssuch. Ssoltino (including the town). Its right wing should be south of the dividing line between itself and Division *Totenkopf*. It is to clear the terrain north of the *LAH's* and 11. Panzer-division's defensive line of enemy forces.

After the *Totenkopf* Division arrives, the defensive line should be called back, and an assault force should be formed in the area around Lutschki. The dividing line runs as follows, with the *Totenkopf* to the right and the *LAH* to the left: Hill 255.9 (held by the *Totenkopf*)— southern edge of the ravine one kilometer south of Mal. Majatschki—the school in Ssuch. Ssoltino (held by the *Totenkopf*).

The start will be ordered for the *Totenkopf* and the *LAH*. It is now planned for 09.00 hours.

Heinrici and Hauck, in *Citadel*, 65, write:

Before the 4th Panzer Army, in cooperation with Armeeabteilung [Army Detachment] Kempf, could remove the enemy on its eastern flank and continue its advance to the northeast, they believed that the threat in the west from the Oboyan and Pena salient area would first have to be eliminated. With the approval of the army group on 9 July, they decided to advance their two panzer corps to the north across the Psel—instead of further to the northeast toward Prokhorovka—in order to gain sufficient space to turn elements to the southwest and destroy the enemy in the Pena salient in cooperation with the LII Corps. This diversion would necessarily cause a two-day delay in the continuation of the attack in the main direction.

140. *Sbornik*, no. 11, pp. 63–64, 145–146; Stadler, *Die offensive gegen Kursk*, 75–82; and Lehmann, *Leibstandarte*, 223–224.

141. During their movement from the Prokhorovka region to the Oboian' road, Vatutin diverted the 10th Tank Corps' 183d and 186th Tank Brigades and sent them to assist the 31st Tank Corps in its planned withdrawal to new defense lines at Kochetovka. The timely arrival of the two brigades prevented the withdrawal from

becoming a rout. Their task complete, the two tank brigades resumed their march to the Oboian' road at nightfall.

142. Stadler, *Die Offensive gegen Kursk,* 75–81. For example, on 9 July *Leibstandarte* reported twelve dead, thirty-four wounded, and two missing. See Lehmann, *Leibstandarte,* 224.

143. *Sbornik,* no. 11, pp. 63–65, 145–146; Babadzhanian, *Liuki otkryli,* 44; and Getman, *Tanki idut,* 101–103.

144. Koltunov and Solov'ev, *Kurskaia bitva,* 158–159.

145. Spaeter, *Grossdeutschland,* 125–127. Although German forces had entered Verkhopen'e on 8 July, it took heavy fighting on 9 July to clear Soviet forces from the entire town. According to archival documents cited in Koltunov, *Kurskaia bitva,* 160, the Germans lost 295 tanks during the fighting on 9 July, most in the XXXXVIII Panzer Corps' sector.

146. Von Mellenthin, *Panzer Battles,* 223–225. See also, Carell, *Scorched Earth,* 71–72.

147. *Sbornik,* no. 11, p. 170.

148. Ibid., 65–66.

149. Carell, *Scorched Earth,* 79.

150. Ibid.

151. Lehmann. *Leibstandarte,* 224–226. See also Stadler, *Die Offensive gegen Kursk,* 81–83.

5. Prokhorovka

1. Gotthard Heinrici and Friedrick Wilhelm Hauck, *Citadel: The Attack on the Russian Kursk Salient,* Joseph Welch, trans., U.S. National Archives, 69, citing *OKW Combat Diary,* vol. 3, entry for 10 July 1943.

2. Albert Seaton, *The Russo-German War, 1941–45* (New York: Praeger, 1970), 365, discusses the traditional Soviet historiography of this matter, which basically claims that Kursk permitted the Allies to achieve victory by keeping the Germans occupied in the east. The converse and equally probable conclusion that Sicily caused Hitler to call off Citadel was rarely discussed by Soviet scholars. Walter Dunn, Jr., has argued in *Kursk: Hitler's Gamble, 1943* (Westport, Ct.: Praeger, 1997), 190–191, that Sicily was, at least in part, an excuse that Hitler used to call off a battle he knew was hopeless.

3. For example, see P. A. Rotmistrov in *The Battle of Kursk* (Moscow: Progress, 1974), 172. Rotmistrov and other Soviet sources claim that 700 German tanks met the 500 tanks of his first echelon corps. Other Soviet sources place 5th Guards Tank Army's total strength at 850 tanks and self-propelled guns. P. P. Vechnyi et al., eds., *Sbornik materialov po izucheniiu opyta voiny* [Collection of materials for the study of war experience], no. 11, March–April 1944 (Moscow: Voenizdat, 1944), 148–149, places German tank strength at 600, including 100 Tigers and the 5th Guards Tank Army (including the 2d and 2d Guards Tank Corps) at 793 tanks and self-propelled guns, including 501 T-34s, 261 T-70s, and 31 Churchills. The Soviet figures count German armor in both the II SS and III Panzer Corps. Paul Carell, *Scorched Earth: Hitler's War on Russia 1941–1943,* Ewald Osers, trans., vol. 2 (London: Harrap, 1970),

80, supports the Soviet view by placing German armored strength at 600 in the II SS Panzer Corps and 300 in the III Panzer Corps and accepting the Soviet figure of 850 tanks and self-propelled guns in the 5th Guards Tank Army. These counts of German armor are clearly inflated.

4. Heinrici, *Citadel*, note 92, places Army Detachment Kempf's tank strength on 11 July at 120 tanks, including 23 Tigers, and about 60 assault guns. At the same time, he places the II SS Panzer Corps operational strength on 12 July at 208 tanks (20 Tigers), 54 assault guns, and 11 captured Soviet T-34 tanks. II SS Panzer Corps' records place corps strength on 10 July at 205 tanks and 67 assault guns, subdivided into 59 tanks and 20 assault guns in *LAH*, 63 tanks and 26 assault guns in *DR*, and 83 tanks and 21 assault guns in *T*. The total figure of around 400 tanks and assault guns for Fourth Panzer Army and Army Detachment Kempf is clearly more accurate than earlier Soviet and German estimates. By 12 July II SS Panzer Corps' strength rose to 293 tanks and assault guns. For details, see Appendix D.

5. Calculated as 172 tanks and assault guns of *Leibstandarte* and *Das Reich* and just over 400 tanks and self-propelled guns of Rotmistrov's 2d, 18th, and 29th Tank Corps.

6. Specifically, Rotmistrov's fresh 18th and 29th Tank Corps, portions of his already depleted 2d Tank Corps, and elements of his 5th Guards Mechanized Corps.

7. Getman's forces were also supported by elements of the 4th Guards, 12th, 35th, and 1837th Antitank Regiments, while the 727th Antitank Regiment supported the 10th Tank Corps.

8. Including 100 tanks in the 5th Guards and 31st Tank Corps, respectively, 50 tanks in the 3d Mechanized Corps, and the remaining 50 in the supporting 180th and 192d Tank Brigades. Antitank support included guns from the 14th, 28th, and 29th Antitank Brigades and the 222d, 1244th, and 869th Antitank Regiments. The 51st and 67th Guards Rifle Divisions retained about 40 percent of their original strength.

9. See, for example, Earl Ziemke, *Stalingrad to Berlin; The German Defeat in the East* (Washington, D.C.: Office of the Chief of Military History, United States Army, 1968), 136, which states, "The Grossdeutschland Division, for instance, had only 87 of its 300 tanks still fit for combat." Most of the remaining tanks were repairable. In total, von Knobelsdorff was able to commit roughly 200 tanks and assault guns in his thrust on 10 July, over half of these against the Soviet 6th Tank Corps. Ziemke's figure appears to reflect *Grossdeutschland's* strength after the intense flank battles. See Appendix D for details.

10. *Sbornik*, no. 11, p. 146, states: "Isolated one from another, separate groups of tanks and motorized infantry of the 200th and 112th Tank Brigades were encircled in the region north of Berezovka, where before nightfall they fought with enemy tanks and infantry, and, with the onset on night, they began to gather in the Berezovka region. As a result of the heavy combat the 6th Tank Corps suffered heavy losses: by the end of 10 July not more than thirty-five tanks and ten antitank guns remained operational. With the onset of darkness, the corps began to assemble the tanks scattered during the day's battles and organized antitank defenses."

11. Ia. Zimin, "Boevye deistviia 1-i tankovoi armii v oboronitel'nom srazhenii pod

Kurskom" [Combat operations of 1st Tank Army in the defensive battle at Kursk], *Voennaia mysl'* [Military thought] 3 (March 1957); 52.

12. A. L. Getman, *Tanki idut na Berlin (1941–1945)* [Tanks advance on Berlin (1941–1945)] (Moscow: Nauka, 1973), 108. A. V. Karavaev's history of the 112th Tank Brigade, *Serdtsa i bronia* [Hearts and armor] (Moscow: Voenizdat, 1971), 30–32, provides an equally vivid picture of the intense combat, which left the brigade with thirteen T-34 and four T-70 tanks by 11 July.

13. M. E. Katukov, *Na ostrie glavnogo udara* [At the point of the main attack] (Moscow: Voenizdat, 1976), 235.

14. Helmuth Spaeter, *The History of the Panzercorps Grossdeutschland*, vol. 2 (Winnipeg, Canada: J. J. Fedorowicz, 1995), 127.

15. Ibid., 128.

16. F. W. von Mellenthin, *Panzer Battles* (Norman: University of Oklahoma Press, 1956), 225–226.

17. Ibid., 226.

18. Spaeter, *Grossdeutschland*, 129.

19. Carell, *Scorched Earth*, 72.

20. *Sbornik*, no. 11, p. 68.

21. Ibid.

22. Ibid., 147.

23. Ibid. By 12 July the combined force of the 5th Guards and 10th Tank Corps numbered about 220 tanks, with another 50 in supporting forces (the 6th Tank Corps and separate tank regiments). The strength of the 3d Mechanized Corps and 31st Tank Corps is more obscure, but probably totaled fewer than 150 tanks.

24. Janusz Piekalkiewicz, *Operation "Citadel"; Kursk and Orel*, Michaela Nierhaus, trans. (Novato, Ca.: Presidio Press, 1987), 168. The author provided no source for this figure. It is probably accurate given that Heinrici, *Citadel*, assesses that on 11 July all of Army Detachment Kempf numbered 120 tanks and 60 assault guns.

25. *Sbornik*, no. 11, p. 70.

26. Rudolf Lehmann, *The Leibstandarte III*, Nick Alcott, trans. (Winnipeg: Fedorowicz, 1993), 227.

27. Ibid., 230, reports that thirty-eight Russian tanks were destroyed by Tigers and tank destroyers, nine by assault guns, and six in close-range fighting. In addition, the Pioneer (Engineer) Battalion reported digging up 336 mines in wooden boxes. The II SS Panzer Corps, as a whole, reported thirty-seven Soviet tanks and thirty-seven antitank guns destroyed on 10 July. See Silvester Stadler, *Die Offensive, gegen Kursk 1943: II. SS-Panserkorps als Stosskeil im Grosskampf* (Osnabruck: Munin verlag GmbH, 1980), 90.

28. During the previous two days, Rotmistrov's army had already traversed 230 to 280 kilometers, some, but not all, of the movement by rail. All accounts indicate that superhuman maintenance efforts kept most of the army's tanks serviceable. Given previous Soviet maintenance problems, it is likely that attrition was heavier than indicated. The 5th Guards Tank Army's assembly areas were in the Bobryshevo, Bol. Psinka, Prelestnoe, Aleksandrovskii, and Bol. Seti region between Oboian' and Prokhorovka.

29. P. A. Rotmistrov, *Stal'naia gvardiia* [Steel guard] (Moscow: Voenizdat, 1984), 180.

30. Ibid., 181.

31. Ibid., 174, 181. Trufanov's force, which had served as army forward detachment during the long march to Prokhorovka, consisted of the 53d Guards Tank Regiment, the 1st Separate Motorcycle Regiment, the 678th Howitzer Artillery Regiment, and the 689th Antitank Artillery Regiment. Thus its nucleus was twenty-one KV heavy tanks and twenty-four antitank guns.

32. *Leibstandarte* committed sixty-seven tanks and ten assault guns to combat on 11 July. See Appendix D for details.

33. I. A. Samchuk and P. G. Skachko, *Atakuiut desantniki* [Airborne forces attack], (Moscow: Voenizdat, 1975), 27–28. The reference to schnapps is a superb case of Soviet mirror-imaging. According to regulations, Soviet forces were "inspired" by a daily vodka ration. See V. V. Veniaminov, "Narkotovskie grammy" [Grams of narcotics], *Voenno-istoricheskii zhurnal* [Military-historical journal] 5 (September–October 1995); 95–96. According to State Defense Committee Order No. 2507, dated 12 November 1942, soldiers in line units were to receive a daily vodka ration of 100 grams.

34. Samchuk and Skatchko, *Atakuiut desantniki*, 29–30.

35. Rotmistrov, *Stal'naia gvardiia*, 181–182.

36. Ibid., 182–183.

37. Lehmann, *Leibstandarte*, 233.

38. Stadler, *Die Offensive*, 99.

39. Lehmann, *Leibstandarte*, 233–234. The 2d SS Panzer Grenadier Regiment accounted for all of the destroyed enemy tanks.

40. Ibid., 234. The panzers included four Panzer IIs, five Panzer IIIs, forty-seven Panzer IVs, and four Panzer VIs.

41. Ibid., 233.

42. *Sbornik*, no. 11, p. 149.

43. Samchuk and Skachko, *Atakuiut*, 33.

44. *Sbornik*, no. 11, p. 149.

45. Rotmistrov, *Stal'naia gvardiia*, 184.

46. Official records place *LAH* strength at sixty-seven tanks (including four Tigers) and ten assault guns. Heinrici, *Citadel*, cites a slightly larger figure by including up to Soviet ten T-34 models in the German division.

47. Franz Kurowski, *Panzer Aces* (Winnipeg, Canada: J. J. Fedorowicz, 1992), 124, quoting from an account by *Obersturmfuehrer* Rudolf von Ribbentrop, commander of the 1st SS Panzer Regiment's 6th Company.

48. Lehmann, *Leibstandarte*, 234.

49. Ibid., 234–235, quoting from an account by Hubert Neuzert, a gunner in the tank destroyer unit.

50. Rotmistrov, *Stal'naia gvardiia*, 186.

51. Carell *Scorched Earth*, 82. The quotation from Rotmistrov provided Carell with his book's title.

52. *Sbornik*, no. 11, p. 150.

53. Lehmann, *Leibstandarte*, 236, provides a vivid eyewitness account of the artillery and tank battle. The Soviet tanks were from the 31st and 32d Tank Brigades.

54. Ibid., 237.

55. Commanded by Lieutenant Colonel M. Gol'dberg, the 55th Guards Tank Regiment belonged to the 12th Guards Mechanized Brigade of 5th Guards Mechanized Corps. It, and the 53d Guards Tank Regiment that went into action late in the afternoon, had been sent forward to compensate for the weakness of Popov's 2d Tank Corps.

56. Ibid., 238.

57. II SS Panzer Corps' records place *DR* armored strength at sixty-eight tanks (including one Tiger and eight T-34s) and twenty-seven assault guns. Heinrici, *Citadel*, note 92, places the total slightly higher.

58. James Lucas, *Das Reich: The Military Role of 2d SS Division* (London: Arms and Armour, 1991), 111.

59. Carell, *Scorched Earth*, 82–83.

60. Ibid., 111, states, "With the onset of darkness, the noise of battle died away, and rain which fell in torrents prevented 2d Guards Tank Corps from attacking *Der Fuehrer's* unprotected right flank; unprotected because Kempf's panzers had still not gained touch with the SS."

61. II SS Panzer Corps records place *T's* armored strength at 101 tanks (including 10 Tigers) and 20 assault guns. Heinrici, *Citadel*, cites a slightly lower total. The division would lose about half this number on 12 July.

62. *Sbornik*, no. 11, p. 151. A II SS Panzer Corps situation report issued at 19.50 hours [2150 Moscow time] stated that *Totenkopf's* panzer group had reached positions astride the Beregovoe-Kartashevka road. See Stadler, *Die Offensive*, 104. For 95th Guards Rifle Division's role in battling *Totenkopf*, see A. I. Oleinikov, *Rozhdennaia na zemliakh zaporozhskikh* [Born on the lands of Zaporozh'e] (Kiev: Politicheskoi literatury Ukrainy, 1980), 70–77.

63. Rotmistrov, *Stal'naia gvardiia*, 189–190.

64. The 11th Motorized Brigade had been left along the Psel River by its parent 10th Tank Corps when it deployed to join the 1st Tank Army. For details on its fight, see I. M. Kravchenko and V. V. Burkov, *Desiatyi tankovyi dneprovskii* [The 10th Dnepr Tank] (Moscow: Voenizdat, 1986), 94–95. During *Totenkopf's* attack the brigade's 2d Motorized Rifle Battalion was encircled in the Psel valley and destroyed. The brigade, which emerged from the day's action with only 30 percent of its personnel and none of its heavy equipment, was withdrawn into reserve the following day.

65. *Sbornik*, no. 11, p. 151.

6. The Germans Halt

1. P. P. Vechnyi et al., eds., *Sbornik materialov po izucheniiu opyta voiny* [Collection of materials for the study of war experience], no. 11, March–April 1944), 71.

2. Ibid.

3. See, for example, "Feindlage am 11.7.1943," *Kreigstagebuchkarte Pz. A.O.K. 4*, in NAM series T-313, roll 369, and analogous maps from the records of Army Detachment Kempf.

4. Paul Carell, *Scorched Earth: Hitler's War on Russia 1941–1943*, Ewald Osers, trans. (London: Harrap, 1970), 84.

5. Ibid., 95–96.

6. Ibid., 86. Janusz Piekalkiewicz, *Operation "Citadel": Kursk and Orel,* Michaela Nierhaus, trans. (Novato, Ca.: Presidio Press, 1987), 204, without citing his source, states, "Fifteen dead and forty-nine seriously injured were the result of this error."

7. Ibid., 86–87.

8. Ibid., 86.

9. *Sbornik,* no. 11, p. 70.

10. P. Ia. Egorov et al., *Dorogami pobed* [On the roads to victory] (Moscow: Voenizdat, 1969), 35–36.

11. P. A. Rotmistrov, *Stal'naia gvardiia* [Steel guard] (Moscow: Voenizdat, 1984), 188–189.

12. A. P. Riazansky, *V ogne tankovykh srazhenii* [In the fire of tank battles] (Moscow: Nauka, 1975), 69. Riazansky's history of the 5th Guards Mechanized Corps provides the most thorough account of its combat role at Kursk.

13. Ibid., 74–75.

14. Helmut Spaeter, *The History of the Panzercorps Grossdeutschland,* vol. 2 (Winnipeg: Fedorowicz, 1995), 129.

15. *Sbornik,* no. 11, p. 147. For the critical action in this sector, see also I. M. Kravchenko and V. V. Burkov, *Desiatyi tankovyi dneprovskii* [The 10th Dnepr Tank] (Moscow: Voenizdat, 1986), 92–95; M. E. Katukov, *Na ostrie glavnogo udara* [At the point of the main attack] (Moscow: Voenizdat, 1976), 237–239; and other Soviet corps and divisional histories.

16. Kravchenko, *Desiatyi tankovyi,* 92.

17. F. W. von Mellenthin, *Panzer Battles* (Norman: University of Oklahoma Press, 1956), 227–228.

18. Spaeter, *Grossdeutschland,* 129–130.

19. *Sbornik,* no. 11, p. 71.

20. G. A. Koltunov and B. G. Solov'ev, *Kurskaia bitva* [The Battle of Kursk] (Moscow: Voenizdat, 1970), 175.

21. G. K. Zhukov, *Reminiscences and Reflections,* vol. 2 (Moscow: Progress, 1985), 190. Stalin telephoned Zhukov on 12 July and ordered him to Kursk now that the Briansk and Western Front offensives were under way.

22. Rotmistrov, *Stal'naia gvardiia,* 192.

23. Rudolf Lehmann, *The Leibstandarte III,* Nick Alcott, trans. (Winnipeg: Fedorowicz, 1993), 239.

24. Out of the 293 tanks and assault guns available on the morning of 12 July. See Appendix D.

25. See Appendix D. On the other hand, Gotthard Heinrici and Friedrich Wilhelm Hauck, *Citadel: The Attack on the Russian Kursk Salient,* Joseph Welch, trans., U.S. National Archives, note 92, places the II SS Panzer Corps strength on 13 July at 157 tanks and assault guns and 11 T-34s.

26. The Soviet 24th Guards Tank Brigade spearheaded the counterattack with the newly arrived 42d Guards Rifle Division in the sector just north of Polezhaev and at least prevented *Totenkopf* forces from entirely clearing Soviet forces from the north bank of the Psel. Elements of the 18th Tank Corps also participated in the counterattack.

27. Riazansky, *V ogne*, 74. The author inflates German strength by incorrectly claiming that the 11th Panzer Division had joined *Totenkopf's* assault.

28. Lehmann, *Leibstandarte*, 240.

29. Ibid.

30. Ibid.

31. Ibid.

32. Rotmistrov, *Stal'naia gvardiia*, 194.

33. *Sbornik*, no. 11, p. 152.

34. See, for example, "Tagliche Lagenkarten vom 10.7–14.7.43," *Kreigstagebuch No. 2, AOK 8, Ia, AOK 8, 44701/14*, in NAM T-312, roll 56, which shows the disposition of Army Detachment Kempf during the period and the movement of XXIV Panzer Corps. The corps assembled in the region east and south of Khar'kov on 12 July and could have been committed into combat two days later. The XXIV Panzer Corps totaled 104 tanks and 7 assault guns (45 tanks in SS *Wiking* and 59 tanks and 7 assault guns in the 23d Panzer).

35. Erich von Manstein, *Lost Victories* (Chicago: Henry Regnery, 1958), 448–449; Earl Ziemke, *Stalingrad to Berlin: The German Defeat in the East* (Washington, D.C.: Office of the Chief of Military History, United States Army, 1968), 137.

36. *Sbornik*, no. 11, pp. 72, 147. Graphic details of the two days of fighting are found in Kravchenko, *Desiatyi tankovyi*, 98–101; and in the 3d Panzer and *Grossdeutschland* unit histories cited above. As usual, these accounts of the operations agree on detail, if not on interpretation.

37. Von Mellenthin, *Panzer Battles*, 228–229.

38. Lehmann, *Leibstandarte*, 243.

39. *Sbornik*, no. 11, p. 72.

40. James Lucas, *Das Reich; The Military Role of 2d SS Division* (London: Arms and Armour, 1991), 112.

41. Ibid.

42. By the evening of 14 July, Group Trufanov was reinforced by the 31st and 32d Antitank Artillery Brigades with over 100 antitank guns.

43. Rudolf Lehmann, *The Leibstandarte III*, Nick Alcott, trans. (Winnipeg: Fedorowicz, 1993), 246–248; and Silvester Stadler, *Die Offensive gegen Kursk 1943* (Osnabruck: Munin Verlag GmbH, 1980), 154. See also Vasilevsky's final report to the *Stavka*, found in A. M. Vasilevsky, *Delo vsei zhizni* [A lifelong cause] (Minsk: Belarus, 1984), 309. See Appendix F.

44. The 4th Guards Tanks Corps had 168 tanks and 21 self-propelled guns, and the 1st Mechanized Corps had 204 tanks.

45. According to Rotmistrov, *Stal'naia gvardiia*, 201–202, and numerous other sources, the offensive, which Zhukov mandated, took place from 17 through 24 July. Rotmistrov later wrote: "After a short, but powerful artillery preparation, 5th Guards Tank Army went over to the offensive. However, the tempo of advance was not high. The enemy held off our formations with strong rear guards that were made up of grenadier regiments, tanks, artillery, mortars, and sappers. They mined the approaches to high ground, population points, forest groves, and road junctions and displayed strong fire resistance. . . . On the night of 24 July, 5th Guards Tank Army without

the 2d Guards Tatsinskaia and 2d Tank Corps, which were transferred to General A. S. Zhadov's 5th Guards Army, withdrew to assembly areas designated by the *front* commander."

It is no coincidence, however, that this period corresponded to the withdrawal of the II SS Panzer Corps and German forces in general to new defense lines north of Belgorod. And the panzer corps did so without any interference from Soviet attacks. As was the case in late February and March 1943 in the Rzhev salient, Soviet historians exploited a German planned withdrawal to take credit for an essentially nonexistent Soviet offensive.

7. Soviet Counteroffensives

1. "Proryv oborony na flange orlovskoi gruppirovki nemtsev" [The penetration of the flank of the German Orel grouping], in *Sbornik materialov po izucheniiu opyta voiny, No. 10 (ianvar'–fevral' 1944g.* [Collection of materials for the study of war experience, No. 10 (January–February 1944)] (Moscow: Voenizdat, 1944), 4. Classified secret; declassified in 1964. Hereafter cited as *Sbornik,* no. 10. This volume details the preparation and conduct of 11th Guards Army's operation north of Orel.

2. G. Zhukov, "Na Kurskoi duge" [In the Kursk bulge], *VIZh,* no. 8 (August 1967); 81.

3. For the details, context, and consequences of Soviet strategic planning for the 1943 summer campaign, see David M. Glantz, "Soviet Military Strategy during the Second Period of War (November 1942–December 1943): A Reappraisal," *Journal of Military History,* no. 60 (January 1996); 115–150.

4. Bagramian's army and supporting tank corps numbered 170,500 men, 648 tanks and self-propelled guns, and almost 3,000 guns and mortars. In his sixteen-kilometer penetration sector alone, Bagramian concentrated 59,777 men, 615 tanks and self-propelled guns, and over 2,900 guns and mortars. For exact figures, see *Sbornik,* no. 10, p. 8; and G. F. Krivosheev, ed., *Grif sekretnosti sniat* [The seal of secrecy removed] (Moscow: Voenizdat, 1993), 189. Boldin's 50th Army consisted of 54,062 men, 236 guns (76mm and over), 241 antitank guns, 50 antiaircraft guns, 594 82mm and 120mm mortars, and 87 tanks and self-propelled guns. Supporting *front* elements brought this total to 62,800 personnel. See Krivosheev, *Grif sekretnosti sniat,* 189. For other details on the 50th Army's composition and role in the operation, see F. D. Pankov, *Ognennye rubezhi: boevoi put' 50-1 armii v Velikoi Otechestvennoi voine* [Firing lines: The combat path of the 50th Army in the Great Patriotic War] (Moscow: Voenizdat, 1984), 128–143. See Appendix B for precise Soviet order of battle and Appendix D for precise army strengths.

5. Fediuninsky's 11th Army was released to Western Front control on 12 July, and Badanov's 4th Tank Army, still forming in the Moscow Military District on 12 July, joined the Western Front six days later. The 11th Army consisted of eight rifle divisions, a tank regiment, and supporting troops and the 4th Tank Army consisted of the combat-seasoned 6th Guards Mechanized and 11th Tank Corps, and the new 30th Tank Corps, the latter formed by volunteers from the Ural tank factories. For further details, see I. I. Iushchik, *Odinnadtsatyi tankovyi korpus v boiakh za rodinu* [The 11th Tank Corps in combat for the homeland] (Moscow: Voenizdat, 1962), 32–

40; and M. G. Fomichev, *Put' nachinalsia s Urala* [The journey began in the Urals] (Moscow: Voenizdat, 1976), 34–45. Major General V. V. Kriukov's 2d Guards Cavalry Corps was also assigned to the Western Front on 18 July to cooperate with the 4th Tank Army in the anticipated exploitation.

6. Soviet sources on the Briansk Front's role in the operation are fewer in number. Among the best are A. B. Gorbatov, *Gody i voiny* [Years and wars] (Moscow: Voenizdat, 1980), 214–229, by the 3d Army commander; V. A. Beliavsky, *Strely skrestilis' na Shpree* [Arrows crisscrossed on the Spree] (Moscow: Voenizdat, 1972), 76–113, about the 63d Army; and L. Sandalov, "Brianskii front v orlovskoi operatsii" [The Briansk Front in the Orel operation], *Voenno-istoricheskii zhurnal* [Military-historical journal; hereafter cited as *VIZh*] 8 (August 1963): 72, by the Briansk Front's chief of staff. Gorbatov's 3d Army consisted of six rifle divisions, two separate tank regiments, and strong supporting artillery, while the 63d Army contained seven rifle divisions and single tank and self-propelled gun regiments. These were supported by the three rifle divisions of the 25th Rifle Corps, five army tank regiments, and three army self-propelled gun regiments. See Appendix B for precise Soviet order of battle.

7. For details on the 3d Guards Tank Army's composition and role in the operation, there are many good sources, including A. M. Zvartsev, ed., *3-ia gvardeiskaia tankovaia: boevoi put' 3-i gvardeiskoi tankovoi armii* [3d Guards Tank: The combat path of 3d Guards Tank Army] (Moscow: Voenizdat, 1982), 61–85; N. G. Nersesian, *Kievsko-Berlinskii: boevoi put' 6-go gvardeiskogo tankovogo korpusa* [Kiev-Berlin: The combat path of 6th Guards Tank Corps] (Moscow: Voenizdat, 1974), 38–60, on 12th Tank Corps during the Orel operation; A. A. Vetrov, *Tak i bylo* [So it was] (Moscow: Voenizdat, 1982), 133–153, on 15th Tank Corps in the Orel operation; and I. Iakubovsky, "3-ia gvardeiskaia tankovaia armiia v bitve pod Kurskom" [3d Guards Tank Army in the Battle of Kursk], *Voennaia mysl'* [Military Thought] 8 (August 1971); 54–76. According to the latter, the 3d Guards Tank Army strength of 731 tanks and self-propelled guns consisted of 475 T-34 medium tanks, 224 T-70 light tanks, and 32 self-propelled guns. Rybalko's tank army was released to Briansk Front control on 14 July.

8. In addition to Sandalov's account, two divisional histories describe action on the Bolkhov axis. Belov's 61st Army, with its longer front, contained the 9th Guards Rifle Corps of three divisions, which was designated to make the army main attack, five additional rifle divisions, a separate destroyer brigade, a separate tank regiment, a self-propelled gun regiment, and supporting units. See Appendix B for full order of battle.

9. Krivosheev, *Grif sekretnosti sniat,* 189, claims that 409,000 men were committed in the operation.

10. For example, according to ibid., 188–189, Central Front strength throughout Citadel was 738,000 personnel. During Operation Kutuzov, the *front* counted a total of 645,300 personnel. Overall, during the Orel operation the three participating Soviet *fronts* committed 927,494 troops to combat out of 1,286,049 personnel available to the three *fronts* (less the 3d Guards and 4th Tank Armies). These troops were supported by 22,075 guns and mortars and 2,192 tanks and self-propelled guns. See Appendix E for details. See G. A. Koltunov and B. G. Solov'ev, *Kurskaia bitva* [The Battle of Kursk] (Moscow: Voenizdat, 1970), 188, for slightly different figures.

11. That is, the 2d Tank Army lost well over half of the 600-plus tanks in the 3d, 16th, and 9th Tank Corps. After Citadel, the 19th Tank Corps was detached to support

the 70th Army and the 9th Tank Corps was retained in the Central Front's reserve. This left the 2d Tank Army with no more than 200 tanks to support the Central Front's main attack by the 13th Army.

12. See Appendix A for full German order of battle.

13. According to Koltunov and Solov'ev, *Kurskaia bitva*, 188, German strength in the Orel operation was 400,000 men, 6,000 guns and mortars, and 1,000 tanks and assault guns, providing a twofold Soviet superiority in manpower and better than threefold in artillery and armor. These figures, however, count total German strength throughout the operation. Initially, the Second Panzer Army fielded about 160,000 men, about 175 tanks, and a like number of assault guns, yielding a Soviet manpower superiority of over seven to one and armor superiority of about eight to one. These figures changed in the Germans' favor as the Ninth Army's forces regrouped to meet the new Soviet threat. Soviet concentration created unprecedented Soviet force superiority in certain sectors. For example, the 59,777 men and 615 tanks and self-propelled guns in the 11th Guards Army's shock group, deployed in a sixteen-kilometer sector, faced two German infantry regiments, backed up by a combat group of the 5th Panzer Division in tactical reserve, or a total of fewer than 10,000 men and 40 tanks. See *Sbornik*, no. 10, p. 8, which counts two full German divisions (28,000) men opposite the shock group.

14. For details, see David M. Glantz, *Soviet Military Deception in the Second World War* (London: Frank Cass, 1989), 160–193.

15. Albert Seaton, *The Russo-German War, 1941–1945* (New York: Praeger, 1971), 366–367.

16. John Erickson, *The Road to Berlin* (Boulder, Colo: Westview Press, 1983), 108. This work contains the best-balanced summary of the Orel operation found in English.

17. For combat details, see *Sbornik*, no. 10, pp. 24–26; Koltunov, *Kurskaia bitva*, 207–212; and numerous German documents, including "Chefkarten, 23 Anlagen, Anlagenband 36 zum KTB, Pz AOK 2, Ia (1 June–13 Aug 1943)," *PZ AOK 2, 37075/49*, in NAM T-313, roll 171; and the associated Second Panzer Army war diaries (*Kreigstagebuchen*).

18. Gorbatov attacked with his 235th and 380th Rifle Divisions abreast in a six-kilometer sector, backed up by his 308th Rifle Division. Kolpakchi arrayed his 129th, 348th, 287th, and 250th Rifle Divisions in first echelon, backed up by the 397th and 5th Rifle Divisions.

19. The KV-1 tanks were probably from the 3d Army's supporting 82d Separate Tank Regiment. The 114th Separate Tank Regiment also supported this army's assault. The 231st Separate Tank Regiment and the 1452d Self-propelled Artillery Regiment supported the 63d Army's first echelon divisions.

20. Sandalov, "Brianskii front," 67. This contains General Popov's report on the first day of his *front's* action and Marshal Zhukov's more optimistic report on the Orel offensive.

21. Seaton, *Russo-German War*, 367.

22. German intelligence reports indicated that the Soviets committed the 4th Guards Army's 3d Guards Tank Corps into the fierce battle east of Orel (from the *Stavka* reserve). This, however, cannot be confirmed by Soviet sources. Both the 4th Guards Army and its associated tank corps did go into action during the latter stages of the subsequent Operation Rumiantsev.

23. For details on the fight east of Bolkhov, see Sandalov, "Brianskii front"; D. K. Mal'kov, *Skvoz' dym i plamia* [Through the smoke and flames] (Moscow: Voenizdat, 1970), 65–79, a history of the 12th Guards Rifle Division; and *Gvardeiskaia chernivskaia: boevoi put' 76-i gvardeiskoi strelkovoi chernigovskoi krasnoznamennoi divizii* [Guards Chernigov: The combat path of the Chernigov Red Banner 76th Guards Rifle Division] (Moscow: Voenizdat, 1976), 124–139.

24. In addition to the other sources on the 3d Guards Tank Army, see Richard N. Armstrong, *Red Army Tank Commanders: The Armored Guards* (Atglen, Pa.: Schiffer Military/Aviation History, 1994), 180–190.

25. The 12th Tank Corps became the 6th Guards Tank Corps, the 15th Tank Corps became the 7th Guards, and the 2d Mechanized Corps was renamed the 7th Guards Mechanized Corps.

26. Earl Ziemke, *Stalingrad to Berlin: The German Defeat in the East* (Washington, D.C.: Office of the Chief of Military History, United States Army, 1968), 138.

27. The Germans also moved the XXXXI Panzer Corps headquarters northward to control the redeployed forces.

28. Janusz Piekalkiewicz, *Operation "Citadel": Kursk and Orel*, Michaela Nierhaus, trans. (Novato, Ca.: Presidio Press, 1987), 251–252.

29. Hermann Plocher, *The German Air Force Versus Russia, 1943* (New York: Arno Press, 1967), 99–100.

30. Fediuninsky's army consisted of eight rifle divisions, a separate tank regiment, and supporting arms. See Appendix B for the army's precise composition. The army moved piecemeal into the growing gap between the 11th Guards and 50th Army, which had been formed when Boldin's advance lagged due to tenacious and skillful resistance by the 5th Panzer Division and several German infantry divisions.

31. Ziemke, *Stalingrad to Berlin*, 139–140; Piekalkiewicz, *Operation "Citadel,"* 258–260.

32. Among the many Soviet sources on this phase of the operation, see Koltunov, *Kurskaia bitva*, 254–257.

33. Plocher, *The German Air Force versus Russia, 1943*, 105.

34. Ibid., 106–107.

35. Krivosheev, *Grif sekretnosti sniat*, 189. According to Krivosheev, Soviet casualties amounted to 112,529 irrevocable losses (killed, severely wounded, missing, and captured) and 317,361 medical losses (wounded or ill). This amounted to well over 33 percent of the approximately 1,286,049 personnel the Soviets ultimately committed to the operation.

36. G. K. Zhukov, *Reminiscences and Reflections*, vol. 2 (Moscow: Progress, 1985), 194, later explained his differences with Stalin:

> After repeated talks, the Supreme Commander reluctantly approved our decision, since this was the only way.
> The operation was planned in great depth and required careful preparation and all-round provisioning, otherwise it might end in failure for us. A well-calculated and prepared offensive should guarantee a definite breakthrough of the enemy's defenses in tactical and operational depth, and such an assault should also provide the right conditions for subsequent offensive operations.
> However, the Supreme Commander was pressing us to start the operation. It took Vasilevsky and myself a great deal of trouble to persuade him that the action should be

mounted when everything was completely ready and all materiel was at hand. The Supreme Commander concurred with us.

Steppe Front commander, Konev, was even more specific:

The ten-day pause from 23 July to 3 August was extremely necessary to prepare our forces for the counteroffensive. First, we had to plan in complex conditions considering that the enemy succeeded in withdrawing his forces to prepared defensive positions. We could not exclude the possibility that the German command could have reinforced his withdrawing forces by transferring divisions from the Donbas and other sections of the Soviet-German front and go over to a counteroffensive. Second, we had to move *front* forces up to positions mandated by the *Stavka*, which required a regrouping that required considerable time. Third, Steppe Front forces had almost no rear services, since a considerable number of its units had been transferred to the Voronezh Front. Therefore, a *Stavka* VGK directive directly stated: "The Chief of Rear Services of the Red Army, Comrade Khrulev, will provide the Steppe Front with necessary rear services by the evening of 18.7." Fourth, the offensives by Southwestern Front forces in the Izium region and by Southern Front forces along the Mius River, which had begun on 17 July, were not fully developed. Fifth and finally, defensive combat was still under way in separate sectors of the Voronezh Front. Thus, to go over to the offensive from the march on the Khar'kov axis in complex operational-strategic conditions was not considered possible. It would have been an unorganized and unplanned offensive, and certainly it would have been difficult to count on its success.

See I. S. Konev, "Na khar'kovskom napravlenii" [Along the Khar'kov axis], *VIZh* 8 (August 1963): 53–54.

37. Many of the Soviet offensives during the summer campaign were named for "Great Captains" of the Russian Empire. P. A. Rumiantsev, whose name was assigned to the Belgorod-Khar'kov operation, had commanded Russian forces in the Russo-Turkish Wars of the later eighteenth century, and M. I. Kutuzov, for whom the Orel operation was named, commanded Russian armies against Napoleon during the 1812 campaign. In addition, the Soviets attached the code-name "Suvorov" to the Western and Kalinin Fronts' Smolensk operation of August 1943. A. V. Suvorov had commanded Russian armies in the Russo-Turkish War and early Napoleonic wars of the late eighteenth century.

38. Zhukov had employed similar offensive techniques at Smolensk in summer 1941, in the Moscow counteroffensive of December 1941 and January 1942, and during Operation Mars in November and December 1942. He would do so again in April 1945 at Berlin.

39. Because of terrain constraints, initially both tank armies were under Voronezh Front control. Once through the German tactical defenses, Rotmistrov's army would revert to Steppe Front control. For details on planning for Operation Rumiantsev and the extensive number of Soviet sources on the topic, see David M. Glantz, *From the Don to the Dnepr: Soviet Offensive Operations, December 1942–August 1943* (London: Frank Cass, 1991), 229–252.

40. Trofimenko's 27th Army consisted of six rifle divisions, a tank brigade, a separate tank regiment, and 189 tanks and self-propelled guns of the 4th Guards Tank Corps; Moskalenko's 40th of six rifle divisions and the 2d Tank Corps; and Chibisov's 38th of five rifle divisions. See Appendix B for the precise composition.

41. The recommendation for a large-scale envelopment was made by General Moskalenko, 40th Army commander. See K. S. Moskalenko, *Na iugo-zapadnom napravlenie* [On the southwestern axis], vol. 2 (Moscow: "Nauka," 1972), 81.

42. For the relationship between the February and July 1943 Soviet offensive operations around Kursk, see David M. Glantz, "Prelude to Kursk: Soviet Strategic Operations, February–March 1943," *Journal of Slavic Military Studies* 8, 1 (March 1995); 1–35.

43. Ultimately, however, most of these mobile groups performed tactical maneuvers since German resistance forced them to be employed in their parent armies' penetration operations.

44. See David M. Glantz, *Soviet Military Operational Art: In Pursuit of Deep Battle* (London: Frank Cass, 1991), 121–138, for a discussion of the evolution of Soviet operational concepts and citations on the many Soviet sources that defined the use of operational maneuver forces.

45. General Malinovsky's Southwestern Front conducted the Izium-Barvenkovo operation with the 1st and 8th Guards Armies and the 23d Tank and 1st Guards Mechanized Corps. General Tolbukhin's Southern Front employed the 5th Shock, 2d Guards, and 28th Armies as his shock group in the Mius operation, supported by the 2d Guards and 4th Guards Mechanized Corps. For details, see A. G. Ershov, *Osvobozhdenie Donbassa* [The liberation of the Donbas] (Moscow: Voenizdat, 1973), 98, 110–112.

46. For a description of the Mius battles, see Ershov, *Osvobozhdenie*, 110–112; and *Sixth Army, Russia*, Ms. no. C-078 (Historical Division, European Command, undated). This manuscript in the Army historical series prepared by German general officers in the postwar years remains the best German account of the Mius defense. See also Ziemke, *Stalingrad to Berlin*, 138.

47. Glantz, *Soviet Military Deception*, 174–177. V. A. Matsulenko, *Operativnaia maskirovka voisk* [Operational deception of forces] (Moscow: Voenizdat, 1975), outlines Soviet deception operations throughout the war. This study is backed up and confirmed by a formerly classified volume, "Dokumenty po voprosam operativnoi maskirovki voisk" [Documents concerning the operational deception of forces], in *Sbornik boevykh dokumentov Velikoi Otechestvennoi voiny, vypusk 27* [Collection of combat documents of the Great Patriotic War, issue 27] (Moscow: Voenizdat, 1956), prepared for publication by the Military-Scientific Directorate of the General Staff.

48. For example, the 1st Tank Army numbered 37,000 men, 542 tanks (including 417 T-34s), and 27 self-propelled guns, while the 5th Guards Tank Army had about the same number of personnel, 503 tanks, and 40 self-propelled guns. For details on the tank armies' operations, see Kh. Babadzhanian et al., *Liuki otkryli v Berline* [They opened the hatchway to Berlin] (Moscow: Voenizdat, 1973), 66–90; and P. Ia. Egorov et al., *Dorogami pobed* [On the roads to victory] (Moscow: Voenizdat, 1969), 66–83.

49. Both the 5th Guards and 6th Guards Armies were organized into two guards rifle corps, each with three Guards rifle divisions. The latter army had an additional rifle division. The Steppe Front's 53d Army fielded seven rifle divisions but had no corps organization. The 69th Army's seven rifle divisions were assigned to two rifle corps, and the 7th Guards Army's eight rifle divisions were organized into three rifle corps.

50. Armstrong, *Red Army Tank Commanders*, 63–64.

51. Throughout the entire operation, the Soviets committed 1,144,400 men and about 2,439 tanks and self-propelled guns in the Belgorod-Khar'kov operation.

Attesting to the heavy fighting, the Soviets suffered 255,566 casualties (71,611 irrevocable and 183,955 medical—wounded and ill). Ultimately, the Germans committed approximately 330,000 men and about 600 tanks and assault guns. See Glantz, *From the Don to the Dnepr*, 399; and Krivosheev, *Grif sekretnosti sniat*, 190.

52. For details on the conduct of the offensive and the hundreds of available Soviet sources, see Glantz, *From the Don to the Dnepr*, 251–365.

53. Ziemke, *Stalingrad to Berlin*, 151–152.

54. By 9 August the 1st Tank Army's strength had fallen from 569 tanks and self-propelled guns to 260 tanks and self-propelled guns, while the 5th Guards Tank Army's strength had eroded from 543 tanks and self-propelled to just over 200. See Glantz, *From the Don to the Dnepr*, 393.

55. For details of the Bogodukhov battle and subsequent fighting, see also Koltunov, *Kurskaia bitva*, 303–352.

56. By 13 August the 1st Tank Army's armored strength had fallen to 134 tanks and self-propelled guns, while the 5th Guards Tank Army retained just over 100 armored vehicles. See Glantz, *From the Don to the Dnepr*, 393.

57. Ziemke, *Stalingrad to Berlin*, 153.

58. For details, see F. Utenkov, "V boiakh pod Akhtyrkoi" [In the battles for Akhtyrka], *VIZh*, no. 8 (August 1982); 38–42; and N. I. Biriukov, *Trudnaia nauka pobezhdat'* [Hard science of prevailing] (Moscow: Voenizdat, 1968), 12–16. Biriukov was a corps commander in the 4th Guards Army.

59. See Appendix B for the precise organization of the 47th Army.

60. Ziemke, *Stalingrad to Berlin*, 156.

61. H. Reinhardt, *German Army Group Operations on the Eastern Front 1941–1943: Southern Area*, Ms. no. P-114C, vol. 5 (USAREUR, Historical Division, 1954), 47.

62. *Unterstellungen und Kampfgruppen Hgr Sud*, Stand. 23.8.43, Stand. 25.8.43. See Appendix E for details.

63. See A. I. Radzievsky, *Tankovyi udar* [Tank strike] (Moscow: Voenizdat, 1977), 212. The over 1,000 lost tanks in the 1st Tank Army included tanks lost on several occasions and reinforcements provided by *front*.

64. Ziemke, *Stalingrad to Berlin*, 157.

8. Conclusions

1. Erich von Manstein, *Lost Victories* (Chicago: Henry Regnery, 1958) 446–447.

2. Ibid., 447.

3. Ibid., 449. In this instance, as in many others, von Manstein was eager to shift any blame from himself to Hitler.

4. Heinz Guderian, *Panzer Leader* (New York: Ballantine, 1965), 244–245.

5. Ibid., 246, 250.

6. F. W. von Mellenthin, *Panzer Battles* (Norman: University of Oklahoma Press, 1956), 214–215.

7. Ibid., 215.

8. Ibid.

9. Ibid., 216.

10. Ibid., 215, 216.

11. Gotthard Heinrici and Friedrick Wilhelm Hauck, *Citadel; The Attack on the Russian Kursk Salient,* Joseph Welch, trans., U.S. National Archives, 16–17.

12. Ibid., 78.

13. Ibid., 82–83.

14. Ibid., 83.

15. Ibid., 83–84.

16. Ibid., 84–85.

17. David M. Glantz, "Prelude to Kursk: Soviet Strategic Operations, February–March 1943." *Journal of Slavic Military Studies* 8, 1 (March 1995); 1–35.

18. P. P. Vechnyi et al., *Sbornik materialov po izucheniiu opyta voiny* [Collection of materials for the study of war experience], no. 11, March–April 1944 (Moscow: Voenizdat, 1944), 20.

19. A. M. Vasilevsky, *Delo vsei zhizni* [A lifelong cause] (Minsk: Belarus, 1984), 312–313.

20. *Sbornik,* no. 11, p. 23.

21. For a detailed Soviet General Staff assessment of the operation, including all technical aspects of tank, antitank, artillery, air defense, air, engineer, and logistical support during combat, see David M. Glantz and Harold Orenstein, eds. and trans., *Classified Secret, Kursk 1943: The Soviet General Staff Study* (London: Frank Cass, forthcoming).

22. *Sbornik,* no. 11, p. 157. Artillery fire (field and antitank) accounted for about 70 percent of German tank losses and 71 percent of Soviet tank losses. Losses to German tanks were assessed at 5 percent for the 2d Tank Army and 13 percent for the 1st Tank Army.

23. Heinrici and Hauck, *Citadel,* 78.

24. Ibid., 79.

25. Ibid., 79–80.

26. G. F. Krivosheev, ed., *Grif sekretnosti sniat* [The seal of secrecy removed] (Moscow: Voenizdat, 1993), 188.

27. For example, in the Voronezh Front from 5 to 18 July, the 6th Guards Army lost 12,810 troops and the 7th Guards Army 11,522 either wounded or burned, which constituted one-third of the *front*'s total casualties of nearly 78,000. These casualties occurred uniformly throughout the duration of the German offensive. On the other hand, between 5 and 18 July, the 40th Army lost 6,289 wounded, primarily after 9 July, when the army's divisions became more heavily engaged. The total of ill generally constituted 13 percent of the total medical casualties, and as a rule, the dead equaled 60 percent of the total number of wounded. In the Central Front during the nine days of defensive combat, the 13th Army suffered 9,500 soldiers wounded and 528 sick. Total killed reached over 80 percent of the number wounded, indicating the ferocity of combat. See E. I. Smirnov, *Voina i voennaia meditsina, 1939–1945 gody* [War and military medicine, 1939–1945] (Moscow: Meditsina, 1979), 289, 294, 296.

28. For example, the 52d and 67th Guards Rifle Divisions and the 15th and 81st Rifle Divisions, which defended tactical positions opposite the German main attacks, suffered between 60 and 70 percent losses. The 90th Guards Rifle Division and the

6th Tank Corps, encircled in the battles around Berezovka, also suffered more than 60 percent losses. The 71st, 73d, and 78th Guards Rifle Divisions, which struggled hard and long on the flanks of the German main thrust, lost between 38 and 45 percent of their strength. The front-line 375th Rifle Division, in the dead space between the II SS and III Panzer Corps, lost almost 40 percent of its strength. Divisions of the 5th Guards and 69th Armies, which were committed to action later in the operation, probably suffered losses of between 20 and 40 percent.

29. Some unofficial sources attribute much higher personnel losses to the Soviets. For example, Boris Sokolov, *Tsena pobedy* [The price of victory] (Moscow: Moskovskii rabochii, 1991), claims the Soviets lost a total of 450,000 killed, 50,000 missing (POWs), and 1.2 million wounded during the three phases of the Kursk operation (against the official figures of 254,470 killed and missing and 608,873 wounded), which amounts to 61 percent of the overall 1.95 million Soviet battle casualties incurred in July and August 1943 on the Eastern Front. While Sokolov's figures are probably somewhat inflated, the official figures are probably conservative. Sokolov places total Soviet tank and self-propelled gun losses at 7,700, somewhat higher than the admitted Soviet figure of 6,064.

30. See Niklas Zetterling, "Loss Rates on the Eastern Front During World War II," *Journal of Slavic Military Studies* 9, 4 (December 1996); 896–906, which quotes from German archival reports. For example, the 320th and 106th Infantry Divisions suffered close to 40 percent losses in the intense fighting along the German right flank.

31. Krivosheev, *Grif sekretnotsti sniat,* 370. For example, the 6th Tank Corps fell in strength from 169 tanks on 6 July to 35 tanks on 11 July. It was subsequently reinforced to a strength of 52 tanks on 18 July. The 3d Mechanized Corps, which had 250 tanks and self-propelled guns on 6 July, had barely 50 remaining on 13 July. The 2d Guards Tank Corps had 174 tanks on 5 July, 100 on 11 July, and fewer than 50 on 14 July. 10th Tank Corps fell in strength from 185 tanks and self-propelled guns on 5 July to 100 tanks and self-propelled guns on 11 July. It lost half of the remainder to the XXXXVIII Panzer Corps' 14 July counterattack. Finally, during the battle for Prokhorovka, the 5th Guards Tank Army lost over 400 of its 840 tanks and self-propelled guns, prompting Stalin reportedly to have asked Rotmistrov, "What have you done to your magnificent tank army?" This quotation is paraphrased from a conversation with Colonel F. D. Sverdlov concerning a correspondence between Stalin and Rotmistrov after the battle.

32. Heinrici and Hauck, *Citadel,* note 91.

33. Krivosheev, *Grif sekretnosti sniat,* 189.

34. Ibid., 370. Tank and self-propelled strength includes 2,893 weapons in the Western, Briansk, and Central Fronts, and the 3d Guards Tank Army's and the 4th Tank Army's 731 and 642 tanks and self-propelled guns.

35. Krivosheev, *Grif sekretnosti sniat,* 190.

36. Based on the conditions, likely enemy, and terrain, Soviet medical authorities projected that the 7th Guards Army would suffer 11,000 wounded and 1,300 ill, or a total of 12,300 medical casualties during ten days of combat. This figure, which amounted to 22.3 percent of total army combat strength, was an accurate projection. During the operation the army lost 13,290 troops, including 11,105 wounded and

2,184 ill, although the operation took twenty-one rather than ten days. See M. F. Voitenko, "Organizatsiia meditsinskogo obespecheniia 7-i gvardeiskoi armii v Belgorodsko-khar'khovskoi nastupatel'noi operatsii" [The organization of medical support of 7th Guards Army in the Belgorod-Khar'kov offensive operation], *Voenno-meditsinskii zhurnal* [Military-medical journal], no. 8 (August 1983): 17.

37. Von Manstein, *Lost Victories,* 450.

38. Guderian, *Panzer Leader,* 251–252.

39. F. W. Von Mellenthin, *Panzer Battles* (Norman: University of Oklahoma Press, 1956), 230.

40. Heinrici and Hauck, *Citadel,* 85.

41. G. K. Zhukov, *Reminiscences and Reflections,* vol. 2 (Moscow: Progress, 1985), 194–195.

42. Vasilevsky, *Delo vsei zhizni,* 340–341.

43. Ibid., 341.

44. Interestingly enough, Western armies went through the same sort of education against blitzkrieg and with mixed results. Having failed to deal with it in 1940, Western armies struggled to overcome it in 1944. The British tried to ape German armored practices at Caen (Operation Goodwood) but failed in the teeth of an effective German antitank defense. In Operation Cobra (St. Lô) the Americans resorted to carpet bombing to smash German defenses and unleash Patton's Third Army for its drive on Paris. At Mortain, American air power combined with determined ground defense sapped the strength and shock power of four attacking German panzer divisions. The same occurred (with the help of weather and terrain) in the Bulge in late 1944, when Hitler unleashed several panzer armies against the Allies. Despite these primarily defensive successes, neither the British nor the Americans were able to mount offensive operations as routinely spectacular as the Germans of 1941 and 1942 or the Soviets of 1943 through 1945, partly because of inexperience and partly because of their less mature force structure and tactical and operational doctrine.

Selective Bibliography

A vast secondary literature exists on the Battle of Kursk, including thousands of books and articles written from the German and Soviet perspectives and a smaller body of literature that attempts to synthesize the two. German sources include memoirs, chapters in numerous accounts of the war on the German Eastern Front, histories of participating units, and a few general studies of the battle. Although less accessible due to limited availability in the West and the language barrier, Soviet sources include an imposing array of memoirs, unit histories, journal articles, and operational studies. Official Soviet military organs prepared a variety of functional studies addressing virtually every aspect of the operation. Because these source materials were hard to obtain and, when available, were considered unreliable, Western authors naturally stressed the German perspective in their work.

In general, sources that have exploited only German archival materials cannot provide accurate Soviet order of battle and sufficient tactical and operational detail on Soviet actions. Of necessity, German interpretation regarding the background, course, and outcome of battles have predominated in these works. On the other hand, while much of their tactical and operational detail is accurate, Soviet sources are often permeated with political biases, exaggeration, and official interpretations, which tend to minimize Soviet mistakes, defeats, command disputes, and combat losses. In short, although they often portray the ebb and flow of combat accurately, they distort the course of battle and show Soviet leaders and forces in the best possible light.

Given the considerable amount of material on the Battle of Kursk, this bibliography includes a selection of the most useful German secondary materials, a more comprehensive list of Soviet secondary sources, and newly available primary source materials.

German Primary Sources

Among the most valuable German primary sources on the Battle of Kursk are the postwar compilations of German archival materials issued in book form and the voluminous German military unit records maintained in Western archives, including the U.S. National Archives in Washington, D.C., and the German Militargeschichtlichen Forschungsamt in Freiberg and Berlin. Surviving OKH (Army High Command) records are fragmentary, since the Soviet Army captured many German unit war diaries, particularly later in the war, and some German forces destroyed their records to prevent them from falling into Soviet hands. Still other unit records were destroyed by Allied fire while being removed from Berlin after the Nazi government's collapse. The most important of these missing records for the Kursk period are many of the records of German Ninth Army. The mass of surviving archival material also includes a significant number of personal diaries interspersed among thousands of unit records at every level of army command, some of which contain information on Kursk.

Among the most important series of OKH and German Army unit records available to scholars on microfilm is the National Archives Microfilm (NAM) series T-78, the records of Foreign Armies East (Fremde Heere Ost). This series contains German wartime intelligence materials and assessments of all aspects of the Soviet Armed Forces and Soviet military-industrial activity. These records provide invaluable materials on the German intelligence picture prior to and during the battle and on the composition of Soviet units. Of equal value are the extensive German unit records. NAM series T-311 contains materials from German Army Groups, NAM series T-312 and T-313 from armies and panzer armies, and NAM series T-314 and T-315 from corps and divisions, respectively.

Even today, new primary source materials that will enrich existing German archival holdings are appearing. Hundreds of postwar memoir studies have lain fallow while accounts by more famous and popular German commanders occupied the historical limelight. These newly discovered memoirs and studies include massive manuscripts written during the immediate postwar years by less famous German military leaders under the auspices of U.S. military historical organizations, in particular, the Historical Division of U.S. European Command. Most prominent in this extensive group of German-language manuscripts is the extensive memoir by the German defensive specialist, G. Heinrici, which has just been rediscovered and is now being prepared for publication. Heinrici's study of the Battle of Kursk is of particular importance for this volume.

Soviet Primary Sources

The closed nature of Soviet society and ideological restrictions on the writing of history have complicated the definition and classification of Russian-language primary source materials. Prior to 1987 the Soviet government limited access to their archives to a handful of "official" historians. When granted, access was carefully controlled. The Soviets limited their official "release" of archival materials to specially selected documents on specific themes, which Party authorities cleared for publication and published to achieve desired political effects. This material was published in historical studies, many of military operational nature, or in the memoirs of notable Soviet wartime leaders. The Party permitted military historians to write on narrow topics from a restricted data base of officially approved sources. While many of the facts contained in these military histories, studies, and memoirs were accurate, certain topics, such as casualties, embarrassing defeats, and the actual correlation of forces between the warring sides were either severely proscribed or routinely distorted. History also served starkly utilitarian ends, such as the advancement of specific political aims or military education. Almost coincidentally, and somewhat ironically, Soviet commitment to sound education in the realm of military science had the beneficial effect of producing even greater candor, although even here within severe constraints.

Because of the unavailability of archival materials, detailed military studies prepared for the purposes of military education and memoir materials, which the Soviets used as vehicles for discussing controversial military and even political issues, fell into a category midway between what Westerners considered as primary and secondary source material. If properly juxtaposed against Western primary sources, these military studies and memoirs served as proxies for actual primary sources—but proxies that had to be handled critically and with care.

The Red Army General Staff Historical Section prepared a variety of studies during and after the war on the basis of archival materials. The Soviet Army used these publications, which were classified as top secret and secret, in army education and training. In the main, these studies incorporated archival materials directly and accurately and were generally honest and primary in nature. Like their unclassified counterpart studies, however, they avoided controversial political issues and tended to avoid politically sensitive defeats. A few of these wartime studies fell into the hands of German intelligence during the war and, hence, into Western hands after the war ended. Many more were released during the Gorbachev period of *glasnost'* and after the fall of the Soviet Union. The Soviet Army General Staff ceased preparation and publication of these studies in the mid-1960s, when the function of historical analysis was passed to the Ministry of Defense's newly created Military History Institute. Henceforth, studies prepared by the politicized institute lacked the depth, accuracy, and candor of their earlier General Staff counterparts.

Another category of primary sources is the numerous classified military publications that were used for educational purposes at the many Soviet military educational institutions, such as the Voroshilov General Staff Academy and the Frunze Academy. Although Soviet authors wrote these studies on the basis of archival materials, they were subject to the same general constraints as General Staff writers, and the studies varied in accuracy based on contemporary political exigencies. The first round of *glasnost'* was in the late 1950s and 1960s. This period is also referred to as the "thaw." When historical *glasnost'* prevailed, these studies were fairly accurate and consistent with archival materials. Ultimately, however, by the mid-1970s, after the Brezhnev regime had discarded *glasnost'*, the accuracy, candor, and value of these materials had declined to the level of standard secondary sources.

Military archival materials released thus far fall into several distinct categories. The first, most accurate, and most useful are series of works that various directorates of the General Staff prepared for publication from 1942 through 1968. While preparing these series, the Red Army (and Soviet Army) General Staff made a genuine attempt to establish the truth about the course and consequences of wartime military operations and to harness that truth in the service of improving future Soviet Army combat performance. For the most part, the accuracy and candor of these studies compare well with German and Japanese archival records. There were, of course, topics that the General Staff could not address, including some of the most sensitive failed wartime operations (such as the Liuban' operation in early 1942 with its Vlasov connection, Operation Mars, the failed companion piece to the Stalingrad operation, and the abortive Belorussian operation of fall 1943). Also prohibited were politically sensitive topics, such as discussions and disputes between *Stavka* members (Stalin in particular), the General Staff, and field commands, which were numerous throughout the war, and the motives for controversial political and military decisions.

The principal and most important General Staff sources are the *Sborniki* (Collections) of materials prepared by the Soviet (Red) Army General Staff. These General Staff studies, prepared by the Directorate for the Study of War Experience and the Military-historical Directorate, include four distinct collections, three of which contain raw materials on wartime tactical issues and processed studies of military operations. The most important of these series is *Sbornik materialov po izucheniiu opyta Velikoi Otechestvennoi voiny* (Collection of materials for the study of the experience of the Great Patriotic War), abbreviated *SMPIOVOV* and classified secret, which contain one volume devoted exclusively to Kursk and several other volumes covering other aspects of the Kursk operation. The fourth series, entitled *Sbornik boevykh dokumentov Velikoi Otechestvennoi voiny, Vypusk 1–43* (Collection of Combat Documents of the Great Patriotic War, Issue 1–43), abbreviated *SBDVOV* and classified secret, supplemented the other war experience volumes and contained directives and orders from the *Stavka* as well as combat documents relating to the activities of all branches and types of Soviet forces. The first thirty volumes (issues) focused on functional combat themes, and three volumes contained key *Stavka* orders.

Unfortunately, the General Staff halted publication of this document series in the mid-1960s. The General Staff also prepared many studies on wartime operations during wartime or during the immediate postwar years. These General Staff materials, prepared and published during or immediately after the war, were all classified, and their high quality, candor, and accuracy reflected the best traditions of General Staff work. They were, in essence, utilitarian and designed to teach the Red Army how to better conduct combat operations. Other General Staff or Ministry of Defense-derived publications, including wartime and postwar issues of journals (*Voennaia mysl'* [Military thought]) and studies prepared by the Voroshilov General Staff Academy and Frunze Academy during and shortly after the war, achieved this same high quality. Although accurate in the main, these works leave out statistical data, in particular relating to correlation of forces and means.

Another vehicle for primary source releases was a variety of military and political journals. The most important is the organ of the General Staff itself, *Voennaia mysl'*, which was published as a controlled publication from 1937 through 1989 and publicly thereafter. Other journals include the open-source *Voenno-istoricheskii zhurnal* [Military-historical journal], the armed forces historical journal that has been published since 1939, and *Izvestiia TsK KPSS* [News of the Communist Party of the Soviet Union's Central Committee], which Party First Secretary Gorbachev used as a prime vehicle for his *glasnost'* program in the late 1980s. Both journals provided a key conduit for the release of documentary archival materials from the mid- and late 1980s.

It is important to note that most of these materials, General Staff studies and books, other institutional studies, and journals alike, although technically archival, are in some way *processed* and that processing has affected their content. In addition, these are *released* materials, which have only recently found their way to the West largely through commercial conduits. Although release of these materials is welcome, the larger question regarding direct archival access in the Western sense of the word remains unanswered. Although Russian authorities have frequently announced that the archives are open for foreign scholars, that access is still severely limited and in no way comparable to access to Western archives.

In general, classified or restricted Soviet studies published between the mid-1960s and the late 1980s, which supposedly exploited archival materials, as well as secondary studies and memoir literature, lacked the substance and accuracy of their wartime and postwar counterparts and their *glasnost'* successors. While many of their operational and tactical details and their narrative account of events were generally accurate, they exaggerated enemy strength and covered up the worst aspects of Soviet combat performance, in particular, specific details regarding the many Soviet combat disasters. Moreover, their political content was far more pervasive and strident than found in the earlier General Staff volumes. This was particularly disturbing regarding educational materials used at the Voroshilov and Frunze Academies up to the late 1980s.

Voroshilov Academy publications, issued since 1942 in a variety of formats under the imprimatur *VAGSh*, include texts, studies, analytical works, and lectures delivered at the academy. Some of these are multivolume surveys of the history of war and military art, such as a two-volume work edited by the eminent military historian I. E. Shavrov, which were published in revised versions every few years. The most interesting and valuable are the wartime volumes and the collections *(Sborniki)* of wartime materials. In general, the Voroshilov materials are more scholarly in nature and, hence, less inaccurate and political. The studies and lectures from the period after 1968, however, contain the same inaccuracies that are found in other Soviet publications. Frunze Academy publications, which have not been released in as great a number as the Voroshilov materials, share the same characteristics of their Voroshilov counterparts. Studies by these military educational institutions prepared after 1989 have corrected many of these earlier deficiencies.

Finally, the collections of selective documents published in recent journals seem to be authentic and represent a genuine effort to begin an increased flow of released archival materials. By their very nature, however, they are selective, and the flow of materials has noticeably decreased since the downfall of Gorbachev and the collapse of the Soviet Union. It remains to be seen whether this trend will be reversed.

Compared with the past state of Soviet historiographical work on the Great Patriotic War, what has transpired in recent years regarding release of archival materials has been revolutionary. But just as the new Russian Revolution is in its infancy, so also is the revolution in historiography. The archival materials that have been released thus far appear prodigious compared with the meager archival materials previously available (through captured German records). They are, however, really very limited compared with what certainly exists behind still-closed doors. Thus, while there is much to celebrate, there is also much to anticipate.

Secondary Sources

Voennaia mysl' (Military thought), abbreviated as *VM*
Voenno-istoricheskii zhurnal (Military-historical journal), *VIZI*,
Voennyi vestnik (Military herald), *VV*

Amirov, K. V. *Ot Volgi do Al'p: boevoi put' 36-i gvardeiskoi strelkovoi verkhned-neprovskoi krasnoznamennoi ordena Suvorova i Kutuzova II stepeni divizii* [From the Volga to the Alps: The combat path of the Upper Dnepr, Red Banner, and Order of Suvorov and Kutuzov II degree 36th Guards Rifle Division]. Moscow: Voenizdat, 1987.

Anan'ev, I. M. *Tankovye armii v nastuplenii: po opytu Velikoi Otechestvennoi voiny 1941–1945 gg.* [Tank armies in the offensive: Based on the experience of the Great Patriotic War]. Moscow: Voenizdat, 1988.

Arkhipilov, T. I., ed. *Kurskaia bitva: vospominaniia uchastnikov* [The battle of Kursk: Recollections of participants]. Voronezh: Tsentral'no-Chernozemnoe, 1968.

Armstrong, Richard N. *Red Army Tank Commanders: The Armored Guards.* Atglen, Pa: Schiffer Military/Aviation History, 1994.

Babadzhanian, A. Kh. *Dorogy pobedy* [The roads to victory]. Moscow: Voenizdat, 1981. The memoirs of the commander of the 3d Mechanized Corps' 3d Mechanized Brigade.

Babadzhanian, A. Kh., Popel', N. K., Shalin, M. A., and Kravchenko, I. M. *Liuki otkryli v Berline: boevoi put' 1-i gvardeiskoi tankovoi armii* [They opened the hatchways to Berlin: The combat path of the 1st Guards Tank Army]. Moscow: Voenizdat, 1973.

Bagramian, I. Kh. *Tak shli my k pobede* [Thus we went on to victory]. Moscow: Voenizdat, 1988. The memoirs of the 11th Guards Army commander.

———. "Udar na severnom fase Orlovskoi dugi" [The attack on the northern face of the Orel salient]. *VM* 9 (September 1973): 65–74.

———. "Flangovyi udar 11–i gvardeiskoi armii" [The flank attack of the 11th Guards Army]. *VIZh* 7 (July 1963): 83–95.

Batov, P. I. *V pokhodakh i boiakh* [In marches and in battles]. Moscow: DOSAAF, 1984. The memoirs of the 65th Army commander.

Bel'dtsev, P. M., ed. *Kurskaia bitva: vospominaniia, stat'i* [The battle of Kursk: Recollections and essays]. Voronezh: Tsentral'no-Chernozemnoe knizhnoe izdatel'stvo, 1982.

Beliavsky, V. A. *Strely skrestilis' na Shpree* [Arrows crisscrossed on the Spree]. Moscow: Voenizdat, 1973. A memoir of the 63d Army.

Bellamy, Chris. *Red God of War: Soviet Artillery and Rocket Forces.* London: Brassey's, 1986.

Bialar, Seweryn, ed. *Stalin's Generals.* New York: Pegasus, 1969.

Boldin, I. V. *Stranitsy zhizni* [Pages of a life]. Moscow: Voenizdat, 1961. The memoirs of the 50th Army commander.

Bragunsky, R. B., Popel'nitsky, N. S., and Usenkov, M. G. *Taktika artillerii v boevykh primerakh (podrazdeleniia i chasti)* [Artillery tactics in combat examples (subunit and unit)]. Moscow: Voenizdat, 1977.

Bulychev, I. "Voiska sviazi v Kurskoi bitve" [Signal forces in the battle of Kursk], *VIZh* 7 (July 1983): 35–42.

Carell, Paul. *Scorched Earth: Hitler's War on Russia 1941–1943.* Translated by Ewald Osers. Vol. 2. London: George Harrap, 1970.

Chaney, Otto P. *Zhukov.* Norman; University of Oklahoma Press, 1971. Expanded second edition in 1996.

Clark, Alan. *Barbarossa: The Russian-German Conflict 1941–45*. New York: William Morrow, 1966.

Davidenko, V. I., and Iashchenko, N. I. *73-ia gvardeiskaia: sbornik vospominanii, dokumentov i materialov o boevom puti 73-i gvardeiskoi strelkovoi stalingradsko-dunaiskoi krasnoznamennoi divizii* [The 73d Guards: A collection of recollections, documents, and materials about the combat path of the Stalingrad-Danube Red Banner 73d Guards Rifle Division]. Alma-Ata: Kazakhstan, 1986.

Demin, V. A., and Portugal'sky, R. M. *Tanki vkhodiat v proryv: boevoi put' 25-go tankovogo korpusa* [The tanks are entering the penetration: The combat path of the 25th Tank Corps]. Moscow: Voenizdat, 1988.

DiNardo, Richard L. *Germany's Panzer Arm*. Westport, Ct.: Praeger, 1997.

Diviziia pervogo saliuta [A division of the first salute]. Moscow: Moskovskii Rabochii, 1984. The history of the 63d Army's 129th Rifle Division.

Dragunsky, D. A. *Gody v brone* [Years in armor]. Moscow: Voenizdat, 1973. The memoirs of the commander of the 3d Mechanized Corps' 1st Mechanized Brigade.

Dunn, Walter S., Jr. *Kursk: Hitler's Gamble, 1943*. Westport, Ct.: Praeger, 1997.

———. *Hitler's Nemesis: The Red Army, 1930–1945*. New York: Praeger, 1994.

Efimov, A., "Primenenie aviatsii v Kurskoi bitve—vazhnyi etap v razvitii operativnogo iskusstva Sovetskikh VVS" [The employment of aviation at Kursk—an important stage in the development of the Soviet Air Force's operational art]. *VIZh* 6 (June 1983): 45–54.

Egorov, P. Ia., Krivoborsky, I. V., Ivlev, N. K., and Rogalevich, A. I. *Dorogami pobed: boevoi put' 5-i gvardeiskoi tankovoi armii* [On the roads to victory: The combat path of 5th Guards Tank Army]. Moscow: Voenizdat, 1969.

Engelmann, Joachim. *Zitadelle: Die grosste Panzerschlacht im Osten 1943*. Friedberg: Podzun-Pallas, 1980.

Erickson, John. *The Road to Berlin*. London: Weidenfeld and Nicolson, 1983.

Erickson, John, and Erickson, Ljubica. *The Soviet Armed Forces, 1918–1992: A Research Guide to Soviet Sources*. Westport, Ct.: Greenwood Press, 1996.

Fedorenko, V. "Deistviia sovetskikh partizan v bitve pod Kurskom" [Actions of Soviet partisans during the battle of Kursk]. *VIZh* 7 (July 1968): 110–116.

Foerster, Roland. *Gezeitenwechsel im Zweiten Weltkreig? Die Schlachten von Charkov und Kursk im Fruhjahr und Sommer 1943 in operativer Anlage, Verlauf und politischer Bedeutung*. Hamburg: Verlag E. S. Mittler & Sohn, 1996.

Fomichev, M. G. *Put' nachinalsia s Urala* [The path began in the Urals]. Moscow: Voenizdat, 1976. The history of the 4th Tank Army's 30th Ural Tank Corps.

Gareev, M. "Oborona na Kurskom duge" [Defense in the Kursk bulge]. *Svobodnaia mysl'* [Free thought] 10 (July 1993): 68–79.

Gavrikov, F. K. "Iugo-vostochnee Orla" [Southeast of Orel]. *VIZh* 7 (July 1988): 61–65.

———. "Oboronialis' stoiko (boevye deistviia 41-i strelkovoi divizii 5 iiuliia 1943 g. v bitve pod Kurskom)" [They defended stoically (the combat actions of the 41st Rifle Division on 5 July 1943 in the battle of Kursk)]. *VIZh* 6 (June 1986): 40–44. A memoir by the 41st Rifle Division chief of operations.

Geschichte der 3. Panzer-Division: Berlin-Brandenburg 1935–1945. Berlin: Buchhandling Gunter Richter, 1967.

Getman, A. L. *Tanki idut na Berlin (1941–1945)* [Tanks advance on Berlin (1941–1945)]. Moscow: Nauka, 1973. The history of the 1st Tank Army's 6th Tank Corps.

Glantz, David M. "Prelude to Kursk: Soviet Strategic Operations, February–March 1943." In *Gezeitenwechsel im Zweiten Weltkrieg?* Hamburg: Verlag E. S. Mittler, 1996.

———. "Soviet Military Strategy during the Second Period of War (November 1942–December 1943): A Reappraisal." *Journal of Military History* 60 (January 1996): 115–150.

———. *The Military Strategy of the Soviet Union*. London: Frank Cass, 1992.

———. *The Role of Intelligence in Soviet Military Strategy in World War II*. Novato, Ca.: Presidio, 1990.

———. *Soviet Military Intelligence in War*. London: Frank Cass, 1990.

———. "Soviet Operational Intelligence in the Kursk Operation, July 1943." *Intelligence and National Security* 5, 1 (January 1990): 5–49.

———. *Soviet Military Deception in the Second World War*. London: Frank Cass, 1989.

———. "Soviet Defensive Tactics at Kursk, July 1943." *CSI Report No. 11*. Fort Leavenworth, Kans.: Combat Studies Institute, 1986.

Glantz, David M., and House, Jonathan. *When Titans Clashed: How The Red Army Stopped Hitler*. Lawrence: University Press of Kansas, 1995.

Golushko, I. "Rabota tyla v vazhneishikh operatsiiakh vtorogo perioda voiny" [Rear service work in the most important operations of the second period of war]. *VIZh* 11 (November 1974): 35–42.

Goncharov, M. *Golubaia pekhota* [Sky blue infantry]. Kishinev: Karta Moldaveniaska, 1979. A memoir of the 4th Guards Airborne Division.

Gorbatov, A. V. *Gody i voiny* [Years and wars]. Moscow: Voenizdat, 1980. The memoirs of the 3d Army commander.

Graser, Gerhard. *Zwischen Kattegat und Kaukasus: Weg und Kampfe der 198. Infantrie-Division, 1939–1945*. Tubingen: Kameradenhilfswerk und traditionsverband der ehemaligen 198 Infantrie-Division, 1961.

The Great Patriotic War of the Soviet Union 1941–1945. Moscow: Progress, 1974.

Guderian, Heinz. *Panzer Leader*. New York: Ballantine, 1965.

Gvardeiskaia chernigovaskaia: boevoi put' 76-i gvardeiskoi strelkovoi chernigovskoi krasnoznamennoi divizii [Guards Chernigov: The combat path of the Chernigov, Red Banner 76th Guards Rifle Division]. Moscow: Voenizdat, 1976.

Hardesty, Von. *The Red Phoenix: The Rise of Soviet Air Power 1941–1945*. Washington, D.C.: Smithsonian Institution Press, 1982.

Healy, Mark. *Kursk 1943: The Tide Turns in the East*. London: Osprey, 1992.

Heinrici, G. *The Campaign in Russia*. Unpublished archival manuscript.

———. "Citadel: The Attack on the Russian Kursk Salient." Manuscript. U.S. National Archives. Based on a postwar debriefing. Order Nr. 5 with notation OKH/GenSt d H/OpAbt (vorg-St) 13.3.43, Nr. 430 163/43 g. Kdos/Chefs, classified Secret Commanders' Eyes Only!

House, Jonathan M. "Waiting for the Panther: Kursk, 1943." In Andrew J. Bacevich and Brian R. Sullivan, eds., *The Limits of Technology In Modern Warfare*. Cambridge: Cambridge University Press, forthcoming.

Iakubovsky, I. "3-ia gvardeiskaia tankovaia armiia v bitve pod Kurskom" [The 3d Guards Tank Army in the battle of Kursk]. *VM* 8 (August 1971), 54–76.

Isaev, S. I. "Vekhi frontovogo puti: khronika deiatel'nosti Marshala Sovetskogo Soiuza G. K. Zhukova v period Velikoi Otechestvennoi voiny 1941–1945 gg." [Landmarks of a front path: Chronicle of the activities of Marshal of the Soviet Union G. K. Zhukov during the Great Patriotic War, 1941–1945]. *VIZh* 10 (October 1991); 23–34. Translated by Stephen Main in *Journal of Slavic Military Studies* 9, 1 (March 1996): 97–119.

Isaev, S. I., and Levchenko, V. N. *Geroi—osvoboditeli Khar'kovshchiny* [Heroes— the liberators of Khar'kov]. Khar'kov: Prapor, 1988.

Istoriia vtoroi mirovoi voiny 1939–1945 [A History of the Second World War 1939– 1945]. 12 vols. Moscow: Voenizdat, 1973–1982.

Iushchuk, I. I. *Odinnadtsatyi tankovyi korpus v boiakh za rodinu* [The 11th Tank Corps in battles for the homeland]. Moscow: Voenizdat, 1962.

Ivanov, S. P. "Zavershenie korennogo pereloma v voine" [The completion of a fundamental turning point in the war]. *VIZh* 6 (June 1983): 12–25.

Ivanovsky, E. F. *Ataku nachinali tankisty* [The tankists began the attack]. Moscow: Voenizdat, 1984. The history of the 2d Tank Corps.

Jentz, Thomas L. *Panzertruppen: The Complete Guide to the Creation and Combat Employment of Germany's Tank Force—1943–1945.* Atglen, Pa.: Schiffer Military History, 1996.

Jukes, Geoffrey. *Kursk: Clash of Armour.* Battle Book No. 7. London: Purnell's History of the Second World War, 1968.

Kachur, V. P., and Nikol'sky, V. V. *Pod znamenem sivashtsev: boevoi put' 169-i strelkovoi rogachevskoi krasnoznamennoi, ordenov Suvorov II stepeni i Kutuzova II stepeni divizii (1941–1945).* [Under the banner of the Sivash: The combat path of the Rogachev, Red Banner, Orders of Suvorov II degree and Kutuzov II degree 169th Rifle Division]. Moscow: Voenizdat, 1989.

Karavaev, A. V. *Serdtsa i bronia: boevoi put' 44-i gvardeiskoi tankovoi brigady* [Hearts and armor: The combat path of the 44th Guards Tank Brigade]. Moscow: Voenizdat, 1971. The history of the 6th Tank Corps' 112th Tank Brigade.

Kardashov, V. *5 iiulia 1943: pamiatnye daty istorii* [5 July 1943: Memorable dates in history]. Moscow: Molodaia Gvardiia, 1983.

Kartashev, L. S. *Ot podmoskov'ia do Kenigsberga: boevoi put' 83-i gvardeiskoi strelkovoi Gorodokskii Krasnoznamennoi, ordena Suvorova divizii* [From the Moscow region to Konigsberg: The combat path of the Gorodok, Red Banner, and Order of Suvorov 83d Guards Rifle Division]. Moscow: Voenizdat, 1980.

Katukov, M. E. *Na ostrie glavnogo udara* [At the point of the main attack]. Moscow: Voenizdat, 1976. The memoirs of the 1st Tank Army commander.

Kichev, P. "V oborone pod Kurskom" [In the defense at Kursk]. *VV* 7 (July 1943); 81–84. The memoir of the chief engineer for the 15th Rifle Division's 321st Rifle Regiment.

Kir'ian, M. M., ed. *Vnezapnost' v nastupatel'nykh operatsiiakh Velikoi Otechestvennoi voiny* [Surprise in offensive operations of the Great Patriotic War]. Moscow: Nauka, 1986.

Knobelsdorff, Otto von. *Geschichte der niedersachsischen 19. Panzer-Division*. Bad Nauheim: Verlag Hans-Henning Podzun, 1958.

Kochetkov, A. D. *Dvinskii tankovyi: boevoi put' 5-go tankovogo korpusa* [Dvina tank: The combat path of the 5th Tank Corps]. Moscow: Voenizdat, 1989.

———. *Ognennyi iiul': dokumental'nye rasskazy i ocherki* [Fiery July: Documentary tales and surveys]. Voronezh: Tsentral'no-Chernozemnoe, 1984.

Kolganov, K. S., ed. *Razvitie taktiki sovetskoi armii v gody Velikoi Otechestvennoi voiny (1941–1945 gg.)* [The development of Soviet Army tactics in the Great Patriotic War (1941–1945)]. Moscow: Voenizdat, 1958.

Kolibernov, E., "Osobennosti organizatsii inzhenernogo obespecheniia v Kurskoi bitve" [The peculiarities in the organization of engineer support in the Battle of Kursk]. *VIZh* 7 (July 1983): 26–34.

Kolomiets, M., and M. Svirin. *Kurskaia duga* [Kuisk bulge]. Moscow: Eksprint HB, 1998.

Koltunov, G. "Kurskaia bitva v tsifrakh (period kontrnastupleniia)" [The Battle of Kursk in numbers (the period of the counteroffensive)]. *VIZh* 7 (July 1968): 77–92.

———. "Kurskaia bitva v tsifrakh (period oborony)" [The Battle of Kursk in numbers (the period of defense)]. *VIZh* 6 (June 1968): 58–68.

Koltunov, G. A., and Solov'ev, B. G. *Kurskaia bitva* [The battle of Kursk]. Moscow: Voenizdat, 1983.

———. *Kurskaia bitva* [The battle of Kursk]. Moscow: Voenizdat, 1970.

Konenenko, A. "Voprosy voennogo iskusstva v bitve pod Kurskom" [Questions of military art in the Battle of Kursk]. *VIZh* 4 (April 1964): 115–119.

Konev, I. S. *Zapiski komanduiushchego frontom* [The notes of a *front* commander]. Moscow: Voenizdat, 1981.

Kovtunov, G. "Na ognennoi duge" [In the fiery bulge]. *VIZh* 7 (July 1981): 57–63. A memoir by the 138th Guards Artillery Regiment chief of staff.

Kozhevnikov, M. N. *Komandovanie i shtab VVS Sovetskoi Armii v Velikoi Otechestvennoi voine 1941–1945 gg.* [The command and staff of the Soviet Air Force in the Great Patriotic War 1941–1945]. Moscow: "Nauka," 1977.

Kozlov, M. A., ed. *V plameni srazhenii: boevoi put' 13-i armii* [In the flame of battle: The combat path of the 13th Army]. Moscow: Voenizdat, 1973.

Kravchenko, I. M., and Burkov, V. V. *Desiatyi tankovyi dneprovskii: boevoi put' 10-go tankovogo Dneprovskogo ordena Suvorova korpusa* [The 10th Dnepr Tank: The combat path of the Dnepr, Order of Suvorov 10th Tank Corps]. Moscow: Voenizdat, 1986.

Krivosheev, G. F., ed. *Grif sekretnosti sniat: poteri vooruzhennykh sil SSSR v voinakh, boevykh deistviiakh i voennykh konfliktakh* [The seal of secrecy removed: USSR armed forces losses in wars, combat operations, and military conflicts]. Moscow: Voenizdat, 1993.

Krivoshein, S. *Ratnaia byl': zapiski komandira mekhanizirovannogo korpusa* [A true war story: Notes of a mechanized corps commander]. Moscow: Molodaia Gvardiia, 1962. The memoirs of the commander of the 1st Tank Army's 3d Mechanized Corps.

Krull, Albert. *Das Hannoversche Regiment 73: Geschichte des Panzer-Grenadier-Regiments 73 (vorm. Inf. Rgt. 73) 1939–1945.* Regimentskameradschaft 73.

Krupchenko, I. E. "Osobennosti primeneniia bronetankovykh i mekhanizirovannykh voisk v Kurskoi bitve" [Peculiarities in the employment of armored and mechanized forces in the Battle of Kursk]. *VIZh* 7 (July 1983): 19–25.

Krupchenko, I. E., ed. *Sovetskie tankovye voiska 1941–1945: voenno-istoricheskii ocherk* [Soviet tank forces 1941–1945: A military-historical survey]. Moscow: Voenizdat, 1973.

Kurowski, Franz. *Panzer Aces.* Winnipeg, Canada: J. J. Fedorowicz, 1992.

Kuznetsov, P. G. *Gvardeitsy-moskvichi* [Moscow Guards]. Moscow: Voenizdat, 1962. A memoir by the 1st Guards Motorized Rifle Division commander.

Larionov, V. V. "Triumf prednamerennoi oborony" [The triumph of premeditated defense]. *VM* 7 (July 1988): 12–21.

Lehmann, Rudolf. *The Leibstandarte III.* Translated by Nick Olcott. Winnipeg, Canada: J. J. Fedorowicz, 1993.

Lobanov, V. *Vosemnadtsataia gvardeiskaia* [The 18th Guards]. Kaliningrad: Kaliningrad, 1975.

Losik, O. A., ed. *Stroitel'stvo i boevoe primenenie sovetskikh tankovykh voisk v gody Velikoi Otechestvennoi voiny* [The formation and combat use of Soviet tank forces in the Great Patriotic War]. Moscow: Voenizdat, 1979.

Lucas, James. *Das Reich: The Military Role of 2d SS Division.* London: Arms and Armour, 1991.

Luchinsky, A. "O nekotorykh voprosakh strategii i operativnogo iskusstva v Kurskoi bitve" [About some questions of strategy and operational art in the Battle of Kursk]. *VIZh* 6 (June 1983): 26–33.

Mackintosh, Malcolm. *Juggernaut: A History of the Soviet Armed Forces.* London: Secker and Warburg, 1967.

Maliugin, N. "Osobennosti tylovogo obespecheniia voisk po opytu Kurskoi bitvy" [Peculiarities of rear support of forces based on the experience of the Battle of Kursk]. *VIZh* 7 (July 1983): 43–49.

Mal'kov. D. K. *Skvoz' dym i plamia: boevoi put' 12-i gvardeiskoi pinskoi krasnoznamennoi ordena Suvorova strelkovoi divizii* [Through smoke and flames: The combat path of the Pinsk, Red Banner, Order of Suvorov 12th Guards Rifle Division]. Moscow: Voenizdat, 1970.

Managarov, I. M. *V srazhenii za Khar'kov* [In the battle for Khar'kov]. Khar'kov: Prapor, 1978.

Manstein, Erich von. *Lost Victories.* Chicago: Henry Regnery, 1958.

Mellenthin, F. W. von. *Panzer Battles.* Norman: University of Oklahoma Press, 1956.

Morozov, I. K. *Ot Stalingrada do Prague: zapiski komandira divizii* [From Stalingrad to Prague: The notes of a division commander]. Volgograd: Nizhne-Volzhskoe, 1976. Tne memoirs of the commander of the 7th Guards Army's 81st Guards Rifle Division.

Moskalenko, K. S. *Na iugo-zapadnom napravlenii, 1943–1945* [On the south western axis]. Vol. 2. Moscow: "Nauka," 1972. The memoirs of the 40th Army commander.

——, ed. *Bitva na kurskoi duge* [The battle in the Kursk bulge]. Moscow: "Nauka," 1975.

Mulligen, Timothy P. "Spies, Ciphers and 'Zitadelle': Intelligence and the Battle of Kursk, 1943." *Journal of Contemporary History* 22 (1987): 235–260.

Mutovin, B. I. *Cherez vse ispytaniia* [Throughout all the trials]. Moscow: Voenizdat, 1986. A history of the 7th Guards Army's 78th Guards Rifle Division.

Nadysev, G. S. *Na sluzhbe shtabnoi* [In staff service]. Riga: Liesma, 1972. Memoirs of the Central Front's chief of artillery.

Nazarov, V. "Muzhestvo i masterstvo v oborone" [Courage and mastery in the defense]. *VIZh* 6 (June 1973): 47–52. A memoir of the actions of the 7th Guards Army's 78th and 73d Guards Rifle Divisions.

Nekhonov, G. "Deistviia tankovoi roty v zasade" [The actions of a tank company in an ambush]. *VIZh* 8 (August 1968): 48–50. Covers the 16th Tank Corps ambush actions.

Nekhonov, G., and Borisov, B. "Kak razvedchiki uveli nemetskii tank" [How scouts stole a German tank]. *VIZh* 6 (June 1963): 43–47.

Nersesian, N. G. *Kievsko-berlinskii: boevoi put' 6-go gvardeiskogo tankovogo korpusa* [The Kiev-Berlin: The combat path of the 6th Guards Tank Corps]. Moscow: Voenizdat, 1974. The history of the 3d Guards Tank Army's 12th Tank Corps.

——. *Fastovskaia gvardeiskaia: boevoi put' ordena Lenina krasnoznamennoi, ordenov Suvorova i Bogdana Khmel'nitskogo 53-i gvardeiskoi tankovoi brigady* [Fastov Guards: The combat path of the Order of Lenin, Red Banner, and Orders of Suvorov and Bogdan Khmel'nitsky 53d Guards Tank Brigade]. Moscow: Voenizdat, 1964. The history of the 12th Tank Corps' 106th Tank Brigade, later redesignated as 53d Guards Tank.

Noskov, E. "Atakuiut tankisti" [Tank troops attack]. *VIZh* 1 (January 1974); 56–60. A memoir of a platoon commander in the 3d Guards Tank Army's 91st Separate Tank Brigade.

Oborona v gody Velikoi Otechstvennoi voiny: sbornik boevykh primerov [Defense in the Great Patriotic War: A collection of combat examples]. Moscow: Izdanie Akademii, 1989. For official use only.

Oleinikov, A. I. *Rozhdennaia na zemliakh zaporozhskikh* [Born in the Zaporozh'e lands]. Kiev: Politicheskoi literatury Ukrainy, 1980. By the commander of the 5th Guards Army's 95th Guards Rifle Division.

Pankov, F. D. *Ognennye rubezhi: boevoi put' 50-i armii v Velikoi Otechestvennoi voine* [Firing lines: The combat path of the 50th Army in the Great Patriotic War]. Moscow: Voenizdat, 1984.

Parotkin, I., ed. *The Battle of Kursk.* Moscow: Progress, 1974.

Parrish, Michael. *The USSR in World War II: An Annotated Bibliography of Books Published in the Soviet Union, 1945–1975. With an Addendum for the Years 1975–1980.* 2 vols. New York: Garland, 1981.

Paul, Wolfgang. *Brennpunkte: Die Geschichte der 6. Panzerdivision (1. leichte), 1937—1945.* Krefeld: Hontges, 1977.

Piekalkiewicz, Janusz. *Operation "Citadel": Kursk and Orel: The Greatest Tank Battle of the Second World War.* Translated by Michaela Nierhaus. Novato, Ca.: Presidio, 1987.

Platonov, S. P., ed. *Vtoraia mirovaia voina 1939–1945 gg.* [The Second World War 1939–1945]. Moscow: Voenizdat, 1958.

Popel', N. K. *Tanki povernuli na zapad* [Tanks turned to the West]. Moscow: Voenizdat, 1960. A memoir by the 1st Tank Army's commissar.

Po prikazu rodiny: boevoi put' 6-i gvardeiskoi armii v Velikoi Otechestvennoi voine, 1941–1945 gg. [In accordance with the Homeland's orders: The combat path of the 6th Guards Army in the Great Patriotic War, 1941–1945]. Moscow: Voenizdat, 1971.

Postnikov, S. I. "Razvitie sovetskogo voennogo iskusstva v kurskoi bitve" [The development of Soviet military art in the Battle of Kursk]. *VIZh* 7 (July 1988): 10–18.

"Rasskazyvaiut komandarmy" [Army commanders speak]. *VIZh* 6 (June 1963): 62–81. Contains interviews with army commanders I. M. Chistiakov (6th Guards), M. S. Shumilov (7th Guards), K. S. Moskalenko (40th), P. A. Rotmistrov (5th Guards Tank), and A. S. Zhadov (5th Guards Army).

Razdievsky, A. I., ed. *Taktika v boevykh primerakh, polk* [Tactics by combat example, regiment]. Moscow: Voenizdat, 1974.

Riazansky, A. P. *V ogne tankovykh srazhenii* [In the fire of tank battles]. Moscow: "Nauka," 1975. The memoirs of the commander of the 5th Guards Tank Army's 5th Guards Mechanized Corps.

———. "Prokhorovka, iiul' 1943–go" [Prokhorovka, July 1943]. *VV* 6 (June 1973), 107–110.

Rokossovsky, K. *A Soldier's Duty*. Moscow: Progress, 1985.

Rotmistrov, P. A. *Stal'naia gvardiia* [Steel guard]. Moscow: Voenizdat, 1984. The memoirs of the 5th Guards Tank Army commander.

Rozhdennaia v boiakh: boevoi put' 71-i gvardeiskoi strelkovoi vitebskoi ordena Lenina krasnoznamennoi divizii [Born in combat: The combat path of the Vitebsk, Order of Lenin, Red Banner 71st Guards Rifle Division]. Moscow: Voenizdat, 1986.

Rudenko, S., and Braiko, P. "16-ia vozdushnaia armiia v bitve pod Kurskom" [The 16th Air Army in the Battle of Kursk]. *VIZh* 7 (July 1963): 21–32. Rudenko was the 16th Air Army commander, and Braiko was the army chief of staff.

Samchuk, I. A. *Trinadtsataia gvardeiskaia: boevoi put' trinadtsatoi gvardeiskoi poltavskoi ordena Lenina dvazhdy krasnoznamennoi ordenov Suvorova i Kutuzova strelkovoi divizii (1941–1945)* [The 13th Guards: The combat path of the Poltava, Order of Lenin, twice Red Banner, Orders of Suvorov and Kutuzov 13th Guards Rifle Division]. Moscow: Voenizdat, 1971.

———. *Gvardeiskaia poltavskaia: kratkii ocherk o boevom puti 97-i gvardeiskoi poltavskoi krasnoznamennoi ordenov Suvorova i Bogdan Khmel'nitskogo strelkovoi divizii* [The Poltava Guards: A short survey of the combat path of the Poltava, Red Banner, Orders of Suvorov and Bogdan Khmel'nitsky 97th Guards Rifle Division]. Moscow: Voenizdat, 1965.

Samchuk, I. A., and Skachko, P. G. *Atakuiut desantniki: boevoi put' 9-i gvardeiskoi krasnoznamennoi, ordena Suvorova i Kutuzova poltavskoi vozdushno-desantnoi divizii* [Airborne troopers attack: The combat path of the Red Banner, Orders of Suvorov and Kutuzov, Poltava 9th Guards Airborne Division]. Moscow: Voenizdat, 1975.

Samchuk, I. A., Skachko, P. G., Babikov, Iu. N., and Gnedoi, I. L. *Ot Volgi do El'bi i Pragi (kratkii ocherk o boevom puti 5-i gvardeiskoi armii)* [From the Volga to the Elbe and Prague: A short survey about the combat path of the 5th Guards Army]. Moscow: Voenizdat, 1976.

Sandalov, L. "Brianskii front v orlovsloi operatsii (zapiski nachal'nika shtaba brianskogo fronta)" [The Briansk Front in the Orel operation (the notes of the Briansk Front chief of staff)]. *VIZh* 8 (August 1963): 62–72.

Sbornik boevykh primerov iz opyta Velikoi Otechestvennoi voiny [A collection of combat examples from the experience of the Great Patriotic War]. Moscow: Voenizdat, 1982.

Seaton, Albert. *The Russo-German War 1941–1945.* New York: Praeger, 1971.

Sekretov, A. N. *Gvardeiskaia postup' (boevoi put' 17–i mozyrskoi krasnoznamennoi ordenov Lenina, Suvorova, i Kutuzova kavaleriiskoi divizii, podshefnoi Tadzhikstanu, v gody Velikoi Otechestvennoi voiny, 1941–1945 gg.)* [Guards gait: the combat path of the Mozyr, Red Banner, Orders of Lenin, Suvorov, and Kutuzov 17th Guards Cavalry Division, sponsored by Tadzhikistan in the Great Patriotic War, 1941–1945]. Dushanbe: Donish, 1985.

Shtemenko, S. M. *The Soviet General Staff at War, 1941–1945.* Translated by Robert Daglish. 2 vols. Moscow: Progress, 1970.

Shukman, Harold, ed. *Stalin's Generals.* London: Weidenfeld and Nicolson, 1993.

Smirnov, A. "Kharakternye cherty operativnogo iskusstva voisk PVO strany v kurskoi bitve" [Characteristic features of the operational art of national air defense forces in the Battle of Kursk]. *VIZh* 6 (June 1983): 56–62.

Smirnov, A. F., and Ogloblin, K. S. *Tanki na Visloi: boevoi put' 31-go tankovogo Vislenskogo korpusa* [Tanks on the Vistula: The combat path of the 31st Vistula Tank Corps]. Moscow: Voenizdat, 1991.

Sokolov, A. "Na kurskom duge" [In the Kursk bulge]. *Kommunist Vooruzhennykh Sil* [Communist of the Armed Forces] 13 (July 1983): 65–71.

Solov'ev, B. G. *Vermakht na puti k gibeli: krushenie planov nemetsko-fashistskogo komandovaniia letom i osen'iu 1943 g.* [The *Wehrmacht* on the path to destruction: The collapse of the plans of the German-Fascist command in the summer and fall of 1943]. Moscow: "Nauka," 1973.

———. "Proval tret'ego nastupleniia vermakhta na Vostoke" [The defeat of the third Wehrmacht offensive in the East]. *VIZh* 7 (July 1970): 33–42.

———. "20-letie velikoi pobedy pod Kurskom (o vliianii strategicheskoi vnezapnosti na vooruzhennouiu bor'bu v bitve pod Kurskom)" [the 20th anniversary of the great victory at Kursk (concerning the influence of strategic surprise on the course of armed struggle in the battle of Kursk)]. *VM* 7 (July 1963): 59–74.

Solov'ev, B. G., and Katukov, A. "Bor'ba za strategicheskuiu initsiativu v bitve pod Kurskom" [The struggle for the strategic initiative in the battle of Kursk]. *VM* 7 (July 1973): 74–88.

Sovetskaia kavaleriia: voenno-istoricheskii ocherk [Soviet cavalry: A military-historical survey]. Moscow: Voenizdat, 1984.

Spaeter, Helmuth. *The History of Panzer Corps Grossdeutschland.* Vol. 2. Winnipeg, Canada: J. J. Fedorowicz, 1995.

Stroeva, Anna. *Komandarm Kravchenko* [Army commander Kravchenko]. Kiev: Polititicheskoi literatury Ukrainy, 1984. A biography of the 5th Guards Tank Corps commander.

Sverdlov, F., "Kurskaia bitva (V takticheskikh primerakh)" [The Battle of Kursk (In tactical examples)]. *VV* 7 (June 1993): 19–22.

———. "Udar po flangu orlovskoi gruppirovki protivnika" [Attack on the flank of the enemy Orel grouping]. *VIZh* 1 (January 1971): 17–28.

Telegin, K. F. *Voiny neschitannye versty* [The countless versts of war]. Moscow: Voenizdat, 1988. The memoirs of the Central Front commissar.

Tsukanov, F. "Manevr silami i sredstvami voronezhskogo fronta v oboronitel'noi operatsii pod Kurskom" [Maneuver of the Voronezh Front's forces and weaponry in the Kursk defensive operation], *VIZh* 6 (June 1963): 35–42.

Vasil'ev, S. I., and Dikan, A. P. *Gvardeitsy piatnadtsatoi: boevoi put' Piatnadtsatoi gvardeiskoi strelkovoi divizii* [15th Guards: The combat path of the 15th Guards Rifle Division]. Moscow: Voenizdat, 1960.

Vasilevsky, A. M. *A Lifelong Cause*. Moscow: Progress, 1976.

Velikaia Otechestvennaia voina Sovetskogo Soiuza. [The Great Patriotic War of the Soviet Union]. 6 vols. Moscow: Voenizdat, 1960–1965.

Venkov, B. S., and Dudinov, P. P. *Gvardeiskaia doblest': boevoi put' 70-i gvardeiskoi strelkovoi glukhovskoi ordena Lenina, dvazhdy krasnoznamennoi, ordenov Suvorova, Kutuzova i Bogdana Khmel'nitskogo divizii* [Guards valor: The combat path of the Glukhov, Order of Lenin, twice Red Banner, Order of Suvorov, Kutuzov, and Bogdan Khmel'nitsky 70th Guards Rifle Division]. Moscow: Voenizdat, 1979.

Vetrov, A. A. *Tak i bylo* [So it was]. Moscow: Voenizdat, 1982. The history of the 3d Guards Tank Army's 15th Tank Corps.

Vitruk, A. "Bronia protiv broni" [Armor versus armor]. *VIZh* 6 (June 1983): 72–79. A memoir of the 2d Tank Army's 16th Tank Corps.

Volkogonov, Dmitri. *Stalin: Triumph and Tragedy*. Edited and translated by Harold Shukman. Rocklin, Calif: Prima, 1992.

———. *Triumf i tragediia: politicheskii portret, I. V. Stalin* [I. V. Stalin: Political portrait, triumph and tragedy]. 2 vols. Moscow: Novosti, 1989.

Volkov, A., "Nekotorye voprosy partiino-politicheskoi raboty v voiskakh voronezhskogo fronta v period kurskoi bitvy" [Some questions of party-political work in the Voronezh Front's forces during the Battle of Kursk]. *VIZh* 7 (July 1983): 50–55.

Vostrov, V. A., ed. *Tematicheskii sbornik boevykh primerov iz opyta Velikoi Otechestvennoi voiny i lokal'nykh voin (polk—armiia)* [Thematic collection of combat examples from the experience of the Great Patriotic War and local wars (regiment and army)]. Moscow: Voenizdat, 1989.

Vysotsky, F. I., Makukhin, M. E., Sarychev, F. M., and Shaposhnikov, M. K. *Gvardeiskaia tankovaia* [Tank Guards]. Moscow: Voenizdat, 1963. The history of the 2d Tank Army.

Werth, Alexander, *Russia at War, 1941–1945*. New York: Dutton, 1964.

Zakharov, M. "O sovetskom voennom iskusstve v bitve pod Kurskom" [About Soviet military art in the Battle of Kursk]. *VIZh* 6 (June 1963): 15–25, and 7 (July 1963): 11–20.

Zaloga, Steven J., and Grandsen, James. *Soviet Tanks and Combat Vehicles of World War II*. London: Arms and Armour Press, 1984.

Zetterling, Niklas. "Loss Rates on the Eastern Front during World War II." *Journal of Slavic Military Studies* 9, 4 (December 1996): 896–906.

Zhadov, A. S. *Chetyre goda voiny* [Four years of war]. Moscow: Voenizdat, 1978. The memoirs of the 5th Guards Army commander.

———. "5-ia gvardeiskaia armiia v kurskoi bitve" [5th Guards Army in the Battle of Kursk]. *VM* 8 (August 1973): 60–77.

Zhukov, G. *Reminiscences and Reflections.* 2 vols. Moscow: Progress, 1985.

———. "Na kurskoi duge" [In the Kursk bulge]. *VIZh* 8 (August 1967): 69–83, and 9 (September 1967): 82–97.

Ziemke, Earl F. *Stalingrad to Berlin: The German Defeat in the East.* Washington, DC: Office of the Chief of Military History, United States Army, 1968.

Zvartsev, A. M., ed. *3-ia gvardeiskaia tankovaia: boevoi put' 3-gvardeiskoi tankovoi armii* [3d Guards Tank: The combat path of the 3d Guards Tank Army]. Moscow: Voenizdat, 1982.

Primary Sources (archival or semi-archival)

"Anlagen 13 zum K.T.B. Lagenkarten. PzAOK 4, Ia, 25.3.43–30.7.43." *PzAOK 4, 34888/17.* NAM T-313, roll 369.

Boevoi sostav Sovetskoi armii [Combat composition of the Red Army]. 3 vols. Moscow: Voenno-nauchnoe upravlenie General'nogo Shtaba [Military-scientific directorate of the General Staff], 1963–1972. Classified secret, declassified in 1964.

"Chefkarten, 23 Anlagen, Anlagenband 36 zum KTB Pz AOK 2, Ia, 1 Jun–13 Aug 1943." *Pz AOK 2, 37075/49.* NAM T-313, roll 171. Contains the operational and intelligence maps of the Second Panzer Army and most of the Ninth Army's sector for the duration of the Battle of Kursk.

"Dokumenty sovetskogo komandovaniia v period Velikoi Otechestvennoi voiny (aprel'–mai 1943 g.)" [Documents of the Soviet command during the Great Patriotic War (April–May 1943)]. Podol'sk: Archives of the USSR Ministry of Defense, undated. Classified secret, declassified in 1963. Contains planning documents associated with the Kursk defense.

"Feindlagenkarten des PzAOK 4 fur die Zeit vom 4.7–31.8.43, Anlage 4 zum Ic-Tatigkeitsbericht." *Pz A.O.K.4.* Originals.

"Feindlagenkarten vom 1.7. 1943 bis 30.9.1943, AOK 2, Ic/AO KTB." *AOK 2, 37418/128.* Part 1, in NAM T-312, roll 1253.

Gurkin, B. "Dokumenty i materialy: "Podgotovka k kurskoi bitve" [Preparations for the Battle of Kursk]. *VIZh*, no. 6 (June 1983), 63–71. Contains key documents associated with the preparation of the Kursk defense.

Gurov, O., and Kovalev, V. "Pobeda na kurskoi duge" [Victory in the Kursk bulge]. *VIZh*, no. 7 (July 1983), 56–64. Contains archival documents related to the Orel and Belgorod-Khar'kov operations.

Iminov, V. T. *Organizatsii i vedenie oborony v bitve pod Kurskom na primer 13-i armii tsentral'nogo fronta (iiul' 1943 g.)* [The organization and conduct of the defense in the Battle of Kursk based on the example of the Central Front's 13th Army]. Moscow: Voroshilov Academy of the General Staff, 1979. Classified secret.

Istoriia voin, voennogo iskusstva i voennoi nauki, T.2: uchebnik dlia Voennoi akademii General'nogo shtaba Vooruzhennykh Sil SSSR [A history of wars, military art, and military science, vol. 2: A textbook for the USSR armed forces General Staff]. Moscow: Voroshilov Academy of the General Staff, 1977.

Komandovanie korpusnogo i divizionnogo zvena Sovetskoi Vooruzhennykh Sil perioda Velikoi Otechestvennoi voiny, 1941–1945 [Corps and divisional commanders of the Soviet armed forces in the Great Patriotic War, 1941–1945]. Moscow: Frunze Academy, 1964. Classified secret, declassified in 1964.

"Kriegstagbuch No. 2, AOK 8, Ia, Tagliche Lagekarten vom 1.7.43–31.12.43." *AOK 8, 44701/14.* NAM T-312, roll 56.

"Lagenkarten. Anlage zu KTB Nr. 8, AOK 9. Ia, 26 Mar–18 Aug 1943." *AOK 9. 35939/7.* NAM T-312, roll 320. Contains the Ninth Army's operational and intelligence maps for the indicated dates.

"Manevr podvizhnymi protivotankovymi rezervami v oboronitel'noi operatsii" [The maneuver of antitank reserves during a defensive operation]. In *Sbornik materialov po izucheniiu opyta voiny, no. 10 (ianvar'–fevral' 1944)* [Collection of materials for the study of war experience, no. 10 (January–February 1944)], 112–126. Moscow: Voenizdat, 1944. Prepared by the Red Army General Staff's Directorate for the Use of War Experience. Classified secret, declassified in 1964, and released to the public in 1990. This section deals with antitank operations during the defensive phase of the Battle of Kursk.

"Nekotorye voprosy boevogo ispol'zovaniia zenitnoi artillerii (po opytu boev na orlovsko-kurskom napravlenii)" [Some questions concerning the combat use of antiaircraft artillery (in battles on the Orel-Kursk axis)]. In *Sbornik materialov po izucheniiu opyta voiny, no. 10 (ianvar'–fevral' 1944)* [Collection of materials for the study of war experience, no. 10 (January–February 1944)], 126–139. Moscow: Voenizdat, 1944. Prepared by the Red Army General Staff's Directorate for the Use of War Experience. Classified secret, declassified in 1964, and released to the public in 1990. This section deals with antiaircraft operations during the defensive phase of the Battle of Kursk.

"Operativnoe maskirovka po opytu voronezhskogo fronta" [Operational deception based on the experiences of the Voronezh Front]. In *Sbornik materialov po izucheniiu opyta voiny, no. 14 (sentiabr'–oktiabr' 1944)* [Collection of materials for the study of war experience, no. 14 (September–October 1944)], 165–180. Moscow: Voenizdat, 1944. Prepared by the Red Army General Staff's Directorate for the Use of War Experience. Classified secret, declassified in 1964, and released to the public in 1990. This section deals with deception during the defensive phase of the Battle of Kursk and the Belgorod-Khar'kov offensive.

"Proryv oborony na flange orlovskoi gruppirovki nemtsev" [Penetration of the defense on the flank of the German Orel grouping]. In *Sbornik materialov po izucheniiu opyta voiny, no. 11 (ianvar'–fevral' 1944)* [Collection of materials for the study of war experience, no. 10 (January–February 1944)], 4–48. Moscow: Voenizdat, 1944. Prepared by the Red Army General Staff's Directorate for the Use of War Experience. Classified secret, declassified in 1964, and released to the public in 1990. This section deals with all aspects of Western Front's assault in the Orel operation.

Reinhardt, H. "German Army Group Operations on the Eastern Front 1941–1943, Southern Area." *MS No. P-114C*. Vol. 6. Historical Division, USAREUR, 1954.

Sbornik materialov po izucheniiu opyta voiny, no. 11 (mart–aprel' 1944) [Collection of materials for the study of war experience, no. 11 (March–April 1944)]. Moscow: Voenizdat, 1944. Prepared by the Red Army General Staff's Directorate for the Use of War Experience. Classified secret, declassified in 1964, and released to the public in 1990. This 215-page volume deals with all aspects of the Battle of Kursk.

"Schematische Kreigsgliederung, Stand: 1.6.43, 7.7.43, 17.7.43, 25.7.43, and 5.8.43." *[OKH] GenStdH, Op.Abt. III*. Originals. Lists German order of battle in Army Group South.

Simakov, E. "Sovetskaia aviatsiia v bitve pod Kurskom" [Soviet aviation in the Battle of Kursk]. *VIZh*, no. 5 (May 1983), 40–44. Contains aviation orders and directives during preparations for the Battle of Kursk.

Simbolokov, V. N. *Bitva pod Kurskom 1943 goda (konspekt lektsii)* [The Battle of Kursk 1943 (conspectus for a lecture)]. Moscow: Voroshilov General Staff Academy, 1950. Classified secret.

"Sommerschlacht um den Orelbogen vom 5. Juli–12 Aug 1943, Pz. A.O.K. 2., Ia Anlagen." *AOK 9. 35939/7*. NAM T-312, roll 320. Contains a detailed account of the Orel operation together with periodic operational and intelligence maps.

Stadler, Silvester. *Die Offensive gegen Kursk 1943: II. SS-Panzerkorps als Stosskeil im Grosskampf*. Osnabruck: Munin Verlag GmbH, 1980. Contains a fairly complete file of documents and maps from the II SS Panzer Corps and its subordinate panzer grenadier divisions related to the Battle of Kursk.

"Tagesmeldungen II. SS Pz.Korps und XXXXVIII Pz.Korps, 1.7.43–13.7.43." *4. Panzerarmee*. NAM T-313, roll 368. Contains the daily armor strength returns from Fourth Panzer Army forces.

"Tagesmeldungen vom 4.7.43–16.7.43," *Generalkommando II.SS-Pz.Korps*. NAM T-354, roll 605. Contains the daily strength returns from II SS Panzer Corps forces.

Zolotarev, V. A., et al., eds. *Russkii arkhiv: Velikaia Otechestvennaia: Kurskaia bitva: Dokumenty i materialy, 27 marta–23 avgusta 1943 g.* [Russian archive: The Great Patriotic: The Battle of Kursk: Documents and materials, 27 March to 23 August 1943]. Vol. 15 (4-4). Moscow: Terra, 1997.

Index